Mr Sraffa on Joint Production
and Other Essays

Mr Sraffa on Joint Production and Other Essays

Bertram Schefold

London
UNWIN HYMAN
BOSTON   SYDNEY   WELLINGTON

Published by the Academic Division of
Unwin Hyman Ltd
15/17 Broadwick Street, London W1V 1FP, UK

Unwin Hyman Inc.,
8 Winchester Place, Winchester, Mass. 01890, USA

Allen & Unwin (Australia) Ltd,
8 Napier Street, North Sydney, NSW 2060, Australia

Allen & Unwin (New Zealand) Ltd in association with the
Port Nicholson Press Ltd,
Compusales Building, 75 Ghuznee Street, Wellington, New Zealand

First publisned in 1989

British Library Cataloguing in Publication Data
Schefold, Bertram
    Mr Sraffa on joint production and other
    essays.
    1. Joint production. Theories
    I. Title
    338'.001
    ISBN 0-04-338150-2

Library of Congress Cataloging in Publication Data
Schefold, Bertram, 1943–
    Mr. Sraffa on joint production and other essays / Bertram
Schefold.
        p.   cm.
    Bibliography: p.
    Includes index.
    ISBN 0-04-338150-2 (alk. paper)
    1. Sraffa, Piero. Production of commodities by means of
commodities.   2. Prices.   3. Production (Economic theory)
I. Title
HB171.S34 1989   88–27733
338'.01——dc 19   CIP

Typeset in 10 on 11 point Times by Mathematical Composition Setters,
Salisbury, Wilts
Printed in Great Britain by the University Press, Cambridge

Contents

Preface

Interest in the application of the classical theory of prices, in its significance for the critique of economic theory, and in the special aspect of joint production has developed slowly but steadily since Sraffa's *Production of Commodities by Means of Commodities* (henceforth to be abbreviated as PCMC) was published in 1960. The core of this book (Part II) consists of my PhD thesis 'Mr Sraffa On Joint Production', which was written in 1969/70 when I was first a Visitor to the Faculty of Economics, then an Advanced Student at King's College, Cambridge. At that time, almost nobody had written about the formal analysis of joint production, and the critique of neoclassical economic theory had only just begun in the form of the debate about the aggregate production function. Following advice – I still do not know whether it was good or bad – I did not immediately attempt a thoroughgoing revision of the book. Instead, I circulated my thesis in English as a private print (with an introduction in German) and set out to make the results available to a wider public by publishing two or three articles about it. As it happened, Sraffa and joint production shortly thereafter came into fashion; copies of the thesis appeared in unexpected places, and the articles (my own included) began to multiply. It became difficult to change the subject of my researches. Indeed, the time to attempt a 'final' textbook has not yet come; the controversy about the revival of classical theory is far from being settled. I have therefore gladly accepted the offer to provide a second edition of this thesis, since the text is often demanded and not generally accessible.

The formal derivations of the original thesis have therefore not been changed but the book has been amended so as to make it easier to follow and to provide an economic interpretation of the mathematical results. References to important later developments and my articles mentioned above have been added. Moreover, additional sections II.9a, 9b, 9c, 11a, 18a, 18b, 19a, 19b, 20a, 20b and a few theorems and notes (which can be recognized by analogous denominations) have been inserted. They were written in different phases in the years after 1971 during which the manuscripts grew while I was, of course, often pursuing different work in pure and applied economics.

Part III is a translation of six essays that I wrote as 'postscripts' to the German edition of Sraffa's *Production of Commodities by Means of Commodities*. Although they date from 1976 and do not always represent the present state of my thinking about the matter, I have left them basically unchanged (except for essay 4a and amendments to essay

6, added 1980) because I believe that they provide useful interpretations of Sraffa's text, which looks extremely abstract at first.

Part I is meant as a very brief introduction to the general problematic of Sraffa's theory, which is discussed extensively in the separate essays in Part III. It also provides a succinct account of the theory of single-product Sraffa systems for those readers who are not familiar with PCMC and gives an outline of problems of joint production that are the topic of the main essay. Some sections of the Introduction may therefore simply be regarded as summaries of corresponding sections of Part III (as indicated in the section headings); other have been added to provide a broader outlook and the motivation to study joint production, which is a ubiquitous phenomenon and yet often unduly (sometimes systematically) neglected. I have also taken the liberty of referring to my later work in the areas concerned.

The problem of the classical theory of prices with joint production has been taken up by several authors since 1971. The theory of fixed capital has been developed in books by Bomel (1976) and van Schaik (1976). Both these issues were treated in more general contexts by Abraham-Frois and Berrebi (1976) and Kurz (1977). Pasinetti (1977) provided a collection of essays. The formal structure of joint-production Sraffa systems has been further clarified in a number of articles (by Salvadori and others). This book is meant to lead from the most abstract and general concepts of the theory of value to economic applications in the areas of the measurement of capital, of growth, of international trade, of natural resources, etc. 'Application' here does not mean confrontation with statistical data but means the use of derived concepts for an understanding of the real world in a way that is – at least in my interpretation – specific to classical theory. An example is the theory of the specialization of land that results from the payment of differential rent. While my interpretation of the relationship between Sraffa's theory on the one hand and that of Ricardo or neoclassical economics on the other corresponds to views generally held by Cambridge economists (Essays 1–3 in part III), my views of the relationship between Sraffa and Marx, of the usefulness of the classical theory of prices for the analysis of accumulation in the modern world and of the systematic foundation of the concept of value in Sraffa (essays 4–6 in Part III) are less orthodox and definitive.

I should like to express first my gratitude to the late Piero Sraffa himself. In many conversations he helped me to better understand the structure, content and meaning of his theory – by means of his short, sharp, but never unfriendly criticisms of my lengthy explanations, by means of illustrations and anecdotes, but never by means of formal arguments and without even once having recourse to a mathematical symbol. I am similarly indebted to the late Joan Robinson. Special thanks are due to G. Bombach and L. Pasinetti who were the referees of my thesis, to J. Eatwell for encouragement and to C. Dziobek for a rough translation of the essays in Part III. In various phases of the development of this book valuable suggestions were also made by K. Bharadwaj, P. Bomel, P. Garegnani, C. Jaeger, M. Nermuth, L.

Pasinetti, A. Roncaglia and others who are too numerous to mention. B. Preissl and a number of assistants and secretaries helped with the typing and editing of the manuscript. The index was prepared by K. Cartensen.

The manuscript as it now stands was ready in August 1983 (apart from section II.9c). Difficulties with different editors, but primarily my involvement with other theoretical issues and with energy policy in Germany, prevented me from giving a technical 'finish' to the text for another five years.

Bertram Schefold
Frankfurt am Main
February 1988

PART I

Introduction

1 Sraffa's First Critique

(See Part III, Essay 1)

Piero Sraffa (born 1898) made his name as a critic of the Marshallian theory of partial equilibrium for the first time in 1925 with an article 'Sulle relazioni fra costo e quantità prodotta' ('On the relationship between costs and output') (Sraffa, 1925). The starting point of his criticism was the distinction between increasing, diminishing and constant returns, which had not received sufficient attention until then. He was opposed to the view that the difficulty involved in verifying this distinction in reality is due to inadequate statistics and attacked the *fundamentum divisionis* itself: whether there are increasing, falling or constant returns in a particular industry depends on the point of view of the observer. Each case may obtain depending on whether the long or the short period, an industry as a whole, or a single firm is taken into account. Moreover, the idea of a dependence of output on costs in conditions of perfect competition is not suggested by experience; rather this dependence was postulated by the theorists of utility who wished to counterpose a rising supply curve to a falling demand curve for reasons of symmetry. They thus took issue with the classicals, in particular Ricardo, whom Sraffa at that time believed to have assumed constant returns for most commodities. Some neoclassicals had only been able to imagine constant returns as a 'cancelling-out' of the opposing tendencies of rising and falling returns. By contrast, Sraffa observed that it is much more natural to conclude that there are constant returns if both tendencies are *absent*. Constant returns are then the rule, not the exception.

He demonstrated further that the theory of partial equilibria in a static system with perfect competition is, apart from certain rare exceptions, compatible only with constant returns so that prices appear to be determined only from the side of cost of production, not by demand. His argument is essentially based on the observation that the interdependence of markets with variable returns runs counter to the independence of supply and demand curves which is necessary for the theory of partial equilibrium. In his article on 'The laws of returns under competitive conditions' in the *Economic Journal* in 1926 (Sraffa, 1926) he considered diminishing costs and admitted that the sales of competing firms depend not on costs alone, but also on demand, as is shown by logic as well as by experience. But if each firm faces an individual demand, it sells in a market on its own in which it is to be considered as a monopolist or – if a minority of customers switches between firms – an oligopolist. It is well known that, as a consequence of Sraffa's articles, economic research turned to the theory of imperfect competition without abandoning the principles of the Marshallian approach.

From 1928 onwards, however, Sraffa undertook something quite different. He examined how the prices of production can be explained precisely by considering the interdependence of markets without regard to returns to scale and demand curves. A combination of the elements of his critique of the prevailing theory provided the foundation for his construction of a new alternative theory – and that alternative theory led to an improved critique.

The execution of this programme required a complete change of view. Sraffa received important stimuli from his reading of the classics, in particular Ricardo; he began to edit Ricardo's works a little later (Sraffa, 1951), encouraged by Keynes. The fundamental ideas leading to *Production of Commodities by Means of Commodities* can be read from Sraffa's preface to his edition of Ricardo's works. Since other publications by Sraffa from that time do not exist, I now want to discuss that introduction in order to arrive at the world of *Production of Commodities by Means of Commodities*.

2   Ricardo and the Surplus Approach

(See Part III, Essay 2)

It is well known that Ricardo considers a closed economy with uniform rates of wages and profits and asks what determines the distribution of the produce between the classes. His method is based on taking the conditions of production and the level of accumulation as given. This determines the level of employment and hence the magnitude of the total product. If the necessary wage of the employed is deducted from the total product, there remains a *surplus* for distribution between two classes – capitalists and landlords – which depends on the conditions prevailing in agriculture. A larger differential in productivity between the best land and the worst still cultivated implies a larger share of rent and therefore a lower share of profits. The uniform rate of profit must fall as the margin of cultivation is pushed out further; in the simplest case no rent is paid on the last land so that lesser productivity at a given wage implies lower profits and an increased outlay per unit of produce.

The classical economists – including Smith, Marx, and Ricardo's more immediate followers – did not agree on the theory of the rate of profit; they had, in fact, rather different theories to link the theory of distribution and that of accumulation. But they did agree on the *method* of connecting their different theories of distribution and of accumulation by means of the notion of the surplus. The magnitude of the surplus depended on the technique in use and the subsistence wage of the workers. As we shall see, this approach admits the existence of institutional determinants in the theory (e.g. regarding the technique in use, the determination of the necessary wage, etc.) and a sequential analysis of the forces of accumulation and distribution through time, whereas the neoclassical theory subsumes the diverse forms of production and distribution under one general law of supply and demand; there is then no given surplus prior to distribution.

The classical method presupposes, first of all, measurement of output and the surplus by means of the price system. We analyse this, setting aside the factors that determine this distribution (productivity of labour on the last land, etc.); rather, we are interested in the natural prices associated with different given distributions. Sraffa himself intended to modernize the theory of 'natural price' – or, as it was also called, 'price of production' – in order to lay the foundation both for a revival of the classical surplus theory and for the advanced critique of the neoclassicals.

The natural price of a commodity is composed of the sum of the values of the means of production entering the production of the commodity, including labour (which itself possesses a value, determined by the workers' conditions of subsistence). The natural price also contains profit (determined by the given rate of profit) and, possibly, rent. Adam Smith's conception of the natural price consisted in 'adding up' these components on the assumption that there existed 'natural rates' for each; i.e. that there were natural rates of wages, profits and rent. The value of a commodity could be calculated by multiplying the number of men, and the amount of capital and of land by the appropriate natural rate and adding them up.

Ricardo criticized Smith's view of the determination of the natural price but he retains the concept. The natural price is, first of all, the average price as it is determined in the long period by competition, which leads to uniform rates of profits and wages. It can be calculated for each commodity provided the technical conditions for the production of each commodity and the 'natural rates' are known. The natural price is to be contrasted with the market price of the short period in which the natural rates – in particular the rates of profit – may not be uniform. But the short period does not concern us here.

Ricardo soon discovered that it would not do to add up the components. In 1816, while working for the first edition of *The Principles*, Ricardo found to his surprise that, in a system in which the natural price of every commodity is given, the prices of those commodities that are chiefly produced by means of machinery and fixed capital will fall relative to the prices of commodities produced mainly by means of direct labour if the real wage rises. An increase in wages does not therefore necessarily imply a rise in all prices (expressed e.g. in terms of gold) as a simple adding-up theory would suggest. How are changes in the distribution between the classes of wage-earners, capitalists and land-owners to be described if the value of the produce to be distributed changes with distribution?

In a preliminary attempt Ricardo had ingeniously bypassed the problem, and, in so doing, he had clarified the fundamental structure of the surplus approach. He used the following model. Suppose that corn – i.e. the subsistence of labour – is used directly or indirectly as a means of production in all industries, while only corn is used in the production of corn itself (as the only means of subsistence of the workers and as seed-corn). If all land is of uniform quality and if more land is available than can be cultivated, there will be no rent under competitive conditions. Profits in agriculture (and therefore in all other industries) will thus be determined by the workers' need for corn, together with the physical rate of reproduction of corn. If there are lands of different quality, the least productive (in terms of corn) of the cultivated lands will pay no rent while the difference between the corn yield and the corn cost of production (including profits according to the average rate) on the other cultivated lands will be paid as rent by farmers to landlords. The rate of profit is then given by the conditions of production on the no-rent land.

At the cost of a drastic simplification, the rate of profit has thus been expressed as the ratio of two homogeneous quantities: profit and capital are both measured in corn in agriculture and all rates of profit in other industries have to be equal to this one. Technical conditions in the production of corn determine the surplus, and the level of the necessary corn wage determines the rate of profit, which can be analysed through time by considering the effect of accumulation on technical conditions and the wage, and by taking into account the feedback between the rate of profit and the rate of accumulation. The rate of profit will fall with the extension to less fertile lands (see Part III, Essay 2). But what if there is a heterogeneous collection of different commodities with their prices in both the numerator and the denominator of the rate of profit? A change in the rate of profit induces changes of prices and *vice versa*. The value of what is given – capital – as well as of what is to be distributed – income – fluctuates.

Ricardo now undertook (and, as Sraffa demonstrated, he never again abandoned the question) to look for a commodity whose price would remain invariant with changes in distribution. Such an invariant measure of value (as he called it) could – if it existed – not only serve as a standard of absolute measurement for different individual commodities. It was also meant to have the advantage of permitting the exact description of changes in distribution by allowing the changes in the amount of total profits or in wages in reaction to a change in the rate of profit to be expressed in terms of a commodity that had itself not changed in value – like corn in the corn model. Ricardo even seems to have hoped to be able to find a standard of absolute value that would, if the values of all other commodities were expressed in terms of it, indicate improvements in methods of production, while it was itself produced at all times with unchanged methods, i.e. requiring the same amount of labour. The value of commodities, expressed in the standard, was thus supposed to fall if their methods of production were improved so that they embodied less labour. Ricardo knew, as is shown in the first chapter of *The Principles*, that such an invariable measure cannot exist in reality. But he believed that he had found at least a good approximation as a standard if a product was taken in whose production the ratio of labour employed to capital used was equal to that of the average of all industries in the economy as a whole. The value of such an average commodity seems to change little with distribution. Moreover, in such a standard, the average price of commodities as well as the aggregate value of their means of production remains nearly invariant to changes in distribution. Whether the standard can also serve as an indicator of the growth of production of other commodities depends on whether the conditions of its own production remain stable through time. Ricardo believed that gold was acceptable as such a standard as far as practical use was concerned, but he never arrived at a completely satisfactory theoretical analysis of the 'invariable measure'.

Ricardo's inconclusive argument is discussed in more detail in Essay 2 in Part III. How Sraffa solved Ricardo's problem – leaving aside, however, the requirement that the standard should allow productivity growth as well as distribution to be expressed – will be shown in a summary fashion below; the intricacies of an adequate mathematical exposition of the relationship between Sraffa's theory of prices and his 'standard commodity' is discussed in Essay 6 in Part Three.

It is Sraffa's great merit to have developed the fundamental concept of value in classical theory into a coherent logical system that provides a real alternative to the marginalists' theory of prices. It does not matter for the logic of the argument how far he developed ideas derived from Ricardo (or Marx; see Part III, Essay 4) or how far he was able to improve our understanding of either because he had arrived at those ideas independently.

3 Single-Product Sraffa Systems: Labour Values

Today, after Leontief and von Neumann, it has become easy to express Ricardo's model of a closed economy without joint production mathematically. Suppose that there are n commodities $j = 1, ..., n$ and that the industries of the country are divided accordingly into sectors $i = 1, ..., n$, each producing commodity i. The i'th industry uses the quantities $a_i^1, ..., a_i^n$ of commodities $1, ..., n$ as inputs and l_i hours of labour per period of production in order to produce one unit of commodity i; symbolically:

$$(a_i^1, ..., a_i^n, l_i) \to (0, ..., 0, 1, 0, ..., 0),$$

or, for all industries taken together:

$$(a_1^1, ..., a_1^n, l_1) \to (1, ..., 0)$$

$$\cdots\cdots\cdots\cdots$$

$$(a_n^1, ..., a_n^n, l_n) \to (0, ..., 1).$$

The condition for reproduction for the economic system as a whole requires that for each single commodity at least as much be produced as is used in the production of all other commodities: if one unit of each commodity j is produced, we must have

$$a_1^j + \cdots + a_n^j \leqslant 1, \qquad j = 1, ..., n$$

We normalize $l_1 + \cdots + l_n = 1$.

In this perspective, the reproduction of commodities by means of commodities and of labour appears as the fundamental reality from which economic reasoning starts. The methods of production of each industry are specified as technical relationships. It should be clear that the technology that they reflect depends on numerous social factors, as is particularly clear if we think of the inputs of labour. The character of the work process and the intensity of labour are clearly not simple matters of engineering requirements. Yet it is useful to start by treating the input–output structure of the economy as a technical datum, and to link the analysis only subsequently with the institutions governing the forms of work, the design of commodities, etc., as will be explained later (sections II.20a, b; Essay 5 in Part III).

The classical economists did not start from the input–output structure as written down above explicitly; rather, they linked commodities and labour by means of the concept of labour values as the quantities expressing the amount of labour embodied directly or indirectly in a unit of any given commodity. Labour values were thus introduced as 'technical' magnitudes in the same sense as the input–output structure of the economy is today regarded as 'technical'. The labour values served as a conceptual tool because they could be used to explain prices at least approximately and because they could be thought of as given, although they could not be calculated mathematically from the input–output structure prior to the development of linear algebra.

However, we are able to calculate labour values by means of a precise definition, which will first be made plausible by means of intuitive reasoning. The quantities $a_i^1, ..., a_i^n$ together with labour l_i have been used during the current period for the production of commodity i. In one unit of commodity i there is therefore contained the direct labour l_i of the current year as well as indirect labour of previous years, which are embodied in the means of production $a_i^1, ..., a_i^n$. How much is this indirect labour? Let us consider a_i^1. a_i^1 is the a_i^1'th part of total production of commodity 1 in the previous year and contains therefore $a_i^1 l_1$ direct labour of the previous year as well as the indirect labour contained in the elements of the vector $(a_i^1 a_1^1, ..., a_i^1 a_1^n)$. These may be further resolved into direct labour of the second but last year and indirect labour contained in the means of production of even older years. (In speaking of previous periods we imagine for the purpose of defining labour values that the same structure of production has always ruled in unchanged form for an infinite number of years and lasts indefinitely into the future, although any actual technology may change between periods so that labour values also change.)

If we denote the direct labour used in the production of commodity i in the current year by $L_i^{(0)}$, the indirect labour entering it from the previous year by $L_i^{(1)}$, the labour of the second but last year by $L_i^{(2)}$, and so on, we have

$$L_i^{(0)} = l_i$$
$$L_i^{(1)} = a_i^1 l_1 + \cdots + a_i^n l_n$$
$$L_i^{(2)} = a_i^1 (a_1^1 l_1 + \cdots + a_1^n l_n) + \cdots + a_i^n (a_n^1 l_1 + \cdots + a_n^n l_n)$$

$$\ldots\ldots\ldots\ldots\ldots,$$

so that the total labour embodied in one unit of commodity i can be resolved into the series

$$L_i = L_i^{(0)} + L_i^{(1)} + L_i^{(2)} + \cdots$$

These formulae can be simplified using matrix notation. For the matrix of inputs (a_i^j) we write $\mathbf{A}$,

$$(a_i^j) = \begin{bmatrix} a_1^1, \ldots, a_1^n \\ \cdots \\ a_n^1, \ldots, a_n^n \end{bmatrix} = \mathbf{A},$$

the output matrix is the unit matrix $\mathbf{I}$.

$$\mathbf{l} = \begin{bmatrix} l_1 \\ \vdots \\ l_n \end{bmatrix}$$

is the vector of direct labour, so that production is symbolically expressed as follows:

$$(\mathbf{A}, \mathbf{l}) \rightarrow \mathbf{I}.$$

With $\mathbf{L}$ as the column vector of direct and indirect labour, and $\mathbf{L}^{(k)}$ as the column vector of labour used k years ago, we obtain, as is easily seen:

$$\mathbf{L}^{(0)} = \mathbf{l}$$
$$\mathbf{L}^{(1)} = \mathbf{A}\mathbf{l}$$
$$\mathbf{L}^{(2)} = \mathbf{A}\mathbf{A}\mathbf{l} = \mathbf{A}^2\mathbf{l}$$
$$\cdots$$
$$\mathbf{L}^{(k)} = \mathbf{A}^k\mathbf{l}.$$

The series $\mathbf{L}^{(0)} + \mathbf{L}^{(1)} + \mathbf{L}^{(2)} + \cdots$ may be interpreted as the vector of the sum of past labour inputs for the net production of one unit of each commodity in the system. These inputs are those that would have been necessary if technology had never changed. Their sum is now *defined* as the vector of labour values. We call this the 'reduction' approach. The labour value of a commodity is thus not to be confused with the amount of labour that somehow may be ascribed to a commodity as having been expended directly and indirectly on its past production under concrete historical circumstances where technology changes all the time.

There are various arguments for using not 'historical' labour values but labour values based on an imagined unchanged technique. The economic reason is that this definition is the direct counterpart to the classical definition of 'natural' price or price of production, as will be seen in the next two sections. A different, more direct argument is that there exists an alternative definition of labour values based on a compelling intuitive consideration, which is compatible only with the 'reduction' approach, not with any attempt at defining 'historical' labour values.

This alternative view is that the total labour L_i embodied in commodity i must be equal to the sum of direct labour entering l_i plus the total indirect labour embodied in the inputs $a_i^1, ..., a_i^n$, which must be equal to $a_i^1 L_1 + \cdots a_i^n L_n$. Therefore (in vector notation):

$$\mathbf{L} = \mathbf{l} + \mathbf{AL}.$$

On this basis labour values $\mathbf{L}$ could be defined as

$$\mathbf{L} = (\mathbf{I} - \mathbf{A})^{-1} \mathbf{l}.$$

The two definitions I have given lead to the same result, if and only if

$$\mathbf{L} = (\mathbf{I} - \mathbf{A})^{-1} \mathbf{l} = \mathbf{l} + \mathbf{A} \mathbf{l} + \mathbf{A}^2 \mathbf{l} + \cdots = \mathbf{L}^{(0)} + \mathbf{L}^{(1)} + \mathbf{L}^{(2)} + \cdots$$

It is intuitively plausible that the equality in the middle must hold. As it happens, it can also be proved mathematically, provided the condition of reproduction $a_1^j + \cdots + a_n^j \leqslant 1$ is fulfilled for all j, with an inequality for at least one j. Note that it is this condition of reproduction that allows us to imagine that the technology of today has been ruling ever since time began.

4   Single-Product Sraffa Systems: Prices

We now turn from 'technical' to 'economic' relations of production.
   Let

$$\mathbf{p} = \begin{bmatrix} p_1 \\ \vdots \\ p_n \end{bmatrix}$$

be the price vector of the n commodities, let w be the rate of wages, and r the rate of profit. Then the equations for prices of production in the Sraffa system are defined as follows:

$$(1 + r)\mathbf{Ap} + w\mathbf{l} = \mathbf{p},$$

or more explicitly:

$$(1 + r)(a_1^1 p_1 + \cdots + a_1^n p_n) + w l_1 = p_1$$

$$\cdots\cdots\cdots\cdots$$

$$(1 + r)(a_n^1 p_1 + \cdots + a_n^n p_n) + w l_n = p_n.$$

Prices are here those of a system in a self-replacing state: prices are equal to unit costs of inputs (valued at the *same* price as outputs) *plus* wages (paid at the end of the period of production, for reasons that I shall discuss), *plus* profits according to a *uniform* rate. Now, although an actual economic system will in all relevant cases fulfil the condition for replacement in that at least as much of every commodity (if not of every item in the natural environment outside the realm of market valuation) is produced as is used, no actual economic system will ever show uniform rates of profit or wages or, indeed, uniform prices. The system under consideration is nevertheless important because the prices of production can be regarded as reference points for economic analysis. As long as the technological data of the economy, the distribution between the classes, the levels of economic activity and the composition of output are not subject to too drastic changes, actual market prices cannot diverge very far from prices of production as defined by the technology and distribution in use in the period under consideration. The rates of profit, the rates of wages and prices are not subject to too much dispersion in reasonably tranquil conditions because of competition. A consideration of prices of production as reference points in this sense is all one needs to answer most of the important questions of classical and neoclassical analysis.

Prices of production have sometimes been regarded as 'centres of gravitation' for market prices or as 'averages' of market prices. These are useful images, but the actual relationship between prices of production and market prices is not as mechanical as the first image suggests. Moreover, to postulate a theory for the weights that would render the notion of 'average' precise is inconsistent with a classical inclination to view the laws underlying the formation of prices of production as fundamental and few in number, because there are countless diverse influences on market prices as 'accidental deviations' from prices of production.

The classical method is thus based on the postulate that the fundamental technical and economic data of an economy in a given period can in principle be specified and must be related as shown in the price equations. The price system is meant to serve for an analysis of change over time, but the method is to treat the system as if it had always been the same in that the prices of outputs are equal to those of inputs. It would transcend the scope of this book to explain the potential and the difficulties involved in this approach fully. The reader can see, however, that the definition of prices of production is analogous to that given for labour values, and there is, as will be shown in the next section, a similar relationship between prices as defined by the equations above and a 'reduction' approach.

A special word is needed to explain why Sraffa does not treat the wage as advanced at the beginning of the period, i.e. why wages are not treated as part of capital on which profits are earned according to the uniform rate. On the one hand, Sraffa may here be seen to prepare the ground for his criticism of neoclassical theory: he aims to show that, even if wages and profits are regarded symmetrically as shares in the net product or in the 'surplus' (here meant in a wider sense than in classical theory proper), the marginal productivity theory of distribution does not hold.

On the other hand, there is also a positive meaning. In the context of agricultural production, with wages remaining at the subsistence level, it makes sense to regard the wage fund as an advance to be made by the capitalists that is similar to the advance of seed-corn. However, the notion of subsistence is a hazy one and there is no wage fund to be advanced in conditions of industrial production where wages are to a large extend paid out of current proceeds and spent on consumption goods that are currently being produced. It would not make much difference if the money wage was regarded as advanced (even the analysis of the standard commodity would essentially remain the same; see Essay 6 in Part III). A different system would emerge only if a subsistence wage had to be advanced as a real basket of commodities, as under agricultural conditions. It would then not be possible to execute Sraffa's thought experiment, i.e. to vary the rate of profit in a given system in order to contemplate the ensuing changes of prices and the wage rate. To this thought experiment we now turn.

The system of n equations in $n + 2$ unknowns $p_1, ..., p_n, w, r$ contains two degrees of freedom. The first is to be interpreted as corresponding to distribution. This is determined exogenously as in Ricardo's corn model. For example, it is given through a fixed real wage from the commodities $b^1, ..., b^n$ by means of an additional equation:

$$b^1 p_1 + \cdots + b^n p_n = w.$$

One might also assume that the wage goods are advanced like a subsistence wage in every industry. The system is then best represented as:

$$(1 + R)\mathbf{Ap} = \mathbf{p},$$

with R being the unique rate of profit obtained by capitalists after distributing the entire surplus to them. However, since there would then not be room for Sraffa's thought experiment of varying the rate of profit in order to criticize neoclassical theory and since the notion of an advanced wage is less appropriate for an industrial economy with its more continuous flow of production than for an agrarian economy with its natural period of production in temperate zones, we continue to assume that the wage is paid at the end of the period.

Various theories have been proposed to explain how the rate of profit might be treated as the independent variable (see Essay 5 in Part III); the wage rate is then a dependent variable.

Given w or r, the remaining system of equations still contains $n + 1$ unknowns and determines relative prices. In order to get from relative prices to what we call 'absolute' prices, an appropriate standard (numéraire) has to be introduced. As we have seen, Ricardo had established certain postulates for such a standard which went too far in some respects. Sraffa shows a construction by means of which his postulates can at least partly be fulfilled. A provisional equation defining a standard may be $p_i = 1$ for some i (e.g. commodity i is gold; prices are then expressed in terms of quantities of gold).

5 Single Product Sraffa Systems: Movement of Relative Prices

I first attempt a discussion of absolute prices, without committing myself to a particular standard. Whatever it is, if a standard of prices and of the wage are given by means of two additional equations, prices can be calculated from

$$(1 + r)\mathbf{A}\mathbf{p} + w\mathbf{l} = \mathbf{p}$$

according to the formula

$$\mathbf{p} = w[\mathbf{I} - (1 + r)\mathbf{A}]^{-1}\mathbf{l}$$

and the rate of profit is determined.

In order to understand the character of the 'natural prices' on which we want to focus, we now change the distribution in a thought experiment by changing w, and we observe the effect of these virtual changes on r and $\mathbf{p}$.

The wage w will have reached its maximum in a certain standard if profits, that is to say r, vanish, i.e. if the entire social product is distributed to the workers:

$$\mathbf{A}\mathbf{p} + w\mathbf{l} = \mathbf{p}.$$

We then have $\mathbf{p}/w = \mathbf{L}$; i.e. prices in terms of the wage rate are equal to labour values. If the wage is lowered, profits rise up to a maximum rate of profit R at which the wage disappears completely. This maximum rate of profit is obviously independent of the standard chosen and (this constitutes one of Sraffa's important discoveries) it is finite, if there exist produced means of production. The maximum rate of profit is a solution to the equation

$$(1 + R)\mathbf{A}\mathbf{p} = \mathbf{p}.$$

Clearly, the system obtained at the maximum rate of profit is analogous to that obtained at the end of section I.4 on the assumption that the wage is included among the means of production in the form of the necessary consumption goods of the workers. In between, w and r are functionally related. It is reasonable to suppose – and can be proved rigorously – that (if there is no joint production) r rises monotonically in every standard if w diminishes (see Figure I.1).

The wage curve is the basis of all subsequent considerations. As w and r change in opposite direction, prices change continuously. This follows

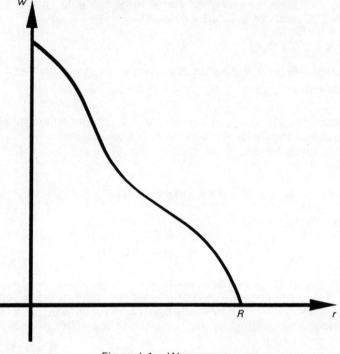

Figure I.1   *Wage curve*

on the one hand directly from

$$\mathbf{p} = w[\mathbf{I} - (1 + r)\mathbf{A}]^{-1}\mathbf{l};$$

on the other hand, this expression can be developed into a series

$$\mathbf{p} = w[\mathbf{I} + (1 + r)\mathbf{A} + (1 + r)^2\mathbf{A}^2 + \cdots]\mathbf{l}.$$

It has an immediate economic interpretation: the coefficients $\mathbf{A}^k\mathbf{l}$ represent, as we have seen, the labour that was employed k years ago and that now enters actual production indirectly:

$$\mathbf{A}^k\mathbf{l} = \mathbf{L}^{(k)}.$$

We thus have

$$p = w[\mathbf{L}^{(0)} + (1 + r)\mathbf{L}^{(1)} + (1 + r)^2\mathbf{L}^{(2)} + \cdots],$$

that is to say, each p_i/w can be represented as the sum of labour used in previous periods for the production of commodity i, where each term is to be multiplied by the power of $1 + r$ that indicates how many years ago the corresponding amount of labour was expended.

This permits a certain number of conclusions:

I p_i/w has the dimension 'time per unit of commodity i'; it is the price of the i'th commodity per wage rate or in terms of the wage rate. Therefore p_i/w indicates the length of time for which a worker has to work at the prevailing w or r in order to earn the value of one unit of commodity i. The labour-time p_i/w is called 'the labour commanded by commodity i'.

From

$$\frac{\mathbf{p}}{w} = \mathbf{L}^{(0)} + (1 + r)\mathbf{L}^{(1)} + (1 + r)^2\mathbf{L}^{(2)} + \cdots$$

follows that this amount of time increases for each commodity as r is raised – or, equivalently, as w diminishes in terms of a commodity standard. Intuitively: as the wage is diminished, each worker has to work longer to acquire any commodity; or, more labour can be bought (commanded) by selling the commodity.

II   This does not contradict Ricardo's astonishing observation that the price of certain commodities may be reduced if the wage is raised, for Ricardo is speaking about absolute prices in terms of a standard that is not the wage rate. As we have seen, r diminishes as w is raised. The individual prices in $\mathbf{p} = w[\mathbf{I} - (1 + r)\mathbf{A}]^{-1}\mathbf{l}$ react with movements of different extent and in different directions to movements of w and the corresponding opposite movements of r.

It is intuitively clear that a (small) increase in w and a corresponding (small) diminution of r will cause the price of a commodity produced by means of much direct labour with very little use of other means of production to rise, whereas that of a commodity produced by means of only a little direct labour but considerable expense on other means of production will fall. One is inclined to call the first process of production 'labour intensive', the second 'capital intensive'.

However, it is possible that one is deceived and that the movements of prices operate in a different fashion. If, for example, the means of production in the second 'capital-intensive' process are particularly 'labour-intensive' commodities, their prices will increase with w and it is conceivable that the effect of their rise with w will prevail over the effect of the diminution of r, so that the produced 'capital-intensive' commodity will, paradoxically, rise in price.

One can thus prove that all prices rise with r in terms of labour commanded, while some may rise and some fall in terms of other standards. Sraffa has provided us with a theory to demonstrate that his particular numéraire ('standard commodity') allows the economic properties of the system to be more transparent than commodity standards chosen at random (see section I.7). He used the standard in particular as a basis for the critique of any concept of capital as a measurable quantity independent of distribution, but the possibility of paradoxical movements of prices and of 'capital' can also be shown using relative prices only, i.e. without committing oneself to a particular numéraire, as we shall see presently.

III   The formula

$$\mathbf{p} = w[\mathbf{L}^{(0)} + (1 + r)\mathbf{L}^{(1)} + (1 + r)^2\mathbf{L}^{(2)} + \cdots]$$

suggests that the movements of prices are visualized better not by means of the relationship between direct labour and other means of production, but by showing the distribution of total labour expended over time, i.e. of direct and indirect labour embodied in the product ('dated quantities of labour'). This may be explained using one of Sraffa's examples (he derived it in turn from another prototype). A bottle of wine (α) incorporates 20 hours of labour expended 8 years ago; an oak chest (β) incorporates just as much labour, but 1 hour was expended 25 years ago

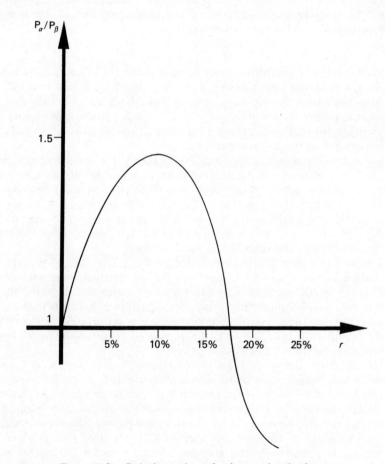

Figure I.2   *Relative price of wine and oak chest*

whereas the 19 remaining are spent in the present period. Therefore:

$$p_\alpha = 20w(1 + r)^8$$
$$p_\beta = w[19 + (1 + r)^{25}].$$

In order to eliminate w, we consider the ratio p_α/p_β,

$$\frac{p_\alpha}{p_\beta} = \frac{20(1 + r)^8}{19 + (1 + r)^{25}}.$$

Wine and oak chest have the same value ($p_\alpha = p_\beta$) at $r = 0$. As r is increased, wine will be more expensive than the oak chest at first, but the price will then fall at 9% and for $r = 17\%$ we again have $p_\alpha = p_\beta$ (see Figure I.2).

Sraffa comments on this observation as follows:

> The reduction to dated labour terms has some bearing on the attempts that have been made to find in the 'period of production' an independent measure of the quantity of capital which could be used, without arguing in a circle, for the determination of prices and of the shares in distribution. But the case just considered seems conclusive in showing the impossibility of aggregating the 'periods' belonging to the several quantities of labour into a single magnitude which could be regarded as representing the quantity of capital. The reversals in the direction of the movement of relative prices, in the face of unchanged methods of production, cannot be reconciled with any notion of capital as a measurable quantity independent of distribution and prices. (PCMC, sec. 48)

6 Single-Product Sraffa Systems: Basics and Non-Basics

The attentive reader will have observed that the maximum rate of profit R did not appear in the example of wine and oak chest. This is to be explained by the fact that wine and oak chest did not here require any means of production other than labour. However, we have been considering systems in which some of the produced commodities are also used as means of production. Then we shall always have a finite maximum rate of profit for the system as a whole.

All commodities can be distinguished according to whether they are used directly or indirectly in the production of all other commodities ('basic commodities') or not ('non-basics'). Non-basics may have the character of pure consumption goods (e.g. 'icecream') or they may enter the production of other non-basics (e.g. 'eggs'). 'Wine' and 'oak chest' in the example above might be considered as non-basics in a system with basics if at least one basic was used in their production jointly with labour. Non-basics are part of the whole circular economic process only in so far as they serve consumption out of wages and profits directly or indirectly. Basics, like 'coal' and 'steel', on the other hand, are in any case directly embedded in the circular process of production. The input matrix $\mathbf{A}$ and the output matrix $\mathbf{I}$ can accordingly be subdivided into submatrices after simultaneous rearrangement of industries and commodities:

$$\mathbf{A} = \begin{bmatrix} \mathbf{A}_1^1 & \mathbf{A}_1^2 \\ \mathbf{A}_2^1 & \mathbf{A}_2^2 \end{bmatrix} = \begin{bmatrix} \mathbf{A}_1^1 & \mathbf{O} \\ \mathbf{A}_2^1 & \mathbf{A}_2^2 \end{bmatrix}, \qquad \mathbf{I} = \begin{bmatrix} \mathbf{I}_1^1 & \mathbf{O} \\ \mathbf{O} & \mathbf{I}_2^2 \end{bmatrix},$$

where $\mathbf{A}_1^1$, $\mathbf{A}_2^2$ are square matrices and $\mathbf{I}_1^1$, $\mathbf{I}_2^2$ unit matrices. $\mathbf{A}_1^1$, $\mathbf{I}_1^1$ is of order m and $\mathbf{A}_2^2$, $\mathbf{I}_2^2$ of order $n - m$. The first m commodities are basic, the last $n - m$ non-basic; therefore $\mathbf{A}_1^2 = \mathbf{O}$. This technical subdivision of the system corresponds to an economic subdivision:

$$(1 + r)\mathbf{A}\mathbf{p} + w\mathbf{l} = \mathbf{p}$$

divides into

$$(1 + r)\mathbf{A}_1^1\mathbf{p}_1 + w\mathbf{l}_1 = \mathbf{p}_1$$
$$(1 + r)(\mathbf{A}_2^1\mathbf{p}_1 + \mathbf{A}_2^2\mathbf{p}_2) + w\mathbf{l}_2 = \mathbf{p}_2,$$

where $\mathbf{p}_1$ denotes the price vector of basics, $\mathbf{l}_1$ the labour vector of basic industries, $\mathbf{p}_2$ the price vector of non-basics, $\mathbf{l}_2$ the labour vector of non-basic industries. It can now be seen that – with given distribution r and a given standard of prices – prices $\mathbf{p}_1$ are determined independently of prices $\mathbf{p}_2$,

$$\mathbf{p}_1 = w[\mathbf{I}_1^1 - (1 + r)\mathbf{A}_1^1]^{-1}\mathbf{l}_1,$$

whereas $\mathbf{p}_2$ can be determined only after calculation of $\mathbf{p}_1$. In order to prevent the economy from falling apart into disconnected systems, one has to assume the existence of at least one basic commodity. In Ricardo's corn model, corn is the only basic commodity.

As we have seen, the 'natural prices' considered here are independent of 'demand' and 'supply', in contrast to 'market prices' and to the conceptions of neoclassical theory, since we start from a given structure of production and a given state of distribution. Commodity demand curves and factor supply curves were not necessary to determine prices. Those trained in neoclassical thinking will therefore be inclined to regard natural prices as derived from costs of production because demand conditions seem to play no role, as in a Marshallian long period in which the structure of production has adapted to demand so that prices are, under competitive conditions, equal to the 'real costs' of labour and 'waiting'.

However, such a view is misleading, and not only because the neoclassicals have, under the influence of the continental schools, abandoned the Marshallian concepts of 'real costs' and 'waiting' and replaced them with the concept of 'opportunity costs'. It is, of course, true that natural prices reflect costs of production in the sense that a uniform rate of profit is assumed to rule, but prices, although *equal* to costs of production, cannot be *explained* by looking at them from the side of costs of production alone. The system of prices of basics is interdependent and unless it is solved for all prices simultaneously, thereby taking into account the quantities produced ('supplied') as well as the quantities used ('demanded'), it cannot be solved at all. Only some non-basics are an exception: after solving the basic system for obtaining the prices of basics, those prices can be used to add up the cost of production for the non-basics that are produced by means of basics alone.

The interdependence of the system of equations means that the objective criterion of the use of a basic commodity in a given self-replacing system therefore contributes to the determination of its price just as much (once distribution is given) as the costs of its inputs.

'Objective criterion' here simply means that the theory starts by taking quantities of commodities as given that are – in principle – objectively measurable. The influences determining the choice of processes of production and the composition of output are not explained, on the other hand, because they are various. We do not have to assume the existence of innate subjective preferences, which are, in neoclassical theory, regarded as given prior to the market process, although we know that preferences cannot become fully known even to the individual through introspection, that individuals' preferences are not independent of one another, that they are affected by the market process, and that they change in the course and under the influence of accumulation. It is the specific cultural development under given historical circumstances, as embodied in the social pattern of production and consumption of commodities, that is of interest here, and not an empty formalism for individual desires. The contention is, therefore, that Sraffa's simple description of demand in the classical tradition of Adam Smith as a definite quantity sold at the 'natural price' allows an easier transition to the consideration of effects of historical modifications of demand than the neoclassical model. The explanation of the character of the change in the demand for luxury goods in the nineteenth century to that for objects of conspicuous consumption in the twentieth, for instance, can by definition not be explained in terms of individual preferences alone. It is true that price elasticities and income elasticities are useful concepts in many instances and that they can sometimes be measured, but the changes of demand involved are small and of a special kind. They do not justify the general use of entire demand functions, let alone the unique 'foundation' of the latter on individual preferences. A classical explanation of the forces governing the composition of output and of demand elasticities has been proposed in Schefold (1985c).

7 Single-Product Sraffa Systems: The Standard Commodity

(See also Part III, Essay 6)

The concept of the basic system was the last link that was still missing before we could approach Ricardo's question of the appropriate standard for absolute value. To this end we are looking for a commodity that is similar to corn in the corn model in so far as the ratio of its value to that of its means of production (without labour) is independent of distribution, irrespective of the standard that is chosen for prices. Such a commodity, if it can be found, will then itself constitute an appropriate price standard, since it will make changes in distribution transparent in a simple fashion: if both the price of the commodity (the commodity is the standard) and the ratio of the price of the commodity to the value of its means of production (without labour) are constant, it is clear that each increase in the wage rate (therefore in the wage) will result in a *proportional* diminution of the rate of profit and *vice versa*. For if the price is by definition invariant (numéraire) and one of its components (the price of its means of production other than labour) happens to be constant as well, a change in the wage entails a change in profits of equal amount but opposite direction, and the change in the rate of profit is proportional to the change in the wage rate. (For a deeper analysis of this point, see Schefold, 1986.)

We have already seen that prices, whatever their standard, will fluctuate in many ways and that the character of the price change will depend on the composition of inputs and therefore on the relationship between direct labour and other means of production. Corresponding movements appear in the proportion of the price of a commodity and the value of the means of production incorporated in it, and this proportion too is different in different industries. But there is one exception: if the wage is zero (at the maximum rate of profit), the ratio of the net values of the products to the capital advanced is the same for all industries in the basic system:

$$(1 + R)\mathbf{A}_1^{\dagger}\mathbf{p}_1 = \mathbf{p}_1,$$

i.e.

$$\frac{p_i - \mathbf{a}_i\mathbf{p}_i}{\mathbf{a}_i\mathbf{p}_i} = R; \qquad i = 1, ..., m.$$

This relationship must also characterize the *standard commodity*.

As soon as the basic system consists of more than one industry, it is inconceivable that a single commodity could serve as standard commodity since all other basic commodities will directly or indirectly enter its production and their prices are subject to fluctuations that can hardly compensate each other as is required. We therefore take a bundle consisting of all basic commodities $q_1, ..., q_m$. (One can show that commodities other than basics do not have to be taken into account. In particular, pure consumption goods cannot enter the standard commodity since they are nowhere used as means of production.) We write $q_1, ..., q_m$ as a row vector $\mathbf{q} = (q_1, ..., q_m)$ and we choose $\mathbf{q}$ such that

$$(1 + R)\mathbf{q}\mathbf{A}_1^1 = \mathbf{q},$$

where $\mathbf{A}_1^1$ denotes the basic system. (This characteristic equation has only one economically significant eigenvalue, which is equal to $1/(1 + R)$ according to theorems by Perron and Frobenius.)

In other words: we do not take the industries of the basic system in the proportions in which they are given originally, but we multiply each (that is to say, we augment or reduce its scale) by such a factor that the aggregate of all inputs, that is to say

$$\mathbf{q}\mathbf{A}_1^1 = q_1(a_1^1, ..., a_1^m) + \cdots + q_m(a_m^1, ..., a_m^m)$$

is proportional to the total product (i.e. $\mathbf{q}\mathbf{A}_1^1 = [1/(1 + R)]\mathbf{q}$).

The vector $\mathbf{q}$ is determined only up to a linear factor. We normalize it by setting $\mathbf{q}\mathbf{l}_1 = 1$.

$\mathbf{q}(\mathbf{I}_1^1 - \mathbf{A}_1^1)$, the net product of the economy in the changed (standard) proportions, is now defined to be the standard commodity, that is to say we normalize $\mathbf{q}(\mathbf{I}_1^1 - \mathbf{A}_1^1)\mathbf{p}_i = 1$ for each state of distribution (for all r or w). In fact, $\mathbf{q}(\mathbf{I}_1^1 - \mathbf{A}_1^1)$ fulfils the requirement that the ratio of the value of the produced commodity to the value of the means of production remains constant for all states of distribution in every standard of prices for

$$\mathbf{q}(\mathbf{I}_1^1 - \mathbf{A}_1^1)\bar{\mathbf{p}} = R\mathbf{q}\mathbf{A}_1^1\bar{\mathbf{p}}$$

for *all*

$$\bar{\mathbf{p}} = \begin{bmatrix} \bar{p}_1 \\ \vdots \\ \bar{p}_m \end{bmatrix}$$

where $\bar{\mathbf{p}}$ are prices in *any* commodity standard (e.g. $\bar{p}_i = 1$).

From

$$(\mathbf{I}_1^1 - \mathbf{A}_1^1)\mathbf{p}_1 = r\mathbf{A}_1^1\mathbf{p}_1 + w\mathbf{l}_1$$

we obtain, if $\mathbf{q}(\mathbf{I}_1^1 - \mathbf{A}_1^1)\mathbf{p}_1 = 1$,

$$1 = \mathbf{q}(\mathbf{I}_1^1 - \mathbf{A}_1^1)\mathbf{p}_1 = r\mathbf{q}\mathbf{A}_1^1\mathbf{p}_i + w\mathbf{q}\mathbf{l}_1 = \frac{r}{R}\mathbf{q}(\mathbf{I}_1^1 - \mathbf{A}_1^1)\mathbf{p}_1 + w,$$

$$1 = \frac{r}{R} + w;$$

there exists therefore a linear connection between wage w and rate of profit r in this standard. The standard can also be used to express prices of non-basics. If the value of the standard commodity $\mathbf{q}(\mathbf{I}_1^1 - \mathbf{A}_1^1)$ is reduced to the labour L_q contained in $\mathbf{q}(\mathbf{I}_1^1 - \mathbf{A}_1^1)$, it resolves ultimately in a series of particular simplicity:

$$
\begin{aligned}
1 &= \mathbf{q}(\mathbf{I}_1^1 - \mathbf{A}_1^1)\mathbf{p}_1 \\
&= \mathbf{q}(\mathbf{I}_1^1 - \mathbf{A}_1^1)w[\mathbf{I}_1^1 - (1+r)\mathbf{A}_1^1]^{-1}\mathbf{l}_1 \\
&= R\mathbf{q}\mathbf{A}_1^1\left(1 - \frac{r}{R}\right)[\mathbf{I}_1^1 + (1+r)\mathbf{A}_1^1 + (1+r)^2(\mathbf{A}_1^1)^2 + \cdots]\mathbf{l}_1 \\
&= \left(1 - \frac{r}{R}\right)\frac{R}{1+R}\,\mathbf{q}[\mathbf{I}_1^1 + (1+r)\mathbf{A}_1^1 + \cdots]\mathbf{l}_1 \\
&= \frac{R-r}{1+R}\left[\mathbf{q}\mathbf{l}_1 + (1+r)\frac{\mathbf{q}\mathbf{l}_1}{1+R} + (1+r)^2\frac{\mathbf{q}\mathbf{l}_1}{(1+R)^2} + \cdots\right] \\
&= \frac{R-r}{1+R}\left[1 + \frac{1+r}{1+R} + \frac{(1+r)^2}{(1+R)^2} + \cdots\right].
\end{aligned}
$$

The dated quantities of labour of the standard commodity therefore diminish like the terms of a geometric series with perfect regularity, and this is not the case for any other commodity (see PCMC, sec. 21).

8 Single-Product Sraffa Systems: Reswitching

(See also Part III, Essay 3)

If in a system – which we shall assume for simplicity is basic (Bharadwaj, 1970) – there exists an alternative method of production for a certain commodity that fulfils the conditions of reproduction

$$
\sum_{i=1}^{n} a_i^j \leqslant 1, \qquad j = 1, \ldots, n,
$$

one may ask which of the two allows a more economical production.

The answer is easy. The standard commodity of the original system can be used to normalize the prices of the system employing the alternative method. We then obtain two diagrams in w and r (see Figure I.3). That of the original system is a straight line going through $(r, w) = (0, 1)$ and $(r, w) = (R, 0)$. It can be proved that the alternative curve w^* will show different maximal rates of wages and profits $\bar{w}$, R, and will cut the straight line in general up to n times; in any case it will fall monotonically. (The use of a different standard of prices would yield analogous results.) For each given rate of wages w_1 the curve lying further to the right belongs to the more economical system, since it implies a higher rate of profit, $r_1 > r_2$. In a neighbourhood of r_1 the same system will *vice versa* imply a higher rate of wages, $w_1 > w_2$. At points of intersection (switch points) r_3, r_4, neither shows an advantage.

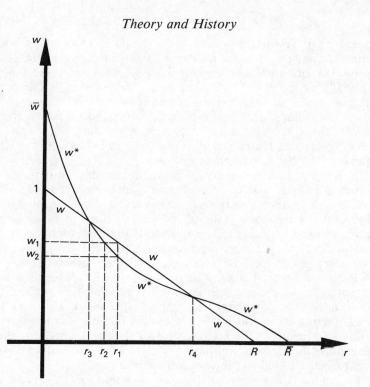

Figure I.3   *Return of technique ('reswitching')*

The observation that the wave curves of alternative techniques intersect in general several times ('reswitching') is a conclusive argument
against any theory of distribution that is based on neoclassical factors of
production. The theory of production functions is completely dependent
on the existence of a monotonic functional relationship between capital
intensity and rate of profit. The existence of several points of intersection
on the other hand is an expression of the return of the same technique at
different values of r and contradicts the hypothesis of a unique and
reversible assignment of techniques to rates of profits. This observation
became the starting point for the critique of neoclassical theory that
Sraffa initiated.

On the other hand, theories of distribution like Kaldor's post-
Keynesian analysis (1956) do not logically contradict the phenomenon
of the return of techniques. This may be asserted, although a truly
comprehensive and consistent representation that would show this
introducing capital accumulation and technical progress is still missing.

9   Theory and History

(See Part III, Essay 5)

Sraffa's book, considered as a contribution to the revival of classical
theory, led to a proliferation of formal analyses of the price and value

systems, their relationships and their significance for the history of economic thought. Much less work was done on the theories of distribution, accumulation, competition, etc. that would be compatible with Sraffa's approach. This is, in a way, to be regretted, but there is also a deeper meaning to the 'omission': Sraffa's theory is inherently more open to institutional data and historical developments, and therefore to a wider range of theoretical approaches in economics, than is the traditional neoclassical doctrine. This is discussed in Essay 5 in Part III. The argument may be introduced as follows.

Modern neoclassical theory aims at the construction of a closed, preferably unique, system of economic equilibrium. It is supposed to show that the market can (given preferences and endowments) mediate between the independent wills of individuals through prices at which exactly as much of each factor and good is supplied as is demanded. In consequence, change takes place only because the parameters of the model change, i.e. because preferences shift and resources alter. The neoclassical economist usually leaves the task of explaining and characterizing change in consumption patterns to sociologists, while distribution is endogenously explained by supply and demand. The market leads to an efficient allocation of resources and fair distribution (given the initial endowments). The methodological separation between the economic analysis of equilibrium and the extra-economic datum of preferences reflects the will to preserve consumer sovereignty.

This contrasts sharply with the classical vision as founded by Adam Smith. The classicals were (apart from Marx, of course) also advocates of *laissez-faire* and market forces, but their economic agents were individuals with historical characteristics as members of classes. Their theory of consumption was based not on utility but on the distinction between the necessaries of life and luxuries. The workers consumed the necessary wage. The division of labour had augmented the productivity of workers but it had (according to Smith) also reduced their intellectual faculties and (in Marx's words) alienated them. The acquisition of luxuries, on the other hand, was seen as directed not uniquely towards the maximization of utility in individual consumption but also towards the display of riches and the exercise of power. The market was seen as an instrument for the promotion of progress, the accumulation of value and riches, and (indirectly) the cultural advance of society that accumulation made possible. This historical perspective emerges from Smith's *Wealth of Nations* read in conjunction with his *Theory of Moral Sentiments*. One can show that not economic freedom and the utility of consumption as such but hope for moral improvement provided the basis of the legitimation of the transition from the feudal and mercantile order to capitalism in Smith (Medick, 1973).

The treatment of the exogenous data of the models and the data themselves are different in the classical theory. A distinction such as that between necessaries and luxuries requires an exogenous specification of the output vector (vector of 'final demand', as the neoclassicals would call it). The view of society as divided into classes requires theories of distribution that reflect the state of development of society and of the specific institutions within which the balance of forces between classes manifests itself. In consequence, even more is treated as exogenous in Sraffa's model. However, his exogenous data for consumption, distribution and technology are not to be left to some other discipline for explanation but to economics. Economic theory then has to be complemented by historical considerations.

Demand patterns are to be derived not so much from individuals as from social strata, and they are associated with the social roles played by individuals who require goods to fulfil their given needs; these needs are shaped by their environment and are different according to status, location in town and countryside, etc. Income changes are associated with migration of people between social strata and the associated demand patterns. Price changes may cause people to use other commodities in their domestic work to fulfil their needs. If wages rise, more aspire to the status of the home-owner with a car − and cities are transformed accordingly − but if the price of bread rises, more turn to potatoes.

Demand is thus responsive to income and price changes in classical theory, but there is a hierarchy of needs (as reflected in the simplest distinction between luxuries and necessaries), and there is no universal substitutability as usually in the neoclassical theory of preferences (Schefold, 1985c) − higher education is no substitute for basic food. It should be noted that the classical view of the forces governing the composition of output not only is closer to the views of modern pyschology than is the conventional representation of preferences but it can also get some support from a study of modern marketing methods, which try to assess the potential for the development of the market for a given group of commodities.

A classical economist may have a poor understanding of extra-economic matters, but his model is open: in order to say anything determinate he *must* ask himself at least: What determines the composition of the product that appears as given in the system? Which forces govern technical change? What determines distribution? The approach undoubtedly favours the explicit treatment of diverse political perspectives within the same fundamental analytical framework.

A very important corollary to what has been said about the 'openness' of the Sraffa model concerns the treatment of the employment of labour, equipment and raw materials. Full employment is not assumed in this type of equilibrium of the economy. Market fluctuations are compatible with fluctuations of the economy, but the techniques used and the fundamental data determining the composition of output and distribution must be more permanent to allow us to speak of a long-period equilibrium (or long-period position). Among the long-run and more permanent data that shape demand patterns one may reckon factors such as technology, population, the trade position of a country, customs and habits, the infrastructure. Short-run fluctuations may be associated with fashions, weather conditions, etc., but also with inventory cycles.

The equipment used must therefore have adapted not only in quality (type of machines, etc.) but also in quantity to the composition of output and its foreseeable changes. This does not imply a stationary state or balanced growth (all industries growing at the same rate). On the contrary, it may be expected that some industries, e.g. those producing rather new commodities, grow faster than others, which are close to reaching saturation levels. But the means of production in each sector must have adapted both to the direct requirements of consumption and to the indirect requirements of other sectors. With constant returns to scale, relative prices can then stay constant, or change slowly with moderate changes of returns (drastic changes imply a different equilibrium). The process may be accompanied by minor fluctuations, primarily in the production of consumer goods and raw materials.

Such a growth process does not in general presuppose or entail full employment of the available labour force. According to the classical view, the supply must adapt through migrations of labour, changes in the rate of participation of labour, agreements about the length of the working week, etc. This picture contrasts with the neoclassical postulate of full employment, achieved through changes in the real wage rate and the capital–labour ratio in the world of the production function with malleable capital; this has, however, been disproved in the reswitching debate (see Essay 3 in Part III). The picture also contrasts with that of a neoclassical general intertemporal equilibrium where the stocks given initially are arbitrary (including labour) and where full employment is reached nevertheless (except in that stocks in excess receive zero prices). The initial endowments of general equilibrium are given, and prices adapt to allow them to get fully employed. In the long-period equilibrium considered here, we consider not the initial endowments but the means of production required to produce the output effectively demanded, using a given technology (Schefold, 1985a). The 'openness' of the model thus allows us to analyse the effects on employment of different states of accumulation.

So far, Sraffa's work has mainly led to a new appraisal of distribution. As it turns out, distribution can, for logical reasons, not be determined by 'supply and demand of capital'.

In some historical periods of steady accumulation of capital it may be meaningful to explain distribution by assuming that the rate of growth is given and (to simplify) that capitalists save all their net profits while workers spend. The rate of profit will then have to be equal to the rate of growth, in accordance with the post-Keynesian theory, which fitted in well with post-war developments. In quite different circumstances it may be better to regard the real wage as given, so that the rate of accumulation depends *vice versa* on the magnitude of the surplus (i.e. it is the rate of profit that limits capitalists' investment, as in Ricardo). Other constellations, and diffuse 'mixtures' of them, are conceivable (see Essay 5 in Part 3). To 'choose' a theory for the explanation of distribution in a historical period is in any case to express an appraisal of the relative social and economic forces in a given framework. According to the post-Keynesian view, the capitalists are able to raise the rate of profit by stepping up investment, while workers are able only to influence the money wage, not the real wage. However, conditions may also be such that the real wage is tied to the money wage (for instance, because foreign competition prevents the rise of the domestic price level and the authorities keep the exchange rate fixed). A rise in the money wage in full employment conditions then increases the real wage and leads to a lower rate of profits, while investment is limited by capacity in a buoyant market so that the pressure on the rate of profit does not immediately lead to a slump. The classical theory of prices must therefore be compatible with various approaches to distribution; each has to be appropriate to the corresponding framework of institutions.

The theory of prices itself may have to be adapted to specific circumstances – for example, in order to take account of permanent obstacles to the equalization of the rates of profit in some industries. This is a special aspect of the forces that cause deviations of market prices from prices of production. It is not difficult to introduce differentials between profit rates in the system.

However, we are interested here in the various contexts in which the pure Sraffa theory of prices of production holds, and not in variants of the theory itself. One may then ask which mechanisms cause the uniformity of the rate of profit, that is, which mechanisms cause market prices to oscillate around prices of production (Schefold, 1981). As we have seen, 'supply and demand' (as derived from preferences of individuals) explain neither the composition of output nor distribution according to the classical approach, but the phrase still provides the best catchword for summarizing the diverse circumstances that cause market prices to deviate from, and approach to, prices of production.

The causes of divergences are various (e.g. shortfall of supply because of bad harvests, excess supply because of overproduction, changes in demand for a commodity in consequence of repercussions from other markets, etc.). But the reason for the 'gravitation' of market prices towards prices of production (Smith [1776] 1976) is essentially only one: the movements of capital equalize rates of profit, which diverge from the normal rate of profit because of oscillations in demand and supply whenever there are no obstacles to the free movement of capital. (Such movements of capital may take various forms and include real and financial transfers. The movements may be inhibited by barriers both to entry and to exit – Semmler, 1982.)

In modern industry, prices are frequently set at levels such that an average rate of profit is earned under normal conditions. This causes capacity used to fluctuate around the normal level while prices are fixed. 'Normal' levels of activity then correspond to 'normal' prices or 'prices of production', and the deviation of capacity utilization from the normal level corresponds to that of market prices from normal prices.

Great traditional causes for fluctuations – such as bad harvests, wars, changes of fashion – still exist, but they have to be supplemented by endogenous economic factors, speculation in particular. They were only cursorily analysed by the classical economists because their discussion seemed to belong not to the core of pure theory but to applied economics, if not to economic history.[1]

We can thus see that the theory of 'natural prices' or – as it is better to call them – prices of production remains topical, although the mechanisms of 'supply and demand' and the forces of competition may have changed as much as the relations governing distribution since the time of the classicals.

Note:

1 Hence, in horses, or wherever it is impossible to equate the supply abruptly with an altered state of the demand, large elongations occur, this way or that, between the oscillating market price (reflecting the cost adfected by the quantity) and the steady central price, or natural price (reflecting the cost only, without regard to quantity). ... As to the manufactured article, there is so little reason for supplying it in any variable ratio, and shoemakers are notoriously such philosophic men, and the demand of the public is so equable, that no man buys shoes or boots at any other than the steady natural price.

(de Quincey [1844], 1970, p. 205)

10   The Problem of Value with Joint Production in a Classical Perspective

We now turn to joint production. Here we encounter many paradoxes. The first is that joint production is – and seems to have always been – a ubiquitous phenomenon of human production: wool and mutton, coke and gas, electric power and hot vapour. Yet the theory of value traditionally focuses on the single-product system, and more so in classical than in neoclassical theory. As a matter of fact, joint production could not play a significant role in the theory of the classicals, as one can see if one analyses their method carefully. The omission of joint production can be traced back to the origin of the classical theory of value. The basic idea of natural price preceded classical theory in the form of the notion of 'just price'. This expression meant at first – from Plato down to the Middle Ages – the postulate that the prices of any commodity should be uniform in a general, accessible market and not dependent on individual, private haggling. Later, the requirement was added that the formation of the just price should be founded on some understandable law (e.g. *labores et expensae* in St Thomas). In attempting to find a clearer concept, Adam Smith hesitated between an 'adding-up theory' of the components of price (wages, profits and rents according to 'natural rates') and a determination in terms of labour values. Ricardo, not knowing matrix algebra, had to start from labour values in order to show that prices can be calculated objectively, given technical methods of production, and that changes in distribution lead only to a modification, not to the overthrow, of the labour theory of value.

Now it was a matter of course in either case (Smith and Ricardo) that the value of a commodity could be ascertained only if the proportions of labour, materials and land that went into it, could be identified. Otherwise Smith could not add up the natural prices of the components and Ricardo could not add up the living labour expended and the labour congealed in the materials (land was free at the margin of cultivation). This procedure could not be applied if several commodities were the joint output of any work. And indeed, in the examples usually given by the classical authors, processes of production are visualized as single-product processes even in cases where we nowadays emphasize the existence of joint costs: the bow used to shoot a deer may also be used to shoot a fox, the saw used to fell a tree may be used to make a boat, etc. The production of wheat is linked to the production of other crops through field rotation. In almost all cases (see Kurz, 1980/1), the joint products that are obviously there and can be turned into commodities were ignored by the classical authors, and the corresponding processes were treated as single-product processes.

The structure of the theory and its analytic tools (the early forms of the labour theory of value) imposed a simplified view of economic reality. In spite of the many concrete examples of joint production, classical authors assumed single-product industries in the main theoretical parts of their works.

Marx explicitly attached a political and economic meaning to the analytic principle of starting from labour values. Production was the 'work process' in which the worker uses his 'tools' to produce an artefact according to a 'conscious plan'. The 'subsumption' of the 'work process' under capitalist conditions had a 'formal' aspect: the product became a 'commodity', the 'worker' was 'exploited', the process of 'value formation' became a process of 'surplus value formation'. There was also a 'real' aspect: the 'work process' itself was transformed, the division of labour increased, the 'tool' was replaced by the 'machine' (Marx, [1890] 1954, vol. I, chapters 5, 12 and 13).

I believe that the Marxian conceptualization of the work process and of the process of value formation (not of surplus value formation, of course) was an adequate expression of classical views that were held generally, but – and this is what matters for us here – it clearly focuses on single-product processes. The worker creates one particular product according to his (or the capitalist's) 'conscious plan', and the labour expended is congealed in the product as value in addition to the labour embodied in the raw material. Hence, when Marx did treat the problem of joint production in vol. III of *Das Kapital*, he distinguished in effect a main product and wastes (which he called 'excretions of production' – note the biological analogy! (Marx, vol. III, 1972, p. 110)). Wastes were sold to contribute additional profits, but Marx was able to assign neither labour values nor prices of production to them because a work process directed at the simultaneous creation of two commodities of equal importance was incompatible with his definition of the work process.

Marx saw this narrow and particular interpretation of the work process, which fits the simple form of the labour theory of value, as the conception of the work process in general. He regarded work as a purposive, goal-oriented activity, and subsumed the artistic, creative work process under it, in conformity with the view of artistic production prevailing between the Renaissance and the nineteenth century.[1]

The Marxian view of work, which may be characterized as one of man as a planning animal (individually and coordinated through the market or collectively), not only represents a widely held ideology but corresponds also in some sense to modern facts. Planning consists essentially in mentally isolating a problem by singling out both a purpose and the domain to be operated on. The plan works if the isolation is feasible, as in a laboratory experiment: if the air disturbs the experimental dropping of balls to test the law of gravity, the experiment is repeated in a vacuum. Economic production does not take place in a vacuum, yet problems are solved as if they could be treated in isolation: people are to be transported from A to B, hence bridges are built and tunnels cut without much regard for the landscape or ecological habitats.

This is 'the problem of the environment' (Schefold, 1985d), but it is also 'the problem of joint production'. Whereas all materials are recycled in the biosphere, so that the excretions of one species are food to others, human production results in both goods to be sold as commodities and wastes, because we do not govern the entire process of reproduction of the biosphere but only the part within which the planned process of production takes place (Marx therefore deplored the fact that the Londoners discharged their excretions into the Thames instead of using them as fertilizer).

We can act according to plans only if we mentally isolate the domain within which the plan is to be executed. If we take 'external effects' into account, we simply admit that we should enlarge the domain; but it always remains limited, whereas nature is the unbounded whole around us.

The classical view of work as a plan was thus a realistic, but simplified, representation of what we do. It was simplified because planning may encompass multiple production of selected goods. We can very well plan to raise sheep and to produce both wool and mutton and not just to slaughter sheep in order to produce mutton. But planning, be it by capitalists or bureaucrats, remains based on the singling out of production processes with (possibly) multiple products and complex domains; it remains something essentially different from an adaptive process of biological growth or from fulfilment of a tradition as in the case of the life of a clan where it is not meaningful to assign specific groups of people to specific products, so that it is not possible to identify separate industries, their products and their workers.

To summarize: joint production of *goods* is a manifestation of the fact that the scope and domain of purposive activity cannot always be isolated at will. Joint production of *commodities* proves that it may pay to enlarge the scope and domain by means of multiple production. External effects are often due to the fact that the joint production of goods and commodities is not planned with sufficient regard for all waste products, so that some of them are harmful and are taken up neither by the economy nor by the biosphere. A list of the waste products of a process may be part of a plan or of a 'book of blueprints', but the list and the 'book' are hardly ever exhaustive.

A historical perspective is implied in this, albeit somewhat speculatively. Planning limits, and allows the separation of, individual processes. The social process fuses into one in the case of primitive communities completely ruled by tradition – one might say that all products are then jointly produced in one process. The genesis of commodity production must logically be associated with single-commodity production. But it is clear that joint production plays an important role under capitalism, and it is plausible that this role has on the whole increased since the industrial revolution, for it appears to be characteristic of the movement of capitalism that first a specific market is entered (e.g. for specific textiles) and only later are outlets for diversification or for selling byproducts found. The organic connection between the artefacts of pre-capitalist modes of production must already have been replaced by commercial and mechanical forms of social integration at the stage of single-product commodity production.

The problem for classical theory (addressed by Marx in the *Grundrisse* – [1857/8] 1953) is to explain how a purely commercial integration of society remains possible with joint production. There are clearly limits to such integration. It suffices to refer here to the procurement of public goods which, if indispensable to production, are joint costs for all processes and provided for by the state. The expansion of the state as a producer of public goods not only reduces the relative importance of the commodity-producing sector, it also means that an increasing share of the costs of production in the wider sense cannot be attributed to specific products and obliges the rationality of commodity production to be transcended as a principle of organization.

Socialism might have meant the extension of the state as a producer of public goods that are so closely related to each other that it was not possible to single out planned activities for their production, as in the case of the primitive community ruled by tradition. But the working mechanism of this kind of socialism on an advanced technological basis has remained obscure, and socialism has in fact almost always been interpreted as the centralization of the task of planning separable activities with separately identifiable goals and a limited number of interdependencies, which were – in principle – known. It should not have – but did – come as a surprise that such a system could – in most cases with greater efficiency – also be regulated by the market.

This broad historical perspective represents my personal view and cannot be expanded here. The story of joint production as part of the history of economic analysis is simpler. As we have seen, the labour theory of value represented a straightforward expression of the classical view of work and production as a set of individually planned processes coordinated through the market. This view conflicted with the fact of joint production even in the narrow sense of joint production of commodities, for it is at once obvious that joint commodity production is not easily explained in terms of a verbally, not mathematically, formulated labour theory of value. If inputs have been bought at 'just' prices, how is the value of the output to be divided among two joint products, such as the traditional wool and mutton? The problem is particularly grave if the products serve as inputs to different other processes – if the value of one basic is indeterminate, those of all other basics will be as well.

For the sake of completeness it must be stressed that the classicals dealt at length with two very special kinds of joint product without, in general, regarding them as such: land, which leaves a process of production in the same condition as it enters it and which has its price determined as a capitalization of the rent; and fixed capital or 'machinery', which leaves the process of production partly used up – the point is to derive the depreciation as the difference between the price of the machine entering the process and that of the machine leaving it in value terms. Even if the classicals proposed (not completely successful) methods to calculate rents and depreciation, there seemed to be no way to explain the relative prices of two joint products resulting from splitting a material in keeping with the logic of labour values. Occasional references to joint production of commodities other than land and fixed capital by Smith and Marx (Kurz, 1986) as mentioned above did not and could not lead to a systematic treatment. J. S. Mill, ([1848] 1970, III, xvi, 1) openly admitted that the classical method (in his case based on costs of production) could not determine the relative prices of joint products.

The neoclassicals seized this opportunity to prove the inevitability of having recourse to supply and demand. Jevons ([1871] 1970, pp. 208–12) made a successful argument for his own theory out of the indeterminacy of the values of joint products according to the old classical approach. Marshall ([1920] 1966, pp. 321–41 and App. Note xxi, p. 703) introduced demand to obtain as many equations as there were prices to be determined. But Marx had – although this was not known – treated joint production in some instances as a contradiction within capitalism, hence as a cause of the capitalist system's increasing difficulty in handling growing forces of production according to the 'law of value'.

Every economist knows that there is indeed much arbitrariness in accounting for depreciation or in the prices set for different derivatives from crude oil. Of course, competition always settles the matter somehow, but whereas it was easy – as de Quincey knew (see note to section I.9) – to predict the value of shoes produced by a shoemaker in the nineteenth century, it is very difficult to predict on the basis of cost calculations how a modern refinery will recover its costs by setting administrated prices for different refined products. Its rate of return for all its processes taken together can in general not deviate much from the rate of profit of the economy, but this observation does not explain how the relative prices of its individual products are set. Is this therefore another area where history must (as in the case of distribution) supplement theory because it is open-ended? The example of public goods as a form of joint social costs proves that there are cases of indeterminacy of possibly growing historical importance, but Sraffa has shown that there is a solution to the problem of the evaluation of joint products that does not require any explicit reference to subjective elements of demand.

Note:

1 This is not the place to enter into a discussion of the Marxian view of human creation, which will remain the subject of important debates (see section II.20b). But just in order to see how peculiar this is, it is instructive to indicate briefly that this view of the work process is not tenable outside specific historical circumstances. For instance, one misses the point if one describes the so-called communal work process in primitive societies in these terms; production based on custom cannot be subdivided into separate work processes each performed according to a specific plan. Nor is there a plan for the execution of social activity as a whole. What appears as a division of labour between men and women, older and younger generation, uncles and parents, in the production of clan houses or in religious ceremonies, makes each member of the community, according to his or her status, directly dependent on the collaboration of every other, and the things produced are part of an organic whole. The clan house cannot be built without the collaboration of all, it must not be built if the appropriate ceremonies do not take place, they in turn require the preparation of all kinds of food, ornaments, etc. Yet there is no planning authority. The organizing principle for this division of labour is neither plan nor market, but tradition. It may result in complicated structures (e.g. gift exchange; see Gregory, 1982), but its objective purpose is neither increased productivity of labour (as under capitalism according to Smith and Marx), nor the improvement of the arts (as, according to Plato, Xenophon and Aristotle) in classical antiquity, but social integration: the clan house cannot be built with everybody participating according to his or her specific role or status unless each member of the clan (which may be dispersed for other activities such as hunting) is there. The task of building results neither from individual nor from collective plans to transform the environment – as when a new factory is built today – but from plans to reproduce the housing of the clan in the place to which it belongs as part of a larger, embracing whole where one is in communication with residing spirits of the ancestors, even with trees and flowers. The building of the house, then, is not so much work in the Marxian or modern sense of the execution of an individual or collective work to realize a preconceived plan; rather it represents the fulfilment of a ceremonial function. Similarly, it seems problematic to reduce the organic harmony of medieval cathedrals merely to the effect of excellent individual or collective planning. Although there were celebrated architects, there must also have been the peculiar 'spirit', that so much fascinated German economists of the nineteenth and early twentieth centuries.

Elements of tradition are present everywhere even in modern society, but no one doubts that they do not constitute the main overall coordinating principle of modern capitalist, socialist or mixed economies.

11 The Fundamental Principle of the Determination of Prices with Joint Production

It is one of Sraffa's major discoveries (perhaps his greatest) that joint production is no obstacle to the determination of prices of production in the classical tradition if certain conditions are met. The intuitive argument runs as follows. There are many more potential processes of production than actual ones. A machine that is usually kept for ten years might be kept for more if it paid to repair it, and it might possibly be kept for less than ten years if wages for repairmen were higher.[1] Sheep can be slaughtered earlier or later and the proportion of wool to mutton can thus be altered; the joint production of heat and electricity can be achieved by means of nuclear power or coal etc. Even the joint products of chemical processes can often be produced by several methods by starting from different basic substances.

However, not all goods are turned into commodities. In so far as old machines and waste goods are costly to remove, they are to be counted as inputs, but many wastes are simply discharged into the environment and thus 'overproduced' and 'free' (these wastes are a disgraceful instance of joint production of goods in the wider sense mentioned above).

In order to simplify, I neglect overproduction in what follows. Any net output composed of n commodities in given quantities will then be produced by n processes. On the one hand, there will be more than n processes potentially available for the production of n commodities, as we have seen. If there is some variability of the returns to scale (constant returns may, but need not, be assumed in Sraffa's theory), at least n processes will in general be needed to produce this given output in the stationary state (or in a state of growth with given and possibly different rates of expansion of different industries). On the other hand, if n such processes are given, they determine relative prices, given the rate of profit, in the same way as they are determined in a single-product system:

$$(1 + r)\mathbf{Ap} + w\mathbf{l} = \mathbf{Bp};$$

and there is no room for more than n processes, because otherwise prices would be overdetermined. (Formally, $\mathbf{B}$ is a square output matrix, and the system is in a self-replacing state with $\mathbf{e(B - A)} \geqslant \mathbf{o}$).

This result constitutes the fundamental principle in the determination of prices with joint production. We get as many processes of production that are actually used as there are commodities actually produced, sold at positive prices and used to be consumed or used in production. The value of the products sold in each process must be equal to their joint cost of production (including profits) so that each process corresponds to one price equation.

Many conceivable economic constellations can lead to this outcome, and they can be formalized on the basis of various assumptions (constant or variable returns, inelastic demand etc.; see e.g. Schefold, 1980). The neoclassicals present an approach that aims at least conceptually at a simultaneous solution of the problems of joint production of goods both in the wider (environment) and in the narrower (joint production of commodities) sense: *all* conceivable processes with all their potential interrelations and – if uncertainty is to be taken into account – all states of nature (Debreu, [1959] 1971) are assumed to be known and given. Prices (as determined by technological conditions and utility) allow the selection of the processes in actual use that take account of the environmental constraint. Transaction costs, in particular costs of information, and possibly some other effects are then invoked to explain the differences between reality and this harmonious picture.

Many criticisms, such as the neglect of increasing returns, have been advanced against the modern general neoclassical equilibrium. One, which is particularly relevant in our context, is only rarely mentioned: it is an essential imperfection of our knowledge that we cannot enumerate the states of nature; the very description of nature in analogy to well-defined engineering technologies is a mistake in view of the objective indeterminacy of very complex systems. The 'goods' and 'processes' operated by 'nature' cannot be represented as a countable set of discrete activities. If they could, many of the most dangerous environmental catastrophes could never have arisen.

Neoclassical theory formalizes the subject of economic activity – or of work, as Marx would have said – so that planning as the achievement of specific goals in isolated domains appears to be possible collectively and individually. It is then quickly admitted that collective planning requires so much information that it is preferable to decentralize the process and to leave it to the market. It is forgotten – or not made explicit in the theory – that the theoretical representation of the activities may itself be misleading.

It might seem that Sraffa's representation of economic activity is similar to that of neoclassical theory, but the point is that he does not attempt to formalize the economic development by which processes or techniques and commodities are selected. The condition of an identity of the number of processes and commodities is simply one of economic consistency. It follows from the uniformity of prices and the rate of profit on the one hand and the necessity of producing a given output on the other. No explicit assumption is made as to whether the activities are not harmful to the environment or optimal in any other sense. They are there because they have been adopted in the working of the economy.

The general equations are the same as those for a single-product system, except that the identity matrix as the output matrix of the single-product system has been replaced by a square matrix $\mathbf{B}$, where b_i^j denotes the quantity of commodity j produced in process i. We assume here that no column and no row of $\mathbf{B}$ vanishes. If m is the number of known processes, n the number of existing commodities, and $m > n$, it is clear that more than one such system could be formed to produce the required output. Which system will turn out to be economically relevant? It is here that optimality can, but need not, be brought into the picture. The relevant criterion to be considered in pure theory is that of profit maximization.

If it were true that each of the potential systems behaved like a basic single-product system, everything would be simple. We could analyse prices for each system in terms of its standard commodity for all rates of profit between zero and the maximum rate of profit by reducing prices to dated quantities of labour. The system that yielded the highest real wage in any standard common to all systems at any given rate of profit would be preferable. More than n methods of production would be compatible at switchpoints where the wage curves of different systems intersected.

If joint-production systems behaved like single-product systems, prices of production would thus be fully determined (given the rate of profit), which implies that any producer would then get to know in the market how his cost of production (including normal profits) was divided between his joint products. Labour values would be similarly determined.

Now it is a fact that a great deal of the literature on business administration is very much concerned with the alleged arbitrariness of setting prices in the presence of joint production. The accountants give many rules (none of which is thought to be completely satisfactory) to explain how joint costs in an enterprise can be ascribed to various joint products or how relative prices of joint products should be set if costs are given. It is fascinating (and should be of great interest to theorists of business administration!) that Sraffa has found a way to determine prices of joint products unequivocally according to a compelling economic logic, provided some conditions are met. In Part II of this book we shall be concerned with showing how exactly prices are determined in various types of joint-production Sraffa systems and, in particular, how they are affected by changes in distribution.

But it may be useful to ask at the very beginning why the difficulties in the setting of prices of joint products arise and have, as it appears, not all definitely been solved with the appearance of Sraffa's book. We shall see that not all of Sraffa's joint-production systems possess economically meaningful solutions. However, satisfactory assumptions can be formulated to ensure such solutions in many important cases so that Sraffa's fundamental principle of price determination is vindicated – though not completely.

It may be the case that the existence of pathological solutions is in part due to the structural complexity of joint-production systems, which we are far from having understood fully. However, I believe that the greater part of the cases encountered in reality where a proper rule for setting the price cannot be found are due to an imperfect working of the mechanism of competition and are, to that extent, not fundamentally different from imperfections in the single-product case. But it is possibly the complexity of joint production that leads to a more frequent occurrence of such cases. Consider a few examples (a more advanced treatment is given in Schefold, 1985b):

(a)   Too few processes are operating to determine the relative price of joint products. Two byproducts in the production of gas from coal – say tar and coke – have been discovered. Their relative price will then be determined as soon as either a second process is found that produces both in different proportions or they are revealed as substitutes of two commodities that are already being produced so that the relative price of the latter codetermines the relative price of the former. These discoveries take time to materialize.

(b)   Too many processes may be operating. This example may also happen with single production. For example, electricity is produced by means of two different methods, say coal-fired and nuclear power stations. One method, say the latter, will then yield a rate of profit above the average. The surplus profit may lead to an elimination of one process (here the former) or to the formation of a rent (say, of uranium producers). Or we may get a differentiation of the product, and hence two commodities with two different prices (e.g. electricity produced at night 'or during daytime). The transitions will again take time.

(c) If a number of commodities, say chemical byproducts, are obtained in a number of processes, the scale of which is mainly determined by the production of other commodities, i.e. by independent circumstances, it may be difficult to adjust outputs and prices in a competitive process so as to achieve a uniform rate of profit.

In the single-product case, the stability of competitive processes is easily confirmed which led from arbitrary initial prices to 'Sraffa' prices with a uniform rate of profit, at least in some cases such as that of a predetermined uniform rate of profit on market prices, according to the self-explanatory formula

$$\hat{\mathbf{p}}_{t+1} = (1 + r)\mathbf{A}\hat{\mathbf{p}}_t + \mathbf{l}, \qquad \hat{\mathbf{p}}_t = \mathbf{p}_t/w_t, \qquad t = 0, 1, 2 \dots .$$

But the convergence of such a process is not assured in the case of joint production, even if the number of processes is already equal to that of commodities, and the conditions under which divergence occurs are related to (though not identical with) those under which there occur counter-intuitive price movements as a function of the rate of profit. These, in turn, are related to, but not identical with, conditions under which the criterion of profit maximization does not give an unambiguous answer to the 'best' combination of processes.

To discuss all this fully is beyond the scope of the present book, but the reader who will perhaps not be completely satisfied with the limitations of the analysis that are shown to exist in the essay 'Mr Sraffa on Joint Production' (Part II) is entitled to know my conclusions. Sraffa's discovery that prices of joint production can, after all, be determined in a system standing in the classical tradition remains startling, but his explicit or implicit assumptions may in reality on occasion not be fulfilled, in that there are not enough or too many processes to determine the prices of all commodities or there may be obstacles in the very structure of production that prevent the competitive mechanism from establishing the 'correct' prices as averages. As a consequence, a strong element of indeterminacy comes in after all. The theory of prices is not as open-ended with respect to joint production as it is with respect to distribution, but it does seem to leave open an area of indeterminacy where the alternatives of business strategies have to be explained in terms of theories of a different kind and where the political character of price setting has to be regarded as inevitable from the point of view of classical theory in its present state. Not all administered prices are arbitrary by comparison with the rule by prices of production.

So-called full-cost prices, for instance, may simply be prices of production calculated with such a mark-up on direct costs that — taking an average over a relatively long period of fluctuations in capacity utilization — average costs are covered with a profit according to the uniform general rate. But sometimes the structure of joint production may be so complex that there is no way of knowing the 'true' rate of profit and hence the price of production.

Note:

1   It must be pointed out, however, that a lower wage in the economy as a whole does not necessarily lead to an increase in the economic life of machines, since a return of the same pattern of lifetimes at different levels of distribution is possible in analogy with reswitching. See Schefold (1978a).

12   The Main Questions to be Answered and the Limits of the Answers Given in this Book

Having tried to give a general idea of the importance of joint production in a much neglected broader setting, I now want to provide a more direct introduction to Part II, which centres around more formal aspects.

Joint-production systems are shown below to have properties that are different from those of single-product systems in Sraffa's own exposition, but the approach does not lead to a radical departure from the argument presented in the first part of Sraffa's book. This is because some additional and rather restrictive assumptions are introduced. These assumptions are easily overlooked, as can be seen by consulting the relevant literature. While the first part of Sraffa's 'Production of Commodities by Means of Commodities' received quite considerable attention when the book was first published, the second passed almost unnoticed for some time. The third part on 'Switching of Techniques' stood at the centre of the most interesting controversy on economic theory of the 1960s, but the discussion was again focused on single-product industries. The first exception to this pattern was Manara's article on 'Il modello di Piero Sraffa per la produzione congiunta di merci a mezzo di merci' in the Italian journal *L'industria*, which appeared in 1968. The author, apart from giving an elegant mathematical formulation for the distinction between basics and non-basics in the case of joint production, pointed to two of the difficulties of joint-production systems: namely the likelihood of negative prices being associated with some labour vectors at some rates of profit in almost any joint-production system and the non-existence of the maximum rate of profit and the standard commodity in certain cases. It was not said whether these were to be considered normal or exceptional. Manara, a mathematician, left the tasks of analysis and interpretation of the 'anomalies' to the economists. Manara failed to note that Sraffa had simply and explicitly assumed that positive prices and a real standard commodity exist (PCMC, sec. 50) – but then Sraffa had failed to indicate under what conditions these assumptions would be fulfilled.

In basic single-product systems, the given surplus of the economy can be shown *always* to be divided between workers and capitalists for all rates of profit between zero and a *finite* maximum rate, provided the condition of self-replacement is fulfilled. Prices are *positive* and the method of production can remain the same at all rates of profit. The standard commodity *always* exists and proves the existence of a linear trade-off.

In order to show that something similar to this picture holds even for joint-production systems, Sraffa assumes that one starts from a given rate of profit at which prices are positive. If the rate of profit is varied in the now-familiar thought experiment, prices will change, but some may turn negative. Sraffa supposes that in this case another method of production is brought in to replace one of those already in existence in such a way that the resulting system will have positive prices. However, at this point an inconsistency not noted by Manara creeps into Sraffa's argument. The switch in the method of production is advantageous if it raises the real wage rate in terms of *any* standard at the given rate of profit. This will be the case for all standards if (as Sraffa assumes in a footnote in his discussion of 'switching' in joint-production systems in his section 96) *all* prices rise monotonically with the rate of profit in terms of labour commanded (as they do in single-product systems). But if a price turns negative before the maximum rate of profit (if that exists) is reached, at least one price in terms of labour commanded does not rise monotonically with the rate of profit. Hence Sraffa should not (as he does) refer to switches in methods of production (according to his own rule for 'switching') in order to be saved from negative prices.

As has been indicated already, Sraffa's theory of joint production cannot be completely rescued from these objections, but my essay on joint production – begun in 1969 and completed in 1970 (with later amendments mentioned in the Preface) – shows that the theory remains fully or partly applicable in important domains. Those readers who do not wish or do not have the time to study the argument in a mathematical exposition are advised to turn to the sections on graphic techniques (sections II.10 and II.11) which have been extended so that they may serve as an outline of most of the argument, but I regard it as more pedagogical to attack the main text first.

Ultimately, the theory of joint production should help to provide conceptual tools to analyse value and prices in long-period equilibria of a modern economy along classical and Keynesian lines. It will, I hope, be seen that insights can be gained not only regarding the properties and the coherence of the logical structure of the theory, but also with a view towards its application, even if not much space will be given to illustrations of possible applications at lower levels of abstraction. For instance, I discuss the formal rules for depreciation derived from the treatment of fixed capital as a joint product (section II.15). It turns out that, in the special case of constant efficiency, depreciation must be progressive with a machine of constant efficiency. Constant quotas for amortization imply rising quotas for depreciation, because the financial charge (proportional to the value of the machine) will decline with its age. Now it is known that depreciation is often regressive, the reasons being that firms wish to secure tax advantages and that depreciation is also influenced (accelerated) by technical progress. It has not been possible to dedicate much room in the text to supplementary explanations of this kind; the reader will have to find them for himself.

Similarly, only little space has been devoted to the detailed confrontation with neoclassical theory. Sraffa's approach to joint production provides a very general framework such that a large variety of the objects of neoclassical theorems and rules are subsumed in the formal apparatus, which may therefore be used to assess their validity. To take again fixed capital: the equality between the cost of production of a machine and its future expected returns in long-run equilibrium is introduced as an obvious necessary condition − in a sense, as an axiom − in the conventional theory. In Sraffa it appears as a theorem to be derived, founded upon the deeper axiomatic structure of joint production.

Or consider the pricing of joint products. The conventional rule is that the relative prices of two joint products are determined by the rate of transformation. Here, this turns out to be a special case of Sraffa's approach. If we suppose constant returns in the production of wool and mutton (both treated as pure consumption goods), there may be two processes − old sheep, say, producing mainly wool over their lifetime, and young sheep producing mutton. We take distribution and hence costs of raw materials and labour as given, including profits, and we denote them by k_1, k_2 for the two processes. They produce quantities w_1, w_2 of wool at price p_w, and amounts m_1, m_2 respectively of mutton at price p_m.

The equations therefore are:

$$k_1 = w_1 p_w + m_1 p_m$$
$$k_2 = w_2 p_w + m_2 p_m;$$

they are similar to equations obtained for differential rent in sections II.19a and II.20. Now, using the assumption that both products are non-basics and do not appear elsewhere in the equations, we may choose, for given distribution, activity levels such that $k_1 = k_2$, and costs can be eliminated. We obtain

$$\frac{p_m}{p_w} = \frac{w_2 - w_1}{m_1 - m_2}.$$

If neither process is to dominate the other, $m_1 > m_2$ must, at equal cost, imply $w_2 > w_1$, and this is exactly the condition for the positivity of the relative price p_m/p_w. This is clearly a rate of transformation. It measures the amount of wool gained in terms of the mutton lost in the transition from the mutton-intensive process 1 to the wool-intensive process 2.

The conventional condition of regarding the relative prices of joint products as determined by their rate of transformation is thus confirmed for a special case. Even the familiar demand condition is reflected in that the two processes will be operated side by side because the proportion in which the two commodities are demanded must lie in between the extremes of the proportions in which they are produced if either process runs in isolation.

But Sraffa's approach is more general and allows the relative prices to be determined even if returns are not constant and/or if the products are basic. In both cases, it will not be possible to eliminate 'costs' from the determination of the relative prices – indeed, if the commodities are basics, they are price-determining as well as price-determined.

Incidentally, the relative prices of two joint products of one process need be determined not through the use of another process that also produces them, though in different proportions, but through their being used elsewhere. If, for instance, a coal-fired power station produces both electricity and heat for district heating, the value of electricity may be regarded as determined, given the cost of operating the plant and the value of the heat, where the value of heat derives from the cost of the main alternative for providing heat, e.g. from the cost of heating by means of oil. This would be an application of the conventional principle of substitution: the value of the main product (electricity) is equal to the costs of production minus the value of the byproduct (heat), and the value of the byproduct is determined by the value of its closest substitute. But again, Sraffa's approach is more general in that the simple criterion of having as many processes as there are commodities will allow the determination of all of the prices in question according to one general rule, of which the conventional principle of substitution is a special case.

One might believe at first sight that the multiplicity of joint products leaves an indeterminacy in that there could not be enough processes to determine the unknowns. But one soon realizes that in reality many processes compete, and the question then becomes which combination of processes is to be chosen as being most profitable (Schefold, 1988; see also sections II.9b and II.9c). At least one determinate solution always exists.

The formal generality of the approach thus conceals the fact that the conventional rules for the determination of relative prices are here contained as special cases, and that they are objects of a criticism that is not always made explicit in the text below. For the task is to discuss not the special applications on their own terms, but the general theory of prices and distribution. The main difference between this and neoclassical theory is to be sought not in any particular principle, such as that yielding the correct formula for depreciation, but in the approach to distribution. While neoclassical economists use supply and demand to explain commodity and factor prices all in the same way, the classical theory has different principles for the formation of commodity prices and for the determination of the distribution of the surplus. It has to be demonstrated that, in this, a theoretical unity can be achieved nevertheless.

Part II therefore starts with the analysis of the most general joint-production systems and gradually introduces more special systems – for instance, those based on the distinction between basics and non-basics. Then, fixed capital and land are explained. Here, we again encounter special systems – for example, those using 'perennial machines' or 'exhaustible resources', but the emphasis is on distinctions related to classical theory, not on practical applications or neoclassical principles. Books treating either in relation to classical theory remain to be written. The final section (20b) concerns the asymmetry in the classical treatment of 'factors'; it is hoped that this, though written some time ago, will still be seen as useful both for a better understanding of the critique and for the representation of the essential traits of an alternative theory.

13 Summary of Results

If an even briefer summary of the chief results is demanded, it may be given as follows. The definition of the basic system turns out to be considerably more complicated in the case of joint production than in the case of single-product systems. However, the definition can be extended to all meaningful systems, although a uniqueness property does not apply to certain exceptions which are akin to one-commodity models in that relative prices are constant (or limited in their movements). Starting from a situation in which prices are positive in a given system in a self-replacing state, the rate of profit may be varied. A (small) class of joint-production systems share all properties of single-product systems ('all-productive systems'), but prices do not remain positive for most with 'large' variations of the rate of profit, and the wage curve does not fall monotonically in all standards. No basic system (including basic single-product systems) has positive prices at all positive rates of profit (including the range between the maximum rate of profit and infinity). Many systems have neither standard commodity nor maximum rate of profit. However, if the rate of profit is equal or superior to the rate of growth, it can be shown that it is almost always possible to delete one process from the system whenever a price turns negative so that the system consisting of the remaining processes overproduces the com- modity that had a negative price. It therefore ceases to be a commodity and there remains a square system with the number of commodities and processes reduced by one. Executing this (and similar) operations wherever necessary, one finds that prices are positive and that the wage in a given standard falls monotonically in the golden rule case as the rate of profit (greater than or equal to the rate of growth at constant returns to scale) rises from zero to a finite maximum. A standard commodity is associated with the system appearing at the maximum rate of profit, and that system is all-productive.

The essential difficulties referred to above do not arise in fixed-capital systems; their analysis therefore forms the central part of the argument. 'Correct' rules for depreciation and the equality of the cost of a machine with the return it generates follow from the treatment of machines as joint products. Finally, land is seen as a most peculiar case of joint production, even if only one product is grown on the land, but the most interesting complications arise in the presence of a multiplicity of agricultural products. One can distinguish rent at the 'extensive' and the 'intensive' margin. The former is analytically quite simple to deal with, but the latter very difficult. Possible applications, especially to the theory of urban rent (where the intensive margin plays a decisive role), are alluded to, and it is shown that the existence of rent enforces specialization of production as a most important consequence of the introduction of capitalism into agriculture. Specialization of land-use is thus engendered by rent, but also by mechanization.

The argument remains at an abstract level throughout. The basic task is humble: to show that the laws of value and distribution derived by Sraffa for single-product systems hold for joint production as well. The proof for this can – with important exceptions – be given, so that the partisan of Sraffian economics who is tired of mathematics and does not wish to enter the complications may be content and leave joint production at rest. But it will also be seen that concrete applications are found (mostly connected with the difficulties mentioned above!) that could as such be of interest both to the theoretical and the applied economist; it is not necessary to leave joint production to the accountants and business administrators.

My essay on joint production reprinted in Part II is in its substance today (1988) eighteen years old and only opens up this area of research. Sections II.9a, 9b, 9c, 11a, 18a, 18b, 19a, 20a and 20b lead up nearer to the present state of the art.

14 Notation and how to Get Started with Joint Production

The reader who wishes to avoid any mathematical presentation to the extent that this is at all possible in our context should study single-product industries (Part III) and, if he insists on joint production, Sraffa's own treatment of it in which the formal apparatus is minimized in a masterly and inimitable fashion. In contrast, the task set in Part II is to prove the verbal arguments about joint production with mathematical rigour. This leads sometimes to questions that an economist would normally not ask because they concern the formal structure of the model and the analytic consistency of definitions. The very beginning is therefore difficult.

After an exposition of basic concepts, it is asked which of several alternative definitions of a basic system is appropriate to joint production. It is shown – by means of a mathematical theorem that was developed specifically for this purpose – that the basic system according to Sraffa's definition has a property of mathematical uniqueness which is not obvious and which alone justifies the definition. The ordinary economist, of course, is usually not interested in such proofs until he gets mixed up with an ambiguous definition that results in a confused discussion. Here, patience is required because the concrete applications follow only at the end of Part II with the section on land (section II.20). An economist who is used to inductive presentations will find this logical ordering strenuous to take in, but he may be comforted first by the thought that a little exercise in mathematical discipline will do him good, second by more relaxing and illustrative sections which have been inserted, and third by any comparison with advanced neoclassical textbooks, which use some really sophisticated mathematical tools for which the mathematical economist who works on classical theory finds (much to his distress!) no economically relevant application.

A word on notation. I am ideologically committed to writing price vectors (columns) on the right, quantity vectors (rows) on the left of matrices – not because of the political connotation but because it seems more appropriate to emphasize the process of production as Sraffa does. In general, a vector with an inferior index is a row vector and one with a superior index a column vector. All other vectors are – with exceptions not leading to confusions – column vectors. The transpose of a vector $\mathbf{x}$ is denoted by $\mathbf{x}'$. A square matrix $\mathbf{A}$ with elements a_i^j, $i, j = 1, ..., n$, can thus be written as composed of its columns $\mathbf{a}^j$, $j = 1, ..., n$, or its rows $\mathbf{a}_i$, $i = 1, ..., n$:

$$\mathbf{A} = (\mathbf{a}^1, ..., \mathbf{a}^n) = \begin{bmatrix} \mathbf{a}_1 \\ \vdots \\ \mathbf{a}_n \end{bmatrix} = (a_i^j).$$

I have – with some exceptions – adopted the convention of using superior and inferior indices, which is standard in tensor analysis and which is – in my view – most appropriate for expressing duality relationships. I have not adopted the Einstein convention for summation as it is too unusual in economics, although it would fit perfectly. The vector

$$\mathbf{e} = (1, ..., 1)'$$

is the sum of all unit vectors $\mathbf{e}^i = (0, ..., 1, ..., 0)'$ and is conveniently used to express the summing-up of the columns of a matrix:

$$\mathbf{e}'\mathbf{A} = (\mathbf{e}'\mathbf{a}^1, ..., \mathbf{e}'\mathbf{a}^n) = \left(\sum_{i=1}^{n} a_i^j \right).$$

$$\mathbf{e} = \underbrace{(1, ..., 1)'}_{n}$$

is an n vector,

$$\mathbf{e}_{(m)} = \underbrace{(1, ..., 1)'}_{m}$$

the analogous m vector. $\mathbf{I}$ is the (n, n) unit matrix, $\mathbf{I}_{(m)}$ the (m, m) unit matrix.

In matrix (vector) inequalities, the sign $\mathbf{A} \geqslant \mathbf{B}$ means $a_i^j \geqslant b_i^j$ and the sign $\mathbf{A} \gneqq \mathbf{B}$ means $\mathbf{A} \geqslant \mathbf{B}$ and $a_i^j > b_i^j$ for some (i, j). $\mathbf{A} > \mathbf{B}$ means $a_i^j > b_i^j$ for all (i, j). $\mathbf{O}$ is a matrix, and $\mathbf{o}$ a vector of zeros.

PART II

Mr Sraffa on Joint Production

A   General Joint-Production Systems

1 The System

Mr Sraffa assumes that great numbers of production processes are
available for the production of n given commodities, that a rate of profit
is given, and that n of these processes (which together form a self-
reproducing system) have been chosen so that the 'prices of production'
(see PCMC, sec. 7) at this one given rate of profit exist, are unique and
are positive. He then considers *hypothetical* variations in the rate of
profit leading to *hypothetical* changes in the price system (changes in
'demand' that might ensue, if the movements were to be real, are
irrelevant in this context).

The equations are written as follows:

$$\mathbf{Bp} = (1 + r)\mathbf{Ap} + w\mathbf{l} \tag{1.1}$$

where $\mathbf{B} = (b_i^j)$, $\mathbf{A} = (a_i^j)$ are two non-negative (n, n) matrices for outputs
and inputs respectively. The inferior index i refers to the processes or
methods of production represented by the rows $\mathbf{a}_i, \mathbf{b}_i$ of $\mathbf{A}, \mathbf{B}$; while the
columns $\mathbf{a}^j, \mathbf{b}^j$ refer to the commodities as inputs and outputs. We
assume $\mathbf{a}_i \neq \mathbf{o}, \mathbf{b}_i \neq \mathbf{o}, i = 1, ..., n$ (every process has an input besides
labour and an output).

$\mathbf{l} = (l_1, ..., l_n)'$ denotes the vector of the labour inputs, r the rate of
profit, w the wage rate. As a convention, we fix $\mathbf{e}'\mathbf{l} = 1$ (total labour-time
expended equals one) and we assume $\mathbf{b}^j \neq \mathbf{o}$; $j = 1, ..., n$; so that we can
measure each good in terms of its total output: $\mathbf{e}'\mathbf{B} = \mathbf{e}'$.[1] The process of
production is symbolized by:

$$(\mathbf{a}_i, l_i) \rightarrow \mathbf{b}_i.$$

Assumptions

The most important general hypothesis we make is

$$\mathbf{e}'(\mathbf{B} - \mathbf{A}) = \mathbf{s}' \geqslant \mathbf{o}, \tag{A.1}$$

that is, $\mathbf{s}$, the vector of net products, shall be semi-positive, i.e. $\mathbf{A}, \mathbf{B}$, is a
system capable of *self-replacement*. The meaning of this condition is that
the economy must have a surplus; the question to be asked is: how is it

distributed? Neoclassical writers like to ignore the concept of surplus. In order to characterize systems of production that have economic meaning, they usually introduce the 'Hawkins–Simon Conditions', which are essentially equivalent to the existence of a surplus without having an independent economic interpretation. But that expedient works only for single-product systems; joint-production systems must be characterized by means of the criterion of self-replacement.

Second, we shall assume that $\mathbf{B} - \mathbf{A}$ is non-singular in the absence of land (for the treatment of land, see section II.19 below):

$$\det(\mathbf{B} - \mathbf{A}) \neq 0, \qquad (A.2)$$

because we assume that the n processes $[\mathbf{a}_i, \mathbf{b}_i]$ are linearly independent and because we must have

$$\mathrm{rk}\,[\mathbf{A}, \mathbf{B}] = \mathrm{rk}\,[\mathbf{A}, \mathbf{B} - \mathbf{A}] = n,$$

where 'rk' means rank and where $[\mathbf{A}, \mathbf{B}] = [\mathbf{a}^1, ..., \mathbf{a}^n, \mathbf{b}^1, ..., \mathbf{b}^n]$ is an $(n, 2n)$ matrix. This assumption is important and quite natural because one cannot (as in the case of single-product industries) distinguish methods by pointing to their respective products; methods are therefore defined to be different (as is clear especially in the case of constant returns to scale) if they are linearly independent.

But how is it possible to have as many processes as there are commodities, and why is production represented by means of linear processes in the first place? In order to answer these questions briefly, we have to anticipate later considerations and discuss the competitive process that forces us to transcend the formal method. An industry, as defined by the statisticians, like the oil industry produces in general many commodities by means of a great number of methods. It would seem that we then have one factory that produces several outputs with the possibility of continuous substitution. This might be interpreted as evidence of only one process (because the amortization of the factory represents an overhead) or of infinitely many because the outputs can be produced in varying proportions. A little reflection shows, however, that the existence of overheads does not preclude the representation of methods by means of several linearly independent equations, since the existence of overheads is not incompatible with the variation of the outputs produced by means of those overheads, raw materials and labour, and since each variation within the technically feasible range represents one process. If the variation through the substitution of outputs is not in itself discrete, the continuum of feasible processes can be approximated by a finite number of them.

Take, for instance, the case of thermal power stations for the production of electricity that are designed to use their waste heat for district heating. Part of the running costs and the amortization of the station add up to the overheads and may be considered as given. In general, one part of such overheads represents the amortization of a plant, which lasts several years; the plant is then formally to be treated like a machine in the Sraffa system (see section II.12 below). Other costs may be due to overhead labour. In the example, the share of electricity in energy delivered will be larger for some power stations than for others, so that the variation of the share leads to many, possibly a continuum of, conceivable processes. However, there will be room for the adoption of only two linearly independent processes if the assumptions about homogeneity of commodities and methods and the assumption about the uniformity of the rate of profit are strictly maintained and if the prices of inputs are given, since only two commodities appear as output: electricity of a certain tension, and heat (vapour) at a certain temperature and a given location. The existence of overheads does not therefore preclude the existence of a multiplicity of linearly independent processes.

Generally, there are more potential techniques than are actually used. There are at least small possibilities for continuous substitution in many cases, even in chemical processes, but it is theoretically preferable to represent the possibility of continuous substitution by means of a 'large' number of processes in a finite, discrete technology. The exclusive assumption of continuous substitution (which is, of course, not always realistic anyway) can be positively misleading, as I have shown elsewhere (see Schefold, 1976a). By contrast, the assumption of discrete technologies is appropriate for many practical cases and adequate as an approximation to deal with continuous substitution where it exists. Of these 'many' potential techniques that can thus safely be assumed to be there, only a few, namely as many as there are commodities, will actually be used, since prices would be overdetermined otherwise (see Schefold, 1978c, 1980, for more details).

Now it is a fact that 'too many' processes are sometimes found in reality because of product differentiation (e.g. temperature of heat delivered) and differing rates of profit. For the energy sector this is discussed in Schefold (1977) and for the appropriate concept of competition see Essay 5 in Part III. The point is that one can then always observe a competitive pressure to eliminate the overdeterminacy of 'too many' processes in actual use, either by increasing product differentiation (thus increasing the number of commodities to match that of processes) or by eliminating supernumerary processes and the quasi-rents or losses to which they give rise in the struggle for markets.

Frequently, 'too few' processes are observed in reality because the potential variations in output do not appear as different methods, realized by different firms, but are concealed in one and the same firm. Such a firm then seems to possess the power to fix relative prices of several outputs at will (or according to 'what the market will bear') within a range without attempting to realize a uniform rate of return. If several firms are involved and some competition rules, prices are occasionally fixed according to a uniform rate of profit, which does not, however, yield a unique determination of output prices since several outputs result from only one process. Economists therefore tend to believe that prices are 'administered arbitrarily', but I suppose that 'potential' techniques could be found in most cases that are responsible for the setting of prices according to the equations used here. In most cases, prices of some joint products are determined by prices of substitutes produced in quite different industries. This may again lead to the appearance of prices fixed arbitrarily, but, mathematically and economically, prices are then fixed 'behind the backs of the producers' by the equality of the number of linearly independent methods and of the number of commodities.

The theory of price movements in consequence of changes in the number of processes and commodities cannot be worked out here in any detail, but what has been said should suffice to indicate that, with joint production, there is a 'law of gravitation' that involves not only price differentials, profits and the amounts produced, but also the number of processes used, and that does not allow 'market prices' to deviate much from the 'prices of production' discussed here. The 'law of gravitation' is analogous to that which applies to single-product industries. Market conditions express the necessity of adapting the number of processes to that of commodities, or *vice versa*.

Clearly, according to the pure logic of the argument, 'counting of equations' is what matters here. By splitting up existing methods into their linearly independent components one can hope to obtain a number of equations sufficiently large to determine the prices of commodities. This splitting up must, on the other hand, be feasible by virtue of a second argument: whatever the nature of the returns to scale involved with variations in output, the commodities could not, except by chance, be produced in the proportion socially required if the number of processes was not as large as that of commodities. It will be necessary to return several times to these important considerations.

To summarize. We assume that in processes commodities are transformed into commodities by means of labour. The system of processes is self-replacing. We observed that the number of commodities is equal to the number of processes because we can see intuitively how competition must have this effect, but the point is that to *assume* this equality suffices to found the theory of prices with joint production.

Prices and their normalization

Starting from the rate of profit $r = r_0$ for which *positive* prices are – to begin with – simply supposed to exist, we can now write our equation (1.1) as

$$w[\mathbf{B} - (1 + r)\mathbf{A}]^{-1}\mathbf{l} = \mathbf{p}. \tag{1.2}$$

This is possible in an open neighbourhood of r_0 where

$$\det[\mathbf{B} - (1 + r)\mathbf{A}] \neq 0.$$

Equation (1.2) determines the relative prices uniquely for given r. They may be normalized in various ways, e.g. either simply by putting $w = 1$, which amounts to expressing prices in terms of the wage rate (labour commanded), or by equalizing a weighted sum of the prices to a given constant, say 1.

We define prices in terms of the wage rate as

$$\hat{\mathbf{p}}(r) = [\mathbf{B} - (1 + r)\mathbf{A}]^{-1}\mathbf{l}.$$

These prices are also called prices in terms of labour commanded (Smith) because $\hat{p}_i(r)$ indicates the amount of labour that can be purchased (commanded) by one unit of commodity i.

We define prices in terms of a given commodity standard $\mathbf{a}$ (where $\mathbf{a} = (a_1, ..., a_n)'$ denotes a vector of commodities) as

$$\mathbf{p}_a(r) = \frac{[\mathbf{B} - (1 + r)\mathbf{A}]^{-1}\mathbf{l}}{\mathbf{a}'\,[\mathbf{B} - (1 + r)\mathbf{A}]^{-1}\mathbf{l}} = \frac{\hat{\mathbf{p}}(r)}{\mathbf{a}'\hat{\mathbf{p}}(r)}.$$

Thus, the wage rate in the standard $\mathbf{a}$ is

$$w_a = \frac{1}{\mathbf{a}'\,[\mathbf{B} - (1 + r)\mathbf{A}]^{-1}\mathbf{l}} = \frac{1}{\mathbf{a}'\hat{\mathbf{p}}(r)};$$

conversely $\hat{\mathbf{p}} = \mathbf{p}_a/w_a = \mathbf{p}/w$, and we have

$$\hat{\mathbf{p}}(r) > \mathbf{o}, \ \mathbf{p}_a(r) > \mathbf{o}$$

with $\mathbf{a}'\mathbf{p}_a(r) = 1$ in a neighbourhood of r_0. The 'basket of goods', $\mathbf{a}$, may e.g. consist of only one good, say i, and may be represented by a unit vector $\mathbf{e}_i$. The sum of prices is formed by putting $\mathbf{a} = \mathbf{e}$ and is used to normalize prices in section II.10 below. Mr Sraffa's standard prices are obtained, if $\mathbf{a}$ equals the standard (net) product. w_a, the wage rate in standard $\mathbf{a}$, is also an indicator for the real wage, but a direct indicator only if the real wage is paid in the same standard $\mathbf{a}$, in which prices are measured. For, if the real wage is $\lambda\mathbf{a}$ ($\mathbf{a}$ is the 'basket of goods'; λ, a scalar factor, expresses the 'number' of 'baskets' per unit of labour), we get $w_a = \lambda\mathbf{a}'\mathbf{p}_a = \lambda$.

An actual payment of the real wage in standard $\mathbf{a}$ presupposes of course

$$\lambda\mathbf{a}' \leqslant \mathbf{s}' = \mathbf{e}'(\mathbf{B} - \mathbf{A}),$$

while the measurement of prices in this standard does not require any such assumption.

Decomposability and all-productive systems

If we want to be guided in our analysis by what we have learned in the case of single-product industries, we have first to extend the distinction between basic and non-basic products (see section I.6). By formal analogy we define:

DEFINITION

The matrices $\mathbf{A}, \mathbf{B}$ form an *indecomposable system*, if no permutation of rows and columns transforms $\mathbf{A}$ and $\mathbf{B}$ simultaneously into almost triangular matrices.

That is to say: The system $\mathbf{A}, \mathbf{B}$ is indecomposable, if and only if no permutation matrices $\mathbf{P}, \mathbf{Q}$ exist,[2] so that

$$\bar{\mathbf{A}} = \mathbf{PAQ} = \begin{bmatrix} \bar{\mathbf{A}}_1^1 & \mathbf{O} \\ \bar{\mathbf{A}}_2^1 & \bar{\mathbf{A}}_2^2 \end{bmatrix} \qquad \bar{\mathbf{B}} = \mathbf{PBQ} = \begin{bmatrix} \bar{\mathbf{B}}_1^1 & \mathbf{O} \\ \bar{\mathbf{B}}_2^1 & \bar{\mathbf{B}}_2^2 \end{bmatrix}$$

where $\bar{\mathbf{A}}_1^1$, $\bar{\mathbf{B}}_1^1$ are square matrices of the same order, say m.

In the single-product case one assumes without loss of generality that $\mathbf{Q} = \mathbf{P}' = \mathbf{P}^{-1}$ (so that single-product systems $(\mathbf{A}, \mathbf{I})$ are indecomposable, if and only if $\mathbf{A}$ is an indecomposable matrix). Self-replacing single-product systems can be shown to be basic in the sense that every commodity enters directly or indirectly the production of every other, if and only if $\mathbf{A}$ is indecomposable (a proof of this is sketched in Essay 6 in Part III). But this definition of basics, which Sraffa uses for single-product industries, is not applicable to joint production: in a decomposable system of the form shown here every commodity may enter the production of every other, if the relevant elements of $\bar{\mathbf{A}}_2^1$ and $\bar{\mathbf{B}}_2^1$ are positive.

Decomposability as defined here has a technical meaning. Let $\mathbf{A}, \mathbf{B}$ be decomposable. $\mathbf{A}, \mathbf{B}, \mathbf{B} - \mathbf{A}$, and $(\mathbf{B} - \mathbf{A})^{-1}$

$$= \begin{bmatrix} \mathbf{B}_1^1 - \mathbf{A}_1^1 & \mathbf{O} \\ \mathbf{B}_2^1 - \mathbf{A}_2^1 & \mathbf{B}_2^2 - \mathbf{A}_2^2 \end{bmatrix}^{-1}$$

$$= \begin{bmatrix} (\mathbf{B}_1^1 - \mathbf{A}_1^1)^{-1} & \mathbf{O} \\ -(\mathbf{B}_2^2 - \mathbf{A}_2^2)^{-1}(\mathbf{B}_2^1 - \mathbf{A}_2^1)(\mathbf{B}_1^1 - \mathbf{A}_1^1)^{-1} & (\mathbf{B}_2^2 - \mathbf{A}_2^2)^{-1} \end{bmatrix}$$

are then, taken together, almost triangular. $\mathbf{A}_1^1$, $\mathbf{B}_1^1$ form a group of m processes that appears to be independent of the rest of the economy. Prices of this part of the decomposed system can be calculated independently of the other equations. If $\mathbf{l}_1$ is the labour vector and $\mathbf{p}_1$ the price vector of the decomposed system, we have

$$(1 + r)\mathbf{A}_1^1\mathbf{p}_1 + w\mathbf{l}_1 = \mathbf{B}_1^1\mathbf{p}_1.$$

However, $(\mathbf{A}_1^1, \mathbf{B}_1^1)$ is in fact a self-reproducing system only if

$$\mathbf{e}'_{(m)}(\mathbf{B}_1^1 - \mathbf{A}_1^1) \geqslant \mathbf{o}.$$

It is clear that $\mathbf{e}'_{(m)}(\mathbf{B}_1^1 - \mathbf{A}_1^1) \geqslant \mathbf{o}$ follows from $\mathbf{e}'(\mathbf{B} - \mathbf{A}) \geqslant \mathbf{o}$, if $\mathbf{B} = \mathbf{I}$, i.e. if $(\mathbf{A}, \mathbf{B})$ is a single-product system. This part of the decomposed system is therefore truly independent of the other processes only if it is assumed that it is by itself self-replacing – and this condition is automatically fulfilled only in single-product systems.

The economic meaning of the decomposition will, among other things, depend on whether wage goods are part of the decomposed part of the system so that the remaining processes produce luxury goods for the consumption of capitalists or whether another separation has been made. The point of the decomposition is at any rate to isolate the core of the economic system where distribution and prices are determined – starting, not as in neoclassical theory from supply of and demand for consumption goods and factors, but from the conditions of reproduction of the core of the economic system.

Decomposability is therefore illustrated best if we assume constant returns to scale and consider variations of production.

We assumed the system to be given in conditions of self-replacement such that $e'(B - A) = s' \geqslant o$. With constant returns to scale we may interpret the summation vector e as the vector of activity levels of the system in the state in which it was given originally with surplus s. We may then *change* the activity levels to some $q \geqslant o$ such that a desired new surplus c is produced:

$$c' = q'(B - A).$$

Taking $c \geqslant o$ as given, c is said to be producible, if $c'(B - A)^{-1} \geqslant o$, for then

$$q' = c'(B - A)^{-1} \geqslant o.$$

Clearly, joint-production systems are decomposable, if and only if an index $k < n$ exists so that (after permutations) for all $q' = (q_1, ..., q_k, o, ..., o)$ it follows

$$c' = q'(B - A) = (c_1, ..., c_k, 0, ..., 0).$$

We shall say that a system is *completely decomposable* if it is decomposable with $A_2^1 = B_2^1 = O$. It then consists of two completely disconnected parts with no exchange of commodities for the purpose of production. Complete decomposability is economically not meaningful and will be ruled out by assumption A.3 below.

ALL-PRODUCTIVE SYSTEMS:

If $(B - A)^{-1} \geqslant o$, (A, B) will form an *all-productive system*. We shall call it *all-engaging* if $(B - A)^{-1} > 0$, for then $q > o$ for any $c \geqslant o$. In an all-engaging system, all activities have to be engaged for the production of any good to take place. In an all-productive system, any surplus can be produced at non-negative activity levels.

It is well known that all single-product systems capable of self-replacement $(A, B) = (A, I)$ are all-productive. A is indecomposable if and only if $(B - A)^{-1} = (I - A)^{-1} > 0$, i.e. if and only if (A, I) is all-engaging. (A, B) is all-productive in a decomposable system only if (A_1^1, B_1^1) is all-productive. For a generalisation, A is replaced by $(1 + r)A$.

It is then seen (see section II.8 below) that joint-production systems are only very rarely all-productive at low rates of profit. The concept is nevertheless important from an analytical point of view because all-productive systems possess the essential characteristics of single-product systems. Moreover, it will turn out (section II.9a) that basic joint-production systems have properties similar to those of all-engaging systems at high rates of profit close to the maximum.

Subsystems and Integrated Systems[3]

The structural properties of a system can be made more transparent by means of various transformations. The first and most important of these involves the construction of the *subsystem* which Sraffa introduced in the Appendix A to his book. What are the activity levels q_i such that a net output e_i of one unit of commodity i is produced? We obviously have

$$q_i = e_i(B - A)^{-1}.$$

A system operating with activity levels q_i thus produces only one unit of one good in the surplus. A system is *all-productive* if and only if all its subsystems have non-negative activity levels. Since these activity levels are not necessarily positive unless (A, B) forms an all-engaging system and since constant returns are irrelevant to the problems of classical price theory anyway, it is best to think of these activity levels as a virtual subdivision of the existing system and not as a transformation that any actual economy could ever undergo. The same subdivision is made with explicit reference to the original surplus in section II.4 below.

The point is that subsystems will allow a better understanding of prices and in particular the proper definition of labour values. They provide, moreover, the starting point for two further transformations: the system of gross integrated industries $(B^{-1}A, I)$ and the system of net integrated industries $[(B - A)^{-1}A, I]$. These systems are formally like single-product systems, although some of their input coefficients will in general be negative. Note that gross integrated industries can be defined only if $\det(B) \neq 0$.

The coefficients z_i^j of the system of *gross integrated industries* indicate the total amount of commodity j required to produce one unit of commodity i in gross output; for if we define

$$x_i = e_i B^{-1},$$

we have

$$x_i A \to x_i B = e_i,$$

i.e. gross output consists of one unit of commodity i, while $x_i A$ represents the vector of inputs, and $Z = B^{-1}A$ with

$$z_i^j = x_i a^j = e_i B^{-1} a^j.$$

The coefficients g_i^j of the system of *net integrated industries* indicate the total input used of commodity j to produce a net output of commodity i (if one prefers: the total input of commodity j to the subsystem i): if $\mathbf{q}_i = \mathbf{e}_i(\mathbf{B} - \mathbf{A})^{-1}$ as above, we have $\mathbf{G} = (\mathbf{B} - \mathbf{A})^{-1}\mathbf{A}$, with

$$\mathbf{q}_i\mathbf{A} = \mathbf{e}_i(\mathbf{B} - \mathbf{A})^{-1}\mathbf{A} = \mathbf{g}_i.$$

The integrated industries (gross and net) help to characterize basics, as we shall see in the following section (theorem 2).

Notes.

1 $\mathbf{e}'\mathbf{B} = \mathbf{e}'$ does, paradoxically, not exclude unproduced goods (i.e. land, mines, etc.; see section II.19), which justifies the assumption $\mathbf{b}^j \neq \mathbf{o}$, $j = 1, ..., n$.

2 Let $\Pi = (k_1, ..., k_n)$ be a permutation of $(1, ..., n)$. Permutation matrices are

$$\mathbf{P} = (p_i^j),\ p_i^j = \delta_{k_i}^j;\ \mathbf{Q} = (q_i^j)\ q_i^j = \delta_i^{k_j};\ \delta_i^j = \begin{cases} 1 \text{ if } i = j \\ 0 \text{ if } i \neq j \end{cases}$$

Notes: (a) $\mathbf{PA}$ is the matrix $\mathbf{A}$ with the rows, $\mathbf{AQ}$ with the columns permuted according to Π.

(b) If $\mathbf{P}$ corresponds to Π, and if Π^{-1} is the inverse permutation to Π, then $\mathbf{P}^{-1}$ corresponds to Π^{-1}.

(c) $\mathbf{P}^{-1} = \mathbf{P}'$ (permutation matrices are orthogonal).

3. This was added 1981. The concept of integrated industries (net only) was introduced by Pasinetti (1973), but the corresponding transformations were used and the relevant theorem 2.1 was proved in Schefold (1971).

2   The Concept of a Basic System

Several equivalent properties can be used to define the basic system in the single-product case (see Schefold, 1978b). Sraffa has chosen the criterion of all commodities entering directly or indirectly the production of all other commodities, while I have chosen that of decomposability because it can more directly be applied to joint production. However, the definition of indecomposability, though useful for the description of technical interdependence, is not satisfactory in joint-production systems from the point of view of prices. Consider the following example:

An indecomposable system of n goods and processes $(\mathbf{A}, \mathbf{B}, \mathbf{l})$ has an $(n + 1)$st process added to it, producing a pure consumption good, say 'gas' (natural gas). The n'th process of the indecomposable system produces 'coke' (used in the production of steel). With the addition of the $(n + 1)$st process, gas, which is always a technical byproduct of coke if made from coal, but which was regarded as a waste in the indecomposable system, becomes a joint product with coke. The n'th and the $(n + 1)$st process differ only in that the n'th process employs a technique aimed at efficient coke production, while in the $(n + 1)$st process the emphasis is perforce on gas because it is a single product. This is shown symbolically in Figure II.2.1.

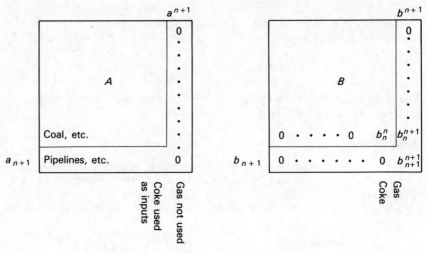

Figure II.2.1

The question now arises whether gas – according to our assumption a pure consumption good – is 'basic' or 'non-basic'. We now have $\mathbf{a}_{n+1} \geqslant \mathbf{o}$, $\mathbf{a}^{n+1} = \mathbf{o}$, $b_n^n > 0$, $b_n^{n+1} > 0$, $b_{n+1}^{n+1} > 0$. Since the system of $n + 1$ processes and commodities is indecomposable like the original system of n processes and commodities, we have to find a new approach in order to show that here gas has a character akin to non-basics in single-product industries, while coke (used in metallurgy) plays the part of a basic. To this end, Mr Sraffa proposes (PCMC sec. 54) to deduct a suitable fraction of the $(n + 1)$st process from the n'th so that gas production is cancelled out in a combined process with a positive output of coke, but possibly some negative inputs. More generally, we define:

Definition

A system $(\mathbf{A}, \mathbf{B})$ is called *non-basic* if a permutation of the columns and a number m exist so that the matrix $[\mathbf{A}^2, \mathbf{B}^2]$ consisting of the last m $(1 \leqslant m \leqslant n - 1)$ columns of $\mathbf{A}$ and of $\mathbf{B}$ has at most rank m.

Thus, gas as a pure consumption good $(\mathbf{a}^{n+1} = \mathbf{o})$ is non-basic. If a system is non-basic in accordance with this definition, combined processes can be formed to eliminate the non-basics:

If $(\mathbf{A}, \mathbf{B})$ is non-basic, $n - m$ rows of the $(n, 2m)$ matrix $[\mathbf{A}^2, \mathbf{B}^2]$ must by definition be linearly dependent on at most m others. If they are the first, we represent them as a linear combination of the last m rows of $[\mathbf{A}_2^2, \mathbf{B}_2^2]$ which are taken as a basis:

$$[\mathbf{A}_1^2, \mathbf{B}_1^2] = \mathbf{H}[\mathbf{A}_2^2, \mathbf{B}_2^2]$$

and we construct a matrix (following Manara, 1968):

$$\mathbf{M} = \begin{bmatrix} \mathbf{I}_{(n-m)} & -\mathbf{H} \\ \mathbf{O} & \mathbf{I}_{(m)} \end{bmatrix}$$

which transforms $(\mathbf{A}, \mathbf{B})$ into a pair of almost triangular matrices:

$$\mathbf{MA} = \begin{bmatrix} \mathbf{A}_1^1 - \mathbf{HA}_2^1 & \mathbf{O} \\ \mathbf{A}_2^1 & \mathbf{A}_2^2 \end{bmatrix}, \qquad \mathbf{MB} = \begin{bmatrix} \mathbf{B}_1^1 - \mathbf{HB}_2^1 & \mathbf{O} \\ \mathbf{B}_2^1 & \mathbf{B}_2^2 \end{bmatrix}.$$

The smallest such system (with the largest m)[1] $\{[\mathbf{A}_1^1 - \mathbf{HA}_2^1], [\mathbf{B}_1^1 - \mathbf{HB}_2^1]\}$ will be called the *basic system*. If it is identical with $(\mathbf{A}, \mathbf{B})$, $(\mathbf{A}, \mathbf{B})$ will be called *basic*. It is at once clear that decomposable systems are non-basic with $\mathbf{H} = \mathbf{0}$.

The usual assumption in single-product systems that there should always be at least one basic good will be replaced by the assumption (missing in Sraffa) that, whenever we have (after permutation) $\mathrm{rk}[\mathbf{A}^2, \mathbf{B}^2] = m$ for the last m columns of a system $(\mathbf{A}, \mathbf{B})$ or for any subsystem decomposed from a larger system $(\mathbf{C}, \mathbf{D})$, it must follow that

$$\mathrm{rk}[\mathbf{A}^1, \mathbf{B}^1] > n - m. \tag{A.3}$$

If (A.3) is not fulfilled, $(\mathbf{A}, \mathbf{B})$ can be made to fall apart into completely disconnected parts.

For if $\mathrm{rk}[\mathbf{A}^1, \mathbf{B}^1] \leqslant n - m$, we get from

$$0 \neq \det(\mathbf{B} - \mathbf{A}) - \det[\mathbf{M}(\mathbf{B} - \mathbf{A})] =$$
$$\det(\mathbf{B}_1^1 - \mathbf{HB}_2^1) - (\mathbf{A}_1^1 - \mathbf{HA}_2^1)\det(\mathbf{B}_2^2 - \mathbf{A}_2^2)$$
$$\mathrm{rk}[\mathbf{A}_1^1 - \mathbf{HA}_2^1, \mathbf{B}_1^1 - \mathbf{HB}_2^1] =$$
$$\mathrm{rk}[\mathbf{A}_1^1 - \mathbf{HA}_2^1, (\mathbf{B}_1^1 - \mathbf{HB}_2^1) - (\mathbf{A}_1^1 - \mathbf{HA}_2^1)] = n - m.$$

Thus, there is $\mathbf{J}$ with $[\mathbf{A}_2^1, \mathbf{B}_2^1] = \mathbf{J}[\mathbf{A}_1^1 - \mathbf{HA}_2^1, \mathbf{B}_1^1 - \mathbf{HB}_2^1]$ and

$$\mathbf{N} = \begin{bmatrix} \mathbf{I}_{(n-m)} & \mathbf{O} \\ -\mathbf{J} & \mathbf{I}_{(m)} \end{bmatrix}, \quad \mathbf{NMA} = \begin{bmatrix} \mathbf{A}_1^1 - \mathbf{HA}_2^1 & \mathbf{O} \\ \mathbf{O} & \mathbf{A}_2^2 \end{bmatrix}, \quad \mathbf{NMB} = \begin{bmatrix} \mathbf{B}_1^1 - \mathbf{HB}_2^1 & \mathbf{O} \\ \mathbf{O} & \mathbf{B}_2^2 \end{bmatrix}$$

Lemma

1 If $\mathbf{A}, \mathbf{B}$ basic, $\mathbf{A} \geqslant \mathbf{0}$, $\mathbf{B} \geqslant \mathbf{0}$, then $\mathbf{e}'\mathbf{A} > \mathbf{o}$, $\mathbf{e}'\mathbf{B} > \mathbf{o}$.[2]
2 If $\mathbf{Bp} = \mu\mathbf{Ap}$, $\mathbf{p} > \mathbf{o}$, then $\mu > 1$.

The first Lemma expresses the fact that only basic systems, not indecomposable ones, exclude pure consumption goods such as gas in the example above. This is a first, weak indication that the definition of basic systems given above represents an improvement over decomposability.

The following theorem shows first that we are dealing with a true generalization from single-product systems; second, that there are transformations of the joint-production system into single-product systems (the gross and net integrated systems) such that the latter is indecomposable if and only if the former is basic. This transformation proves very useful and could also have been used as a starting point for defining basic joint-production systems. Its intuitive significance follows from the interpretation of integrated systems. The third statement is an obvious consequence of the two that precede it.

Theorem 2.1

1   Single-product systems are basic (in the sense of the definition just given), if and only if they are indecomposable.

   1   Assume $\det(\mathbf{B}) \neq 0$, $\det(\mathbf{B} - \mathbf{A}) \neq 0$. The systems of gross and net integrated industries $(\mathbf{B}^{-1}\mathbf{A}, \mathbf{I})$ and $[(\mathbf{B} - \mathbf{A})^{-1}\mathbf{A}, \mathbf{I}]$ are indecomposable, if and only if $(\mathbf{A}, \mathbf{B})$ is basic.

   2   $(\mathbf{B}^{-1}\mathbf{A}, \mathbf{I})$ and $[(\mathbf{B} - \mathbf{A})^{-1}\mathbf{A}, \mathbf{I}]$ are completely decomposable, if and only if (A.3) does not hold.

   3   All-engaging systems are basic.

   Proof (Lemma):

   1   Trivial.

   2   Normalize $\mathbf{p}$, so that $\mathbf{e}'\mathbf{p} = 1$. With $\mathbf{e}'(\mathbf{B} - \mathbf{A}) = \mathbf{e}' - \mathbf{e}'\mathbf{A} \geqslant \mathbf{o}$ we get $1 = \mathbf{e}'\mathbf{p} = \mathbf{e}'\mathbf{B}\mathbf{p} = \mu\mathbf{e}'\mathbf{A}\mathbf{p} < \mu\mathbf{e}'\mathbf{p} = \mu$.

   Proof (Theorem):

   1   If $(\mathbf{A}, \mathbf{I})$ is non-basic, we get (after permutation) for the last m columns $\mathrm{rk}[\mathbf{A}^2, \mathbf{I}^2] \leqslant m$. From $\mathrm{rk}\,\mathbf{I}_2^2 = m$ follows $\mathrm{rk}[\mathbf{A}^2, \mathbf{I}^2] = m$, hence $\mathbf{A}_1^2 = \mathbf{O}$, since $\mathbf{I}_1^2 = \mathbf{O}$. Thus $\mathbf{A}$ is decomposable. The converse is obvious.

2   If $(\mathbf{A}, \mathbf{B})$ is non-basic, permutation matrices $\mathbf{P}, \mathbf{Q}$ and a non-singular matrix $\mathbf{M}$ exist, so that $\mathbf{MPAQ}$ and $\mathbf{MPBQ}$ are almost triangular. Thus, the matrix $(\mathbf{MPBQ})^{-1}\mathbf{MPAQ} = \mathbf{Q}^{-1}\mathbf{B}^{-1}\mathbf{P}^{-1}\mathbf{M}^{-1}\mathbf{MPAQ} = \mathbf{Q}^{-1}\mathbf{B}^{-1}\mathbf{AQ}$ is almost triangular as the product of two almost triangular matrices and so is $\mathbf{Q}^{-1}\mathbf{IQ} = \mathbf{I}$.

   Conversely, if $(\mathbf{B}^{-1}\mathbf{A}, \mathbf{I})$ is decomposable, $(\mathbf{A}, \mathbf{B})$ is non-basic; for $\mathbf{Q}^{-1}\mathbf{B}^{-1}\mathbf{AQ}$ is almost triangular (the last m columns are zero in the first $n - m$ rows), thus

$$m = \mathrm{rk}[\mathbf{Q}^{-1}\mathbf{B}^{-1}\mathbf{AQ}^2, \mathbf{I}^2] = \mathrm{rk}[(\mathbf{BQ})\{\mathbf{Q}^{-1}\mathbf{B}^{-1}\mathbf{AQ}^2, \mathbf{I}^2\}]$$
$$= \mathrm{rk}[\mathbf{AQ}^2, \mathbf{BQI}^2] = \mathrm{rk}[\mathbf{AQ}^2, \mathbf{BQ}^2],$$

thus m columns of $\mathbf{A}$ and $\mathbf{B}$ form together an $(n, 2m)$ matrix of rank m. The proofs for $(\mathbf{B} - \mathbf{A})^{-1}\mathbf{A}$ and theorem 2.1.2' are similar.

3   Since $\mathbf{e}'\mathbf{B} = \mathbf{e}'$, $\mathbf{B} \geqslant \mathbf{O}$, we have $(\mathbf{B} - \mathbf{A})^{-1}\mathbf{B} > \mathbf{O}$, if $(\mathbf{B} - \mathbf{A})^{-1} > \mathbf{O}$. Thus $(\mathbf{B} - \mathbf{A})^{-1}\mathbf{B}$ is an indecomposable matrix, $[(\mathbf{B} - \mathbf{A})^{-1}\mathbf{B}, \mathbf{I}]$ an indecomposable system, $[(\mathbf{B} - \mathbf{A})^{-1}\mathbf{B}, \mathbf{I}]$ and $(\mathbf{A}, \mathbf{B})$ basic systems.

q.e.d.

Multiplication by $\mathbf{M}$ decomposes our original equation (1.1) into two separate expressions:

$$(1 + r)(\mathbf{A}_1^1 - \mathbf{HA}_2^1)\mathbf{p}_1 + w(\mathbf{l}_1 - \mathbf{Hl}_2) = (\mathbf{B}_1^1 - \mathbf{HB}_2^1)\mathbf{p}_1$$
$$(1 + r)(\mathbf{A}_2^1\mathbf{p}_1 + \mathbf{A}_2^2\mathbf{p}_2) + w\mathbf{l}_2 = \mathbf{B}_2^1\mathbf{p}_1 + \mathbf{B}_2^2\mathbf{p}_2. \tag{2.1}$$

The first of these equations can be solved independently of the second; both taken together give the same result as (1.1). Equations (1.1) and

(2.1) are therefore equivalent for the determination of relative prices and the wage rate, given the rate of profit. The question to be asked is: why is the definition 2.1 the best of several possible extensions of the definitions of the basic system known for single-product systems? (The main alternative definitions are mentioned in Schefold, 1978b.)

It should be made clear that several properties can be associated with the intuitive notion of a 'basic'. One might intuitively think of a commodity as 'basic' if its supply was most essential to production in an emergency such as a war, and this property leads to the definition of a commodity as 'basic' if it enters directly or indirectly all other commodities, i.e. to Sraffa's first definition. However, the two properties of 'basics' most relevant to our context are (a) *technical* independence of one set of *processes* from the rest of the economy, and (b) *economic* independence of one set of *commodities* from the others in that influences on prices of the 'independent' commodities affect the prices of the others, but not *vice versa*.

With our definition, we are back to (technical) decomposability in the sense defined above if $\mathbf{H} = \mathbf{O}$. $(\mathbf{A}_1^1, \mathbf{B}_1^1)$ then form a system by themselves, if $\mathbf{e}_{(k)}(\mathbf{B}_1^1 - \mathbf{A}_1^1) > \mathbf{o}$. The technical independence of $\mathbf{A}_1^1$, $\mathbf{B}_1^1$ is here reflected in the fact that one need not know the processes $(\mathbf{A}_2, \mathbf{B}_2, \mathbf{l}_2)$ to determine prices in the system $(\mathbf{A}_1^1, \mathbf{B}_1^1, \mathbf{l}_1)$.

$(\mathbf{A}_2, \mathbf{B}_2, \mathbf{l}_2)$ on the other hand should not be viewed as a block of interdependent processes or as a system in the same sense as $(\mathbf{A}_1^1, \mathbf{B}_1^1, \mathbf{l}_1)$ may be viewed as a self-replacing system, but rather as a collection of disconnected industries producing a set of 'luxury goods' none of which is technically essential or economically relevant for the basic part of the system.

However, technical decomposability has its ambiguities in joint-production systems. We have already noted one reason: $(\mathbf{A}_1^1, \mathbf{B}_1^1)$ has to be self-replacing in order to qualify as an 'independent set of processes'. The second ambiguity is equally important: the essential wage-goods should be produced in $(\mathbf{A}_1^1, \mathbf{B}_1^1)$; bread is as essential to production as fuel. In the intuitive sense of 'basic', necessaries of life (of which the 'subsistence wage' of the workers consists) are 'basic goods' *par excellence*. They include whatever is considered indispensable for the maintenance of the customary way of life of the labour force, and they ought therefore to be implicit in the inputs of the whole economy and the outputs of the basic system.

But this would involve splitting the wage into a basic part and a surplus part – a step that Mr Sraffa is reluctant to take for the reasons expounded in PCMC, sec. 8. We shall leave the question of 'splitting' open since it is largely a matter of interpretation and does not affect the mathematical structure of the model. The reader should simply pay attention to the fact that a few of the propositions that we prove make more sense if the distinction between a 'basic wage' (to be advanced) and a 'surplus wage' (share in the surplus) is acceptable. The former can be thought to be implicit in the input matrix. One may assume 'splitting' whenever one pleases.

'Technical independence' thus becomes a gradual concept: one could construct a hierarchy of processes depending on how vital they are for the remainder of the economy; decomposability and self-replacement would be the leading ideas in the construction.

But these more technical notions serve only as an introduction to the understanding of the form and causes of the economic independence of the prices of basic commodities. We return to the equations (2.1). If $\mathbf{H} \neq \mathbf{O}$, it is definitely not possible any more to say that a group of processes is technically independent of the others: the expressions $\mathbf{A}_1^2 = \mathbf{H}\mathbf{A}_2^2$, $\mathbf{B}_1^2 = \mathbf{H}\mathbf{B}_2^2$ show that some goods produced and/or used in the non-basic processes (the non-basics) are also used and/or produced in some basic processes. However, although the prices of the first $n - m$ commodities are thus not independent of the last m processes $(\mathbf{A}_2, \mathbf{B}_2, \mathbf{l}_2)$, we have at least constructed an imaginary system

$$(\overline{\mathbf{A}}_1^1, \overline{\mathbf{B}}_1^1, \overline{\mathbf{l}}_1) = (\mathbf{A}_1^1 - \mathbf{H}\mathbf{A}_2^1, \mathbf{B}_1^1 - \mathbf{H}\mathbf{B}_2^1, \mathbf{l}_1 - \mathbf{H}\mathbf{l}_2)$$

that determines the prices of the first $n - m$ commodities for all rates of profit in such a way that they appear to be independent of the movements of the prices of the last m commodities.

That this formal appearance has a sound economic meaning follows from the fact that a tax on basic commodities or a change in the rate of profit for the basic system affects all prices, while a tax on non-basics or a change in the rate of profit confined to the non-basic part of the system leaves prices of basics unchanged. Since Sraffa is concerned with showing that what happens with distribution in the basic part is what really matters, we are justified, from his point of view, in adopting the definition given above.

Other questions require other definitions. If we are interested in the relationship between prices and technology, decomposability is the appropriate concept and does not require any consideration of replacement conditions. For a change in a method of production of the decomposable part of a decomposable system does not affect prices of basics, while prices of basics *may* be (but need not be) affected if a method of production of a non-basic changes with $\mathbf{H} \neq \mathbf{O}$.

My procedure will eventually be justified by the demonstration (given in the next section) that, except for flukes, no mathematical procedure exists with which it is possible to decompose the system, by means of linear methods, further than into basics and non-basics. Moreover, it will be shown that the set of basic commodities is uniquely determined, while the set of basic processes is determined only up to linear combinations.

This indeterminacy concerning the processes does not matter, however. We have seen that the uses of linear combinations of methods are characteristic for firms operating under joint production, and that methods are here only distinguished by being linearly independent of another. It is conceivable that a firm operates with one method in the basic part of the system, and with another in the non-basic part. Hence we are here concerned with showing that no method for linear combinations of methods exists that allows the number of basic commodities or their identity to be changed.

In intuitive terms: we found two 'megacorporations' using the existing processes at positive or, by going into debt for outputs and 'selling' inputs, negative activity levels such that the first megacorporation, if taxed, influences the prices of the second through changed prices of the commodities that it delivers, while the second, if taxed, does not influence the first at all. The point is then that the products are uniquely defined while the activities of the 'corporations' are defined only up to linear 'superpositions'.

Notes

1 There may, however, be more than one possible combination of processes to represent the basic system, while basic commodities are, as we shall see, unique. For the problem of uniqueness see section II.3; for examples see section II.20.
2 Not true, if only indecomposability is assumed.

3   The Uniqueness of the Basic System

The uniqueness of the basic system has to be proved in a double sense. First we have to show that only one basic system exists (up to linear combinations of processes), if the Sraffa–Manara definition is accepted. Second, we have to solve the problem set out in the last section; that is, we have to justify the definition itself and show that no other definition of the basic system could be given (in a sense still be to specified in precise mathematical terms). Broadly speaking, it will be proved that two Sraffa systems with the same number of commodities yield – flukes apart – the same vector of relative prices at 'many' rates of profit, if and only if they are identical up to linear combinations of processes. Any process designated to isolate basic commodities while preserving the structure of prices must therefore lead to the essentially same result as the definition that I have given above.

We take the second problem first and begin by analysing any two matrices $\mathbf{F}$, $\mathbf{G}$ with a labour vector, $\mathbf{m}$, satisfying the same price system as equation (1.1)

$$[\mathbf{G} - (1 + r)\mathbf{F}]\hat{\mathbf{p}}(r) = \mathbf{m} \qquad (3.1)$$

where

$$\hat{\mathbf{p}}(r) = [\mathbf{B} - (1 + r)\mathbf{A}]^{-1}\mathbf{l}. \qquad (3.2)$$

$(\mathbf{F}, \mathbf{G}, \mathbf{m})$ shall fulfil the same assumptions as $(\mathbf{A}, \mathbf{B}, \mathbf{l})$. In particular $\det(\mathbf{B} - \mathbf{A}) \neq 0$, $\det(\mathbf{G} - \mathbf{F}) \neq 0$.

Write $\mathbf{A}_{Ad}$ for the adjoint of a matrix $\mathbf{A}$. If $\det(\mathbf{A}) \neq 0$, $\mathbf{A}_{Ad} =$

$\mathbf{A}^{-1}\det(\mathbf{A})$, if $\det(\mathbf{A}) = 0$, $\mathbf{A}\mathbf{A}_{Ad} = \mathbf{O}$. (3.1), (3.2) are equivalent to

$$\det[\mathbf{B} - (1 + r)\mathbf{A}]\mathbf{Dl} = [\mathbf{G} - \mathbf{F} - r\mathbf{F}][\mathbf{B} - \mathbf{A} - r\mathbf{A}]_{Ad}\mathbf{l} \qquad (3.3)$$

where we choose $\mathbf{D}$ to be any non-singular matrix mapping $\mathbf{l}$ onto $\mathbf{m}$:

$$\mathbf{m} = \mathbf{Dl}.$$

$[\mathbf{B} - (1 + r)\mathbf{A}]_{Ad}$ is a polynomial matrix of degree $n - 1$ in r. Expand the two sides of (3.3) to get

$$\sum_{v=0}^{n} \beta_v r^v \mathbf{Dl} = [(\mathbf{G} - \mathbf{F}) - r\mathbf{F}](\mathbf{z}^0 + \mathbf{z}^1 r + \cdots + \mathbf{z}^{n-1}r^{n-1}) \qquad (3.4)$$

with constant vectors $\mathbf{z}^i$ and constants β_v, and with

$$\beta_0 = \det(\mathbf{B} - \mathbf{A})$$
$$\mathbf{z}^0 = (\mathbf{B} - \mathbf{A})_{Ad}\mathbf{l}.$$

Since (3.1), (3.2) shall hold for a full neighbourhood of r_0, (3.4) will hold identically in r and is equivalent to the equations

$$\beta_0 \mathbf{Dl} = (\mathbf{G} - \mathbf{F})\mathbf{z}^0$$
$$\beta_1 \mathbf{Dl} = (\mathbf{G} - \mathbf{F})\mathbf{z}^1 - \mathbf{F}\mathbf{z}^0$$
$$\cdots \qquad\qquad (3.5)$$
$$\beta_{n-1} \mathbf{Dl} = (\mathbf{G} - \mathbf{F})\mathbf{z}^{n-1} - \mathbf{F}\mathbf{z}^{n-2}$$
$$\beta_n \mathbf{Dl} = -\mathbf{F}\mathbf{z}^{n-1}$$

which we write in matrix form:

$$[\mathbf{G} - \mathbf{F}, -\mathbf{F}]\begin{bmatrix} \mathbf{z}^0, \mathbf{z}^1, ..., \mathbf{z}^{n-1}, \mathbf{o} \\ \mathbf{o}, \mathbf{z}^0, ..., \mathbf{z}^{n-2}, \mathbf{z}^{n-1} \end{bmatrix} = [\beta_0 \mathbf{Dl}, ..., \beta_n \mathbf{Dl}] \qquad (3.6)$$

We ask, now, to what extent $[\mathbf{G} - \mathbf{F}, -\mathbf{F}]$ is determined by (3.6). This will depend on the rank of the (n, n) matrix $[\mathbf{z}^0, ..., \mathbf{z}^{n-1}]$.

First, it is clear that

$$[\mathbf{G} - \mathbf{F}, -\mathbf{F}] = \mathbf{D}[\mathbf{B} - \mathbf{A}, -\mathbf{A}] = [\mathbf{DB} - \mathbf{DA}, -\mathbf{DA}] \qquad (3.7)$$

can be taken as a particular solution of (3.6), since $\mathbf{D}$ was chosen to be invertible. The complete set of solutions to (3.6) can be represented as the sum of this particular solution (3.7) plus *all* the solutions of the corresponding homogeneous equation, written as

$$[\mathbf{X}, -\mathbf{Y}]\begin{bmatrix} \mathbf{z}^0, ..., \mathbf{z}^{n-1}, \mathbf{o} \\ \mathbf{o}, \mathbf{z}^0, ..., \mathbf{z}^{n-1} \end{bmatrix} = \mathbf{O}. \qquad (3.8)$$

Any $\mathbf{X}$ and $\mathbf{Y}$ for which

$$\mathbf{X}[\mathbf{z}^0, ..., \mathbf{z}^{n-1}] = \mathbf{o}, \qquad \mathbf{Y}[\mathbf{z}^0, ..., \mathbf{z}^{n-1}] = \mathbf{o}$$

that is to say, for which $\mathbf{X}\hat{\mathbf{p}}(r) \equiv \mathbf{o}$, $\mathbf{Y}\hat{\mathbf{p}}(r) \equiv \mathbf{o}$ identically in r, will satisfy this equation, but these are not all the solutions. We get a complete survey as follows:

Consider any $\mathbf{X}$ fulfilling

$$\mathbf{Xz}^0 = \mathbf{X}(\mathbf{B} - \mathbf{A})_{Ad}\mathbf{l} = \mathbf{o} \qquad (3.9)$$

to be given. (3.8) will then determine $\mathbf{Y}$:

$$\mathbf{X}[\mathbf{z}^1, ..., \mathbf{z}^{n-1}, \mathbf{o}] = \mathbf{Y}[\mathbf{z}^0, ..., \mathbf{z}^{n-1}] \qquad (3.10)$$

but not fully, unless $\det[\mathbf{z}^0, ..., \mathbf{z}^{n-1}] \neq 0$.

Retracing our path to the original equations, we find from

$$(\mathbf{X} - r\mathbf{Y})[(\mathbf{B} - \mathbf{A}) - r\mathbf{A}]^{-1}\mathbf{l} = \mathbf{o}$$

that

$$\mathbf{Y}_0 = \mathbf{X}(\mathbf{B} - \mathbf{A})^{-1}\mathbf{A} \qquad (3.11)$$

is a particular solution to (3.8), because

$$[\mathbf{X} - r\mathbf{Y}_0][\mathbf{B} - \mathbf{A} - r\mathbf{A}]^{-1}\mathbf{l} = \mathbf{X}[\mathbf{I} - r(\mathbf{B} - \mathbf{A})^{-1}\mathbf{A}][\mathbf{B} - \mathbf{A} - r\mathbf{A}]^{-1}\mathbf{l}$$
$$= \mathbf{X}(\mathbf{B} - \mathbf{A})^{-1}\mathbf{l} = \mathbf{o}.$$

To get the full set of solutions to (3.10) and (3.8), we have again to add to $\mathbf{Y}_0$ the solutions $\mathbf{Y}_1$ of the homogeneous equation

$$\mathbf{Y}_1[\mathbf{z}^0, ..., \mathbf{z}^{n-1}] = \mathbf{O}.$$

These solutions are the same as the ones for which

$$\mathbf{Y}_1\hat{\mathbf{p}}(r) \equiv \mathbf{o} \qquad (3.12)$$

holds identically in r.

Our matrices $\mathbf{F}$, $\mathbf{G}$ with the labour vector $\mathbf{m}$ are now seen to be related to the original $\mathbf{A}$, $\mathbf{B}$, $\mathbf{l}$ by

$$\mathbf{G} - \mathbf{F} = \mathbf{D}(\mathbf{B} - \mathbf{A}) + \mathbf{X}$$
$$\mathbf{F} = \mathbf{D}\mathbf{A} + \mathbf{Y}_0 + \mathbf{Y}_1 \qquad (3.13)$$

where $\mathbf{X}$ is any matrix satisfying (3.9), $\mathbf{Y}_0$ is related to $\mathbf{X}$ by (3.11), and $\mathbf{Y}_1$ satisfies (3.12). Define

$$\mathbf{M} = \mathbf{D} + \mathbf{X}(\mathbf{B} - \mathbf{A})^{-1}$$

and (3.13) becomes

$$G - F = M(B - A)$$
$$F = MA + Y_1$$

and

$$Ml = Dl + X(B - A)^{-1}l = m,$$

where $\det(M) \neq 0$, for $\det(G - F) \neq 0$, $\det(B - A) \neq 0$. Since our derivation can be reversed we have found:

Theorem 3.1[1]

Prices are the same in two systems (F, G, m), (A, B, l) for all rates of profit, i.e.

$$\hat{p}(r) = [G - (1 + r)F]^{-1}m = [B - (1 + r)A]^{-1}l,$$

if and only if matrices M, Y with $\det(M) \neq 0$, $Y\hat{p}(r) \equiv o$, exist so that

$$F = MA + Y, \quad G = MB + Y, \quad m = Ml.$$

COROLLARY:

Prices $\hat{p}(r)$ are the same in two systems (F, G, m), (A, B, l) for all rates of profit, if they coincide in $n + 1$ different points $r_0, ..., r_n$ $(r_i \neq r_j)$.

PROOF (OF COROLLARY):

Immediate by application of the theorem of identity for polynomials (equation (3.4) holds in $n + 1$ points).

The two matrices M and Y, by which (F, G, m) and (A, B, l) are related to each other, have straightforward economic interpretations. To pre-multiply A, B, l by M means to form n new processes f_i, g_i, m_i by linear combination from the original a_i, b_i, l_i. To add Y with $Y\hat{p}(r) \equiv o$ means to add artificially to each process a set of inputs and outputs whose value is zero at all rates of profit. Thus, in the first case, new industries are formed by linear combination; in the second, industries 'exchange' goods in such quantities that the value of the goods exchanged is zero at all rates of profit and in every industry.

To illustrate the second operation, which one might think impossible, take an indecomposable matrix as the input matrix of a single-product system (A, I, l) and assume the labour vector to be the positive eigenvector belonging to the dominant root $(1 + R)^{-1}$ of A. This is the famous special case for which the 'organic composition of capital' is the same in all industries and independent of the rate of profit so that prices are proportional to labour values. If

$$(1 + r)Ap + wl = p$$

and

$$\mathbf{Al} = \frac{1}{1 + R}\, \mathbf{l},$$

it follows

$$\mathbf{p}(r) = \mathbf{l}$$

for $w = (R - r)/(1 + R)$.
  Define

$$\mathbf{y}^1 = -\frac{1}{l_1}(\mathbf{a}^2 l_2 + \cdots + \mathbf{a}^n l_n), \qquad \mathbf{y}^2 = \mathbf{a}^2, \dots, \mathbf{y}^n = \mathbf{a}^n,$$

$$\mathbf{Y} = [\mathbf{y}^1, \dots, \mathbf{y}^n].$$

In the system

$$(1 + r)\overline{\mathbf{A}}\mathbf{p} + w\mathbf{l} = \mathbf{p}$$

with

$$\overline{\mathbf{A}} = \mathbf{A} - \mathbf{Y} = \begin{bmatrix} a_1^1 - y_1^1, 0, \dots, 0 \\ \cdots\cdots \\ a_n^1 - y_n^1, 0, \dots, 0 \end{bmatrix}$$

which is equivalent with $(\mathbf{A}, \mathbf{I}, \mathbf{l})$ in that prices are the same as in $(\mathbf{A}, \mathbf{I}, \mathbf{l})$, $n - 1$ goods are 'non-basics' despite the indecomposability of $\mathbf{A}$. In fact, all goods, except one, turn out to be pure consumption goods!

It is worth while to ponder a little on this discovery before proceeding further with the argument. We have found that an economy in which prices are proportional to labour values is equivalent to a one-commodity world! This sheds some light on the classical assumption of the labour theory of value, which assumed that prices did not deviate much from values (depending on the time it takes to bring a commodity to market in Ricardo, or on the migration of capital following the prospect of higher rates of profit in Marx's transformation of values into prices). Here we are about to show not only that a direct proportionality of prices and values is highly exceptional, but also, and more specifically, what the exception means: the absence of the central problem of capital theory, namely, the measurement of capital.

This does not mean that the assumption of prices proportional to values cannot be useful in some cases, but it should be clear that Samuelson's (1962) construction of the surrogate production function was not among them. His aim was to prove that the neoclassical production function – in which one good is the capital good as well as the consumption good – could be shown to result from a process of aggregation. To this end he represented different techniques by means of different wage curves, but, by drawing them as straight lines, he implied a uniform composition of capital for the industries of each technique and in this way unknowingly presupposed the one-commodity world that his construction was supposed to overcome.

Next, we show that one is justified in neglecting matrices $\mathbf{Y}$ with $\mathbf{Y}\hat{\mathbf{p}}(r) \equiv \mathbf{o}$, for such matrices $\mathbf{Y} \neq \mathbf{O}$ cannot exist unless $(\mathbf{A}, \mathbf{B})$ is a mathematically and economically exceptional system and/or $\mathbf{l}$ is in a very special relationship with $(\mathbf{A}, \mathbf{B})$. Such exceptional systems can only be constructed on purpose and will never be encountered in actual situations or in systems with coefficients chosen at random. The proof of this contention is absolutely decisive for demonstrating that the isolation of an essentially unique basic system can — except for mathematical flukes — be effected by means of linear combinations of processes.

In slight modification of the conventional terminology, we call a root R of $\det[\mathbf{B} - (1 + r)\mathbf{A}] = 0$ semi-simple, if $\operatorname{rk}[\mathbf{B} - (1 + R)\mathbf{A}] = n - 1$. Whether R is a simple root or not: if R is semi-simple, there is (up to a scalar factor) one and only one 'eigenvector' $\mathbf{q}$ with $\mathbf{q}'[\mathbf{B} - (1 + R)\mathbf{A}] = \mathbf{o}$.

Theorem 3.2

Let $R_1, ..., R_t$ be the roots of $\det[\mathbf{B} - (1 + r)\mathbf{A}] = 0$, with multiplicities $s_1, ..., s_t$; $(s_1 + \cdots + s_t = n)$.[2] The price vector $\hat{\mathbf{p}}(r)$ assumes n linearly independent values $\hat{\mathbf{p}}(r_1), ..., \hat{\mathbf{p}}(r_n)$ at any n different rates of profit $r_1, ..., r_n (r_i \neq r_j, r_i \neq R_j)$, if all t roots $R_1, ..., R_t$ of the equation $\det[\mathbf{B} - (1 + r)\mathbf{A}] = 0$ are semi-simple and if $\mathbf{q}_i\mathbf{l} \neq 0$; $i = 1, ..., t$; for the associated 'eigenvectors' with $\mathbf{q}_i\mathbf{B} = (1 + R_i)\mathbf{q}_i\mathbf{A}$. Conversely, if one root $\bar{R}$ is not semi-simple or if $\mathbf{q}_i\mathbf{l} = 0$ for some i, it follows that $\hat{\mathbf{p}}(r_1), ..., \hat{\mathbf{p}}(r_n)$ are linearly dependent for any $r_1, ..., r_n (r_i \neq R_j)$. If $\bar{R}$ is real, there is an associated real eigenvector $\bar{\mathbf{q}}$ with $\bar{\mathbf{q}}\hat{\mathbf{p}}(r) = 0$ for all r.

PROOF:

Let s_i be the multiplicity of R_i, R_i semi-simple, $\sum_{i=1}^{t} s_i = n$. According to Jordan's theory of Normal Forms (see, e.g. Gröbner, 1966, pp. 201–5), there exist n linearly independent vectors

$$\mathbf{q}_{i,1}, ..., \mathbf{q}_{i, s_i}; \qquad i = 1, ..., t;$$

with

$$\mathbf{q}_{i,1} = \mathbf{q}_i,$$
$$\mathbf{q}_i = R_i\mathbf{q}_i\mathbf{A}(\mathbf{B} - \mathbf{A})^{-1},$$
$$\mathbf{q}_{i,\sigma}[\mathbf{B} - (1 + R_i)\mathbf{A}](\mathbf{B} - \mathbf{A})^{-1} = \mathbf{q}_{i,\sigma}[\mathbf{I} - R_i\mathbf{A}(\mathbf{B} - \mathbf{A})^{-1}]$$
$$= -R_i\mathbf{q}_{i,\sigma-1};$$

where

$$\sigma = 2, ..., s_i.$$

It follows that

$$\mathbf{q}_{i,\sigma}[\mathbf{I} - r\mathbf{A}(\mathbf{B} - \mathbf{A})^{-1}] = \mathbf{q}_{i,\sigma}\left[1 - \frac{r}{R_i}\right] - r\mathbf{q}_{i,\sigma-1}$$

and this formula holds for $\sigma = 1, \ldots, s_i$, if we define $\mathbf{q}_{i,0} = \mathbf{o}$ for all i.
With this we get

$$\begin{aligned}
\mathbf{q}_{i,\sigma}(\mathbf{B} - \mathbf{A})\hat{\mathbf{p}}(r) &= \mathbf{q}_{i,\sigma}(\mathbf{B} - \mathbf{A})[\mathbf{B} - (1 + r)\mathbf{A}]^{-1}\mathbf{l} \\
&= \mathbf{q}_{i,\sigma}[\mathbf{I} - r\mathbf{A}(\mathbf{B} - \mathbf{A})^{-1}]^{-1}\mathbf{l} \\
&= \frac{R_i}{R_i - r}\,\mathbf{q}_{i,0}\mathbf{l} + \frac{rR_i}{R_i - r}\,\mathbf{q}_{i,\sigma-1}[\mathbf{I} - r\mathbf{A}(\mathbf{B} - \mathbf{A})^{-1}]^{-1}\mathbf{l} \\
&= \frac{R_i}{R_i - r}\,\mathbf{q}_{i,0}\mathbf{l} + \frac{rR_i}{R_i - r}\frac{R_i}{R_i - r}\,\mathbf{q}_{i,\sigma-1}\mathbf{l} + \frac{(R_i r)^2}{(R_i - r)^2} \\
&\quad \times \mathbf{q}_{i,\sigma-2}[\mathbf{I} - r\mathbf{A}(\mathbf{B} - \mathbf{A})^{-1}]^{-1}\mathbf{l} \\
&= \frac{R_i}{R_i - r}\,\mathbf{q}_{i,0}\mathbf{l} + \frac{rR_i^2}{(R_i - r)^2}\,\mathbf{q}_{i,\sigma-1}\mathbf{l} \\
&\quad + \cdots + \frac{R_i}{R_i - r}\left[\frac{rR_i}{R_i - r}\right]^{\sigma-1}\mathbf{q}_i\mathbf{l};
\end{aligned}$$

$$\sigma = 2, \ldots, s_i; \; i = 1, \ldots, t;$$

$$\mathbf{q}_i(\mathbf{B} - \mathbf{A})\hat{\mathbf{p}}(r) = \frac{R_i}{R_i - r}\,\mathbf{q}_i\mathbf{l}.$$

Define

$$\begin{aligned}
\mathbf{Q} &= [\mathbf{q}'_{1,1}, \ldots, \mathbf{q}'_{1,s_1}, \ldots, \mathbf{q}'_{t,1}, \ldots, \mathbf{q}'_{t,s_t}]', \\
\mathbf{T} &= \mathbf{Q}(\mathbf{B} - \mathbf{A}).
\end{aligned}$$

The vector

$$\mathbf{v}(r) = \mathbf{T}\hat{\mathbf{p}}(r)$$

assumes in n points $r_1, \ldots, r_n (r_i \neq r_j, r_i \neq R_j)$ n linearly independent values, if and only if $\mathbf{q}_i\mathbf{l} \neq 0$; $i = 1, \ldots, t$. The necessity of this latter condition is obvious, for $\mathbf{q}_i(\mathbf{B} - \mathbf{A})\hat{\mathbf{p}}(r) = 0$ if $\mathbf{q}_i\mathbf{l} = 0$. To verify that $\mathbf{q}_i\mathbf{l} \neq 0$ is sufficient, consider the matrix

$$\mathbf{C} = [\mathbf{c}(r_1), \ldots, \mathbf{c}(r_n)]$$

where $\mathbf{c}(r) = \det[\mathbf{B} - (1 + r)\mathbf{A}]\mathbf{v}(r)$. Assume that $\mathbf{C}$ (consisting of the values of n polynomials at n points) is singular, i.e. assume, to begin with, that the s_1'th row is equal to a linear combination of the first $s_1 - 1$ and the last $n - s_1$ rows. Since the values in n points fully determine a polynomial of $(n - 1)$st degree (and none of the polynomials is of higher degree), the polynomial in the s_1'th row would have to be equal to the linear combination of the first $s_1 - 1$ and the last $n - s_1$ rows not only in $r_1, ..., r_n$, but everywhere. But this is impossible since the s_1'th polynomial does not vanish at $r = R_1$, while the $n - 1$ other polynomials and hence their linear combination are zero at $r = R_1$. If $\mathbf{C}$ is singular and the s_i'th row cannot be represented as a linear combination of the other rows, the proof has, by means of an obvious extension, to be completed by induction (see Schefold, 1976a, or, for an alternative proof, 1976c). Thus $\mathbf{C}$ is non-singular and

$$\hat{\mathbf{p}}(r) = \mathbf{T}^{-1}\mathbf{v}(r)$$

assumes n linearly independent values at n different points, if the R_i are semi-simple, and if and only if $\mathbf{q}_i\mathbf{l} \neq 0$, $i = 1, ..., t$. The necessity of the R_i being semi-simple remains to be shown. Suppose R is a multiple root of $\det[\mathbf{B} - (1 + R)\mathbf{A}] = 0$ and $\mathrm{rk}[\mathbf{B} - (1 + R)\mathbf{A}] < n - 1$. There are then two linearly independent $\mathbf{q}_1, \mathbf{q}_2$ with

$$\mathbf{q}_i[\mathbf{B} - (1 + R)\mathbf{A}] = \mathbf{o}; \qquad i = 1, 2; \qquad \mathbf{q}_i\mathbf{l} \neq 0.$$

We get as above

$$\mathbf{q}_i(\mathbf{B} - \mathbf{A})[\mathbf{B} - (1 + r)\mathbf{A}]^{-1}\mathbf{l} = \mathbf{q}_i[\mathbf{I} - r\mathbf{A}(\mathbf{B} - \mathbf{A})^{-1}]^{-1}\mathbf{l} =$$

$$\frac{R}{R - r}\mathbf{q}_i\mathbf{l}; \ i = 1, 2;$$

thus

$$(\mathbf{q}_1 - \lambda\mathbf{q}_2)(\mathbf{B} - \mathbf{A})\hat{\mathbf{p}}(r) = 0, \qquad \lambda = \frac{\mathbf{q}_1\mathbf{l}}{\mathbf{q}_2\mathbf{l}},$$

identically in r with $(\mathbf{q}_1 - \lambda\mathbf{q}_2)(\mathbf{B} - \mathbf{A}) \neq \mathbf{o}$. This is impossible, if $\hat{\mathbf{p}}(r)$ assumes n linearly independent values in any n points. $\bar{\mathbf{q}} = \mathbf{q}_1 - \lambda\mathbf{q}_2$ is a real vector, if R is real.

q.e.d.

Multiple roots that are not semi-simple are mathematically rather exceptional,[3] and the careful examination of examples suggests that they are hardly more than flukes in any system from the economic point of view. We exclude them therefore at present from our consideration but shall revert to them in section II.7.

As regards the condition that $\mathbf{q}_i\mathbf{l} \neq 0$ for all eigenvectors $\mathbf{q}_i$ (the roots being semi-simple), there is because of $\mathbf{l} > \mathbf{o}$, apart from a finite number of classes of mathematical flukes,[4] again no economically relevant case except the one we dealt with separately above where $\mathbf{l}$ is equal to the prices at the maximum rate of profit and the organic composition is constant: if $\mathbf{l}$ is an eigenvector with $\mathbf{A}\mathbf{l} = (1 + R)^{-1}\mathbf{l}$, in a single-product system $(\mathbf{A}, \mathbf{I}, \mathbf{l})$, it follows $\mathbf{q}_i\mathbf{l} = 0$ for all $\mathbf{q}_i$ belonging to different eigenvalues $R_i \neq R$.[5]

Barring this. $\hat{\mathbf{p}}(r)$ assumes n linearly independent values for any n

different given rates of profit, whether $(\mathbf{A}, \mathbf{B})$ is basic or not. If we visualize the price vector as a curve in n-dimensional space as a function of the rate of profit, we have thus proved that it is nowhere contained in a hyperplane through the origin.

We shall call systems with this property of prices 'regular' and the exceptions 'irregular'. Prices change direction *erratically* (and yet continuously) in regular systems. Moreover, one can show that neither absolute (normalized) nor relative prices are constant for any interval, be it ever so small, in regular systems. Prices of irregular systems are contained in a hyperplane, as further analysis reveals. In the extreme case of a uniform organic composition of capital mentioned above (single-product system with $(1 + R)\mathbf{Al} = \mathbf{l}$), relative prices p_i/p_j are constant; the price vector $\mathbf{p}$ is confined to a straight line and is, given an appropriate normalization, constant and proportional to labour values. It is argued in Schefold (1976a) that the irregular systems of given order are of measure zero in the space of all possible Sraffa systems of the same order. This is perhaps the most precise formulation of the exceptional character of irregular systems.

A number of results spring from the unexpected properties of prices in regular Sraffa systems. It follows, e.g., that relative prices $(p_1/w)/(p_2/w) = p_1/p_2$ in a regular two-sector model rise (or fall) monotonically with r. Or we have:

COROLLARY TO THEOREMS 3.1 AND 3.2

Two regular single-product systems $(\mathbf{A}_1, \mathbf{I}, \mathbf{l}^1)$, $(\mathbf{A}_2, \mathbf{I}, \mathbf{l}^2)$ whose price vectors coincide at $n + 1$ rates of profit are identical.

Proof:
The coincidence of the prices at $n + 1$ points is sufficient to allow the application of theorem 3.1. Therefore $\mathbf{A}_1 = \mathbf{M}\mathbf{A}_2 + \mathbf{Y}$. $\mathbf{Y} = \mathbf{O}$, because prices assume linearly independent values at any n of the $n + 1$ points. $\mathbf{M} = \mathbf{I}$, because the output matrices are both unit matrices. Thus $\mathbf{A}_1 = \mathbf{A}_2$.
q.e.d.

Equipped with this notion of regularity let us return to the discussion of the definition of a basic system. Suppose $(\mathbf{F}, \mathbf{G}, \mathbf{m})$ is a joint-production system yielding the same prices as $(\mathbf{A}, \mathbf{B}, \mathbf{l})$, and that $(\mathbf{F}, \mathbf{G}, \mathbf{m})$ is decomposable. We show that $(\mathbf{F}, \mathbf{G}, \mathbf{m})$ is then non-basic and, in general (i.e. in the regular case), related to $(\mathbf{A}, \mathbf{B}, \mathbf{l})$ through a transformation that is essentially identical with the one that I have used in the definition of the basic system.

In fact, if $(\mathbf{A}, \mathbf{B}, \mathbf{l})$ is regular, $(\mathbf{F}, \mathbf{G}, \mathbf{m})$ is regular, no $\mathbf{Y} \neq \mathbf{O}$ with $\mathbf{Y}\mathbf{p}(r) \equiv \mathbf{o}$ can exist and $\mathbf{F} = \mathbf{M}\mathbf{A}$, $\mathbf{G} = \mathbf{M}\mathbf{B}$, and $\mathbf{m} = \mathbf{M}\mathbf{l}$, $\det [\mathbf{M}] \neq 0$, for any two systems with $\hat{\mathbf{p}} = [\mathbf{B} - (1 + r)\mathbf{A}]^{-1}\mathbf{l} = [\mathbf{G} - (1 + r)\mathbf{F}]^{-1}\mathbf{m}$. Assume now, $\mathbf{F} = \mathbf{M}\mathbf{A}$, $\mathbf{G} = \mathbf{M}\mathbf{B}$ are almost triangular, i.e. assume the last m columns are zero in the first $n - m$ rows. Since $\mathbf{M}$ is non-singular,

$$\text{rk}\,[\mathbf{M}\mathbf{A}^2, \mathbf{M}\mathbf{B}^2] = \text{rk}\,[\mathbf{A}^2, \mathbf{B}^2] \leqslant m.$$

Thus, $(\mathbf{A}, \mathbf{B})$ is non-basic and the multiplication by $\mathbf{M}$ that turned $(\mathbf{A}, \mathbf{B})$ into almost triangular matrices could also be effected by a matrix of the form

$$\begin{bmatrix} \mathbf{I}_{(n-m)} & -\mathbf{H} \\ \mathbf{O} & \mathbf{I}_{(m)} \end{bmatrix}$$

as used in the definition of the basic system.

Note that any system decomposed in this way from a regular system is itself regular.

Proof:
The goods belonging to the decomposed system are uniquely determined and so are its prices $\mathbf{p}_1(r)$ (using the usual notation). If the decomposed system of $n - m$ goods were not regular, a not necessarily real $(n - m)$ vector $\mathbf{q}_1 \neq \mathbf{o}$ would exist such that $\mathbf{q}_1 \mathbf{p}_1 = 0$. But then

$$[\mathbf{q}_1, \mathbf{o}] \begin{bmatrix} \mathbf{p}_1(r) \\ \mathbf{p}_2(r) \end{bmatrix} = 0$$

for the n vector $[\mathbf{q}_1, \mathbf{o}] \neq \mathbf{o}$ in contradiction to the assumption that the system is regular, i.e. that $\hat{\mathbf{p}}(r)$ assumes n linearly independent values for any n rates of profit.

Thus we have proved:

Theorem 3.3

Any system decomposed (i.e. by means of $\mathbf{M}$ and $\mathbf{Y}$ matrices) from a regular system is itself regular and is (up to the permutations and linear combinations of processes) identical to one that can be arrived at by means of the procedure used in the Sraffa–Manara definition of the basic system in section II.2.

The second of the two problems set at the beginning of this section is now solved for regular systems. We have shown that by no other definition than the one given in section II.2 we can decompose a regular system further than into a basic system and a group of non-basic processes. For, if a second decomposition were possible, it could also be effected by the Sraffa–Manara construction, and the result of the first decomposition could not have been the basic system, since the basic system was defined as the smallest system arrived at this way (its uniqueness remains to be shown). Since the decomposed system of a regular system is regular, the same argument applies if a decomposed system is decomposed once more in itself.

As we can see from the example after the corollary of theorem 3.1, the assumption of regularity is also essential in this context: a non-regular basic system can sometimes be decomposed by means of the $\mathbf{Y}$ matrices (see also section II.7). We therefore call a regular basic system *truly basic* and an irregular basic system *pseudo-basic*.

COROLLARY:

The basic system of a regular non-basic system is truly basic.

As regards irregular systems, the Sraffa–Manara definition has not been justified by our considerations (except in that irregular systems have mathematically and economically the character of exceptions). The decomposition of a basic system by means of **Y** matrices as shown above (industries 'exchange' a set of goods of zero value) is economically less meaningful than the construction of the basic system (linear combination of industries), and it is not very relevant anyway because of the rarity of irregular systems. The only economically relevant irregular systems are those with prices that are proportional to labour values. They have often been discussed, but not from the point of view of decomposability. A discussion of other irregular systems from an economic or indeed any other point of view is not known to me. They have here been discovered only thanks to the application of mathematical methods. I shall nevertheless return to pseudo-basic systems in section II.7 in order to be methodologically complete. I take pains to consider the exceptions carefully so that others may be free to disregard them.

I have finally to prove an assertion I have often made (although of course not used in proofs), namely that the Sraffa–Manara construction leads to a uniquely determined basic system in both the regular and the irregular case.

Theorem 3.4

Two basic systems derived from the same system $(\mathbf{A}, \mathbf{B}, \mathbf{l})$ by means of the Sraffa–Manara construction (section II.2) consist of the same goods (with the same prices for all r) and are identical up to linear combinations of the processes.

PROOF:

Following theorem 2.1 it is evidently sufficient to show that the basic part of $[(\mathbf{B} - \mathbf{A})^{-1}\mathbf{B}, \mathbf{I}]$ is unique. Following Gantmacher (1966, XIII, §4), the system $[(\mathbf{B} - \mathbf{A})^{-1}\mathbf{B}, \mathbf{I}]$ can be decomposed after simultaneous permutations of rows and columns in the following manner:

$$\mathbf{D} = (\mathbf{B} - \mathbf{A})^{-1}\mathbf{B} = \begin{bmatrix} \mathbf{D}_1^1 & \mathbf{0} & \cdots & \mathbf{0} & \mathbf{0} & \cdots & \mathbf{0} \\ \mathbf{0} & \mathbf{D}_2^2 & \cdots & \mathbf{0} & \mathbf{0} & \cdots & \mathbf{0} \\ \cdots\cdots\cdots\cdots\cdots\cdots\cdots\cdots\cdots\cdots \\ \mathbf{0} & \mathbf{0} & \cdots & \mathbf{D}_g^g & \mathbf{0} & \cdots & \mathbf{0} \\ \mathbf{D}_{g+1}^1 & \mathbf{D}_{g+1}^2 & \cdots & \mathbf{D}_{g+1}^g & \mathbf{D}_{g+1}^{g+1} & \cdots & \mathbf{0} \\ \cdots\cdots\cdots\cdots\cdots\cdots\cdots\cdots\cdots\cdots \\ \mathbf{D}_s^1 & \mathbf{D}_s^2 & \cdots & \mathbf{D}_s^g & \mathbf{D}_s^{g+1} & \cdots & \mathbf{D}_s^s \end{bmatrix}$$

with each $\mathbf{D}_1^1, ..., \mathbf{D}_s^s$ indecomposable and so that in each sequence $\mathbf{D}_f^1, ..., \mathbf{D}_f^{f-1}$ ($f = g + 1, ..., s$) at least one matrix is different from zero.

The number g is then uniquely determined. With theorem 2.1 it follows from assumption (A.3), applied to the completely decomposable system

$$\begin{bmatrix} \mathbf{D}_1^1, \mathbf{O}, ..., \mathbf{O} \\ \mathbf{O}, \mathbf{D}_2^2, ..., \mathbf{O} \\ .... \\ \mathbf{O}, \mathbf{O}, ..., \mathbf{D}_g^g \end{bmatrix}, \begin{bmatrix} 1, 0, ..., 0 \\ 0, 1, ..., 0 \\ .... \\ 0, 0, ..., 1 \end{bmatrix},$$

that $g = 1$. Thus

$$\mathbf{D} = \begin{bmatrix} \mathbf{D}_1^1 & \mathbf{O} \\ \mathbf{D}_2^1 & \mathbf{D}_2^2 \end{bmatrix}$$

with $\mathbf{D}_1^1$ indecomposable and uniquely determined. The rest is obvious.

q.e.d.

Land at the intensive margin will be seen to be the most important non-basic in indecomposable systems. In the corresponding section (II.20) I shall give an example of a system of three goods and three processes which can be constructed by subtracting any of the three processes from the two others. That example will make it plain that the Sraffa–Manara construction can indeed lead to basic systems involving the same goods but identical only up to linear combinations of the processes.

Notes

1 A more direct proof is in Schefold (1976c).
2 To assume (as we do) that the degree of the polynomial $\det[\mathbf{B} - (1 + r)\mathbf{A}]$ is not smaller than n, implies the assumption that $\det(\mathbf{A}) \neq 0$. The only economically meaningful reason for $\det(\mathbf{A}) = 0$ is the existence of pure consumption goods. To exclude them is justified since we are talking about basic systems.
3 Even multiple roots are exceptional, for it follows from the theory of algebraic functions that every multiplicity of roots is unstable, in that any small change or perturbation of the coefficients of a system $(\mathbf{A}, \mathbf{B}, \mathbf{l})$ with a multiple root will lead to a system with n distinct simple roots. A precise analysis of this point requires, however, a more detailed analysis, if the perturbations are to be confined to the positive elements of the matrices $(\mathbf{A}, \mathbf{B})$.
4 To obtain an exception, one of at most n eigenvectors would have to be contained in the hyperplane which is orthogonal to $\mathbf{l}$.
5 This follows from

$$\frac{1}{1 + R_i} \mathbf{q}_i \mathbf{l} = \mathbf{q}_i \mathbf{A} \mathbf{l} = \frac{1}{1 + R} \mathbf{q}_i \mathbf{l}, \quad R_i \neq R.$$

4 Labour Values

In single-product systems, $\hat{\mathbf{p}}_i(0) = \mathbf{u}_i$ is interpreted as the amount of direct and indirect labour embodied in one unit of good i. The same can be said in the case of joint production: $\mathbf{a}_i\mathbf{u} + l_i$ is the amount of direct and indirect labour embodied in process i. This labour is expended in different proportions on the products that constitute the output of process i:

$$\mathbf{a}_i\mathbf{u} + l_i = \mathbf{b}_i\mathbf{u}$$
$$\mathbf{A}\mathbf{u} + \mathbf{l} = \mathbf{B}\mathbf{u}$$

hence

$$\mathbf{u} = (\mathbf{B} - \mathbf{A})^{-1}\mathbf{l}.$$

Mathematically speaking, this is a *definition* of a vector $\mathbf{u}$, which we call 'the vector of labour values'. Economically speaking, there are several justifications for this definition, which are sometimes erroneously interpreted as 'proofs' of a 'theorem' that $\mathbf{u}$ is the vector of labour values. The simplest definition is the direct one.

The total labour value produced in a process is equal on the one hand to the sum of the labour values of the commodities produced in it, on the other to the labour values of the commodities used up in it *plus* the direct labour expended in it. If the vector of labour values is denoted by $\mathbf{u}$, it is seen to be determined uniquely in a square system where the number of commodities is equal to that of independent processes, for $\mathbf{A}\mathbf{u} + \mathbf{l} = \mathbf{B}\mathbf{u}$ yields $\mathbf{u} = (\mathbf{B} - \mathbf{A})^{-1}\mathbf{l}$.

The definition is economically not quite satisfactory, however, since the traditional notion of labour value as the amount of labour embodied in 'the' product of the labour process seems to rest on single-product industries. Labour values are introduced by means of an implicit equation. Are there other, intuitively more appealing, ways of defining labour values that do not require us to have recourse to an implicit definition in order to allocate labour expended in a process between several outputs?

In the single-product system, $\mathbf{u}$ can be resolved into the sum of past labour inputs: $\mathbf{A}\mathbf{l}$ is the labour being embodied in the current period; $\mathbf{A}^2\mathbf{l}$ the labour embodied in the preceding period, and so on:

$$\mathbf{u} = \mathbf{l} + \mathbf{A}\mathbf{l} + \mathbf{A}^2\mathbf{l} + \cdots.$$

This formula is mathematically proved by matrix expansion

$$(\mathbf{I} - \mathbf{A})^{-1} = \mathbf{I} + \mathbf{A} + \mathbf{A}^2 + ...,$$

valid, as is well known, for all $\mathbf{A}$ whose eigenvalues are all smaller than one in absolute value and in particular for all matrices representing self-reproducing single-product systems. The definition of labour values by summing up all past labour inputs on the assumption of a technology that does not change through time is perhaps the one most appropriate from the classical point of view.

However, a similar expansion is not always possible if $\mathbf{B} \neq \mathbf{I}$, nor is there an economic reason to expect it (see e.g. section II.19 on land). It is true that – with $\det(\mathbf{B}) \neq 0$ – we can form the series

$$(\mathbf{I} - \mathbf{B}^{-1}\mathbf{A})^{-1} = \mathbf{I} + \mathbf{B}^{-1}\mathbf{A} + \cdots,$$

if $\det[\mathbf{B} - \lambda_i\mathbf{A}] = 0$ entails $|\lambda_i| > 1$ for all n roots of the equation; for $\det[\mathbf{B} - \lambda_i\mathbf{A}] = 0$ entails $\det[(1/\lambda_i)\mathbf{I} - \mathbf{B}^{-1}\mathbf{A}] = 0$.

The expansion of the labour vector

$$\mathbf{u} = (\mathbf{I} - \mathbf{B}^{-1}\mathbf{A})^{-1}\mathbf{B}^{-1}\mathbf{l} = \mathbf{B}^{-1}\mathbf{l} + \mathbf{B}^{-1}\mathbf{A}\mathbf{B}^{-1}\mathbf{l} + \cdots$$

is to dated quantities of labour of the transformed system $(\mathbf{B}^{-1}\mathbf{A}, \mathbf{I}, \mathbf{B}^{-1}\mathbf{l})$ of gross integrated industries. No similar series exists for net integrated industries. The series shows that the conventional definitions of labour values can be extended to joint production, provided that the system is transformed.

This definition is, however, only satisfactory if mathematically and economically sufficient conditions can be found to guarantee the convergence of the series, which is, unfortunately, problematic.

A third way of accounting labour values is the so-called subsystems approach (PCMC, Appendix A), which we have already used in a simplified form in section II.1. It provides a satisfactory solution:

Write $\mathbf{S}$ for the diagonal matrix derived from the surplus vector and assume the surplus to be strictly positive:

$$\mathbf{S} = \begin{bmatrix} s_1 & & 0 \\ & \ddots & \\ 0 & & s_n \end{bmatrix}; \qquad \mathbf{s}' = (s_1, \dots, s_n) = \mathbf{e}'(\mathbf{B} - \mathbf{A}) > \mathbf{o}.$$

We determine activity levels $\mathbf{q}_i$ by which the surplus s_i of good i and nothing else is produced:

$$\mathbf{q}_i = s_i[\mathbf{e}_i(\mathbf{B} - \mathbf{A})^{-1}], \qquad \mathbf{e}_i = (0, \dots, 0, 1, 0, \dots, 0),$$

or

$$\mathbf{Q} = \begin{bmatrix} \mathbf{q}_1 \\ \vdots \\ \mathbf{q}_n \end{bmatrix} = \mathbf{S}(\mathbf{B} - \mathbf{A})^{-1}.$$

$$\mathbf{e}'\mathbf{Q} = \mathbf{e}'\mathbf{S}(\mathbf{B} - \mathbf{A})^{-1} = \mathbf{s}'(\mathbf{B} - \mathbf{A})^{-1} = \mathbf{e}'$$

means that we may interpret $\mathbf{Q}$ as a virtual subdivision of the actual activity levels $\mathbf{e}$. Since $\mathbf{q}_i$ are the activity levels appropriate for the production of s_i,

$$\bar{u}_i = \mathbf{q}_i \mathbf{l}$$

must be the amount of work expended on the isolated production of s_i and $\tilde{u}_i = (1/s_i)\bar{u}_i$ expresses the amount of direct and indirect labour embodied per unit of good i.

We have

$$\tilde{\mathbf{u}} = \mathbf{S}^{-1}\bar{\mathbf{u}} = \mathbf{S}^{-1}\mathbf{Q}\mathbf{l} = \mathbf{S}^{-1}\mathbf{S}(\mathbf{B} - \mathbf{A})^{-1}\mathbf{l} = (\mathbf{B} - \mathbf{A})^{-1}\mathbf{l} = \mathbf{u},$$

as was to be expected.

If we do not insist on visualizing the subsystems as a subdivision of the system as a whole, we can define it more directly by

$$\mathbf{q}_i = \mathbf{e}_i(\mathbf{B} - \mathbf{A})^{-1},$$

as in section II.1 above, and labour values are directly given by

$$\mathbf{q}_i\mathbf{l} = u_i.$$

It is then not necessary to assume the surplus to be strictly positive.

The point is that a subsystem produces period for period a *net* product of one unit of one commodity which therefore incorporates all the living labour in the subsystem. This provides a definition of labour values that is at once applicable to single-product and to joint-production systems and that does not require us to introduce the concept of indirect labour at the level of the definition.

An Apparent Paradox (see PCMC, sec. 70)

Labour values are paradoxically not always positive. Suppose that $(\mathbf{A}, \mathbf{B}, \mathbf{l})$ is such that one of the prices $\hat{\mathbf{p}}(0)$ at $r = 0$ or 'labour values', say $\hat{p}_1(0) = u_1$, is negative. Consider an expansion of the production of good 1 by some small amount δ_1. $\mathbf{q}$ is the vector of activity levels by which the ordinary activity levels $\mathbf{e}$ have then to be augmented:

$$\mathbf{e}' + \mathbf{q}' = (\mathbf{s}' + \delta_1\mathbf{e}_1)(\mathbf{B} - \mathbf{A})^{-1} = \mathbf{e}' + \delta_1\mathbf{e}_1(\mathbf{B} - \mathbf{A})^{-1}$$

(δ_1 should be chosen sufficiently small to have $\mathbf{e} + \mathbf{q} \geqslant \mathbf{o}$). As stated in the subsystems approach, we interpret $\mathbf{q}'\mathbf{l}$ as the additional labour that is consumed in the production of δ_1. We find:

$$\mathbf{q}'\mathbf{l} = \delta_1\mathbf{e}_1(\mathbf{B} - \mathbf{A})^{-1}\mathbf{l} = \delta_1\mathbf{e}_1\mathbf{u} = \delta_1 u_1 < 0,$$

that is to say, we find that the increase in the production of good 1 does not require an increase in the consumption of productive labour, but that, on the contrary, it seems to have set labour free.

Such a state of affairs looks very paradoxical at first sight. We shall see, however, not only that it occurs frequently, but even that it is typical for joint production (see sections II.9a and II.9b, and, in particular, for a certain type of inefficient machinery sections II.15 and II.16).

Suffice it to say at present that negative prices at $r = 0$ are perfectly compatible with positive prices for some $r > 0$ which conceal the inefficiency implied in negative labour values: an economy working at $r = 0$ would not indulge in producing good 1 in ever-increasing quantities simply because this could be done without engaging more labour, but it would switch to new techniques, which allow positive $\hat{\mathbf{p}}(0)$. As it turns out, the good in question may well be produced in ever greater quantities after the switch, but as a waste product, not as a commodity; thus outside the system.

5   Distribution and the Standard Commodity

Assuming that the workers' subsistence wage is not already implicit in the input matrix $\mathbf{A}$, we introduce it as follows: if labour is unskilled and interchangeable between industries, it is consistent to regard the labour force as homogeneous in the consumption pattern. Assume that the whole wage is for subsistence. If the wage rate is uniform, the workers in every industry will buy a fraction of the total wage $\mathbf{d}^1 = (d_1, ..., d_n)$ proportional to their number or (what amounts to the same thing) proportional to the labour-time necessary in that industry so that the matrix

$$\mathbf{D} = \mathbf{ld'} = \begin{bmatrix} l_1 d_1, & ..., & l_1 d_n \\ \vdots & & \vdots \\ l_n d_1, & ..., & l_n d_n \end{bmatrix}$$

represents the real wage consumed by the workers in every industry. It depends on the existence of a uniform wage rate but not of a uniform rate of profit.

$\mathbf{l}_w = \mathbf{Du}$, $\mathbf{u} = (\mathbf{B} - \mathbf{A})^{-1}\mathbf{l}$, is then the labour-time the workers spend in each industry on earning their living. From

$$\mathbf{l}_w = (\mathbf{ld'})\mathbf{u} = \mathbf{l}(\mathbf{d'u}) = \alpha\mathbf{l}$$
$$\alpha = \mathbf{d'u} \leqslant \mathbf{s'u} = \mathbf{e'}(\mathbf{B} - \mathbf{A})(\mathbf{B} - \mathbf{A})^{-1}\mathbf{l} = 1$$

it follows that the time they have to work for themselves is (if $\mathbf{u} \geqslant \mathbf{o}$) a positive fraction of the time they spend working for the capitalists – that is to say, Marx's rate of surplus value $\varepsilon = (1 - \alpha)/\alpha$ is uniform and positive irrespective of the rates of profit (Morishima and Seton, 1961; Okishio, 1963).

The rate of surplus value is a concrete measure for income distribution, but Mr Sraffa chooses another one – partly because the wage, as soon as it exceeds the subsistence level, cannot be determined before prices are known, partly because he considers the rate of profit as the independent variable, and regards it as prior to the distribution of physical income.

I overlooked the consequences of negative labour values for the Marxist concept of exploitation when I wrote this in 1970. They have since been pointed out by Ian Steedman (1975):

If prices are positive at some positive rate of profit while some labour values are negative, and if the commodities with negative values constitute the major part of the share of the surplus going to the capitalists, surplus value will be negative while profits are positive. Hence it is even more difficult to see how profits could, in accordance with Marx, be explained as a redistribution of surplus value in joint-production systems than it is in single-product systems where surplus value is always positive, if and only if profits are positive. The Marxian concepts of surplus value and exploitation are useless if positive profits can coexist with a negative or zero rate of exploitation.

Those who wish to rescue that concept in order to use it outside the framework for which it was originally conceived (an ingenious, but simplified model of nineteenth-century capitalism with single-product industries and fixed capital) should, in my view, try to show that wage goods have positive labour values in the relevant cases (as in the case of fixed capital). It seems to me at any rate erroneous to tamper instead with the concept of labour values, which is perfectly straightforward thanks to the subsystems approach.

The standard commodity as the explanatory concept introduced by Mr Sraffa for the understanding of the movements of relative prices and the wage rate in function of the rate of profit is briefly explained in Part I and extensively in Essay 6 in Part III; there is no difference here between the case of joint-production and single-product systems, if the standard commodity exists. Here we list briefly its main features. To make an easy start we postulate that the polynomial

$$\det\left[\mathbf{B} - (1 + r)\mathbf{A}\right] = 0,$$

has one and only one simple root $R > 0$ in $\{r \mid r \geqslant 0\}$. The real 'eigenvector' $\mathbf{q}$

$$(1 + R)\mathbf{q}'\mathbf{A} = \mathbf{q}'\mathbf{B}$$

associated with it is normalized by

$$\mathbf{q}'\mathbf{l} = 1.\,^{[1]}$$

$\mathbf{q}$ are the 'standard multipliers', $\mathbf{t}' = \mathbf{q}'(\mathbf{B} - \mathbf{A})$ the standard commodity.[2] We use it to define standard prices

$$\mathbf{p}_t = \frac{\left[\mathbf{B} - (1 + r)\mathbf{A}\right]^{-1}\mathbf{l}}{\mathbf{t}'\left[\mathbf{B} - (1 + r)\mathbf{A}\right]^{-1}\mathbf{l}}, \qquad \mathbf{t}'\mathbf{p}_t = 1.$$

The relation

$$1 = \frac{r}{R} + w_t$$

which follows from

$$1 = \mathbf{q}'(\mathbf{B} - \mathbf{A})\mathbf{p}_t(r) = \mathbf{q}'\,[r\mathbf{A}\mathbf{p}_t(r) + w_t\mathbf{l}]$$

$$= \frac{r}{R}\,\mathbf{q}'(\mathbf{B} - \mathbf{A})\mathbf{p}_t(r) + w_t$$

has become very famous. Because

$$\frac{r}{R} = \frac{r\mathbf{q}'\mathbf{A}\mathbf{p}}{\mathbf{q}'(\mathbf{B} - \mathbf{A})\mathbf{p}},$$

it shows how the shares of profits and wages (wages are equal to the wage rate for $\mathbf{e}'\mathbf{l} = 1$) vary *linearly* in an economy in standard proportions, that is, in an economy for which $\mathbf{q} = \mathbf{e}$ ($\mathbf{e}$ is always assumed to denote the actual proportions).

If $\mathbf{e} \neq \mathbf{q}$, $1 = (r/R) + w_t$ still holds as a relation between the rate of profit r and the wage rate:

$$w_t = 1 - \frac{r}{R} = \frac{1}{\mathbf{t}'\hat{\mathbf{p}}(r)}.$$

The real wage may consist of any basket of goods with $w_t = \bar{\mathbf{a}}'\mathbf{p}_t$, $\bar{\mathbf{a}}' \leqslant \mathbf{e}'(\mathbf{B} - \mathbf{A})$. If the real wage is a fraction $\lambda(r)$ of a given basket $\bar{\mathbf{a}}$ in some range of r and if $\hat{\mathbf{p}}(r)$ (prices in terms of the wage rate) rise monotonically with r, $w_{\bar{a}}(r)$ will fall, whatever $\bar{\mathbf{a}}$.

If some $\hat{p}_i(r)$ do not rise with r, the value of the wage in terms of the standard commodity, $w_t = \lambda(r)\,\bar{\mathbf{a}}'\mathbf{p}_t(r)$, will fall with r, but not necessarily $\lambda(r)$, i.e. the wage in terms of basket r (see below, section II.9b).

The standard prices

$$\mathbf{p}_t(r) = \left(1 - \frac{r}{R}\right)[\mathbf{B} - (1 + r)\mathbf{A}]^{-1}\mathbf{l} = \left(1 - \frac{r}{R}\right)\hat{\mathbf{p}}(r)$$

tend for $r \to 0$ to labour values

$$\mathbf{p}_t(0) = (\mathbf{B} - \mathbf{A})^{-1}\mathbf{l} = \mathbf{u}.\,[3]$$

They make the value of the national product at $r = 0$ equal to one (equal to the value of the standard commodity):

$$\mathbf{e}'(\mathbf{B} - \mathbf{A})\mathbf{p}_t(0) = \mathbf{e}'(\mathbf{B} - \mathbf{A})\mathbf{u} = \mathbf{e}'\mathbf{l} = 1$$

and possess, unlike $\hat{\mathbf{p}}(r)$, a limit for $r = R$; for the limit

$$\boldsymbol{\pi} = \lim_{r \to R} \mathbf{p}_t(r) = \lim_{r \to R} \left[\frac{(R - r)(\mathbf{B} - (1 + r)\mathbf{A})_{\mathrm{Ad}}\mathbf{l}}{R \det[\mathbf{B} - (1 + r)\mathbf{A}]} \right]$$

exists, because R is a simple root of $\det[\mathbf{B} - (1 + r)\mathbf{A}] = 0$, and it can be shown (see section II.9b below) that $\boldsymbol{\pi} = \mathbf{p}_t(R)$, with $\mathbf{p}_t(R)$ defined by

$$(1 + R)\mathbf{A}\mathbf{p}_t(R) = \mathbf{B}\mathbf{p}_t(R), \qquad \mathbf{t}'\mathbf{p}_t(R) = 1.$$

The real wage $\bar{\mathbf{a}}$ ($\bar{\mathbf{a}}'\mathbf{p}_t(r) = w_t$) is zero at $r = R$, whatever $\bar{\mathbf{a}} \geqslant \mathbf{o}$, if $\mathbf{p}_t(R) > \mathbf{o}$.

Notes

1 Remember $\mathbf{e}'\mathbf{l} = 1$. We shall tacitly assume from now on (in line with the conclusions of sections II.3 and II.7) that $\mathbf{q}'\mathbf{l} \neq 0$.
2 $\mathbf{t}' \geqslant \mathbf{o}$, if $\mathbf{q}' \geqslant \mathbf{o}$; for $\mathbf{t}' = \mathbf{q}'(\mathbf{B} - \mathbf{A}) = R\mathbf{q}'\mathbf{A}$.
3 $\mathbf{p}_t(r)$ can be constant, therefore equal to values, if and only if

$$(1 + r)\mathbf{A}(\mathbf{B} - \mathbf{A})^{-1}\mathbf{l} + \left(1 - \frac{r}{R}\right)\mathbf{l} = \mathbf{B}(\mathbf{B} - \mathbf{A})^{-1}\mathbf{l};$$

therefore if and only if $\mathbf{l}$ is an eigenvector in the equation

$$R\mathbf{A}(\mathbf{B} - \mathbf{A})^{-1}\mathbf{l} = \mathbf{l},$$

as is confirmed by a short calculation.

6 Expansions of the Price Vector

We continue to assume that $\det[\mathbf{B} - (1 + r)\mathbf{A}] = 0$ has a simple positive root. The smallest is denoted by R. Moreover, we assume that $(\mathbf{A}, \mathbf{B})$ is basic.

In single-product systems the standard prices could be reduced to a series of 'dated quantities of labour':

$$\mathbf{p}_t(r) = \left(1 - \frac{r}{R}\right)[\mathbf{I} - (1 + r)\mathbf{A}]^{-1}\mathbf{l}$$

$$= \left(1 - \frac{r}{R}\right)[\mathbf{l} + (1 + r)\mathbf{A}\mathbf{l} + (1 + r)^2\mathbf{A}^2\mathbf{l} + \cdots]. \qquad (6.1)$$

In section II.4 the $\mathbf{A}^n\mathbf{l}$ were recognized as dated labour terms. The reduction to dated quantities of labour is important in so far as it represents (together with the standard commodity) one of the most important concepts for the explanation of prices in Sraffa systems. If the reduction exists, its function will be the same as in the single-product case, but does it exist?

The expansion $(\det(\mathbf{B}) \neq 0!)$

$$\mathbf{p}_t(r) = \left(1 - \frac{r}{R}\right)[\mathbf{B} - (1 + r)\mathbf{A}]^{-1}\mathbf{l}$$

$$= \left(1 - \frac{r}{R}\right)[\mathbf{I} - (1 + r)\mathbf{B}^{-1}\mathbf{A}]^{-1}\mathbf{B}^{-1}\mathbf{l}$$

$$= \left(1 - \frac{r}{R}\right)[\mathbf{I} + (1 + r)\mathbf{B}^{-1}\mathbf{A} + (1 + r)^2(\mathbf{B}^{-1}\mathbf{A})^2 + \cdots]\mathbf{B}^{-1}\mathbf{l} \qquad (6.2)$$

(where it is admissible) represents a reduction to dated quantities of labour, for joint-production systems, transformed into gross integrated industries. We can also use the net integrated industries. The series is then different in that it depends on r, not on $1 + r$, and converges always for a sufficiently small neighbourhood of zero.

$$\hat{\mathbf{p}}(r) = [\mathbf{B} - (1 + r)\mathbf{A}]^{-1}\mathbf{l}$$

$$= [\mathbf{I} - r(\mathbf{B} - \mathbf{A})^{-1}\mathbf{A}]^{-1}(\mathbf{B} - \mathbf{A})^{-1}\mathbf{l}$$

$$= [\mathbf{I} + r(\mathbf{B} - \mathbf{A})^{-1}\mathbf{A} + r^2[(\mathbf{B} - \mathbf{A})^{-1}\mathbf{A}]^2 + \cdots]\mathbf{u}. \qquad (6.3)$$

Theorem 6.1

The series (6.2), [(6.3)], converges for $0 \leqslant r < R$, if $\mathbf{B}^{-1}\mathbf{A} \geqslant \mathbf{O}[(\mathbf{B} - \mathbf{A})^{-1}\mathbf{A} \geqslant \mathbf{O}]$. If $\mathbf{B}^{-1}\mathbf{A} \not\geqslant \mathbf{O}[(\mathbf{B} - \mathbf{A})^{-1}\mathbf{A} \not\geqslant \mathbf{O}]$, it converges in no larger neighbourhood of zero than $0 \leqslant r < R$. While the series 6.2 may not converge for any $r \geqslant 0$, there is $\bar{R} > 0$ such that 6.3 converges for all $0 \leqslant r < \bar{R}$, and $\bar{R} \leqslant R$, if a maximum rate of profit exists.

PROOF:

We have to see whether a positive limit to r exists so that the absolute values of all complex eigenvalues of $(1 + r)\mathbf{C} = (1 + r)\mathbf{B}^{-1}\mathbf{A}$ are smaller than one. If a positive limit exists, (6.2) will be valid within that range.

Replace the elements of $\mathbf{C} = \mathbf{B}^{-1}\mathbf{A}$ by their absolute values and denote the ensuing semi-positive matrix by $|\mathbf{C}|$. $|\mathbf{C}|$ is indecomposable (theorem 2.1) and has a maximal positive eigenvalue λ with which $\mathbf{q} > \mathbf{o}$, $\mathbf{q}'|\mathbf{C}| = \lambda\mathbf{q}'$ is associated. Let $\mu, \mathbf{x}$ be any (complex) eigenvalue and eigenvector of $(1 + r)\,\mathbf{C}$:

$$(1 + r)\mathbf{C}\mathbf{x} = \mu\mathbf{x}.$$

$|\mathbf{x}|$ is the vector of absolute values of the components of $\mathbf{x}$. From

$$|\mu\mathbf{x}| = |\mu|\,|\mathbf{x}| = (1 + r)\,|\mathbf{C}\mathbf{x}| \leqslant (1 + r)\,|\mathbf{C}|\,|\mathbf{x}|$$

$$|\mu|\,\mathbf{q}'\,|\mathbf{x}| \leqslant (1 + r)\mathbf{q}'\,|\mathbf{C}|\,|\mathbf{x}| = (1 + r)\lambda\mathbf{q}'\,|\mathbf{x}|$$

and $\mathbf{q} > \mathbf{o}$, $\mathbf{x} \geqslant \mathbf{o}$, it follows that

$$|\mu| \leqslant (1 + r)\lambda.$$

Thus, $|\mu| < 1$ if $(1 + r)\lambda < 1$. Distinguish:

(a) $\mathbf{B}^{-1}\mathbf{A} \geqslant \mathbf{O}$. Then $\mathbf{B}^{-1}\mathbf{A} = |\mathbf{B}^{-1}\mathbf{A}|$, $\mathbf{q}'\mathbf{B}^{-1}\mathbf{A} = \lambda\mathbf{q}'$ and $\mathbf{B}^{-1}\mathbf{Ap} = \lambda\mathbf{p}$ with $\mathbf{p} > \mathbf{o}$. From Lemma, section II.2, we have $\lambda < 1$. According to the Frobenius theorem, λ is the greatest real root of $\mathbf{B}^{-1}\mathbf{A}$. R was defined as the smallest real root of $\det[\mathbf{B} - (1 + r)\mathbf{A}] = 0$. Thus $\lambda = 1/(1 + R)$ which proves the first assertion.
(b) $\mathbf{B}^{-1}\mathbf{A} \not\geqslant \mathbf{O}$. The series converges for $0 \leqslant r < (1/\lambda) - 1$, if $\lambda < 1$. This may be the case, but since $1/(1 + R)$ is one of the eigenvalues of $\mathbf{B}^{-1}\mathbf{A}$, we have from $|\mu| \leqslant (1 + r)\lambda$ for $r = 0$ $1/(1 + R) \leqslant \lambda$. An example for $\lambda > 1$ may be constructed by means of the graphic technique (section II.11).

The proof for (6.3) is analogous, except in that (6.3) converges for $0 \leqslant r < \bar{R}$ where $1/\bar{R}$ is equal to the largest absolute value of the eigenvalues of $(\mathbf{B} - \mathbf{A})^{-1}\mathbf{A}$.

q.e.d.

There is therefore always a series available that helps to explain how relative prices deviate from labour values at least at small rates of profit. Space prevents consideration of concrete applications; the reader will have to work them out for himself.

7 Peculiarities of Joint-Production Systems: Existence of the Standard Commodity

The standard commodity represents a splendid didactical device for the explanation of the fundamental properties of prices of production. It is, in itself, by no means indispensable to Mr Sraffa's theory, but it provides such useful insights that we shall begin our analysis of the existence, positivity and uniqueness of prices, their movement as a funcion of the rate of profit and the properties of the wage curve in joint-production systems in this section by examining the conditions under which the concept of the standard commodity and of the maximum rate of profit can be extended to joint production – and what happens, if they cannot.

The question of the existence and uniqueness of the standard commodity is mathematically and in economic interpretation intricately linked to the notion of basics. First, because the characteristic polynomial of a non-basic system falls apart

$$\det[\mathbf{B} - (1 + r)\mathbf{A}] = \det(\mathbf{M})\det[\mathbf{B} - (1 + r)\mathbf{A}] = \det[\mathbf{MB} - (1 + r)\mathbf{MA}]$$
$$= \det[\mathbf{B}_1^1 - \mathbf{HB}_2^1 - (1 + r)(\mathbf{A}_1^1 - \mathbf{HA}_2^1)]$$
$$\times \det[\mathbf{B}_2^2 - (1 + r)\mathbf{A}_2^2].$$

Roots of the second part of this equation (roots of $\det[\mathbf{B}_2^2 - (1 + r)\mathbf{A}_2^2] = 0$) yield eigenvectors totally irrelevant from the economic point of view, if the interpretation of non-basics given in section II.2 is accepted. This is obvious if a root $\tilde{R}$ of $\det[\mathbf{B}_2^2 - (1 + r)\mathbf{A}_2^2] = 0$ is greater than the maximum rate of profit R in the basic system which we here suppose to exist: prices cannot rise beyond R, because $\hat{\mathbf{p}}_1(R)$ diverges. In the opposite case, all one can say is that a uniform rate of profit for all processes $\mathbf{A}_2, \mathbf{B}_2, \mathbf{l}_2$ is impossible at or around $r = \tilde{R}$; for

$$[\mathbf{B}_2^2 - (1 + r)\mathbf{A}_2^2]\hat{\mathbf{p}}_2 = \mathbf{l}_2 + [\mathbf{B}_2^1 - (1 + r)\mathbf{A}_2^1]\hat{\mathbf{p}}_1$$

is not solvable for $\hat{\mathbf{p}}_2$ at $r = \tilde{R}$. Thus, if r is to remain uniform, some non-basic processes have to be replaced (see PCMC, Appendix B).

We now turn to the basic system $(\bar{\mathbf{A}}_1^1, \bar{\mathbf{B}}_1^1)$ and to the roots of $\det[\bar{\mathbf{B}}_1^1 - (1 + r)\bar{\mathbf{A}}_1^1] = 0$. If there are several positive roots, we define the smallest of them to be the relevant maximum rate of profit for the intuitive reasons given in PCMC, sec. 64. The question is whether it exists and whether the standard commodity associated with it is unique.

In order to solve the problem of uniqueness we have again to recall our discussion of the basic system. Although we argued there that multiple eigenvalues are extremely exceptional, we propose here the following solution for the sake of completeness: If the smallest positive root of $\det[\bar{\mathbf{B}}_1^1 - (1 + r)\bar{\mathbf{A}}_1^1] = 0$ is semi-simple, [1] only one eigenvector and therefore a uniquely defined standard commodity exist. If the system is not truly basic and the root is not semi-simple, it follows from theorem 3.2 in section II.3 that some $\bar{\mathbf{q}}$, $\bar{\mathbf{q}}$ real, $\bar{\mathbf{q}} \neq \mathbf{o}$, with $\bar{\mathbf{q}}\hat{\mathbf{p}}(r) = 0$ exists. Suppose that the i'th component of $\bar{\mathbf{q}}$ does not vanish. Without loss of generality $(\bar{\mathbf{A}}_1^1, \bar{\mathbf{B}}_1^1, \bar{\mathbf{l}}_1) = (\mathbf{A}, \mathbf{B}, \mathbf{l})$. Define

$$\mathbf{Y} = \frac{1}{q_i}\begin{bmatrix} a_1^j\bar{q}_1, ..., a_1^j\bar{q}_n \\ ..... \\ a_n^j\bar{q}_1, ..., a_n^j\bar{q}_n \end{bmatrix} = \frac{1}{q_i}\mathbf{a}^j\bar{\mathbf{q}},$$

where $\mathbf{a}^j$ is *any* column of $\mathbf{A}$. Since $\mathbf{Y}\hat{\mathbf{p}}(r) = \mathbf{o}$, we find that the system $(\mathbf{A} - \mathbf{Y}, \mathbf{B}, \mathbf{l})$ has the same prices as $(\mathbf{A}, \mathbf{B}, \mathbf{l})$ for all rates of profit, but it differs from our original system in that $(\mathbf{A} - \mathbf{Y}, \mathbf{B}, \mathbf{l})$ is non-basic because the j'th column of the input matrix consists of zeros; commodity j has been turned into a pure consumption good. Either this non-basic will have to be eliminated and the procedure if necessary repeated until the disturbing multiple roots have disappeared. Or else, if this extension of the concept of a basic system seems to lead too far away from economic intuition, this sudden and unexpected appearance of a non-basic will induce one to rule out *a priori* all systems with non-semi-simple roots of $\det[\mathbf{B} - (1 + r)\mathbf{A}] = 0$.

We conclude at any rate that we have either a maximum rate of profit with which a unique standard commodity is associated or no maximum rate of profit and no standard commodity at all. Roots with several eigenvectors, or ambiguities about which of several roots should be chosen, may be ruled out.

We now have identified the basic system in the regular as well as in the irregular case. We have defined labour values, and have seen that a (restricted) analogon to the reduction to dated quantities of labour exists. Finally, we have seen that the standard commodity (if it exists) allows distribution and price movements to be explained as in the single-product case.

Our concern in the next two sections will be to find sufficient conditions, first for the existence of the maximum rate of profit and a standard commodity in the basic system (having excluded all sorts of pseudo-maximum rates of profit), and second for prices to be positive. Such conditions by no means spring directly from the concept of a basic system as is the case with single-product systems. Nor is there a comprehensive and straightforward mathematical theory. We shall therefore have to add further restrictions to Sraffa's method and introduce balanced growth in a later section, which will finally allow us to draw the proper wage curve for any joint-production system.

We first have to specify particular joint-production systems by economic criteria, if we want to get anywhere. The specifications are restrictive in relation to our discussion of the basic system, but it will be seen that these particular cases are contained in the later analysis of balanced growth and help to illuminate it. Before we start, we prove a rather trivial, but nevertheless very important theorem. We show that in no economic system are prices positive and finite for all rates of profit. If $\hat{\mathbf{p}}(r) > \mathbf{o}$ at $r = r_0$ and the rate of profit rises, there must come a point $r = r_1$ at which either prices in terms of the wage rate become infinite and the wage falls to zero $- r_1 = R$ is then the maximum rate of profit $-$ or some prices turn negative. Systems without a maximum rate of profit are not absurd because in them, too, there is a limit to the rise in the rate of profit and the viability of the system, in the shape of negative prices. Systems with a maximum rate of profit (and standard commodity) are on the other hand not immune from negative prices. The point of the theorem is to show in the most direct possible way that there is a finite range to the rate of profit (or the wage rate) in which the surplus can be economically meaningfully divided between profits and wages.

Theorem 7.1

Let $(\mathbf{A}, \mathbf{B}, \mathbf{l})$ be a basic system, $\mathbf{A} \geqslant \mathbf{O}$, $\mathbf{B} \geqslant \mathbf{O}$. Either a maximum rate of profit and a standard commodity exist and/or prices in any standard do not remain positive for all positive r. (The theorem asserts that it is impossible for a system without a standard commodity to have non-negative prices at all rates of profit.)

PROOF:

Suppose $\hat{\mathbf{p}}(r) = [\mathbf{B} - (1 + r)\mathbf{A}]^{-1}\mathbf{l} \geqslant \mathbf{o}$, $\det[\mathbf{B} - (1 + r)\mathbf{A}] \neq 0$ for $r \geqslant r_0 \geqslant 0$. Since $\mathbf{e}'\mathbf{A} > \mathbf{o}$ (according to the Lemma in section II.2) and since $\mathbf{e}'\mathbf{B} = \mathbf{e}'$ (the usual normalization) and since $\mathbf{e}'(\mathbf{B} - \mathbf{A}) \geqslant \mathbf{o}$, we can write

$$\mathbf{e}'\mathbf{A} = \gamma\mathbf{e}' + \mathbf{f}', \qquad \mathbf{f}' \geqslant \mathbf{o}, \qquad 0 < \gamma < 1,$$

and get for all $r \geqslant r_0 \geqslant 0$

$$\mathbf{B}\hat{\mathbf{p}}(r) - (1 + r)\mathbf{A}\hat{\mathbf{p}}(r) = \mathbf{l}$$

$$\mathbf{e}'\mathbf{B}\hat{\mathbf{p}}(r) - (1 + r)\mathbf{e}'\mathbf{A}\hat{\mathbf{p}}(r)$$

$$= \mathbf{e}'\hat{\mathbf{p}}(r) - (1 + r)\gamma\mathbf{e}'\hat{\mathbf{p}}(r) - (1 + r)\mathbf{f}'\hat{\mathbf{p}}(r)$$

$$= \mathbf{e}'\hat{\mathbf{p}}(r)[1 - (1 + r)\gamma] - (1 + r)\mathbf{f}'\hat{\mathbf{p}}(r) = \mathbf{e}'\mathbf{l} = 1.$$

Since $\mathbf{e}'\hat{\mathbf{p}}(r)$ and $\mathbf{f}'\hat{\mathbf{p}}(r)$ remain positive for all r, the left-hand side of the last equation must have turned negative for $r > (1/\gamma) - 1$, which is a contradiction. Either or both of the assumptions must therefore be false. The extension to other price standards is immediate.

q.e.d.

In particular, we conclude: if prices $\hat{\mathbf{p}}(r)$ (prices in terms of the wage rate) do not fall as r rises from some r_0 with $\hat{\mathbf{p}}(r) > \mathbf{o}$, they must diverge to infinity at some *finite* rate of profit which is the maximum rate of profit.

We shall soon be able to show that such a maximum rate of profit will in all relevant cases always be reached if commodities with negative prices and processes producing them are properly eliminated. But first we turn to certain special cases.

Note

1   R with $\det[\mathbf{B} - (1 + R)\mathbf{A}] = 0$ is called semi-simple if $\operatorname{rk}[\mathbf{B} - (1 + R)\mathbf{A}] = n - 1$ (see section II.3).

8   All-productive and Related Systems

We transform $(\mathbf{A}, \mathbf{B}, \mathbf{l})$ as in section 6:

$$\hat{\mathbf{p}}(r) = [\mathbf{B} - (1 + r)\mathbf{A}]^{-1}\mathbf{l} = [\mathbf{I} - r(\mathbf{B} - \mathbf{A})^{-1}\mathbf{A}]^{-1}(\mathbf{B} - \mathbf{A})^{-1}\mathbf{l}.$$

If $(\mathbf{A}, \mathbf{B})$ is all-productive $((\mathbf{B} - \mathbf{A})^{-1} \geqslant \mathbf{O})$, it has all the essential properties of a single-product system.

The main difference is that a basic all-productive system is not necessarily all-engaging, while a basic single-product system is always all-engaging. Otherwise we have:

If $(\mathbf{A}, \mathbf{B})$ is basic, $(\mathbf{B} - \mathbf{A})^{-1}\mathbf{A}$ is indecomposable. There is a simple root $R > 0$ of $\det[\mathbf{I} - r(\mathbf{B} - \mathbf{A})^{-1}\mathbf{A}] = 0$, which is also a simple root of $\det[\mathbf{B} - (1 + r)\mathbf{A}] = 0$ and the eigenvector associated with it is positive:

$$(1 + R)\mathbf{A}\mathbf{p} = \mathbf{B}\mathbf{p}, \qquad \mathbf{p} > \mathbf{o},$$

because $(\mathbf{B} - \mathbf{A})^{-1}\mathbf{A}$ is indecomposable and

$$\mathbf{p} = R(\mathbf{B} - \mathbf{A})^{-1}\mathbf{A}\mathbf{p}.$$

The standard multipliers

$$(1 + R)\mathbf{q}'\mathbf{A} = \mathbf{q}'\mathbf{B}$$

and the standard commodity $\mathbf{t}' = \mathbf{q}'(\mathbf{B} - \mathbf{A}) = R\mathbf{q}'\mathbf{A}$ are at least semi-positive because $\mathbf{A}(\mathbf{B} - \mathbf{A})^{-1} \geqslant \mathbf{O}$. From the expansion of the price vector in system II.6 it is seen that all-productive systems have positive prices for $0 \leqslant r < R$. They are also alone in being immune against the inefficiency mentioned in section II.4 which is connected with negative labour values.

Unfortunately, all-productive systems are as such quite untypical for joint production: in a two-sector model where two goods are produced by two processes it is necessary and sufficient for all-productivity that each process produces more of one commodity than it uses and uses more of the other than it produces. More convincing examples exist for $n > 2$, but one does not get very far.

It is, however, possible to find some meaningful, though related generalizations from all-productive systems:

(1) $[\mathbf{B} - (1 + \bar{r})\mathbf{A}]^{-1} \geqslant \mathbf{O}$ for some $\bar{r} \geqslant 0$. $[\mathbf{B} - (1 + \bar{r})\mathbf{A}]^{-1} \geqslant \mathbf{O}$ for some $\bar{r} \geqslant 0$ is a condition considerably weaker than $(\mathbf{B} - \mathbf{A})^{-1} \geqslant \mathbf{O}$. Such systems are called *almost all-productive*. Economically, it means that no price $\hat{p}_i(\bar{r})$ in terms of the wage rate falls as a result of any partial increase of the wage or of working hours $l_j \to l_j + \delta l_j$ at any rate of profit in any one industry j (see example in section II.11). The system $[(1 + \bar{r})\mathbf{A}, \mathbf{B}, \mathbf{l}]$ fulfils the same conditions as an all-productive system. In particular, maximum rate of profit and standard commodity exist and prices $\mathbf{p}_t(r)$ are positive for $\bar{r} \leqslant r \leqslant R$.

It is a most surprising result that essentially all systems turn out to be almost all-productive at high rates of profit (see section II.9b) after the elimination of commodities with negative prices and of the processes producing them.

(2) $\mathbf{A}(\mathbf{B} - \mathbf{A})^{-1} \geqslant \mathbf{O}$. If $\mathbf{A}(\mathbf{B} - \mathbf{A})^{-1}$ is positive and indecomposable, a maximum rate of profit and positive standard multipliers exist without any commodity or process having to be eliminated, for

$$\mathbf{q}' = R\mathbf{q}'\mathbf{A}(\mathbf{B} - \mathbf{A})^{-1},$$
$$(1 + R)\mathbf{q}'\mathbf{A} = \mathbf{q}'\mathbf{B}.$$

Because of

$$\mathbf{A}(\mathbf{B} - \mathbf{A})^{-1} = \mathbf{Q} \geqslant \mathbf{O},$$
$$\mathbf{A} = \mathbf{Q}(\mathbf{B} - \mathbf{A}), \qquad \mathbf{Q} \geqslant \mathbf{O}$$
$$\mathbf{a}_i = \mathbf{q}_i(\mathbf{B} - \mathbf{A}), \qquad \mathbf{q}_i \geqslant \mathbf{o}.$$
$$\mathbf{Q} = [\mathbf{q}'_1, ..., \mathbf{q}'_n]',$$

this condition means that, if constant returns to scale prevail, all goods can be produced independently in the proportions in which they are required as inputs for production, since the production of the inputs does not lead to any negative activity level. Again, this condition is weaker than $(\mathbf{B} - \mathbf{A})^{-1} \geqslant \mathbf{O}$, for it does not imply that all semi-positive net outputs are producible at non-negative activity levels; it implies only that all convex combinations of the vectors $\mathbf{a}_1, ..., \mathbf{a}_n$ are producible.

If $\mathbf{q}_i = \mathbf{a}_i(\mathbf{B} - \mathbf{A})^{-1} \geqslant \mathbf{o}$, $i = 1, ..., n$, the production of the commodities $\mathbf{a}_i$ required as inputs in process i for the production of output $\mathbf{b}_i$ can be increased without contracting any process in the system. Thus, although a system with $\mathbf{A}(\mathbf{B} - \mathbf{A})^{-1} \geqslant \mathbf{O}$ is not always capable of producing a net output of commodities in all conceivable combinations, it is at least capable of expanding all lines of production independently of each other in so far as no contractions leading to negative activity levels are involved. Such systems will be called *flexible*. It is conceivable that flexible systems could play a part in a dynamic theory that does not presuppose a uniform rate of profit but shows how it comes about. One of the mechanisms involved in the process of equalization is the free flow of circulating capital. However, additional assumptions are required to reach determinate conclusions about the positivity of prices in flexible systems. One can show that they are not necessarily all-productive near the maximum rate of profit (example in section II.11a).

(3) *Integrated industries*. Similar properties can be proved to exist for systems where the corresponding integrated industries (gross and net as defined in section II.1) have non-negative input coefficients. In particular, it was shown in section II.2 that $\mathbf{B}^{-1}\mathbf{A}$ and $(\mathbf{B} - \mathbf{A})^{-1}\mathbf{A}$ will be indecomposable, if $(\mathbf{A}, \mathbf{B})$ is a basic system. The detailed investigation of prices, standard commodity, etc., is left as an exercise to the reader.

The interest in the systems considered in this section lies not so much in their immediate empirical relevance (real systems are typically neither all-productive nor dominated by single-product industries), as in their providing an extension of the norm given by single-product systems against which the difficulties of joint production proper can be measured. E.g. if joint-production systems are characteristically not flexible, this means that – against the intuition one obtains in the study of single-product systems – a process cannot expand without forcing another to contract. If coke and gas are jointly produced from coal, while there is also separate production of natural gas, and if coke is uniquely used in certain foundries, these foundries cannot expand *ceteris paribus* unless the production of natural gas is reduced in order to compensate for the increased production of gas from coal that will accompany increased coke production for foundries. A systematic survey of difficulties of joint production proper is – even at the time of writing the second edition of this essay – still lacking, but the field of application of Sraffa's concepts (basics, standard commodity) can fortunately be expanded by introducing concepts of efficiency, and it turns out that almost-all-productive systems eventually come back in again. To this we turn in section II.9b.

9 The Standard Commodity and the Possibility of Balanced Growth

Consider $\mathbf{A} \geqslant \mathbf{O}$, $\mathbf{B} \geqslant \mathbf{O}$ as von Neumann matrices (assuming that constant returns to scale prevail) and assume that $\mathbf{A}$ includes the subsistence part of the workers' wage so that we may conceive of an actual rise in the rate of profit up to what corresponds to the maximum rate of reproduction in a state of balanced growth.

The maximum rate of balanced growth α cannot be pushed up indefinitely; there is an upper limit to the α for which

$$\alpha \mathbf{q}' \mathbf{A} \leqslant \mathbf{q}' \mathbf{B}, \qquad \mathbf{q} \geqslant \mathbf{o};$$

this is the condition of expanded reproduction. Von Neumann and his followers have shown how a semi-positive price vector can be associated with the maximum rate of growth

$$\alpha \mathbf{q}' \mathbf{A} \leqslant \mathbf{q}' \mathbf{B}, \qquad \mathbf{q} \geqslant \mathbf{o},$$

so that

$$\alpha \mathbf{A} \mathbf{p} \geqslant \mathbf{B} \mathbf{p}, \qquad \mathbf{p} \geqslant \mathbf{o},$$

and so that

$$\alpha \mathbf{q}' \mathbf{A} \mathbf{p} = \mathbf{q}' \mathbf{B} \mathbf{p},$$

i.e. so that overproduced goods fetch zero prices and unprofitable activities are at standstill. (Profits here are at most 'normal' profits, the rate of profit is the maximum rate of profit and equals the rate of balanced growth.)

These α, $\mathbf{q}$ and $\mathbf{p}$ must exist for our system $\mathbf{A}$, $\mathbf{B}$ ($\mathbf{A} \geqslant \mathbf{O}$, $\mathbf{B} \geqslant \mathbf{O}$, $\mathbf{a}_i \neq \mathbf{o}$, $\mathbf{b}^i \neq \mathbf{o}$, $i = 1, ..., n$),[1] since all the assumptions conventionally used to prove von Neumann's theorem are fulfilled.

(I) If $\alpha \leqslant 1$, $\mathbf{A}, \mathbf{B}$ is inefficient because it is incapable of expanded reproduction in a state of balanced growth.

(II) If $\alpha > 1$ and the strict inequality holds in either $\alpha \mathbf{q}' \mathbf{A} \leqslant \mathbf{q}' \mathbf{B}$ and/or $\alpha \mathbf{A} \mathbf{p} \geqslant \mathbf{B} \mathbf{p}$ in some component, $\mathbf{q}$ and $\mathbf{p}$ cannot both be positive for $\alpha \mathbf{q}' \mathbf{A} \mathbf{p} = \mathbf{q}' \mathbf{B} \mathbf{p}$. Thus, some activities must be unprofitable at that rate of profit and/or there are overproduced goods.[2]

If both these inefficiencies (I and II) are ruled out, we have $\alpha \mathbf{q}' \mathbf{A} = \mathbf{q}' \mathbf{B}$, $\alpha = 1 + R$, $R > 0$, $(1 + R)\mathbf{A}\mathbf{p} = \mathbf{B}\mathbf{p}$. $\mathbf{q}$ may be interpreted as standard multipliers. Thus, $\mathbf{t}' = \mathbf{q}'(\mathbf{B} - \mathbf{A})$, the standard commodity, exists and is, together with $\mathbf{p}_t(R)$ where $(1 + R)\mathbf{A}\mathbf{p}_t = \mathbf{B}\mathbf{p}_t$, semi-positive.

It is possible to give a more specific sufficient condition for this:

Gale (1956) has shown that the maximum rate of expansion can be defined as

$$\alpha = \underset{\mathbf{q} \geqslant \mathbf{o}}{\text{Max}} \underset{j}{\text{Min}} \frac{\mathbf{q}'\mathbf{b}^j}{\mathbf{q}'\mathbf{a}^j}$$

$$(\mathbf{A} = [\mathbf{a}^1, ..., \mathbf{a}^n],$$
$$\mathbf{B} = [\mathbf{b}^1, ..., \mathbf{b}^n]),$$

where

$$\alpha(\mathbf{q}) = \underset{j}{\text{Min}} \frac{\mathbf{q}'\mathbf{b}^j}{\mathbf{q}'\mathbf{a}^j}$$

is a continuous function in the interior of the compact set $\{E \mid \mathbf{q} \geqslant \mathbf{o},$ $\mathbf{q}'\mathbf{e} = 1\}$. Balanced growth occurs at the point $\bar{\mathbf{q}}$ where $\alpha(\bar{\mathbf{q}})$ attains its maximum on E. If there are uneconomic activities, the maximum $\alpha(\bar{\mathbf{q}})$ is attained on the boundary of E. If there is overproduction,

$$\underset{j}{\text{Min}} \frac{\bar{\mathbf{q}}'\mathbf{b}^j}{\bar{\mathbf{q}}'\mathbf{a}^j}$$

will be smaller than some

$$\frac{\bar{\mathbf{q}}'\mathbf{b}^j}{\bar{\mathbf{q}}'\mathbf{a}^j}$$

(the overproduced goods). The latter is *not* the case if the highest rate of reproduction for each good is found in a different process, so that there is a one-to-one correspondence between the n processes and the n goods in terms of the highest rate of reproduction. Each process will then contribute for some good to the attaining of the maximum rate of growth.

Conditions sufficient for balanced growth without overproduction are slightly more stringent:

Theorem 9.1

If permutations of goods and processes and a constant $\alpha >$ can be found so that $\mathbf{e}(\mathbf{B} - \alpha\mathbf{A}) \geqslant \mathbf{o}$ and for all $a_i^j \neq 0 \ i \neq j$

$$0 \leqslant \frac{b_i^j}{a_i^j} < \alpha < \frac{b_j^j}{a_j^j} \leqslant \infty$$

and so that $b_i^j = 0$ for $a_i^j = 0$, $i \neq j$, it follows that a maximum rate of profit R and a standard commodity exist.

NOTE:
The assumption

$$0 \leqslant \frac{b_i^j}{a_i^j} < \alpha < \frac{b_j^j}{a_j^j} \qquad (i \neq j)$$

is necessary: if only

$$\frac{b_i^j}{a_i^j} < \frac{b_j^j}{a_j^j}$$

is assumed, overproduction is not ruled out, as examples with $n \geqslant 3$ show. For $n = 2$ however, the assumption is sufficient (see also section II.11).

The *proof* of Theorem 9.1 may either be based on von Neumann's theorem, using Gale's method (1956), or we may proceed as follows: $\mathbf{B} - \alpha\mathbf{A}$ has positive elements in the diagonal and negative elements outside. After multiplying $\mathbf{A}, \mathbf{B}$ from the right with the diagonal matrix

$$\mathbf{D} = [d_i^j] = \left[\frac{1}{b_j^j - \alpha a_j^j} \, \delta_i^j \right], \qquad \delta_j^j = 1, \, \delta_i^j = 0 \ (i \neq j),$$

we can decompose $\mathbf{BD} - \alpha\mathbf{AD}$ into

$$\mathbf{BD} - \alpha\mathbf{AD} = \mathbf{I} - \mathbf{C}$$

with $\mathbf{C} \geqslant \mathbf{O}$. Thus, $(\mathbf{BD} - \alpha\mathbf{AD})^{-1} \geqslant \mathbf{O}$ and $(\mathbf{B} - (1 + r)\mathbf{A})^{-1} \geqslant \mathbf{O}$ for $1 + r = \alpha$. The rest is obvious.

q.e.d.

The systems defined by the assumptions of theorem 9.1 might be called *balanced*. It is clear from the proof that balanced systems are almost all-productive. The main insight obtained in this section is the one derived from the von Neumann model: systems without a semi-positive standard commodity and semi-positive $\mathbf{p}_t(R)$ suffer from specific inefficiencies revealed at $r = R$, much in the same way as systems that are almost all-productive are susceptible to suffer from inefficiencies revealed at $r = 0$, but covered at $r = \bar{r} > 0$. Both these inefficiencies occur in systems where the possibility of substitution is inherent: they are not all-engaging and yet basic.

Notes

1 These assumptions were stated in section II.1. They are sufficient for von Neumann according to Kemeny, Morgenstern and Thompson (1956). For the reasons given in section II.2 we suppose that $\mathbf{A}, \mathbf{B}$ are basic.
2 A striking example of case II is given in section II.17 on fixed capital where the standard commodity $\mathbf{t}$ exists for some $r = R$, but with $\mathbf{p}_t(R) \geqslant \mathbf{o}$. The

maximum rate of growth cannot be equal to $1 + R$. It turns out that α can be increased beyond $1 + R$ by abandoning processes using old equipment so that the old machines appear as overproduced goods and processes using them as uneconomic (see also section II.9b).

9a   Residual Commodities and Dispensable Processes

The preceding sections focused on special joint-production systems which – by means of one property or another – allowed the retention of characteristic features of single-product systems. Section II.9b will show how these assumptions can be dropped and how joint production in general can be analysed, provided a different set of assumptions – namely, balanced growth at constant returns to scale and the equality of the rate of growth and the rate of profit – is adopted.

Before we turn to that, it may be useful to consider typical instances of joint production that are not observed in the all-engaging or flexible systems of section II.8, or the balanced system of section II.9, in order to realize the importance of the more general forms of joint production. The analysis extends observations made in sections II.7 and II.8 and is complementary to Schefold (1978b). For the present purpose of illustration, it suffices to assume a stationary system where the rate of profit is equal to zero.

If a productive system $(\mathbf{A}, \mathbf{B}, \mathbf{l})$ is given, we shall say that commodity i is *separately producible*, if the i'th row of $(\mathbf{B} - \mathbf{A})^{-1}$, i.e. the vector $\mathbf{q}_i = \mathbf{e}_i(\mathbf{B} - \mathbf{A})^{-1}$ is semi-positive; if $\mathbf{q}_i$ contains at least one negative element, we shall say that i is a *residual commodity*. A process j will be said to be *indispensable* if the j'th column of $(\mathbf{B} - \mathbf{A})^{-1}$ or the vector $\mathbf{q}^j = (\mathbf{B} - \mathbf{A})^{-1}\mathbf{e}^j$ is positive; if $\mathbf{q}^j$ contains zeros or negative elements, process j will be said to be *dispensable*.

The first of these two definitions is straightforward: a commodity is separately producible if and only if the corresponding subsystem operates at non-negative 'activity levels' $\mathbf{q}_i$, i.e. if and only if (assuming constant returns) a net output of one unit of commodity i can be produced without activating any processes at a negative level. Clearly all commodities are separately producible in all-productive systems. However, it is typical for joint-production systems to contain residual commodities, i.e. commodities with subsystems involving negative activity levels. If commodity i is a residual commodity (i.e. not separately producible) with $\mathbf{q}_i = \mathbf{e}_i(\mathbf{B} - \mathbf{A})^{-1}$ not semi-positive, and if $\varepsilon > 0$ is small so that $\mathbf{e}' + \varepsilon\mathbf{q}_i > \mathbf{o}$ with

$$\mathbf{o} \leqslant (\mathbf{e}' + \varepsilon\mathbf{q}_i)(\mathbf{B} - \mathbf{A}) = \mathbf{s}' + \varepsilon\mathbf{e}_i,$$

we have the economy that produces the original surplus $\mathbf{s}$ at unit activity levels $\mathbf{e}$ in a modified form such that the surplus is increased by a small amount of commodity i through a *reduction* of some activities. Hence the name 'residual commodity': it is obtained as a left-over by contracting some processes. It is intuitively plausible that a *pure residual commodity*, i.e. one with $\mathbf{q}_i = \mathbf{e}_i(\mathbf{B} - \mathbf{A})^{-1} \leqslant \mathbf{o}$ or one that required no increase in any activity level to be produced, cannot exist. Otherwise there would have to be at least one rate of profit at which all prices, including that of commodity i, p_i, would be positive so that

$$0 < p_i = \mathbf{e}_i\mathbf{p} = \mathbf{q}_i(\mathbf{B} - \mathbf{A})\mathbf{p}$$
$$= r\mathbf{q}_i\mathbf{A}\mathbf{p} + w\mathbf{q}_i\mathbf{l},$$

which is a contradiction since $\mathbf{A}\mathbf{p} > \mathbf{o}$, $\mathbf{l} > \mathbf{o}$, hence $r\mathbf{q}_i\mathbf{A}\mathbf{p} < 0$, $\mathbf{q}_i\mathbf{l} < 0$ with $\mathbf{q}_i \leqslant \mathbf{o}$.

Pure residual commodities cannot exist for economic reasons, but the worst environmental problems may well be concerned with something like 'pure residual goods'! If all economic activities require directly or indirectly the burning of fossil fuels and if these are separately producible, all economic activities (except the planting of trees, etc.) increase the amount of carbon dioxide in the atmosphere with possibly catastrophic consequences for the world climate. As long as capturing and storing carbon dioxide by means of planting and storing more trees than are being burnt or other favourable measures to act on global weather conditions are not undertaken, the good 'stable world climate' can – given the energy system based on fossil fuels – be increased only by reducing the activity levels in the production of *all* basic goods.

Similar arguments could be made about the good 'not dissipated lead content of the earth crust' or – with present technologies – 'wilderness', but not e.g. about 'health'. In a way the argument rests on a trick: the production of more stability of the world climate depends on the negative production of the good 'atmospheric carbon dioxide', which in turn depends on the negative production of the commodities coal, oil and gas.

We may note in passing that a neoclassical economist would hardly present the argument in this way in theory-oriented expositions, since he would from the outset introduce the possibility of substitution in the energy sector. But, whichever way we put it: the advantage of the classical approach is that it focuses unequivocally on the techniques that are there in use without prejudicing the question of substitution possibilities that might be realized by internalizing external effects. There is no way in the classical approach to put a shadow price on the stability of the world climate, nor can it, for logical reasons, ever become a commodity (it is a public good, and a pure residual). This is as it should be, in that – according to the classical view – social and political conditions determine the few distinct techniques that come about as alternatives to those already in existence in the process of technical progress. One of them is then adopted according to profitability, if competition has its way, but this is not simply substitution owing to externally imposed or internally generated price changes. The opposition between both schools is not absolute: the classical economist can take substitution into account and the neoclassical political forces; only the emphasis is very different.

We leave environmental problems and joint production of goods and return to the world of commodities. Pure residual commodities are thus impossible, but residual commodities are ubiquitous with joint production. As we shall see, old machines are typically such, but other examples are readily found: if electricity is on the one hand produced jointly with hot vapour for heating in thermal power stations and on the other produced in hydroelectric power stations, the net output of hot vapour can be increased with an unchanged level of electricity production by raising the number of thermal power stations and reducing that of hydroelectric ones.

Only residual commodities can have negative labour values (see the 'Apparent Paradox' concerning labour values in section II.4 above, which involved a residual commodity). The labour value u_i will in fact be negative if, in the subsystem for the production of commodity i, more labour is employed in those processes that have to be contracted in order to obtain a net output of one unit of commodity i than in those that have to be expanded. This is the meaning of

$$u_i = \mathbf{e}_i\mathbf{u} = \mathbf{e}_i(\mathbf{B} - \mathbf{A})^{-1}\mathbf{l} = \mathbf{q}_i\mathbf{l} < 0.$$

Similarly, in systems with a positive total labour value of the means of production in each industry, i.e. in systems with $\mathbf{Au} > \mathbf{o}$, only the price of residual commodities can fall in terms of the wage rate at low rates of profit. By differentiating the equation for prices in terms of the wage rate (labour commanded)

$$\frac{\mathrm{d}}{\mathrm{d}r}\,\mathbf{B}\hat{\mathbf{p}}(r) = \frac{\mathrm{d}}{\mathrm{d}r}\,[(1 + r)\mathbf{A}\hat{\mathbf{p}}(r) + \mathbf{l}]$$

one obtains for $r = 0$

$$\left.\frac{\mathrm{d}\hat{\mathbf{p}}(r)}{\mathrm{d}r}\right|_{r=0} = (\mathbf{B} - \mathbf{A})^{-1}\mathbf{A}\hat{\mathbf{p}}(0),$$

therefore one obtains as an expression for the change of the labour commanded of commodity i

$$\frac{\mathrm{d}\hat{p}_i(0)}{\mathrm{d}r} = \mathbf{e}_i\,\frac{\mathrm{d}\hat{\mathbf{p}}(0)}{\mathrm{d}r} = \mathbf{e}_i(\mathbf{B} - \mathbf{A})^{-1}\mathbf{A}\hat{\mathbf{p}}(0)$$

$$= \mathbf{q}_i\mathbf{Au}.$$

In other words: the labour commanded by commodity i (which is at $r = 0$ equal to its labour value) increases with a small increase in the rate of profit with a rate equal to the labour embodied in the means of production of its subsystem. If $\mathbf{Au} > \mathbf{o}$, the price in terms of labour commanded therefore always rises at small rates of profit, if commodity i is separately producible, whereas it falls for those residual commodities i for which the value of the means of production in the processes that have to be contracted to obtain one more unit of commodity i is greater than that of the means of production in the processes that have to be expanded.

Simplifying matters a little: if paper and tables are made from trees and equivalent tables are also made from steel and plastics, an increase in the rate of profit will reduce the price of paper in terms of the wage rate if the raw material cost of trees is less than that of steel and plastics.

Prices of separately producible goods, of course, will always rise in terms of labour commanded at $r = 0$, provided the values of their means of production are positive. (This result applies to the products of fixed capital at all rates of profit below the maximum; see section II.14, theorem 14.1.)

We now turn to dispensable processes. Process j was said to be indispensable if the j'th column of $(\mathbf{B} - \mathbf{A})^{-1}$ is positive, because that implies that no net output whatever can be produced without activating process j. This follows from the fact that if the j'th element of

$$\mathbf{q}' = \mathbf{c}'(\mathbf{B} - \mathbf{A})^{-1}$$

is to be positive for all $\mathbf{c} \geqslant \mathbf{o}$, we must have

$$\mathbf{q}'\mathbf{e}^j = \mathbf{c}'(\mathbf{B} - \mathbf{A})^{-1}\mathbf{e}^j > 0$$

for all $\mathbf{c} \geqslant \mathbf{o}$, i.e. $(\mathbf{B} - \mathbf{A})^{-1}\mathbf{e}^j > \mathbf{o}$.

While all processes are indispensable in basic single-product or in all-engaging systems, it is the essence of joint-production systems that they can contain dispensable processes. In the example above, different types of electric power stations can permanently coexist, partly because of rents (a feature of joint production, too, as we shall see), partly because joint products such as hot vapour for heating yield a positive contribution towards the covering of the costs of production. But this coexistence implies that, technically speaking, some types of power stations – i.e. the corresponding methods of production – could be dispensed with from the point of view of electricity generation.

Processes that are not indispensable are called dispensable because it is possible to obtain at least one non-negative net output without activating them. For if $(\mathbf{B} - \mathbf{A})^{-1}\mathbf{e}^j$ contains a zero, say in row i, the i'th subsystem $\mathbf{e}_i = \mathbf{q}_i(\mathbf{B} - \mathbf{A})$ does not use process j:

$$\mathbf{q}_i\mathbf{e}^j = \mathbf{e}_i(\mathbf{B} - \mathbf{A})^{-1}\mathbf{e}^j = 0$$

so that one unit of commodity i is produced without utilizing process j, if $\mathbf{q}_i \geqslant \mathbf{o}$.

If some elements of $(\mathbf{B} - \mathbf{A})^{-1}\mathbf{e}^j$ are positive while the others are all negative and/or if $\mathbf{q}_i$ is not non-negative, we can find i, j with

$$q_i^j = \underset{k,l}{\text{Min}}\ \mathbf{q}_k^l = -\varepsilon, \qquad \varepsilon > 0$$
$$(\varepsilon\mathbf{e}' + \mathbf{q}_i)\mathbf{e}^j = (\varepsilon\mathbf{s}' + \mathbf{e}_i)(\mathbf{B} - \mathbf{A})^{-1}\mathbf{e}^j = 0$$

with $\varepsilon\mathbf{e}' + \mathbf{q}_i \geqslant \mathbf{o}$, $\varepsilon\mathbf{s}' + \mathbf{e}_i \geqslant \mathbf{o}$. This means that a non-negative surplus $\varepsilon\mathbf{s}' + \mathbf{e}_i$ can be produced by means of non-negative activity levels $\varepsilon\mathbf{e}' + \mathbf{q}_i$

without using process j at all, where process j is one of the dispensable processes of the system.

If all processes are indispensable, the system is all-engaging and all commodities are separately producible, but the converse is not true. For instance, non-basics are separately producible in single-product systems while the corresponding processes are dispensable.

Some introductory remarks to explain the purpose of applying the concept of dispensable processes may be useful. The concept of residual commodities was defined to illustrate why negative values and falling prices in terms of labour commanded may obtain. This raises the question of how negative values can be eliminated (since negative prices cannot occur in practice) and how we can show that the wage curve falls in terms of suitable commodity standards although some commodities may not rise in terms of the wage rate with an increase in the rate of profit. It will be shown in section II.9b how the properties of single-product systems (positive prices, falling wage curve, standard commodity) can continue to hold although the existence of typical features of joint-production systems such as residual commodities is admitted. The method will rely on the truncation of dispensable processes.

Another characteristic of joint production is the curious effects arising in the context of the introduction of new methods of production and new commodities. We shall now illustrate these effects by means of the concept of dispensable processes; and we shall see in section II.9b that some general statements about changes in techniques continue to hold nevertheless.

The crucial difference between single-product and joint-production systems is that the equality between the number of processes and commodities is automatically re-established as a technical datum in single-product systems if a new process is introduced, whereas it can come about only as a result of an economic process in joint-production systems. In fact, whenever a new method for the production of several commodities is adopted, the change of several prices must be analysed to find the combination of methods that is preferable. It is shown in section II.9b that the existence of surplus profits or losses yields an unambiguous criterion for this choice of technique in a comparison of the long-run prices, but it is easy to visualize that the process of transition between the techniques may be complicated; proper research into the question of how market prices and quantities adjust to new conditions has not been undertaken.

However, we may now consider the discovery of a new consumption good as an illustrative first step. We can prove:

Let a productive joint-production system with n processes and n commodities $(i = 1, ..., n)$ be given. If an $(n + 1)$st commodity (a pure consumption good $i = n + 1$) is introduced and manufactured in some of the processes that are indispensable, its price $\hat{p}_{n+1}$ will – whatever is charged – contribute towards covering the expenses of production in such a way that all other prices $\hat{p}_1, ..., \hat{p}_n$ will fall in terms of the wage rate, whereas some of them may rise and some fall if commodity $n + 1$ is produced by dispensable processes.

This illustrates, first of all, the point that prices are (relative to our theory) indeterminate if the number of commodities exceeds that of processes. When the new consumption good is introduced, the entrepreneurs will of course charge a determinate price for it, but we cannot predict from the structure of production what that will be.

The price will be set so that entrepreneurs producing the new commodity jointly with pre-existing outputs will make surplus profits. If competition works, the rate of profit will return to uniformity and (as we shall assume) stay the same through a change of (in the case of the basic system) all prices and a rise of the real wage. Workers will get more at an unchanged rate of profit because prices $\hat{p}_1, ..., \hat{p}_n$ fall in terms of the wage rate. Prices $\hat{p}_1, ..., \hat{p}_n$ are thus determined, given the rate of profit and price $\hat{p}_{n+1}$, while the latter is arbitrary (or corresponds to 'what the traffic will bear') within a range defined by the requirement that all prices remain positive.

To see this, we assume that the rate of profit is zero, so that we have

$$(\mathbf{B} - \mathbf{A})\hat{\mathbf{p}} = \mathbf{l}$$

before the introduction of the new good. Afterwards we get

$$\mathbf{B}\hat{\mathbf{p}} + \mathbf{b}^{n+1}\hat{p}_{n+1} - \mathbf{A}\hat{\mathbf{p}} = \mathbf{l}$$

or

$$(\mathbf{B} - \mathbf{A})\hat{\mathbf{p}} = \mathbf{l} - \mathbf{b}^{n+1}\hat{p}_{n+1},$$

where $\mathbf{b}^{n+1}$ is the vector of outputs of the new consumption good. Hence prices $\hat{\mathbf{p}}$ are now given by

$$\hat{\mathbf{p}} = (\mathbf{B} - \mathbf{A})^{-1}\mathbf{l} - (\mathbf{B} - \mathbf{A})^{-1}\mathbf{b}^{n+1}\hat{p}_{n+1}$$

where $\hat{p}_{n+1}$ can, from a formal point of view, be at any level between zero and the first value for which $\hat{p}_i$, $i = 1, ..., n$, turns negative. The vector $\hat{\mathbf{p}}$ thus becomes a linear function of $\hat{p}_{n+1}$.

The point is that all prices $\hat{\mathbf{p}}$ will be the more diminished the more is charged for the new commodity (the greater $\hat{p}_{n+1}$) if it is produced by indispensable processes, because $(\mathbf{B} - \mathbf{A})^{-1}\mathbf{b}^{n+1}$ then represents a positive linear combination of positive vectors, whereas the effect is indeterminate otherwise.

In terms of the example above: if the hydroelectric power stations are turned to additional uses by making them collect water, which is – after purification – used for personal consumption, this will contribute towards covering their expenses of production. The price of electricity can thus be lowered, but thermal power stations will then be compelled to charge more for their hot vapour because they get less for their electricity.

The next step in this approach could consist of an analysis of the introduction of a new process for which room has been made by the introduction of the new consumption good – say, wells for drilling water which complement the dams and pre-existing natural sources which earn rents. After this, the joint-production system will again be determinate in that the set of prices compatible with a uniform rate of profit will be unique. It is possible to derive conditions that this additional method of production would have to fulfil in order to fit with those already in existence, but we shall not pursue the matter.

This should suffice to illustrate some effects of joint production proper that seem at least to be counter to intuition and that have to this day remained largely unexplored.

The neoclassical economist will regard our account of the introduction of a new consumption good as quite unsatisfactory – much in the same way as he will frown upon our treatment of the external effects of the burning of fossil fuels above. Here he will miss any reference to the conditions of demand for the new consumption goods and to the interaction of supply and demand conditions with distribution.

He will, of course, be quite right in postulating that demand conditions be examined. The story of the transition as presented here is incomplete, and it is of no avail to point to a new method of production that will ultimately restore the determinacy of the solution of the price system, since the process of transition deserves to be analysed. However, the classical approach really only asks for caution in this matter. On the one hand demand depends on social conditions and is not only derived from mutually independent tastes of individuals; on the other, demand depends on the conditions of supply ('sales promotion'). The formula 'what the market will bear' refers to the diversity of these influences, and the forces governing the rate of profit (which we supposed to remain unchanged) are yet another matter. While the neoclassical economist is, in principle, not prevented from taking all sorts of economic and institutional data into account, his education will lead him to reduce most of them to independent preferences, which are revealed by whatever happens. We prefer to leave a gap that must be filled by complementary considerations.

We have now touched the limits of classical analysis. The reader will have to decide for himself whether he wants to retreat to those elements of neoclassical theory that survive the classical critique or whether he wants to supplement the latter with models of a different kind and with historical and institutional approaches (see Part III). Meanwhile, we return with the following analysis to a more traditional perspective where it is shown that basic propositions about single-product systems concerning the positivity of prices, the wage curve, etc. can be extended on the basis of the unsatisfactory assumptions of constant returns and an equality of the rate of growth with the rate of profit, afterwards (section II.9c) allowing for more general assumptions.

9b Balanced Growth and Truncation

When I wrote section II.9 in 1970, it did not occur to me that the method of considering balanced growth might be a great help for the analysis, although both balanced growth and truncation (in reference to fixed capital) were mentioned.

The main reason for this omission was that balanced growth presupposes constant returns and a particular specification of the composition of net output– or, if the rate of profit equals the rate of growth, the wage – so that several aspects of Sraffa's method are affected and in particular the distinction between the basic and the non-basic part of the system is blurred. Only fixed capital does not require such a specification (except in that old machines do not enter the wage) and I therefore concentrated my efforts on fixed capital. I now insert this section in order to show the power of the analysis in terms of balanced growth. The presentation will be simplified and proofs will not always be rigorous, in particular in that certain irregular exceptions in the sense of section II.3 will be disregarded. For a rigorous and more comprehensive analysis the reader is referred to my article 'On counting of equations' (Schefold, 1978c). The presentation used here is perhaps closer to Sraffa (linear programming is avoided) and certainly easier to follow.

The literature on truncation (see Nuti, 1973, for references) is still largely confined to fixed capital, but wage curves for different subsystems of von Neumann systems can also be drawn.

The fundamental ideas are quite simple. If a price turns negative with a change in the rate of profit, a rearrangement of the system will be found such that more of the commodity in question is produced. It is then overproduced, receives a zero price, ceases to be a commodity and drops – together with some process using it – from the system, which has one process and one commodity less than before. This is truncation, and it involves (at $r = g = 0$) clearly residual commodities and dispensable processes. Changes in methods of production are here analysed, by using the criterion not whether they lead to a fall of all prices in terms of labour commanded (they do not – see section II.9a), but whether they lead to surplus profits. The intuitive difficulties arise only with the corresponding dual concepts.

Despite the fact that they have no obvious application in reality, the concepts of 'dual truncation' and 'commodity switch' are also introduced because logical and mathematical completeness require it.

We assume that the real wage is given and serves as the only standard of prices. Since it will for the greater part consist of pure consumption goods, the distinction between the basic and the non-basic part of the system must at least initially be disregarded in what follows because the wage curve will now depend on non-basics as well as on basics.

The system $(\mathbf{A}, \mathbf{B}, \mathbf{l})$ is complemented by a vector $\mathbf{d}$ and written $(\mathbf{A}, \mathbf{B}, \mathbf{l}, \mathbf{d})$; $\mathbf{d}$ denotes at the same time the composition of the real wage, of the vector of total consumption, and of the standard of prices. A system will now be called regular if both $(\mathbf{A}, \mathbf{B}, \mathbf{l})$ and the transposed system $(\mathbf{A}', \mathbf{B}', \mathbf{d})$ are regular in the sense of section II.3.

Let a rate of growth, g, be given. The equation

$$\mathbf{q}' [\mathbf{B} - (1 + g)\mathbf{A}] = \mathbf{d}'$$

expresses the fact that a basket of goods, $\mathbf{d}$, remains for consumption out of the net product of the economy $\mathbf{q}'(\mathbf{B} - \mathbf{A})$ after the investment of $g\mathbf{q}'\mathbf{A}$ for growth at rate g with activity levels $\mathbf{q}$. Combining this with the equation

$$[\mathbf{B} - (1 + r)\mathbf{A}]\mathbf{p} = w\mathbf{l},$$

where prices are expressed in terms of $\mathbf{d}$, $\mathbf{d}'\mathbf{p} = 1$, $w = 1/\mathbf{d}'\hat{\mathbf{p}}$ (index d in $\mathbf{p}_d$, w_d is omitted in this section), we see that $\mathbf{d}$ is the real wage of a unit of labour if $r = g$ and if capitalists only save while workers only consume.

The curve of consumption per head, c, i.e. of consumption $\mathbf{d}'\mathbf{p}$ divided by labour employed $\mathbf{q}'\mathbf{l}$ at rate of growth g

$$c(g) = \frac{\mathbf{d}'\mathbf{p}}{\mathbf{q}'\mathbf{l}} = \frac{1}{\mathbf{d}'[\mathbf{B} - (1 + g)\mathbf{A}]^{-1}\mathbf{l}}$$

coincides geometrically with the wage curve w because $w(r) = c(g)$ at $g = r$.

The vector of activity levels will have negative components (and the wage curve is not economically meaningful) with $r = g$ beyond some finite maximum rate of growth $\hat{g}$; if it was, $\mathbf{q}'[\mathbf{B} - (1 + g)\mathbf{A}] = \mathbf{d}'$ could be solved with non-negative $\mathbf{q}$ for all $g > 0$, but then the equation $\mathbf{q}'[\mathbf{B} - (1 + g)\mathbf{A}]\mathbf{e} = \mathbf{d}'\mathbf{e}$ would be valid for all $g > 0$, although $[\mathbf{B} - (1 + g)\mathbf{A}]\mathbf{e}$ will be a negative vector for large g because no row of $\mathbf{A}$ vanishes (section 1). Hence $\mathbf{q}' = \mathbf{d}'[\mathbf{B} - (1 + g)\mathbf{A}]^{-1} \geqslant \mathbf{o}$ is impossible for large g.

If systems are not all-productive, $\mathbf{q}$ and $\mathbf{p}$ need not be positive, even for small $r = g$. Wage curves not only may rise in some ranges, but will even diverge to infinity if $\mathbf{d}'\hat{\mathbf{p}} = \mathbf{q}'\mathbf{l} = 0$. The systems are not economically meaningful in such intervals; the point will be to eliminate the commodities and processes causing negative prices and activity levels.

The wage curve will, on the other hand, always tend to zero at points R_i with $\det[\mathbf{B} - (1 + R_i)\mathbf{A}] = 0$ in the regular case, since an eigenvector $\mathbf{q}_i$ will be associated with R_i such that $(R_i - r)^{s_i}\mathbf{d}'[\mathbf{B} - (1 + r)\mathbf{A}]^{-1}$ will tend to become proportional to $\mathbf{q}_i$ with $r \to R_i$ (according to an analysis as in the proof of theorem 3.2), and $\mathbf{q}_i\mathbf{l} \neq 0$, so that w tends to zero at R_i with the power of s_i, where s_i is the multiplicity of R_i as a root of the characteristic equation $\det[\mathbf{B} - (1 + r)\mathbf{A}] = 0$. The wage curve is therefore everywhere well defined except in a (in the regular case) finite number of points with $\mathbf{d}'\hat{\mathbf{p}} = \mathbf{q}'\mathbf{l} = 0$, and activity levels and prices are well defined except at points R_i where the wage curve vanishes. The smallest $R_i > 0$ (if it exists) is the maximum rate of profit in the sense of section II.7; but it will soon be seen that the wage curve can sometimes be meaningfully extended beyond R by means of truncation and 'dual' truncation until a 'true maximum rate of profit' is reached.

The wage curve w falls strictly monotonically at points $r = g$ where both activity levels and prices are positive, for − according to the formula for the differentiation of a matrix – if $\mathbf{q} > \mathbf{o}$, $\mathbf{p} > \mathbf{o}$,

$$
\begin{aligned}
w'(r) &= \{w(r)[\mathbf{d}'(\mathbf{B} - (1+r)\mathbf{A})^{-1}\mathbf{l}]^{-1}\}' \\
&= -w^{-2}(r)\mathbf{d}'[(\mathbf{B} - (1+r)\mathbf{A})^{-1}]'\mathbf{l} \\
&= w^{-2}(r)\mathbf{d}'[\mathbf{B} - (1+r)\mathbf{A}]^{-1}(-\mathbf{A})[\mathbf{B} - (1+r)\mathbf{A}]^{-1}\mathbf{l} \\
&= -w^{-2}(r)\mathbf{q}'\mathbf{A}\hat{\mathbf{p}} < 0.
\end{aligned}
$$

We now consider a Sraffa system capable of balanced growth at rate of growth g with positive prices and activity levels at $r = g$. We were used to hypothetical movements of the rate of profit; let now both rates $r = g$ vary simultaneously. It is characteristic for joint production that one of the prices or activity levels may fall to zero. Consider a point $r_1 = g_1$ at which a price, p_1, say, vanishes as $r = g$ is, say, increased, while the other prices and activity levels are positive. Increase $r = g$ further to $r_2 = g_2$ by any amount so small that p_1 turns negative while all other prices and activity levels remain positive. (Exceptions such as cases where p_1 reaches a minimum at r_1 and is positive both for $r < r_1$ and $r > r_1$, or where several prices vanish simultaneously or a divergence to infinity at a point where the net product of the corresponding commodity happens to be zero (see Schefold, 1989), need not detain us here.)

Define $\mathbf{C}(r) = \mathbf{B} - (1+r)\mathbf{A}$, $\hat{\mathbf{C}}(r) = [\mathbf{C}(r)]^{-1}$, so that $\hat{\mathbf{c}}_1(r)\mathbf{C}(r) = \mathbf{e}_1$. For all r we have

$$
(\mathbf{q}' + \varepsilon\hat{\mathbf{c}}_1)\mathbf{C} = \mathbf{d}' + \varepsilon\mathbf{e}_1
$$

where $\varepsilon > 0$ and $\mathbf{q}' = (q^1, ..., q^n)$. It is clear that $\hat{\mathbf{c}}_1$ contains negative elements for $r_1 \leqslant r \leqslant r_2$ since

$$
\hat{\mathbf{c}}_1(r)\mathbf{l} = \hat{p}_1(r) \leqslant 0.
$$

Hence ε may, starting from zero, gradually be increased until one component of $\mathbf{q}' + \varepsilon\hat{\mathbf{c}}_1$, say the n'th, vanishes so that $\varepsilon = -q^n/\hat{c}_1^n$ with $\hat{c}_1^n < 0$ and the corresponding process n is put to rest for any given r in $r_1 \leqslant r \leqslant r_2$. The production of commodity one rises at the same time by an amount equal to ε, since output net of investment rises to $\mathbf{d}' + \varepsilon\mathbf{e}_1$. Hence commodity one is overproduced and ceases to be a commodity. This operation, by which a commodity and a process are eliminated from the system, is called *truncation*.

Truncation leads to an increase in the real wage since $(\mathbf{q}' + \varepsilon\hat{\mathbf{c}}_1)\mathbf{l} = \mathbf{q}'\mathbf{l} + \varepsilon\hat{p}_1$, labour employed has diminished by the absolute amount of $\varepsilon\hat{p}_1$, and the real wage $w = 1/(\mathbf{d}'\hat{\mathbf{p}}) = 1/(\mathbf{q}'\mathbf{l})$ is increased to $1/(\mathbf{q}'\mathbf{l} + \varepsilon\hat{p}_1) = 1/(\mathbf{q}'\mathbf{l} - \varepsilon|\hat{p}_1|)$ for $r_1 < r \leqslant r_2$, while the real wage stays constant at r_1 and is lower in the similarly truncated system for $r_0 \leqslant r < r_1$, $r_1 - r_0$ sufficiently small.

The truncation constructed at r_1 defines a truncated system $(\bar{\mathbf{A}}, \bar{\mathbf{B}}, \bar{\mathbf{l}}, \bar{\mathbf{d}})$ capable of self-replacement with the number of commodities and activity levels reduced by one. We assume it to be regular. The truncated system yields a higher real wage $\bar{w} = 1/(\bar{\mathbf{d}}'\bar{\mathbf{p}})$ for $r_1 < r \leqslant r_2$, because $\hat{p}_1(r_2) < 0$, and its use is therefore advantageous there, but it will also be necessary to use it because an economic system with a negative price cannot exist in reality. Prices for commodities $2, \ldots, n$ vary continuously as we move in our mental experiment from $r < r_1$ to $r > r_1$, while commodity one of the original system is an overproduced good in (or, rather, outside) the truncated system at r_2. The prices $\bar{p}$ of the commodities $2, \ldots, n$ of the truncated system in terms of labour commanded are thus positive for reasons of continuity, while positive activity levels $\bar{q}$ have been proved to exist by construction at r_1 (we have $\bar{q}^i = q^i - (q^n/\hat{c}_1^n)\hat{c}_1^i$; $i = 1, \ldots, n-1$ in $r_1 \leqslant r \leqslant r_2$), hence $\bar{p} > 0$, $\bar{q} > o$ in the entire interval $r_0 \leqslant r \leqslant r_2$ if $r_1 - r_0$ and $r_2 - r_1$ are sufficiently small.

Figure II.9b.1 shows the two wage curves considered (drawn as heavy lines where the corresponding system is to be adopted at each $r = g$). We want to compare the incentives and disincentives of moving between the original system and its truncation at r_0 and r_2. From $\bar{q}'\bar{l} = q'l + \varepsilon\hat{c}_1 l = q'l + \varepsilon\hat{p}_1$, we obtain

$$\hat{p}_1 = \frac{\bar{q}'\bar{l} - q'l}{\varepsilon}.$$

Since $\bar{p}_1 > 0$ at r_0, an amount of labour is saved, in moving from the truncated system to the original system, equal to the labour commanded

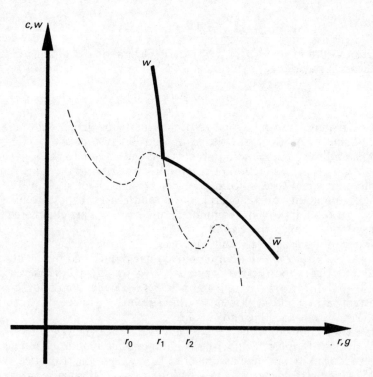

Figure II.9b.1   *Wage curves of system and truncation*

by the quantity of commodity one that is, as it were, 'erroneously' overproduced in the truncated system and evaluated in the original system at r_0. But this overproduction is 'correct' at r_2, and the labour commanded by the overproduced amount of commodity one is, in absolute terms, equal to the labour saved in moving from the original system to the truncation at r_2. This solves the 'paradox of negative labour values' observed in section 4 at $r = g = 0$: if a labour value is negative at $r = 0$, we are dealing with a residual commodity (section II.9a). The system ought to be truncated at $g = 0$ in order to increase net product per worker, and labour can be saved by shifting employment from the process using the residual commodity as a mean of production to other processes so that the residual commodity is overproduced; its overproduction allows labour to be saved by an amount equal to the absolute value of the overproduced commodity. The limit of the overproduction of the residual commodity is given by the requirement that activity levels be positive in the truncated system and are such that the required surplus is produced.

Apart from the criterion of the level of the real wage and of the negative price in the original system at r_2, there is the question of costs. If the process truncated at r_1 (without loss of generality process n) was operated at the level at which it was used in the original system and evaluated at the prices ruling in the truncated system, it would yield surplus profits or losses relative to normal profits (in terms of labour commanded) equal to the amount of work saved or lost in the transition from the truncated system to the original system at any r in $r_0 \leqslant r \leqslant r_2$. The criterion of cost and of the real wage therefore coincide because the real wage rate is the inverse of labour employed to produce the basket of the real wage: it appears profitable to use the truncated process from the point of view of the truncated system (and hence to make the transition to the original system) at r_0 where $w > \bar{w}$, and that process leads *vice versa* to a loss if evaluated at r_2 where $\bar{w} > w$. These assertions all follow from the formula:

$$
\begin{aligned}
\frac{1}{\bar{w}} - \frac{1}{w} &= \bar{\mathbf{d}}'\bar{\mathbf{p}} - \mathbf{q}'\mathbf{l} \\
&= \mathbf{q}'\mathbf{C}[0, \bar{\mathbf{p}}']' - \mathbf{q}'\mathbf{l} \\
&= \sum_{j=1}^{n-1} q^j \left(\sum_{k=2}^{n} c_j^k \bar{p}_k - l_j \right) + q^n \left(\sum_{k=2}^{n} c_n^k \bar{p}_k - l_n \right) \\
&= q^n \sum_{k=2}^{n} c_n^k \bar{p}_k - l_n
\end{aligned}
$$

hence, in obvious notation, 'difference in employment' is equal to 'surplus profits/losses in terms of labour commanded'

$$
\bar{\mathbf{q}}'\bar{\mathbf{l}} - \mathbf{q}'\mathbf{l} = q^n(\bar{\mathbf{c}}_n\bar{\mathbf{p}} - l_n)
$$

or, after multiplication by the wage rate $\bar{w}$, a 'difference of total money wage' is equal to 'monetary quasi-rents', if we want to adopt the Marshallian term to denote the profit differential due to the transition. This differential is also equal to $\varepsilon\hat{p}_1$.

We summarize in intuitive terms. Suppose we are in r_2 in the original system. Commodity one has to be subsidized because its price is negative. If the transition to the truncation is made, the entrepreneurs of process n will make a loss, and the amount of labour saved is equal to the negative amount of labour commanded by the overproduced commodity and to the losses that would be made in process n if it .was run at the 'old' activity level and evaluated at 'new' prices.

So much for truncation. There is no incentive to truncate the original system as long as $\mathbf{p} > \mathbf{o}$, $\mathbf{q} > \mathbf{o}$, for the required basket is produced and processes break even. Nothing is to be gained by means of truncation because, if any commodity i is to be overproduced according to the formula used above, one obtains

$$(\mathbf{q}' + \varepsilon\hat{\mathbf{c}}_i)\mathbf{C} = \mathbf{d}' + \varepsilon\mathbf{e}_i,$$

but this overproduction of commodity i with $\varepsilon > 0$ reduces the real wage because

$$(\mathbf{q}' + \varepsilon\hat{\mathbf{c}}_i)\mathbf{l} = \mathbf{q}'\mathbf{l} + \varepsilon\hat{p}_i > \mathbf{q}'\mathbf{l}$$

for $\hat{p}_i > 0$. This is the theorem of *'non-substitution'* for joint production: if $\mathbf{p} > \mathbf{o}$, no 'substitution' is required if the composition of $\mathbf{d}$ is varied as long as $\mathbf{q}$ remains positive.

However, a *method switch* to an alternative method of production may be profitable. If an $(n + 1)$st method of production $(\mathbf{a}_0, \mathbf{b}_0, l_0)$ is given that is linearly independent of $(\mathbf{a}_i, \mathbf{b}_i, l_i)$, $i = 1, ..., n$, it may represent an alternative to one, several or possibly all n of the other methods of production $1, ..., n$. We denote by $\mathbf{q}_{(i)}$, $\mathbf{p}^{(i)}$ and $w^{(i)}$ the activity levels, prices and wage rate of the system that *omits* method i and consists of methods $1, ..., i - 1, i + 1, ..., n$. Only systems i with positive prices and activity levels are of interest, and any two from those will (if they do not happen to be equally profitable) be related by (in obvious notation with $\mathbf{c}_k = \mathbf{b}_k - (1 + r)\mathbf{a}_k$, $k = 0, 1, 2, ..., n$):

$$q^j_{(i)}(\mathbf{c}_j\hat{\mathbf{p}}^{(j)} - l_j) = -q^i_{(j)}(\mathbf{c}_i\hat{\mathbf{p}}^{(i)} - l_i) = \mathbf{q}_{(j)}\mathbf{l}^{(j)} - \mathbf{q}_{(i)}\mathbf{l}^{(i)},$$

for

$$\mathbf{q}_{(j)}\mathbf{l}^{(j)} - \mathbf{q}_{(i)}\mathbf{l}^{(i)} = \sum_{k \neq j} q^k_{(j)}l_k - \mathbf{d}'\hat{\mathbf{p}}^{(i)}$$

$$= \sum_{k \neq i,j} q^k_{(j)}\mathbf{c}_k\hat{\mathbf{p}}^{(i)} - \mathbf{d}'\hat{\mathbf{p}}^{(i)} + q^i_{(j)}l_i$$

$$= -\left\{\left(\mathbf{d}' - \sum_{k \neq i,j} q^k_{(j)}\mathbf{c}_k\right)\hat{\mathbf{p}}^{(i)} - q^i_{(j)}l_i\right\}$$

$$= -q^i_{(j)}(\mathbf{c}_i\hat{\mathbf{p}}^{(i)} - l_i),$$

and similarly with i and j reversed.

System i of two systems i, j with positive prices will therefore yield a higher real wage $w^{(i)} = 1/\mathbf{q}_{(i)}\mathbf{l}$, if and only if it employs less labour to produce $\mathbf{d}$, and that will happen if and only if the labour commanded by the losses that would be made in process i – if it was activated at activity levels of system j and evaluated at prices of system i – are equal to the amount of labour saved, and this would happen if and only if the surplus profits that would be made in process j – if it was activated at activity levels of system i and evaluated at prices of systems j – are again equal to the amount of labour saved in the transition from system j to system i.

The combination of processes to be used is therefore found by first eliminating those with negative prices and activity levels. Among the remaining systems $i = 0, 1, 2, ..., n$ (where i is, as before, the process omitted by system i) the process will be chosen that yields the highest real wage. This system will be found because the method omitted in any system will yield surplus profits in 'current' prices as long as the method omitted in the 'current' system is not the one omitted by the 'optimal' system; the method omitted by the optimal system is unique in showing losses. The optimal system represents, in that sense, the only 'stable' solution, because there is no incentive to make a transition to another system (see Schefold, 1980, for the discussion of the neoclassical versus the classical interpretation of this result).

We can thus draw the wage curve for any system with positive prices and activity levels for given $g = r$, and replace the system by the wage curve of its truncation wherever a price turns negative. The envelope of the wage curves of systems producing the same net output but differing in some of their methods of production shows the combination of methods to be used (see Figure II.9b.2). The criterion of surplus profits and losses that leads to the choice of the optimal system for each $r = g$ is seemingly independent of the composition of the real wage, but in reality the composition matters because the criterion of surplus profits and losses (or of costs) has been formulated on the assumption that activity levels are positive.

Of course, it is also at least formally possible that an activity level turns negative; we then have the dual phenomenon to truncation, i.e. *dual truncation*. The formal procedure to derive its properties is analogous to that employed to discuss truncation; Table II.9b.1 below gives a comparison of the results on the assumption that $q^1 > 0$ at r_0, $q^1 = 0$ at r_1, $q^1 < 0$ at r_2 so that process one must be truncated, which leads, without loss of generality, to the overproduction of commodity n for $r_1 \leqslant r \leqslant r_2$. We abbreviate $\bar{\mathbf{c}}^1 = (c_2^1, ..., c_n^1)'$, $\bar{\mathbf{c}}_n = (c_n^1, ..., c_n^{n-1})$, $\bar{\mathbf{c}}^n = (c_2^n, ..., c_n^n)'$, $\bar{\mathbf{c}}_1 = (c_1^1, ..., c_1^{n-1})$. The letter ε in the last row of the table denotes the amount by which commodity one must be overproduced at r_1 until one activity level (here the n'th) vanishes according to the formula $(\mathbf{q}' + \varepsilon \hat{\mathbf{c}}_1)\mathbf{C} = \mathbf{d}' + \varepsilon \mathbf{e}_1$ explained above; the derivation of the corresponding dual formulae involves some complications, however. Assume $\mathbf{d}'\hat{\mathbf{c}}^1 = q^1 = 0$ at r_1. Hence $\delta(r) \geqslant 0$ can in the relevant cases be defined such that – apart from flukes – one and only one component (the n'th, say) of $\hat{\mathbf{p}} - \delta\hat{\mathbf{c}}^1$ vanishes in a neighbourhood of r_1 containing two points $r_0 < r_1$, $r_2 > r_1$; one then has $\mathbf{C}(\hat{\mathbf{p}} - \delta\hat{\mathbf{c}}^1) = \mathbf{l} - \delta\mathbf{e}^1$ and $\hat{\mathbf{p}} - \delta\hat{\mathbf{c}}^1 = (\bar{\mathbf{p}}', 0)'$, $\bar{\mathbf{p}} > \mathbf{o}$.

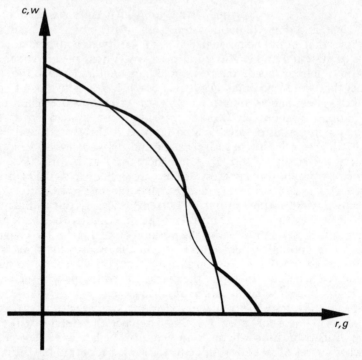

Figure II.9b.2   *Envelope of wage curves of system and truncation*

There are two particular difficulties arising with dual truncations. The first concerns those cases where $\mathbf{d}$ is not strictly positive in contrast to the analogous formula for truncations with $\hat{\mathbf{e}}_1 \mathbf{l} = 0$ and $\mathbf{l} > \mathbf{o}$. We neglect this possibility in this simplified presentation. Second, whereas it was at once clear that ε had to be positive in order to ensure production and overproduction of $\mathbf{d}$, we shall yet have to justify our choice of $\delta > 0$ for dual truncation. It implies $\delta = \hat{p}/\hat{c}_n^1$, $\hat{c}_n^1 > 0$, for $r_0 \leqslant r \leqslant r_2$.

The dual truncation so defined leads to a loss in process one for $\mathbf{C}(\hat{\mathbf{p}} - \delta\hat{\mathbf{e}}^1) = \mathbf{l} - \delta\mathbf{e}^1$ for all r, $r_0 \leqslant r \leqslant r_2$. It will turn out that we must have a negative sign in the dual, and that surplus profits are not possible on either side of r_1. The difference between the inverse of the real wage of the dual truncation and that of the original system follows from $\bar{\mathbf{d}}'\bar{\mathbf{p}} = \mathbf{d}'(\hat{\mathbf{p}} - \delta\hat{\mathbf{e}}^1) = \mathbf{d}'\hat{\mathbf{p}} - \delta q^1$, where δq^1 will turn out to be the labour commanded of the overproduction. Hence $\bar{\mathbf{d}}'\bar{\mathbf{p}} - \mathbf{d}'\hat{\mathbf{p}} = -\delta q^1 < 0$ for $q^1 > 0$ in $r_0 \leqslant r < r_1$, and *vice versa* for $r_1 < r \leqslant r_2$. The activity levels of the truncated system, $\bar{\mathbf{q}}$, are defined by $\bar{\mathbf{q}}'\bar{\mathbf{C}} = \bar{\mathbf{d}}$, $\bar{\mathbf{C}} = c_j^i$; $i = 2, ..., n$; $j = 1, ..., n - 1$. Since $(0, \bar{\mathbf{q}}') \doteq \mathbf{q}'$ at r_1, we have $\bar{\mathbf{q}} > \mathbf{o}$ for $r_2 - r_1$ sufficiently small, and we obtain

$$-\delta q^1 = \bar{\mathbf{d}}'\bar{\mathbf{p}} - \mathbf{d}'\hat{\mathbf{p}}$$
$$= \bar{\mathbf{q}}'\bar{\mathbf{l}} - \mathbf{d}'\hat{\mathbf{p}}$$
$$= (0, \bar{\mathbf{q}}')\mathbf{C}\hat{\mathbf{p}} - \mathbf{d}'\hat{\mathbf{p}}$$

$$= \sum_{j \ne n} (\bar{\mathbf{q}}' \bar{\mathbf{c}}^j - d^j)\hat{p}_j + (\bar{\mathbf{q}}' \bar{\mathbf{c}}^n - d^n)\hat{p}_n$$

$$= (\bar{\mathbf{q}}' \bar{\mathbf{c}}^n - d^n)\hat{p}_n.$$

The first activity level, q^1, is by assumption negative for $r_1 < r \le r_2$, hence $-\delta q^1 > 0$ and $\bar{\mathbf{q}}' \bar{\mathbf{c}}^n > d^n$ in $r_1 < r \le r_2$. We have overproduction of commodity n in the dual truncation at positive activity levels in that interval where the original system is, because of $q^1 < 0$, technically not feasible. We have, *vice versa*, $\bar{\mathbf{q}}' \bar{\mathbf{c}}^n < d^n$ in $r_0 \le r < r_1$. The truncation is therefore technically not feasible − and indeed not necessary − where the original system has positive prices and activity levels.

This confirms at the same time that we had to choose $\delta > 0$ and explains why the truncated process can show losses on both sides of r_0: the overriding criterion is that of technical feasibility, which prevents any use of the truncation at r_0, while the original system is impossible at r_2.

A second truncation with non-negative activity levels and prices, involving the overproduction of a different commodity, could have been constructed with $\delta < 0$, i.e. $-\delta > 0$. We shall come back to it, but it would not be relevant to our present discussion − nor would the other $n - 2$ truncations that could, in a similar way, be constructed (with all wage curves crossing at r_1) be of interest, because they would each have some negative prices or activity levels.

The structure of all wage curves of all subsystems or truncations of a given joint-production system is in fact very complex, but all important results of our investigation are contained in Table II.9b.1. The formal symmetries of the table are easily recognized, but it may be found surprising that the system yielding the lower real wage is chosen on both sides of the point of intersection of the wage curves in the case of dual truncation (see Figure II.9b.3). This is again possible simply because the dual truncation at r_0 does not produce a sufficient amount of one commodity at r_0, while the original system has a negative activity level at r_2 so that both systems are not admissible for technical reasons at r_0, r_2 respectively. The criterion that the system with the highest real wage be chosen can be applied only to systems that fulfil the precondition of productivity, i.e. that are technically feasible.

This also explains why the rule that processes involving losses should not be activated is violated at r_0 in so far as process one, if evaluated in prices of the dual truncation, shows a loss and yet must be used because the original system is the only one that is technically feasible.

In other words: the well-known criteria of adopting processes yielding surplus profits and systems yielding the highest real wage can be retained but only if the application of the rule is restricted to systems for which technical feasibility is assured. If this restriction does not seem to fit in well with Sraffa's theory, it should be stressed that dual truncation does not appear to be a plausible occurrence from the point of view of economic intuition. There is no dual truncation in pure fixed-capital systems, and *relevant* examples involving pure joint production are difficult to imagine.

This is even more true of *commodity switches*, the dual to the method

Table II.9b.1   Table for comparison of truncation and dual truncation

		Truncation			Dual truncation		
		r_0	r_1	r_2	r_0	r_1	r_2
Original system	Prices	$\mathbf{p} > 0$	$p_1 = 0$	$p_1 < 0$	$\mathbf{p} > 0$	$\mathbf{p} > 0$	$\mathbf{p} > 0$
	Activity levels	$\mathbf{q} > 0$	$\mathbf{q} > 0$	$\mathbf{q} > 0$	$\mathbf{q} > 0$	$q^1 = 0$	$q^1 < 0$
	Overproduction						
	Surplus		none				
	profits/losses		processes break even				
Truncated system	Prices			positive			
	Activity levels			positive			
	Overproduction	$\bar{\mathbf{q}}'\bar{\mathbf{c}}^1 > d^1$	$\bar{\mathbf{q}}'\mathbf{c}^1 > d^1$	$\bar{\mathbf{q}}'\mathbf{c}^1 > d^1$	$\bar{\mathbf{q}}'\bar{\mathbf{c}}^n < d^n$	$\bar{\mathbf{q}}'\bar{\mathbf{c}}^n = d^n$	$\bar{\mathbf{q}}'\bar{\mathbf{c}}^n > d^n$
	Surplus profits/losses	$\bar{\mathbf{c}}_n\bar{\mathbf{p}} > l_n$	$\bar{\mathbf{c}}_n\bar{\mathbf{p}} = l_n$	$\bar{\mathbf{c}}_n\bar{\mathbf{p}} < l_n$	$\bar{\mathbf{c}}_1\bar{\mathbf{p}} < l_1$	$\bar{\mathbf{c}}_1\bar{\mathbf{p}} < l_1$	$\bar{\mathbf{c}}_1\bar{\mathbf{p}} < l_1$
Comparison	Wage	$w > \bar{w}$	$w = \bar{w}$	$w < \bar{w}$	$w < \bar{w}$	$w = \bar{w}$	$w > \bar{w}$
	Continuity		$\bar{\mathbf{p}} = (p_2,\dots,p_n)'$			$\bar{\mathbf{q}}' = (q^2,\dots,q^n)$	
Difference in labour employed = labour commanded by loss in truncated process			$\bar{\mathbf{q}}'\bar{\mathbf{l}} - \mathbf{q}'\mathbf{l} = \varepsilon\hat{p}_1 = q^n(\bar{\mathbf{c}}_n\bar{\mathbf{p}} - l_n)$			$\mathbf{d}'\bar{\mathbf{p}} - \mathbf{d}'\mathbf{p} = (\bar{\mathbf{q}}'\bar{\mathbf{c}}^n - d^n)\hat{p}_n = -\delta q^1$	
Product value difference = value of overproduction			$\varepsilon = -\dfrac{q^n}{\hat{c}_1^n}$			$\delta = \dfrac{\hat{p}_n}{\hat{c}_n^1}$	
system adopted if $r = q$		w	w or $\bar{w}$	$\bar{w}$	w	w or $\bar{w}$	$\bar{w}$

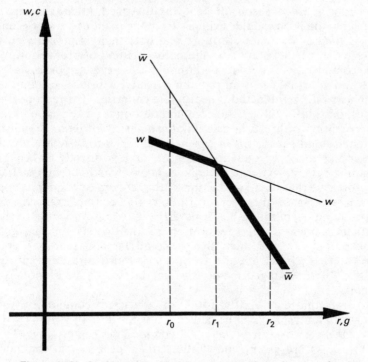

Figure II.9b.3   *Wage curve of system and dual truncation*

switches discussed above. Formally, a commodity switch takes place at $r_1 = g_1$ if the system containing n processes and n goods with positive prices (commodities) involves the production of an $(n + 1)$st good that is not a commodity at one rate of growth g_0 where it is overproduced, while another good, the first say, is overproduced at another rate of growth g_2, so that good one ceases to be a commodity at an intermediate rate of growth g_1 where good $n + 1$ is turned into a commodity.

The formal symmetry with method switches is clear, but economically there is a difference. One now requires each system to produce or overproduce $n + 1$ goods. With the same n methods of production, a different good is overproduced at different rates of growth, while the remaining goods are not overproduced and are commodities at positive prices at all rates of growth. In discussing commodity switches, one thus postulates by assumption that the production or overproduction of $n + 1$ goods is a *technical* requirement of growth of the system, whereas in the case of method switches the $(n + 1)$st method may be used or not used according to *economic* considerations as an alternative to n existing processes with n commodities. One is so much interested in the economic mechanism of method switches precisely because one has first to prove that the economic criteria for choice exist and can function, while the technical requirements of reproduction with commodity switches are economically more trivial, not although but because they are technically vital.

There is another reason for believing that method switches are more interesting than commodity switches from the point of view of economic theory. Method switches are more plausible than commodity switches because the specification of an alternative method of production for the same composition of output is – although it is never as precise as that of a method in actual use – an economic reality; it suffices to point to the existence of different methods in different countries. The reproduction of 'goods' outside the universe of commodities, on the other hand, is indeed a precondition of life; a largely unknown variety of living organisms in ecosystems and substances in geochemical cycles must reproduce themselves, and their reproduction is more or less directly linked to the economic system, whether or not we know it and care about it. It is therefore true that the reproduction of the economic system presupposes a much larger natural 'system' with flows that can be arranged in some sort of an input–output table. It nevertheless seems rather far-fetched to postulate a meaningful specification of the 'goods' in this gigantic input–output 'system' such that it could be said that one good is overproduced at one rate of growth, and another at a different rate of growth, with unchanged methods of production in the economic 'sub-system'.

However that may be: the formal properties of commodity switches are easy to derive and can be contrasted with those of method switches above. If n processes involving $n + 1$ commodities (a_i^j, b_i^j, l_i), $i = 1, ..., n$; $j = 0, 1, ..., n$; are given, and if the letter j denotes the commodity j omitted in system j producing commodities $0, 1, ..., j - 1, j + 1, ..., n$ without overproduction and overproducing good j, one has, in analogous notation to that employed above,

$$\mathbf{d}_{(i)}\hat{\mathbf{p}}^{(i)} - \mathbf{d}_{(j)}\hat{\mathbf{p}}^{(j)} = \mathbf{q}_{(i)}\mathbf{l} - \sum_{k \neq j} d^k \hat{p}_k^{(j)}$$

$$= \mathbf{q}_{(i)}(\mathbf{l} - \sum_{k \neq i,j} \mathbf{c}^k \hat{p}_k^{(j)}) - d^i \hat{p}_i^{(j)}$$

$$= (\mathbf{q}_{(i)}\mathbf{c}^i - d^i)\hat{p}_i^{(j)}.$$

The formula shows that, of two systems i and j with positive prices and activity levels, only one can be technically feasible and overproduce the good outside the system, here good i, and that it will then employ more labour (both sides of the equation positive). This implies again that the system to be chosen among those with positve prices and activity levels will be the one with the lowest real wage, as the only one fulfilling the technical condition of reproduction. It is thus again confirmed that the criterion of cost minimization and the related criterion of maximization of the real wage apply only in a comparison of systems that are technically feasible – here, among those with positive prices, only one is.

We have been discussing the changes in the utilization of methods of production in the provision of a given net output as the rate of growth and the rate of profit vary simultaneously, starting from a situation in which prices and activity levels are positive. We have distinguished four possible types of change: truncation, method switches, dual truncation, and commodity switches. This distinction and the description of the cases can be shown to be complete apart from flukes owing to irregular systems. (Important exceptions may, however, be due to the pattern of zeros in $\mathbf{A}$, $\mathbf{B}$ and — especially — $\mathbf{d}$, as I have indicated in Schefold, 1978c.)

Starting from a given Sraffa system with positive prices and activity levels at $r = g$, the relevant wage curve can thus be drawn by executing truncation, methods switches, etc. This involves going both backwards to $r = g = 0$ and forwards to a *true maximum rate of profit* $\hat{R}$, i.e. not to the maximum rate of profit of any single given system or truncation, but to the one that is the maximum rate of profit of the system that appears *last* on the envelope of the wage curves of technically feasible systems derived by means of truncation, method switches, etc. A finite $\hat{R} > 0$ exists for the 'last system' (except for flukes); it is such that the real wage vanishes and a standard commodity exists, as we shall presently see.

Wage curves of systems that are not technically feasible are not to be considered for the economic comparison of wage curves; they may be above the envelope of the wage curves of technically feasible systems that represents the relevant wage curve. The envelope of technically feasible wage curves $w_e(r)$ falls monotonically as long as prices and activity levels are positive, and they remain (apart from the said flukes) positive up to a finite $\hat{R}$ where w_e vanishes, i.e. $w_e(\hat{R}) = 0$.

Flukes are possible if a system appearing on the envelope does not allow any increase in $g = r$ without an activity level turning negative at some $\hat{g}$ where $w_e(\hat{g}) > 0$, and if a dual truncation is not feasible at $\hat{g}$, e.g. because a mean of production j with $d^j = 0$ happens to be indispensable for the reproduction of the system, but is used and produced in only one process i and has an own rate of reproduction equal to $\hat{g}$. With $(1 + \hat{g})a_i^j = b_i^j$, the system can then obviously not expand at rates of growth higher than $\hat{g}$; a negative quantity of good j will be produced if $g > \hat{g}$. Yet consumption per head may be positive at $\hat{g}$ so that $w_e(\hat{g}) > 0$. The rate of profit cannot be raised beyond $\hat{g}$, but there is no standard commodity associated with $\hat{g}$ (see Schefold, 1989).

If this kind of occurrence is ruled out (for a sufficient condition see Schefold, 1978b), one has $\hat{g} = \hat{R}$, $w_e(\hat{R}) = 0$, and the last truncation appearing on the envelope at $\hat{R} - \varepsilon$, $\varepsilon > 0$ sufficiently small, will, if it is regular and basic, have a unique, positive standard commodity, and will be almost all-productive. This is a rather surprising little result, which was announced in section II.8.

We give only a sketch of a proof of these assertions (for a complete proof, see Schefold, 1978b) on the additional hypothesis (which could be eased) that the system $(\mathbf{A}, \mathbf{B}, \mathbf{l}, \mathbf{d})$ appearing last on the envelope has strictly positive prices and activity levels. For the system then has a unique positive standard commodity simply by assumption, because there is $\mathbf{q} > \mathbf{o}$ with $\mathbf{q}' \mathbf{C}(\hat{R}) = \mathbf{o}$, $\mathbf{C}(r) = \mathbf{B} - (1 + r)\mathbf{A}$, $\mathbf{a}^j \neq \mathbf{o}$; $j = 1, \ldots, n$; therefore $\mathbf{q}' (\mathbf{B} - \mathbf{A}) = \hat{R}\mathbf{q}\mathbf{A} > \mathbf{o}$. Let H be the interior of the convex hull of the $\mathbf{c}^j(\hat{R})$ and define $X(r) = \{\mathbf{x} \mid \mathbf{x}' \mathbf{c}^j \geqslant 0$, all $j\}$. If $X(\hat{R} - \varepsilon)$ did contain no positive points for each ε, $\varepsilon > 0$, there would be $\bar{\mathbf{x}}, \bar{\mathbf{x}} \not> \mathbf{o}$, $\bar{\mathbf{x}}' \mathbf{c}^j(\hat{R}) \geqslant 0$, hence $\bar{\mathbf{x}}' \mathbf{h} \geqslant 0$ for all $\mathbf{h} \in H$, in contradiction to the fact that the vectors $\mathbf{c}^j(\hat{R})$ are in a hyperplane with a normal $\mathbf{q} > \mathbf{o}$ in $\mathbb{R}^n_+$ and that the origin lies in H because $\Sigma \mathbf{c}^j(\hat{R})p_j(\hat{R}) = \mathbf{o}$, $\mathbf{p}(\hat{R}) > \mathbf{o}$, so that the intersection of any two-dimensional plane containing $\mathbf{q}$ with H will have points on both sides of a straight line through the origin in common with H, and only for a point $\mathbf{h}$ on one side can it be true that $\bar{\mathbf{x}}'\mathbf{h} \geqslant 0$. Hence $\mathbf{x} > \mathbf{o}$ for all $\mathbf{x} \in X(\hat{R} - \varepsilon)$ and some $\varepsilon > 0$, so that $[\mathbf{C}(\hat{R} - \varepsilon)]^{-1} > \mathbf{O}$ for all sufficiently small $\varepsilon > 0$.

We have thus found that a monotonically falling wage curve in terms of standard $\mathbf{d}$ can be constructed starting from any Sraffa system with positive prices and activity levels at some $r = g > 0$, if $r = g$ are varied simultaneously, and that the simplest type of Sraffa system is finally encountered as the wage curve approximates the true maximum rate of profit, namely one that is akin to single-product Sraffa systems in all essential aspects.

This result would be perfectly satisfactory if we had not been compelled to assume that golden rule conditions $(r = g)$ obtain everywhere. But if this assumption is dropped, and if e.g. $g = 0$, and only r is varied, the foregoing analysis still provides a starting point. The wage curves originating from truncation, alternative methods, etc. have to be drawn as above. Additions to our normal rules of choice may now be necessary, however. Take e.g. the case of a dual truncation. According to the case expounded in Table II.9b.1 above and shown here again in Figure II.9b.4 in a similar diagram, the truncation $\bar{w}$ has to be chosen at

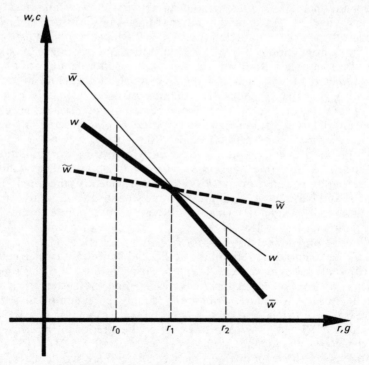

Figure 11.9b.4   *New constellations if* **g** < **r**

$r_2 = g_2$, because only the truncation $\overline{w}$ is technically feasible at g_2. But if $r \neq g$, and $r_2 \geqslant r \geqslant r_1$ while $r_0 \leqslant g < r_1$, it is clear that the original system must be chosen – it is alone in being technically feasible at g and has the additional advantage of allowing the highest real wage to be paid, with all processes breaking even and positive activity levels. In the reverse case ($g = r_2$, $r = r_0$), the truncation must be chosen because of a negative activity level at $g = r_2$; the process to be truncated yields losses at $r = r_0$.

This particular constellation raises no new problems as long as we consider w and $\overline{w}$, but we mentioned a second truncated system with non-negative prices and activity levels that can be generated – apart from the one that we have chosen – at each r_1 where a dual truncation occurs. It is the one obtained by looking for a $-\delta = \lambda > 0$ in the above analysis of dual truncation. With $q^1 = 0$ at r_1, $q^1 < 0$ at r_2, etc., as above, there is $\lambda > 0$ such that $\hat{\mathbf{p}} + \lambda \hat{\mathbf{c}}^1 \geqslant \mathbf{o}$, and $\hat{p}_1 + \lambda \hat{c}_1^1 = 0$, say, and thus, without loss of generality, the first commodity is overproduced. One obtains for the corresponding 'second dual truncation', which we denote by $\tilde{\mathbf{C}}, \tilde{\mathbf{q}} > \mathbf{o}, \tilde{\mathbf{p}}$ with $(0, \tilde{\mathbf{p}}') = (\hat{\mathbf{p}} + \lambda \hat{\mathbf{c}}^1)'$ etc.:

$$\lambda q^1 = \tilde{w}^{-1} - w^{-1} = (\tilde{\mathbf{q}}' \tilde{\mathbf{c}}^1 - d^1)\hat{p}_1$$

and

$$\mathbf{c}_1 \tilde{\mathbf{p}} > l_1$$

We now have $\lambda q^1 < 0$ and $\tilde{w} > w$ at r_2, and $\lambda q^1 > 0$ with $\tilde{w} < w$ at r_0. The 'second dual truncation' is economically irrelevant if the rate of growth is equal to the rate of profit, because it does not produce or overproduce the first commodity d^1 at r_2, while we have $\tilde{w} < w$ at r_0. Moreover, although the second dual truncation is technically feasible at r_0, it will not be used because the first process yields surplus profits ($\mathbf{c}_1 \tilde{\mathbf{p}} > \tilde{l}_1$) if evaluated in prices of the truncation. The second dual truncation will therefore not be chosen on either side of r_1, if $g = r$.

But if we have, for instance, a rate of growth equal to r_0 and a rate of profit equal to r_2, a new problem results because, on the one hand, the second dual truncation is technically feasible at r_0 and yields a higher real wage at r_2, while, on the other hand, there are surplus profits to be earned in the operation of the first process if evaluated in prices $\tilde{\mathbf{p}}$, which implies that there would be an incentive to return to the original system w or to the dual truncation $\overline{w}$, once $\tilde{w}$ was introduced. Fortunately, the 'return' would solve the dilemma. The original truncation is technically feasible at $g = r_0$ and yields positive prices at a uniform rate of profit $r = r_2$. The point therefore is that the system to be chosen must be characterized by the property that no extra profit at r can be earned by making the transition to some other process, while it must be technically feasible at g. The wage, then, can be maximized only among systems that fulfil both conditions. (Example: cf. Fig. 11.9c.1 at $r = 0.198$).

We therefore find the solution even if $g \neq r$. However, a complete analysis requires a consideration of all truncations, including the second dual truncation. This will be done in the next section, which is based on an extended equilibrium concept and on linear programming.[1]

It may be noted that a simpler analysis suffices for systems such that all truncations are technically feasible for all rates of growth between zero and the maximum rate of profit (Sec 18a). It will be seen that fixed-capital systems are technically feasible whenever they are on the envelope of the wage curves, if the real wage does not, as is plausible, contain old machines. Fixed-capital systems have the additional advantage that the truncation chosen does not then depend otherwise on the composition of the real wage. Dual truncations and commodity switches do not obtain; fixed-capital systems therefore conform to a simple extension of the ordinary rules of economic rationality of single-product systems. The analysis of fixed-capital systems below shows that they are the really relevant special case of the perhaps too abstract analysis presented here.

Note

1   Section II.9c is the latest addition to this book. It is based on Schefold (1988), which in turn owes a great deal to Lippi (1979), Salvadori (1982) and Bidard (1984).

9c   Beyond the Golden Rule

The analysis of the previous section was based on the assumption that the rate of growth equals the rate of profit according to the so-called Golden Rule. To the economic optimality conditions that it implies (the technique chosen at ruling rate of profit is the one that yields the maximum consumption per head at the rate of growth equal to the rate of profit) there corresponds a simplified mathematical structure.

However, golden rule conditions obtain only if total investment is equal to total profits. The condition is fulfilled for the classical assumption about savings: all profits are saved and all wages spent. The hypothesis is noteworthy more for its elegance than for its realism.

In order to bring the difficulties associated with the deviation from golden rule conditions into focus, we reconsider the analysis of the previous section in terms of the linear programming method. Mathematically speaking, it is the impossibility of an immediate application of the duality relationships that causes the difficulties in the case where $r > g$ because capitalists consume some part of their profits.

The linear programming approach, which is essentially equivalent to the analysis of section 9b, has two parts. On the one hand, there is the dual

$$\text{Min } \mathbf{q}'\mathbf{l}! \qquad \text{S.T.} \qquad \mathbf{q}'[\mathbf{B} - (1 + g)\mathbf{A}] \geqslant \mathbf{d}', \mathbf{q} \geqslant \mathbf{o}.$$

The dual means that the labour input is to be minimized by choosing appropriate activity levels $\mathbf{q}$, subject to the condition that a vector of requirements for consumption $\mathbf{d}$ be produced or overproduced at rate of growth g. The vector $\mathbf{d}$ is assumed to be independent of r and g. If $g = r$, solutions to the dual exist if and only if there are solutions to the primal:

$$\text{Max } \mathbf{d}'\mathbf{p}! \qquad \text{S.T.} \qquad [\mathbf{B} - (1 + r)\mathbf{A}]\mathbf{p} \leqslant \mathbf{l}, \mathbf{p} \geqslant \mathbf{o}.$$

The primal means that, at equilibrium prices, no process will make extra profits. To simplify we write $\mathbf{p}$ for $\hat{\mathbf{p}}$. If $\mathbf{q}$ and $\mathbf{p}$ are optimal solutions,

$$\mathbf{q}'\mathbf{l} = \mathbf{q}'[\mathbf{B} - (1+r)\mathbf{A}]\mathbf{p} = \mathbf{d}'\mathbf{p}.$$

It follows that overproduced commodities are free, and processes involving losses are not used:

$$\mathbf{q}'[\mathbf{b}^j - (1+g)\mathbf{a}^j] > d^j \Rightarrow p_j = 0,$$

$$[\mathbf{b}_i - (1+r)\mathbf{a}_i]\mathbf{p} < l_i \Rightarrow q^i = 0.$$

It can then be shown (Schefold, 1978c) that square truncated systems or truncations emerge as solutions in the regular case. A square truncation is here a system consisting of a combination of processes of $\mathbf{A}$, $\mathbf{B}$, $\mathbf{l}$ producing or overproducing the goods in vector $\mathbf{d}$; it is called 'square' because the number of goods with positive prices ('commodities') is assumed to be equal to the number of processes that have been activated. The optimum is associated with a maximization of $1/\mathbf{q}'\mathbf{l} = w$, i.e. with a maximum of the real wage among those systems that are feasible in the dual by producing or overproducing the requirements for consumption $\mathbf{d}$. The optimality condition of the primal, on the other hand, may be interpreted as a minimization of the real wage among those processes that do not yield extra profits at equilibrium prices (because prices are expressed in terms of labour commanded). However, what matters is the well-known maximization of the real wage that occurs among systems fulfilling the quantity conditions. We are used to maximizing the real wage among competing systems, given the rate of profit, because this normally means choosing the most profitable system, given the wage rate.

We may again observe that these rules do not need to be modified in the case where the rate of profit exceeds the rate of growth, if it is known that all relevant truncations are able to produce $\mathbf{d}$ at non-negative activity levels for rates of growth smaller than the rate of profit. For to those truncations there then correspond vectors of activity levels that are feasible in the dual both at r and at g. If the truncation on the envelope is not chosen according to the primal, although a truncation below the envelope leads to a smaller real wage, this can only be the case because the associated price vectors are not feasible in the primal, and they can be not feasible only because they involve extra profits. These extra profits will be made precisely because the application of the price vectors associated with a sub-optimal truncation to the optimal technique yields extra profits causing the adoption of that technique. The application of the conventional rule of choice therefore remains valid for single-product and fixed-capital systems (which have this property of semi-positive activity levels being associated with rates of growth lower than the rate of profit), although the technique chosen on the envelope at the rate of profit r is not necessarily optimal, in that consumption per head is not necessarily maximized at the lower rate of growth g.

However, in the general case we have to take the possibility into account that a system that appears to be optimal (in some sense) from the point of view of prices at r would have negative activity levels if the rate of growth were as high as r. It might also be possible with some such systems that negative prices would obtain if the rate of profit were as low as g while in fact activity levels are positive at g. The duality relationships of linear programming then cannot be applied. Meaningful solutions are provided by extended von Neumann systems, as discussed by Łoś (1976) or *cost minimizing systems* (CMS) as discussed in Salvadori (1982). Given the activities represented by an input matrix $\mathbf{A}$, an output matrix $\mathbf{B}$, a labour vector $\mathbf{l}$ and the requirements of consumption $\mathbf{d}$, a CMS is represented by a vector of activity levels $\mathbf{q}$ and a vector of prices $\mathbf{p}$ such that $\mathbf{d}$ is produced or overproduced at activity levels $\mathbf{q}$ at the rate of growth g, such that no process yields extra profits at prices $\mathbf{p}$ at the rate of profit r, and such that overproduced goods are free and loss-making processes are not used.

Our formal definition is as follows. Let g and r be given, $0 \leqslant g \leqslant r$, let

$$\mathbf{p} \in P = \{\mathbf{p} \geqslant \mathbf{o} \mid [\mathbf{B} - (1 + r)\mathbf{A}]\mathbf{p} \leqslant \mathbf{l}\},$$
$$\mathbf{q} \in Q = \{\mathbf{q} \geqslant \mathbf{o} \mid \mathbf{q}'[\mathbf{B} - (1 + g)\mathbf{A}] \geqslant \mathbf{d}\}.$$

A CMS is then given by a pair of vectors $\bar{\mathbf{p}} \in P$, $\bar{\mathbf{q}} \in Q$ such that

$$\bar{\mathbf{q}}'[\mathbf{B} - (1 + g)\mathbf{A}]\bar{\mathbf{p}} = \mathbf{d}'\bar{\mathbf{p}},$$
$$\bar{\mathbf{q}}'[\mathbf{B} - (1 + r)\mathbf{A}]\bar{\mathbf{p}} = \bar{\mathbf{q}}'\mathbf{l}.$$

With this definition, one has the following theorem (the proof is obvious):

Theorem 9c.1

If and only if $\mathbf{p}$, $\mathbf{q}$ represent a CMS, one has $\mathbf{p} \in P$, $\mathbf{q} \in Q$, and

$$\mathbf{q}'[\mathbf{b}^j - (1 + g)\mathbf{a}^j] > d^j \Rightarrow p_j = 0,$$
$$[\mathbf{b}_i - (1 + r)\mathbf{a}_i]\mathbf{p} < l_i \Rightarrow q_i = 0.$$

A CMS may be interpreted in terms of the theory of games (Łoś, 1976). We have:

Theorem 9c.2

Let $\bar{\mathbf{p}}$, $\bar{\mathbf{q}}$ be a CMS. Then we have

$$\bar{\mathbf{q}}'[\mathbf{B} - (1 + g)\mathbf{A}]\bar{\mathbf{p}} \leqslant \mathbf{q}'[\mathbf{B} - (1 + g)\mathbf{A}]\bar{\mathbf{p}} \text{ for all } \mathbf{q} \in Q,$$
$$\bar{\mathbf{q}}'[\mathbf{B} - (1 + r)\mathbf{A}]\bar{\mathbf{p}} \geqslant \bar{\mathbf{q}}'[\mathbf{B} - (1 + r)\mathbf{A}]\mathbf{p} \text{ for all } \mathbf{p} \in P.$$

PROOF:

From the definition we obtain

$$\bar{q}'\,[B - (1 + g)A]\bar{p} = d'\,\bar{p} \leqslant q'\,[B - (1 + g)A]\bar{p} \text{ for all } q \in Q, \text{ and}$$
$$\bar{q}'\,[B - (1 + r)A]\bar{p} = \bar{q}'\mathbf{l} \geqslant \bar{q}'\,[B - (1 + r)A]p \text{ for all } p \in P$$

q.e.d.

In terms of the theory of games this means that one player will, given $\bar{p}$, choose activity levels q so as to minimize $q'\,[B - (1 + g)A]\bar{p}$, while the other player will, given $\bar{q}$, choose p so as to maximize $\bar{q}'\,[B - (1 + r)A]p$.

I propose the following interpretation of the rules of this game. Let us denote, for any $q \in Q$, $q'\,[B - (1 + g)A] = d^{+}$. The vector d^{+} may be interpreted as the vector of goods available for consumption, given activity levels q, while d are the requirements for consumption. The game in the CMS then obviously is such that activity levels are chosen so as to minimize the value of the excess of d^{+} over d; this minimization of excess production is what remains of the minimization of the labour input at g according to the dual under golden rule conditions.

On the other hand, let $[B - (1 + r)A]p = \mathbf{l}^{+}$ for any $p \in P$ be the vector of what remains in each sector for the payment of the wage (in terms of labour commanded) after other inputs have been paid for (including normal profits) at a given vector of prices p. The second player then tries to find prices p such that the excess of $\mathbf{l}$ over $\mathbf{l}^{+}$ is minimized, i.e. the second player tries to raise the wage in each sector up to its required maximum. In this restricted sense, the maximization of the real wage at r survives.

Theorem 9c.3

Let $0 \leqslant g \leqslant r < R$ be given, where R is the maximum rate of balanced growth (the true maximum rate of profit of the system $(A, B, \mathbf{l}, d)$ in the sense of section II.9b). Then there exists a CMS.

PROOF:

We follow Lippi (1979). Consider the linear programme

$$\text{Min } q'\mathbf{l}! \text{ S.T. } q'\,[B - (1 + r)A] \geqslant d, q \geqslant o.$$

According to the assumption about R, this linear programme has a semi-positive solution $\bar{q}$. Define the sets

$$U = \{u \geqslant o \mid u'\mathbf{l} \leqslant \bar{q}\mathbf{l}\},$$
$$X(u) = \{x \geqslant o \mid x'\,[B - (1 + r)A] \geqslant d - (r - g)u'A\}$$

and let $T(u)$ represent the set of solutions of the linear programme

$$\text{Min } x'\mathbf{l}, x \in X(u), u \in U.$$

$T(\mathbf{u})$ is non-empty, for $\tilde{\mathbf{q}} \in X(\mathbf{u})$ and $\mathbf{l} > \mathbf{o}$ so that the dual and the primal have, with $\tilde{\mathbf{q}}$ and with $\mathbf{p} = \mathbf{o}$ respectively, each feasible vectors.

$T(\mathbf{u})$ is bounded because $\mathbf{l} > \mathbf{o}$, it is closed and convex; one can show that it is an upper semi-continuous mapping.

Finally we have $T(\mathbf{u}) \subset U$, for we have $X(\mathbf{o}) \subseteq X(\mathbf{u})$ for all $\mathbf{u} \in U$, hence $\mathbf{x}'\mathbf{l} \leqslant \tilde{\mathbf{q}}'\mathbf{l}$ for $\mathbf{x} \in T(\mathbf{u})$.

It follows that we may apply the fixed point theorem of Kakutani; there is therefore a fixed point $\mathbf{q}$ of the mapping $T(\mathbf{u})$, and a price vector $\mathbf{p}$ as the solution of the primal programme associated with $\mathbf{u} = \mathbf{q}$. We have

$$\mathbf{q}'\,[\mathbf{B} - (1 + r)\mathbf{A}] \geqslant \mathbf{d}' - (r - g)\mathbf{q}'\mathbf{A},$$

and

$$\mathbf{q}'\,[\mathbf{B} - (1 + g)\mathbf{A}] \geqslant \mathbf{d}', \quad [\mathbf{B} - (1 + r)\mathbf{A}]\mathbf{q} \leqslant \mathbf{l},$$

and

$$\mathbf{q}'\mathbf{l} = \mathbf{q}'\,[\mathbf{B} - (1 + r)\mathbf{A}]\mathbf{p} = \mathbf{d}'\mathbf{p} - (r - g)\mathbf{q}'\mathbf{A}\mathbf{p},$$

hence

$$\mathbf{q}'\,[\mathbf{B} - (1 + g)\mathbf{A}]\mathbf{p} = \mathbf{d}'\mathbf{p},$$

which completes the proof that $\mathbf{q}$, $\mathbf{p}$ represent a CMS.

This proves the existence of a meaningful solution that generalizes our consideration of the golden rule·case within the relevant range, i.e. for rates of growth and rates of profit smaller than the maximum obtainable under golden rule conditions.

Examples show that such solutions may also exist for some range of rates of profit exceeding R, if we are dealing with general joint-production systems involving dual truncations or commodity switches. For such systems may allow solutions to the primal for $r > R$ while solutions to the dual must fulfil $g < R$ since R is the maximum rate of expansion.

The solutions are, exceptions apart, square Sraffa systems or truncations as in previous sections of this book. For suppose we had for some r and g, $g < r$, a 'rectangular' solution, e.g. one with more processes than there are commodities. This means that, without loss of generality, $(q^1, ..., q^{m+1})$ and $(p_1, ..., p_m)$ would be strictly positive vectors while the other activity levels and prices would be zero. Ignoring degenerate solutions, the first $m + 1$ processes would then break even, the others would make losses. Similarly, the first m commodities of the vector of final demand $\mathbf{d}$ would be produced in exactly the required amounts; the others would be overproduced.

Obviously, such a solution may obtain at a switchpoint such that two or more truncations, e.g. consisting of processes $(1, ..., m)$ and $(2, ..., m + 1)$, yield the same price vector at r while $\mathbf{d}$ may be produced by either truncation or a combination of both, as in the previous section.

If the two truncations are regular and different, their wage curves can coincide only in a finite number of discrete points, hence it is clear for this constellation that the solution must be square, except for points where wage curves cross or if irregularities arise. A similar reasoning holds for the other constellations (note that points of truncation and dual truncation involve a local degeneracy).

One can thus show, by suitable extensions of the argument, that the solutions to the linear programming problem may be given as follows. First one lists all possible square *truncations*, i.e. all possible subsystems of $(\mathbf{A}, \mathbf{B}, \mathbf{l}, \mathbf{d})$, which are composed of coefficients a_i^j, b_i^j, l_i, d^j, taken from an equal number of corresponding rows and columns of $(\mathbf{A}, \mathbf{B}, \mathbf{l}, \mathbf{d})$ respectively. A truncation $(\bar{\mathbf{A}}, \bar{\mathbf{B}}, \bar{\mathbf{l}}, \bar{\mathbf{d}})$ of order m consists of coefficients (a_i^j, b_i^j, l_i, d^j) with $i \in \{i_1, ..., i_m\}$; $j \in \{j_1, ..., j_m\}$; $1 \leqslant i_1 < \cdots < i_m \leqslant n$; $1 \leqslant j_1 < \cdots < j_m \leqslant \mathrm{n}$. It generates a truncated price vector $\bar{\mathbf{p}} = (\bar{p}_{i_1}, ..., \bar{p}_{i_m})'$ at r such that

$$(1 + r)\bar{\mathbf{A}}\bar{\mathbf{p}} + w\bar{\mathbf{l}} = \bar{\mathbf{B}}\bar{\mathbf{p}},$$

and a corresponding truncated vector of activity levels at g. Obviously, the curves $1/\bar{\mathbf{d}}'\bar{\mathbf{p}}$ and $1/\bar{\mathbf{q}}'\bar{\mathbf{l}}$ are geometrically the same $(1/\bar{\mathbf{d}}'\bar{\mathbf{p}} = 1/\bar{\mathbf{q}}'\bar{\mathbf{l}}$ for $r = g$). Hence there is one wage curve to each truncation (provided $\bar{\mathbf{B}} - (1 + r)\bar{\mathbf{A}}$ is not singular and $\bar{\mathbf{q}}$ and $\bar{\mathbf{l}}$ or $\bar{\mathbf{d}}$ and $\bar{\mathbf{p}}$ are not orthogonal). A vector of prices, with components p_i equal to $\bar{p}_i$ if i is in the truncation and equal to zero if i is outside the truncation, will be called the *augmented* price vector to $\bar{\mathbf{p}}$; similarly for activity levels.

Suppose that we have a truncation such that its augmented price vector $\mathbf{p}$ at r is in P and its augmented vector of activity levels $\mathbf{q}$ is in Q at g, $g < r$ given. It follows that $\mathbf{p}$ and $\mathbf{q}$ then form a CMS since $\bar{\mathbf{q}}'[\bar{\mathbf{B}} - (1 + g)\bar{\mathbf{A}}] = \bar{\mathbf{d}}'$, hence $\mathbf{q}'[\mathbf{B} - (1 + g)\mathbf{A}]\mathbf{p} = \mathbf{d}'\mathbf{p}$, and $[\bar{\mathbf{B}} - (1 + r)\bar{\mathbf{A}}]\bar{\mathbf{p}} = \bar{\mathbf{l}}$, hence $\mathbf{q}'[\mathbf{B} - (1 + r)\mathbf{A}]\mathbf{p} = \mathbf{q}'\mathbf{l}$.

Truncations with $\mathbf{p} \in P$ at r will be called *p*-feasible at r (prices are semi-positive at r, processes in the truncation break even and processes outside do not make surplus profits). Truncations with $\mathbf{q} \in Q$ are called *q*-feasible. (They produce, but do not overproduce goods for final demand in the truncation, and they produce or overproduce those outside.) Imagine the wage curve of each *p*-feasible truncation (with $\mathbf{p} \in P$) at any r to be coloured green at r, and those of *q*-feasible truncations (with $\mathbf{q} \in Q$) at any g to be coloured red at g.

We have found:

Theorem 9c.4

Given $(\mathbf{A}, \mathbf{B}, \mathbf{l}, \mathbf{d})$ and $g < r$, all CMS will be given exactly by those truncations the wage curves of which are red at g and green at r.

One curve will have been coloured both red and green at each point between zero and R. This wage curve is, after a little reflection, found to be on the lower envelope of the green wage curves and on the upper envelope of the red ones. It may be called the *golden rule curve* because it is composed of connected pieces of the wage curves of truncations that are a CMS for each $r = g$. The CMS is therefore uniquely defined if $r = g$ except in that wage curves may be crossing at $r = g$ (to be precise: the amount of the wage to be paid in standard **d** is always uniquely defined under golden rule conditions).

If golden rule conditions are not fulfilled, it is possible that several CMSs will be found. One may then argue that the one yielding the highest real wage should be chosen as the dominating technique, i.e. as the most profitable technique, given the real wage. However, the competitive process need not lead to the emergence of this *dominant technique* because any CMS is stable, in that processes not used in the CMS will not be profitable if evaluated in terms of the prices of the CMS.

While the golden rule curve can be shown to be continuous if regularity is assumed, one may have to 'jump' in isolated points from the wage curve of one CMS to that of another if $g < r$ and if r is varied with given g, or if g is varied with given r. Moreover, the wage curve of a given CMS need not be monotonically falling as r is increased, with given g. However, I have tentatively argued in Schefold (1988) that both these possibilities are not really harmful to the analysis (although they are aesthetically not appealing) and that they are not very likely to be encountered in actual economic systems anyway. For these contain many sectors with industries in which multiple production is confined to groups of commodities produced by groups of processes such that an aggregation of groups yields a single-product system, with discontinuities and non-monotonicities disappearing in the aggregate. It has to be admitted that this argument is not rigorous. A rather dramatic set of exceptions has been presented by d'Agata (1983). His analysis, however, involves differential rent of the intensive kind, which causes a variety of difficulties because of the emergence of negative entries in the basic system, as we shall see in sections II.19 and II.20.

We find, at any rate, that the CMS always exists and is normally given by one definite truncation. This is remarkable in view of the many problems with joint production encountered in the previous sections.

It may be useful to conclude this section with a numerical example. The numbers in Table II.9c.1 have been chosen so as to yield a diagram of wage curves that illustrate all the difficulties that have been mentioned. There are three processes, numbered 1, 2, 3, which produce two goods; final demand is (6, 6.5). Units have been chosen such that labour inputs are equal to unity in all processes for convenience of calculation. The input and the output coefficients then are as shown in the table. There are three possible truncations of order two, composed of

Table II.9c.1

Processes	Inputs		Outputs	
	1	2	1	2
1	16/3	16	37/3	36
2	6	3/2	16	53/4
3	1/10	4/5	79/10	23/2

two out of three processes and denoted $(1, 2)$, $(2, 3)$, $(1, 3)$. Moreover, there are six truncations of order one, composed of one process and one good (with, if the truncation is q-feasible, overproduction of the other good), denoted by $1, 1$ for the truncation consisting of process 1 and good 1, by $1, 2$ for process 1 and good 2, etc.

Figure II.9c.1 shows the most interesting details of the system of wage curves to be calculated from Table II.9c.1 in the area given by $0 \leqslant r \leqslant 1.1$ and $1.4 \leqslant w \leqslant 2$. It can be seen that two truncations of order two are a CMS at least in some intervals. $(1, 2)$ is a CMS for $0 \leqslant g \leqslant 0.198$ and $0 \leqslant r \leqslant 0.198$ (golden rule curve), but $(1, 2)$ is also a CMS for $0 \leqslant g \leqslant 0.198$ and $0.198 \leqslant r \leqslant 0.569$. Curiously, $(1, 2)$ turns red (q-feasible) once more for $1.202 \leqslant g \leqslant 1.39$ (not shown in the diagram). $(1, 3)$ is a CMS for $0 \leqslant g \leqslant 0.198$ and for $0.373 \leqslant r \leqslant 1.5$; (1.3) is the golden rule curve for $0.836 \leqslant g = r \leqslant 1.5$. $(2, 3)$ is only q-feasible for $0.836 \leqslant g \leqslant 1.202$.

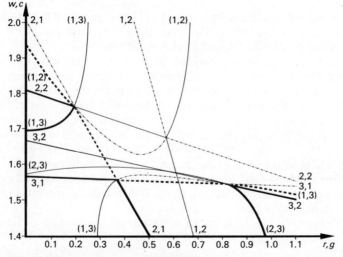

Figure II.9c.1. *Wage curves to table II.9c.1*
Bold lines = wage curves of **q**-feasible truncations ('red'). Dotted lines = wage curves of **p**-feasible truncations ('green'). Dotted and bold lines = golden rule curve. Weak black lines = other wage curves.

As was to be expected, the golden rule curve is continuous and strictly monotonically falling. It is composed of the following truncations: $(1, 2)$ for $0 \leqslant g = r \leqslant 0.198$; $2, 1$ for $0.198 \leqslant g = r \leqslant 0.373$, $3, 1$ for $0.373 \leqslant g = r \leqslant 0.836$; $(1, 3)$ for $0.836 \leqslant g = r \leqslant 1.5$ and (outside the diagram) $3, 2$ for $1.5 \leqslant g = r \leqslant 13.375$. It is easy to see why we have such a high rate of balanced growth. We are dealing with a joint-production system with strictly positive coefficients such that all rates of reproduction of goods $b_{ij}/a_{ij} - 1$ may be calculated; they are highest (and equal to 13.375 and 78 respectively) in process 3.

Next we consider the dominant technique, i.e. the CMS that yields the highest real wage. If $0 \leqslant g \leqslant 0.198$, it is, of course, given by the golden rule curve $(1, 2)$ for $0 \leqslant r \leqslant 0.198$, but this may now be extended for $0.198 \leqslant r \leqslant 0.569$. It is then given by $2, 2$ and, finally, by $3, 1$ up to $r = 78$. This very high rate of profit with low rates of growth is possible because of the high rate of reproduction of the first commodity in process 3. The example should not be interpreted to imply the possibility of similarly high rates of profit in real systems. It is true that the rates of reproduction of actual systems may be quite large e.g. for some agricultural commodities. But the corresponding processes cannot be run in isolation, as in this example, for they require inputs from other processes with lower rates of reproduction of individual commodities. If all goods are demanded, each process can be run on its own only in a joint-production system with strictly positive inputs and outputs and with each rate of reproduction positive.

The dominant technique is different for $0.198 < g < 0.373$ and given by 2.1 and 3.1 successively. For $0.373 < g < 0.836$, 3.1 is dominant. For $0.836 < g < 1.5$, $(1, 3)$ is dominant if also $0.836 < r < 1.5$, but if $1.5 < r < 13.375$, $3, 2$ is dominant. For $1.5 < g < 13.375$, the rate of profit must remain in the same range (if $g < r$), and the curve of the dominant technique is reduced to the golden rule curve.

The complications of this example are connected with the multiplicity of CMSs. For instance, $(1, 2)$, $(1, 3)$ and $3, 1$ are each a CMS if $g = 0$ and $r = 0.5$. We can have discontinuities of wage curves. At a switchpoint between two single-product systems, differing in one process of production, the wage $w(r)$ and prices change continuously with r, although the change of the process and hence of the system implies a change of employment, i.e. $w(g)$ is different for the two systems if the given rate of growth is not equal to the rate of profit. Most changes of the wage in consequence of changes of r, with g given and fixed, similarly do not imply a discontinuous change of $w(r)$. The dominant technique, with g given, is continuous here in this sense.

But there is a CMS such that a variation of r with g given leads to a discontinuous change of $w(r)$. If $g = 0$ and $r = 0.5$, $(1, 3)$ is a CMS. If r is now lowered to 0.373 and beyond, $(1, 3)$ ceases to be p-feasible. The wage curve of $2, 1$ – which looks like a continuous extension – is not q-feasible at $g = 0$, while that of $3, 1$ – also a seemingly continuous extension – is not p-feasible for $r < 0.373$. Hence it is necessary, at $r = 0.373$, to 'jump' to the dominant technique $(1, 2)$. A dual phenomenon is the discontinuity of $w(g)$ on the wage curve of the dominant technique, with r fixed at 0.7 and g rising from zero beyond 0.198.

Another 'anomaly' is the rise of the wage curve of the dominant technique for $g = 0$ and r slightly smaller than 0.569. Such non-monotonicities are generally ruled out for single-product and fixed-capital systems and in the golden rule case. Similarly, $w(g)$ rises for g below 0.198 and r fixed e.g. at 0.5 on curve $(1, 3)$.

It should be stressed that the example has been constructed – not without difficulties – so as to exhibit the 'anomalies'. It is rather contrived in that a dozen or so other examples, based on joint-production systems with strictly positive coefficients generated at random, yielded none of the 'anomalies'. Finally, there are the reasons — which have been mentioned — for not expecting to encounter them in reality where strictly positive joint-production systems are not found and where there is, on the contrary, the tendency to produce joint products in groups with little overlap, which motivates the traditional focus on single production. However, as formal possibilities, the 'anomalies' undoubtedly exist without being unlikely in a strict mathematical sense like the irregular systems that are of measure zero in the set of possible systems. On the other hand, they represent, although they are aesthetically not pleasing, no substantial obstacles to the theory. For this, the existence of the dominant technique and of the associated prices of production is essential. The mechanism that may or may not lead market prices to 'gravitate' to such prices of production, which may or may not lead to the establishment of uniform rates of profit (and possibly of growth), which regulate effective demand and distribution, are matters to be investigated subsequently and by means of quite different methods.

10 Graphic Techniques Method

The patient reader will probably be longing for concrete examples. In order to avoid lengthy calculations they will be given graphically. The reader is advised to redraw the graphs for himself. The figures are explained in the text.

The system $\mathbf{p}_t = w[\mathbf{B} - (1 + r)\mathbf{A}]^{-1}\mathbf{l}$ has 21 fixed and 5 variable coefficients for $n = 3$. A proper graphic representation is therefore not trivial.

The common procedure is to measure goods on the axes of the coordinate system. One unit of length on the abscissa represents one physical unit of good 1, one unit of length on the ordinate represents one physical unit of good 2. One then has to take $\mathbf{a}_i$, $\mathbf{b}_i$, i.e. the processes, as vectors and interpret $\mathbf{a}_i\mathbf{p}$, etc., as scalar products ($\mathbf{p}$ is also a vector; each component can be measured on the corresponding axis because prices are normalized by reference to goods).

While this approach is more satisfactory from the point of view of linear and multilinear algebra, it proves less cumbersome to draw the column vectors $\mathbf{a}^i$, $\mathbf{b}^i$ of the goods and of labour on axes that represent the processes. The measure of goods and of labour is given by the familiar normalization

$$\mathbf{e}'\mathbf{B} = \mathbf{e}'(\mathbf{b}^1, ..., \mathbf{b}^n) = \mathbf{e}', \qquad \mathbf{e} = (1, ..., 1)',$$

i.e. total output of each good equals one unit. The normalization allows us to draw vectors of different goods i, $i = 1, 2$, with different physical dimensions in the same diagram because the abscissa now measures the fraction of the output of good i produced in process 1, while the ordinate measures the fraction of good i produced in process 2. If good 1 is pigs, and 5 pigs are produced in process 1 and 10 pigs in process 2, and if good 2 is iron, and 20 tons are produced in process 1 and 5 tons in process 2,

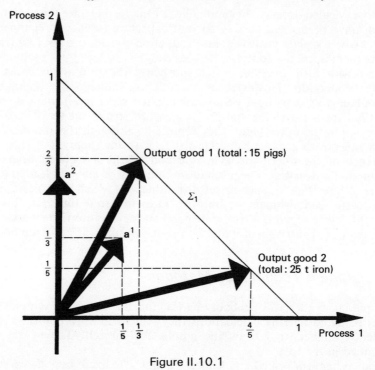

Figure II.10.1

the diagram looks as in Figure II.10.1. An input of 3 pigs in process 1 and of 5 pigs in process 2 is represented by vector $\mathbf{a}^1$; an input of 16 tons of iron to process 2 and no iron to process 1 is represented by vector $\mathbf{a}^2$ in Figure II.10.1.

The conditions $\mathbf{e}'\mathbf{B} = \mathbf{e}'$, $\mathbf{e}'\mathbf{l} = 1$, $\mathbf{B} \geqslant \mathbf{O}$, $\mathbf{l} > \mathbf{o}$ mean that the $\mathbf{b}^1, \dots, \mathbf{b}^n$, $\mathbf{l}$ are points on the simplex

$$\Sigma_1 = \{\mathbf{x} \mid \mathbf{e}'\mathbf{x} = 1, \mathbf{x} \geqslant \mathbf{o}\},$$

$\mathbf{e}'(\mathbf{B} - \mathbf{A}) \geqslant \mathbf{o}$ means that the $\mathbf{b}^i - \mathbf{a}^i$ are 'to the right of and above'

$$\Sigma_0 = \{\mathbf{x} \mid \mathbf{e}'\mathbf{x} = 0\}.$$

For a two-commodities/two processes system the diagram looks as in Figure II.10.2, if commodity 1 is produced in both processes and if commodity 2 is a product of process 1 only.

Instead of standard prices $\mathbf{p}_t$ or prices in terms of the wage rate $\hat{\mathbf{p}}$ we use unit sum prices $\mathbf{p}_e$:

$$\mathbf{p}_e = \frac{[\mathbf{B} - (1 + r)\mathbf{A}]^{-1}\mathbf{l}}{\mathbf{e}'\,[\mathbf{B} - (1 + r)\mathbf{A}]^{-1}\mathbf{l}} = w_e\hat{\mathbf{p}}(r)$$

$$w_e = \frac{1}{\mathbf{e}'\,[\mathbf{B} - (1 + r)\mathbf{A}]^{-1}\mathbf{l}} = \frac{1}{\mathbf{e}'\hat{\mathbf{p}}(r)}, \qquad \mathbf{e}'\mathbf{p}_e = 1.$$

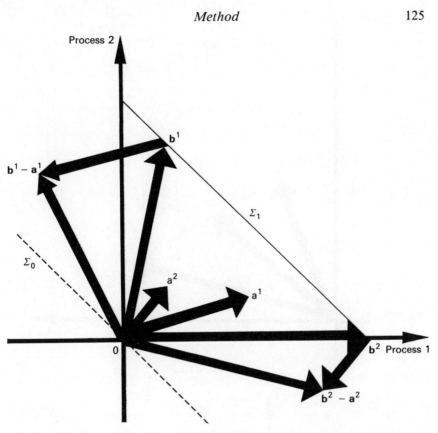

Figure II.10.2

The normalization of prices allows us to interpret prices as weights. In two dimensions $p_1 = \lambda$, $p_2 = 1 - \lambda$, $0 < \lambda < 1$. If $\mathbf{c}^1$ and $\mathbf{c}^2$ are vectors, $\mathbf{c}^1 p_1 + \mathbf{c}^2 p_2 = \lambda \mathbf{c}^1 + (1 - \lambda)\mathbf{c}^2 = \mathbf{c}^3$ is a vector which is the centre of gravity of vectors $\mathbf{c}^1$ and $\mathbf{c}^2$ with weights p_1 and p_2, or, geometrically, a point on the straight line between $\mathbf{c}^1$ and $\mathbf{c}^2$ as in Figure II.10.3, with $p_1 + p_2 = 1$. We thus interpret $\mathbf{B}\mathbf{p}_e$, $\mathbf{A}\mathbf{p}_e$, $[\mathbf{B} - (1 + r)\mathbf{A}]\mathbf{p}_e$ in n dimensions as the weighted sum of the vectors $\mathbf{b}^1, ..., \mathbf{b}^n$, where $[\mathbf{b}^1, ..., \mathbf{b}^n] = \mathbf{B}$, of $\mathbf{a}^1, ..., \mathbf{a}^n$, where $[\mathbf{a}^1, ..., \mathbf{a}^n] = \mathbf{A}$, and of $\mathbf{b}^1 - (1 + r)\mathbf{a}^1, ..., \mathbf{b}^n - (1 + r)\mathbf{a}^n$ where $[\mathbf{b}^1 - (1 + r)\mathbf{a}^1, ..., \mathbf{b}^n - (1 + r)\mathbf{a}^n] = \mathbf{B} - (1 + r)\mathbf{A}$. The set

$$\{\mathbf{x} \mid \mathbf{x} = \mathbf{A}\mathbf{p}_e, \mathbf{p}_e \geqslant \mathbf{o}, \mathbf{e}'\mathbf{p}_e = 1\}$$

is the simplex spanned by $[\mathbf{a}^1, ..., \mathbf{a}^n]$.

In two dimensions, the set

$$\{\mathbf{x} \mid \mathbf{x} = [\mathbf{b}^1 - (1 + r)\mathbf{a}^1]p_1 + [\mathbf{b}^2 - (1 + r)\mathbf{a}^2]p_2, p_1 + p_2 = 1, (p_1, p_2) \geqslant \mathbf{o}$$
$$= \{\mathbf{x} \mid \mathbf{x} = [\mathbf{B} - (1 + r)\mathbf{A}]\mathbf{p}_e, \mathbf{e}'\mathbf{p}_e = 1, \mathbf{p}_e \geqslant \mathbf{O}\}$$

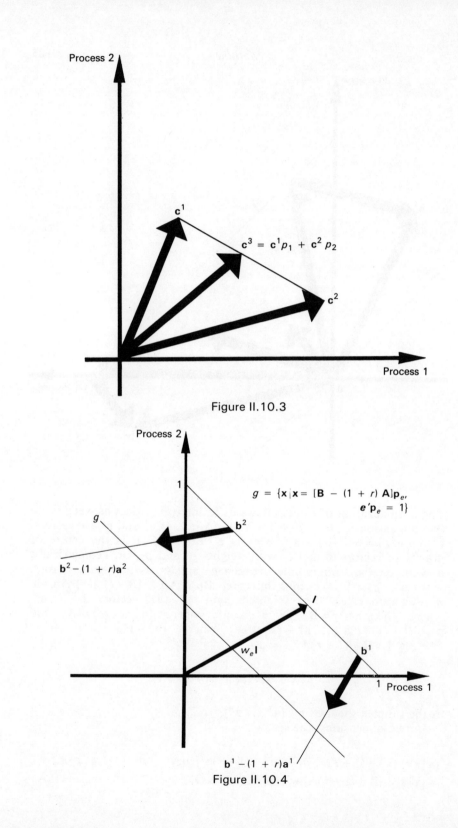

Figure II.10.3

$$g = \{\mathbf{x} \mid \mathbf{x} = [\mathbf{B} - (1 + r)\,\mathbf{A}]\mathbf{p}_e,$$
$$\boldsymbol{e}'\mathbf{p}_e = 1\}$$

Figure II.10.4

is represented (Figure II.10.4) by the straight line *g* through

$$[\mathbf{b}^1 - (1 + r)\mathbf{a}^1], \qquad [\mathbf{b}^2 - (1 + r)\mathbf{a}^2].$$

If the reader has carefully followed up to here, he will now realize that the price equations can conveniently be summarized in a two-dimensional diagram (for the two-dimensional case), because the solution of the equation

$$[\mathbf{B} - (1 + r)\mathbf{A}]\mathbf{p}_e = w_e\mathbf{l}, \qquad \mathbf{e}'\mathbf{p}_e = 1,$$

is represented by the intersection of that line, *g*, with **l** in the point $w_e\mathbf{l}$ (no lines for $\mathbf{b}^i$ or $\mathbf{a}^i$ are drawn, only $\mathbf{b}^i - \mathbf{a}^i$ as the vector pointing from $\mathbf{b}^i$ to $\mathbf{b}^i - \mathbf{a}^i$).

The price ratios themselves can be shown in the diagram (Figure II.10.5). Define

$$\mathbf{c}^1 = [\mathbf{b}^1 - (1 + r)\mathbf{a}^1]p_1,$$
$$\mathbf{c}^2 = [\mathbf{b}^2 - (1 + r)\mathbf{a}^2]p_2,$$

where $p_1 + p_2 = 1$, $(p_1, p_2) \geqslant \mathbf{o}$. The point $\mathbf{c}^3 = \mathbf{c}^1 + \mathbf{c}^2$ equals $w_e\mathbf{l}$. The price ratios can now be introduced.

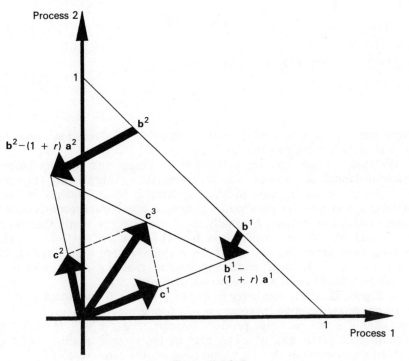

Figure II.10.5

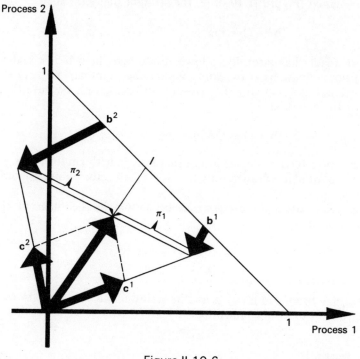

Figure II.10.6

One reads from Figure II.10.6:

$$\frac{\pi_1}{\pi_2} = \frac{p_2}{p_1}.$$

Note the inverse relationship: if $\mathbf{l}$ is closer to $\mathbf{b}^1 - (1 + r)\mathbf{a}^1$ than to $\mathbf{b}^2 - (1 + r)\mathbf{a}^2$, it follows that $p_2 > p_1$.

We first consider the representation of inputs and outputs alone, ignoring labour and prices. The following four examples are (Figures II.10.7–10): a basic single-product system; a basic joint-production system; a non-basic single-product system; a non-basic (decomposable) joint-production system. Normally, as r increases, w diminishes until $r = R$ and $w_e = 0$ are reached and $\mathbf{b}^1 - (1 + R)\mathbf{a}^1$, $\mathbf{b}^2 - (1 + R)\mathbf{a}^2$ are linearly dependent. We show this for a basic single-product system in Figure II.10.11. It is geometrically evident that the price ratio is a monotonic function of r in the two-dimensional case.

In Figure II.10.12, one price is negative for $r = 0$ and small r, then both prices are positive (beyond $r = r_1$). It is geometrically evident that this cannot occur in single-product systems, because $\mathbf{b}^1 - (1 + r)\mathbf{a}^1$ is then in the fourth and $\mathbf{b}^2 - (1 + r)\mathbf{a}^2$ in the second quadrant of the coordinate system, so that they cannot be on the same side of $\mathbf{l}$.

We now turn to activity levels. We represent them as vectors. $\mathbf{q}'\mathbf{b}^i$

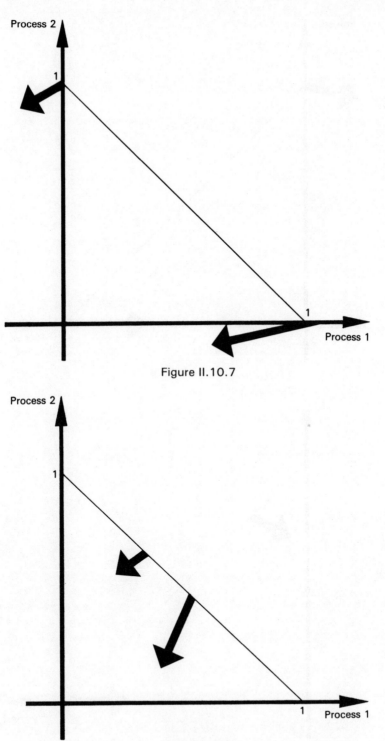

Figure II.10.7

Figure II.10.8

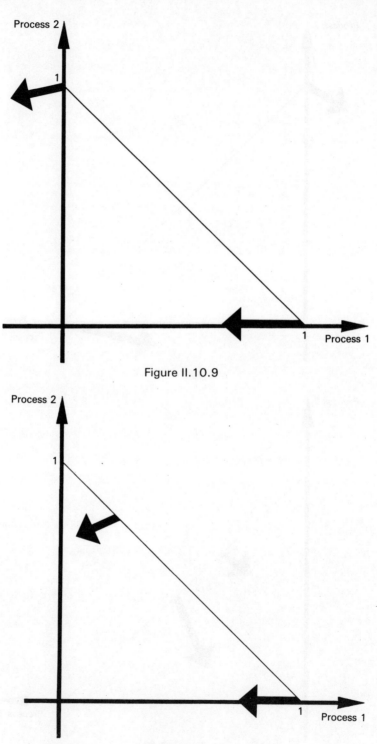

Figure II.10.9

Figure II.10.10

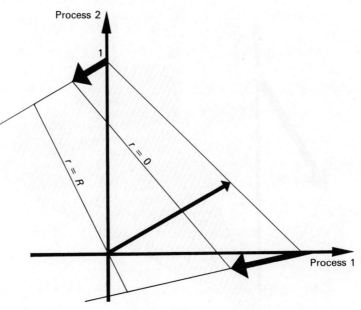

Figure II.10.11

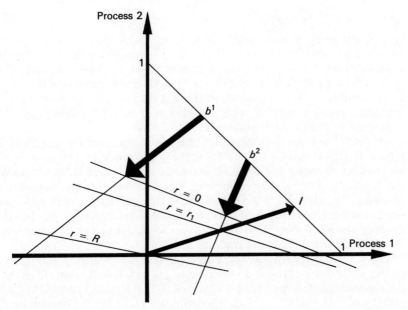

Figure II.10.12

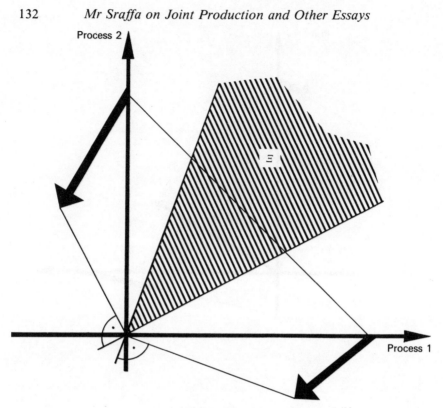

Figure II.10.13

($\mathbf{q}$ activity level, $\mathbf{b}^i$ vector of outputs in commodity i) is interpreted as a scalar product (Figure II.10.13). The shaded cone Ξ is the set of all activity levels producing a non-negative surplus, i.e. with $\mathbf{c}' = \mathbf{q}'(\mathbf{B} - \mathbf{A}) = [\mathbf{q}'(\mathbf{b}^1 - \mathbf{a}^1), \ \mathbf{q}'(\mathbf{b}^2 - \mathbf{a}^2)] > \mathbf{O}$. It contains $\mathbf{e} = (1, 1)'$. A single-product system as shown in this diagram is capable of producing any semi-positive surplus with semi-positive activity levels since Ξ is contained in the positive quadrant.

$(\mathbf{B} - \mathbf{A})^{-1} > \mathbf{O}$ means that Ξ lies in the (strictly) positive quadrant. In Figure II.10.14, this is not the case; the joint-production system is not all-productive, but it is almost all-productive. In Figure II.10.15, $\mathbf{A}, \mathbf{B}$ is basic, the system is all-productive, i.e. $(\mathbf{B} - \mathbf{A})^{-1} \geqslant \mathbf{O}$, but not all engaging, i.e. $(\mathbf{B} - \mathbf{A})^{-1} \not> \mathbf{O}$. Evidently, this cannot happen with basic single-product systems. The corresponding diagram for single-product systems shows at once that $(\mathbf{I} - \mathbf{A})^{-1} > \mathbf{O}$ if the system is basic while $(\mathbf{I} - \mathbf{A})^{-1} \geqslant \mathbf{O}$ if it is non-basic.

The standard multipliers form a vector $\mathbf{q}$ which is orthogonal on each of the vectors $\mathbf{b}^i - (1 + R)\mathbf{a}^i$ because $\mathbf{q}'[\mathbf{B} - (1 + R)\mathbf{A}] = \mathbf{o}$. Thus, $\mathbf{q}$ is orthogonal on the hyperplane containing the origin and spanned by those vectors $\mathbf{b}^i - (1 + R)\mathbf{a}^i$, $i = 1, 2$. First (Figure II.10.16) we determine the

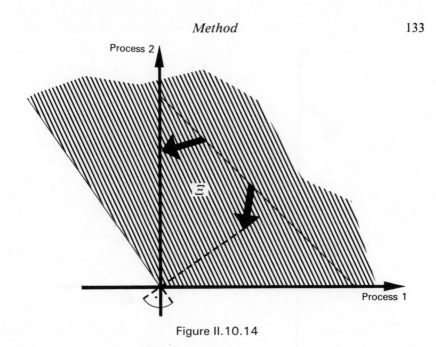

Figure II.10.14

direction of the vector of standard multipliers: $\mathbf{n}$ is the normal on the hyperplane spanned by $\mathbf{b}^j - (1 + R)\mathbf{a}^j$, $j = 1, 2$. Second, the length of $\mathbf{q}$ is determined by $\mathbf{q}'\mathbf{l} = 1$. $\mathbf{q}$ can be obtained geometrically by mirroring the projection of $\mathbf{l}$ on $\mathbf{n}$ at the unit circle (Figure II.10.17).

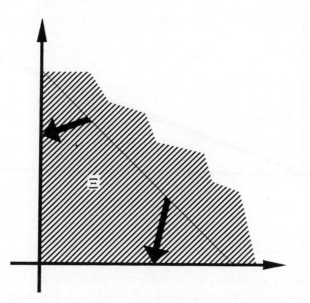

Figure II.10.15

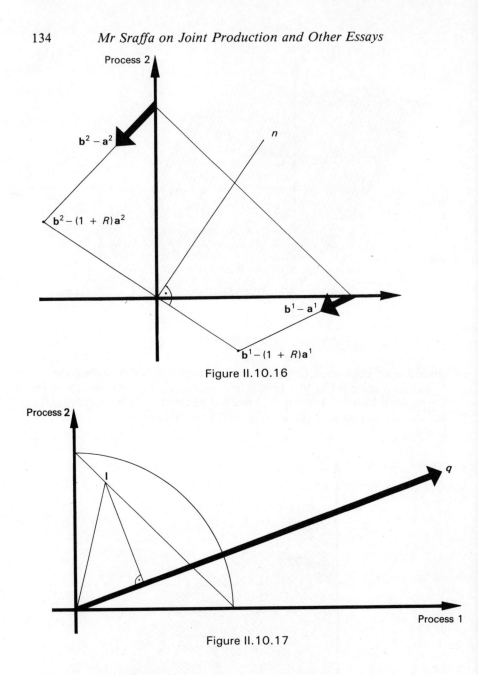

Figure II.10.16

Figure II.10.17

11   Applications

It is now evident from the geometry that $\mathbf{p}_e(r) > \mathbf{o}$, $\mathbf{p}_e(R) > \mathbf{o}$, $\mathbf{q} > \mathbf{o}$ for all single-product systems and $\mathbf{q} > \mathbf{o}$, $\mathbf{p}_e(R) > \mathbf{o}$ and $\mathbf{p}_e(r) > \mathbf{o}$ for $r > \bar{r}$ for systems with $[\mathbf{B} - (1 + \bar{r})\mathbf{A}]^{-1} > \mathbf{O}$. An all-productive system, i.e. $[\mathbf{B} - \mathbf{A}]^{-1} \geqslant \mathbf{O}$ is shown in Figure II.11.1, while an almost all-

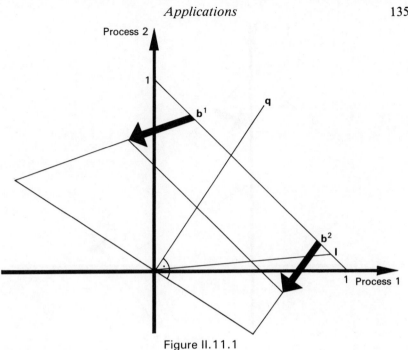

Figure II.11.1

productive system, i.e. $[\mathbf{B} - (1 + r)\mathbf{A}]^{-1} \geqslant \mathbf{O}$ for $r \geqslant \bar{r}$ is shown in Figure II.11.2.

The standard multipliers may not be positive (Figure II.11.3) and may not exist at all (see Manara, 1968, for the first numerical example). To 'show' the standard multipliers that do not exist (Figure II.11.4), one draws the straight lines $\{\mathbf{x} \mid \mathbf{x} = [\mathbf{B} - (1 + r)\mathbf{A}]\mathbf{p}, \mathbf{e}'\mathbf{p} = 1\}$ for 'many' rates of profit. The straight lines cover the plane up to an area bounded by a curve to which the straight lines are tangential. If one of these lines hits the origin for $r = \widetilde{R}$, it follows that $\mathbf{b}^1 - (1 + \widetilde{R})\mathbf{a}^1$ and $\mathbf{b}^2 - (1 + \widetilde{R})\mathbf{a}^2$ are linearly dependent for $r = \widetilde{R}$. If the origin happens to lie in the area that is left free by the lines

$$\{\mathbf{x} \mid \mathbf{x} = [\mathbf{B} - (1 + r)\mathbf{A}]\mathbf{p}, \mathbf{e}'\mathbf{p} = 1\}$$

no standard multipliers exist, nor does a standard commodity as real numbers or vectors. (The complex solutions have never been shown to have an economic meaning.)

In general, there are two eigenvectors in a two-sector model, even in single-product systems. But only one of them, $\mathbf{q}$, has positive components: the one corresponding to the lower rate of profit $r = R$. The other, $\widetilde{\mathbf{q}}$, associated with the eigenvalue belonging to the higher rate of profit $r = \widetilde{R}$, has no economic meaning (Figure II.11.5).

Many other special cases could be considered. In particular, the irregular system can be represented. The system can be irregular because it has a multiple root (here at $R = \widetilde{R} = 1$); relative prices are then

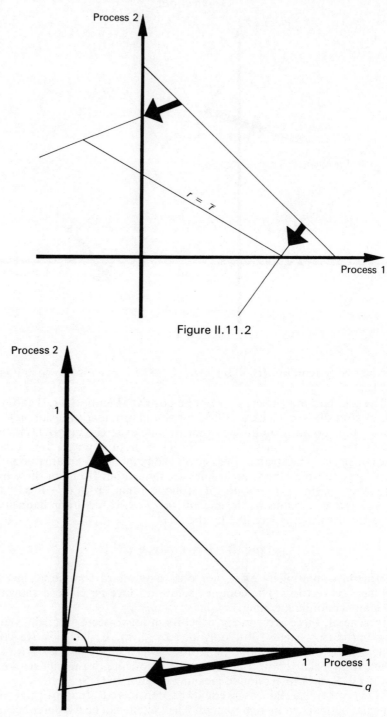

Figure II.11.2

Figure II.11.3

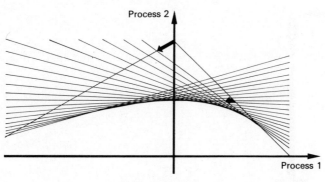

Figure II.11.4

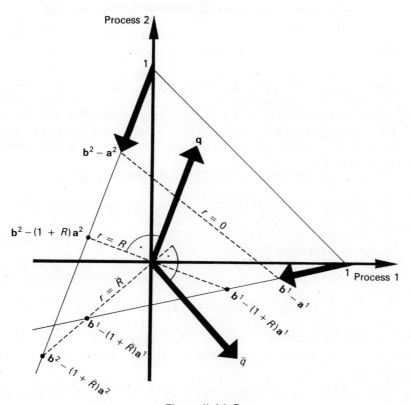

Figure II.11.5

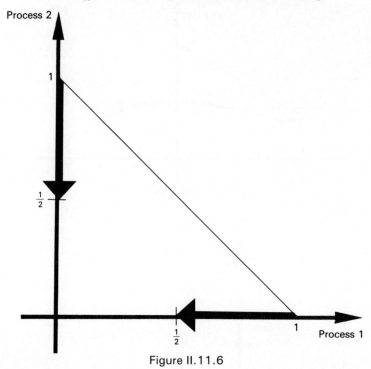

Figure II.11.6

evidently constant for any labour vector **l** (Figure II.11.6). Or **l** may be orthogonal to the eigenvector $\tilde{\mathbf{q}}$, belonging to $\tilde{R}$, so that relative prices are again constant and **l** is an eigenvector of the system (Figure II.11.7).

Other examples may be constructed by the reader, but one inefficiency is worth dealing with in particular: the one that corresponds to theorem 9.1 in section II.9.

Consider (it makes sense for $n = 2$) systems with $\mathbf{A} > \mathbf{O}$.

$$g_i^j = \frac{b_i^j}{a_i^j} \qquad (i, j = 1, 2)$$

is the rate of reproduction of good j in process i.

We define: a system involving two goods and two processes is *imbalanced* if one process is better than the other for both goods in that

$$(g_i^1, g_i^2) > (g_j^1, g_j^2) \text{ for } (i, j) = (1, 2) \text{ or } (2, 1).$$

The example proposed by Professor Manara is inefficient in this sense.

Theorem

If the inefficiency above (imbalance) is ruled out, a positive standard ratio R and a positive **q** and $\mathbf{p}(R)$ exist.

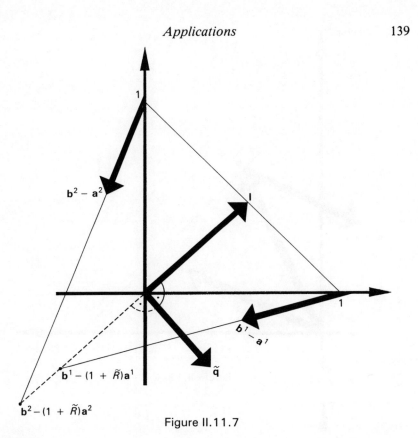

Figure II.11.7

PROOF:

If the system is not imbalanced, we have, without loss of generality,

$$g_1^1 > g_2^1 \text{ and } g_1^2 < g_2^2,$$

i.e.

$$\frac{b_1^1}{a_1^1} > \frac{b_2^1}{a_2^1} \text{ and } \frac{b_1^2}{a_1^2} < \frac{b_2^2}{a_2^2},$$

therefore

$$\frac{b_1^1}{b_2^1} > \frac{a_1^1}{a_2^1} \text{ and } \frac{b_1^2}{b_2^2} < \frac{a_1^2}{a_2^2}.$$

Now

$$\frac{b_1^i}{b_2^i} = \cot \beta^i, \qquad \frac{a_1^i}{a_2^i} = \cot \alpha^i$$

where β^i, α^i are the angles between the axis representing the first process and vector $\mathbf{b}^i$, $\mathbf{a}^i$. The rest is evident from the geometry as illustrated by Figures II.11.8–10.

q.e.d.

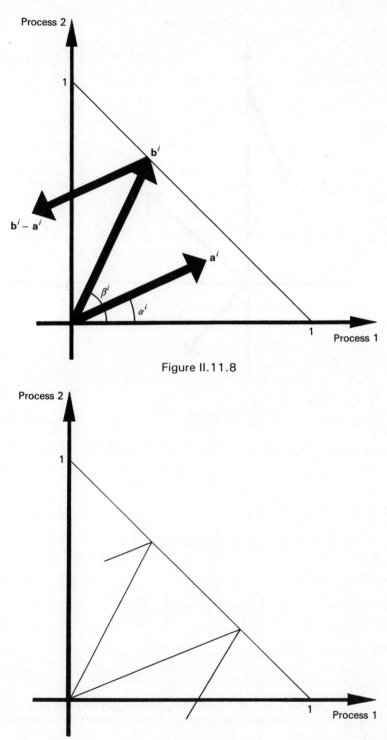

Figure II.11.8

Figure II.11.9

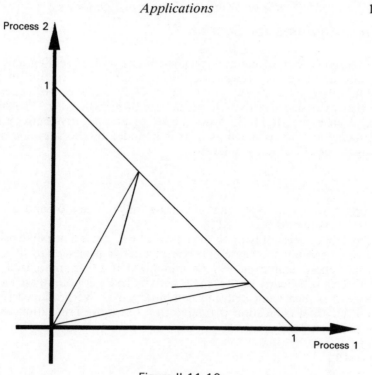

Figure II.11.10

An imbalanced system may nevertheless possess positive prices for low r, if the labour vector is appropriate, that is to say, if the less efficient technique employs less labour (note that we draw only $\mathbf{c}^i$, no $\mathbf{b}^i$ and $\mathbf{a}^i$). If $\mathbf{l} = \mathbf{l}^1$, prices are positive for $0 \leqslant r < \bar{r}$. If $\mathbf{l} = \mathbf{l}^2$, one price is negative for all r (Figure II.11.11).

Three-dimensional examples will be considered later.

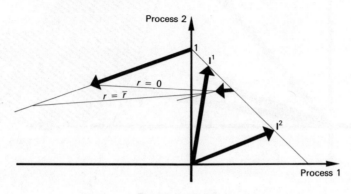

Figure II.11.11

11a   Diagrams for Section 9b

The representation of method switches in terms of these diagrams does not appear to be very rewarding, but a graphic construction of truncation is useful. Let $\mathbf{c}^i = \mathbf{b}^i - (1 + r)\mathbf{a}^i$, $i = 1, 2$, and $\mathbf{q}'\mathbf{c}^i = d^i$, where $\mathbf{d}$ is the real wage and $\mathbf{q}$ activity levels at rate of growth $g = r$. The shaded area X in Figure II.11a.1 shows the set of non-negative activity levels producing at least as much as $\mathbf{d}$. It is bounded by the axes and by the straight lines Γ_i of activity levels

$$\Gamma_i = \{\mathbf{x} \mid \mathbf{x}'\mathbf{c}^i = d^i\}, \; i = 1, 2,$$

passing through $\mathbf{q}$. Note that we draw only $\mathbf{c}^i$, not $\mathbf{b}^i$ and $\mathbf{a}^i$. This diagram assumes $\mathbf{d} > \mathbf{o}$.

Any labour vector $\mathbf{l}$ lying to the left of $\mathbf{c}^1$ will cause a negative price p_2 (see the diagrammatic representation of relative prices p_1/p_2 in section II.10). Labour employed will be minimized if $\mathbf{x}'\mathbf{l}$ is minimized, with $\mathbf{x} \in X$. This will clearly be the case if activity levels at point $\bar{\mathbf{q}}$ are chosen; process 2 is then truncated and commodity 1 is overproduced (Figure II.11a.2). Dual truncation is treated in a like way. Truncation ensures that prices remain positive.

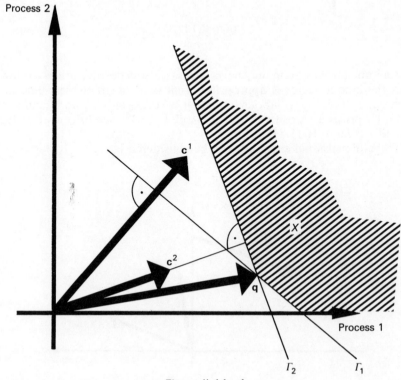

Figure II.11a.1

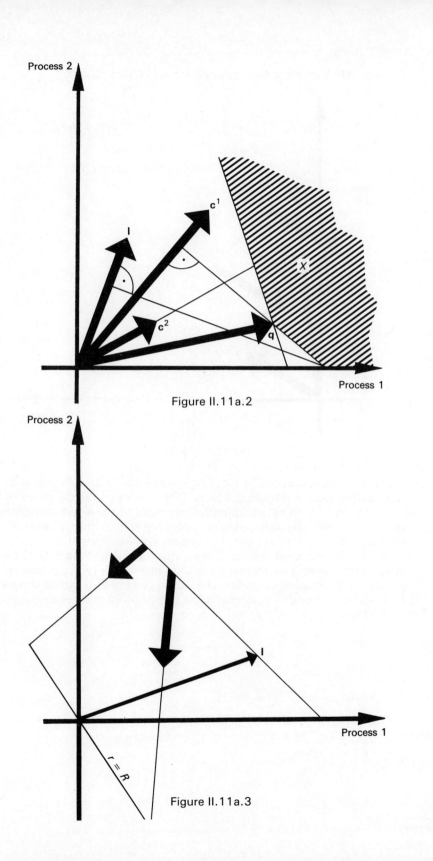

Process 2

c¹

l

X

c²

q

Process 1

Figure II.11a.2

Process 2

l

r = R

Figure II.11a.3

Process 1

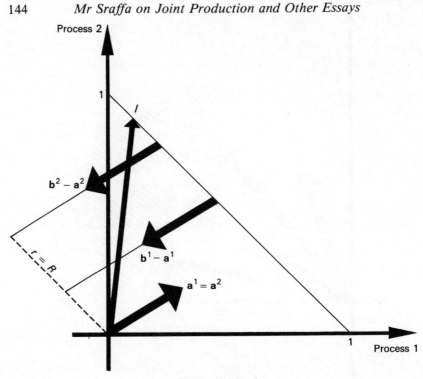

Figure II.11a.4

It is geometrically clear that the 'last system' (see section 9b) must be almost all-productive (Figure II.11a.3). The maximum rate of profit of the last system is the true maximum rate of profit of the original system.

However, if only the standard commodity is positive while prices at the maximum rate of profit are not, the system requires truncation at high rates of profit and need not be almost all-productive. Figure II.11a.4 illustrates this point, and represents at the same time a rather pathological instance (mentioned in section II.8) of a system which can be shown to be flexible, with positive prices at a low rate of profit and negative ones at high rates.

B   Specific Joint-Production Systems

12   Definition of a Pure Fixed-Capital System

As the reader will remember, Mr Sraffa concentrates in his Chapter X ('Fixed Capital') on the changes in value of single machines of different ages. In his presentation a commodity i with price p_i is produced by a new machine M_0, circulating capital goods which we here omit, to begin with, and labour. The whole output of commodity i is produced during T_i years (the lifetime of the machine) at constant efficiency, i.e. Sraffa assumes that the relation of the output to each input of the machine is constant in the examples he examines. Old machines are treated as joint products; a machine of age $\tau - 1$ with price $p_{m,\tau-1}$ produces in the τ'th process a T_i'th of the output of commodity i plus a τ years old machine with price $p_{m,\tau}$ so that we have T_i equations to determine the prices of the old machines $M_1, \ldots, M_{T_i-1}$ and the price of commodity i; the price of M_0 is, to begin with, regarded as given. Ignoring all inputs except machines and labour we have:

$$(1 + r)M_0 p_{m0} + \frac{wl_i}{T_i} = \frac{1}{T_i} p_i + M_1 p_{m1}$$

$$(1 + r)M_1 p_{m1} + \frac{wl_i}{T_i} = \frac{1}{T_i} p_i + M_2 p_{m2}$$

$$\ldots$$

$$(1 + r)M_{T_i-1} p_{m,\tau-1} + \frac{wl_i}{T_i} = \frac{1}{T_i} p_i.$$

$M_{\tau-1} p_{m,\tau-1} - M_\tau p_{m,\tau}$ represents depreciation of the machine in year τ, and a profit of $r M_{\tau-1} p_{m,\tau-1}$ has to be earned on the value of the machine $M_{\tau-1} p_{m,\tau-1}$.

Taking that analysis for granted, we inquire into the interaction between fixed capital and the economy as a whole, confining ourselves to '*pure fixed-capital systems*'. We allow for machines that follow any pattern of efficiency.

In order to facilitate the discussion, we introduce the following terminology: in any fixed-capital system it shall always be possible to distinguish between *finished goods* or products (circulating capital and new machines) and *intermediate goods* or products (old machines of various ages). In the normal case, corresponding to secs 76–78 in

PCMC, each process produces one and only one finished good (no *superimposed* joint production) together with one, several or possibly no intermediate products. For each finished product shall exist one *primary process* producing it by means of finished goods alone. The 1-year-old machines that the primary process turns out as intermediate goods are completely used up in *secondary processes* with no other intermediate goods as means of production. The secondary processes produce the same finished good and possibly intermediate goods. The latter are again used in secondary processes producing the same finished good and possibly intermediate goods. The pattern repeats itself until after several stages all intermediate inputs are used up and processes are reached with the finished good as the single product.

The total output of one finished good in the economy (equal to one for $\mathbf{e}'\mathbf{B} = \mathbf{e}'$) is thus produced by a *group* of one primary and several, say α, secondary processes, involving, we assume, no more than α intermediate goods, which are all produced and used up within the group. [1]

This definition broadens the scheme given in PCMC, sec. 76, not only because it allows for varying efficiency and the use of several machines, but also because new machines may be brought in at any stage and old machines may be used in different ways. Suppose e.g. a good G is produced by two machines (N, M) lasting two (N_0, N_1) and three years (M_0, M_1, M_2) respectively.

If the group is to determine the price p_g of the one finished good G plus the prices p_{n1}, p_{m1}, p_{m2} of the three intermediate goods N_1, M_1, M_2, it must consist of four processes. Ignoring all inputs except M, N and labour, we have:

primary process:
$$(1 + r)(M_0 p_{m0} + N_0 p_{n0}) + w l_1 = G_1 p_g + M_1 p_{m1} + N_1 p_{n1}$$

secondary processes:
$$(1 + r)(M_1 p_{m1} + N_1 p_{n1}) + w l_2 = G_2 p_g + M_2 p_{m2},$$
$$(1 + r)(\tfrac{1}{2} M_2 p_{m2} + \tfrac{1}{2} N_0 p_{n1}) + w l_3 = G_3 p_g + \tfrac{1}{2} N_1 p_{n1}$$
$$(1 + r)(\tfrac{1}{2} M_2 p_{m2} + \tfrac{1}{2} N_1 p_{n1}) + w l_4 = G_4 p_g.$$

Total input of finished goods used up is $M_0, \tfrac{3}{2} N_0$. The particular combination of the machines in this group makes it possible to reduce the four equations to one by multiplying them by $\tfrac{1}{2}[(1 + r)^3 + (1 + r)^2]$, $\tfrac{1}{2}[(1 + r)^2 + (1 + r)]$, $(1 + r)$, 1, respectively, and adding them as in PCMC, sec. 76, so that intermediate goods cancel out:

$$
\begin{aligned}
(1 + r)\tfrac{1}{2}\{ & [(1 + r)^3 + (1 + r)^2] M_0 p_{m0} + [(1 + r)^3 + (1 + r)^2 \\
& + (1 + r)] N_0 p_{m0}\} + w\{\tfrac{1}{2}[(1 + r)^3 + (1 + r)^2] l_1 + \tfrac{1}{2}[(1 + r)^2 \\
& + (1 + r)] l_2 + (1 + r) l_3 + l_4\} \\
= & \{\tfrac{1}{2}[(1 + r)^3 + (1 + r)^2] G_1 + \tfrac{1}{2}[(1 + r)^2 + (1 + r)] G_2 + (1 + r) G_3 \\
& + G_4\} p_g.
\end{aligned}
$$

In this 'pure' case, the transfer of intermediate goods between groups (*interlocked systems*) has been excluded.

We also exclude *perennial machines*, i.e. machines whose lifetime is physically indefinite (infinite), provided that they are adequately maintained. The columns $\mathbf{a}^j, \mathbf{b}^j$ representing a perennial machine j in a joint-production system $\mathbf{A}, \mathbf{B}$ are characterized by positive elements in pairs in the same line of production (e.g.

$$a_1^1 = b_1^1 > 0, \ a_2^1 = b_2^1 > 0, \ a_j^1 = b_j^1 = 0, 3 < j \leqslant n),$$

while there is one line i for which $b_i^1 > 0$, $a_i^1 = 0$ (e.g. $a_3^1 = 0$, $b_3^1 > 0$), so that the machine is produced somewhere (process i) and any input reappears on the right-hand side of the equation if it has been used on the left. It cannot be said whether such perennial machines are finished or intermediate goods and they are therefore not to be considered as an instance of pure fixed capital. They constitute the borderline between fixed capital and land, giving rise to a sort of hire-price. We shall deal with them in a separate section.

We shall not deal at all, however, with superimposed joint production and interlocked systems although their exclusion can at least partially be relaxed by combining the results of part A and part B of this book.

The intuitive description of pure fixed-capital systems is now replaced by a more workable mathematical definition. It looks prohibitively complicated at first, but an intuitive explanation of the axioms will be given here, and deeper reasons for preferring this formulation to simpler ones will be advanced in section II.18a.

Definition

A pure fixed-capital system is given by a basic joint-production system $\mathbf{A}, \mathbf{B}, \mathbf{l}$ ($\mathbf{A}, \mathbf{B}$ are (n, n) matrices); together with an (n, n) matrix $\mathbf{Q}(r) \geqslant \mathbf{O}$ subdivided as follows ($m < n$):

$\mathbf{Q}_1^1 = \mathbf{J}$	$\mathbf{Q}_1^2 = \mathbf{K}$	$\}m$
$\mathbf{Q}_2^1 = \mathbf{O}$	$\mathbf{Q}_2^2 = \mathbf{I}_{(n-m)}$	$\}n - m$

$\mathbf{A}_1^1$	$\mathbf{A}_1^2 = \mathbf{O}$
$\mathbf{A}_2^1$	$\mathbf{A}_2^2$

$\mathbf{B}_1^1$	$\mathbf{B}_1^2$
$\mathbf{B}_2^1$	$\mathbf{B}_2^2$

and with

(a) $\mathbf{A}_1^1 \neq \mathbf{O}$, $\mathbf{A}_1^2 = \mathbf{O}$. $\mathbf{B}_1^1 \geqslant \mathbf{O}$ and diagonal.
(b) $\mathbf{Q}_2^1 = \mathbf{O}$, $\mathbf{Q}_2^2 = \mathbf{I}_{(n-m)}$.
(c1) $\mathbf{Q} = (q_i^j)$. If $q_i^j \neq 0$, q_i^j is a polynomial $q_i^j(r)$ with positive coefficients in $1 + r$, and with $q_i^j(0) = 1$.
(c2) $\mathbf{Q}_1^1(r) = \mathbf{J}(r)$ is diagonal (thus $\mathbf{J}(0) = \mathbf{I}_{(m)}$).
(c3) $\mathbf{Q}_1^2(r) = \mathbf{K}(r) = [\mathbf{k}^1, ..., \mathbf{k}^{n-m}]$. All elements of $\mathbf{k}^j$ except one vanish.

(c4) $\mathbf{Q}_1^2(r) = \mathbf{K}(r) = [\mathbf{k}_1', ..., \mathbf{k}_{n-m}']'$. The degree of the polynomials $j_i^i(r)$ on the diagonal of $\mathbf{J}(r) = \mathbf{Q}_1^1(r)$ exceeds the degree of all other polynomials on the same row of $\mathbf{Q}_1$, i.e. it exceeds the degrees of all polynomials of $\mathbf{k}_i(r)$.

(d) $\mathbf{KB}_2^1$ is a diagonal matrix.

(e) $\mathbf{Q}_1[\mathbf{B}^2 - (1 + r)\mathbf{A}^2] = \mathbf{JB}_1^2 + \mathbf{K}[\mathbf{B}_2^2 - (1 + r)\mathbf{A}_2^2] = \mathbf{O}$ for all r.

(*f*) If $k^{j1}, ..., k^{j\alpha}$ are the positive elements of $\mathbf{k}_i$ and if Δ_i is the $(n - m, n - m)$ diagonal matrix with the elements of $\mathbf{k}_i$ on the diagonal, the matrix

$$\begin{bmatrix} \Delta_i \mathbf{A}_2^2 \\ \Delta_i \mathbf{B}_2^2 \end{bmatrix}$$

has not more than α semi-positive columns.

We translate this definition back into intuitive language:

$$\mathbf{A}^1 = \begin{bmatrix} \mathbf{A}_1^1 \\ \mathbf{A}_2^1 \end{bmatrix}, \qquad \mathbf{B}^1 = \begin{bmatrix} \mathbf{B}_1^1 \\ \mathbf{B}_2^1 \end{bmatrix}$$

are the finished, $\mathbf{A}^2, \mathbf{B}^2$ the intermediate goods. The matrices

$$\mathbf{A}_1 = [\mathbf{A}_1^1, \mathbf{A}_1^2] = [\mathbf{A}_1^1, \mathbf{O}] \text{ (see (a)),}$$
$$\mathbf{B}_1 = [\mathbf{B}_1^1, \mathbf{B}_1^2]$$

represent the primary, $\mathbf{A}_2, \mathbf{B}_2$ the secondary processes. $\mathbf{A}_1^2 = \mathbf{O}$ implies that finished goods can be produced by means of finished goods alone, and $\mathbf{B}_1^1$ is diagonal because each primary process produces only one finished good.

$\mathbf{Q}$ is the matrix that effects the summing-up of the secondary processes and the (one) primary process (see (b), (c)) belonging to the same group (d). (e) means that the intermediate goods cancel out. The summing-up effected by matrix $\mathbf{Q}_1$ can be illustrated by means of the example, discussed above, involving two machines lasting two and three years respectively. The four equations were to be multiplied by $\frac{1}{2}[(1 + r)^3 + (1 + r)^2]$, $\frac{1}{2}[(1 + r)^2 + (1 + r)]$, $(1 + r)$, 1, respectively. These four coefficients represent the four elements of a row of matrix $\mathbf{Q}_1$; the first coefficient is on the diagonal of $\mathbf{J}$, the three others are elements of $\mathbf{K}$. They are normalized polynomials according to (c1). It is clear that $\mathbf{J}$ must be diagonal (assignment of primary processes to the finished goods that are their products). (c3) assures that groups do not interlock: each secondary process is combined with one and only one group. (c4) means that the operation of a group 'starts' with the primary process and with finished goods alone (highest power of $1 + r$).

(*f*) is the optional condition which may be replaced according to the note following on theorem 13.2. It means that if α secondary processes are in the group belonging to finished good i, at most α intermediate goods are involved. Although the formula looks a little difficult, it is intuitively easy to grasp. If there are more intermediate goods (more than

α, say β) involved in the group of secondary processes, than there are processes in it (i.e. α), there will remain $\beta - \alpha$ prices of intermediate goods which are not determined within the group. Such an occurrence is undesirable in itself, and it will later be seen that it is only compatible with the other axioms if the group is related with another with which it has some intermediate goods ($\beta - \alpha$) in common. It is interesting to note for which of the following theorems this has to be ruled out.

Obviously, determinant $\det \mathbf{Q}(r) = \det \mathbf{J}(r)$ does not vanish for $r \geq 1$. The matrix $\mathbf{Q}$ has therefore not only a form but also an effect similar to $\mathbf{M}$ in sections II.2 and II.3: it generates a system where the prices of finished goods are, like basics, seemingly independent of intermediate goods. The axiomatic presentation has been chosen, among other things, in order to establish this analogy between finished products and basics and between the $\mathbf{Q}$ matrix and the $\mathbf{M}$ matrix (see also section 18a). But here the coefficients are variable:

$$\mathbf{p}(r) = w[\mathbf{B} - (1 + r)\mathbf{A}]^{-1}\mathbf{l} = w[\widetilde{\mathbf{B}}(r) - (1 + r)\widetilde{\mathbf{A}}(r)]^{-1}\widetilde{\mathbf{l}}(r)$$

with

$$\widetilde{\mathbf{B}}(r) = \mathbf{Q}(r)\mathbf{B}, \ \widetilde{\mathbf{A}}(r) = \mathbf{Q}(r)\mathbf{A}, \ \widetilde{\mathbf{l}} = \mathbf{Q}(r)\mathbf{l}.$$

Because of (e) the system decomposes:

$$\{[\mathbf{J}(r)\mathbf{B}_1^1 + \mathbf{K}(r)\mathbf{B}_2^1] - (1 + r)[\mathbf{J}(r)\mathbf{A}_1^1 + \mathbf{K}(r)\mathbf{A}_2^1]\}\mathbf{p}_1 = w(\mathbf{J}\mathbf{l}_1 + \mathbf{K}\mathbf{l}_2)$$
$$[\mathbf{B}_2^1 - (1 + r)\mathbf{A}_2^1]\mathbf{p}_1 + [\mathbf{B}_2^2 - (1 + r)\mathbf{A}_2^2]\mathbf{p}_2 = w\mathbf{l}_2.$$
$$\widetilde{\mathbf{B}}_1^1 = \mathbf{J}(r)\mathbf{B}_1^1 + \mathbf{K}(r)\mathbf{B}_2^1$$

is a diagonal matrix with non-vanishing diagonal.[2] We divide the equations by

$$j_i^i(r) + [\mathbf{k}_i(r)\mathbf{b}^i]$$

and denote the resulting matrices and the labour vector by:

$$\hat{\mathbf{A}}(r) = (\widetilde{\mathbf{B}}_1^1)^{-1}\widetilde{\mathbf{A}}_1^1 = (\mathbf{J}\mathbf{B}_1^1 + \mathbf{K}\mathbf{B}_2^1)^{-1}(\mathbf{J}\mathbf{A}_1^1 + \mathbf{K}\mathbf{A}_2^1),$$
$$\mathbf{I}_{(m)} = (\widetilde{\mathbf{B}}_1^1)^{-1}\widetilde{\mathbf{B}}_1^1,$$
$$\hat{\mathbf{l}} = (\widetilde{\mathbf{B}}_1^1)^{-1}\widetilde{\mathbf{l}} = (\mathbf{J}\mathbf{B}_1^1 + \mathbf{K}\mathbf{B}_2^1)^{-1}(\mathbf{J}\mathbf{l}_1 + \mathbf{K}\mathbf{l}_2).$$

Thus, we get the following system determining the prices $\mathbf{p}_1$ of finished products:

$$\mathbf{p}_1 = w[\mathbf{I}_{(m)} - (1 + r)\hat{\mathbf{A}}]^{-1}\hat{\mathbf{l}}.$$

It has the property that $\hat{l}_i$, $\hat{a}_i^j(r)$ are rational functions in $(1 + r)$ with non-negative coefficients. We call this system $(\hat{\mathbf{A}}(r), \hat{\mathbf{l}}(r))$ of variable coefficients the *centre* of the fixed-capital system.

According to a conventional amortization formula, to which Sraffa refers in his sec. 75 and which he proves in his own framework in sec. 76, this rational function, multiplied by $1 + T$, equals

$$\frac{r(1 + r)^{T}}{(1 + r)^{T} - 1}$$

for a machine with 'a lifetime of T years and constant efficiency'. This means that

$$(1 + r)\hat{a}_i^j(r)p_j = (1 + r)M_{\tau-1}p_{m,\tau-1} - M_{\tau}p_{m,\tau}$$

for a machine j of constant efficiency as discussed at the beginning of this section; i.e. it is the *amortization* which equals the sum of *depreciation* $M_{\tau-1}p_{m,\tau-1} - M_{\tau}p_{m,\tau}$ plus the profits, or (if the rate of interest equals the rate of profit) the *financial charge* of the value of the capital advanced in the form of the machine. Thus $(1 + r)a_i^j(r)p_j$ is, in the case of constant efficiency, the total charge (amortization as sum of interest and depreciation) of the machine to be earned in each year.

It is to be noted that the part of the amortization charge which is due to interest must fall as the machine grows older because the machine falls in value. Since the relation of output to each input stays constant with constant efficiency, the total charge for amortization is the same in every year. But the value of the machine, and hence the interest charge, diminishes. Thus the part of the charge due to depreciation must rise, which implies that the value of the machine must fall faster than in proportion to its age, if the exact balance between costs and proceeds is to be struck in each year (PCMC, sec. 84).

It is thus logically to be expected that depreciation rises with the age of the machine, but in reality there is an opposite tendency to let the book value of machines depreciate fast at the beginning of their life and more slowly afterwards. That opposite tendency is due to technical progress: machines installed today depreciate not only because of wear and tear, as examined here, but also because the machines of tomorrow will be more productive. Often, linear depreciation is used as a convention, which may, as a compromise between these two tendencies, be quite reasonable. We could bring the effect of technical progress into our story, but we will not since we cannot deal with all complications at the same time. The effect of technical progress is mentioned only in passing in order to warn the reader not to regard the centre coefficients as a normative concept capable of immediate application. (In reality, of course, taxation also plays a major role.)

We revert to the centre of pure fixed-capital systems. The formula showing the relative price movement of the machine and depreciation is given below in section 15 (theorem 15.3). Generalizing that result, one may interpret $\hat{a}_i^j(r)$, the centre coefficient, also in the case of varying efficiency as an artificially constructed average charge of interest and depreciation, if j is a machine. But the point to be observed is that the coefficients representing circulating capital goods become functions of the rate of profit, too, if the efficiency of the machine varies (Schefold, 1976b).

NOTE

To conclude this section, I give two examples that are useful for the discussion of the axiomatic system.

(1)   The first example is of a complete fixed-capital system fulfilling all axioms except $(^*f^*)$. There are two kinds of machines, blast-furnaces M and lorries N, each growing 2 years old $(M_0, M_1; N_0, N_1)$ and producing together steel (G) by which they are also produced. Old and new lorries are then used to produce corn (X).

$$(1 + r)G_1 p_g + wl_1 = M_0 p_{m0}$$
$$(1 + r)G_2 p_g + wl_2 = N_0 p_{n0}$$
$$(1 + r)(M_0 p_{m0} + N_0 p_{n0}) + wl_3 = G_3 p_g + M_1 p_{m1} + N_1 p_{n1}$$
$$(1 + r)(M_1 p_{m1} + N_1 p_{n1}) + wl_4 = G_4 p_g$$
$$(1 + r)(N_0 p_{n0} + X_1 p_x) + wl_5 = X_2 p_x + N_1 p_{n1}$$
$$(1 + r)(N_1 p_{n1} + X_3 p_x) + wl_6 = X_4 p_x.$$

The system is basic, yet in the 'centre' corn emerges as a self-reproducing non-basic (X):

$$(1 + r)G_1 p_g + wl_1 = M_0 p_{m0}$$
$$(1 + r)G_2 p_g + wl_2 = N_0 p_{n0}$$
$$(1 + r)^2(M_0 p_{m0} + N_0 p_{n0}) + w[(1 + r)l_3 + l_4] = [(1 + r)G_3 + G_4]p_g$$
$$(1 + r)^2 N_0 p_{n0} + [(1 + r)^2 X_1$$
$$+ (1 + r)X_3]p_x + w[(1 + r)l_5 + l_6] = [(1 + r)X_2 + X_4]p_x.$$

This example shows that the axiom $(^*f^*)$ is independent of (a), ..., (e). Counting of equations shows that each group containing α intermediate goods allows at most $\alpha + 1$ processes, if (a), ..., (e) hold. With $(^*f^*)$, the group will consist of exactly $\alpha + 1$ equations. $(^*f^*)$ thus ensures that prices of intermediate goods are determined in the one group in which they occur. In this example, the corn-producing processes are basic, because they help to determine the price of N_1, i.e. of old lorries, which are clearly basic.

(2)   The second example shows the transfer of an intermediate good from one group to another ('interlocked system'), e.g. of race-horses (M) from racing (G) to breeding (X):

$$(1 + r)M_0 p_{m0} + wl_1 = G_1 p_g + M_1 p_{m1}$$
$$(1 + r)M_1 p_{m1} + wl_2 = G_2 p_g + M_2 p_{m2}$$
$$(1 + r)M_2 p_{m2} + wl_3 = X_3 p_x + M_3 p_{m3}$$
$$(1 + r)M_3 p_{m3} + wl_4 = X_4 p_x.$$

Such transfers have been excluded, since they lead to joint production in the centre:

$$(1 + r)^4 M_0 p_{m0} + w \sum_{v=0}^{3} l_{4-v} (1 + r)^v$$
$$= [G_1(1 + r) + G_2](1 + r)^2 p_g + [(1 + r)X_3 + X_4]p_x.$$

Genuine examples for such transfers are hard to find in industry if the time-structure of processes is taken literally: lorries do not start as carriers of wood and then are used for carrying stones later; they are used for carrying wood and stones *alternately*. The real problem therefore concerns superimposed joint production rather than interlocked systems.

Notes

1   This last condition is optional and can be replaced by another. See Notes at the end of next section and after theorem 13.2.
2   For $\mathbf{Q}_1^1 = \mathbf{J}(0)$, $\mathbf{B}_1^1$ and $\mathbf{KB}_2^1$ are diagonal. Since $\mathbf{e}_{(m)}' \widetilde{\mathbf{B}}_1^1(0) = \mathbf{e}_{(m)}' \mathbf{Q}_1(0)\mathbf{B}^1$ $= \bar{\mathbf{e}}_{(m)}' [\mathbf{J}(0), \mathbf{K}(0)]\mathbf{B}^1 = \mathbf{e}'\mathbf{B}^1 = \mathbf{e}_{(m)}'$, it follows $\widetilde{\mathbf{B}}_1^1(0) = \mathbf{I}_{(m)}$.

13   The Centre of Fixed-Capital Systems

We analyse first the system $\hat{\mathbf{A}}(r)$, $\mathbf{I}_{(m)}$, $\hat{\mathbf{I}}(r)$ that I have called the centre of the fixed-capital system.

Theorem 13.1

For the centre $\hat{\mathbf{A}}(r)$, $\mathbf{I}_{(m)}$ we have

1. $\mathbf{e}_{(m)}' [\mathbf{I}_{(m)} - \hat{\mathbf{A}}(0)] \geqslant \mathbf{o}$.
2. $\det [\mathbf{I}_{(m)} - \hat{\mathbf{A}}(0)] \neq 0$.

PROOF:

1   This is nothing other than the familiar condition

$$\mathbf{e}' (\mathbf{B}^1 - \mathbf{A}^1) \geqslant \mathbf{o},$$

for

$$\mathbf{e}_{(m)}' \mathbf{Q}_1(0) = \mathbf{e}_{(m)}' [\mathbf{J}(0), \mathbf{K}(0)] = [\mathbf{e}_{(m)}', \mathbf{e}_{(n-m)}'] = \mathbf{e}' ; \widetilde{\mathbf{B}}_1^1(0) = \mathbf{I}_{(m)}.$$

2
$$0 \neq \det \mathbf{Q}(0)\det(\mathbf{B} - \mathbf{A}) = \det [\mathbf{Q}_1(\mathbf{B}^1 - \mathbf{A}^1)]\det(\mathbf{B}_2^2 - \mathbf{A}_2^2)$$
$$= \det(\widetilde{\mathbf{B}}_1^1 - \widetilde{\mathbf{A}}_1^1)\det(\mathbf{B}_2^2 - \mathbf{A}_2^2)$$
$$= \det(\widetilde{\mathbf{B}}_1^1)\det(\mathbf{I} - \hat{\mathbf{A}})\det(\mathbf{B}_2^2 - \mathbf{A}_2^2). \qquad \text{q.e.d.}$$

We want to prove that the centre is basic. This is not trivial. Whole columns of $\mathbf{A}_1^1$ may be zero, because some finished goods are used only in conjunction with intermediate goods, e.g. *'spare parts'* for old machines.

Theorem 13.2

The centre $\hat{\mathbf{A}}(r)$, $\mathbf{I}_{(m)}$ is a basic system for $r \geqslant 0$.

PROOF:

(It is interesting to note that some assumptions could be relaxed to allow for superimposed joint production[1]). Without loss of generality, we assume $r = 0$, therefore $\mathbf{J} = \mathbf{J}(0) = \mathbf{I}_{(m)}$, $\mathbf{K} = \mathbf{K}(0)$,

$$\tilde{\mathbf{B}}_1^1 = \mathbf{J}\mathbf{B}_1^1 + \mathbf{K}\mathbf{B}_2^1 = \mathbf{I}_{(m)}.$$

We have to show that if $(\tilde{\mathbf{A}}_1^1, \tilde{\mathbf{B}}_1^1)$ is non-basic, or with the notation:

$(\tilde{\mathbf{A}}_1^1)_1^1$	$(\tilde{\mathbf{A}}_1^1)_1^2$	$(\tilde{\mathbf{A}}_1^2)_1$
$(\tilde{\mathbf{A}}_1^1)_2^1$	$(\tilde{\mathbf{A}}_1^1)_2^2$	$(\tilde{\mathbf{A}}_1^2)_2$
$(\tilde{\mathbf{A}}_2^1)^1$	$(\tilde{\mathbf{A}}_2^1)_1^2$ $\Big\}\alpha$ $\overline{}$ $(\tilde{\mathbf{A}}_2^1)_2^2$	$\tilde{\mathbf{A}}_2^2$

		$\mathbf{K}_1$	$\Big\}$
	$\mathbf{J}$	$\mathbf{K}_2$	m
		$\overbrace{}$ α	
	$\mathbf{0}$	$\mathbf{I}_{(n-m)}$	$\Big\} n-m$

(and ignoring trivial permutations) that if $(\tilde{\mathbf{A}}_1^1)_1^2 = (\tilde{\mathbf{B}}_1^1)_1^2 = \mathbf{O}$, it follows that $\tilde{\mathbf{A}}, \tilde{\mathbf{B}}$ is non-basic. For if $\tilde{\mathbf{A}}, \tilde{\mathbf{B}}$ is non-basic, $\mathbf{A}, \mathbf{B}$ is also non-basic, because $\tilde{\mathbf{A}} = \mathbf{Q}(0)\mathbf{A}$, $\tilde{\mathbf{B}} = \mathbf{Q}(0)\mathbf{B}$, $\det\mathbf{Q}(0) = 1 \neq 0$, in contradiction to our assumption that pure fixed-capital systems are basic.

We show that the assumptions $(\tilde{\mathbf{A}}_1^1)_1^2 = (\tilde{\mathbf{B}}_1^1)_1^2 = \mathbf{O}$ and $\tilde{\mathbf{A}}, \tilde{\mathbf{B}}$ is basic lead to a contradiction. We distinguish three cases according to whether (1) all, (2) some or (3) no column of $\mathbf{K}_1$ vanishes.

(1) Not all the columns of $\mathbf{K}_1$ vanish, for if we have $\mathbf{K}_1 = \mathbf{O}$, we get

$$[(\tilde{\mathbf{A}}_1^2)_1, (\tilde{\mathbf{B}}_1^2)_1] = [\mathbf{K}_1\mathbf{A}_2^2, (\mathbf{B}_1^2)_1 + \mathbf{K}_1(\mathbf{B}_2^2)]$$
$$= [\mathbf{O}, (\mathbf{B}_1^2)_1] = [\mathbf{O}, \mathbf{O}]$$

(using (e)), and $\tilde{\mathbf{A}}, \tilde{\mathbf{B}}$ is non-basic.

(2) Assume that the first α columns of $\mathbf{K}_1$ vanish, while the remaining $\beta = n - m - \alpha > 0$ do not, and assume $\alpha > 0$. From this and (*f*) it follows first that (using (e)) the last β rows of $[\mathbf{A}_2^2, \mathbf{B}_2^2]$ are such that the a_i^j, b_i^j are zero in at least $\alpha = n - m - \beta$ columns of $\mathbf{A}_2^2$ and $\mathbf{B}_2^2$, say in the first α of each, or, extending the notation,

$$(\mathbf{A}_2^2)_2^1 = (\mathbf{B}_2^2)_2^1 = \mathbf{O}.$$

It follows secondly that

$$(\widetilde{\mathbf{A}}_2^2)_2^1 = (\widetilde{\mathbf{B}}_2^2)_2^1 = \mathbf{O}$$

and this entails (using (e) again):

$$[(\widetilde{\mathbf{A}}_1^2)_1^1, (\widetilde{\mathbf{B}}_1^2)_1^1] = [\mathbf{K}_1^1(\mathbf{A}_2^2)_1^1 + \mathbf{K}_1^2(\mathbf{A}_2^2)_2^1, (\mathbf{B}_1^2)_1^1 + \mathbf{K}_1^1(\mathbf{B}_2^2)_1^1 + \mathbf{K}_1^2(\mathbf{B}_2^2)_2^1]$$
$$= [\mathbf{O}, (\mathbf{B}_1^2)_1^1]$$
$$= \mathbf{O}.$$

Since all the columns of $\mathbf{K}_1^2$ have a positive element and since

$$\mathbf{O} = [(\widetilde{\mathbf{A}}_1^1)_1^2, (\widetilde{\mathbf{B}}_1^1)_1^2] = [(\mathbf{A}_1^1)_1^2, (\mathbf{B}_1^1)_1^2] + \mathbf{K}_1^2[(\mathbf{A}_2^1)_2^2, (\mathbf{B}_2^1)_2^2],$$

we get

$$[(\mathbf{A}_2^1)_2^2, (\mathbf{B}_2^1)_2^2] = [(\widetilde{\mathbf{A}}_2^1)_2^2, (\widetilde{\mathbf{B}}_2^1)_2^2] = \mathbf{O}.$$

Thus we have, taken together:

$$[(\widetilde{\mathbf{A}}_1^1)_1^2, (\widetilde{\mathbf{B}}_1^1)_1^2] = \mathbf{O}, \quad [(\widetilde{\mathbf{A}}_1^2)_1^1, (\widetilde{\mathbf{B}}_1^2)_1^1] = \mathbf{O},$$
$$[(\widetilde{\mathbf{A}}_2^1)_2^2, (\widetilde{\mathbf{B}}_2^1)_2^2] = \mathbf{O}, \quad [(\widetilde{\mathbf{A}}_2^2)_2^1, (\widetilde{\mathbf{B}}_2^2)_2^1] = \mathbf{O}.$$

This is sufficient to show $\widetilde{\mathbf{A}}, \widetilde{\mathbf{B}}$ is non-basic if $\alpha > 0, \beta > 0$.

(3) If $\alpha = 0$ and no column of $\mathbf{K}_1$ vanishes we can, from

$$\mathbf{O} = [(\widetilde{\mathbf{A}}_1^1)_1^2, (\widetilde{\mathbf{B}}_1^1)_1^2] = [(\mathbf{A}_1^1)_1^2, (\mathbf{B}_1^1)_1^2] + \mathbf{K}_1[(\mathbf{A}_2^1)^2, (\mathbf{B}_2^1)^2],$$

conclude that

$$[(\mathbf{A}_2^1)^2, (\mathbf{B}_2^1)^2] = [(\widetilde{\mathbf{A}}_2^1)^2, (\widetilde{\mathbf{B}}_2^1)^2] = \mathbf{O},$$

i.e. that $\widetilde{\mathbf{A}}, \widetilde{\mathbf{B}}$ is non-basic. This completes the proof.

q.e.d.

NOTE:

The proof of this theorem makes use of condition (*f*). Some condition of the sort is required to avoid the possibility that the system $\mathbf{A}, \mathbf{B}$ decomposes once the basic intermediate goods are eliminated.[2] Several alternatives to (*f*) are conceivable, of which the following is obviously the simplest. On the basis of results obtained later it could be argued that the centre that appears here as an artificial construction is in fact from the economic point of view at least as important a category as the system itself. It might not only be more expedient but even more economic to assume directly that the centre is basic and to drop the assumption that $\mathbf{A}, \mathbf{B}$ is basic together with (*f*). But then it is also interesting to analyse the conditions under which the basicness of the system as a whole implies that of the centre. For a partial reversal of the problem see Schefold (1974, theorem 3.iv), where it is shown (on the basis of more restrictive assumptions) that, if all primary processes are indispensable, $\mathbf{A}$, $\mathbf{B}$ form an indecomposable system.

Theorem 13.3

A pure fixed-capital system $\mathbf{A}$, $\mathbf{B}$ has a standard ratio R and a standard commodity. The standard ratio R is a root of the equation $\det[\mathbf{B} - (1 + r)\mathbf{A}] = 0$, the standard commodity t is given by

$\mathbf{t}' = \mathbf{q}'(\mathbf{B} - \mathbf{A}) > \mathbf{o}$ where $\mathbf{q}$, the standard multipliers, are uniquely defined and positive: $\mathbf{q} > \mathbf{o}$.

The proof of this theorem relies on theorem 13.4, which we prove first.

Theorem 13.4

There is a unique $\hat{\mathbf{q}} > \mathbf{o}$ and a $R > 0$ which is a root of the equation $\det[\mathbf{I}_{(m)} - (1 + r)\hat{\mathbf{A}}(r)] = 0$ so that $(1 + R)\hat{\mathbf{q}}'\hat{\mathbf{A}}(R) = \hat{\mathbf{q}}'$ (the centre has a standard ratio and a standard commodity).

PROOF:

1   $\hat{\mathbf{A}}(r)$ is a semi-positive, indecomposable matrix and so is $(1 + r)\hat{\mathbf{A}}(r)$ for $r \geqslant 0$. There is therefore, for each $r \geqslant 0$, a uniquely defined $\lambda(r) > 0$ and $\mathbf{x}(r) > 0$ with

$$\lambda(r)\mathbf{x}(r) = (1 + r)\hat{\mathbf{A}}(r)\mathbf{x}(r)$$

and

$$\mathbf{e}'_{(m)}\mathbf{x}(r) = 1.$$

2   We have $\lambda(0) < 1$ from the Lemma in section II.2 and from theorem 13.1.

3   On the other hand $\lambda(r) \to +\infty$ for $r \to +\infty$. To see this, consider

$$\lambda(r) = \lambda(r)\mathbf{e}'_{(m)}\mathbf{x}(r) = (1 + r)\mathbf{e}'_{(m)}\hat{\mathbf{A}}(r)\mathbf{x}(r).$$

$\mathbf{e}'_{(m)}\hat{\mathbf{A}}(r)$ is a row vector of rational functions in $1 + r$. $\mathbf{e}'_{(m)}\mathbf{a}^j(r)$ (which itself is a sum of rational functions) tends to a positive value (finite or infinite), if and only if there is i ($1 \leqslant j \leqslant m$, $1 \leqslant i \leqslant m$) so that $a_i^j \neq 0$, for then and only then is the degree of the numerator with certainty at least equal to that of the dominator[3] for at least one of the rational functions added up to $\mathbf{e}'_{(m)}\hat{\mathbf{a}}^j(r)$ (namely $\hat{a}_i^j(r)$). If no such $a_i^j \neq 0$ exists, the commodity j does not appear as an input in the primary processes although it is a finished good. Such a good j has therefore the character of a 'spare part', being used only as an input together with old machines.

If no spare parts exist, $(1 + r)\mathbf{e}'_{(m)}\mathbf{a}^j(r)$ tends to infinity for all j, thus $\lambda(r) \to +\infty$ for $r \to \infty$.

But even if some spare parts exist, or, more generally, if $\mathbf{A}_1^1$ is decomposable ($\mathbf{A}_1^1 \geqslant \mathbf{O}$, $\mathbf{A}_1^1 \neq \mathbf{O}$ following (a)), there is (after suitable rearrangement) an indecomposable (s, s) matrix $(\mathbf{A})_1^1$, $0 < s \leqslant m$, contained in $\mathbf{A}_1^1$.

$$\mathbf{d}' = [\mathbf{e}_{(s)}, \underbrace{0, ..., 0}_{m-s}]$$

is an m vector, the first s components of which are equal to one. We use it to normalize $\mathbf{x}(r)$: $\mathbf{d}'\mathbf{x}(r) = 1$ and get (with the usual notation):

$$\begin{aligned}\lambda(r) &= \lambda(r)\mathbf{d}'\mathbf{x}(r) = (1 + r)\mathbf{d}'\hat{\mathbf{A}}\mathbf{x}(r) \\ &\geqslant (1 + r)\mathbf{d}'[\hat{\mathbf{a}}^1(r), ..., \hat{\mathbf{a}}^s(r)][x_1(r), ..., x_s(r)]' \\ &= (1 + r)\mathbf{e}'_{(s)}\hat{\mathbf{A}}_1^1\mathbf{x}^1(r).\end{aligned}$$

Since $(\mathbf{A}_1^1)_1^1 \geqslant \mathbf{O}$ and indecomposable and since $\hat{a}_i^j(r)$ tends at least to a finite positive value if $a_i^j > 0$, $\mathbf{e}'_{(s)}\hat{\mathbf{A}}_1^1(r)$ tends in each component to a positive finite value or to $+\infty$. Thus, there is r_1, $\varepsilon > 0$ so that

$$\mathbf{e}'_{(s)}\hat{\mathbf{A}}_1^1(r) \geqslant \varepsilon\mathbf{e}'_{(s)}$$

for $r > r_1$.

From

$$\begin{aligned}\lambda(r) &\geqslant (1 + r)\mathbf{e}'_{(s)}\hat{\mathbf{A}}_1^1(r)\mathbf{x}^1(r) \\ &\geqslant (1 + r)\varepsilon\mathbf{e}'_{(s)}\mathbf{x}^1(r) = (1 + r)\varepsilon\end{aligned}$$

for $r > r_1$, it follows $\lambda(r) \to \infty$ for $r \to \infty$.

4   $\lambda(r)$ is a continuous function of r, $r \geqslant 0$, since the $\hat{a}_i^j$ are continuous functions of r and since the dominant root of an indecomposable semi-positive matrix is a continuous function of the elements of the matrix.

5   Since $\lambda(0) < 1$, $\lambda(r) > 1$ for sufficiently great r and since $\lambda(r)$ is continuous, there must be a definite smallest $R > 0$ for which $\lambda(R) = 1$, so that

$$\mathbf{x}(R) = (1 + R)\hat{\mathbf{A}}(R)\mathbf{x}(R)$$

and

$$\det[\mathbf{I}_{(m)} - (1 + R)\hat{\mathbf{A}}(R)] = 0.$$

6.   Since the root R of $\det[\mathbf{I}_{(m)} - (1 + r)\hat{\mathbf{A}}(R)] = 0$ (R fixed) is simple, $\hat{\mathbf{A}}(R)$ being indecomposable, it follows that there is a unique $\hat{\mathbf{q}} > \mathbf{o}$ with

$$(1 + R)\hat{\mathbf{q}}'\hat{\mathbf{A}}(r) = \hat{\mathbf{q}}'.$$ q.e.d.

The proof of the preceding theorem is now fairly obvious: $\det[\mathbf{I}_{(m)} - (1 + R)\hat{\mathbf{A}}(R)] = 0$ is equivalent to $\det[\widetilde{\mathbf{B}}_1^1 - (1 + R)\widetilde{\mathbf{A}}_1^1(R)] = 0$. Since R is a simple root of $\det[\widetilde{\mathbf{B}}_1^1 - (1 + r)\widetilde{\mathbf{A}}_1^1(R)] = 0$, there is a unique $\tilde{\mathbf{q}}$ so that

$$(1 + R)\tilde{\mathbf{q}}'\ \widetilde{\mathbf{A}}_1^1(R) = \tilde{\mathbf{q}}'\widetilde{\mathbf{B}}_1^1(R)$$

or

$$R\tilde{\mathbf{q}}' = \tilde{\mathbf{q}}'\ \widetilde{\mathbf{A}}_1^1(R)[\widetilde{\mathbf{B}}_1^1(R) - \widetilde{\mathbf{A}}_1^1(R)]^{-1}$$
$$= \tilde{\mathbf{q}}'\ \widetilde{\mathbf{A}}_1^1(R)[\mathbf{I}_{(m)} - \hat{\mathbf{A}}(R)]^{-1}[\widetilde{\mathbf{B}}_1^1(R)]^{-1}.$$

$\hat{\mathbf{A}}(R)$ is indecomposable and its dominant root is $(1 + R)^{-1} < 1$. The inverse $[\mathbf{I}(R) - \hat{\mathbf{A}}(R)]^{-1}$ does therefore exist and is positive. Since $\widetilde{\mathbf{A}}_1^1(R)$, $[\widetilde{\mathbf{B}}_1^1(R)]^{-1}$ (the latter is diagonal) are non negative and have (as is easily proved with 13.2) at least one positive element in every row and column, $\widetilde{\mathbf{A}}_1^1(R)[\mathbf{I}_{(m)} - \hat{\mathbf{A}}(R)]^{-1}[\widetilde{\mathbf{B}}_1^1(R)]^{-1}$ is positive, hence indecomposable, and $\tilde{\mathbf{q}}$ must be positive. Define[4]

$$\mathbf{q}' = \tilde{\mathbf{q}}'\mathbf{Q}_1(R) = \tilde{\mathbf{q}}'\ [\mathbf{J}(R), \mathbf{K}(R)]$$

and we get (using (e), p. 148):

$$\begin{aligned}
(1 + R)\mathbf{q}'\mathbf{A} &= (1 + R)\tilde{\mathbf{q}}'\mathbf{Q}_1(R)\mathbf{A} \\
&= [(1 + R)\tilde{\mathbf{q}}'\widetilde{\mathbf{A}}_1^1(R), \tilde{\mathbf{q}}'(1 + R)\widetilde{\mathbf{A}}_1^2(R)] \\
&= [\tilde{\mathbf{q}}'\widetilde{\mathbf{B}}_1^1(R), \tilde{\mathbf{q}}'\widetilde{\mathbf{B}}_1^2(R)] \\
&= \tilde{\mathbf{q}}'\mathbf{Q}_1(R)\mathbf{B} \\
&= \mathbf{q}'\mathbf{B}.
\end{aligned}$$

Obviously $\mathbf{q} > \mathbf{o}$.

The uniqueness follows from the fact that each eigenvector $\mathbf{p}$ of $\mathbf{A}$, $\mathbf{B}$ at R yields an eigenvector for the centre at R.

q.e.d.

Theorem 13.5

The standard prices $\mathbf{p}_{t1}$ of the finished goods of a pure fixed-capital system are positive for all rates of profit.

PROOF:

Almost obvious from $\mathbf{p}_{t1}(r) = w[\mathbf{I}_{(m)} - (1 + r)\hat{\mathbf{A}}]^{-1}\hat{\mathbf{I}}$. We have $\hat{\mathbf{I}} > \mathbf{o}$ and $\mathrm{dom}(1 + r)\hat{\mathbf{A}}(r) < 1$[5] for $r < R$, since R was defined as the lowest value for which $\mathrm{dom}(1 + r)\hat{\mathbf{A}}(r) = 1$. Thus, $[\mathbf{I}_{(m)} - (1 + r)\hat{\mathbf{A}}]^{-1} > \mathbf{O}$ and $\mathbf{p}_{t1}(r) > \mathbf{o}$ for $0 \leqslant r < R$ whatever the normalization. Moreover, we have $(1 + R)\hat{\mathbf{A}}(R)\mathbf{x}(R) = \mathbf{x}(R)$ with $\mathbf{x}(R) > \mathbf{o}$. It remains to be shown that $\mathbf{p}_{t1}(r)$ tends to the solution of $(1 + R)\hat{\mathbf{A}}(R)\mathbf{x}(R) = \mathbf{x}(R)$, provided $\mathbf{p}_{t1}$ and $\mathbf{x}$ are normalized with the same vector $\mathbf{t}' = \hat{\mathbf{q}}'[\mathbf{I}_{(m)} - \hat{\mathbf{A}}(R)]$. We omit the proof which is similar to the one given in section 5.

q.e.d.

Theorem 13.6

The centre is all-engaging.

NOTE:

By this we mean the assertion that all activities (including the secondary processes) can and have to be engaged for the production of any finished good to take place (if the maximum lifetimes of machines, i.e. the secondary processes to be employed in conjunction with the primary processes, are given).

PROOF:

Assume $\mathbf{c}' = (c_1, 0, ..., 0) \geqslant \mathbf{o}$ is to be produced. $\mathbf{c}_1 = (d_1, ..., d_m)$ is a vector of finished goods. (No intermediate goods shall appear in the surplus: the last $n - m$ components of the vector $\mathbf{c}$ vanish.) We have to show that the activity levels appropriate for the production of $\mathbf{c}'$ are positive:

$$\mathbf{q}'(\mathbf{B} - \mathbf{A}) = \mathbf{c}', \mathbf{q}' > \mathbf{o},$$

i.e.

$$\mathbf{q}' = \mathbf{c}'(\mathbf{B} - \mathbf{A})^{-1} > \mathbf{o}, \text{ if } \mathbf{c}' \geqslant \mathbf{o}.$$

This follows from

$$
\begin{aligned}
\mathbf{q}' &= \mathbf{c}'(\mathbf{B} - \mathbf{A})^{-1} = \mathbf{c}'(\mathbf{B} - \mathbf{A})^{-1}[\mathbf{Q}(0)]^{-1}\mathbf{Q}(0) \\
&= \mathbf{c}'(\mathbf{QB} - \mathbf{QA})^{-1}\mathbf{Q} \\
&= (c_1, \mathbf{o})\begin{bmatrix} \mathbf{I} - \hat{\mathbf{A}}(0) & \mathbf{O} \\ \mathbf{B}_2^1 - \mathbf{A}_2^1 & \mathbf{B}_2^2 - \mathbf{A}_2^2 \end{bmatrix}^{-1}\mathbf{Q} \\
&= \{c_1[\mathbf{I}_{(m)} - \hat{\mathbf{A}}(0)]^{-1}, \mathbf{O}\}\begin{bmatrix} \mathbf{J}(0) & \mathbf{K}(0) \\ \mathbf{O} & \mathbf{I}_{(n-m)} \end{bmatrix} \\
&= \{c_1[\mathbf{I}_{(m)} - \hat{\mathbf{A}}(0)]^{-1}\mathbf{J}(0), c_1[\mathbf{I}_{(m)} - \hat{\mathbf{A}}(0)]^{-1}\mathbf{K}(0)\},
\end{aligned}
$$

from $[\mathbf{I}_{(m)} - \hat{\mathbf{A}}(0)]^{-1} > \mathbf{o}, c_1 \geqslant \mathbf{o}, \mathbf{J}(0) = \mathbf{I}_{(m)}$, and the fact that $\mathbf{K}(0)$ has a positive element in each column.

q.e.d.

COROLLARY:

The centre is all-productive.

Notes

1   No use is made of (c2) and (d).
2   See example (1) in Note to section II.12.
3   The degree is higher in the numerator if $a_i^j > 0$, $b_i^i = 0$ for some i, given j (axiom (c4)).

4 In accordance with PCMC, sec. 84.
5 domM denotes the dominant root of an indecomposable matrix **M**.

14 Price Movements of Finished Goods

Although the centre $\hat{\mathbf{A}}, \mathbf{I}_{(m)}, \hat{\mathbf{I}}$ looks now, formally and with its positive prices, very much like a single-product system, one can prove, using the methods of section 3, that there is no single product system equivalent to it. Such a proof is, however, not necessary. The main difference between the behaviour of prices in an ordinary single-product system and in the centre of a fixed-capital system is that in the former case $\hat{\mathbf{p}}(r)$ (prices in terms of the wage rate) rise monotonically for $0 \leqslant r < R$ while this is not necessarily so for the latter, despite $\mathbf{p}_{t1}(r) > \mathbf{o}$ for $0 \leqslant r \leqslant R$.

As an example consider the following simple fixed-capital system:

$$(1 + r)K_0\hat{p}_k + l_0 = M_0\hat{p}_{m0}.$$
$$(1 + r)(K_1\hat{p}_k + M_0\hat{p}_{m0}) + l_1 = K_1'\hat{p}_k + M_1\hat{p}_{m1}$$
$$(1 + r)(K_2\hat{p}_k + M_1\hat{p}_{m1}) + l_2 = K_2'\hat{p}_k.$$

In the first process, the new machine is produced by means of corn (K); in the second, corn and a 1-year-old machine are produced by means of corn and a new machine; in the third, corn by means of an old machine. (In Figure II.14.1 the system is drawn with $l_0 = 0$).

If the processes, particularly the first, use little corn and if the second process produces more corn than the third, while the third employs more labour than the second, and the first employs very little labour, it follows from ($M_0 = M_1 = 1$)

$$\hat{p}_k = \frac{(1 + r)^2 l_0 + (1 + r)l_1 + l_2}{(1 + r)K_1' + K_2' - (1 + r)[(1 + r)^2 K_0 + (1 + r)K_1 + K_2]}$$

that $\hat{p}_k(r)$ may fall over some range of r, for in the extreme case of $K_0 = K_1 = K_2 = \varepsilon$, $l_0 = \delta$; ε, δ small, therefore

$$p_k \approx \frac{(1 + r)l_1 + l_2}{(1 + r)K_1' + K_2'},$$

$\hat{p}_k$ falls for $(l_1/l_2) < (K_1'/K_2')$. However, Figure II.14.1 (it represents the three-dimensional model belonging to this system projected on the plane) shows that the price of the (inefficient) 1-year-old machine is negative in this case. It turns out that $\hat{\mathbf{p}}_1(r)$ will rise monotonically with r at all rates of profit where the fixed-capital system is viable, i.e. where $\hat{\mathbf{p}} > \mathbf{o}$, i.e. in particular where the prices of *all* intermediate goods are positive ($\hat{\mathbf{p}}_2 > \mathbf{o}$). This result should be interpreted in relationship with those of section 9a: old machines are obviously residual commodities, while primary processes are indispensable.

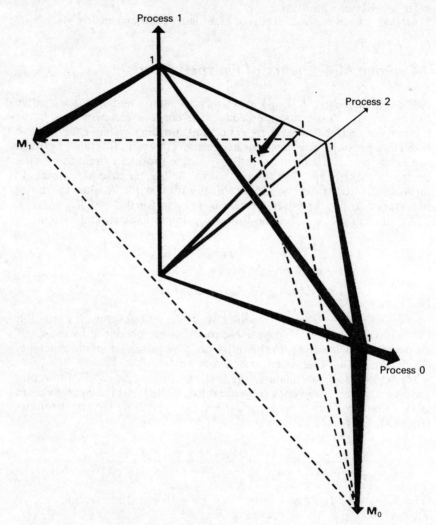

Figure II.14.1

Theorem 14.1

The prices $\hat{\mathbf{p}}_1 = [\mathbf{I}_{(m)} - (1 + r)\hat{\mathbf{A}}(r)]^{-1}\hat{\mathbf{l}}(r)$ are monotonically rising in a neighbourhood of $r = r_0$ if $\hat{\mathbf{p}}_2(r_0) > \mathbf{o}$.

PROOF:

By differentiation of

$$\mathbf{B}\hat{\mathbf{p}}(r) = (1 + r)\mathbf{A}\hat{\mathbf{p}}(r) + \mathbf{l}$$

with respect to r, we get

$$\mathbf{B}\frac{\mathrm{d}}{\mathrm{d}r}\hat{\mathbf{p}}(r) = (1+r)\mathbf{A}\frac{\mathrm{d}}{\mathrm{d}r}\hat{\mathbf{p}}(r) + \mathbf{A}\hat{\mathbf{p}}(r),$$

$$[\mathbf{B} - (1+r)\mathbf{A}]\frac{\mathrm{d}}{\mathrm{d}r}\hat{\mathbf{p}} = \mathbf{A}\hat{\mathbf{p}}.$$

We premultiply this equation by $\mathbf{Q}_1(r)$:

$$\mathbf{Q}_1[\mathbf{B} - (1+r)\mathbf{A}]\frac{\mathrm{d}}{\mathrm{d}r}\hat{\mathbf{p}} = \mathbf{Q}_1\mathbf{A}\hat{\mathbf{p}}$$

and use axiom (e):

$$[\widetilde{\mathbf{B}}_1^1 - (1+r)\widetilde{\mathbf{A}}_1^1]\frac{\mathrm{d}}{\mathrm{d}r}\hat{\mathbf{p}}_1 = \widetilde{\mathbf{A}}_1\hat{\mathbf{p}},$$

$$[\mathbf{I} - (1+r)\hat{\mathbf{A}}_1^1]\frac{\mathrm{d}}{\mathrm{d}r}\hat{\mathbf{p}}_1 = (\widetilde{\mathbf{B}}_1^1)^{-1}\widetilde{\mathbf{A}}_1\hat{\mathbf{p}}.$$

Since $[\mathbf{I} - (1+r)\hat{\mathbf{A}}]^{-1} > \mathbf{O}$, $(\widetilde{\mathbf{B}}_1^1)^{-1} \geqslant \mathbf{O}$, $\widetilde{\mathbf{A}}_1 \geqslant \mathbf{O}$, $\hat{\mathbf{p}}(r) > \mathbf{o}$ at $r = r_0$ and since $\hat{\mathbf{A}}$ is indecomposable, the theorem follows from

$$\frac{\mathrm{d}}{\mathrm{d}r}\hat{\mathbf{p}}_1(r_0) = [\mathbf{I} - (1+r_0)\hat{\mathbf{A}}]^{-1}(\widetilde{\mathbf{B}}_1^1)^{-1}\widetilde{\mathbf{A}}_1\hat{\mathbf{p}}$$

$$= [\mathbf{I} - (1+r_0)\hat{\mathbf{A}}]^{-1}[\hat{\mathbf{A}}, (\widetilde{\mathbf{B}}_1^1)^{-1}\widetilde{\mathbf{A}}_1^2]\hat{\mathbf{p}}(r_0) > \mathbf{o}.$$

q.e.d.

NOTE:

We have thus proved that prices of finished goods not only will be positive, but they also rise in terms of the wage rate, provided the prices of intermediate goods are positive. The underlying reason is that the activity levels to produce one unit of a finished good would, if we had a rate of growth g equal to r, always be positive. If we thus extended the considerations of section 9a to balanced growth with $g = r$, we could state that finished goods are separately producible at g, $0 \leqslant g = r < R$, while intermediate goods, although residual goods, are assumed to have positive prices, so that theorem 14.1 would follow from section 9a by this extension to balanced growth with $g = r$. But it is the main interest of fixed-capital systems that a satisfactory analysis of them is possible without any reference to growth, balanced or not.

Another sufficient condition ensures rising $\hat{\mathbf{p}}(r)$. In our example, $\hat{p}_k$ fell in a case where the old machine M_1 was inefficient: though more labour was used in conjunction with M_1, less was produced than with M_0.

In order to illustrate this concept of efficiency, we have to reinterpret our construction of the centre. As in section 12, there are two machines

N, M lasting two years (N_0, N_1) and three years (M_0, M_1, M_2), respectively. For a change we combine them into a different group of (of course again) four equations:

$$(1 + r)(M_0p_{m0} + N_0p_{n0}) + wl_1 = G_1p_g + M_1p_{m1} + N_1p_{n1}$$
$$(1 + r)(M_0p_{m0} + N_1p_{n1}) + wl_2 = G_2p_g + M_1p_{m1}$$
$$(1 + r)(2M_1p_{m1} + 2N_0p_{n0}) + wl_3 = G_3p_g + 2M_2p_{m2} + 2N_1p_{n1}$$
$$(1 + r)(2M_2p_{m2} + 2N_1p_{n1}) + wl_4 = G_4p_g.$$

Multiplying these equations successively by $(1 + r)^3$, $(1 + r)^2$, $\frac{1}{2}[(1 + r)^2 + (1 + r)]$, $\frac{1}{2}[(1 + r) + 1]$ and adding we again get an equation in which G appears as single product:

$$(1 + r)\{[(1 + r)^3 + (1 + r)^2]M_0p_{m0} + [(1 + r)^3 + (1 + r)^2 + (1 + r)]N_0p_{n0}\}$$
$$+ w[(1 + r)^3l_1 + \cdots + \tfrac{1}{2}l_4] = [(1 + r)^3G_1 + \cdots + \tfrac{1}{2}G_4]p_g.$$

The mathematical operation by which all intermediate goods were eliminated to determine the price p_g in one equation can now be made concrete as follows: instead of thinking of the four processes as of four industries running side by side at the same time, imagine an entrepreneur producing G in four successive years. He will start with buying two new machines M_0, N_0. At the beginning of the second year he will be left with M_1, N_1, having produced G_1. In the second year, he combines a new M_0 with N_1 and a new N_0 with M_1 and produces $\frac{1}{2}G_3$, G_2, M_1, M_2, N_1. In the third year he produces with another new N_0 and with M_1 again $\frac{1}{2}G_3$, M_2, N_1 and, with M_2 and N_1, $\frac{1}{2}G_4$. Without buying any new machine he can repeat the last step with M_2, N_1 producing another $\frac{1}{2}G_4$ and nothing else.

In this way the production of four successive years appears as an *integrated process* (not to be confused with the 'integrated industries' of section 1) using 'dated inputs' and producing a flow of one single output. The equation

$$(1 + r)\{[(1 + r)^3 + (1 + r)^2]M_0p_{m0} + [(1 + r)^3 + (1 + r)^2 + (1 + r)]N_0p_{n0}\}$$
$$+ w[(1 + r)^3l_1 + \cdots + \tfrac{1}{2}l_4] = [(1 + r)^3G_1 + \cdots + \tfrac{1}{2}G_4]p_g$$

represents a single-product price equation for this integrated process. Each input and output is dated by the appropriate power of $1 + r$.

Nothing prevents us from applying this interpretation to the coefficients of the polynomials in $(1 + r)$ in the system $(\tilde{\mathbf{A}}^1_1, \tilde{\mathbf{B}}^1_1, \tilde{\mathbf{I}})$ which appear as nominators and denominators in the centre $(\hat{\mathbf{A}}, \mathbf{I}, \hat{\mathbf{I}})$. Write

$$\hat{a}^j_i(r) = \frac{\sum_{\nu=1}^{N} \alpha^j_{i,\nu}(1 + r)^{N-\nu}}{\sum_{\nu=1}^{N} \beta_{i,\nu}(1 + r)^{N-\nu}}, \qquad \hat{l}_i(r) = \frac{\sum_{\nu=1}^{N} \alpha^0_{i,\nu}(1 + r)^{N-\nu}}{\sum_{\nu=1}^{N} \beta_{i,\nu}(1 + r)^{N-\nu}}.$$

$\alpha^j_{i,1}$, $j = 0, ..., m$, represent the inputs of finished goods and labour to the output $\beta_{i,1}$ of good i in the first year. $\alpha^j_{i,N}$, $\beta_{i,N}$ are inputs and outputs of the last year of the integrated process lasting N years (thus the N'th is the current year).

With this, we can state a sufficient condition for rising $\hat{p}_1(r)$ in the whole range $0 \leqslant r < R$.

Theorem 14.2

The prices $\hat{p}_1(r)$ do not fall with r for $0 \leqslant r < R$, if $\alpha^j_{i,\nu}\beta_{i,\mu} \geqslant \alpha^j_{i,\mu}\beta_{i,\nu}$, or (provided $\alpha^j_{i,\mu}, \alpha^j_{i,\nu} \neq 0$) if

$$\frac{\beta_{i,\mu}}{\alpha^j_{i,\mu}} \geqslant \frac{\beta_{i,\nu}}{\alpha^j_{i,\nu}} \text{ for } j = 0, ..., m;$$

$$\text{for } i = 1, ..., m; \text{ and } \mu > \nu.$$

That is to say, $\hat{p}_1(r)$ rises if the relation of output to input is less favourable at the beginning of the integrated process than at its end. If there is only one machine, it means that all proportions of the output to each input increase as the machine grows older. Or we may also say $\hat{p}_1(r)$ rises if the efficiency of the machines employed does not fall with the age of the machines.

PROOF:

Since $\hat{A}(r)$ is indecomposable, $\hat{p}_1$ will rise if all $\hat{a}^j_i(r)$ and $\hat{l}_i(r)$ are rising functions of r. The condition of the theorem can be derived as a sufficient condition by means of a short calculation and some simplifications from the requirement

$$\frac{\mathrm{d}}{\mathrm{d}r}\, \hat{a}^j_i(r) \geqslant 0, \frac{\mathrm{d}}{\mathrm{d}r}\, \hat{l}_i(r) \geqslant 0.$$

q.e.d.

As a result, we have seen that the movement of the price of a finished good depends on the viability of the processes using the intermediate goods ($\hat{p}_2 > o$) and on the changing input–output pattern (efficiency pattern) of the corresponding integrated process. In the following section we shall give a precise definition of rising and falling efficiency and we shall analyse the interrelations between these problems by examining the behaviour of prices of intermediate goods. In contrast to $\hat{p}_1$, prices $\hat{p}_2$ are capable of turning negative and *a fortiori* of fluctuating in $0 \leqslant r \leqslant R$. This follows from the fact that intermediate processes are dispensable (see section 9a).

NOTE:

$\hat{p}_1(0)$ is the vector of the sums of direct and indirect labour (section 4) embodied in the finished goods. If the equations in the centre are interpreted as integrated processes, the series

$$\hat{\mathbf{p}}_1(r) = [\mathbf{I} - (1+r)\hat{\mathbf{A}}(r)]^{-1}\hat{\mathbf{l}}(r)$$
$$= \{\mathbf{I} - (1+r)[\tilde{\mathbf{B}}_1^1(r)]^{-1}\tilde{\mathbf{A}}_1^1(r)\}^{-1}[\tilde{\mathbf{B}}_1^1(r)]^{-1}\tilde{\mathbf{l}}(r)$$
$$= \{\mathbf{I} + (1+r)(\tilde{\mathbf{B}}_1^1)^{-1}\tilde{\mathbf{A}}_1^1 + (1+r)^2[(\tilde{\mathbf{B}}_1^1)^{-1}\tilde{\mathbf{A}}_1^1]^2 + \cdots\}(\tilde{\mathbf{B}}_1^1)^{-1}\tilde{\mathbf{l}},$$

which converges for some rates of profit $r \geq 0$, is akin to a reduction to 'dated quantities of labour' (section 6). The normal reduction to dated quantities of labour of the fixed-capital system as a whole, in accordance with PCMC, sec. 79, is not always possible for the whole fixed-capital system. (*Proof:* If, in the first example of section 14, $K_2 = K_3 = 0$ and if $K_3^1 < K_2^1$, i.e. if the machine is of falling efficiency, the equation $\det[\mathbf{B} - (1+r)\mathbf{A}] = 0$ will have a negative root which is smaller in absolute value than standard ratio R.) It is therefore of some interest to note that a reduction exists for the centre of fixed-capital systems, but it is intuitively not surprising since the centre operates like a single-product system for any given r.

15   The Value of Machines

We return to the 'microeconomic' point of view discussed at the end of section 12. A more detailed exposition is to be found in Schefold (1974).

To simplify matters, we consider *one* machine M with a total physical lifetime T at its $T-1$ vintages $M_1, ..., M_{T-1}$. $M_0, ..., M_{T-1}$ produce the same finished good, say $\mathbf{b}^1$ with price $\hat{p}_1$. M_0 is the new machine (finished good), $\hat{p}_{m0}, ..., \hat{p}_{m,T-1}$ are the prices of $M_0, ..., M_{T-1}$. We assume that there is only one machine ($M_0, ..., M_{T-1}$) engaged in the production of $\mathbf{b}^1$. The T equations

$$(1+r)\mathbf{a}_1\hat{\mathbf{p}}_1 + (1+r)M_0\hat{p}_{m0} + l_1 = b_1^1\hat{p}_1 + M_1\hat{p}_{m1}$$
$$(1+r)\mathbf{a}_2\hat{\mathbf{p}}_1 + (1+r)M_1\hat{p}_{m,1} + l_2 = b_2^1\hat{p}_1 + M_2\hat{p}_{m2}$$
$$\vdots$$
$$(1+r)\mathbf{a}_T\hat{\mathbf{p}}_1 + (1+r)M_{T-1}\hat{p}_{m,T-1} + l_T = b_T^1\hat{p}_1$$

are part of the basic system $\mathbf{A}, \mathbf{B}$. $\hat{p}_{m0}$ as the price of a finished good is determined in the system of finished goods – the centre $\hat{\mathbf{A}}, \mathbf{I}, \hat{\mathbf{l}}$ – relative to which we now treat the old machine as a sort of non-basic by assuming the prices of finished goods to be given. We shall use the properties that finished goods are known to possess to discuss the prices of intermediate goods. With $\hat{\mathbf{p}}_m = (\hat{p}_{m0}, ..., \hat{p}_{m,T-1})'$, $\hat{\mathbf{p}} = \hat{\mathbf{p}}_1 =$ price vector of finished goods, $\mathbf{b}_T = (b_T^1, 0, ..., 0)$, our equations can be written

$$\hat{p}_{m0} - \frac{M_1}{(1+r)M_0}\hat{p}_{m,1} = \{[\mathbf{b}_1 - (1+r)\mathbf{a}_1]\hat{\mathbf{p}} - l_1\}\frac{1}{(1+r)M_0}$$
$$\vdots$$

$$\hat{p}_{m,T-2} - \frac{M_{T-1}}{(1+r)M_{T-2}}\hat{p}_{m,T-1} = \{[\mathbf{b}_{T-1} - (1+r)\mathbf{a}_{T-1}]\hat{\mathbf{p}} + l_{T-1}\}\frac{1}{(1+r)M_{T-2}}$$

$$\hat{p}_{m,T-1} = \{[\mathbf{b}_T - (1+r)\mathbf{a}_T]\hat{\mathbf{p}} - l_T\}\frac{1}{(1+r)M_{T-1}}$$

or, assuming without loss of generality $M_0 = M_1 = \cdots = M_{T-1} = 1$, and with the matrix

$$\mathbf{N}(r) = \begin{bmatrix} 1 & \dfrac{-1}{1+r} & 0 & \cdots & 0 \\ & 1 & \dfrac{-1}{1+r} & & \vdots \\ & & \cdot & \cdot & 0 \\ & & & 1 & \dfrac{-1}{1+r} \\ \mathbf{0} & & & & 1 \end{bmatrix}$$

and the vector

$$\mathbf{L}(r) = \frac{1}{1+r} \begin{bmatrix} (\mathbf{b}_1 - (1+r)\mathbf{a}_1)\hat{\mathbf{p}} - l_1 \\ \vdots \\ (\mathbf{b}_T - (1+r)\mathbf{a}_T)\hat{\mathbf{p}} - l_T \end{bmatrix}$$

as

$$\mathbf{N}(r)\hat{\mathbf{p}}_m = \mathbf{L}(r).$$

Since (proof by induction)

$$[\mathbf{N}(r)]^{-1} = \mathbf{D}(r),$$

$$\mathbf{D}(r) = \begin{bmatrix} 1 & \dfrac{1}{1+r} & \dfrac{1}{(1+r)^2} & \cdots & \dfrac{1}{(1+r)^{T-1}} \\ & 1 & \dfrac{1}{1+r} & \cdots & \dfrac{1}{(1+r)^{T-2}} \\ & & 1 & \ddots & \vdots \\ & & & \ddots & \dfrac{1}{1+r} \\ \mathbf{0} & & & & 1 \end{bmatrix},$$

we get finally

$$\hat{\mathbf{p}}_m = (\mathbf{D}(r)\mathbf{L}(r).$$

Thus, we have at once:

Theorem 15.1

If $\mathbf{L}(r) > \mathbf{o}$, $\hat{\mathbf{p}}_m(r) = \mathbf{D}(r)\mathbf{L}(r) > \mathbf{o}$.

This result is hardly surprising, since $(1+r)L_\tau(r)$, $1 \leqslant \tau \leqslant T$, represents current output minus input of the τ-year-old machine. The machine has positive value as long as the L_τ are positive, i.e. as long as the value of current net output is positive.

We distinguish three types of *efficiency*, defined as *constant*, if $L_1(r) = L_2(r) = \cdots = L_T(r)$ for a *given r, rising* if $L_1(r) \leqslant \cdots \leqslant L_T(r)$, *falling* if $L_1(r) \geqslant \cdots \geqslant L_T(r)$ for *given r.*

Theorem 15.2

The relations

$$\mathbf{b}_1 = \cdots = \mathbf{b}_T, \qquad \mathbf{a}_1 = \cdots = \mathbf{a}_T, \qquad l_1 = \cdots = l_T$$
$$\mathbf{b}_1 \leqslant \cdots \leqslant \mathbf{b}_T, \qquad \mathbf{a}_1 \geqslant \cdots \geqslant \mathbf{a}_T, \qquad l_1 \geqslant \cdots \geqslant l_T$$
$$\mathbf{b}_1 \geqslant \cdots \geqslant \mathbf{b}_T, \qquad \mathbf{a}_1 \leqslant \cdots \leqslant \mathbf{a}_T, \qquad l_1 \leqslant \cdots \leqslant l_T$$

are sufficient for the efficiency in this sense to be constant, rising and falling respectively for *all r*, $0 \leqslant r < R$.

PROOF:
Obvious, since $\hat{\mathbf{p}} = \hat{\mathbf{p}}_1(r) > \mathbf{o}$ for $0 \leqslant r < R$.

q.e.d.

Theorem 15.3

1^1.

$$\frac{p_{m,\tau-1}(r)}{p_{m,0}(r)} = \frac{(1+r)^T - (1+r)^\tau}{(1+r)^T - 1}, \quad 0 < r < R, 0 \leqslant \tau \leqslant T,$$

$$\frac{p_{m,\tau}(0)}{p_{m0}(0)} = 1 - \frac{\tau}{T}, \quad r = 0, 0 \leqslant \tau \leqslant T,$$

$$\text{if } \mathbf{b}_1 = \cdots = \mathbf{b}_T,$$
$$\mathbf{a}_1 = \cdots = \mathbf{a}_T$$
$$l_1 = \cdots = l_T$$

2. $\hat{\mathbf{p}}_m(\bar{r}) > \mathbf{o}$, if the efficiency is constant or rising at $r = \bar{r}$.
3. If the efficiency of M is falling at $r = \bar{r}$, $\hat{p}_{m1}(\bar{r}), \ldots, \hat{p}_{m,T-1}(\bar{r})$ may be negative and $\hat{p}_{m,\tau+1}$, if $p_{m,\tau}(r) < 0$.

PROOF:

1

$$\frac{\hat{p}_{m,\tau}}{\hat{p}_{m0}} = \frac{1 + \dfrac{1}{1+r} + \cdots + \dfrac{1}{(1+r)^{T-\tau-1}}}{1 + \cdots + \dfrac{1}{(1+r)^{T-1}}}$$

$$= \frac{(1+r)^T - (1+r)^\tau}{(1+r)^T - 1}.$$

The limit $r \to 0$ is obtained by differentiation.

2
$$\hat{p}_{m0}(\bar{r}) = L_1(\bar{r}) + \cdots + \frac{1}{(1+\bar{r})^{T-1}} L_T(\bar{r})$$

is positive, M_0 being a finished good. Thus

$$(1+\bar{r})\hat{p}_{m,0}(\bar{r}) = (1+\bar{r})\left[L_1(\bar{r}) + L_2(\bar{r}) + \cdots + \frac{1}{(1+\bar{r})^{T-2}} L_T(\bar{r})\right]$$

$$= (1+\bar{r})L_1(\bar{r}) + p_{m1} > 0.$$

If $L_1(\bar{r})$ is positive, $\hat{p}_{m1}(\bar{r})$ is positive because $L_\tau(\bar{r}) > 0$, $\tau \geqslant 2$. If $L_1(\bar{r})$ is negative or zero, $\hat{p}_{m1}(\bar{r}) \geqslant (1+\bar{r})\hat{p}_{m0}(\bar{r}) > 0$, etc.

3   The reader may construct an example; one was given using the graphic technique in section 14. The rest follows, using a similar argument as in (2).

NOTE 1:

Efficiency, as defined in this paragraph, is dependent on the rate of profit: a machine that is of falling efficiency at one rate of profit may be of rising efficiency at another; theorem 15.2 gives the only obvious and simple condition under which efficiency of a machine has a technical meaning independent of distribution.

NOTE 2:

$(M_\tau \hat{p}_{m\tau})/(L_{\tau+1})$ is the capital–net output ratio for machine M_τ. For machines with constant efficiency at all rates of profit the 'capital–net output ratio' is

$$K_\tau(r) = \frac{M_\tau \hat{p}_{m\tau}}{L_{\tau+1}} = 1 + \frac{1}{1+r} + \cdots + \frac{1}{(1+r)^{T-\tau-1}}, \qquad 0 \leqslant \tau \leqslant T-1.$$

(The machine has a lifetime of T years). K_τ falls monotonically with increasing r and age. Falling efficiency lowers, rising efficiency raises the capital–net output ratio with respect to K_τ. The average capital–net output ratio for a machine of constant efficiency is:

$$\bar{K}_T(r) = \frac{1}{T} \sum_{\tau=0}^{T-1} K_\tau(r).$$

We get

$$\bar{K}_T(0) = \frac{T+1}{2}.$$

A simple straightforward relationship between the capital–output ratio and the length of life of the machine therefore exists only at $r = 0$.

NOTE 2a:

The charge $[r(1 + r)^T]/[(1 + r)^T - 1]p_{m0}$, derived for the case of constant efficiency, is equal to $(1 + r)p_{m,\tau-1} - p_{m,\tau}$ as was asserted at the end of section 12. Depreciation as a percentage of the total amortization charge of the machine, i.e.

$$\frac{p_{m,\tau-1} - p_{m,\tau}}{(1 + r)p_{m,\tau-1} - p_{m,\tau}},$$

rises geometrically with the age τ of the machine according to 15.3.1, if $r > 0$. Needless to say, there are only constant depreciation quotas at $r = 0$ and no interest charge.

The centre coefficient for a machine of constant efficiency j

$$\hat{a}_i^j = \frac{r(1 + r)^{T-1}}{(1 + r)^T - 1}$$

tends to $1/T$ for $r \to 0$ (one T'th of the machine has to be renewed per year and this depreciation is the only cost, if no interest is charged). If the rate of interest rises, it remains true that the value of all the depreciation

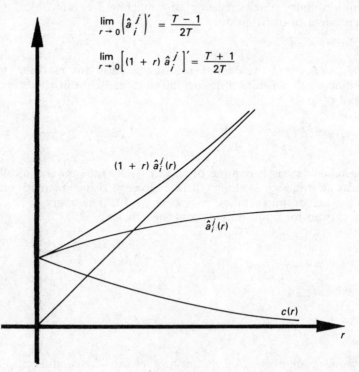

$$\lim_{r \to 0} \left(\hat{a}_i^{\,j}\right)' = \frac{T - 1}{2T}$$

$$\lim_{r \to 0} \left[(1 + r)\,\hat{a}_i^{\,j}\right]' = \frac{T + 1}{2T}$$

$(1 + r)\,\hat{a}_i^j\,(r)$

$\hat{a}_i^j\,(r)$

$c(r)$

r

Figure II.15.1

paid is equal to the value of the new machine, but the formula

$$\lim_{r \to \infty} \hat{a}_i^j = 1$$

shows that, with rising r, the interest cost of the amortization to be advanced increases until it is – at rates of interest much higher than those prevailing in reality – as high as if a new machine had to be bought every year. (It is clear that the centre coefficient cannot rise beyond one, for if the sum to be advanced for amortization each year were higher, a new machine would in fact be bought.) The total amortization $(1 + r)\hat{a}_i^j$ per unit then diverges to infinity; it can be written as

$$(1 + r)\hat{a}_i^j = \frac{r(1 + r)^T}{(1 + r)^T - 1} = r + \frac{r}{(1 + r)^T - 1}.$$

The total amortization is thus divided into the interest cost of a perennial machine and a term $c(r)$ which tends to $1/T$ for $r \to 0$ and to zero both for $r \to \infty$ and, given r, for $T \to \infty$. This is shown graphically in Figure II.15.1.

NOTE 2b:

Linear depreciation means that a fraction $1/T$ of the new machine p_0 is written off each year so that $p_t = (1 - t/T)p_0$ is the price of the machine at age t, and

$$b_t = (1 + r)p_{t-1} - p_t = \left[r\left(1 - \frac{t - 1}{T}\right) + \frac{1}{T} \right] p_0$$

is the amortization in year t. The linear depreciation rule is, strictly speaking, incompatible with a uniform rate of profit and constant efficiency except at $r = 0$, but it represents an approximation frequently used in practice. It overestimates amortization for $t = 1$ (with $p_0 = 1$, $b_1 > (1 + r)\hat{a}_i^j$ for $r > 0$), there is an intersection of $(1 + r)\hat{a}_i^j$ and b_t, with $b_t > (1 + r)\hat{a}_i^j$ for $t < \frac{1}{2}(T - 1)$ and small r, and an underestimation $b_t < (1 + r)\hat{a}_i^j$ for larger t and all $r > 0$. Total amortization for a *balanced stock of machines* (one machine of each age, with a new machine entering and a T years old machine leaving the stock each year) will be equal to $A(r) = T(1 + r)\hat{a}_i^j$ according to the 'correct' formula and equal to $B(r) = 1 + (r/2)(T + 1)$ according to linear depreciation so that $A(r) > B(r)$ for a stock in stationary conditions and $r > 0$.

However, the remarkable result is that $B(r)$ is equal to $A(r)$ in zero *and* first approximation with $A(0) = B(0)$ *and* $A'(0) = B'(0)$, whereas the latter is not true for the single amortization coefficients in each year; we have $b_t = (1 + r)\hat{a}_i^j$ for $r = 0$ but $b_t'(r) = 1 - (t/T)$ while $((1 + r)\hat{a}_i^j)' = (T + 1)/2T$ at $r = 0$. The underestimation by means of linear depreciation, which is slight for $0 < r \ll 2/(T - 1)$, is further mitigated or reversed for a growing stock of machines and $r > 0$.

If one approximates $A(r)$ by means of $B(r)$ for $0 \leqslant r < 2/(T - 1)$ and by means of Tr for $r > 2/(T - 1)$, the relative deviations $[A(r)/B(r)] - 1$

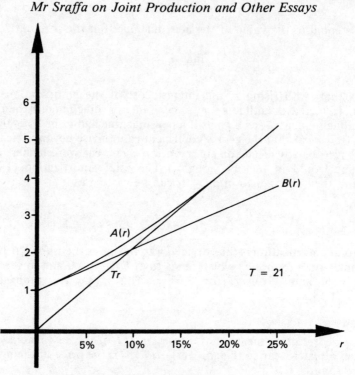

Figure II.15.2

and $[A(r)/Tr] - 1$ are largest at $r = \bar{r} = 2/(T-1)$ where $T\bar{r} = B(\bar{r})$. Hence, the deviations are bounded by

$$\frac{A(\bar{r})}{T\bar{r}} - 1 = \frac{\left(1 + \dfrac{2}{T-1}\right)^T}{\left(1 + \dfrac{2}{T-1}\right)^T - 1} - 1 = \frac{1}{1 - \left(1 - \dfrac{2}{T+1}\right)^T} - 1$$

which is between 15 per cent and 15.7 per cent for all $T \geqslant 5$ and converges to $1/(e^2 - 1)$ for $T \to \infty$. Figure II.15.2 for $T = 21$ is therefore essentially the same for all $T \geqslant 5$ (except in that $\bar{r}$ diminishes for larger T).

Note

1   This result is from PCMC, sec. 83 (with diagram).

16   Efficiency and Age of Machines

The results of section II.15 require some comment. While it is perfectly obvious that ageing machines retain certain positive values as long as they work profitably ($\hat{\mathbf{p}}_m > \mathbf{o}$ if $\mathbf{L}(r) > \mathbf{o}$), it is more difficult to accept the results of the last theorem with the startling asymmetry between rising and falling efficiency. Prices of machines with rising efficiency are positive under all circumstances, even if the new machines do not seem to work profitably (e.g. $L_1(r) < 0$, $L_2(r) < 0$, etc.); but machines of falling efficiency may be worthless, or even of negative value, from a certain age onwards. Given the expectation of an average profit, that is to say, given r, the latter have to be subsidized if they are to be kept running up to the end of their physical lifetimes.

An intuitive explanation would have to run roughly as follows. Prices of joint products cannot be reduced to cost of production alone.[1] While the value of the whole product of an industry is equal to the 'cost of production', this value is embodied in the various products according to the uses to which they are put as means of production. In the particular case of fixed capital, the value of a machine depends essentially on the return obtained in its later use. According to the traditional definition, the value of an asset is equal to the value of the correctly anticipated and properly *discounted net returns*. To calculate the return L_τ in year τ, one has to deduct current costs A_τ from current revenue B_τ. If the discount factor is $1 + r$, one gets as the value $p_{m,t-1}$ of a $t - 1$-year-old machine M with lifetime T,

$$p_{m,t-1} = B_t - A_t + \frac{B_t - A_t}{1 + r} + \dots\frac{B_T - A_T}{(1 + r)^{T-t}}, \qquad t = 1, \dots, T.$$

This formula is identical with the one above:

$$\hat{\mathbf{p}}_m = \mathbf{D}(r)\mathbf{L}(r),$$

because current costs A_τ are equal to $\mathbf{a}_\tau\hat{\mathbf{p}}(r) + [1/(1 + r)]l_\tau$ and revenue to $[1/(1 + r)]\mathbf{b}_\tau\hat{\mathbf{p}}(\tau)$. We have to conclude that the traditional method of evaluating capital goods is a special case of the 'joint production' approach. Note here in particular that p_{m0} is, on the one hand, equal to the 'price of production' in the centre and on the other to 'discounted net returns'. This equality, although most natural from the economic point of view, had to be proved and not simply assumed. The 'price of production' in the centre explains the price of the product from the point of view of past costs (that is the meaning of the 'integrated processes' in section II.14). Here, in section II.16, we explain the price of a machine from the point of view of the future income it generates.

The puzzle of rising and falling efficiency is now easily understood. The case of rising efficiency corresponds to 'learning by doing', 'work in progress', etc. The extreme case of the latter is a plant whose construction takes several years, during the first of which no product is obtained. If efficiency does not fall, as assumed in theorem 15.3.2, nothing could be gained by shortening or truncating the economic life of the plant. Since there is no alternative to the plant, in that its product cannot be produced by any better means, a positive value is assigned even to the plant under construction. This must be so because the system is basic, and in particular because the centre is indecomposable, i.e. each finished product is essential to the running of the system. If efficiency rises, the last processes are indispensable, even if a positive net output appears only in later processes, hence they will not be truncated.

The case of falling efficiency is quite different: prices may turn negative (economic death may occur before physical obsolescence is reached), because the old machines are in fact not indispensable. We have seen earlier that negative prices can occur only if some processes in the system can be discarded without the system becoming totally unproductive (see section 8). This is indeed the case if efficiency falls: total net output of the system can be kept constant by increasing the number of new machines and shortening the average lifetime.

By reducing the lifetime of inefficient machines we arrive eventually at a system with positive prices (provided the fundamental condition $\mathbf{e}'(\mathbf{B} - \mathbf{A}) \geqslant \mathbf{o}$ holds for some reduced system – if it does not, the system is not viable under any circumstances). The formal presentation of how the method of truncation can be extended to the case where the rate of growth falls short of the rate of profit for fixed capital will be given in section 18a.

'Rising' and 'falling' efficiency refer mostly to stages in the life of a machine or – since we are speaking here of the group of processes producing a finished good by means of a combined machine – of a plant. The efficiency of most real machines will at first rise and later fall. The efficiency pattern of actual machines may be seen as the superimposition of rising and falling trends, for a machine will hardly rise forever in efficiency. On the other hand, a machine of rising efficiency is not likely to suffer a sudden death. Thus our definition of rising efficiency is only an analytical concept. Machines of rising efficiency may be supposed to turn, after a finite time, into machines of constant or falling efficiency.

Note

1   Not even the prices of basics in single-product systems can be explained by cost of production alone. The term can be applied only by abstraction from the interdependence of markets, i.e. by considering the good in question as a non-basic whose price is unequivocally equal to its cost of production (see PCMC, sec. 9).

17   Perennial and Obsolete Machines in Long-Period and Short-Period Analysis

A machine M with constant efficiency[1] and a lifetime of T years enters the centre with the production equation

$$M_0 p_{m0} \frac{r(1 + r)^T}{(1 + r)^T - 1} + (1 + r)\mathbf{a}_i \mathbf{p} + w l_i = b_i^j p_j$$

(see sections II.12 and II.15 above and PCMC secs 75/76).

The expression $[r(1 + r)^T]/[(1 + r)^T - 1]$ tends to r as T tends to infinity and we get for a capital good with a very long lifetime at constant efficiency:

$$rM_0 p_{m0} + (1 + r)\mathbf{a}_i\mathbf{p} + wl_i = b_i^j p_j.$$

The equation can also be written as

$$(1 + r)[M_0 p_{m0} + \mathbf{a}_i\mathbf{p}] + wl_i = b_i^j p_j + M_0 p_{m0}.$$

In this form, the equation is equally reasonable, since it represents the equation for a machine that is perfectly maintained so that it leaves the production process in the same condition in which it entered it, i.e. undeteriorated. In consequence, the price of the machine in use is the same as the price of the new machine. This second equation is more natural from the point of view of joint production and is valid also for $r = 0$, but the first expresses a perhaps more familiar economic approach, for we can interpret $rp_{m,0} = \rho_0$ for $r \neq 0$ as hire-price[2] and the equation reads as follows:

$$\rho_0 M_0 + (1 + r)\mathbf{a}_i\mathbf{p} + wl_i = b_i^j p_j.$$

Every reference to depreciation has vanished in the expression $rp_{m0} = \rho_0$; only the part of interest has remained in the total charge of a machine $(1 + r)p_{m,\tau-1} - p_\tau$. The price p_{m0} of the *perennial machine* is determined from the side of cost of production in the process that produces the machine.

Since the produced machine lasts forever, and since it can clearly not be treated as a consumption good, any perennial machine produced in the surplus must be absorbed by the growth of the system; perennial machines have no room in stationary systems as produced commodities, only as instruments of production that have, like land, always been there. The price of a perennial machine in a stationary system can therefore only be determined through capitalization of its hire-price, and the latter must be determined like the rent of land. But the production of perennial machines is conceivable in growing systems, and the hire-price is then *vice versa* determined by the cost of production of a new perennial machine.

It is an economic and not a technical consideration whether a particular machine is used as a permanent capital good (which may involve a permanent, high level of maintenance cost, provided it is at all feasible) or as a machine with a finite lifetime. The single parts of many machines are of finite duration at constant efficiency. Machines can in principle be perennial if those parts are replaced periodically. If technical progress goes on, only the largest 'machines' have a chance of being made perennial. Thus, a railway-line may be genuinely everlasting, because the rails are periodically replaced. But even a knife may be allowed to last forever (and this is no paradox because we are speaking of the knife's economic identity) if the handle is replaced every six and the

blade every two months.[3] Whether these constant repairs are worth-
while, or whether it is advantageous to rely on periodic replacement of
the entire machine, and the extent to which the two are to be combined,
are matters of the choice of techniques in a system without technical
progress, and depend very much on expectations if technical progress is
present.

Although permanent goods cannot be determined as either finished
or intermediate goods, they fit into a slightly generalized concept of
fixed-capital systems – not surprisingly, since they are the limit case for
machines of finite age and constant efficiency. The reader will verify that
all propositions proved about the centre still hold,[4] if coefficients
representing the use of permanent goods are included in $\hat{A}(r)$ in the form
$[r/(1 + r)]M$. In particular, prices of commodities produced by means of
permanent goods rise automatically with r in terms of the wage rate if all
other prices do the same.[5]

If technical change is the essence of capitalist development, there
cannot be much room for perennial machines since the productivity of
perennial machines does not grow and since they are by definition never
replaced; strictly speaking, they cannot exist. But they represent an
interesting limit case between machines and land, and it is quite
conceivable that long-lasting machines are sometimes treated as if they
were everlasting.

These considerations suggest a few remarks about change. The formal
structure of our model allows only one representation of *technical
progress*: the replacement of some processes by others which allow a
reduction in the cost of production by lowering prices in terms of the
wage rate. This is discussed under 'switching of techniques' in the next
section. It is introduced at first only to compare techniques at different
rates of profit, but the analysis can be used for the discussion of technical
progress, provided care is taken to respect the conditions of accumulation: the erratic character of switches must be thought to be evened up
in the flow of technical progress where the single changes are random,
but where the overall effects are regular on average and are such that
productivity rises at a constant rate and allows wages and profits
to rise at rates that in turn are compatible with the ruling laws of
distribution.

Technical progress in the machine-producing industry leads at once to
the replacement of primary processes when a new machine has been
invented and introduced, but the old machine can continue to remain in
use for some secondary processes. Relative prices will, however, shift in
accordance with the growth of productivity in the industry considered
and the economy as a whole. The price of the finished good produced by
the old machine will be determined by the cost of production in the
processes using the new. The old machine can be used as long as the value
of its product, as determined by the new machine, exceeds its cost of
production using the old machine (and excluding the cost of production
of the old machine itself). The difference is called *quasi-rent*. Quasi-rent
is different from hire-price in that *obsolete machines* are not produced,
unlike perennial machines, and it is different from land in that obsolete

machines usually do not last forever. We do not attempt a precise formalization of quasi-rents of obsolete machines; it is rather obvious, as we shall see.

The simplest case is that of an obsolescent machine that lasts forever. It is then to be treated like a perennial machine in a stationary system because it has, being obsolescent, no price of production while the price of the product of the machine must be supposed to be known. If Φ is the quasi-rent of the obsolescent machine M, with price p_m, the price results *ex post* from a capitalization of the quasi-rent:

$$Mp_m = \Phi/r.$$

Or the machine lasts only for one year. Then, since there will be no machine left as a joint product at the end of the period, we must have $\Phi = (1 + r)Mp_m$ so that the machine price is *ex post*

$$Mp_m = \Phi/(1 + r).$$

Finally, we may have the intermediate case of an obsolescent machine that lasts for a certain number of years, possibly with varying efficiency. The formulae for machines as finished goods derived in section II.15 may then be used, except that the price of the 'new' obsolescent machine is not given like the price of production of a new machine as a finished good. Instead, we know the price of the finished good produced as an output by means of the obsolescent machine, because the output is produced also by the new machine that has superseded the obsolescent one as an element of the socially necessary technique. The obsolescent machine can still be used if the prices of the goods in the socially necessary technique are such that positive prices result *ex post* for the obsolescent machine at all its ages.

It follows that different obsolescent machines may be used side by side even if they are of widely different efficiency because different values can be ascribed to them. They are therefore like land, not only in that the quasi-rent is analogous to rent but also in that, like different lands, different obsolescent machines may coexist which derive from different *'vintages'* of techniques that had previously been socially necessary. Such quasi-rents are therefore frequent.

It should be observed that, in spite of the potential multitude of machines of different vintages that will possibly each exist in various ages, the rate of profit will be uniform. The reason is that the prices ascribed to the machine not in the socially necessary technique adapt – this is why the expression '*ex post*' is used. But the uniformity is not, as the expression might suggest, artificial, although this determination of prices looks odd for those used to mixing up 'cost of production' and 'subjective determination' through supply and demand in an unfortunate Marshallian tradition.

Our survey of the forms of capital is now complete; we may use it to discuss the time-honoured question of whether capital should be viewed as a *stock* or as a *flow*. The subdivision of time into periods seems to stand in the way of an answer in the present framework. But the joint production approach implies a treatment of capital that is close to that of a flow: the best proof of this is given by the possibility of transforming the fixed-capital system into the centre. This replaces depreciation by a coefficient which is like a flow magnitude in that it is 'used up' during one period of production and such that it equals depreciation plus the financial charge on the stock. The longer a machine lasts, on the other hand, the smaller the element of depreciation, the larger the financial charge and the more the physical input is like a perennial machine.

The rate of profit is always equal to net profits (revenue minus circulating capital cost, minus wages, minus depreciation) divided by the capital stock, but each can be calculated in different ways. Let **a** be the vector of circulating capital (finished) goods, **b** that of outputs of finished goods in one process; **p** is the corresponding price vector. In obvious notation, the rate of profit then is:

$$r = \frac{[\mathbf{b}(t) - \mathbf{a}(t)]\mathbf{p} - wl(t) - (M_{t-1}p_{t-1} - M_t p_t)}{M_{t-1}p_{t-1} + \mathbf{a}(t)\mathbf{p}}$$

which is, for a machine of constant efficiency and a lifetime of T years, transformed into

$$r = \frac{(\mathbf{b} - \mathbf{a})\mathbf{p} - wl - \alpha M_0 p_0}{\alpha M_0 p_0 + \mathbf{a}\mathbf{p}},$$

where

$$\alpha = \frac{r(1 + r)^{T-1}}{(1 + r)^T - 1}$$

is the familiar centre coefficient. Similar formulae can be derived for perennial machines and in the presence of quasi-rents. If a perennial machine is produced in a growing system, its price p_0 is known and the rate of profit is

$$r = \frac{(\mathbf{b} - \mathbf{a})\mathbf{p} - wl}{M_0 p_0 + \mathbf{a}\mathbf{p}},$$

while in a stationary system there is only a hire-price, so that we have, if Φ represents the total hire-cost,

$$r = \frac{(\mathbf{b} - \mathbf{a})\mathbf{p} - wl - \Phi}{\mathbf{a}\mathbf{p}}.$$

The latter two formulae look like ratios of flows, but if both the hire-cost and the price of the perennial machine are regarded as given, we may write

$$r = \frac{\Phi}{M_0 p_0}$$

so that we have a ratio of a flow to a stock. The same formula is obtained for an obsolescent machine that yields a quasi-rent and is of everlasting constant efficiency. (One can also work out formulae for obsolescent machines of variable efficiency and finite lifetime; the theory of machines of variable efficiency applies except that we have the quasi-rent in place of the cost of production of the new machine.)

Shall we regard fixed capital as a stock or as a flow? I believe that both points of view can be justified, but I have not been able to convince Joan Robinson. Marshallians and Keynesians favour the stock approach, Böhm-Bawerkians and Marxists the flow approach. The formal equivalence of the approaches in the present framework does not mean that there is no issue at stake in a dynamic world:

(a) The idea of fixed capital as a stock pertains mainly to *macro-economics*. The reproduction conditions of fixed capital are at most of subsidiary interest in the short period. Changing efficiency matters little. Especially large aggregates of capital, such as plants, are regarded as perennial, because they are maintained. If market prices of finished goods are fairly constant as determined by prices of production – and not too distant from –. and if the same holds true for hire-prices and quasi-rents (*mutatis mutandis*), the prices of capital goods in use must in the short run be regarded as deriving from the capitalization of hire-prices and quasi-rents, inverting the formula above. This yields

$$M_0 p_0 = \frac{\Phi}{r}.$$

However, the rate of discount to be used here, in the short period, is clearly the rate of interest, which may diverge from the long-run rate of profit. If it does, the well-known drastic revaluation of fixed-capital assets takes place which plays an important role in Keynesian and post-Keynesian economics. For instance, a fall in the rate of interest raises the prices of assets (land, as we shall see, would be affected in the same way) and thus gives a spur to the production of new capital goods, i.e. it is an incentive to investment. The possibility of seemingly independent movements of capital goods prices and consumer goods prices – which is a special aspect of the phenomenon under consideration – has been regarded as the expression of a fundamental opposition between a rudimentary 'Keynesian' theory of prices and the classical one. We have now seen that the two are perfectly compatible.

(b) The flow approach is more congenial to a *classical theory of growth and structural change*. Technical progress implies changes of the socially necessary technique. The corresponding prices of production can only be calculated if fixed capital is regarded as produced, with new machines making their appearance as finished goods. Perennial machines are then an exceptional limit case. Obsolescent machines, although ubiquitous in reality, are unimportant in so far as they are only price-determined, not price-determining. Marx took this view of fixed capital in the process of accumulation, and he therefore treated constant capital as a flow magnitude (depreciation in terms of labour value plus the value of materials used up). Böhm-Bawerk's stance was similar, taking the length of roundabout production as the measure for the amount of capital temporarily bound.

But neither found a correct treatment. The reason is to be sought not only in Marx's known difficulties in transforming values into prices (see Essay 4 in Part III below) and in the inconsistency of the neoclassical theory of distribution (see Essay 3 in Part III below), with Böhm-Bawerk's special problem of the neglect of compound interest in the calculation of the period of production, but also in the fact that the correct treatment of fixed capital involves an aspect both of a stock and of a flow. Ultimately, the stock aspect predominates in that the qualitative change of the physical stock must be known in order to calculate the quantitative flows of depreciation and amortization.

Notes

1 With constant input and output coefficients.
2 Hire-price, not quasi-rent. The latter term should be reserved for the obsolete machines discussed below.
3 The overall period of production is assumed to be one year. The contention would then strictly be true if the replacement period of the handle could be said to be an irrational multiple of the replacement period of the blade.
4 With the exception that the centre may not be 'basic' at $r = 0$. Moreover, it should be assumed that some finished goods exist, that the rate of growth is positive and that the perennial machines are produced.
5 To see this, one has to start the proof of 14.1 from an equation

$$\mathbf{B}\hat{\mathbf{p}}(r) = (1 + r)\mathbf{A}\hat{\mathbf{p}}(r) + r\mathbf{C}\hat{\mathbf{p}}(r) + \mathbf{l}$$

where $\mathbf{A}$ represents the matrix of all inputs of finished and intermediate goods, where $\mathbf{C}$ is equal to $\mathbf{A}$ augmented by perennial machines, and where $\mathbf{B}$ is the matrix of all outputs.

18 Fixed Capital, Switching of Techniques and the von Neumann Model

We return to the pure fixed-capital system as defined in section II.12 in order to examine it with respect to *switches of technique*. Fixed capital will again be seen to lie in between the simple features of single-product industry systems and the intricacies of joint production.

Let us first restate the argument about 'switching' in basic single-product systems and all-engaging systems:

Theorem 18.1

If we are given an all-engaging system with an alternative method of production in one industry, it follows for any given rate of profit, r, smaller than both maximum rates of profit:

1 All prices $\hat{\mathbf{p}}$ (prices in terms of the wage rate) are lower for one of the two techniques (the 'superior') – or else they are all equal. [1]
2 Wage rate and real wage are higher for the superior technique at the given rate of profit.
3 The inferior technique, if it is at all capable of reaching this highest real wage, reaches it at a lower rate of profit. (See Figure II.18.1.)

We *prove* this theorem as follows:

(1) $(\mathbf{A}, \mathbf{B}, \mathbf{l})$ denotes our original system. The question is whether it is advantageous to replace a method say the first $(\mathbf{a}_1, \mathbf{b}_1, l_1)$ by $(\mathbf{a}_0, \mathbf{b}_0, l_0)$ – it is assumed, of course, that this replacement is technically feasible. Write

$$\mathbf{C} = \begin{bmatrix} \mathbf{b}_2 - (1 + r)\mathbf{a}_2 \\ \mathbf{b}_n - (1 + r)\mathbf{a}_n \end{bmatrix}, \qquad \mathbf{c}_0 = \mathbf{b}_0 - (1 + r)\mathbf{a}_0,$$

$$\mathbf{C}_0 = \begin{bmatrix} \mathbf{c}_0 \\ \mathbf{C} \end{bmatrix}, \qquad \mathbf{c}_1 = \mathbf{b}_1 - (1 + r)\mathbf{a}_1,$$

$$\mathbf{C}_1 = \begin{bmatrix} \mathbf{c}_1 \\ \mathbf{C} \end{bmatrix}, \qquad \mathbf{m} = (l_2, ..., l_n)',$$

$$\mathbf{m}^0 = (l_0, \mathbf{m}')',$$
$$\mathbf{m}^1 = (l_1, \mathbf{m}')',$$

and let $\hat{\mathbf{p}}^0, \hat{\mathbf{p}}^1$ denote the two possible price vectors in terms of the wage rate, so that

$$\mathbf{C}_0 \hat{\mathbf{p}}^0 = \mathbf{m}^0, \qquad \mathbf{C}_1 \hat{\mathbf{p}}^1 = \mathbf{m}^1.$$

Thus $\mathbf{C}\hat{\mathbf{p}}^0 = \mathbf{C}\hat{\mathbf{p}}^1 = \mathbf{m}$, $\mathbf{C}(\hat{\mathbf{p}}^1 - \hat{\mathbf{p}}^0) = \mathbf{o}$.

Consider the set of all vectors $\mathbf{x}$ for which $\mathbf{C}\mathbf{x} = \mathbf{o}$. Since $\mathrm{rk}\mathbf{C} = n - 1$, it is a straight line g through the origin. In particular, the $\mathbf{x}_0$ for which

$$\mathbf{C}_0\mathbf{x}_0 = \begin{bmatrix} \mathbf{c}_0\mathbf{x}_0 \\ \mathbf{C}\mathbf{x}_0 \end{bmatrix} = \begin{bmatrix} 1 \\ 0 \\ \vdots \\ 0 \end{bmatrix} = \mathbf{e}^1$$

is on this line. Since $(\mathbf{C}_0)^{-1} > \mathbf{O}$ (we are in an all-engaging system), $\mathbf{x}_0 = (\mathbf{C}_0)^{-1}\mathbf{e}^1 > \mathbf{o}$ and all points on g are positive, negative or zero. [2]

Thus we have either $\hat{\mathbf{p}}^1 > \hat{\mathbf{p}}^0$, $\hat{\mathbf{p}}^1 = \hat{\mathbf{p}}^0$ ('switchpoint'), or $\hat{\mathbf{p}}^1 < \hat{\mathbf{p}}^0$.

(2) Follows immediately from (1).

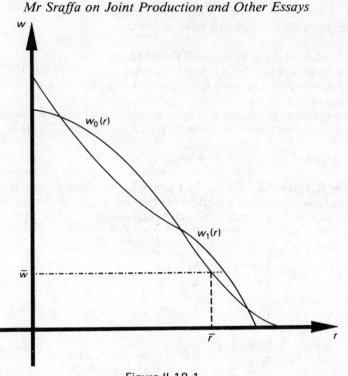

Figure II.18.1

(3)   If **a** is the standard in which prices are measured,

$$w_a = \frac{1}{\mathbf{a}'\,[\mathbf{B} - (1+r)\mathbf{A}]^{-1}\mathbf{l}} = \frac{1}{\mathbf{a}'\,\hat{\mathbf{p}}(r)}$$

is the wage rate corresponding to this standard. It falls monotonically with rising r, since $\hat{\mathbf{p}}(r)$ rises monotonically with r and it is a straight line $w = 1 - (r/R)$, if $\mathbf{a}' = \mathbf{q}'(\mathbf{B} - \mathbf{A})$ (standard commodity). w_a is smaller for the inferior technique at the rate of profit at which the comparison is made and w_a falls for higher rates of profit.

q.e.d.

COROLLARY:

Prices of non-basics are, at a given rate of profit, also lower in terms of the wage rate in the system with a superior method for the production of a basic commodity.

The *proof* of the corollary follows by direct extension from the proof of the theorem. The analysis of switches of technique between methods producing only non-basics is trivial. This theorem is important because it shows that once the distribution between profits and wages is given — be it specified by means of r, w, or whatever — the technique that will be adopted under conditions of perfect competition because prices in terms of the wage rate are lowest is also the one most advantageous for the capitalist class as a whole (given the wage, profits are highest) and for the class of wage-earners (given r, wages are highest).

The choice between technically alternative systems for which the assertions of theorem 18.1 hold will be called *neutral*.

The case of fixed-capital systems is complex, because only the centre, not the whole system, fulfils the condition $[\mathbf{I}_{(m)} - (1 + r)\hat{\mathbf{A}}(r)]^{-1} > \mathbf{O}$. With this, the first and second parts of theorem 18.1 hold if none other than finished goods are taken into account and if the methods using intermediate goods are considered only to the extent that they influence the production of finished goods.

Since wage goods are, as a matter of course, finished products, the third part of 18.1 holds for fixed-capital systems in those ranges of the rate of profit where prices of finished goods in terms of the wage rate rise monotonically with the rate of profit, i.e. in those ranges where the system is viable because all prices are positive (see theorem 14.1).

Theorem 18.2

If prices $\hat{\mathbf{p}}_2(r) > \mathbf{o}$ for $r_1 \leqslant r \leqslant r_2$, prices $\hat{\mathbf{p}}_1$ of finished goods rise monotonically with r and the choice of techniques is neutral in the centre of the fixed-capital system for $r_1 \leqslant r \leqslant r_2$.

This result is not quite as concise as the one obtained for single-product systems, because the superior technique entails lower prices in terms of the wage rate only for finished products, not necessarily for intermediate goods (that they are positive should and can be assumed in any case beforehand – see section II.18a). It is as a matter of fact quite easy to construct examples where the price $\hat{p}_{m\tau}$ of an intermediate good M_τ rises in consequence of an 'invention' that lowers the prices of finished goods.

It is nevertheless an important argument for the superiority of a technique under competitive conditions that it entails lower prices in terms of the wage rate, because surplus profits earned in the production of a finished good will lead to the adoption of the method of production that allows production of the finished good most cheaply in terms of the wage rate. This follows from the application of the following theorem to the centre:

Theorem 18.2a

If an all-engaging system with an alternative method of production for one industry is given such that prices in terms of the wage rate are lower for the alternative system, prices in terms of any standard of the original system will show surplus profits if applied to the alternative method, and prices in terms of any standard of the alternative system will show losses if applied to the original system.

PROOF:

Using the notation of 18.1, one has, treating process $(\mathbf{a}_0, \mathbf{b}_0, l_0)$ as the alternative, $\hat{\mathbf{p}}^0 < \hat{\mathbf{p}}^1$ and $\mathbf{C}\hat{\mathbf{p}}^0 = \mathbf{C}\hat{\mathbf{p}}^1 = \mathbf{m}$. If 'original' prices $\hat{\mathbf{p}}^1$ applied to the alternative process did not show extra profits, we should have $c_0 \hat{p}^1 \leqslant l_0$, therefore $C_0 \hat{p}^1 \leqslant m^0$ and $\hat{p}^1 \leqslant (C_0)^{-1} m^0 = \hat{p}^0$ contradicting $\hat{p}^0 < \hat{p}^1$. Similarly for the converse case and for other price standards. The proof rests on $(C_0)^{-1} > O$.

Theorem 18.2a can at once be applied to the centre or rather to the integrated processes of a fixed-capital system; the point is that surplus profits and losses will, irrespective of the standard of prices, lead to the adoption of the integrated process which is superior at the given rate of profit.

As a matter of fact, one can also prove that the price of the finished good whose method of production is improved falls in terms of all other prices (Schefold, 1978b). This additional result is of importance for the understanding of the functioning of commodity price standards. If prices are, e.g., expressed in terms of gold, and surplus profits lead to the adoption of a new method for producing copper, the gold price of copper will fall while other gold prices will partly rise and partly fall. If progress takes place in gold mining, gold becomes cheaper in terms of all other commodities, which implies that the gold price of copper and of all other finished goods will *rise* in terms of gold. Marx therefore thought that inflations under the gold standard that seemed to be related to the discovery of new gold fields were due not to the increased quantity of gold produced as such, but to its diminished cost of production.

Prices of old machines have not explicitly been taken into account here, but the choice of technique in fixed-capital systems concerns the entire group of processes producing a finished good. Indeed, one might believe that the choice of technique concerns finished goods alone, since it is not only a feature of our mathematical construction that the determination of prices of finished products precedes the determination of prices of intermediate goods. Prices of finished goods are determined in an actual market and the value of a finished good is realized in money, while the prices of old machines often exist only as book values and reflect estimates of expected returns the accuracy of which may only be tested upon the failure of an enterprise.

But the conditions of production of intermediate goods are reflected in integrated processes – the secondary processes can in fact in most cases be reconstructed from the integrated process. The formal pre-eminence of finished goods in our presentation is only justified in so far as prices of finished goods furnish the direct criterion for finding the superior technique.

In particular, this criterion will enable us to determine the optimal life time for all machines in the system for given r, for with theorem 18.2 we have proved that, for all possible combinations of lifetimes of machines in a given system fulfilling the basic condition $e'(B - A) > o$ and $\hat{p} > o$ ($\hat{p}_2 > o!$), there exists a technique whose prices $\hat{p}_1$ are lower than the ones of all other combinations. Since the centre is all-productive, this is independent of the proportions in which finished goods are produced. The truncation of old machines will lead to a truncated system which is also a pure fixed-capital system, if groups have the simple structure shown in section 15. If several machines are engaged in the production of one finished good, it will also be possible to determine the best of several possible combinations of the ageing machines into a group as described in sections 12 and 15, using the analysis of 9b and 9c.

We end this section with a comment on the von Neumann model. We have proved that there exists a maximum rate of profit with which a positive vector **q** is associated so that

$$\mathbf{q}'\,[\mathbf{B} - (1 + R)\mathbf{A}] = \mathbf{o}$$

(**A, B** is a pure fixed-capital system).

Assume **p**$(R) >$ **o**. We have then

$$[\mathbf{B} - (1 + R)\mathbf{A}]\mathbf{p} = \mathbf{o}$$

and **q** and **p** may be interpreted as von Neumann activity and price vectors, if $1 + R$ is the maximum rate of growth in the economy. But what if $\mathbf{p}_t(R) \ngeq \mathbf{o}$? We have seen that this is possible only if the efficiency of the machines involved does not rise with age (or remains constant). We know on the other hand that unprofitable activities are not used in the von Neumann model.

Since a von Neumann solution must exist for a basic system **A, B** $(\mathbf{A} \geqslant \mathbf{O}, \mathbf{B} \geqslant \mathbf{O})$, we conclude that there must be some unprofitable activities and that the unprofitability is due to inefficient machines. The condition that the von Neumann expansion factor is equal to the maximum possible rate of growth ensures that new machines are used in greater proportion than the inefficient old machines in such a way that the von Neumann **q** gives the proportions of the fastest possible balanced growth. Some inefficient intermediate goods are still produced, but not used; they will appear as overproduced goods in a von Neumann activity and their von Neumann prices will be zero.

Thus we find that overproduced goods in a basic system are not only waste products, or miraculously abundant commodities, but old machines whose continued use would impede the growth of the system.

The inefficiency expressed in a negative labour value (see section II.4) and discussed as a property of residual goods in section II.9a is now also easily illustrated. An old machine, M_T, cannot be of rising efficiency if it has a negative labour value. It will therefore be possible to keep the net output of the system (apart from M_T) constant by using the processes employing the new machine to a greater extent and by reducing the use of M_T. This will save labour. At the same time, M_T will not be used up any more – hence the appearance of M_T as a product in the output of the system, produced by a negative amount of labour. In the example in Figure II.18.2 (for the explanation, see section II.14) prices are positive for small rates of profit and negative afterwards, if corn inputs and outputs are given by $\mathbf{k}^1, \mathbf{l} = \mathbf{l}^1$. They are negative first and positive up to R if corn is represented by $\mathbf{k}^2$, labour by $\mathbf{l}^2$. In the first of these two cases, the process employing M_1 would be abolished if $r \approx R$ and would thus not enter the von Neumann system; in the second it would be abolished at $r = 0$.

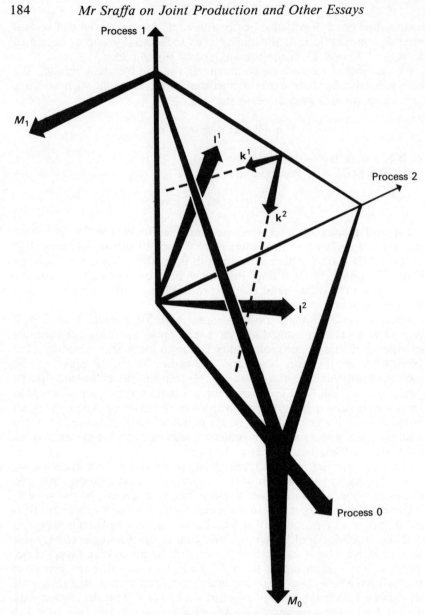

Figure II.18.2

Notes

1 Equality occurs at most at *n* rates of profit: the 'switch points'.
2 $\hat{\mathbf{p}}^0 = \hat{\mathbf{p}}^1$ (switchpoint), if and only if $l_0 = \mathbf{c}_0\hat{\mathbf{p}}^0 = \mathbf{c}_0\hat{\mathbf{p}}^1 = \mathbf{c}_0(\mathbf{C}_1)^{-1}\mathbf{m}^1$, therefore at most at *n* points.

18a   Fixed Capital and Truncation if $g < r$

We have seen that the fixed-capital model exhibits all desirable properties, in particular a falling wage curve, if machines with negative prices can be ruled out, and this irrespective of whether the golden rule conditions are fulfilled. This can also be illustrated by means of the graphic technique.

Figure II.18a.1 shows the truncation of a fixed-capital system of the type

$$\overset{\mathbf{A}}{\begin{bmatrix} \frac{1}{4} & 0 \\ 0 & 1 \end{bmatrix}} \quad \overset{\mathbf{l}}{\begin{bmatrix} \frac{1}{10} \\ \frac{9}{10} \end{bmatrix}} \Rightarrow \overset{\mathbf{B}}{\begin{bmatrix} \frac{2}{5} & 1 \\ \frac{3}{5} & 0 \end{bmatrix}}; \quad \overset{\mathbf{d}}{[\tfrac{3}{5}, 0]};$$

at $r = g = 0$ (diagrams with $r = g > 0$ can also be drawn). Clearly $\bar{q}\bar{l} = 2/5 < \mathbf{q}'\mathbf{l} = 4/5$. The second process yields a positive price p_2, and is therefore worth using, only at high rates of profit and low wage rates where its relative high labour requirement is less important than its low (actually zero) direct requirement of raw materials.

One may ask whether the properties of fixed capital also apply to more general systems. In this section we shall try to define the most general class of joint-production systems for which these properties hold, and we shall show in particular that prices can be made positive by means of truncation for all systems in this class. This point of view will enable us to see the axioms in perspective that we have used to define fixed capital and to relate sections II.12–II.18 on fixed capital of the original thesis

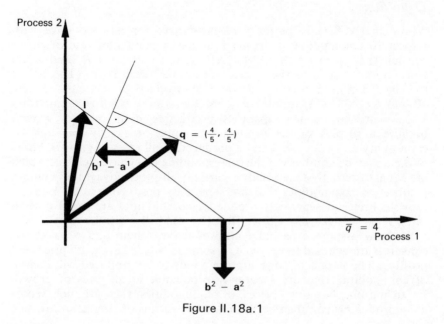

Figure II.18a.1

(which have been changed very little) with the discussion of section II.9b (written later) on the one hand and with the old concepts of section 8 on the other.

The wage curve falls monotonically at r if and only if

$$\frac{dw}{dr} = -\frac{1}{w^2}\,\mathbf{d}'\,[\mathbf{B}-(1+r)\mathbf{A}]^{-1}\mathbf{A}[\mathbf{B}-(1+r)\mathbf{A}]^{-1}\mathbf{l}$$

as we have seen in section II.9b by differentiating the price equations; $\mathbf{d}$ is the standard of prices. The transformation

$$\frac{dw}{dr} = -\frac{1}{w^2}\,\mathbf{d}'(\mathbf{B}-\mathbf{A})^{-1}[\mathbf{I}-r\mathbf{A}(\mathbf{B}-\mathbf{A})^{-1}]^{-1}$$

$$\mathbf{A}(\mathbf{B}-\mathbf{A})^{-1}[\mathbf{I}-r\mathbf{A}(\mathbf{B}-\mathbf{A})^{-1}]^{-1}\mathbf{l}$$

shows that systems with $\mathbf{A}(\mathbf{B}-\mathbf{A})^{-1} \geqslant \mathbf{O}$, i.e. flexible systems as defined in section II.8, will have monotonically falling wage curves for all compositions of the real wage which can be produced in the stationary state at positive activity levels. The same is true, of course, for all-productive systems. No assumption about the equality of the rate of growth and the rate of profit is required.

Fixed-capital systems are neither flexible nor all-productive, but they possess both properties in, as it were, a reduced form. Their outstanding feature seems to be that the centre consisting of finished goods is all-engaging. We define:

Definition

A system $(\mathbf{A}, \mathbf{B}, \mathbf{l})$ is *partially all-productive* (or all-productive with respect to commodities $1, \ldots, m$) if it has a maximum rate of profit R such that $\mathbf{q}_i(r) = \mathbf{e}_i[\mathbf{B}-(1+r)\mathbf{A}]^{-1} \geqslant \mathbf{o}$ for $0 \leqslant r < R$, and if all consumption goods of the system are among the first m. (This is not to be confused with almost all-productive systems where $[\mathbf{B}-(1+r)\mathbf{A}]^{-1} \geqslant \mathbf{O}$ for all $r, \bar{r} \leqslant r < R$ and some $\bar{r} \geqslant 0$.) Commodities $1, \ldots, m$ are now called separately producible at all rates of growth because a surplus or net product consisting of exactly one unit of commodity $i, i = 1, \ldots, m$, can be produced at all rates of growth. Some of them may be non-basic if the corresponding $\mathbf{q}_i(r)$ have elements which are equal to zero. Systems are thus partially all-productive if they contain a subset of commodities that are separately producible at all rates of growth. Prices of separately producible commodities are positive at all rates of profit since $\hat{p}_i = \mathbf{e}_i\hat{\mathbf{p}} = \mathbf{e}_i[\mathbf{B}-(1+r)\mathbf{A}]^{-1}\mathbf{l} = \mathbf{q}_i(r)\mathbf{l} > 0$.

We now assume a partially all-productive system and a basket of consumption goods $\mathbf{d}$ to be given at some $r_0 > 0$ such that *all* prices are positive. The basket of consumption goods to be produced will consist of commodities that are separately producible at all rates of growth by definition. Negative prices of commodities that are not separately producible can then be eliminated by means of truncation: if, say,

$\hat{p}_n = 0$ at r_1, $\hat{p}_n < 0$ at r_2, while all other prices are positive at r_0, r_1, r_2, $r_0 < r_1 < r_2$, and if $\hat{\mathbf{C}}(r) = [\mathbf{C}(r)]^{-1} = [\mathbf{B} - (1 + r)\mathbf{A}]^{-1}$, ε units of commodity n can be overproduced at r_1, because

$$[\mathbf{q}'(r_1) + \varepsilon \hat{\mathbf{c}}_n(r_1)]\mathbf{C}(r_1) = \mathbf{d}' + \varepsilon \mathbf{e}_n$$

where $\mathbf{d}$ is the standard of prices in terms of any basket of separately producible commodities n with $\mathbf{q}'(r)\mathbf{C}(r) = \mathbf{d}'$. Since $\hat{\mathbf{c}}_n(r_1)\mathbf{l} = \hat{p}_n(r_1) = 0$, $\hat{\mathbf{c}}_n(r_1)$ has negative elements and $\varepsilon > 0$ can be increased until one component of $\mathbf{q}(r) + \varepsilon \hat{\mathbf{c}}_n(r)$ vanishes. Thus a truncation $(\bar{\mathbf{A}}, \bar{\mathbf{B}}, \bar{\mathbf{l}}, \bar{\mathbf{d}})$ is defined with prices in terms of the wage rate $\bar{\mathbf{p}}$ and activity levels $\bar{\mathbf{q}}$ which differs from the original system by the deletion of one process and of commodity n which is overproduced. The wage rate is increased at r_2 since $\hat{p}_n(r_2) < 0$ and

$$1/\bar{w}(r_2) = \bar{\mathbf{d}}'\bar{\mathbf{p}} = \bar{\mathbf{q}}'\bar{\mathbf{l}} = [\mathbf{q}'(r_2) + \varepsilon \hat{\mathbf{c}}_n(r_2)]\mathbf{l} = \mathbf{q}'(r_2)\mathbf{l} + \varepsilon \hat{p}_n(r_2) < 1/w(r_2).$$

It can further be proved, as in section 9b, that the truncated process yields surplus profits at r_0 and losses at r_2 if evaluated in terms of $\bar{\mathbf{p}}(r_0)$ and $\bar{\mathbf{p}}(r_2)$, respectively.

The point is now that these relationships remain valid for partially all-productive systems even if the rate of growth is lower than the rate of profit. For if the truncations are also partially all-productive with respect to the same separately producible commodities, the wage curves for the original system and its truncations can be drawn as a function of the rate of profit between zero and the true maximum rate of profit, and each wage curve will fall monotonically at each rate of profit r where prices are positive, since $\mathbf{d}'[\mathbf{B} - (1 + r)\mathbf{A}]^{-1} \geqslant \mathbf{o}$ by definition of partially all-productive systems in the formula

$$\frac{dw}{dr} = -\frac{1}{w^2}\, \mathbf{d}'\,[\mathbf{B} - (1 + r)\mathbf{A}]^{-1}\mathbf{A}\,[\mathbf{B} - (1 + r)\mathbf{A}]^{-1}\mathbf{l} = -\frac{1}{w^2}\, \mathbf{q}(r)\mathbf{A}\hat{\mathbf{p}}(r).$$

The truncation to be adopted will be on the envelope of these wage curves, but it does not have to be assumed that the rate of growth equals the rate of profit: every truncation or system on the envelope at r will be capable of growth at rates of growth lower than r since $\mathbf{q}(g) \geqslant \mathbf{o}$, $0 \leqslant g < R$.

It is thus found that all the essential properties of fixed-capital systems are reproduced for systems that are, *together with their relevant truncations*, partially all-productive. Now it is clear that the truncation of a fixed-capital system is also a fixed-capital system — at least if each group consists of one machine only — so that the questions arise: what is the most general structure of a pure fixed-capital system such that all its truncations are also pure fixed-capital systems, and are these systems essentially the only partially all-productive systems or are there any others? How can a survey of these systems be given?

A differentiated answer to these questions leads to a rather complex theory for which the axiomatic system of section 12 should provide the starting point. Consider e.g. the system

$$\mathbf{A} = \begin{bmatrix} \frac{1}{4} & 1 & 1 \\ \frac{1}{4} & 0 & 0 \\ \frac{1}{4} & 0 & 0 \end{bmatrix} \rightarrow \begin{bmatrix} \frac{3}{5} & 0 & 0 \\ \frac{1}{5} & 1 & 0 \\ \frac{1}{5} & 0 & 1 \end{bmatrix} = \mathbf{B}$$

This system is basic and partially all-productive since the vector $\mathbf{q}'(r) = [1, 1 + r, 1 + r]$ shows that the first commodity is separately producible at all rates of growth below the maximum rate of profit: $\mathbf{q}'(r)[\mathbf{B} - (1 + r)\mathbf{A}] = \lambda \mathbf{e}_1$. This vector can be used to construct a $\mathbf{Q}$ matrix

$$\mathbf{Q} = \begin{bmatrix} 1 & 1 + r & 1 + r \\ 0 & 1 & 0 \\ 0 & 0 & 1 \end{bmatrix}$$

which fulfils axioms (b), (c1), (c2), (c3), (d), (e) but not $\mathbf{A}_1^2 = \mathbf{O}$, i.e. (a), or (c4). In fact, this is not a fixed capital system since primary and secondary processes cannot be distinguished. Yet prices for this system may be positive at all rates of profit depending on the distribution of labour requirements, so that the question whether truncations are also partially all-productive does not necessarily arise.

On the other hand one can now prove that all partially all-productive systems possess a $\mathbf{Q}$ matrix fulfilling some of the axioms of section 12, for let $(\mathbf{A}, \mathbf{B}, \mathbf{l})$ be a system that is partially all-productive with respect to commodities $1, \ldots, m$.

Define

$$(\mathbf{I}_{(m)}, \mathbf{O})[\mathbf{B} - (1 + r)\mathbf{A}]^{-1} = [\mathbf{X}(r), \mathbf{Y}(r)].$$

By assumption $(\mathbf{X}, \mathbf{Y}) \geqslant \mathbf{O}$; $0 \leqslant r < R$; the coefficients of $(\mathbf{X}, \mathbf{Y})$ are rational functions of r, and define

$$[\tilde{\mathbf{J}}(r), \tilde{\mathbf{K}}(r)] = \det [\mathbf{B} - (1 + r)\mathbf{A}][\mathbf{X}(r), \mathbf{Y}(r)]$$

$$\tilde{\mathbf{Q}} = \begin{bmatrix} \tilde{\mathbf{J}} & \tilde{\mathbf{K}} \\ \mathbf{O} & \mathbf{I}_{(n-m)} \end{bmatrix}.$$

$\tilde{\mathbf{Q}}$ is then a matrix consisting of polynomials fulfilling at least axioms (b), (c1) (apart possibly from $q_i^j(0) = 1$ if $q_i^j \neq 0$), and (in part) (e). Since $\mathbf{X}(-1)\mathbf{B}_1^1 + \mathbf{Y}(-1)\mathbf{B}_2^1 = \mathbf{I}_{(m)}$, $\mathbf{B}_1^1$ and $\tilde{\mathbf{K}}\mathbf{B}_2^1$ must, apart from permutations, be diagonal, if we add the assumption $\mathbf{X}(-1) \geqslant \mathbf{O}$, $\mathbf{Y}(-1) \geqslant \mathbf{O}$ (see axioms (a) and (c)). Hence all partially all-productive systems fulfil some of the axioms of section 12, and, by adding additional assumptions the set of partially all-productive systems is narrowed down to the set of pure fixed-capital systems.

However, as has been shown by means of an example, partially all-productive systems need not have the structure of pure fixed-capital systems in that primary and secondary processes cannot necessarily be distinguished, although it is one of the intuitively most plausible characteristics of fixed capital that there are processes producing finished goods by means of finished goods alone. Moreover, it had to be assumed that truncations of partially all-productive systems were also partially all-productive.

Let us therefore start from the other side and assume that the partially all-productive system can be stripped by means of truncations of all commodities that are not separately producible and of a corresponding number of processes, that the resulting system $(\mathbf{A}_1^1, \mathbf{B}_1^1)$ remains all-productive, and that we even have $[\mathbf{B}_1^1 - (1 + r)\mathbf{A}_1^1)]^{-1} > \mathbf{O}$ for $-1 \leqslant r < R$, therefore $(\mathbf{B}_1^1)^{-1} > \mathbf{O}$. This implies $\mathbf{B}_1^1 = \mathbf{I}_{(m)}$ (Schefold, 1978b). If the truncated processes and commodities are now brought back one by one and not in blocks, one can arrive at a pure fixed-capital system where each group consists of one machine only, if it is assumed that the commodity 'grafted' on to a truncation $\overline{\mathbf{A}}$, $\overline{\mathbf{B}}$ is produced by one of the processes in $\overline{\mathbf{A}}$, $\overline{\mathbf{B}}$, and used by the new process; symbolically

$$\overline{\mathbf{A}} \rightarrow \overline{\mathbf{B}}$$

becomes, through adding a commodity (old machine) and a process using it which produces the same finished good as the other processes in the group:

$$[\overline{\mathbf{A}}_{\bullet}] \rightarrow [\overline{\mathbf{B}}_{\bullet}]$$

One machine here does nót mean that we must imagine that physically only one instrument is used in each group. A complex of several 'machines' can enter the primary process and they can then grow older together. Provided there is no trade of old machines between groups, the complex of machines can remain united, and there is no need to determine the relative prices of the components of the complex in secondary processes since there is no trade, while the components have separate prices in so far as they enter the primary process as separate finished goods. This type of fixed-capital system has been examined by several authors, and by myself (Schefold, 1974).

Our considerations suggest that the axiomatic system set out in section II.12 describes a structure that lies in between the simplest type of fixed capital where old machines form a complex such that the relative prices of its components cannot be determined, and the abstract partially all-productive systems. The axiomatic system is identical neither with the latter (as has been shown by means of the example in this section) nor with the former, as follows from the very first example of section 12 where it was possible after all to determine relative prices of a complex of machines – see also the first example in the Note to section II.12, which showed that axiom ($^*f^*$) was independent of the other axioms. To start from partially all-productive systems as in this section would have meant renouncing a construction of fixed-capital systems with their characteristic distinction between primary and secondary processes and retaining only that between finished and intermediate goods. To start from fixed-capital systems where relative prices of machines in a complex within a group are not distinguished means accepting an unnecessary restriction. I do not know whether the axiomatic system proposed here is the most appropriate, i.e. whether it is the most general which retains the specific features of fixed capital from the point of view of the technical structure of production and which exhibits the desirable economic properties of positive prices, falling wage curve, etc. However, when I worked it out, attempts by trial and error seemed to show that the axiomatic system that I had chosen eventually represented an interesting compromise between generality on the one hand (in the sense of capturing as many systems as possible in the set of those that share the main properties of fixed-capital systems) and specificity on the other (in the sense of a construction of fixed-capital systems from groups of processes that each employ one machine).

Only further research can show whether the compromise was really a good one. The structure of joint-production systems is generally not well understood. Here, the specific form of the axioms does not allow the *time structure* inherent in fixed-capital systems to be easily recognized. 'Time structure' has been emphasized in the 'neo-Austrian' literature on capital theory following Hicks (Hicks, 1970). It has been made explicit by means of the concept of the 'integrated processes' in section II.14, and has been applied to an example involving machines employed in one group, but it is more – indeed trivially – obvious if one machine is operated in each group. The powers of $1 + r$ in the coefficients of the $\mathbf{Q}$ matrix express the element of time in the more general case, but a further analysis of the rather complicated time structure in cases with not just one machine per group in the $\mathbf{Q}$ matrix would be desirable.

18b Fixed Capital and Joint Production in a Growing Economy

This book is primarily concerned with the theory of prices of a system in a given state of reproduction, and not with the growth and change of that system. Some very brief remarks on accumulation and technical progress are nevertheless appropriate. They will be inserted here, before we turn to land, because growth with scarce (not produced) resources requires a specific kind of structural change: the output of fully cultivated lands stagnates (to the extent that there is no growth of productivity) while expansion takes place either on 'marginal' land, which pays no rent, or on rent-paying land if a more productive technique gradually replaces one that is less productive.

If this particular kind of structural change is excluded – we shall turn to it later – there remains balanced growth as the simplest prototype of a process of accumulation. This has already been considered. A uniform rate of growth leads – if it is equal to the rate of profit – to duality relationships, which are pleasing to the theorist.

However, *structural change* is a permanent feature of the process of accumulation because the composition of output alters. It may have two distinct causes:

(a) The *composition of demand* for consumption goods changes with rising incomes. This is not a difficult problem because the change is, by its nature, smooth. To the extent that the rise of incomes is steady, a gradual and foreseeable rise of workers in low-wage groups to higher-wage groups with the associated consumption pattern takes place, and a similar transformation will be observed with capitalist (rentier) consumption. It is, in my view, more in the spirit of the classical tradition to express the shift thus in terms of a migration between social groups than in terms of income elasticities of demand of individuals (Engel curves), but the smooth character of the transition is preserved either way and could be formalized within our model in a variety of manners. A particular phase of development could, for example, be characterized by stagnant production of bread and expanding production of meat. The output of any period has to contain the increments of the means of production of the next period. Although the rates of growth of the different sectors are therefore different, the rate of profit remains uniform. That is to say, we should still feel entitled to define prices of production on the basis of a uniform rate of profit since market prices could not deviate much from these prices of production as centres of gravitation in a tranquil environment where the structural change is foreseen.

The classical image of the economy is thus preserved: the rate of profit is uniform and considerably exceeds the average of the (differing) rates of growth of the various sectors. Because of analytical convenience, undue emphasis has been given to balanced growth lately. Ricardo did not assume a 'steady state' or 'golden age', with agriculture expanding at the same rate as manufacturing. Structural change was, in itself, no obstacle to regarding the system of prices of production as a long-period equilibrium. Only the difficulties with neoclassical representation of long-period equilibria and the formal elegance of duality relationships have led to the recent emphasis on 'steady states' and an erroneous association of Sraffa's theory with activity analysis.

(b) However, such structural change presupposes also *technical progress* and changing methods of production – the rise of income per head is tied to the rise of productivity. Here we have to face a more fundamental difficulty: technical progress can be thought to proceed fairly steadily at a highly *aggregated* level. Countless improvements (and possibly also a number of mistaken changes) of methods of production result on average in a continuous rise in the productivity of labour. Hence it is possible to discuss the macroeconomic interaction between changes in the level of productivity and the rate of growth, the capital–output ratio and the rate of profit, etc., and to analyse the conditions under which a certain level of employment can be maintained, or technological unemployment and a crisis are introduced.

However, technical progress sometimes comes in the form of a *'shock'* at a disaggregated, *sectoral* level. It is true that, even at the level of the firm, one form of technical progress consists in the gradual intensification of labour, but others result from fundamental changes of methods of production involving changes in raw materials and machines. It is impossible to represent technical progress in this sense through a gradual change of input–output coefficients in a Sraffa system, e.g. by replacing constant input–output coefficients by input–output coefficients that diminish steadily at an exponential rate. The problem with this type of technical progress is precisely that e.g. labour is saved by building larger ships and by replacing wood and sails by steel and engines so that some input coefficients rise and others fall; the problem in the analysis of prices is then to determine whether such changes lead to reductions in the cost of production and whether the reduction in the cost of production corresponds to a real gain in some sense. Technical progress may be represented in terms of falling input–output coefficients in input–output analysis in the sense of Leontief where 'sectors' are highly aggregated, but not in a Sraffa type of model, which should explain prices of commodities. The analysis of switches of techniques between known methods of production which result in the thought experiment where we change the rate of profit can be used to represent technical progress if we ask whether a newly invented method of production can be introduced at a given rate of profit. We are then not talking about a thought experiment, but we try to determine the conditions under which a new method is *eligible* to be introduced (falling prices of finished goods in terms of the wage rate, rise in the real wage, surplus profits accruing to the entrepreneurs who were first to use the new method). The question is then whether we are entitled to say that the system incorporating the newly invented method represents the state to which the economy will be tending without further change or whether the invention must be regarded as a shock that causes other alterations, in particular of distribution and the level of employment.

There are several methods to deal with the problem of *'transition'* in the face of changing methods of production. It is often said that transitions cannot be discussed at all because the processes involved are too complicated. It is certainly true that discussion of processes of transition requires a change in the level of abstraction.

There is, to begin with, no general theory of *market prices* and of quantity changes outside 'normal' conditions. As a matter of fact, the concept of 'price of production' was invented and opposed to 'market price' precisely because we know of fundamental laws only in regard to long-period equilibria, while the circumstances governing market prices are diverse and vary with the particular situation under consideration. It is therefore argued that we should only 'compare' different positions of the economy.

It is true that we cannot do more than 'compare' positions in those cases where we know that the transition from one equilibrium to the other necessarily involves changes in parameters such that the new equilibrium shifts or is unstable. This objection to the attribution of a causal direction in the comparison of equilibria is frequently valid when we compare two macroeconomic growth paths, say one with, the other without a tax on profits. Since the imposition of the tax may well affect the inducement to invest, it is likely that the system will, after the imposition of the tax, differ from the original state with respect to not only the tax, but also the level of activity, income and employment.

The comparison of equilibria therefore yields causal relationships only if such effects are not present because the conditions defining the equilibrium are sufficiently stable. Traditional neoclassical theory was based on such forces since the theory of utility started from properties of individuals that were thought to be invariant to changes of the equilibrium position.

It is clear that an equilibrium is not stable in this sense whenever a speculative element comes in through changes of expectations, which in turn affect the equilibrium position. It is then at best possible to describe what happens in terms of a process, and sometimes only a very broad description is appropriate: 'The stock market collapsed' or 'The discovery of gold mines led to a boom'.

This does not mean that we should forbid any attribution of a causal significance to comparisons wholesale. If we compare a Sraffa system at two different rates of profit, we should in most cases not interpret the comparison as a change that might take place in an economy, but if we compare two situations in which the labour requirements differ in all sectors by 5 per cent, we may say that an intensification of labour is a plausible kind of change that may take place and that may, but need not, be accompanied by a corresponding rise of the real wage. Or we may follow Ricardo in safely concluding from a comparison of Sraffa systems that a tax on rent falls on landlords (because land is non-basic, as we shall see), whereas it is not so clear whether a tax on profits falls on capitalists without further repercussions.

The difficulty in analysing technical progress is that it is not clear *a priori* whether or not the change is of a character that violates stability conditions. However, there are methods for analysing it at a sectoral level in terms of input–output coefficients and yet preserving a smoothness in the transitions such that in some – but not all – cases we may regard one equilibrium as the 'beginning', the other as the 'end' of a process of transition of which we do not – and need not – know the details.

The least complicated situation is one in which – assuming single-product industries – two methods of production for the same commodity coexist in time, an old and a new. There are then, as we have seen, two vectors of prices of production; we shall show that the surplus profits are in some way analogous to rent. *The socially necessary technique is*, following Ricardo (though he did not use the term), *that which can be generalized to satisfy demand at the corresponding price of production.* It is therefore the new technique, if technical progress takes place in industry, and it is the technique employed on the no-rent land in the case of differential rent.

However, if we want to focus on the process of transition, we may also say that the socially necessary technique (in the sense of Marx) is – at any time – a *moving average* between the conditions of production corresponding to the old and those corresponding to the new method so that prices of production during the transition are derived from an average of the old and of the new method. The weights to be used in forming the average are themselves to be derived at any time from the percentage of output that is produced by firms having already made the transition and those that have not.

It is likely that methods change in several industries, and it is characteristic for technical progress that these changes are related in technological waves.

We generalize to joint production. If $\mathbf{A}, \mathbf{B}, \mathbf{l}$ is the system of the past and $\bar{\mathbf{A}}, \bar{\mathbf{B}}, \bar{\mathbf{l}}$ that of the future, the 'average system' is

$$(1 + r)(\mathbf{D}\mathbf{A} + \bar{\mathbf{D}}\bar{\mathbf{A}})\mathbf{p} + w(\mathbf{D}\mathbf{l} + \bar{\mathbf{D}}\bar{\mathbf{l}}) = (\mathbf{D}\mathbf{B} + \bar{\mathbf{D}}\bar{\mathbf{B}})\mathbf{p},$$

where $\mathbf{D}, \bar{\mathbf{D}}$ are diagonal matrices representing weights for each process such that $\mathbf{D} + \bar{\mathbf{D}} = \mathbf{I}$ ($\mathbf{I}$ unit matrix), and each d_i^i indicates the share of production still produced according to the old, and $\bar{d}_i^i$ that produced according to the new method in industry i. These prices of production, although derived from a moving average, may still be regarded as centres of gravitation in that market prices will deviate from them to the extent that there are temporary discrepancies of supply and demand.

It becomes possible in this way to visualize smooth transitions with a changing technological structure in the course of accumulation – provided the macroeconomic conditions (in particular regarding the balance of investment and saving, and the given state of distribution) are met.

For reasons of simplicity and conceptual clarity one may prefer the definition of 'socially necessary technique', which I would like to associate with the name of Ricardo since the formula for prices of production derived from 'average conditions' above seems to blur the concept of rate of profit and of price of production. But the Marxian definition clearly represents a generalization from that given by Ricardo. Surplus profits and losses are implicit in it. The equation

$$(1 + r)(d_i^i\mathbf{a}_i\mathbf{p} + \bar{d}_i^i\bar{\mathbf{a}}_i\mathbf{p}) + w(d_i^i l_i + \bar{d}_i^i \bar{l}_i) = (d_i^i\mathbf{b}_i + \bar{d}_i^i\bar{\mathbf{b}}_i)\mathbf{p}$$

can be rewritten as

$$(1 + r)\bar{\mathbf{a}}_i\mathbf{p} + w\bar{l}_i + \bar{\rho}_i = \bar{\mathbf{b}}_i\mathbf{p}$$

where

$$\bar{\rho}_i = -\frac{d_i^i}{\bar{d}_i^i} \{[\mathbf{b}_i - (1 + r)\mathbf{a}_i]\mathbf{p} - wl_i\}$$

represents the surplus profit $\bar{\rho}_i$ made in industry i by using the new method, and

$$\rho_i = -\frac{\bar{d}_i^i}{d_i^i} \{[\bar{\mathbf{b}}_i - (1 + r)\bar{\mathbf{a}}_i]\mathbf{p} - w\bar{l}_i\}$$

the losses made in industry i ($\rho_i < 0$) if the old method is used at prices corresponding to the average:

$$(1 + r)\mathbf{a}_i\mathbf{p} + wl_i + \rho_i = \mathbf{b}_i\mathbf{p}.$$

Since the Marxian definition of the socially necessary technique is not all that close to the approach that we have pursued so far, we do not analyse the conditions under which the new technique in fact yields positive surplus profits and the old one losses relative to normal profits, i.e. $\bar{\rho}_i > 0$, $\rho_i < 0$; rather, we return to the 'Ricardian' approach where the socially necessary technique in manufacturing is the latest technique available, and where prices are defined accordingly.

If there are two single-product techniques $\mathbf{A}, \mathbf{l}$ and $\bar{\mathbf{A}}, \bar{\mathbf{l}}$, and if it is possible to get from technique $\mathbf{A}, \mathbf{l}$ on to $\bar{\mathbf{A}}, \bar{\mathbf{l}}$, with $\mathbf{A}, \mathbf{l}$ and $\bar{\mathbf{A}}, \bar{\mathbf{l}}$ differing with respect to several methods, there must be a *chain of technologies* $\mathbf{A}^{(t)}, \mathbf{l}^{(t)}$; $t = 1, ..., T$; with $(\mathbf{A}^{(1)}, \mathbf{l}^{(1)}) = (\mathbf{A}, \mathbf{l})$ and $(\mathbf{A}^{(T)}, \mathbf{l}^{(T)}) = (\bar{\mathbf{A}}, \bar{\mathbf{l}})$ such that technologies t and $t + 1$ differ only with respect to one method of production. The price vectors associated with technologies t will then fall monotonically in terms of the wage rate as t increases:

$$\hat{\mathbf{p}}_t > \hat{\mathbf{p}}_{t+1}$$

and surplus profits are earned in those methods of production where technology $t + 1$ differs from t if prices $\hat{\mathbf{p}}_t$ are used for evaluation; *vice versa*, losses obtain in the same process if it is evaluated at prices $\hat{\mathbf{p}}_{t+1}$. If the analysis is executed in terms of joint-production systems, the existence of surplus profits and losses furnishes the sole criterion of 'progress'; the price vector need not fall.

Whichever procedure is chosen – the 'Marxian moving average' or the 'Ricardian chain of socially necessary techniques' – there is no presumption in either case that the processes of transition can be captured in detail. However, it is contended that their essential features (surplus profits and losses as driving forces) can thus be understood.

It is to be noted that technical progress usually appears as a series of related switches of methods of production. This is illustrated by the possibility of *'trigger effects'* (Morishima, 1964): if a new method is invented in, say, the first industry of a single-product system, its introduction at a given rate of profit may trigger off switches in other industries to other methods of production that had already been known, but that had previously not been profitable. For instance, it may pay to install heat pumps for the heating of houses as soon as a cheap method for producing electricity has been introduced. The heat pump may have been known prior to the invention, but fossil fuels had to be used as long as electricity remained expensive.

Another reason for technical progress not usually being linked to one industry alone is that inventions are based on advances in technical knowledge, and any important advance may give rise to several applications.

If technological development thus has to be thought of as a sequence of waves of method changes, with switches grouped in clusters linked by related advances in knowledge and trigger effects, the analysis in terms of comparisons of 'blueprints' of technologies may be misleading if insufficient attention is paid to the interaction between the dynamics of the investment implied by a wave of technical changes and macro-economic conditions. For instance, technological unemployment caused by rationalization may have unforeseeable repercussions on the growth process of the economy as a whole.

But here we are more interested in what happens at a sectoral level, where there is also an interaction between technical progress, investment and profitability.

We may illustrate it by means of the problem of capital gains and losses. If a method employing fixed capital in an industry is replaced by a new one, so that the price of the finished good in terms of the wage rate is lowered, the machines of the old method will survive for a while even if no new ones of the old type are produced any more. The dynamic of the transition from the old to the new method may now be quite different depending on how the old machines are treated. Their cost of production may be written off so that they can be used for continued production of the finished good at prices of the new method; the old machine will then yield a quasi-rent (PCMC, sec. 91). Or the old method and the new method coexist for a while at market prices close to the old prices of production. In the former case, unused amortization funds and quasi-rents, in the latter case the surplus profits are available to finance the investment in the spreading of the new method. Whether they will so be used is an open question; the answer is crucial if one wants to know something about the speed and the character of the transition.

It is well known that the existence of surplus profits associated with innovations may lead to cumulative effects at the sectoral (but also at the macroeconomic) level if they are used to generate further advances in knowledge, further inventions and innovations. As a result, technical progress may proceed much faster in some sectors than in others. The corresponding relative cheapening of products facilitates the expansion of the market for the firms participating in the process and this in turn leads to economies of scale. *Cumulative processes* in the sense of a regional concentration of production with positive external effects will also follow. The forces of competition that otherwise make for greater homogenization and uniformity in respect to prices, wage rates, rates of profit, qualities of commodities, may thus also lead to differentiation and growing disparities.

This, together with the macroeconomic instability of the process of accumulation has led some authors (notably Robinson, 1979) to conclude that the classical analysis in terms of prices of production, based on a uniform rate of profit, and regarded as 'centres of gravitation' was irrelevant to the modern world. It is certainly true that a description of the phases of processes of transition between different methods of production requires a change of abstraction and the introduction of considerations with which we are not concerned in the other parts of this book. But it should have become clear that the comparison of different equilibrium positions of the economy represents a valid start for each such analysis and that we can go beyond mere comparisons and infer something about cause and effect by looking at the surplus profits and losses implied. Finally, the two methods (of 'moving average' and of 'chains') are useful tools in that the first allows the transition to be viewed as smooth and the second allows technological changes to be seen not as isolated events, but as related.

The discussion of accumulation and technical progress has mainly been confined to fixed-capital or even single-product systems. This was necessary because the analysis of switches of technique with perfectly general joint-production systems had been based on balanced growth, which is a convenient and sometimes inevitable assumption, but not satisfactory in a discussion of technical progress.

The next section is dedicated to the problem of land, which is also incompatible with steady growth (except on the basis of very artificial assumptions).

19 'Extensive' and 'Intensive' Diminishing Returns

Definitions

Unproduced means of production that, by 'being in short supply, enable their owners to obtain a rent' (PCMC, sec. 85) can be described as goods that leave every process in exactly the same condition as they enter it and that are nowhere produced. They present far greater difficulties than either pure consumption goods, which are also non-basics but are produced and not used in production, or permanent capital goods, which also leave the production process as they enter it but are produced.

One might think it impossible that means of production do not change at all in the process of production. For example, mines are gradually exhausted as they are exploited and even agricultural land is improved or deteriorates in the course of cultivation. But the capital invested or disinvested in land must, at least conceptually, be distinguished from the abstract space or territory occupied by that capital. This is clear in the case of buildings occupying space. The rent paid for the building should be split into true rent for the occupation of space and amortization for the building to be paid until the building is abandoned. The separation of both elements is often not easy because buildings are 'machines' of rather constant efficiency and a potentially very long life. The uncertainties surrounding the notion of a lifetime of a building are one of the reasons for the creeping-in of speculative elements in the theory of rent, which ought to be, one might believe, as static as its object, land. The distinction between rent and amortization is nevertheless a matter of the logic of the market, not a fancy of the theorist, and it will here be presupposed.

We similarly assume that improvements in agriculture are also to be treated as investments in fixed capital. This concerns not only the digging of drains and the planting of trees, but even fertilization. Field rotation should not be regarded as a transformation of the land either. We shall not say that the seeding of clover transforms clover-bearing land into land suitable for wheat, but rather that one type of land is suitable for the combined (joint) production of clover and wheat, which are planted alternately in successive years, in much the same way as a confectioner produces his outputs jointly, by using the oven alternately to bake either tarts or cakes. Only mines seem to introduce a new element because, unlike ploughing or building, the process of exploiting a mine cannot be repeated on the same spot after its exhaustion. However, we abstract here, in accordance with an age-old deplorable practice of our civilization, from permanent and irreversible changes such as exhaustion of mines, first because classical theory is functional and descriptive, not normative, secondly because the exhaustion of a mine, if it is to be treated (cf sec 19b), should be regarded as the depletion of a capital stock used in conjunction with the land as the space occupied by the mine.

But, in order to simplify, we shall also assume that only circulating capital is used on the land; the problem of singling out amortization, which is frequently almost impossible to solve in reality, does not then arise. There are many techniques that can potentially be used on land. Each *'type' of land* is assumed to be *homogeneous*, that is to say, each technique that can be used anywhere on any given land can be used in each of its parts with the same physical efficiency. Land is then also said to be of the same *'kind'* or *'quality'*. Two types of land are different only if they differ in physical productivity with respect to at least one technique (say, heavy as opposed to light ploughs) and one product (say, wheat). In defining types of land one has thus to take all existing techniques into consideration. If, for instance, an invention is made that renders absolutely flat land more productive, two acres of land – one flat and one hilly territory – that were classed as the same type of land according to previous uses and known possibilities will now have to be classed as different, independently of whether the new technique will actually be used on the flat acre of land (whether it will depends on prices, and these depend on the rate of profit). The understanding of most of what follows depends on the understanding of this point. *Transport costs* and *building regulations* are institutional forms differentiating types of land; they, too, are 'techniques' defining types of land, in that eight-storey buildings are allowed in one area, three-storey buildings in another. One of the main results of rent theory (to be derived presently) is that one or, at most, two techniques for the production of one commodity can coexist on the same land, while most land is usually completely specialized. Building regulations, which are another important cause for speculation, often only legalize an existing tendency for specialization. The model assumes, however, that such regulations can be considered as given, and that they define a type of land in the same way as physical characteristics do.

Formally, good k is an unproduced good or mean of production ('land' for short), if $\mathbf{a}^k = \mathbf{b}^k = (\lambda_1^k, ..., \lambda_n^k)'$. A typical equation reads (λ denotes 'land'):

$$(1 + r)(\mathbf{a}_i\mathbf{p} + \lambda_i^k p_\lambda) + wl_i = b_i^j p_j + \lambda_i^k p_\lambda$$

($\mathbf{a}_i$ is a vector of various inputs, b_i^j the crop produced).

It is more usual to write this equation as Mr Sraffa does,

$$(1 + r)\mathbf{a}_i\mathbf{p} + \lambda_i^k \rho_k + wl_i = b_i^j p_j,$$

with $\rho_k = rp_\lambda$ as the rent accruing to the owner of the land. The coefficient λ_i^k denotes the amount of land of type k that is required in process i to produce b_i^j units of commodity j. The normalization $\mathbf{e}'\mathbf{B} = \mathbf{e}'$ can be maintained, i.e. $\lambda_1^k + \cdots \lambda_n^k = 1$. Rent exists whether land is traded or not. If it is, its price is determined by capitalization of the rent at the current rate of interest and this price may be identified with the price entering the equations in the first form if we assume, for simplicity's sake, that the rate of profit and the rate of interest are the same.

Whichever expression is chosen, it is clear that rent and price of land cannot be determined before other prices are known. We shall show that land is a non-basic, even if its product enters the basic system.

To conclude these introductory remarks we note how the normalizations ·adopted in section II.1 have to be modified to allow for land.

Our theory of the basic system (sections 1–3) was based on the assumption $\det(\mathbf{B} - \mathbf{A}) \neq 0$ and on the normalization $\mathbf{e}'\mathbf{B} = \mathbf{e}'$. In order to keep the normalization and in order to show that the results of section II.1–3 apply to land, it is best to write the equations for land in the first form (where land appears both as an input and as an output) and to replace the input matrix $\mathbf{A}$ by $\bar{\mathbf{A}} = (1 + \bar{r})\mathbf{A}$, where $\det[\mathbf{B} - (1 + \bar{r})\mathbf{A}] \neq 0$. If one then transforms the rate of profit accordingly:

$$1 + r \to \frac{1 + r}{1 + \bar{r}},$$

all the results of sections 1–3 apply to the transformed system $(\bar{\mathbf{A}}, \mathbf{B}, \mathbf{l})$.

However, the transformation to integrated industries with the accompanying reduction to dated quantities of labour is not possible in the presence of land. Land as a non-basic has first to be eliminated. The first of the two reductions considered in sections II.4 and II.6 — that based on gross integrated industries — is impossible because $\det \mathbf{B} = 0$ if the second form is chosen, while $\mathbf{B}^{-1}\mathbf{A}$ has an eigenvector with eigenvalue of one if the first form is chosen, so that the series $\mathbf{l} + \mathbf{B}^{-1}\mathbf{A}\mathbf{l} + (\mathbf{B}^{-1}\mathbf{A})^2\mathbf{l} + \cdots$ does not converge. Similarly, the reduction to net integrated industries will not work because $\det (\mathbf{B} - \mathbf{A}) = 0$ if the first form is chosen while $\mathbf{l} + (\mathbf{B} - \mathbf{A})^{-1}\mathbf{A}\mathbf{l} + [(\mathbf{B} - \mathbf{A})^{-1}\mathbf{A}]^2\mathbf{l} + \cdots$ will not converge if the second form is chosen because there is also an eigenvector with an eigenvalue of minus one.

We now turn to the two main forms of rent and to the elimination of land as a non-basic.

(I) Differential Rent of the First Kind (DRI):

In the simplest case there is only one product grown on m different types of land. To begin with, we assume that only one, the last, is not in short supply while all the other land is fully cultivated. Then we get m equations, assuming that we now have m different types of land, each used in a separate process; together, say the first m:

$$
\begin{aligned}
(1+r)\mathbf{a}_1\mathbf{p} &+ \lambda_1^j\rho_1 &+ wl_1 &= b_1^j p_j \\
(1+r)\mathbf{a}_2\mathbf{p} &+ \lambda_2^2\rho_2 &+ wl_2 &= b_2^j p_j \\
&\vdots &\vdots \\
(1+r)\mathbf{a}_{m-1}\mathbf{p} &+ \lambda_{m-1}^{m-1}\rho_{m-1} &+ wl_{m-1} &= b_{m-1}^j p_j \\
(1+r)\mathbf{a}_m\mathbf{p} &+ &wl_m &= b_m^j p_j
\end{aligned}
$$

The last of these equations determines p_j, the others determine the $m - 1$ rents $\rho_\mu = rp_{\lambda\mu}$.

In order to understand why one particular land is not in short supply, assume tentatively that none of the land is in short supply, while no selection of $m - 1$ land is sufficient to produce the total output required. That is to say, assume that each of the m lands is cultivated partially. The assumption leads immediately to a nonsensical conclusion, for rents would still occur as an expression of surplus profits obtained on superior land at the given rate of profit, so that part of the rent-yielding lands would be cultivated and part not. This is impossible whether land is owned by landlords or by the producers. If it is owned by producers or free, producers will crowd into rent-yielding lands and appropriate the rents as surplus profits. If lands are owned by landlords, they will compete for farmers, letting out lands at low rents and offering farmers an opportunity to produce at extra profits until all rent-bearing lands are occupied and rents have been bid up to absorb all surplus profits. Hence the fact that one and only one of the cultivated lands will appear not to be in short supply – the others either being fully cultivated or not cultivated at all.

Since rents depend on the rate of profit, it is not only not feasible to order the sorts of land according to productivity before the distribution between profits and wages is known, but even impossible to tell beforehand which land will not be in short supply. This complicates the choice of techniques as we shall see (section II.20a), but it may already be said that the equation for the land paying no rent enters the basic system if the product of the land is a basic commodity.

As for the choice of this land, suffice it to say at present that production is expanded by cultivating ever new types of land, and this expansion at constant returns to scale on each land and for each technique must satisfy two requirements: output must grow at the required rate and the lands must be chosen in such a combination that (in ideal circumstances) costs of production are lowest for the cultivated no rent land. The sequence of expansion seems to define an order of 'fertility', but the ordering of the land really depends on the rate of profit. Output rises continuously, while the new areas come gradually under cultivation. Whenever a new area has been covered fully, prices and some rents rise.

All this is rather obvious if the produce of the land is non-basic. If it is basic, a different equation (that of the new no-rent land) enters the basic system with each change of the no-rent land in the course of expansion. If the basic processes represent a single-product system, all prices in terms of the wage rate will rise with this change of technique, for they must all either rise or fall according to theorem 18.1, but if they fell, the technique would have been feasible for a lower level of output and would therefore have been introduced before, for reasons of profitability. The transition from the utilization of land m as marginal land to that of land $m + 1$ with rising output can thus be analysed by observing that the replacement of process m by process $m + 1$ in the standard system operates like a 'reversed technical progress' or − in Ricardo's terminology − an increase in the 'difficulty of production'.

The formal analogy between the transition from one no-rent land to the next and the return from a superior technique to an inferior one at a given rate of profit thus entails that the wage rate falls in terms of any commodity standard (theorem 18.1).

Further, we have proved that surplus profits are earned by those entrepreneurs who adopt the 'new' superior method, while 'old' prices of the inferior technique are still ruling (theorem 18.2a). Applied to the transition from land m to land $m + 1$ this means that 'surplus profits' arise in the use of the process on land m as soon as land $m + 1$ had entered the basic system and determines the prices of basics, but these 'surplus profits' now accrue as rents to the owners of land m. The equations now are (with 'new' prices denoted by $\tilde{\mathbf{p}}$):

$$(1 + r)\mathbf{a}_1\tilde{\mathbf{p}} + \tilde{w}l_1 + \lambda_1^1\tilde{\rho}_1 = b_1^j\tilde{p}_j$$

$$\cdots\cdots$$

$$(1 + r)\mathbf{a}_m\tilde{\mathbf{p}} + \tilde{w}l_m + \lambda_m^m\tilde{\rho}_m = b_m^j\tilde{p}_j$$

$$(1 + r)\mathbf{a}_{m+1}\tilde{\mathbf{p}} + \tilde{w}l_{m+1} = b_{m+1}^j\tilde{p}_j.$$

It can be shown (see section II.18) that the price of the product rises more than all other prices since the reverse is true for technical progress; the agricultural product becomes more expensive in terms of all other commodities.

From a formal point of view, it is fairly obvious (and can be shown by means of examples) that not all rents on lands $1, \ldots, m - 1$ will rise as output and its price rise because the change in *relative* prices may affect different lands unequally so that an existing 'order of fertility' of different lands may in principle be changed not only through changes of the rate of profit but also through changes in output.

However, neither effect is likely to be observed in practice in pure form. Changes in the uniform rate of profit are only conceptual experiments. And the growth of output is, in real systems, accompanied by technical progress, with more important effects on relative prices. The methods used in agriculture, on the other hand, are usually rather similar for the production of one and the same commodity. Inferior land often requires more seed corn, more labour, more machinery and more space per unit of output so that rents are, after all, not unlikely to rise with the price of the output. Ricardo's insistence on an order of fertility was not unfounded as an empirical generalization, but as a theoretical postulate.

As an example outside agriculture for this type of rent (DRI) we mention the surplus profits obtained on a patented cheap method of production that allows a restricted group of entrepreneurs to produce at lower costs than all other manufacturers in the same business during the period for which the patent is granted and on the assumption that the privileged entrepreneurs are unable or unwilling to supply the whole of the market. The patent derives a definite value from the capitalization of the surplus profit.

(II) Differential Rent of the Second Kind (DRII)

Mobility and competition ensure that rent is uniform on land of given quality. Yet, it is possible that more than one technique for the production of the same commodity is used on one land. To see this assume that land is of only one type; we write λ_i for the amount of land of this type used in process i. Two techniques can then determine rent ρ and price p_j simultaneously without the intervention of a 'no-rent land'.

$$(1 + r)\mathbf{a}_1\mathbf{p} + wl_1 + \lambda_1\rho = b_1^j p_j$$
$$(1 + r)\mathbf{a}_2\mathbf{p} + wl_2 + \lambda_2\rho = b_2^j p_j.$$

Assume first for simplicity that j is non-basic and does not enter its own production. Write:

$$k_i = (1 + r)\mathbf{a}_i\mathbf{p} + wl_i$$

for the unit cost of production and normalize $b_1^j = b_2^j = 1/2$ to get

$$k_1 + \lambda_1\rho = \frac{p_j}{2}$$

$$k_2 + \lambda_2\rho = \frac{p_j}{2}.$$

Rent and price are positive if $k_i < k_j$ implies $\lambda_j < \lambda_i$, since $\rho = (k_1 - k_2)/(\lambda_2 - \lambda_1)$ and since $p_j = 2(k_1\lambda_2 - k_2\lambda_1)/(\lambda_2 - \lambda_1)$. The two techniques are compatible if one is relatively more capital-intensive, the other more land-intensive (given r).

For a closed two-sector model, k_1, k_2 cannot be considered as given, but the price behaviour as a function of the rate of profit may be studied by means of a diagram. The graphic technique of sections 10 and 11 can be applied if land is treated as a joint product (Figures II.19.1a and b),

$$(1 + r)(a_1 p + \lambda_1\pi) + wl_1 = \tfrac{1}{2}p + \lambda_1\pi$$
$$(1 + r)(a_2 p + \lambda_2\pi) + wl_2 = \tfrac{1}{2}p + \lambda_2\pi$$

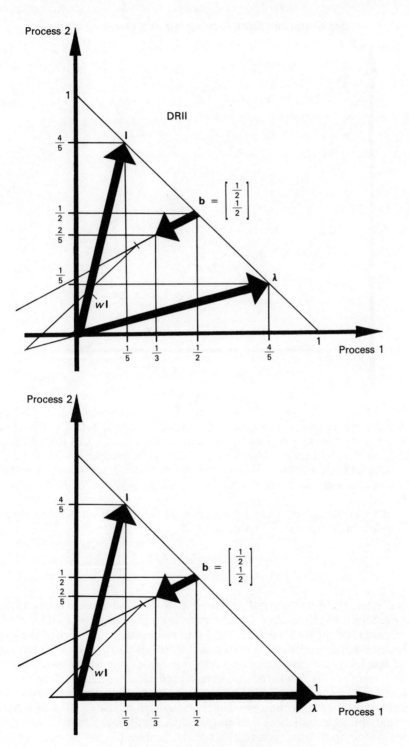

Figure II.19.1a and II.19.1b

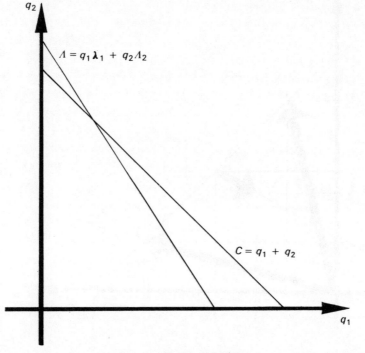

Figure II.19.2

with $p + \pi = 1$, $r\pi = \rho$, $l_1 + l_2 = 1$, $a_1 + a_2 < 1$, $\lambda_1 + \lambda_2 = 1$. For DRI, we have e.g. $\lambda_1 = 1$, $\lambda_2 = 0$. Land price and rent are positive at low rates of profit in both examples. The diagram cannot be used at $r = 0$.

Assuming constant returns to scale, we now determine to what extent the two techniques are to be used if total output is given (see PCMC, sec. 88).

Let total output be C and total area of land Λ. With activity levels q_1, q_2 we must have (see Figure II.19.2):

$$q_1\lambda_1 + q_2\lambda_2 = \Lambda$$
$$q_1 + q_2 = C.$$

As C rises, the more 'capital'-intensive and less land-intensive technique (the technique with smaller λ_i and higher a_i)[1] covers a greater and greater percentage of the total surface. Rent and price change only when the rise in output enforces the introduction of a third yet more 'capital'-intensive and less land-intensive technique that supersedes one of the two others. DRII thus results from the successive application of more 'capital' — 'doses' of raw material and labour — to the same piece of land. In agriculture, the two techniques can be thought to be 'close' to each other, in that the inputs of both techniques differ only marginally. One then obtains the traditional picture of an intensification of cultivation. But the two techniques may also be radically different: we may think of the coexistence of traditional and modern farming methods which has been a persistent feature in some regions for a long time. Further, we mention two different types of housing in a geographically restricted urban area as an example outside argriculture. Ground rents are reflected in land values; the price of the product is – by an unfortunate confusion of terms – the rent requested for letting a unit of a building (a floor of offices, for example). The two techniques find a visible expression in the height of houses. The expansion of dwelling-space is effected by pulling down low houses and replacing them gradually by higher ones. The prices and rents stay constant as long as the same two techniques coexist; both rise when the transition to a third, more 'capital'-intensive and less land-intensive technique is made.

Specialization

Bearing the two basic patterns of DRI and DRII in mind, we consider heuristically more general cases; excluding multiple-product processes (joint production) – apart from land itself, of course. We want to find out how many techniques can coexist on a given number of lands when several heterogeneous products are produced. It will be seen that rent leads to a certain specialization of the land. We shall then examine the theoretical consequences of the introduction of land for the basic system in the general case in section II.20 while particular aspects will be discussed in section II.20a.

If, with agriculture, mining, forestry, tourism, etc., there are k types of products to be 'grown' on m types of land, they will allow up to $m + k$ different processes; not more. This is *enforced specialization*. It arises because there are k prices and m rents to be determined, which allows only $m + k$ equations (except at switchpoints and assuming other prices as given and determined by other equations).

Simple counting of equations does not suffice to determine the number t of processes used exactly if one does not know whether all land is in short supply or not. In fact, if $m = 1$ (one land), we have $t = k + m - 1 = k$ if the land is not in short supply because prices of k products are to be determined; we have $t = k + m = k + 1$ otherwise, if there is a positive rent to be determined along with the prices of k products.

Suppose now that all m lands, $m > 1$, are in short supply; we must then have $t = m + k$. If $(m, k) = (2, 2)$, it is not necessary for any product to be grown on either land by two different methods, for if there are two crops to be grown on two types of land, both in short supply, it may be that both products will be grown on both lands so that both rents will be positive and one technique is used for each product on each land. But it is also possible that each product is produced by means of two techniques on only one land. Whether specialization takes place or not depends here on the choice of techniques.

However, at least partial specialization must take place, even if the number of products k exceeds the number of lands m, as soon as the number of products and of goods are both at least equal to 2 and either or both exceed 2. If there are e.g. three products to be grown on two lands, one land will always appear to be unsuited for at least one of the crops. Except for flukes, no two crops can be grown together on more than two lands; we would have six equations for five unknowns if each crop was to be grown on both lands and if $k = 3$, $m = 2$.

The strict requirement of a uniform rate of profit and uniform rents thus enforces a certain specialization of the land (with single-product processes), in that it will look as if it was impossible to grow a certain crop on all lands. For if all crops were to be grown on all lands (no specialization at all), we should have mk processes, but there is room for only $m + k$ and $mk > m + k$ if $(m, k) \geqslant (2, 2)$.

A land is completely specialized if only one crop can be grown on it. If $m \gg k$ (say 100 lands, e.g. because transportation is taken into account, and, say, 15 agricultural and 5 other products, i.e. 20 commodities), at least $m - k$ lands (i.e. 80 or 80 per cent) will be completely specialized for single-product processes, since even the artificial assumption of having – wherever feasible – only two processes on one land leads only to k lands (here 20) being used doubly. Forty processes on 20 lands then determine 20 rents and the prices of all 20 products; the remaining 80 processes determine the rents of the remaining 80 lands, and on each of these lands only one crop can be grown.

To illustrate this further, assume that all k products are grown on a no-rent land (DRI). Each rent-paying land will then in general allow only one crop; exceptions indicate 'switchpoints' and do not even allow small variations in the rate of profit. Similarly, if all land is in short supply (DRII) (rent is to be paid everywhere) and if all products are grown on one of them, two products will be compatible on one other land while all the remaining lands will be completely specialized. It is intriguing to think that any pattern of enforced specialization may be changed completely by a simple change in the rate of profit!

Two applications may here be distinguished. First, the classical case determined in a less stylized form by Adam Smith: wheat, the 'leading produce' is grown on all lands (distinguished partly by natural qualities, partly by their distance from the centres of consumption) and all other crops are grown each on one land jointly with wheat (sheep in the North, legumes in the South, cattle in between); the hierarchy of rents is then primarily determined by the conditions of wheat production, and on several lands a second crop is grown apart from wheat.

At the other extreme, all land is specialized except one where all crops are grown together on one land, and one of them by means of two methods. This is the central land, the centre of a city, for example, with offices, housing, some industry, etc. The two techniques might be offices in sky-scrapers and old residential buildings. The higher the difference in 'capital' intensity between the high running costs (mainly amortization) of sky-scrapers and the low running costs of residential buildings (mainly maintenance), and the greater the difference in land intensity (office room provided per unit area of land), the greater the ground rent and hence the price of real estate according to our formula for rent with DRII above.

The coexistence of techniques leads to intensive rent. Here, we show in concrete terms how the rent of land may be given in the centre so that – to the extent that other functions of the city are also partly provided in the centre – the surrounding areas of the city must be specialized: there is an industrial area, several housing areas, a subordinate administrative centre, etc. It is clear that the demarcations between areas result to an important extent from political decisions and that the commodities in this market are not as homogeneous in reality as in the model. On the one hand, there is differentiation because of traffic conditions, noise, aesthetic considerations, etc. On the other, lower prices and rents in suburban areas are balanced by higher transportation costs in terms of money and time. But the point is that – in so far as there is homogeneity – the demarcations, once introduced, will reproduce themselves and appear to be rational, because, with given land values and prices for housing, it will be too expensive – and not even attractive – e.g. to move with ordinary houses into the subordinate administrative area, while it is forbidden to move conversely with offices into residential areas because that would tend to raise land prices. The mixture of functions in a traditional town can, to the distress of planners, not be reproduced on its outskirts and it tends to disappear in the centre itself with rising land prices.

The same examples will be taken up once more in section II.20a where we discuss them in a dynamic context. The various forms of specialization, which we have found by means of counting equations, result from the uniformity of prices and of the rate of profit and from the consequent uniformity of rent on each land.

Such specialization does not take place in the same way if the crops are joint products linked by technical production conditions such as rotating crops. One could still elaborate a theory of enforced specialization by classifying joint products into partly overlapping groups, but it is perhaps more instructive to consider the opposition between single-product systems on the one hand and systems where each process produces every good on the other.

We discuss the contrast by means of an example. Rotating crops are joint products despite the fact that the plants do not grow together in the same place at the same time, because the alternation increases the fertility of the soil and makes the production of the crops concerned technically interdependent. As we saw, a cycle of, say, wheat, clover and pasture applied on the same field in successive years makes these three crops and the cattle on the pasture joint products in a three-year period in the same way as different kinds of bread baked in the same oven are joint products of the oven in one morning.

If the period of production is shorter than the period of rotation, inputs and outputs can be dated and premultiplied by the appropriate power of $(1 + r)$ as was done for the integrated processes in the case of fixed capital. If wheat a_1^1 is planted in the first year, yielding wheat b_1^1 by means of labour l_1, and clover a_2^2, yielding clover b_2^2 by means of labour l_2, is planted in the second year in a two-year cycle, we get an equation of the following type:

$$(1 + r)^2 a_1^1 p_1 + (1 + r)a_2^2 p_2 + (1 + r)wl_1 + wl_2 + (1 + r)\lambda_1^1 \rho_1 + \lambda_2^1 \rho_1$$
$$= (1 + r)b_1^1 p_1 + b_2^2 p_2.$$

It has lately been suggested that this equation be derived from a combination of two processes of the following type (see Gibson and McLeod, 1980):

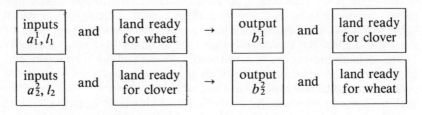

If the two corresponding price equations are added up (after premultiplying the first by $1 + r$), the same equation as before is reached, although we now have two types of land (land ready for wheat and land ready for clover) instead of one. By combining the processes, one land (land ready for clover) is eliminated with its rent so that the procedure is mathematically equivalent to ours. The procedure has its conceptual advantages, but care has to be taken to make it compatible with the proper definition of the type of land according not only to its actual, but also to its potential uses. The practical drawback is that rent does not vary with the stage of crop rotation in reality, whereas this is suggested by Gibson and McLeod's procedure.

My own approach has been to introduce fictitious commodities representing the substances that are added and subtracted from the soil through cultivation. The most important here would be nitrogen, which is lost in wheat production but recovered through nitrogen fixation of clover; we then get:

clover + labour + land → clover + (fixed nitrogen)

wheat + labour + land + (fixed nitrogen) → wheat.

This seems to confirm that improvements of land can be treated like fixed capital, because 'fixed nitrogen' can be eliminated from the equations like a machine. However, since 'fixed nitrogen' can by definition not become a saleable commodity and since more complicated biochemistry is involved anyway, it is better to reserve this traditional trick of introducing 'machines' for irrigation, dams and other long-lasting improvements of land. At any rate, we shall for simplicity assume here that the period of rotation is equal to the period of production.

Traditional farming leads to a great diversity of products, not only because of the advantages of crop rotation, but also because the farmer must keep himself busy throughout the year, i.e. allocate his labour time in many activities. Even so the intensity of his work and the return to his effort will vary during the year. There were other elements of joint costs to several outputs on a traditional farm. This diversity is being destroyed today because artificial fertilizers and insecticides reduce the incentive for rotation, because the adoption of labour-saving machinery changes the allocation of time and because the machines are often not suitable for more than one crop. All these effects taken together entail a reduction of the number of products grown on each farm. It is this that leads to regional specialization and the ruin of the landscape to which we were used.

As a matter of fact, the law of rent need not entail any specialization at all if all products are produced jointly on each land. For it remains true with joint production that the number t of processes used on m lands in short supply for the production of k products equals $m + k$, but fewer than mk processes are needed if each product is to be produced on each land. Suppose for instance that five products (three kinds of crops and two kinds of cattle) are being produced jointly on the no-rent land by means of five methods, or rather five systems of rotation, such that the relative prices are determined. For this the methods need differ only slightly so as to satisfy demand. The five products can then be grown jointly by means of similar or quite different methods on any number of rent-bearing lands and the diversity of products can on a small plot be the same as in a large region. The example is perhaps far-fetched, but suffices to illustrate the fact that – theoretically – no specialization at all needs to take place with joint production for any value of m and k; specialization is shown to result from the dissolution of social and ecological bonds leading to joint production.

Diversity

From a local point of view, land rents appear to limit heterogeneity. In most cases, only one of many potential uses of land is realized. In a historical perspective, this is the replacement of local diversity by specialization.

But just the opposite conclusion is reached if we look at the matter from a global point of view. Land is an obstacle to the adoption of a unique process of production in single-product industries on the lands within the system taken together. Whereas competition ideally allows only one method of production in, say, the steel industry (where land plays no role), several are allowed in agriculture, for example in the production of cattle, for there may be $m + 1$ methods of raising cattle in use if there are m types of land (humid land, arid land, mountainous land, etc.). The homogenization of the market process leads to a homogenization of the process of production, with single-product industries for each commodity on each type of land (excepting the intensive margin where two processes for the production of the same commodity may coexist) but not *across* lands.

If land is absent, only the most advanced method of production survives. If land is present, the border of each type of land indicates the area within which only one method is used in most cases. In this sense, land implies a *diversity* of the processes of production, which is to be contrasted with the specialization of each land.

All this merely follows from the counting of equations. The interesting questions regard cause and effect: is the payment of rent a consequence or a cause of this diversity? We shall turn to that question in section 20a, and we shall find that the answers differ for DRI and DRII.

To conclude this section, we have to consider a difficulty in the analysis of rent which sometimes leads to confusion. It is due to the fact that the area within which only one method is used does – in spite of special-ization – sometimes not coincide with the area of 'land of one type'. Several different crops (case I) or even the same crop by means of two different methods (case II) can be grown on a territory that must analytically be defined to represent one type of land, while it is also possible that the same crop is grown by the same method on a territory consisting of two analytically different types of land (case III) (see, however, Cartelier, 1979).

To see this, remember that a territory represents land of the same type if it is homogeneous with respect to the application of all known methods of production. Hence, of *all* commodities of the economy that can be grown on it, each can in principle be grown on it everywhere by means of the same method of production. It is thus possible that a product is actually grown on two lands by one and the same method so that the two lands appear as one, although they are analytically distinct because they differ in productivity with respect to at least one crop that can potentially be grown on them but that actually grows on some other land (case III). A forest growing over a known coal-field is different from an ordinary forest, even if the coal-field is not being exploited. The space occupied by a three-storey building in an area where ten-storey buildings are permit-ted is different from one in a zone where only three storey buildings are allowed.

Conversely, what is analytically one and the same type of land can look as if there were two lands because of differential rent of the second kind (case II), or even as if there were many because the land in question may be the one on which relative prices of different crops are determined so that each other land is specialized (case I; see the example above where all m crops were grown on the marginal n'th of n lands so that the remaining $n - 1$ lands were completely specialized).

Our theory of specialization thus implies that, for a land to be of one type, it is neither necessary nor sufficient that exactly one crop is grown on it by exactly one method, although the law of enforced specialization entails that this will be true for most lands if the numbers of land and products are large.

Note

1   Land-intensity, but not 'capital'-intensity, has here a meaning independent of the rate of profit.

19a A Digression on International Trade

In so far as DRI is only a reflection of surplus profits, it can be applied to problems of international trade.[1] A brief digression on this is warranted, not only because it enhances our understanding of DRI, but also because the subject merits special attention. We look at it from a peculiar point of view: that of specialization. The positive theory of international trade is, of course, beyond the scope of this book. But we may consider an instructive particular case by assuming that the flow of financial capital establishes a uniform rate of profit in and across all countries.

If it were not for surplus profit, it seems to follow from the theory of prices of production either that all countries are completely alike or that specialization with free trade in commodities takes place. To prove this (at a high level of abstraction, of course), we have to assume that the rate of profit is equalized between two countries that trade all the commodities they produce, and that all commodities are produced in both countries. If the rate of profit moves without loosing its uniformity, relative prices must also change and must be the same in both countries. This implies – if they are regular economies and single-product systems – that both countries have proportional price vectors at each rate of profit, hence proportional labour vectors and the same input–output matrix according to an obvious generalization of the corollary to theorems 3.1 and 3.2. The labour vectors can then be said to be equal in terms of efficiency units. Instead of trade equalizing factor prices, we here have trade at equal factor prices equalizing countries!

Although this implication of the classical approach (exogenons distribution) is contrary to the traditional view, I want to analyze it in some detail. A special case where two countries use the same technology, have the same rate of profit and differ only in that the labour vector of one country is proportionally greater than that of the other, with the wage just compensating for the difference, is not entirely fanciful: two countries with similar technologies can trade at equal rates of profit if a lower wage is paid in the country with the lesser productivity of labour in each industry.

Of course, methods of production will tend to be the same in two countries that both produce and trade n commodities at the same rate of profit even if the rate of profit is fixed, because $n + 1$ methods of production are – in regular systems – possible only at a switchpoint, and even then two different methods would be available for only one commodity in single-product systems, except by a further fluke.

'Being made equal' is, fortunately, not the inescapable fate of all countries. There are several simplified assumptions in the model, and the relaxation of any allows an escape from such a brutal conclusion: trade does not take place in all commodities, commodities and labour are not homogeneous, the rate of profit is not uniform, and even if it is it does not change sufficiently to cause shifts of relative prices that enforce either the adoption of identical methods of production in both countries or their complete specialization. Moreover, there are transport costs and

tariffs, and there are those causes that lead to a multiplicity of the processes of production of a good, even within one country, i.e. land rents.

Yet there remains some force in the argument of 'equalization'. In
order to put it into perspective, we attempt to explain the coexistence
of different methods of production in several countries in terms of
differentials of the rate of profit. The scenario is then as follows: there is
a uniform rate of profit, in that there is a uniform rate of return equal to
a global rate of interest in each country, and there is trade in many
commodities, but some processes of production are specific to specific
countries and accordingly give rise to surplus profits and losses. The
specificity of processes may be due to natural conditions (e.g. climate) or
to historical forces (e.g. skill of labour).

Suppose, for instance, that countries A and B are identical apart from
the steel industry, which is more productive in B because workers and
managers stick to old habits in A. We conclude from the results of
section 9b that the losses made in country A's steel industry are – if
country B's prices rule – in terms of labour commanded equal to the
labour-power of the workers who are not made redundant by keeping the
traditional method going. Since we assume $r = g$ in both countries, the
steel industry's loss in country A must be compensated for through a
subsidy, which will ultimately fall on workers if capitalists save and
workers spend. Conversely, if A's prices rule, the corresponding surplus
profits increase consumption in country B.

We may now imagine many countries, and each may have a different
method of production for some of the commodities. If the advanced
countries impose their prices, the backward ones will make losses and
will ultimately have to adapt. But the surplus profits that arise in the
opposite case with the use of new methods at old prices are analogous
to rents if differences in methods persist. In either case we can start
counting equations.

Before we do so, we have to reflect on the transitory nature of surplus
profits and losses. In so far as there is no limit to the level at which an
industry operates in any country, the choice of technique is not analogous to that involving scarce land. The share of production in each
industry is not determined between 'advanced' and 'backward' countries. Scarce land is the reason why different methods of production for
the same commodity can persist indefinitely as long as there is no
technical progress. The output to be produced on each land is then also
determined. If there is no land constraint, competition will allow only
one method to survive in each single-product industry within one
country. In the international context, competition also operates and
results, as we saw, eventually either in the equalization of countries or
in their specialization; the coexistence of countries with 'advanced
methods' and with 'backward methods' is a transitory phenomenon;
surplus profits and losses must disappear as long as they are not
converted into some kind of rent.

However, various forms of 'consolidation' of surplus profits and
losses are conceivable, and the 'transitory' situation of competition
between 'backward' and 'advanced' countries can be made semi-
permanent by introducing appropriate assumptions about growth.

A neat and convenient introductory hypothesis is that all differentials are reflected in different national wage levels of advanced countries, which persist because the methods of production cannot be transferred from one country to the other, although the rate of profit is uniform because of the mobility of financial capital. The amounts of labour available in each country operate as constraints analogous to land. Then we have, instead of m products to be grown on k lands, m commodities to be produced in k countries. Since the international rate of profit is given, there are $m + k - 1$ prices and real wage rates to be determined in terms of a given international monetary standard which leaves room for $m + k - 1$ processes.

The ensuing distribution of processes over countries is seen to be analogous to that of land by means of a simple reinterpretation: the assumption of wage rates alone making good for productivity differentials at a uniform rate of profit leads to a system that is formally equivalent to one where land rents make good for productivity differentials at a uniform rate of profit and zero wages, with a vector of land inputs equal to the labour vector. The equations

$$(1 + r)\mathbf{a}_i^{(j)}\mathbf{p} + w_{(j)}l_i^{(j)} = p_i,$$

where

$$\mathbf{a}_i^{(j)}, \, l_i^{(j)}$$

are the input vector of raw materials and labour to the production of commodity i in country j; $i = 1, ..., m$; $j = 1, ..., k$; and where $w_{(j)}$ is the wage rate of country j, are exactly analogous to the equation

$$(1 + r)\mathbf{a}_i^{(j)}\mathbf{p} + \rho_{(j)}\lambda_i^{(j)} = p_i$$

for production in one country with k types of land, rents $\rho_{(j)}$ and zero wages.

Below we shall say more about the analogy between land and labour; it is characteristic for the classical theory of value that the analogy can come up only in the international context, whereas it exists within each nation for the neoclassical approach. The reason is that classical theory assumes some kind of homogeneity of labour in each country, but heterogeneous labour for different countries. However, even in the theory of international trade the analogy is close only if full employment is assumed, as we shall see, and this assumption will be dropped in due course.

A simple, but not the most meaningful, solution is, as above, obtained if we assume a large country in which all m commodities are produced with wages at the subsistence level so that the wage rate is zero (the necessary wage is treated like the raw materials, see section II.2 on the 'splitting of the wage'). The rate of profit and prices are then determined. There is room for the production of only one commodity by means of one different process in each of the remaining countries, and each of these processes then determines one 'surplus wage rate' $w_{(j)}$. The 'large country' is analogous to the no-rent land; there is full employment in the 'small countries' where wage rates are positive in analogy to the positive rents on lands that are cultivated fully because of lower costs. Needless to say, this model brings out only a very special aspect of international trade.

It is useful, however, in that it permits a simple and direct criticism of the neoclassical theory of international trade. Since the system is formally analogous to that of rent with DRI, we know that a rise of the real wage in the large country and a consequent fall of the general rate of profit will cause variations of the wage rates in the small countries. If we order the countries according to the level of the real wage in any given state of distribution, we notice that this order will change with a change of distribution in exactly the same way as 'fertility' changes with distribution in the case of land. It follows that the 'comparative advantage' of any country is not defined independently of distribution. Similarly, the gain from trade in terms of consumption per head relative to a situation of autarky may, if golden rule conditions are not fulfilled, be negative and fluctuate with profit rates. Distribution and 'gains from trade' are not regulated by quantities of 'factor endowments'. Hence we consider instead the impact of trade on technology.

The model is adequate for making this point, but it gives a poor representation of the problems of international trade because we have assumed full employment in the 'small' countries – an assumption that allows us to by-pass the problem of growth since world demand was taken to be satisfied by fully using the resources (i.e. labour) of the small countries, with the large country taking up the slack. The small countries were technologically more advanced. This is arbitrary.

An alternative model requires an explicit consideration of the growth process to explain the share of world production accruing to each country if the techniques employed in each country differ. It is the essential characteristic of international trade that there are limits to the competitive equalization of productive conditions between 'nations'. To the extent that labour is not internationally mobile, there are wage differentials between nations. Rates of profit will not be uniform either, if flows of financial capital do not equalize them. The consequent inequalities in the conditions of production and distribution must be stable and durable to allow an analysis in terms of long-period equilibrium as is implied in a system of prices of production. We distinguish two cases:

(a)   Each country follows its own dynamic in its growth process and the rate of profit is determined in each according to the post-Keynesian theory of distribution, i.e. the rate of profit of country j, r_j, is equal to g_j/s_j, where g_j is the rate of growth and s_j the propensity to save out of profits. A certain specialization of production will then result even if all countries have access to the same technology, simply because of the different states of distribution. The country with the largest rate of growth will end up being the largest in terms of output. If we assume that it produces all commodities and imposes its prices on the rest of the world, the logic of the counting of equations forces us to admit that each other country will again only admit one different industry: that which allows payment of the highest real wage at the rate of profit $r_j = g_j/s_j$. The coexistence of several methods of production for one commodity is here made possible because the rates of growth act as a constraint in a similar way as labour did above and land did in the case of rent.

But we shall not analyse this case in detail because the assumption of balanced growth in each country combined with unbalanced growth in the world is analytically cumbersome and because there is little reason not to assume a free flow of financial capital, and hence a uniform world rate of profit, if there is free trade in goods.

(b)   The importance of unbalanced growth has been discussed in a previous section (II.18b); that analysis may be combined with this to yield a more realistic model with unbalanced growth within countries. But here we shall consider a further possibility: both the rate of profit and the rate of growth are uniform across countries – though possibly unequal – and not all goods are traded between countries. It is this assumption that will provide us with a sophisticated argument to escape from the unfortunate conclusion that international trade results in almost complete specialization or 'equalization'.

There may be different reasons why some goods are not traded: transport costs may be prohibitive or certain goods may be consumed or used only in some countries. Let the real wage in terms of commodities be given in each country j, $j = 1, ..., k$, and let us simplify by assuming that n commodities are traded in the whole world while m_j commodities are traded only within country j (no overlap between countries). We then expect to have (except at switchpoints)

$$n + m_1 + \cdots + m_k$$

methods of production for the same number of commodities to be distributed over the world. This appears to prove that, if one country produces all internationally traded commodities, the other countries will either have to adopt the same methods or have to specialize in not traded commodities. But this means that they would have to be autarkic since they would not offer anything in international exchange.

However, the point is that the rules for the counting of equations must here be changed. It is – theoretically at least – conceivable that all n commodities that are internationally traded will be produced in each country by means of different methods, although both the rate of profit and even the wage rate may be uniform throughout the world. This may happen provided a sufficient number of the not internationally traded commodities are basics. If, for example, corn and steel are the two international commodities, and if they are produced in country A by means of horses, coal, ships, etc., and in country B by means of tractors, electricity, railways, etc., it is possible that the relative price of corn in terms of steel will be the same in both countries at all rates of profit (and not only by accident at a switchpoint). Different levels of productivity could be compensated through paying efficiency wages.

The formal condition is proved in (3.10) in (Schefold, 1978c). If two regular single-product systems $(\mathbf{A}, \mathbf{l})$ and $(\mathbf{F}, \mathbf{m})$ with t commodities are given such that they yield the same prices in terms of labour commanded for commodities $1, \ldots, s$ (where $1 \leqslant s \leqslant t$) in an interval of the rate of profit, the input–output matrices and the labour vector will be related by

$$\mathbf{F} = \mathbf{NAN}^{-1}$$
$$\mathbf{m} = \mathbf{Nl}$$

where (after permutation)

$$\mathbf{N} = \begin{bmatrix} \mathbf{N}_1^1 & \mathbf{O} \\ & \mathbf{N}_2 \end{bmatrix} \begin{matrix} \}s \\ \}t-s \end{matrix}$$

and $\mathbf{N}_1^1 = \mathbf{I}$ ($=$ unit matrix). Since the converse is also true, we can, if $(\mathbf{A}, \mathbf{l})$ is given, construct an infinity of systems $(\mathbf{F}, \mathbf{m})$ yielding the same prices as $(\mathbf{A}, \mathbf{l})$ for commodities $1, \ldots, s$, provided $s < t$. If we partition matrixes $\mathbf{A}$ and $\mathbf{F}$ like $\mathbf{N}$, we obtain

$$\mathbf{F}_1^1 = \mathbf{A}_1^1 - \mathbf{A}_1^2 (\mathbf{N}_2^2)^{-1} \mathbf{N}_2^1.$$

It follows from this formula that two countries must employ the same methods of production if the internationally traded commodities $1, \ldots, s$ happen to be the only basics, for then $\mathbf{A}_1^2 = \mathbf{O}$ and $\mathbf{F}_1^1 = \mathbf{A}_1^1$. But if some not internationally traded commodities are basics, we have $\mathbf{A}_1^2 \neq \mathbf{O}$ and the degrees of freedom in constructing an arbitrary $\mathbf{F}_1^1$ from a given $\mathbf{A}_1^1$ depend on the one hand on the distribution of the positive elements of $\mathbf{A}_1^2$, but on the other on the number of elements of $\mathbf{N}_2^1$ and $\mathbf{N}_2^2$ which is $t(t-s)$ and, given t, largest for $s = 1$. We should therefore expect that it is more likely (or less unlikely) that some internationally traded commodities are produced by means of different methods in different countries and yet have the same relative prices, if internationally traded commodities are basics and if their number is small in relation to that of not internationally traded basics.

Of course, we do not know how many actually feasible methods of production can be found in the set of imaginary methods of production engendered by the variations of the coefficients of matrix $\mathbf{N}_2$. But neither can we say that the number of processes used in k countries with n internationally traded commodities and m_j not internationally traded commodities in country j, $j = 1, \ldots, k$, is, except at switchpoints and barring irregular systems, necessarily equal to $n + m_1 + \cdots + m_k$. Rather, we should say that this number represents the lower bound, and the upper is given by

$$kn + m_1 + \cdots + m_k,$$

i.e. by the case where all internationally traded commodities are being produced in all countries by means of different methods.

With this we have shown that international trade tends to impose a specialization on different countries, or else they have to use the same methods of production as their competitors. But we have also seen that limitations on the number of commodities exchanged – transport costs, tariffs, rents, wage payments, which have the character of rents or residuals – all mitigate this tendency. Moreover, if one is close to a switchpoint, two methods are almost equally profitable and may therefore coexist in the real world, even if only one is to be adopted in theory. The argument that trade enforces an equalization not only of factor prices, but of the production methods of countries themselves, remains, in my eyes, strong and impressive nevertheless.

It may be remarked that the introduction of joint production would alter the argument in one respect: as in the case of the parallel argument for the specialization of land, it would, if a large country imposed its price for all commodities, formally remain possible for any small country to produce all commodities in one different joint-production process if the real wage adapted to the conditions given by international trade like rent in the case of land. But only one process would be admissible in each small country! The situation, although formally identical with that observed in the case of land, appears to be rather different in that joint production is the natural result of crop rotation and therefore of an organic combination of natural processes, whereas it would be misleading to consider diverse internationally traded goods such as copper, steel, rubber, etc. as joint products. This could be done only by a socialist society that had given up the rational evaluation of the various industries domestically and lumped them all together by considering the collective production of literally every domestic good as one gigantic overhead. While this procedure might correspond to some extreme socialist ideals, it would hardly stand the test of international competition which imposed the 'law of value' and the rule of efficiency.

The assumptions we have made could be varied a great deal because there is no single, archetypal model for international trade; international trade means precisely that the conditions of a closed system of production with homogeneous labour do not exist. But here we do not even survey the main theories of international trade; what has been said suffices to illustrate the contention that the essential phenomena of DRI transcend the familiar setting of Ricardian landlords. Differentials arise with any diversity of methods in the production of a commodity in single-product systems. If they are due to technical progress in competitive conditions, they pass away, but land is only the most obvious cause for lasting differentials. The transformation of profit differentials into land-rents, their capitalization as land prices, their skimming-off by wage-earners or the state in other cases: these are all devices that allow the diversity of methods of production to persist while the uniformity of the rate of profit is formally restored. Much of what has been said about international trade is in fact also applicable to regional analysis within nations.

Matters are quite different with DRII, which seems to apply only to land. With DRII, diversity of methods of production is the consequence, not the cause of the existence of rent. This will be shown in section II.20a, where we shall look at processes of transition in order to separate cause and effect. But first we consider a second digression.

Note

1 Joan Robinson suggested to me in 1970 that I should apply the above theory of specialization to international trade. A pioneering work in the area was that by Parrinello (Parrinello, 1970). The first textbook of the neo-Ricardian theory of international trade was published by Steedman (Steedman, 1979a), who also published a collection of essays on the subject (Steedman, 1979b).

19b   A Digression on Exhaustible Resources[1]

Ricardo treated the extraction of ores and coal from mines not like the depletion of a known stock, but like the application of capital and labour to land, which yields a regular flow of agricultural commodities. In the same way as the extension of cultivation may lead to a rise of prices because less fertile lands have to be used, the exhaustion of single mines or the physical constraints on the rate of extraction may make necessary the exploitation of less accessible mines. The mine working at any one time at highest unit costs of extraction paid no rent. Technical progress and discoveries would cause the costs to fall, but Ricardo held the view that the costs of extraction, at least of precious metals, were sufficiently constant that gold could come near to being an 'invariable standard of value', not only because the composition of capital corresponded to that of the average of the economy, but also because the productivity of labour in gold mining was thought to be roughly constant.

At a time when the exhaustion of key resources seems to be imminent as a result of a period of unprecedented growth, Ricardo's views can be seen to reflect the optimism of an era in which it was not possible to think through the consequences of the generalization of the industrial system to the world as a whole. But his formal analysis only requires some modification to take account of the fact that minerals are exhaustible.

An exhaustible resource could be exhaustible in the strict sense that all accessible deposits where it was found could be depleted within a foreseeable future and that it was indispensable to production. We call this an irreplaceable commodity.

An *irreplaceable commodity* is therefore a commodity that is basic within all known techniques of production $\mathbf{A}, \mathbf{B}, \mathbf{l}$ and that can itself not be produced after a given initial stock of it has been used up so that all known systems are then no longer viable with $\mathbf{q}'(\mathbf{B} - \mathbf{A}) \geqslant \mathbf{s}$; $\mathbf{q} \geqslant \mathbf{0}$; where $\mathbf{s}$ is the surplus to be produced.

The exhaustion of an irreplaceable commodity would be a catastrophe by definition since it would mean the collapse or at least the contraction of the system. But it would not necessarily be obvious for the members of the society beforehand which commodity was irreplaceable. Since a growing industrial society uses more and more materials that end up dissipated in the environment and that are not recycled through natural processes, increasing amounts of energy and labour have to be devoted to the recovery of such materials and to the correction of disturbed natural processes in soils, lakes, even the ocean and the air. If, for example, a densely populated world should choose a future based on total industrialization, where total industrialization meant reliance on industrial processes for recycling and the maintenance of artificially transformed ecological systems, the corresponding path of economic development might prove not to be viable, i.e. some commodities (energy or other) might turn out to be irreplaceable. If we disregard the possibility of the exhaustion of irreplaceable commodities (not because it might not be relevant, but because the consequences are beyond the scope of theorizing) and if we disregard the possibility of complete exhaustion of non-basics such as leopards (not because it would not be sad, but because we could live without them), the notion of 'exhaustible resource' takes on a different meaning. The exhaustion of a commodity then only means that the system can switch to a substitute without losing its viability as it did in the past (e.g. from timber to coal and from coal to oil).

At any one time the future substitute must be more expensive than the cost of production (including profits) of the commodity currently being produced – otherwise it would already be used. The availability of the exhaustible resource is gradually modified by its extraction. This causes a slow rising of prices, which will affect all prices in the system.

The neoclassical economist is inclined to determine the time-path of exhaustion as a problem of intertemporal resource allocation with a given utility function which expresses time preference. But purely subjective determinants of demand are – though never irrelevant – rarely the dominating influence on the composition of output. Social, political and historical influences shape consumption patterns and are in any case needed to *explain* the subjective element. It is clear that this also applies to questions of intertemporal allocation. The political element in particular is likely to play an even greater role in cases where decisions have to be taken under uncertainty about unknown risks, e.g. concerning future conditions of ownership.

The long-period position and the price system are therefore expected to be modified gradually in the course of extraction.

The reader should note that the change of technology between periods and the consequent change of prices are not a peculiarity of the theory of exhaustible resources. On the contrary, relative prices always change; they tend to fall with technical progress and to rise with the extension of cultivation to inferior lands in a given state of technological knowledge. Exhaustible resources are peculiar only in so far as the level and the rate of change of prices in the present depends not only on the change of present conditions between this period and the next but also on the entire sequence of technical changes and price changes between now and the point in time when the substitute for the exhaustible resource will be introduced.

We are concerned with prices of production, not with market prices.

We therefore *define* the price of production for each period of production in the same way as we have been defining prices elsewhere in this book, i.e. by assuming that prices of inputs and of outputs are the same in each period. We do not ask whether the ensuing stepwise change of prices of production between periods due to the gradual exhaustion of the resources leads to a smooth drift or to violent jumps of market prices.

In a given state of the economy the industries $i = 1, ..., n - 1$ and the commodities $j = 1, ..., n - 1$ are not thought to be exhaustible. Industry n produces the exhaustible commodity n (there is no substantial difficulty in generalizing to several exhaustible commodities). Since the state of the economy is expected to shift, in so far as exhaustion takes place, we have to use an index for time t. The equations for the first $n - 1$ industries are as usual (except for the time index t):

$$(1 + r)\mathbf{a}_1\mathbf{p}(t) + w(t)l_1 = \mathbf{b}_1\mathbf{p}(t)$$

$$...$$

$$(1 + r)\mathbf{a}_{n-1}\mathbf{p}(t) + w(t)l_{n-1} = \mathbf{b}_{n-1}\mathbf{p}(t).$$

Technology is assumed to be independent of time, except in the last industry n. The time index has therefore so far been applied only to prices, not to inputs and outputs of the first $n - 1$ industries.

The *exhaustible resource* is commodity n (possibly a basic that enters the production of the $n - 1$ other commodities). Its value in use is the same as that of its future substitute in that both render the same services to all consumers or other users of the commodity. (In reality, substitutes usually render the same services only to some users. For example, coal and oil may be equivalents as fuels but not as chemical raw materials.)

At the beginning of period t there is a stock $s_n(t)$. The stock may consist of ore *in situ* underground (in the case of a mine) or above (in the case of rare trees in a tropical forest which is possibly not reproducible, except in a geological life-span). Cases where there is a natural rate of reproduction that is, however, lower than that of extraction, might also be considered as a further complication. We shall speak of 'mines' in what follows. The amount of the stock in the mine may be difficult to estimate in practice, but either we assume it to be known as a measurable quantity of ore of given quality, crude oil, etc., or we suppose that (what amounts to the same thing) successive states $s_n(t)$ of the mine can be distinguished such that one unit of the commodity can be produced in each period t; $t = 1, 2. ...$ from the mine in its corresponding state. There is no rational basis for calculating prices unless the rhythm of extraction leading to eventual substitution is defined in terms of quantities (but the assumption that one unit is extracted each year is not essential and has been made only in order to simplify the notation).

One unit of commodity n is obtained from the stock at price $p_n(t)$. The physical transformation involved in obtaining the commodity may simply consist in pumping – as in the case of crude oil – but the equation for the extraction may also represent a more complex mechanical and chemical process. At the end of the period the stock has been reduced to $s_n(t+1)$. The values ascribed to the stock are $z(t)$, $z(t+1)$, respectively; the materials and labour used in the extractive industry are $\mathbf{a}_n(t)$, $l_n(t)$. Machines and joint products could be superimposed on this analysis along the lines of previous sections.

Several such processes of extraction may be operated on different lands; let us assume that there is an $(n+1)$st, which, being cheaper, allows payment of rent $\rho(t)$ for the use of λ units of land per unit of output. The land price is $\pi(t)$, with $\rho(t) = r\pi(t)$. We may therefore add two equations to our system:

$$(1+r)[s_n(t)z(t) + \mathbf{a}_n(t)\mathbf{p}(t)] + w(t)l_n(t)$$
$$= p_n(t) + s_n(t+1)z(t+1)$$

$$(1+r)[s_{n+1}(t)z(t) + \mathbf{a}_{n+1}(t)\mathbf{p}(t) + \lambda\pi(t)] + w(t)l_{n+1}(t)$$
$$= p_n(t) + s_{n+1}(t+1)z(t+1) + \lambda\pi(t).$$

Technology is not constant here because the degree of exhaustion may affect the amount of raw materials and labour required for extraction. This conceptualization of the problem is, I believe, correct, but it is difficult to explain it because of its complexity. We may note first that the system of $n+1$ equations is underdetermined. We simplify it in order to show how it may be closed in the general case.

We may abstract from the $(n+1)$st process involving a rent to begin with. The character of the rent, the treatment of the land price, the reasons why the stocks $s_{n+1}(t)$, $s_{n+1}(t+1)$ of the rent-paying mine are evaluated at the same prices $z(t)$, $z(t+1)$ as those of mine n will be explained later.

Consider process n. The input and the output coefficients depend on time, hence prices have a time index, and this is the reason why prices – but not coefficients – in processes $1, 2, ..., n-1$ also depend on time.

We link the different periods between now and the future substitution by assuming that the stock and its price at the end of each period are equal to the stock and its price at the beginning of the next, so that we have

period t		period $t+1$		
stock		stock		stock
$s_n(t)$	production	$s_n(t+1)$	production	$s_n(t+2)$
price	prices $p(t)$	price	prices $p(t+1)$	price
$z(t)$		$z(t+1)$		$z(t+2)$

According to this view, prices of production of commodities are thought to be a constant average of market prices of each period. The dwindling stock has to be evaluated at the beginning and at the end of each period in order to form those prices of production. It is best to regard $z(t)$, $z(t+1), ...$ as book values; a market price for the stock does not

necessarily exist since the stock is usually sold not as a separate commodity but rather as part of a piece of land, as we shall see.

Those who also are familiar with the neoclassical theory of exhaustible
resources, which is more directly oriented towards an explanation of
market prices, might prefer to define not only the price of the stock but
also prices of commodities with reference to the beginning and the end of
each period. In fact, one could distinguish input and output prices so
that one would get, instead of equation n, an equation of the type

$$(1 + r)[s_n(t)z(t) + \mathbf{a}_n(t)\mathbf{p}(t)] + w(t)l_n(t) = p_n(t + 1) + s_n(t + 1)z(t + 1) \tag{*}$$

for each time period t.

The solution to the system of prices can be found recursively, starting
from the price of the future substitute (which is supposed to be known).
We shall show this for the system of equations with prices of production,
but the reader may verify that essentially the same result is obtained on
the basis of equation (*), in which input prices and output prices are
different for each period. We shall not use equation (*) because it blurs
the classical notion of the rate of profit. Moreover, it suggests a simplistic
and mechanical image according to which production takes place during
the period and exchange 'between' periods. This image is useful as an
expository device – it is, in fact, used by Sraffa himself at the beginning
of his book ('market held after the harvest') when changes in methods of
production are not considered. But a more advanced treatment is to be
based on the distinction between market prices and prices of production.

The n'th process may also be written as

$$p_n(t) = [(1 + r)\mathbf{a}_n(t)\mathbf{p}(t) + w(t)l_n(t)]$$
$$+ [(1 + r)s_n(t)z(t) - s_n(t + 1)z(t + 1)]$$

where the first term on the right-hand side represents the technical cost of
extraction and the second the royalty of the mine composed of the
financial charge $rs_n(t)z(t)$ on the stock $s_n(t)$ to be advanced and the
depreciation (or appreciation, as we shall see!) $s_n(t)z(t) -$
$s_n(t + 1)z(t + 1)$ of the stock, which is reduced from $s_n(t)$ to $s_n(t + 1)$.

The n'th equation can be solved (jointly with equations $1, ..., n - 1$) by
assuming that the stock happens to get exhausted in the period T. For
then $s_n(T + 1) = 0$, $s_n(T + 1)z_n(T + 1) = 0$, and $p_n(T)$ is known because
the substitute of commodity n will start to be produced in period T by
means of a known substitute method $(\bar{\mathbf{a}}_{n+1}, \bar{l}_{n+1})$ which is, for simplicity,
assumed to be a single-product process.

The system of period T is

$$(1 + r)\mathbf{a}_i\mathbf{p}(T)w(T)l_i = \mathbf{b}_i\mathbf{p}(T), \qquad i = 1, ..., n - 1$$
$$(1 + r)\bar{\mathbf{a}}_n\mathbf{p}(T) + w(T)\bar{l}_n = p_n(T)$$

and determines $p_1(T), ..., p_n(T)$. But there is a second method for
producing commodity n in period T, which must be equally profitable; it

consists of depleting the mine. If $s_n(T+1) = 0$, we have

$$(1 + r)[s_n(T)z(T) + \mathbf{a}_n(T)\mathbf{p}(T)] + w(T)l_n(T) = p_n(T).$$

The value $z(T)$ to be ascribed to the quality of ore $s_n(T)$ (or to the mine in the state $s_n(T)$) can therefore be determined as a residual: the *'substitute equation'* determines $p_n(T)$, given the solution of the system in period T, and this in turn allows the determination of $z(T)$ in conjunction with equations $1, ..., n - 1$ of the system of period T on the assumption that $s_n(T+1) = 0$:

$$z(T) = \frac{p_n(T) - (1 + r)\mathbf{a}_n(T)\mathbf{p}(T) - w(T)l_n(T)}{(1 + r)s_n(T)}.$$

The value of the stock $s_n(T)$ is positive so long as the price of the commodity produced exceeds its costs of extraction.

It is now easy to see how this solution may be extended further back.

The owner of the mine can always expect his stock of ore to appreciate at a rate equal to the rate of interest since the price of the substitute is above the current price of the commodity produced, so that the price of the latter must go up if he withholds production, whereas an even steeper rise is incompatible with competition. If ore is measurable, we may say that any unit quantity of ore appreciates and $z(t + 1) = (1 + r)z(t)$, but if ore is not measurable, we still have $z(t + 1) = (1 + r)z(t)$, for it is then the mine as a whole that must appreciate when it is transformed from state $s_n(t)$ into $s_n(t + 1)$ with $s_n(t)$ unchanged, i.e. with $s_n(t)z(t + 1) = (1 + r)s_n(t)z(t)$.

Using the formula for $z(T)$ as a residual, we have $z(t) = (1 + r)^{t-T}z(T)$, and the price of the commodity is given by

$$p_n(t) = w(t)l_n(t) + (1 + r)\{\mathbf{a}_n(t)\mathbf{p}(t) + [s_n(t) - s_n(t + 1)]z(T)(1 + r)^{t-T}\}.$$

If the n'th commodity is a basic, it is clear that only the substitute equation can enter the basic system, in much the same way as only the equation for the production of corn on the 'last' land enters the basic system. Ore (or the mine in its various states) is also a non-basic. We analyse first the case where the commodity n itself is a non-basic under special assumptions.

If commodity n is a pure consumption good (or non-basic that does not enter directly or indirectly its own reproduction) its cost of production is given and may be written as

$$p_n(t) = k(t) + c(t)$$

where

$$k(t) = w(t)l_n(t) + (1 + r)\mathbf{a}_n(t)\mathbf{p}(t)$$

is the cost of raw materials and labour and

$$c(t) = [s_n(t) - s_n(t+1)]z(T)(1+r)^{t-T+1}$$

is the user cost of the mine (both including profits).

If the technique used in industry n is constant (like the techniques used in other industries) and if a constant amount is extracted in each period, $k(t)$ and $s_n(t) - s_n(t+1)$ are constant and we may write

$$p_n(t) = k + c(1+r)^{t-T}$$

where $k = k(t)$ and $c = (1+r)[s_n(t) - s_n(t+1)]z(T)$.

In particular

$$p_n(0) = k + \frac{c}{(1+r)^T}$$

so that we obtain a reformulation of Hotelling's (Hotelling, 1931) famous rule

$$p_n(t) = k + [p_n(0) - k](1+r)^t.$$

The cost of production of the commodity is equal to its cost of extraction plus a user cost (due to the prospective exhaustion of the ore in the ground) which rises at a rate equal to the rate of interest.

Consider the value of the total stock of ore *in situ* at the beginning of each period

$$S(t) = s(t)z(t).$$

If one unit of ore is extracted per period from a stock that initially contains T units, we have $z(t) = (1+r)^t z(0)$ and

$$\frac{S(t)}{S(0)} = \left(1 - \frac{t}{T}\right)(1+r)^t,$$

The formula shows that the value of the stock diminishes linearly if $r = 0$, in the same way as a machine depreciates linearly if $r = 0$. We saw above that the user cost $p_n(t) - k$ is equal to the royalty $(1+r)s_n(t)z(t) - s_n(t+1)z(t+1)$ that must be paid to the owner of the mine. Under the assumption of linear depletion, it is equal to $(1+r)(T-t)z(t) - [T - (t+1)]z(t+1) = (1+r)z(t)$, and this is again the cost (including profits) of the quantity of ore used up. But whereas the value of an old machine $p_{m,t}$ always falls monotonically relative to that of a new machine p_{m0} according to the formula

$$\frac{p_{m,t}}{p_{m0}} = \frac{(1+r)^T - (1+r)^t}{(1+r)^T - 1}$$

(see theorem 15.3 above), with

$$\frac{p_{m,t}}{p_{m0}} = 1 - \frac{t}{T}$$

for $r = 0$, $S(t)$ may rise initially relative to $S(0)$ for r and T sufficiently large, as Figure II.19b.1 shows.

The maximum of $S(t)/S(0)$ is reached at

$$t = T - 1/\log(1 + r) \simeq T - 1/r.$$

This appreciation of a dwindling stock is a distinguishing feature of the theory of exhaustible resources; it may be asked, however, why it is so little observed in practice.

Some numerical values are given in Table II.19b.1. It can be seen that the rise to the maximum is very slow and gradual if lower rates of interest are — as they must be — associated with long time-periods, but the last line shows that a high rate of interest of 4 per cent for 100 years would curiously be associated with an almost five-fold rise of the value of the stock at a time when the stock has physically become depleted by three-quarters!

A strong appreciation of the stock presupposes high rates of interest over very long time-periods. This is not plausible.

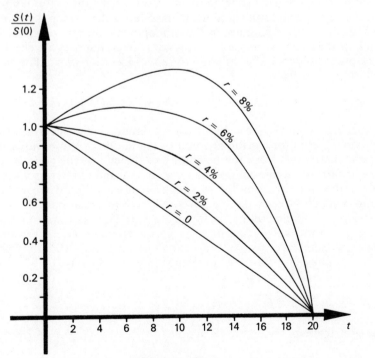

Figure II.19b.1

Table II.19b.1   *The maximum value of a stock of ore with linear depletion over T years, reached at t years, with a rate of interest of r per cent*

T	r	t	$S(t)/S(0)$
20	7	5.210	1.052
30	5	9.504	1.086
50	4	24.503	1.333
80	3	46.169	1.655
100	2	49.502	1.346
150	1.5	82.835	1.537
200	1	99.501	1.352
100	4	74.503	4.737

We now consider *monopoly control* of the mine. This causes the price to rise faster than under competitive conditions, where the price of the ore rises at a rate equal to the rate of interest, but where the price of the commodity itself rises more slowly because its rise is dampened by the cost of extraction. Monopoly control can be checked somewhat if the buyers of the commodity store it artificially. A partially competitive equilibrium is reached if the price of the commodity is − by means of slow extraction − made to rise so fast as to make artificial storage profitable in a steady state (and not only as a buffer for temporary disturbances). This is an equilibrium in so far as the monopolistic owners of the mines then find allies in the monopolistic owners of the artificial stocks if the rate of increase of prices goes down, but they are checked by the storage holders if they attempt to raise prices even more. The *'storage equation'* then reads

$$(1 + r)p_n(t) + (1 + r)\mathbf{a}_0(t)\mathbf{p}(t) + w(t)l_0(t) = p_n(t + 1)$$

where $\mathbf{a}_0$, l_0 is the cost in terms of labour and materials (tanks, containers, etc.) for storing one unit of commodity n (to be advanced at capital cost $rp_n(t)$ from the beginning to the end of the period). If this (precarious) economic constellation can be expected to last, $z(T)$ is to be determined as above, and the appreciation of each unit of ore and of the commodity is in each period governed by *two* equations: the storage equation, which determines $p_n(t)$, given $p_n(t + 1)$, and the equation for the extraction, which determines $z(t)$, given $z(t + 1)$. In the case of constant technical costs of storage q and of extraction (including profits) in the production of a pure consumption good, we have

$$p_n(t + 1) = (1 + r)p_n(t) + q$$
$$p_n(t) + s_n(t + 1)z(t + 1) = (1 + r)s_n(t)z(t) + k.$$

The first formula yields the recursion

$$p_n(t) = (1 + r)p_n(t - 1) + q = (1 + r)^2 p_n(t - 2) + (1 + r)q + q$$

hence

$$p_n(t) = (1 + r)^t p_n(0) + q \frac{(1 + r)^t - 1}{r}$$

$$\frac{p_n(T)}{(1 + r)^T} = p_n(0) + q \frac{(1 + r)^T - 1}{r(1 + r)^T}$$

so that the discounted value of the commodity in period T exceeds at the beginning of extraction its current value by an amount which, multiplied by the amortization of a machine of constant efficiency equals the cost of technical storage each year. One can see that, according to a modification of Hotelling's rule, $p_n(t)$ rises faster than the rate of interest, if there are technical costs to artificial storage, i.e. if $q > 0$.

The right-hand side of the expression

$$p_n(t) - k = (1 + r)s_n(t)z_n(t) - s_n(t + 1)z_n(t + 1),$$

i.e. the royalty or user cost, may also be looked at as an 'amortization' of the mine, i.e. as the sum of its capital cost $rs_n(t)z_n(t)$ *plus* its depreciation $s_n(t)z_n(t) - s_n(t + 1)z_n(t + 1)$, but − in analogy with a machine of rising efficiency − the left-hand side, i.e. the excess of the value of the commodity over its 'technical' cost of extraction, rises monotonically with t, so that there is even more room for the value of the mine to appreciate (instead of depreciate) relative to the value of the new mine in the first phase of extraction than in the previous case where the possibility of storing the ore in the mine led to the condition $z_n(t + 1)$ $= (1 + r)z_n(t)$ and hence to the rise of $p_n(t)$ slower than compound interest. The exact formula is obtained by multiplying each of the equations

$$p_n(\tau) - k = (1 + r)s_n(\tau)z_n(\tau) - s_n(\tau + 1)z_n(\tau + 1),$$

$\tau = t, ..., T$, by $(1 + r)^\tau$ and adding them so as to eliminate $z_n(t + 1), ..., z_n(T)$ as in the case of a machine. However, we shall not pursue the matter since the introduction of a storage equation is a less natural (though not inconceivable) solution to the problem of exhaustible resources than the assumption that the rhythm of extraction leads to the appreciation of the ore at a rate equal to the rate of interest.

It has already been recalled that the appreciation of an exhaustible resource (which was discovered by Hotelling in this century) was not admitted by Ricardo. It would be a mistake to think that the omission was due to the fact that the change of prices, in particular of the value of the stock, was in conflict with the classical notion of equilibrium at a uniform rate of profit. Price changes accompanying structural change are inevitable and perfectly compatible with the concept of normal profits, the classical examples being the tendency of prices of agricultural commodities to increase and of manufactured products to diminish. But ve shall give four reasons why the theory of exhaustible resources that has received so much attention lately is of practical relevance only under exceptional circumstances, so that the classicists may be excused for having ignored it by subsuming the incomes of mine owners to the general theory of rent.

The first and most fundamental objection concerns the possibility of perfect foresight. It is clear and has often been observed that the anticipation of the price of a future substitute is different in an uncertain world, but it has hitherto not been stressed sufficiently that the very rise of the price of the exhaustible commodity itself will cause complex price changes in the entire economy, if we are dealing with a basic commodity. It is true that, in principle, the future system based on the substitute may be thought to provide a firm frame of reference to assess prices; but in the course of the depletion of the mine the commodity is sold at actual prices. It is then problematic to assume that the future price systems $\mathbf{p}(1), ..., \mathbf{p}(T+1)$ can be anticipated with all the feedbacks of $p_n(t)$ or the prices $p_1(t), ..., p_{n-1}(t)$ for $t = 1, ..., T+1$. Some justification might be sought in the assumption that the long-period position, which extends over many periods, is modified only slowly by the change of $p_n(t)$, which governs that of $\mathbf{p}(t)$. But it follows from the above equation that the user cost included in $p_n(t)$ rises with $(1+r)^t$, and this entails that all other prices $\hat{p}_i(t)$, $i = 1, ..., n-1$, will also rise in terms of the wage rate if the system is all-engaging. One might then conjecture that the change of *relative* prices will be moderate. However, there is no reason for this. If commodity n is oil, and its price $\hat{p}_n$ (in terms of the wage rate) rises, all other prices go up in terms of the wage rate in a system of single-product industries, but relative prices may fluctuate. To see this, the first $n-1$ equations may be written as follows

$$(1+r)(\overline{\mathbf{A}}\overline{\mathbf{p}} + \overline{\mathbf{a}}^n \hat{p}_n) + \overline{\mathbf{l}} = \overline{\mathbf{p}}$$

where $\overline{\mathbf{A}} = (a_i^j)$; $i, j = 1, ..., n-1$; $\overline{\mathbf{a}}^n = (a_1^n, ..., a_{n-1}^n)'$, $\overline{\mathbf{l}} = (l_1, ..., l_{n-1})'$, $\overline{\mathbf{p}} = [1/(w(t))][p_1(t), ..., p_{n-1}(t)]'$, and where we assume $b_i^j = \delta_i^j$; $i, j = 1, ..., n-1$.

The prices of commodities $1, ..., n-1$ are therefore in terms of the wage rate in period t

$$\overline{\mathbf{p}} = [\mathbf{I} - (1+r)\overline{\mathbf{A}}]^{-1}[\overline{\mathbf{l}} + (1+r)\overline{\mathbf{a}}^n \hat{p}_n]$$

so that a rise in the price of oil, i.e. of $\hat{p}_n$, operates like a rise in labour requirements which affects the sectors very unequally. The price changes may be complex (by analogy with Wicksell effects) in the case of a constant technology for commodities $1, ..., n-1$. They will be very complex (by analogy with reswitching) if they lead to technological change. It follows that it is a very bold hypothesis, admissible purely for analytical reasons, to suppose that the appreciation of the value of an exhaustible commodity is governed by correct expectations. This objection to the theory is reduced in importance if the commodity produced plays no very significant role as a means of production (so that it may be treated as if it was a non-basic) and/or if the substitute is already being used in the current period, either because the mine is near exhaustion or because the difference between the cost of extraction of the commodity and the cost of production of the substitute is small. But then the royalty is already similar to a temporary rent!

The second objection concerns the influence of technical progress on the process of extraction. The rise in the productivity of labour in mines counteracts the tendency of the price of the commodity to rise. A fall in the prices of the output of the mine leads to a situation in which it is not possible to cover the capital cost of storage even within the mine (let alone the capital cost of artificial storage).

Third, even if productivity is constant and if we are dealing with a non-basic produced under competitive conditions in many mines that are all alike, the royalty to be paid for each mine as a whole will tend to rise or fall only moderately during about the first half of the process of extraction, if depletion is linear. For, as we saw above, the appreciation of each unit of ore at positive rates of interest is counterbalanced by the diminution of the stock, so that the total royalty will look like a roughly constant 'absolute' rent to be paid for the permission to extract from the mine. (There is not necessarily a 'marginal' mine, hence no 'differential' rent.) That the phenomenon is rather different from both absolute and differential rent will only be seen in the second phase when the value of the old mine falls precipitately relative to that of the new. (There is some similarity between this and the fact that the lifetime of machines may also be divided into several phases: construction, slow depreciation offset by rise in efficiency, eventual rapid fall in value – Schefold, 1974.)

Fourth, it should not be forgotten that many mines coexist with different costs of extraction. If the ores can be compared and their quality evaluated at ore prices $z(t)$, the ensuing cost differentials between mines must be regarded as differential rents. It is likely that – before the last phase of extraction of an individual mine begins with the corresponding strong rise in the price of the product – other mines will start operating because they have become profitable.

This provides the last reason for the classical neglect of the exhaustion problem. The difference between the productivity of various mines was a far greater influence on the residual income of mine owners after the payment of materials and wages and after the accounting of normal profits than the extremely slow tendency of the total reserves of any commodity to get exhausted. Ricardo thus regarded the analysis of mines as analogous to the extension of cultivation to inferior lands. The uncertainty concerning the future course of prices (which is a matter of principle in a basic system), the unpredictability of technical progress and the likelihood that the slow change of total royalties in any one mine is dominated by cost differentials between mines may still provide a pragmatic justification for preferring a direct simplifying analysis in terms of rents to a complicated and essentially futile endeavour to deal with these uncertainties in terms of subjective expectations and probabilities. With many mines, it is at any rate likely that there will be 'marginal' mines paying very little rent or royalty. These may serve the purpose served by the last land in Ricardo: to provide a reference point for the analysis of the effects of changing conditions of demand, cost, etc., on quantities, prices and rents.

Nevertheless, for the sake of theoretical rigour, we introduce the analysis of mine rents not as an alternative, but as a supplement to the analysis of royalties. We therefore now add the equation for the $(n + 1)$st process that yields a rent. The determination of the rent is trivial, given the price of commodity n, and is in principle the same whether we derive a formula for the royalty of the mine on the basis of its potential exhaustion or whether we assume that $s_n(t) - s_n(t + 1)$ is so small as to be negligible.

The crucial question is whether it is admissible to assume that the values ascribed to the stocks in the ground of the second mine are in each period the same as those ascribed to the stocks of the first mine. Is there a value to, say, $5 \cdot 10^7$ barrels of oil undergound of given chemical quality, but irrespective of location, so that differences in the cost of access, production and transportation can be interpreted as rents? This is a theoretical question since the scientific definition of 'quality' is solvable. The distinction between rent and royalty that follows from the assumption of uniform accounting prices for stocks should be attempted because the material existence of a perfect market for the stocks *in situ* is not required to allow mine owners to ascribe correct values to them. If there is a change in commodity prices between periods because the exhaustion is near, if that is foreseeable and if storage technologies exist, the ascription of values to stocks is theoretically feasible and may be tested in an actual market for claims to the resources. If any of these conditions is not fulfilled, only current differentials of costs are observable; then all extra profits of owners must be lumped together into one rent. In those cases, the rents of mines are formally indistinguishable from differential rent of the ordinary kind and from absolute rent.

A more detailed analysis would require a specific assumption regarding the determinants of the rates of exhaustion. If ordinary rents occur in mines, it must be asked why the cheapest mine is not exhausted first. The answer is that faster extraction may render the cheapest mine more expensive because of deteriorating working conditions, as in mining proper, or because of increasing irrecoverable losses, as in the case of oil fields where fast depletion may dangerously reduce the pressure of the oil spring. It is well known that increases in the degree of monopoly tend to reduce rates of extraction. In our analysis this was illustrated by the extreme possibility of introducing artificial storage.

If the rates of extraction are given, the various mines give rise to rents that may be distinguished from royalties under the conditions cited above. The question then is whether these rents are simply to be regarded as surplus profits of the mine as an enterprise or even – as sometimes in current language with reference to oil companies – as windfall profits or whether they are rents related to space so that they may be expressed in terms of value per area and are payable to the owners of the land.

The answer depends not just on institutional facts and ownership, but also on how the use of the land for mining competes with alternative uses.

If, for instance, the land is a forest, which yields a rent, and the resource is lignite, which can be obtained by means of surface mining, the rent of the latter operation must exceed that of the forest to allow mining; the land rent goes to the owner of the land. The royalty will be appropriated by the authority that authorizes the exploitation of the mine (it may be the state), but the entrepreneur of the mine, the land-owner and the receiver of the royalty may also coincide in one person.

With all this happening on the land, the land itself remains the same to the extent that the changes that it undergoes are reversible. This definition of types of land is in accordance with that adopted in section II.19, where it was stressed that reversible changes such as those during field rotation should not be expressed as transformations of the land (although land may be viewed as a joint product), but should be treated as investment in analogy to machines on the land.

We may therefore distinguish four types of land: a forest (a), a forest with coal beneath (b), land with surface mining going on (c), and the waste land that results from that (d). Lands (a) and (b) pay the same rent as long as they are used as forests, but they have to be distinguished from each other. When the mine is opened up, land (b) is transformed into (c), later into (d) in modern practice, but the state might require the mine owner to form a reserve from which the eventual restoration of land (d) into a land of type (a) (but never (b)) will be paid, with the cost ultimately falling on the buyer of the commodity (lignite). In either case, the irreversibility of the change results in a transformation of land such that it here really appears as a joint product in some equations. The transformation changes the properties of the land, which is no longer simply the area where 'rent is paid for the undestructible powers of the soil'.

Note

1   This section owes its first inspiration to work by S. Parrinello (1982).

20   Effects of the Presence of Land on the Basic System

We return to more technical matters and consider the influence of the presence of land on the basic system. The general case has been dealt with in sections II.2 and II.3; in this section we discuss only single-product processes using land, with DRI and DRII.

There is a sharp contrast in the way DRI and DRII affect the basic system. If a basic good is grown on a no-rent land (DRI), there is no problem, because it will enter the basic system represented in a single-product process. If all land is in short supply, however, negative multipliers will inevitably come into play, as is shown by the example in Table II.20.1 of two goods grown in single-product processes on two lands both in short supply.

Table II.20.1

Corn		Cattle		Land I		Land II		Labour		Corn		Cattle
$(a_1^1$	,	a_1^2	,	1	,	0	,	$l_1)$	$\rightarrow$	$(b_1^1$	,	0)
$(a_2^1$	,	a_2^2	,	1	,	0	,	$l_2)$	$\rightarrow$	$(0$	,	$b_2^2)$
$(a_3^1$	,	a_3^2	,	0	,	1	,	$l_3)$	$\cdot \rightarrow$	$(b_3^1$	,	0)
$(a_4^1$	,	a_4^2	,	0	,	1	,	$l_4)$	$\rightarrow$	$(0$	,	$b_4^2)$

Note: For convenience the coefficients of land are taken to be equal to one.

The basic system involves not only negative multipliers – it leads to a sort of joint-production system with some negative elements:

$$(a_1^1 - a_2^1, a_1^2 - a_2^2, l_1 - l_2) \rightarrow (b_1^1, -b_2^2)$$
$$(a_3^1 - a_4^1, a_3^2 - a_4^2, l_3 - l_4) \rightarrow (b_3^1, -b_4^2).$$

The conditions for rent and prices to be positive in certain ranges of the rate of profit and for the standard commodity to exist are now different. Our results derived for general joint-production systems are not applicable because of the negative coefficients.

A three-sector model is sufficient to illustrate that, although the goods that enter the basic system are unique, the basic processes are determined only up to linear combinations of processes (compare section II.3 above).

Corn		Cattle		Land		Corn		Cattle
$(a_1^1$	,	a_1^2	,	1)	$\rightarrow$	$(b_1^1$	,	0)
$(a_2^1$	,	a_2^2	,	1)	$\rightarrow$	$(0$	,	$b_2^2)$
$(a_3^1$	,	a_3^2	,	1)	$\rightarrow$	$(b_3^1$	,	0)

The basic system can be formed by subtracting any one of the three equations from the two others. The resulting three systems will look different but give of course the same prices for all r.

Even if the basic system is a single-product system in all respects except that it shows one negative coefficient, all sorts of difficulties may arise. If in the example

Ploughs		Corn		Land		Labour		Ploughs		Corn
$(m_1$	,	k_1	,	0	,	$l_1)$	$\rightarrow$	$(1$	,	0)
$(m_2$	,	k_2	,	λ_2	,	$l_2)$	$\rightarrow$	$(0$	,	1)
$(m_3$	,	k_3	,	λ_3	,	$l_3)$	$\rightarrow$	$(0$	,	1)

the particular values

Ploughs		Corn		Land		Ploughs		Corn
$(\tfrac{2}{5}$	,	1	,	0)	$\rightarrow$	(1	,	0)
$(\tfrac{1}{10}$	,	$\tfrac{2}{5}$	,	1)	$\rightarrow$	(0	,	1)
$(\tfrac{2}{5}$	,	$\tfrac{1}{5}$	,	2)	$\rightarrow$	(0	,	1)

are taken, no standard commodity exists, for the standard system (the second row is doubled, which does not alter price relations)

$$(\tfrac{2}{5}, 1) \rightarrow (1, 0)$$
$$(-\tfrac{1}{5}, \tfrac{3}{5}) \rightarrow (0, 1)$$

has a characteristic equation

$$\tfrac{11}{25}(1 + r)^2 - (1 + r) + 1 = 0$$

with negative discriminant

$$1 - \tfrac{44}{25} = -\tfrac{19}{25}$$

and thus no real, let alone positive, solution for $1 + r$ or r.

The example is striking, since neither of the two corn-producing processes seems at first sight distinctly superior to the other. The second process employs fewer ploughs and is more land-intensive, while the corn rate of reproduction is higher for process 3. However, on closer examination, one discovers that process 3 requires four times more ploughs and since plough production has a very great input of corn one expects that l_2 must be considerably greater than both l_1 and l_3 if the two processes are to be compatible.

One finds that both prices and rent are positive for $r = 4\%$, if $l_1 : l_2 : l_3 = 2 : 25 : 1$. The proportion of the labour inputs cannot be altered much, lest the rent turn negative.

The non-existence of the standard commodity in this case is as such no important result; the standard commodity is merely an analytical tool that facilitates and illuminates the explanation of the properties of self-reproducing systems. As an explanatory device for the interpretation of price movements, it has a didactic function. As soon as price movements in single-product systems are understood, it has served its main purpose (see Part III, Essay 6). As a standard of the real wage, it is a conceptual aid in single-product and related systems, like fixed-capital systems where the relation

$$1 = \frac{r}{R} + w_t$$

has an unambiguous meaning because the wage falls with a rise in the rate of profit, whatever the wage goods, for it is then the simplest representation for a wide class of falling wage curves. But as soon as prices of wage goods in terms of the wage rate fluctuate, it is not certain any more that the wage will fall with a rise in r. Nor is it certain any more that one of the two alternative techniques will be advantageous for both classes only because it implies a higher wage in terms of the standard commodity.

The possibility of the lack of these two properties is more important than the possibility of the lack of the standard commodity in systems where differential rent of the second kind occurs. (That $\hat{p}$ may fluctuate is proved *a fortiori* by the non-existence of the maximum rate of profit; see section II.7.)

Its lack comes perhaps as less of a surprise if it is remembered that the laws of income distribution are here (DRII) complicated by the presence of a third class of income receivers (landlords, land-owning capitalists, etc.).

It is thus on the one hand clear that the existence of a third form of revenue (rent) will not invariably destroy the simple laws of income distribution that govern single-product industries. We have seen this in the case of differential rent of the first kind with single-product processes. It is equally clear that the rationality of single-product systems is destroyed in the case of intensive diminishing returns. While this was clear to me and noted when I wrote sections II.19 and II.20 in 1970 (only section II.19 has here been amended to emphasize points that had formally already all been made in the first version), I have been unable to reduce this contrast substantially since; the next section represents only a later attempt (basically dating from 1972) to improve matters by showing that the technical difficulties are related to the fact that the dynamic of DRII is very different from that of DRI and involves a different kind of distributional conflict.

20a   Differential Rent, Absolute Rent and the Choice of Techniques

I have argued elsewhere in this book (see Part I, Ch. 9 and Part III, Essay 5) that it is one of the peculiar advantages of Sraffa's system that it leaves room for a determination of 'demand' and the 'socially necessary' method of production that need not, in most cases will not, and at the macroeconomic level cannot, conform to the neoclassical version of economic rationality. Distribution and the employment of produced means of production cannot be determined by supply and demand for capital (the model is not closed with respect to distribution), the choice of techniques need not be competitive, and demand depends only to a negligible extent on innate preferences and mainly on other factors. The theory of rent is particularly well suited to illustrate each of these points.

We shall not dwell now on the fact that the growth of demand is a function of the level of accumulation and of distribution rather than of shifts in preferences; the point will be taken up later. We can deal quickly with the extension of the critique of the marginal productivity theory of capital to the case of land: if Sraffa's basic assumption about land is accepted, the rent of any land cannot vary at a constant rate of profit and of wages; there is only one degree of freedom as soon as prices have been normalized. Usually the rate of profit is taken as the independent variable. If we take the rate of rent of one land instead as formally variable, the curves showing the amount of land used per man employed and output per man as a function of rent will look as pathological as the functions of capital per man and output per man as a function of the rate of profit, but the difficulty will be compounded by the fact that rent is in general not a monotonic function of the rate of profit. This should suffice to discourage any attempt at a construction of a surrogate production function involving land.

The really interesting questions to be examined concern the choice of techniques, however. One might believe at first sight that simple assumptions suffice for a treatment of the choice of techniques according to the method known from the single-product case. If m lands are given some of which are in short supply, the wage curve may in fact be drawn for each on the assumption that it is the no-rent land. (The corresponding equation enters the basic system and determines prices for basic commodities if the produce of land is basic.) However, of these wage curves only those are admissible at rate of profit r that are such that an area of lands, which must each be fully cultivated and entail lower costs of production than the no-rent land, exists and is, together with the cultivated part of the no-rent land, just sufficient to produce the required output. The pattern of cultivation may therefore have to change drastically at a switchpoint between two such wage curves because the cost of production on the no-rent land Λ_1 in use at rate of profit r_1 may be lower at r_2 than that of a land Λ_2 that had lower costs and paid rent at r_1 but which must become the no-rent land at r_2. The first land, Λ_1, will then pay rent at r_2. It follows that Λ_1 must be cultivated fully at r_2 while Λ_1 is cultivated only partially at r_1. It therefore does not suffice to consider only the level of unit costs in the comparison of different combinations of lands at different rates of profit; it has always to be assumed that the combinations compared allow production of the required output, and the growth of output will alter the combinations used. There are diminishing returns in the extension of production to inferior qualities of land, although the homogeneity of each type of land ensures constant returns or unit costs in the gradual extension of production over its surface as long as it remains marginal.

A similar phenomenon occurs if DRII intervenes in the extension of production of a fully cultivated isolated piece of land. In order to exclude the difficulties discussed in section II.20 due to negative coefficients in the basic system, one conveniently assumes that the combined processes that enter the basic system in the case of DRII do not contain negative elements because the process that needs less land per unit of output in the pair of processes to be combined requires more of each mean of production and labour. The condition $k_i < k_j$, $\lambda_j < \lambda_i$ which is necessary and sufficient for the positivity of rent (section II.19) is thus extended to each mean of production; if $k_\mu = (1 + r)\mathbf{a}_\mu \mathbf{p} + w l_\mu$, $\mu = i, j$, $\lambda_i < \lambda_j$ must entail $a_i^v \geqslant a_j^v \geqslant 0$, for all v, and $l_i \geqslant l_j$. The assumption is reasonable in the classical case of the intensive margin in agriculture where only one product is involved and intensification is a continuous or almost continuous process of applying more corn and labour per acre in successive doses for the production of more corn per unit area. Guichard (1979) has shown that a slight generalization of this condition allows discussion of the choice of technique as a function of both the level of production and the rate of profit for DRI and DRII with the result that all relevant wage curves are continuous, fall monotonically and allow a standard commodity to be defined for each of the basic systems. The latter thus depends on the level of production, but this is no anomaly because the same is true in single-product systems if there are no constant returns to scale.

The assumption of allowing only combined processes with positive coefficients in the standard system is in fact less natural in the urban example of DRII discussed above. But it remains true that the marginal dose of 'capital' applied pays no differential rent as in the case of DRI. The example may be recalled. The growth of demand for offices at price p requires the construction of sky-scrapers to replace gradually existing lower old buildings by pulling them down and building the sky-scrapers in their place. The cost of production of an office room is equal to the amortization and maintenance of the corresponding building (represented here by circulating capital items and labour k_1, k_2). The cost of an office room (amortization of construction and maintenance) produced in the sky-scrapers is, per unit area, equal to $k_1/\lambda_1 = p/\lambda_1 - \rho$, that of an office in a low old building is equal to $k_2/\lambda_2 = p/\lambda_2 - \rho$, so that the increase in cost incurred on one unit area by turning to the more intensive technique equals $p/\lambda_1 - p/\lambda_2 = k_1/\lambda_1 - k_2/\lambda_2$. $1/\lambda_i$ is the output (number of offices) produced per unit area; the formula of section II.19 (with changed normalization)

$$p = \frac{k_1\lambda_2 - k_2\lambda_1}{\lambda_2 - \lambda_1} = \frac{k_1/\lambda_1 - k_2/\lambda_2}{1/\lambda_1 - 1/\lambda_2}$$

therefore represents the increase in cost divided by the increase in output per area or the cost of the marginal unit produced. It is negative if the intensification is not real ($k_i/\lambda_i > k_j/\lambda_j$ but $\lambda_i > \lambda_j$) so that the lower-cost technique should be used alone. A negative labour value ($p < 0$ at $r = 0$) of offices signifies, as before (sections II.4, II.9a, II.9b, II.18, II.18a) that a waste of social labour is taking place, for the lower-cost technique should then be used alone in the stationary state.

This process of raising output per area which gives rise to DRII will be called '*intensification*'. To assume as above that $\lambda_j < \lambda_i$ entails $a_j^v \geqslant a_i^v$ for all v means restricting it to a limited number of cases, but the definition then has the great advantage of being independent of prices and of the level of the rate of profit. The process of intensification can therefore be contrasted with various forms of technical progress, which are also defined in real terms, such as the saving of labour (a reduction of coefficients of the labour vector), saving of raw materials (a reduction of coefficients of the input matrix of a single-product system) or mechanization.

Before we compare, let us recall that *mechanization* means the introduction of a machine for the saving of labour at the expense of using more of each raw material. As is explained in Essay 4 in Part III (see also Schefold, 1976b), Marx's famous theory of the falling rate of profit and of the rising organic composition of capital can be formalized consistently if new machines are assumed to be produced in new processes and used to mechanize existing processes for the production of a given commodity in such a way that the amount of each raw material used in the production of one unit of the commodity is not diminished whereas labour is saved and the total use of raw materials is increased because raw materials are consumed in the production of the machine. The maximum rate of profit of the system will then fall if the commodity in question is basic, and mechanization will be advantageous at low rates of profit where the saving of labour leads to a saving of wages that is sufficiently important to offset the increased costs of raw materials. (The point is that mechanization of e.g. weaving does not, as such, reduce the requirement of the raw material yarn for weaving, but increases the requirements of steel and fuel for the consumption and use of the machine.)

Intensification in the restricted sense of the above definition is similar to mechanization in that it reduces the maximum rate of profit, but it also raises prices at all rates of profit if the commodity produced is basic. It is thus the reverse of a type of technical progress such as a uniform saving of raw materials, which is advantageous at all rates of profit, or a proportionate saving of labour requirements in all processes, which is advantageous at all rates of profit except the maximum. Intensification in the restricted sense lowers the wage curve at all rates of profit; it is therefore introduced only under the pressure of increased demand.

The increased use of raw materials and labour in any one process without a reduction of any input other than land leads to an increase of all prices in terms of the wage rate because some coefficients of the input–output matrix and of the labour vector are increased and none are reduced with intensification in the restricted sense where only the amount of land used per unit of output is diminished.

An example. If one unit of corn is grown per acre by means of corn (with price p) on part of one type of land according to the equation

$$p = (1 + r)\tfrac{1}{4}p + \tfrac{1}{4}w,$$

two processes are used as soon as the extension of the first process to the whole land does not satisfy demand. From

$$p = (1 + r)\tfrac{1}{4}p + \tfrac{1}{4}w + \rho$$
$$p = (1 + r)\tfrac{1}{2}p + \tfrac{1}{2}w + \tfrac{1}{2}\rho$$

one obtains the basic system

$$p = (1 + r)\tfrac{3}{4}p + \tfrac{3}{4}w.$$

The wage curve in terms of corn $w/p = 3 - r$ is therefore reduced to $w/p = (1/3) - r$.

An analogous result obtains in the case of DRI if new land has to be cultivated in order to satisfy increased demand, and if the process on this new no-rent land requires more of each input and labour per unit of output than the process that it replaces in the basic system. The new land is then unambiguously less fertile.

We observe, therefore, that the growth of output on land by extensive and intensive methods unequivocally lowers the rate of profit for any given level of the real wage in accordance with classical views, if we assume that the extension of cultivation on less fertile land and the intensification of production are defined in real terms so as to render their meaning independent of the rate of profit. Analogous results hold for attempts to formulate classical theories of technical progress in the framework of Sraffa systems.

In the same way as there is no meaning of the quantity of capital independently of the rate of profit, fertility and intensification cannot be defined independently of the rate of profit if some inputs rise and some fall in the process.

But this point has been raised so often as to have become tedious. We now want to examine the processes of transition associated with an increase in production. There is a crucial difference between differential rent of the first and of the second kind in regard to this question.

Suppose that demand for, say, corn rises so that a new type of inferior land must be cultivated in order to produce the quantity socially required. If there are capitalists ready to invest at the normal rate of profit, the new type of land will be cultivated as soon as the market price begins to oscillate around a level that is sufficient to cover the cost of production on the new no-rent land.[1]

From the point of view of the logic of the argument, it is clear that the simple rise in demand and in the price is sufficient to warrant the cultivation of the new marginal land. New surplus profits then arise on the lands already cultivated. Whether and when these surplus profits are turned into increases in rent does not affect what happens on the marginal land. The owners of rent-bearing lands will of course want to turn the surplus profits into rents as soon as possible so that the value of these lands as capitalized rents rises, whereas the farmers will try to conceal the surplus profits, but all this does not affect the increase in production and of price.

Matters are quite different with differential rent of the second kind (intensification). In this case, two techniques must come to coexist on the same land, paying a uniform rent per acre, of which one (the less intensive, say technique 1) is cheaper in terms of capital and labour per unit of output but requires more land; we had $p = k_1 + \rho\lambda_1$ and $p = k_2 + \rho\lambda_2$, hence

$$p = \frac{k_2\lambda_1 - k_1\lambda_2}{\lambda_1 - \lambda_2}, \qquad \rho = \frac{k_2 - k_1}{\lambda_1 - \lambda_2}$$

with $\lambda_1 > \lambda_2$, $k_1 < k_2$; $k_i = \Sigma a_i^j p_j + wl_i$; $i = 1, 2$. Suppose that the land is first cultivated only in part, using technique 1. We then have $p = k_1$, and the land pays no rent. Suppose that the price rises above k_1 as soon as the whole land is cultivated and demand rises further. No other land is available for the product in question; the land is an 'oasis'. Even if the *price* now rises up to

$$p = \frac{k_2\lambda_1 - k_1\lambda_2}{\lambda_1 - \lambda_2} > k_1$$

or even beyond, this is in itself *not* sufficient to cause capitalists to use technique 2 in order to increase production on the 'oasis' as long as *rents* do not rise. For as long as rents or a payment for the soil are not demanded, the surplus profits will be higher for those capitalists who continue to use technique 1 than for those who use technique 2. These surplus profits are equal to $p - k_1$ which is greater than $p - k_2$. Only as soon as rents must be paid (or as soon as these surplus profits are capitalized as the price of the soil) will the capitalists be indifferent as to whether they use technique 1 or technique 2, for their 'costs' then include rents (or interest at a rate equal to the rate of profit on the price of the soil π), hence $p = k_1 + \rho\lambda_1 = k_2 + \rho\lambda_2$ (with $\pi = \rho/r$).

In the case of rent of the second kind, the surplus profits accompanying the increase in price must therefore appear as a *cost* to the capitalist, otherwise the rise in price will not lead to an increase in production, whereas no such condition is required in the case of differential rent of the first kind. Here we come to the confirmation of the fundamental difference in the functioning of DRI and DRII which was alluded to at the ends of sections II.19 and II.20. With DRI, the diversity of methods gives origin to profit differentials and hence rents. With DRII, rent causes the duplicity of methods on one land for the production of one commodity. This difference can only become manifest in disequilibrium situations, and in different ways according to the institutional set-up. We confront the two characteristic cases.

If the growing population of an industrialized 'old' land has to be fed by the cultivation of 'new' territories (colonies), the price of bread may rise, if it includes increased costs of transportation for example. However, it may take some time before the landlords in the 'old' land will be able to turn the surplus profits of the capitalists in the old land into increased rents, because, for example, the differential is at first appropriated by traders and intermediaries or because the rent contracts have a long duration. (The initial advantage relative to the eventual equilibrium situation is conversely on the side of the landlords if the importation of cheap corn cheapens the price of bread — as in the case discussed by Ricardo himself — because rents fall only as soon as rent contracts have expired.)

The point is that the pressures on rent-bearing land that follow the change in the price of the commodity produced leave the expansion of production on the no-rent land, i.e. of the process entering the basic system, unaffected. But such pressures arise in the 'combined process' of DRII which enters the basic system. This, our second case, illustrates the curious fact that the presence of DRII may upset the simple laws of distribution, as we saw in section II.20.

Further complications arise if the demarcation of the land and the techniques to be used are subject to political influences. Consider once more the urban example. The possibility of changing building regulations leads to speculation and many owners of houses and of the ground they occupy are inert. They can enjoy rising surplus profits owing to the rising rents paid for the increasing use of office space, so that it takes time for intensification to start. Urban ground rent also rises in the form of a rising price of the soil, but not many houses change hands and not much building takes place before a *political* decision as to the height of the next generation of buildings is reached. If the buildings of the next generation are too low, they will have to displace existing buildings too fast, causing great inconvenience, while too tall buildings are expensive. A theoretical solution involving time preferences to find the 'correct' height may exist in a model of partial equilibrium in neoclassical theory, but it is likely to be rendered irrelevant by speculative forces. A conflict results for which a political solution must be found. There are political limits to the rate at which old buildings can be pulled down, and demand for office space increases at a certain rate (it is the rate of increase of demand that must here be regarded as given in the classical tradition, not a certain quantity demanded). The lower the former rate and the higher the latter, the higher must the new buildings be.

The difficulties of finding the 'correct' equilibrium will be compounded if we think of a whole region with several urban centres. There is some autonomy in the determination of land rents in each city centre in accordance with the local dynamic of growth, yet the land rents of all kinds of land between various city centres must be compatible in such a way that − setting aside other differences in the quality of land − lower land prices at greater distance from any centre will compensate for higher costs of transportation to the centre. It is not likely that a perfect spatial equilibrium will be found and one therefore expects to encounter an abrupt change in land prices at some distance from any city. Rents 'within' the city are determined through the 'autonomous' mechanism of DRII. The price of housing depends in the centre on cost of production *plus* rent, which is determined by the commercial use of the centre, and falls off − other things being equal − in proportion to costs of transportation in terms of money and time. Rents on the agricultural land 'outside' also reflect cost of transportation, but primarily agricultural productivity. Hence the marked discontinuity of land prices at the border line between the two zones, which is a further cause of speculation.

But let us look at the determination of the techniques to be employed in the centre itself from a theoretical point of view. The relationship between price, rent, costs and land requirements can be represented in a diagram (always assuming that the product in question is a non-basic); see Figure II.20a.1. The straight lines represent techniques according to the formula $k_i + \rho \lambda_i = p$, $i =$ I, II, III, IV. The low old buildings (large λ_I, small k_I) coexist with tall buildings at price p_1 and rent ρ_1. Technique IV

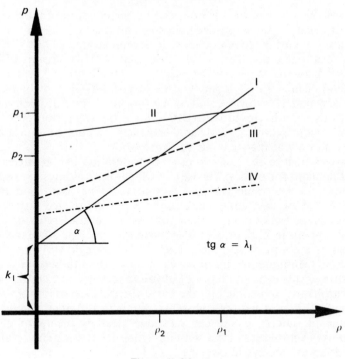

Figure II.20a.1

would be preferable to II in combination with I in any case if it existed. Suppose it does not. Technique III would then represent the dilemma which we have discussed: if III is chosen instead of II, price p_2 and rent ρ_2 are lower than p_1, ρ_1, but III implies a faster replacement of old buildings by new ones because $\lambda_{III} > \lambda_{II}$.

The rates of replacement are not constant but they follow from the given rate of growth g of demand. If techniques I, II are activated in period t with activity levels $q_I(t)$, $q_{II}(t)$ and if the total area of land is Λ, we have the condition for land use $q_I(t)\lambda_I + q_{II}(t)\lambda_{II} = \Lambda$ and the condition for demand $q_I(t) + q_{II}(t) = s(1 + g)^t$ (s constant), therefore

$$q_I(t) = \frac{\Lambda - \lambda_{II}s(1 + g)^t}{\lambda_I - \lambda_{II}}, \qquad q_{II}(t) = \frac{\lambda_I s(1 + g)^t - \Lambda}{\lambda_I - \lambda_{II}}$$

with $\lambda_I s = \Lambda$ and $q_{II}(0) = 0$, if the process of replacement begins at $t = 0$. Technique II replaces the 'old' technique at the rate

$$g_{II}(t) = \frac{q_{II}(t + 1) - q_{II}(t)}{q_{II}(t)} = \frac{g}{1 - \dfrac{\Lambda}{(1 + g)^t \lambda_I s}},$$

i.e. very fast in the early stage ($g_{II}(0) = \infty$) with $g_{II}(t)$ falling to g as t

increases. But the rise of g is bounded by the condition that $q_I(t)$ must not turn negative, i.e. t must remain so small that $\Lambda \geqslant \lambda_{II}s(1 + g)^t$. (An even more intensive technique must intervene at greater t.)

The formulae make it strikingly clear that DRII is incompatible with balanced growth. Whereas the problems of all other kinds of joint production can – if only formally – be solved satisfactorily by assuming a rate of balanced growth equal to the (positive!) rate of profit (section II.9b), this road is closed with DRII where the expansion even 'at the margin' involves both growth and contraction. This structural change disappears only at higher levels of aggregation.

But we return to the 'microscopic' consideration of the effects of the rate of demand for offices. The rate at which old buildings are ceded has been seen to determine the new technique to be used, and the two techniques in use determine rent and price. Several related distributional conflicts shape the outcome: one concerns the level of rents or price of the soil, one the level of prices (or of the letting-price of office space), one speculative extra profits and losses, etc. The strategic variable is always the second technique, for its choice determines the equilibrium situation. In this sense this is not a theory of absolute rent where a certain level of rent is arbitrarily demanded on the basis of a position of power. There is a formal difference between absolute rent and differential rent of the second kind (DRII), which can be made clear by means of counting equations – yet there is also a sense in which DRII *is* similar to absolute rent (see several essays in Arena *et al.*, 1982).

Consider the formal argument first: I should speak of absolute rent[2] if an exogenously determined rate of rent ρ is charged per unit of land (e.g. in terms of labour commanded). If then a single-product system $(\mathbf{A}, \mathbf{I}, \mathbf{l})$ is given, and if $\boldsymbol{\lambda}$ denotes a vector of land of one kind, we should have

$$(1 + r)(a_1^1 p_1 + \cdots + a_1^n p_n) + l_1 + \rho\lambda_1 = p_1$$

$$\cdots\cdots$$

$$(1 + r)(a_n^1 p_1 + \cdots + a_n^n p_n) + l_n + \rho\lambda_n = p_n$$

so that absolute rent operates as if labour l_i in process i was increased by a quantity $\rho\lambda_i$ that depends on the amount of land used in process i (as if land was labour) and on the amount of rent charged by the owners of the land (on the basis of their monopoly power). It is this concept of absolute rent that establishes a formal analogy between land and labour and that seems to justify the neoclassical assertion that there is a symmetry between land theories and labour theories of value. But this assertion rests on an approach to rent which is not the classical theory of rent. Land and labour are not symmetric as 'factors of production' in classical theory (see section II.20b).

We now measure in terms of the standard commodity (introducing the real wage w) and extend the analysis to m kinds of land with m rents being charged:

$$(1 + r)(a_1^1 p_1 + \cdots + a_1^n p_n) + wl_1 + \rho_1\lambda_1^1 + \cdots + \rho_m\lambda_1^m = p_1$$

$$\cdots\cdots$$

$$(1 + r)(a_n^1 p_1 + \cdots + a_n^n p_n) + wl_n + \rho_1\lambda_n^1 + \cdots + \rho_m\lambda_n^m = p_n.$$

If $\mathbf{q}'(\mathbf{I} - \mathbf{A}) = R\mathbf{q}'\mathbf{A}$ is the standard commodity, and if we normalize $\mathbf{q}'\mathbf{1} = 1$, and $\mathbf{q}'\boldsymbol{\lambda}^i = 1$, $i = 1, ..., m$, for each type of land, we obtain

$$r\mathbf{q}'\mathbf{A}\mathbf{p} + w\mathbf{q}'\mathbf{1} + \rho_1\mathbf{q}'\boldsymbol{\lambda}^1 + \cdots + \rho_m\mathbf{q}'\boldsymbol{\lambda}^m = \mathbf{q}'(\mathbf{I} - \mathbf{A})\mathbf{p} = 1,$$

hence the formula

$$\frac{r}{R} + w + \rho_1 + \cdots + \rho_m = 1,$$

which renders the trade-off between the real wage and rent rates ρ_i (given the rate of profit) perspicuous.

Absolute rent in this sense could result from imperfect competition and also from a system of land taxes. It may be important in some real cases but it is structurally different from differential rent. The latter is due to the coexistence of more processes than there are commodities so that rents can be determined as differentials in cost, whereas rents appear as independent elements of cost in the case of absolute rent. A rise in absolute rent does not presuppose a rise in demand. Both forms can be combined: for example, it is possible that the marginal land pays absolute rent so that the differential rents are in the normal case increased accordingly.

Now we compare this to DRII. It is clear that DRII is formally different from absolute rent, yet it seems to me that the dynamic of DRII that we have discussed will often operate as if DRII was absolute. For we have seen that the more cost-intensive technique (in terms of capital and labour) will be adopted by capitalists no sooner than it has been made as profitable as the cheaper technique by the rise in the rent. A speculative rise in the price of the product and in rent must therefore take place – possibly in the form of a speculative trade of parcels of land – before the second technique is actually introduced. As soon as it is installed, it will – if expectations were not false – 'justify' the extent of the rise in prices and rent.

The rise in price may thus exceed the differential that is warranted because of the rise in demand. After the event, everything will look as if the structure of costs derived from the methods of production determined price and rent alone, but the economic causality may more often work the other way round, especially in the case of the urban example: costs in terms of capital and labour are allowed to rise in the choice of the second method until (given rent) only normal profits remain. The equilibrium constellation looks as if costs (including profits) determined the price at which a quantity is demanded that can be produced at no lesser costs, but this may be mistaken: the combination of methods will not necessarily represent a least-cost technique if there is an exogenous (political) influence on the choice of technique.

The neoclassicist would explain the process of rising prices in terms of a diagram of the type shown in Figure II.20a.2. There is a supply curve for the product which rises in steps, each step corresponding to a combination of two methods on the 'oasis'. The rise in demand is

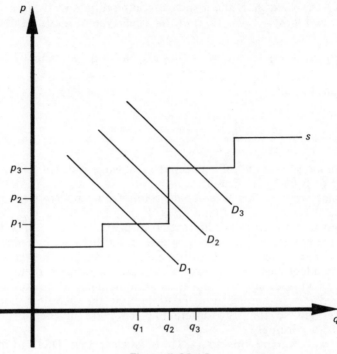

Figure II.20a.2

expressed in terms of a shift of the demand curve to the right. There are constant costs with rising output in the vicinity of q_1, the rise in demand is checked by the rise in price at q_2, given D_2, and the price rises with demand until a higher level is reached with a different combination of two techniques (q_3).

There are several objections to this kind of interpretation from the classical point of view. Sraffa's fundamental argument concerns the interdependence of supply and demand if the product is basic; independent curves of supply and demand can then not be drawn. But even if the product is non-basic and if demand curves are accepted (although points on them out of equilibrium are difficult to identify by rigorous and objective analysis), the situation at q_2 cannot be analysed at the same level of abstraction as that at q_1 and q_3 because the rate of profit cannot be uniform in the system at q_2.

According to the classical method one assumes given techniques at a given rate of profit. Their determination at q_1 and q_3 is a question of a historical process. But the situation at q_2 is transitory; it can be left open whether the transition is characterized mainly by speculative and disorderly or by steady movements of market prices. The extent to which preferences change, income increases or population grows, as explanations of the rise in demand, the importance of imperfect competition, the role of expectations: all these have to be analysed in the concrete context of that transition. The same is true of the question of the relationship between market prices and prices of production in situations such as those at q_1 and q_3. The point is, then, that p_1 and p_3 represent prices of production, while p_2 is something different: a market price.

Attempts to explain processes in terms of supply and demand as derived from preferences and in terms of power (absolute rent) appear from this point of view not as altogether wrong but as partial truths and auxiliary constructions which can sometimes be used to good purpose in applied economies. Their relevance cannot be judged independently of the institutional context. There is essentially one straightforward axiomatic theory of prices of production, and there are many incomplete and complicated approaches to the explanation of market prices.

The model of rent in general, and of DRII and the urban example in particular, do not here require a methodology that would be different from that appropriate to other applications of Sraffa's theory of single or of joint production. Classical theory always starts from the assumption of given methods of production and derives prices that seem to reflect only costs of production. But it is also true that the determination of techniques is subject to influences of varied character. The view of competition explained in Essay 5 in Part Three is compatible with the assumption that there is a tendency to equalize the rates of profit even if there are market imperfections. Big corporations tend to understate their profits *ex post* because most of their profits are hidden in depreciation allowances, costs of representation, and the like. This means that the methods of production they use are in part chosen so as to allow the concealment of profits as costs. The rise in price and rent that we have discussed here is a similar phenomenon – irrespective of whether the rise in rent in the case of DRII is explained as in part imposed or only as demand determined: it is true in any case that the second technique that comes in will justify this rise in price and rent.

In essence, we have found that rents arise because of cost differentials which cannot be eliminated through an extension of the least cost technique since land is scarce. Wages and relative wage rates have a different explanation in classical theory because labour is usually not in short supply. Often, even if effective demand is such that full employment of labour could be reached, the constraint may be overcome through migration and changes in the participation rate. The macroeconomic theory of distribution here has to deal with a variety of possible cases, while different skills of labour are, unlike land, producible – at least in principle. The ensuing asymmetry in the treatment of land and labour will be analysed in the next section.

Notes

1 Cost of production may here include a payment for monopoly rent, that is required to induce the owners (perhaps the state) of the marginal land to allow production on a soil previously reserved for non-commercial use.

   Geographical hazards, political and military conditions and other obstacles to colonization were often the cause of an occupation of territories not according to the hierarchy of costs of production. But reasons similar to those precluding our discussion of the determinants of monopoly rent prevent us from analysing the reasons for violations of the 'Ricardian rule' of cultivating lands with cheapest cost of production first. There is, however, in my opinion no *theoretical* difficulty involved in modifying the Sraffian framework according to concrete historical circumstances to take account of elements of monopoly rent and of violations of the 'Ricardian rule'.

2　To repeat: the term 'absolute rent' is synonymous with what is called by others 'monopoly rent' and has nothing to do with Marx's dubious concept of absolute rent, which is based on the idea that techniques used in agriculture may imply low organic compositions of capital and, therefore, high profits in the early stages of a historical transformation of values into prices of production so that parts of these high profits can be retained as rents by land-owners if their power inhibits the free inflow of capital to agriculture and the corresponding reduction of prices.

20b　Homogeneity and Heterogeneity of Capital, Land and Labour

In section II.20a it has for the first time become useful to employ marginalist expressions. This should come as no surprise since marginalist theory originated from an unwarranted generalization of Ricardo's theory of rent at the intensive margin. The treatment of rent is nevertheless substantially different in Sraffa and in neoclassical models insofar as 'absolute rent', as introduced in the last section, could result from increased demand in neoclassical theory, whereas it would be regarded as temporary or as imposed by exogenous forces in the classical approach. The structure of a Sraffa system with land, fixed and circulating capital, non-basics and labour shows clearly that each 'factor' appears with a distinct structure in the model, whereas neoclassical theory gives a symmetrical treatment to each of the traditional factors land L, labour N and capital K in a production function $F(L, N, K)$. No wonder that neoclassicals feel justified to extend this to n factors (including intangibles such as entrepreneurship) once these totally heterogeneous objects (space, work and commodities or money) have been assimilated. Capital, land and labour are treated in an analogous manner in models of general equilibrium. The means of production in a general equilibrium system are given as a list of heterogeneous objects such as stocks, machines, parcels of land of different types, and classes of labour of different skills. Supply and demand relationships are derived for each of them and these determine the rental rates of each stock, machine, parcel of land and type of labour. The fact that machines are produced is taken into account, but the produced machines are different commodities from the machines inherited from the past and used at the beginning of the period under consideration, so that there is no general rate of profit on produced means of production. The leading models of neoclassical theory therefore introduce capital, land and labour either as three homogeneous quantities or as three sets of heterogeneous objects. The interchangeability of the factors of production in neoclassical theory due to the analogous treatment they receive is, for example, reflected in the fact that production functions for capital and labour are structurally identical with production functions for land and labour. Differences appear in the theory of growth (capital is invested, population increases, land is fixed), but not in static equilibrium.

Matters are quite different in classical theory as represented in Sraffa's model. Here capital is a homogeneous quantity in so far as there is a uniform rate of profit on the value of the produced means of production, which are, however, heterogeneous as use values. The homogenization of the means of production as capital is the result of the evaluation of commodities, which is the main theme of the book. No corresponding homogenization of land takes place; on the contrary, it is the essence of differential rent that different lands yield different incomes per acre. Land is treated in a special manner, even if it is regarded as a joint product because it is then the defining characteristic of land that the amount appearing as an output is equal to the amount used as an input. Each land is in any case a non-basic and may as such be eliminated from the system. Finally, the treatment of labour exhibits a curious mixture. Labour is introduced as something homogeneous; the process of homogenization that permits the use of only one variable for the wage rate takes place prior to the determination of prices and is hardly discussed at all. This final section of Part II is dedicated to answering the question as to what justifies the assumptions which led to this structural difference in the treatment of the so-called 'factors of production'. We shall mainly be concerned with the treatment of labour, for while capital and land have been discussed extensively, the homogeneity of labour has been accepted as if it was a matter of course.

The assumption that labour is 'all of one kind' is just as unreal as the assumption that capital is perfectly malleable. Yet it is made by people who fiercely attack the latter hypothesis. Why is one of these hypotheses a convenient and permissible simplification while the other is not?

It is helpful to discuss first the homogeneity of commodities in order to solve this puzzle. As a matter of fact even the assumption of homogeneous commodities represents an abstraction. It is *not* simply justified because 'the market' classes objects that are sold as 'homogeneous' commodities (e.g. apples of a certain type), rather we have to explain why 'the market' can do this. The answer is that there are objective criteria for classification, deriving in part from biological taxonomy (species, race), in part from quality of preservation. Matters are easy with inorganic materials: there are some commodities, for example metals, which are physically homogeneous to such an extent that any bar, e.g. of copper of given fineness, serves any conceivable purpose just as well as any other bar. Some commodities are homogeneous with respect only to special uses, while they differ for others. Which uses matter for classification depends on the function of the commodity in the system of production and on their role in consumption as a social activity. One buys food not only for oneself, but also for one's guests, and one buys clothes not to suit one's own taste, but that of others.

The main problem of the social theory of consumption consists not so much in the analysis of the *freedom* of choice as in analysing and explaining the *constraints* on consumption that are given with the task of reproducing a household in a given social environment: in surburbs cars are a necessity for the middle class; elsewhere they are a luxury used by the upper class, etc.

To work out a phenomenology of the social formation of use values is a formidable task to which the less was contributed lately, the more economists got lost in the neoclassical theory of preferences. Meanwhile, we observe that commodities are differentiated according to their uses, and differences of quality are – in accordance with costs – reflected in prices, but commodities that are physically homogeneous can be assumed to have uniform prices as a result of competition.

Capital goods have very different uses. But as means of production of saleable outputs they yield uniform profits on their costs, if there is equilibrium. The level of the general rate of profit is the strategic variable of capitalist development and whatever affects it adversely (for example, real wages rising faster than productivity) was, in the view of Ricardo and his followers, an incentive for capitalists to act jointly as a class, and this in spite of the heterogeneity of capital goods.

This needed not be so with land. Traditional sociological bonds uniting landlords may be stronger than those uniting capitalists in countries where class divisions have a long history reaching far back into pre-capitalist conditions. But, from what we have seen in section II.19, it follows that landlords, mine owners, modern estate agents, cannot operate like a class united through a common revenue paid according to a common rate; however united they are through social traditions – economically they are divided because the laws of commodity production lead to specialization in the use of land. The opposition between landlords and capitalists often concerns only parcels of land and even can all but disappear if rents and surplus profits cannot be properly distinguished and/or if the capitalist owns the land. Landlords can in any case have no more unity from the economic point of view, however strong social and political bonds may have been in earlier times, than derives from the linkage, if it exists, between different products grown on different lands. The lords of wheat-producing lands in England were once united because of the corn laws, but that did not unite them with mine owners; the rents of the latter did not necessarily move in relationship with those of the former. Rents were a macroeconomic problem for Ricardo only because of the uniformity of the product, corn, that represented the main element of wages, and because the predominance of corn meant that agricultural rents in general were determined by the conditions of corn production. Because of this heterogeneity of land it does not make much sense to draw a curve showing the relationship between rents and the wage rate or rents and the rate of profit in analogy with the curve showing the trade-off between the rate of profit and wages. Whereas a monotonically falling wage curve is a natural result, so that the exceptions that occur in the context of a joint production have to be explained, there is no reason to expect a monotonically falling rent curve as a function of the rate of profit if wages are also present.

What now of labour? The wage curve would not make sense if labour was not in some sense homogeneous or if relative wage rates were not constant. There are quite different reasons for the heterogeneity of labour. We have to consider which of them might be relevant for classical theorizing.

Various social prejudices lead to artificial segmentations of the working class. There is or ought to be compensation for dangerous or dirty work or work that is despised (Smith's public executioner). Pure theory interprets such attitudes to work in principle as given, but the economist should explain the origin, the use and abuse of tastes in a historical context. This task does not concern economists exclusively. It is a legitimate simplification to abstract from it for theoretical purposes.

Next we come to skills that are produced. The usual assumption here is that the cost of production of these skills is known, so that relative wage rates can (in so far as they relate to skills) be explained through costs of production in the same way as prices of produced means of production. (It is clear that the caveat that cost of production is a one-sided expression because it neglects the influence of the uses of skilled people as inputs applies here just as well as in the case of commodities.) Many difficulties beset this conception: the time-lags involved are very long, important skills are provided outside the commodity-producing system (e.g. in the family) and tastes and prejudices in practice often play an overriding influence. I nevertheless see no fundamental objection to the classical approach, which – like neoclassical theories – regards the skill of labour as in some way analogous to capital.

It goes almost without saying that natural skills like artistic talents, dexterity, body size or body strength may yield scarcity rents which are left aside in the classical approach by way of a legitimate abstraction.

There remains then what I regard as the fundamental question of whether different kinds of unskilled work that do not require special skills (produced or natural) and that are not subject to special prejudices can be considered as homogeneous in the same way as e.g. gold is homogeneous. Therefore one may ask why different kinds of labour that require only a negligible time of apprenticeship can and are compared although the outputs produced are heterogeneous, say window-cleaning and shovelling. The market provides a measure in that the output produced (measured in terms of prices) can be compared to wages paid, but this measure functions only to the extent that net output can be calculated and is priced in the market (which is not the case if the work process produces only part of the final product). Moreover, our concern is really with the question why the window-cleaner and the shoveller receive equal pay for equal hours. What then is the reason why it makes sense in classical theory to equalize different kinds of unskilled work *prior* to the determination of prices?

The hypothesis of homogeneity is so difficult to swallow because it can in no model involving different capital goods be assumed that labour is all of one kind since there are work processes that are specific to each commodity. Shovelling and window-cleaning may occur in several industries, but no two industries are alike in their labour requirements.

The basic answer to our puzzle is simply this: if one asks under what conditions the wage differentials disappear, one is led to the conclusion that conventions define 'normal effort' which are made operative through free or enforced mobility of labour. Gold has the same value in coins and in bars if both can be converted into each other at negligible cost and without changing the fineness. The same is true of the window cleaner and the shoveller. Apprenticeship corresponds to recasting and normal effort to the normal standard of fineness.

However, any convention as to the units of length to be employed under various circumstances exist only because there are universal procedures for measuring length. The fineness of gold is determined by objective chemical measurement. What about labour? The question has two aspects. First one has to explain why labour is measurable. The answer: 'because it is executed in real time, which is measurable' leads at once to the second question: why should different kinds of work performed during the same time count as equivalent? It is obviously the notion of 'normal effort' introduced above that is crucial. It has been treated in different ways by different authors.

The deepest philosophical – though not necessarily correct – analysis of the homogeneity of labour was given by Marx, and I have amended the essay on Marx in Part III in this direction in order to render my interpretation of this procedure. But Sraffa has by-passed the analysis of the homogeneity of labour, and all we can do here is to show how he did it.

There are two conceptions of simple (unskilled) labour, which I should like to call 'strong' and 'weak' homogeneity. 'Strong homogeneity' is what we find in Marx. He supposes that 'normal effort' is *physiologically* measurable, so that we can – at least in principle – ascertain – even if practical measurements are not precise – whether the window-cleaner and the shoveller expend labour with equal effort in a given amount of time, much in the same way as we can ascertain whether the same amount of gold is contained in a ring and in a coin. Different kinds of labour are thus strongly homogeneous because the commodity labour power is homogeneous and has the (in principle measurable) use value of yielding homogeneous labour, even if this labour is put to different uses, like gold which is cast in different forms. Marx sought the conceptual cause of 'homogeneous labour' in 'abstract labour', and this is discussed in Essay 4 of Part III below.

Ricardo assumed 'weak homogeneity' in section II of the first chapter of his *Principles*: 'The estimation in which different qualities of labour are held, comes soon to be adjusted in the market with sufficient precision for all practical purposes, and depends much on the comparative skill of the labourer, and intensity of the labour performed'. Without really trying to analyse 'skill and intensity', Ricardo concludes with a quotation from Smith which asserts that the 'proportion' between wage rates in 'different employments' is not altered for any considerable time, even 'by revolutions in the public welfare' which affect distribution or 'the proportion between different rates of wages and profits'. Weak homogeneity thus entails the hypothesis that wage differentials may be taken as data from the market to reduce different kinds of labour to an arbitrary common unit.

Sraffa similarly does not simply assume homogeneous labour for he postulates in section 10 that differences in the quality of work have been expressed as differences in the quantity of labour: 'We ... assume any differences in quality to have been previously reduced to equivalent differences in quantity' (PCMC, sec. 10). Since we abstract here from skills, this means in our context that he accepts wage differentials unexplained and uses them for aggregation. The only alternative assumption – that labour is trivially homogeneous through being all of one kind – is, though not impossible to conceive, not to be taken very seriously since it is as difficult to imagine that the same kind of concrete labour, e.g. shovelling, is the only form of labour in all industries as it is to imagine a capitalist one-commodity world. It is therefore certainly not 'trivial homogeneity' which Sraffa has in mind, although it 'amounts to the same thing' (PCMC, sec. 10).

There is good institutional evidence that wage differentials are constant, but very little good theory to explain this fact (leaving aside theories based on the reduction of skilled to unskilled labour, which is here taken for granted because we are concerned only with the questionable homogeneity of unskilled labour in different occupations). Sraffa's acceptance of wage differentials is not blind, however, but in keeping with what I take to be his general philosophy that there is no universal economic theory of capitalism that would derive from an ahistorical rationality of economics. All theories are crude in that their assumptions can only be simplified idealizations of a more differentiated reality, but they are refined if the conceptual superstructure built on those assumptions shows a compelling inner logic. Since it is Sraffa's aim to question the idea of a general rationality of the capitalist framework by analyzing the key concept of the neoclassical theory of *capital*, it is not surprising that *labour* is treated in a simple fashion. But it is a momentous question to ask why such an approach should work and why Sraffa's assumptions about the homogeneity of labour can be simpler even than his assumptions about demand for consumption goods: whereas only the result of the social determination of the composition of output is assumed to be given and prices of outputs are derived in the system, both the composition and the evaluation of the various inputs of labour are taken to be known and left unexplained. The manifold labour processes represent a very differentiated reality which seems to obey no general law. At any rate, Sraffa does not explain it.

I shall not attempt an explanation, and the open-endedness of Sraffa's theory is discussed elsewhere in this book. But the treatment of labour may be formalized. This will allow us to return to the main theme, that is to say, to showing how the treatment of labour in Sraffa is structurally different from that of capital and land.

We consider a single-product system with n industries. There are m kinds of labour, distinguished not by the produce of each industry, but by the operations to be performed. Some kinds of workers occur in virtually all industries (e.g. cleaners), some in many (e.g. electricians), some are specific (e.g. composers). The number of occupations m may exceed the number of industries, or it may be smaller; $m = 1$ is theoretically conceivable.

For the sake of argument we assume (although these are by no means simple matters) that it is possible to reduce differences in skill to differences in labour time (through the costs of training in so far as the skills are accessible to the average individual, or through scarcity rents in so far as special talents, special preferences or special monopolies are concerned).

The system can then be written as follows:

$$l_1^1 w_1 + \cdots + l_1^m w_m + (1 + r)\mathbf{a}_1 \mathbf{p} = p_1$$

$$\cdots$$

$$l_n^1 w_1 + \cdots + l_n^m w_m + (1 + r)\mathbf{a}_n \mathbf{p} = p_n$$

where w_i is the wage rate of labour of type i, $\mathbf{a}_i$ the vector of inputs to process i, and $\mathbf{p}$ the price vector. If prices are expressed in terms of money, the dimension of w_i is 'money per unit of labour of type i'. Hence it seems impossible to set wage rates equal, e.g. $w_1 = w_2$, or to add types of labour, e.g. $l_1^1 + l_1^2$. Yet this is precisely what Marxian theory does. Strong homogeneity means that two different activities l_1^1 and l_1^2 may be of equal dimension as expenditures of homogeneous labour power.

One may postulate that there are coefficients α_i, $i = 2, ..., m$, of the dimension 'type of labour 1, divided by type of labour i'. Such coefficients result from wage differentials:

$$\alpha_i = \frac{w_i}{w_1}, \qquad i = 2, ..., n.$$

If the wage differentials are invariant, the coefficients α_i allow labour to be expressed in terms of labour of type 1. With $w = w_1$, and $\mathbf{l}^1 + \alpha_2 \mathbf{l}^2 + \cdots + \alpha_m \mathbf{l}^m = \mathbf{l}$ one may write

$$w_1 \mathbf{l}^1 + \cdots + w_m \mathbf{l}^m = w_1 \left(\mathbf{l}^1 + \frac{w_2}{w_1} \mathbf{l}^2 + \cdots + \frac{w_m}{w_1} \mathbf{l}^m \right) = w\mathbf{l},$$

an equation that is dimensionally correct and in which the dimension of vector $\mathbf{l}$ is that of $\mathbf{l}^1$.

This is what I take to be Sraffa's procedure, which may be justified pragmatically, as we have seen. We have called it 'weak homogeneity'. Since Sraffa does not say how the differences in the quality of labour are to be reduced to differences in quantity, one cannot prove that he means to take wage differentials as his basis for aggregation, but no other weights have been proposed.

Marx emphatically postulates a different intellectual operation, which would allow one to write $1 = \alpha_2 = \cdots = \alpha_m$ and $\mathbf{l} = \mathbf{l}^1 + \cdots + \mathbf{l}^m$ ('strong homogeneity'). For Marx it was more than an assumption made for the sake of simplicity. His equations are conceptually correct, but not economically meaningful if they are defended only on grounds of the argument that all types of human activity are performed in real time.

That is why Marx added the requirement that all simple labour be of an average quality. There seems to be some foundation for this view in the competitive process. Since it is clear that labourers move from less agreeable jobs to more agreeable ones (if they can) and that employers select the more industrious (where they can find them), competition equalizes 'something'.

Whatever it is, it must be assumed to have already been equalized when labour is introduced in classical theory as a concept that is supposed ultimately to explain competition. It is either the marginal disutility of work or it is the intensity of work. Workers have – given equal remuneration per hour – individually no incentive to move from shovelling to window-cleaning, if the marginal disutility of one hour of shovelling is equal to the marginal disutility of one hour of window-cleaning. There is no social pressure to make workers move between shovelling and window-cleaning, if both types of work yield the same hourly wage and are performed – according to the prevailing view – with equal intensity. The former interpretation is subjective, the latter supposedly objective and physiological. The former view would lead to the abandonment of classical theory, the latter is not rigorous in that the results of modern medicine and economic practice do not substantiate it at all: no national wage agreement contains a measure of the intensity of work that would be applicable to all professions, although the collective wage bargain would become much simpler if it existed.

I therefore do not believe that the assumption of strong homogeneity would be compatible with Sraffa's methodology. To adopt the subjective view would be contrary to his critique of neoclassical theory, to adopt the postulate of a social notion of 'intensity' across professions would be contrary to his consistent reliance on data that are, in principle, objectively measurable, and there is no trace of any attempt by him to found a concept of 'intensity' on a prior concept of the formation of 'labour power' and 'abstract labour' as in Marx. However, there is no firm proof of this. Since one may formally put the differentials equal to unity ($\alpha_1 = \alpha_2 = \cdots = \alpha_m = 1$), there is here the possibility of considering Sraffa both as a Marxist who believes in exploitation of labour power and as a neo-Ricardian. Strong homogeneity leads to the vision that economic forces tend to create unity among unskilled labourers. Weak homogeneity allows for the possibility that rivalry between different segments of the working class develops and may appear to dominate distribution although the theory shows that, given the rate of profit, the share of total wages is determined.

If this agnostic position is maintained, justice is done to historical forces which render conflict as likely as peaceful bargaining in the formation of wage rates.

The structural similarity of the theories of land and labour has now been revealed as a false trail because the wage differentials are assumed to be given from outside while the rates of differential rent are determined within the model. We can use the standard commodity $\mathbf{q}'(\mathbf{I} - \mathbf{A})$, with $\mathbf{q}'(\mathbf{I} - \mathbf{A})\mathbf{p} = 1$, in order to show possible movements of wage differentials explicitly: in now familiar notation (and using the normalization $1 = \mathbf{q}_1\mathbf{l}^1 = \cdots = \mathbf{q}_m\mathbf{l}^m$ for each type of labour) one obtains

$$\mathbf{q}'\,(\mathbf{I} - \mathbf{A})\mathbf{p} - r\mathbf{q}'\mathbf{A}\mathbf{p} = w_1\mathbf{q}_1\mathbf{l}^1 + \cdots + w_m\mathbf{q}_m\mathbf{l}^m$$

therefore

$$1 - \frac{r}{R} = w_1 + \cdots + w_m.$$

The quantities $w_1, \ldots, w_m$, r/R denote fractions of the standard product. Relative wages w_i/w_j are normally supposed to be constant. But if they are not, the formula shows that, given the rate of profit, the real wage of each type of labour can only be increased if the sum of all other wages is reduced by the same amount. This may be said to represent the distributional conflict between sections of the working class which are segmented according to the kind of work they perform and which receive relative wages according to exogenous rules (which may reflect trade union power). Constant relative wages allow the formal aggregation of heterogeneous unskilled labour in accordance with the principle of weak homogeneity. However, they express in general not social homogeneity, but a segmentation of the working class. Each interest group of workers defends its share against all others in a wage bargain that appears to be between labour and employers, but that is in reality more often between the sections of the working class themselves to the extent that the rate of profit is already given.

Note that the relationship between the rate of profit and wages $w_1, \ldots, w_m$ remains the same if relative wages change, as long as we reckon in terms of the standard commodity. On the other hand, different curves for relative prices are obtained as a function of the rate of profit for different relative wages because the vector of aggregate labour

$$\mathbf{l} = \mathbf{l}^1 + \alpha_2\mathbf{l}^2 + \cdots + \alpha_m\mathbf{l}^m$$

depends on relative wage rates since $\alpha_i = w_i/w$. This shows – in my view decisively – that Sraffa's analysis is based on weak homogeneity and presupposes constant wage differentials, for, if differentials were allowed to vary, $\mathbf{l}$ would change in response to changes of r.

If, on the other hand, real wages are expressed in terms of commodity baskets $\mathbf{d}_i$ that are specific for each kind of labour, one obtains for relative real wages the function

$$\frac{\mathbf{d}_i\mathbf{p}}{\mathbf{d}_j\mathbf{p}} = \frac{\mathbf{d}_i[\mathbf{I} - (1 + r)\mathbf{a}]^{-1}(\mathbf{l}^1 + \alpha_2\mathbf{l}^2 + \cdots \alpha_m\mathbf{l}^m)}{\mathbf{d}_j[\mathbf{I} - (1 + r)\mathbf{A}]^{-1}(\mathbf{l}^1 + \alpha_2\mathbf{l}^2 + \cdots + \alpha_m\mathbf{l}^m)},$$

which shows that relative real wages vary with the rate of profit, even if wage differentials (i.e. the coefficients α_i) are fixed and given.

It follows that, as an alternative to taking the wage differentials w_i as given (which may be interpreted as real wage rates expressed in terms of any standard common to all segments of the labour class), one might also take relative real wages in terms of specific standards d_i as given, and try to derive the aggregation coefficients α_i on that basis. However, it is more convenient to retain at least the idea of a common standard of the real wage (e.g. the standard commodity) that is used to express wages of all segments of the labour force, since relative wage differentials have to be kept constant for the type of analysis we have undertaken. It is clear, on the other hand, that the assumption of different wage baskets that are specific for each kind of labour would destroy even the semblance of a homogeneity of labour.

The comparison with land is now simple. Formulae of the same type as above were obtained in the case of absolute rent, but the formulae for different kinds of labour remain different from those for differential rent, even if wage rates vary.

A clear analogy between differential rent and wage differentials occurs only in those exceptional cases where the same product is produced by means of two methods that differ in the proportions in which they use different kinds of labour. If three exceptionally strong men are able to dig a pit faster than three average workers and get more pay accordingly, the extra wage bears a similarity to a differential rent, but such examples seem rather artificial in an industrial society. The case of piece wages is more to the point. If workers are paid per unit of output, it is not altogether impossible for employers to let slow work go by since proportionately less wages have to be paid. However, a proportionate reduction of the wage for slow work does not cover overheads of any kind, it is in conflict with the idea of a minimum wage, which (even if it does not exist in the economy as a whole) nevertheless has some meaning in each trade and, last but not least, piece wages are paid in a dynamic process in which employers pay more attractive wages to the better workers in order to raise the intensity of work in a given occupation (where its evolution over time is measurable).

A strict analogy between wage rates and the rentals of land was found in the section on international trade (see Part II, Ch. 19a) on the assumption of full employment, with labour acting as a constraint analogous to land. But this compensation of differences in the efficiency of work through differences of wages could be permanent and was not subject to reduction under competitive pressure because labour was assumed not to be mobile in the international context and because technologies were specific for different countries.

The analogy between land and labour is not compelling even in the international context as soon as the full employment condition is dropped. Moreover, it is not clear what the differentials reflect, if at least two entire hierarchies of wage rates and work intensities in two different countries are involved. If efficiency is different in the North and in the South, how is it to be decided whether this difference, which certainly reflects differences in the productivity of work (technology), is also affected by a difference in the average intensity of work (assiduity)? A precise measurement of the average intensity of work is clearly not possible in the international context, since it does not even exist on a national scale. As a matter of fact, the phrase perhaps is often used only for ideological purposes.

After considering this and other examples, one must conclude that wage differentials bear only a rare and superficial resemblance to rents as derived in Sraffa. The fundamental reason is that labour is in the long period, unlike the relatively more fertile lands, in general not in short supply: not in the aggregate, if we do not assume full employment, and not at the level of different skills, to the extent that these are producible. The analogy is close with surplus profits and quasi-rents as discussed in the section on rent (see Part II, Ch. 20a), but neither phenomenon would destroy the structural dissimilarity in the treatment of profits, wages and rents in Sraffa, which contrasts with the analogous treatment of all three in static neoclassical theory.

This much can be said: the positive theory of the regulation of wage conflicts and of the stability of relative wages in a long period analysis, the historical account of the very slow change of standards of distributive justice regarding different kinds of work and the extension of the 'macro' critique of the marginal productivity theory of the wage to that of wage differentials all transcend the formal confrontation of the treatment of land and labour and hence the scope of this essay on joint production.

PART III

Other Essays

Essay 1 Production Costs in Neoclassical Theory

In 1925 Sraffa published his first attempt at a critique of the neoclassical theory of equilibrium under the title 'Sulle relazioni fra costo e quantità prodotta' (Sraffa, 1925) ('On the relationship between costs and output'). The attack was directed against the Marshallian theory of partial equilibrium; the Walrasian theory was hardly mentioned. Marshall's analysis rests upon the presupposition of perfect competition and the *ceteris paribus* clause: the prices of products are determined by the equilibrium of the collective supply and demand curves in individual markets in which individual buyers or sellers cannot influence the price. Since all economic transactions are interconnected, however, supply and demand in an individual market are indirectly connected; partial analysis can therefore only be meaningfully carried out when it is established that the quantitative influence of the indirect connection of supply and demand is so small that it may be ignored and both curves can be constructed independently of one another. But this condition, as Sraffa shows, is essentially fulfilled only when each individual commodity is produced under conditions of constant returns to scale – that is exactly under the conditions that leave no room for the neoclassical influence of utility on price.

The modern reader might now regard this discussion as obsolete since Walras's system of general economic equilibrium appears to have overtaken Marshall's. But the situation is not so simple. On the one hand Walras and his successors did not succeed in comprehending satisfactorily the connection between prices and output of capital goods already produced and in the process of being produced (that is the typical problem of interdependence of capitalistic production);[1] on the other hand, Walras was unable to incorporate increasing returns and the elements of a dynamic macroeconomic accumulation theory contained in the Marshallian conception. Moreover, partial analysis in the Marshallian tradition lives on in modern textbooks on microeconomics, because Walrasian theory does not explain the position of the individual firm. It is therefore not only of historical interest to study Sraffa's critique of Marshall today, to consider whether partial analysis since then has been placed on a better footing and to ask to what extent modern theory is able to answer Marshall's questions, taking into account the whole wealth of phenomena he tried to grasp.

The context of Sraffa's article of 1925, which was the first in a small but important series of contributions of his, was as follows. Marshallian theory had been seriously questioned in 1922 in an article by J. C. Clapham in the *Economic Journal* with the curious title 'Of Empty Economic Boxes' (Clapham, 1922). On the surface, Clapham's article seemed only to question the empirical applicability of a particular Marshallian distinction for the analysis of the conditions of supply in particular industries. Clapham, so it seemed (especially since this was the point taken seriously by Pigou in his reply to Clapham in the same issue of the journal), asked how industries such as hat-making or coal-mining could be classed as obeying the 'laws' of diminishing, increasing or constant returns. Increasing returns could confidently be expected to prevail in manufacturing industries, but did not the growth of productivity let it appear doubtful whether even coal-mining should also be classed as an industry with increasing returns? And were constant returns not altogether improbable as the result of counteracting tendencies to increasing and diminishing returns which just balanced each other?

Clapham's question as to the applicability of the basic concepts underlying the construction of the supply curve were uncomfortable and his emphasis on increasing returns was disturbing and led to a long debate because increasing returns are not generally compatible with perfect competition. Moreover, the article had deeper layers because its subtle and ironic references to the endless geographical and historical variety of the institutions of economic life reflected the historian's (for Clapham was a most eminent economic historian) traditional distrust of the abstractions of economic theory. There is no explicit reference in the article to the continental *Methodenstreit* between the German 'Historical School' (with whose work Clapham was well acquainted) and the 'Austrians' as the defenders of (neoclassical) economic theory, although some aspects of Clapham's article are reminiscent of that important debate about the correct method for arriving at statements about economic matters – from generalized observations, as the historians emphasized, or from *a priori* reasoning based on a preconceived notion of economic rationality, as the neoclassicists (in the continental case, the Austrians) have always maintained. English neoclassicism, as represented by Marshall and as developed by Pigou, seemed misleading to Clapham, because it did not allow the transition to be made from theory to the real historical world.

I surmise that the English debate that followed Clapham's contribution was, not really paradoxically, less acute at the *methodological* level than the German debate because Marshall's writings had always been closer to empirical and historical reality than the purer continental theories. Marshall liked to wrap up his analytical apparatus with concrete historical illustrations because he wanted economics to remain an applied science and because he had the ambition to find a neoclassical view of the economic history of mankind that would serve as an alternative to the socialist historical perspective. These were valid reasons for strewing an analytical treatise with innumerable illustrations, but there was also another, mentioned by Joan Robinson: many illustrations or, rather, images were introduced simply to divert from analytical defects such as the incompatibility of his notion of competition with increasing returns by means of fables (cf. the story of the 'trees in the forest' and the surrogate notion of a 'representative firm').

The latter 'concept' figured prominently in the debate in the *Economic Journal* that followed Clapham's seemingly innocent initial question. Sraffa observed (see 'Symposium', 1930, p. 90). 'At the critical point of his [D. H. Robertson's] argument the firms and the industry drop out of the scene, and their place is taken by the trees and the forest, the bones and the skeleton, the waterdrops and the wave − indeed all the Kingdoms of nature are drawn upon to contribute to the wealth of his metaphors.' As Sraffa rightly noted, the participants in the debate had recourse to vague analogies and unclear modifications of Marshall's analytical framework in order to evade rather than to confront Clapham's questions.

Sraffa's contribution was, then, to mercilessly isolate the central logical arguments. His own famous closing remark was (ibid, p. 93):

> I am trying to find what are the assumptions implicit in Marshall's theory; if Mr Robertson regards them as extremely unreal, I sympathise with him. We seem to be agreed that the theory cannot be interpreted in a way which makes it logically self-consistent and, at the same time, reconciles it with the facts it sets out to explain. Mr. Robertson's remedy is to discard mathematics, and he suggests that my remedy is to discard the facts; perhaps I ought to have explained that, in the circumstances, I think it is Marshall's theory that should be discarded.

This insistence on the pure logic of economic theory was not, in my view, caused by a refusal to see the changing forms of economic life; rather it reflected, in Sraffa's case, the desire to isolate the narrow logical construction, which can be based on plausible fundamental assumptions, in order to confront it with a reality that is on the surface much more varied. He did not wish 'to discard the facts' to take sides with the theorists to defend them from the historians' attacks; nor did he take sides with the historians to attack deductive theorizing in economics. But he attacked the leading species of a large genus of false theories in order to make room for a different kind of theory with a different relation to factual history. Indeed, the theory he came up with eventually in 'Production of Commodities by Means of Commodities' is in my view distinguished because it suggests how facts and specific historical developments are to be integrated with pure theory. The point is that his model is open with respect to parameters for which a complete deductive theory cannot exist because there would otherwise be no degree of freedom for historical action. The neoclassical opponents, on the other hand, start from assumptions about a kind of general economic rationality which functions as a system in a competitive market only under unreal conditions and which is nevertheless claimed to be perfectly general and to apply essentially to all historical epochs.

Sraffa's ultimate aim was not visible to the participants of the debate (and perhaps it was not even clear to himself when he first took part in it). Before the publication of PCMC, readers of Sraffa's early works saw in his contribution a critique of Marshall and a hint for a construction of a theory of imperfect competition but no systematic new approach to the theory of value. It is, then, the purpose of this essay to work over Sraffa's early articles, which were written in the context of the debate initiated by Clapham, in order to detect the arguments that point towards PCMC. The later work may then be better understood.

The Italian article of 1925 (Sraffa, 1925) is less well known than the English of 1926 but it is more important – even Schumpeter liked it better. Every textbook, begins the essay, suggests that, for each commodity at each point in time, we can determine whether increased production of the commodity must lead to rising, falling or constant average costs. Because of the difficulty of verifying such a hypothesis empirically the textbooks refer to the future, which is to bring better statistics. But Sraffa tackles the *fundamentum divisionis* itself: there are no 'laws of return' *inherent* in an industry; whether costs rise, fall or are constant depends essentially on the observer's point of view, that is on how the term 'industry' is defined and on the length of the period of time under consideration. Sraffa concentrates on the long period in order to be able to contrast the classical and neoclassical theories with one another.[2]

The classicals (by this is meant principally Ricardo and his school) dealt with the problem of rising output with reference to the division of labour. In general, says Sraffa, they took production costs to be constant. If they were rising, as in the case of agriculture, they were discussed in connection with the resulting change in distribution and if they were falling, they were discussed in connection with the general technical progress that they represented. The idea of encompassing rising and falling returns in one single law is, by contrast, new – that is, neoclassical – and corresponds to an attempt to subordinate the problems of production and distribution to those of price theory by means of opposing a falling demand curve symmetrically to a supply curve that is, in general, rising and derived from costs. This modification of cost analysis originated simultaneously with the reduction of value to utility.

While rising average returns are typical for the expansion of an industry under simultaneous extension of the use of *all* factors,[3] diminishing average returns emerge as typical when only one factor is extended while the others remain constant. The conditions under which both tendencies are produced are therefore qualitatively substantially different from one another. In an industry both can occur at the same time or separately. The question is whether analogous or qualitatively different causes are the basis of these two laws.

Let us take agriculture as an example of diminishing returns and, derived from this, rising costs by variation of one factor. There is a homogeneous piece of land for cultivation with corn. Then at first glance it seems a law of nature that

1   with increasing intensity of cultivation of the ground the corn crop

will at first increase, then decrease, so that successive 'doses of capital' (labour, seed, equipment) bring first increasing, then diminishing returns;

2 different, though in themselves homogeneous, pieces of land can be ordered according to fertility;

3 the ordering of lands according to their fertility is dependent on the total quantity produced since the expenditure of capital varies with the quantity produced and its allocation to different lands.

The attentive reader of PCMC will be able to criticize each of these statements from his advanced standpoint since he knows that relative prices are dependent on the rate of profit and so the alternative techniques on the different lands are to be arranged in different orders according to different rates of profit. The less radical critique of 1925 establishes the following: To begin with, it is in no way correct that, on given ground, it is a matter of first rising, then diminishing returns. For the isolated producer will, if he has only little capital, choose the technique that yields the highest average return (see point M of Figure III.1.1), cultivating to begin with only a part of the land at his disposal. When production expands further he will cultivate more land, always applying the method that will yield the highest average return until the entire piece of land is fully sown and production can be further increased

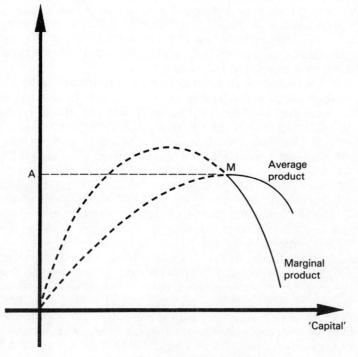

Figure III.1.1

only by taking into account a falling average return. The maximum average return is equal to the marginal return. Only those points on the return curve that lie to the right of this point are economically relevant.

Rising returns to the left of the maximum are often assumed in the literature since Turgot. They correspond to a uniform use of capital on the entire area (dotted lines in Figure III.1.1). But economically that has no meaning if the constant factor (here 'land') can be divided. We learn the absurdity of a rising average return to the variable factor (capital), used with constant land, from the fact that the marginal return to land would be negative if one adds more land in this situation. To the left of M the 'true' return curve (average and marginal), given the divisibility of land, is represented by means of the dotted straight line AM in Figure III.1.1. It is now a question of why the curve falls to the right of the maximum.

One is inclined to regard it as a natural law when marginal output lies below average output. Similarly one is inclined (and here Sraffa criticizes Wicksteed who is named in the introduction to PCMC) to take the expenditure of the successive 'injections (doses) of capital', as a homogeneous magnitude where increasing use leads to diminishing marginal returns. But Sraffa shows that the interposed 'natural law' is only a reflection of the rational economic choice of alternative techniques by producers. The producer will choose (for the amount of 'capital' that is given to him in the form of money) the combination of land, labour and means of production that (if he is 'isolated') brings him the greatest return, that is, the greatest profit, if he is a tenant farmer. So the fall of the curve reflects nothing more than the conscious arrangement of alternative techniques according to their productivity; in this way the techniques are homogeneous only in that the means of production are purchased, that is, represented in money.[4]

Now let the output curve deriving from the producers' choice for each of many different pieces of land be given. The pieces of land can then be ordered according to their fertility, independently of the production level, by regarding each of them in terms of the maximum of its average productivity. The extension of production proceeds from fertile to less fertile ground, with each piece of ground being cultivated with such intensity that the marginal output is the same for all cultivated ground. The cultivated lands (in general even the last) then yield Ricardian 'extensive' and 'intensive' rents. According to this definition, the expansion of cultivation does not change the order of productivity. What it *can* change is the order of rents; the rents do not always need to fall in the order of cultivation.

The Ricardian theory of rents, well known in its main features, is in principle sharply delineated by Sraffa to make it clear why the neoclassical application of this theory to manufacturing industry is permissible only under the most limiting conditions. And indeed it is Ricardo's *intensive* rent, which originates with expansion of production on given ground by an increase in the use of capital, that concerns neoclassicism, and not the extensive rent, for which the diverse productivity of different plots of land is responsible. Ricardo attributed greater significance to the law of diminishing (falling) returns by extension of cultivation than to that by intensification (Sraffa, 1925, p. 291) because cultivation of inferior ground does not in general affect the conditions of production on better ground (if we exclude transport), while the use of previously applied doses of capital alters the quality of the land so that (to use a modern turn of phrase) the marginal output curve generated by the use of successive injections of capital is not 'reversible'. If some doses were again removed, in certain circumstances irreversible changes (i.e. *improvements*) would remain behind in the ground. Even with a reversible curve the use of an additional dose of money capital can mean that the preceding doses of finance are to be used for other capital goods than in the case of the additional dose not being available.[5]

Moreover, the use of the additional 'doses of capital' can lead to increasing returns in cases of indivisibilities which make it impossible to apply the more productive technique on a smaller scale.

Ricardo was therefore cautious when postulating a law of diminishing returns for additional doses of capital on a given piece of land. For his theory of distribution, based on the principle of surplus, the intensive rent was also much less important than the extensive. On the other hand, the law of diminishing returns with a given amount of a constant factor plays the main part in the neoclassical theories of marginal productivity and price: on it alone are based the concept of the 'marginal product of capital' and the rising supply curve of an industry that has a constant factor at its disposal (e.g. land or labour of a given type).

We see that Sraffa already undermines this construction with the arguments that in PCMC arrive at formal perfection: he calls the homogeneity of the variable capital factor into question by pointing to the heterogeneous methods of production that are used by spending money capital. In the 1925 article of course he does not yet allude to an insurmountable logical contradiction at the core of neoclassical theory as he does in PCMC.

Now the main question is: can the law of diminishing returns be applied in industry? Irreversibilities and indivisibilities (already referred to) obviously play an important role in manufacturing.

The point of departure for the application of the law of diminishing returns to industry in the long run must be that the expansion of industry with diminishing returns comes about through the entry of new firms into the same business. Barone therefore tried (Sraffa, 1925, p. 298) to apply the law to industry by interpreting the process of the addition of new firms in a manner akin to Ricardo's transition to ever more inferior ground. However, the dubious character of this interpretation can be seen immediately. By a, to a certain extent, literal transfer of the theory of rents to industry one must presume that the newly entering firms are less productive than those already resident in the business. That is improbable. The majority of newly entering firms will start, for the very reason that they are new, with a more advanced technique so that in the long term, which is the sole concern here, additional firms are not analogous to less and less productive land. Thus, the supply curve for all firms of the industry cannot be constructed in the same way as that for a particular agricultural product, because the 'order of productivity' in industry does not correspond to the order of entry of new firms. [6]

The question then is whether the law of diminishing returns in analogy with the model of intensive rent can, on certain conditions at least, be applied to industry (Marshall, [1920] 1966, p. 687). The only significant case (as will be shown below) is found in an industry where all firms produce the same product and all firms need a certain quantity of the same factor, which is not utilized in any other industry. The exclusiveness of the use of this factor means (its divisibility taken for granted) that for the industry as a whole the returns are diminishing, i.e. that the costs and the collective supply curve of the firms must rise. The individual supply curves of the single firms are of course, in contrast for instance to normal demand curves, in this case not independent of each other, since the cost curve of the individual firm is dependent on the share (quota) of the constant factor at its disposal. In order to be able to sum up the marginal cost curves of the individual firms, the cause of the rise in costs for the collective whole (that is, the limited factor) must affect all firms in the same way, i.e. the prerequisite must be that each firm in the collective is given a constant fixed share of the factor at the disposal of the whole industry. Hence, it is possible that, while the costs for the whole industry rise, the individual can reduce his production costs to a minimum on the one hand by utilizing the advantages of mass production and on the other hand by obtaining a certain share of the constant factor without being compelled to use it more intensively (Marshall, [1920] 1966, p. 301).

For an individual firm, which is small in comparison with the whole industry but large in the face of its competitors, increasing returns to scale can hold within certain limits. Since a factor is limited for the whole branch of industry, the supply curves are dependent on the distribution of the constant factor to the firms. This distribution must therefore be predetermined. As we shall see, in 1926 Sraffa drew from such discussions the conclusion that the Marshallian theory can only preserve a certain realism when it abandons the condition of perfect competition. In the 1925 article it is only a matter of setting out the possible scope of application of the theory. The assumption, described by Sraffa himself as 'artificial', that the shares of each firm in the constant factor are given allows the rigorous construction of the supply curve of the industry from the aggregate of the supply curves of the individual firms; but in this way the condition of perfect competition is already implicitly undermined.

Sraffa neglects the question of how the price of the constant factor, from the industry's point of view in short supply, is here determined. The assumption prevents the supply of the scarce factor from being completely elastic and thus its price from being given. Let us take the case of a completely inelastic supply of 'land'. As in the textbook, we could first postulate constant returns to scale with respect to land, as far as it extends, and to other factors, let us say 'capital'. The factor price of the capital, to be considered as given, and the amount of land available for the industry then determine, simultaneously with the demand for corn, the amount of capital to be used, the land rent and the corn price by equating the prices of the factors with the values of their marginal products. However, this simple extension of the partial analysis for coping with the determination, here necessarily simultaneous, of the prices of factor and product, leaves the size of firms indefinite on account of the given linear-homogeneous production function.

In order to allow for the possibility hinted at by Sraffa of increasing returns for the (not too large) individual firm, U-shaped cost curves are drawn for individual firms according to the neoclassical theory of the firm and, if necessary, imperfect competition and price differentials between firms are taken into consideration. But then the land rent is ignored and the distribution of the factor among the firms is assumed exactly as in Sraffa.

The third modern alternative consists in having recourse to Walras–Debreu (Debreu, [1959] 1971, p. 41). There the ownership by individuals of firms and factors is separate from the firms' disposition of factors of production so that the allocation of factors to firms is not *a priori* given but calculated. Firms, on the other hand, differ from the first in their production possibilities, so that, though differences between firms are taken into account, factor prices, factor distribution and production prices can be determined simultaneously. But the mathematical solution lacks economic content. According to Debreu, the prices emerging from the equilibrium are only signals that indicate for a whole branch of industry the production quantity corresponding to the profit maximum. The prices give no clue as to how the quantity produced by the industry, along with the factor distribution to the individual firms, should be determined. An infinite number of divisions of the total turnover of the branch to the individual firms is in general mathematically compatible with equilibrium. So Sraffa's problem is not solved even in the framework of the modern theory of general economic equilibrium of the short period in perfect competition; that is, Sraffa's critique of 1925 is today as topical as it was then because the modern neoclassical theory of the firm must be based on Marshall.

Let us now look at the case of 'increasing returns' as they occur through a proportional increase in the use of all factors. We have mentioned above the case of the increase in the use of one factor while maintaining the others constant; it causes falling returns in the case of a divisible constant factor. The so-called 'increasing returns to scale' often lead to a terminological dilemma: if the divisibility of all factors and products was unlimited, returns to scale would not occur, since the most productive technique would have to be applicable even on the smallest scale. But if some factors or products are indivisible, we get constant returns to scale through multiplication of the indivisible units, and the 'increasing returns to scale' seem to be due only to a sloppy application of the factor concept; if 'larger' units are more productive than 'smaller', one is forced to describe the larger units as different factors on account of their special use value. Example: steamships cannot be made as small as one likes, the larger steamships are more efficient than smaller ones. If steamships of a certain size are considered as a factor, then constant returns prevail and steamships of another size are different factors. If we start from merely one aspect of the use value and count all steamships as part of a factor, then we get increasing returns, but the units of the factor are no longer homogeneous. This state of affairs has created much confusion (cf. Chamberlin, [1948] 1962, Appendices B and H, in particular pp. 235–44). The only clear case of increasing returns to scale is Adam Smith's classical division of labour in which mass employment of labour becomes more efficient – simply by reorganization of labour processes without changing the average expenditure of raw materials and tools per man. Here we can speak of increasing returns to scale without straining the factor concept.

But, however we define increasing returns to scale, it is well known that increasing returns are in the long term incompatible with perfect competition, when they can be obtained *within* each firm of the industry. Marshall had therefore criticized Cournot's attempt to aggregate, by simple addition, the supply curves of a great number of firms with internal falling costs. According to Marshall's definition of perfect competition, the equilibrium price is given for each firm and it can sell any chosen quantity at this price. Now, when production costs within a firm can be reduced by unlimited expansion of all factor inputs, the firm will produce more and more at the given price (theoretically an infinite amount), which means in practice that the assumption of perfect competition is violated and that the firm that starts from the lowest cost position eventually gains the monopoly of the whole branch of industry while constantly enlarging its production facilities and finally alone satisfying the entire market need – provided, of course, that a single firm or a group of firms does not procure new cost advantages through a new discovery monopolized by them.

There is, in Marshall's work, a most remarkable development from his early writings, in which he acknowledges the great importance of internal returns to scale and links them with general technical progress and the possibilities inherent in each individual firm to utilize (to the full) the advantages of better division of labour by expansion of production, up to the late writings in which internal returns to scale and the resulting difficulties of neoclassical theory are almost passed over in silence; instead, the whole emphasis is on the curious construction of 'external' returns to scale. According to Sraffa, Marshall showed great skill in concealing this change in his thinking.[7] External returns to scale occur if each individual firm of a certain minimal size, taken in isolation, shows increasing costs while the average costs of the industry, taken together, fall with the increase in the number of firms within it.

Indeed we find in the main text of Marshall's *Principles* no real analysis of internal returns to scale but only the cautious hint that internal increasing returns to scale are only with difficulty compatible with competition – a hint that is then further developed in Appendix H (Marshall, [1920] 1966, p. 664). Here Marshall draws a falling supply curve, which is supposed to represent falling costs, in intersection with a demand curve falling similarly from left to right so that both curves repeatedly intersect each other. In this way he regards as stable the points of intersection where the demand curve intersects the supply curve from the upper left because an expansion of production is profitable as long as the amount produced is less than what corresponds to the point of intersection, whereas the quantity produced cannot be sold at normal profits if it is more than what corresponds to the point of intersection. But here the argumentation breaks down completely. As Joan Robinson has emphasized (Robinson, 1971, p. 54, p. 58), Marshall tries to represent the expansion of an industry as a shift of demand along the falling supply curve instead of acknowledging that in this case a long-term, stable, perfectly competitive equilibrium does not exist. The short-term expansion of each firm may be limited by capacity; but already here it is not clear how demand is divided among the individual firms under competitive conditions. In the long term, as we have seen, no equilibrium exists in perfect competition because this implies that each firm can market an unlimited amount at the current price. Since costs can, by the expansion of one individual firm, be reduced at will, the growth of the individual firm is unrestricted. Secondly, even if competition is less than perfect, the argument is inadmissible because (as Marshall himself points out one page further on – [1920] 1966, p. 666) the supply curve, which is thus traced through historical time, is irreversible: the advantages of mass production occur in improvements in equipment, which are not lost with a falling-off in demand; so the supply curve is not unambiguously defined. When Marshall limits production by bringing a falling supply curve of an individual industry, obtained by aggregating falling supply curves of individual firms, to intersection with the demand curve, he has implicitly surrendered the conditions of competition, the notion of long-term equilibrium and with it his theory of value for this case.

It is true that external returns to scale can be dealt with in the framework of Marshallian analysis: for every firm, there exists an ordinary U-shaped average cost curve as a function of output. It falls initially, since otherwise in the long term the size of the firms would have to tend to zero; it reaches a minimum at which average costs are equal to marginal costs, and it finally rises with the marginal costs. According to the theory, a long-term equilibrium can exist only when the price corresponds to the minimum of the average costs; at a lower price the firm makes losses, at a higher price a profit would be made that would have to be due to a particular factor. This factor should be counted among the costs since the payment of all factors is counted with the costs (including entrepreneurial profits). If present-day neoclassical theory allows such profits, they are to be understood as surplus profits accruing in the short period and due to particular production advantages of individual firms. In the long run, such profits are incompatible with the Marshallian definition of perfect competition since, with perfect competition, each special advantage must be able to be approximated by all firms so that it becomes a factor of production.

This argumentation displays the peculiar tautological character of the neoclassical factor concept. However, Sraffa does not dwell on this observation but completes the construction of the collective supply curve with external returns. External returns mean that the height of the cost curve of each individual firm is dependent on the whole output of the industry concerned. The output amount Z of the industry as a whole is equal to the sum of the outputs produced by each firm in operation at minimal unit costs of all firms. These unit costs fall with increasing output Z because the minima of the cost curves of individual firms fall as a result of external effects as total output and hence the number of firms in operation increases. The minimum average cost of the firm that is typical (representative) of the firms operating if total output produced is Z gives the point on the curve for the average costs of the total industry at output Z; it falls and thus lies above the marginal cost curves for the whole industry. So the average cost curve of the industry is the aggregate total supply curve. If the demand curve intersects it from the upper left (which by no means needs to be the case since both curves fall), the point of intersection represents an equilibrium, because at this point each individual firm operates at the minimum of its average costs and therefore has no motive or possibility to change the quantity it produces. With an increase in the total demand the price sinks since the existing firms experience a reduction in production costs as a result of external effects and the addition of new firms.

Sraffa quite rightly points out that this case is, in reality, met very rarely; while external effects may not be a rare occurrence, the construction (here only hinted at), on account of the *ceteris paribus* clause, assumes that the external effects are to be attributed to the effect of a production advantage enjoyed only by this industry, as defined by its product. For example, clockmakers: the more clocks are made in a region in small craft workshops, the better and the sooner all children will learn the village craft. So the effects are external from the standpoint of the individual firm but internal from the standpoint of the branch of industry.

For each individual firm marginal costs are equal to average costs. For the whole industry, however, marginal costs are less than total average costs because the reduction in costs for the industry effected by production expansion, cannot be appropriated by individual firms. The situation is compatible with perfect competition but not Pareto-optimal since the (social) marginal costs lie below the individual marginal costs that determine the price.

Marshallian partial analysis of falling returns cannot, as we shall now show, be separated from the assumption that the industry showing falling returns is characterized by the fact that it utilizes only one factor of production, which is specific to it. Sraffa, by analogy, shows by means of an analysis of the problems of interaction that Marshall's construction of the supply curve with external returns to scale is dependent on the assumption, made by us above, that all firms in the industry produce the same commodity and no other industry participates in the production advantage that causes the external effects. The problem of interaction may be represented in the light of the analysis of falling returns as a result of a constant factor.

Let there be given a scarce factor that is used by several industries producing one product each. If the individual industries using it are numerous and small in comparison with the total number of industries and if, in order to exclude external effects, the individual firms are independent of one another, each of the branches of industry works approximately with constant returns. If, however, the number of industries using the factor (let us say 'crude oil') is small, then an increase in demand for the produce of one of the industries (let us say: private cars) will change the use of the factor inputs of that industry and therefore the factor price changes. This change in factor price will have an effect on the prices of products of other industries (let us say: buses), whereby in general the demand curve belonging to the first product (private cars) is altered. But this must not be: the *ceteris paribus* analysis demands that supply and demand curves that are each individually brought to the intersection are independent of each other. The following dilemma thus occurs (Sraffa, 1925; see also Robinson, 1972a, pp. 116–19): if the number of industries requiring the factor is large – as with, say, the factor 'electrical energy' – then the returns from the point of view of the individual industries are constant; or, if the number of industries is small, then the equilibrium price cannot be constructed according to Marshall's method.

Sraffa further concludes that constant returns to scale have to be considered as the normal case in the Marshallian framework. If theorists think of constant returns to scale only as an accidental result of opposed and superimposed rising and falling tendencies, he replies that it is much more natural to base the hypothesis of constant returns to scale on the absence of any tendencies to non-proportional returns. From the standpoint of Marshall's partial analysis, constant returns emerge as soon as each factor is divisible, used by a large number of small industries and the individual firms are independent of one another.

Marshall's theory of perfect competition strives for a determination of quantity of production, of commodity and factor prices, of national product and of distribution through an analysis of the interaction of the supply curves of factors of production and demand functions, derived from cost of production and utility theory. According to Marshall's parable of the scissors (Marshall, [1920] 1966, p. 290), the 'subjective' factors (demand) and the 'objective' ones (production costs) should influence price formation in the same way as both blades of a pair of scissors move in the cutting process – or if only one blade moves, the stationary blade remains at all events necessary for cutting. But if Sraffa's critique is justified and almost only constant returns are compatible with perfect competition, the symmetry of 'subjective' and 'objective' factors is lost. The only cases where non-constant returns are compatible with perfect competition in partial analysis occur, according to Sraffa, when an industry, defined by the product common to the firms, alone uses a factor, or in the case of external effects that are internal to an industry.

Even these two cases show that the symmetrical determination of supply and demand meets difficulties, since the construction of the supply curves seems curiously to be dependent on the point of view of the observer. If we view an industry primarily as a group of firms that jointly utilize a factor of production, with this factor not being used by other industries (e.g. agriculture), then we will expect increasing costs. If one retains the definition of 'industry' according to the product, one expects, in perfect competition, if not constant then at least falling costs (effects that are external to the firms and internal to the industry). The ambiguity is caused by the fact that increasing costs originate chiefly from variations in the proportion of factor utilization, while falling costs are due to a change in the quantity of employment of all factors with more efficient utilization. Classification becomes even more indefinite with reference to different periods of time. Rising costs predominate in the short term and falling costs in the long term. Sraffa thus proposes to take constant production costs as a first approximation to reality until the theory of interdependence of the different markets, i.e. the theory of general economic equilibrium, is further advanced (Sraffa, 1925, p. 328). However, he proposes the hypothesis of constant production costs, without enthusiasm, not because he finds it realistic but because Marshall's theory with its double condition of perfect competition and the *ceteris paribus* clause permits the rigorous analysing of no other relevant cases.[8]

The enthusiasm is that much less as Marshall – as we saw above in the impressive example of rent – is not in the position to provide an objective basis for the theory of production costs since a variable 'capital input' corresponds to an unforeseeable change between different methods of production.

The reader, schooled in modern neoclassical analysis, will perhaps be surprised at the emphasis on partial analysis and may regard Sraffa's critique as irrelevant since the theory of equilibrium according to Walras and Pareto permits us to take into consideration the interdependence of the different markets. However, it may be remembered *first* that (as we saw above) Walrasian equilibrium does not clearly determine the size of firms; Marshallian partial analysis therefore lingers on in modern textbooks as the only neoclassical theory of the firm. *Second*, Walrasian theory becomes entangled in unrealistic assumptions allowing no productive theoretical developments. Sraffa wrote to Keynes in the summer of 1926:

Some of such connected variations [of costs and quantity produced] must be regarded as a part of the simultaneous equilibrium of all industries (Pareto's point of view). For others, perhaps the most important, it must be recognized that the assumption that perfect competition may be taken as an hypothesis well representative of the multiplicity of independent producers, is untenable. (Roncaglia, 1978, p. 13)

The Walrasian theory is thus taken into consideration, but immediately rejected, since there can be a great number of competitors without perfect competition being prevalent among them. If one has not already guessed, the continuation of the letter makes it clear what Sraffa is thinking of: in the reality of industrial production, falling production costs are of enormous importance; they are analysed satisfactorily by neither Marshall nor Walras.

Internal returns are not compatible with perfect competition. Sraffa therefore looks for a theory that allows not only Marshall's *ceteris paribus* clause but also his conception of perfect competition to be overcome. In this, he takes Marshall as his starting point and not Walras[9] because in Marshall's work a rich variety of economic questions is unfolded, using simple analytical tools, with numerous allusions to problems that really go beyond the framework of his assumptions, whereas Walras proceeds in a formal and deductive way within a narrow horizon, so that a *logical* critique cannot show how many *real* phenomena remain poorly understood in his work. Modern economic theory requires less a grasp of reality than remaining consistent in argumentation. Logical criticism is therefore more respectable and effective than substantial criticism: Sraffa, who wanted to preserve the substance and further knowledge by criticism, had to criticize a Marshall, not a Walras.

Sraffa's 1925 critique leaves the Marshallian structure in ruins: with constant returns to scale Marshall's efforts to procure, under his assumptions, equal right for subjective evaluation by utility as for objectively given production costs are completely wrecked. Sraffa's article, which does not contain one single polemic sentence, shows great polemical strength[10] by the unprecedented consistency with which he subdivides Marshall's arguments by rigorous classification and reduces his theory of value step by step to a triviality.

Looking back, we recognize today in Sraffa's critique of Marshall the start of a continuing critique of the factor concept (especially with application to 'capital') and the germ of the thoughts that led on to PCMC when Sraffa reduces the 'natural law' of diminishing marginal output by the use of successive 'doses of capital' to economic calculation by the use of different production techniques. The real point of PCMC is, of course, still not seen: relative prices are already determined when only the amounts to be produced, the input of commodities and labour, and the rate of profit are given.

PCMC shows that the question of returns to scale is irrelevant for the question of whether utility has an influence on the formation of price. Much more relevant is what determines the amount of production and the rate of profit. To the extent that consumer preferences influence the determination of input and output quantities, they determine prices indirectly; but other forces can also contribute. In the 1925 article, on the other hand, the derivation of the price of a commodity is still directly dependent on consumer preferences if the commodity is not produced under constant returns to scale; Sraffa shows solely that Marshallian analysis can only seldom take this case into consideration.

To arrive at PCMC Sraffa had, above all, to examine the interdependence between industries. He had to dissolve the factor concept and give up the *ceteris paribus* clause. But in his next publication he directed himself first to the theory of imperfect competition under the title of 'The laws of returns under competitive conditions'. In this, he summarizes in a few pages in English the main results of his Italian work. He describes the abandonment of the *ceteris paribus* clause, i.e. of the analysis of the interdependence of the markets, as too difficult to be applied to 'real conditions' in a 'protective way'.[11] Therefore he carried his ideas on in the direction of an analysis of imperfect competition, on the one hand by demonstrating that increasing returns must lead to an abandonment of the postulate of perfect competition, on the other hand by discussing empirical observations of the market behaviour of real firms. He shows that each firm in practice has a nucleus of customers who, for reasons of situation or the special make-up of the product or personal relations, always buy their goods from this firm while, over and above, a larger market of customers exists who have no such fixed preference for a certain firm. In consequence, firms are in competition with one another in relation to the additional groups of buyers while they appear as monopolists in the smaller customer circles. Firms must take into account this split in their markets for determining price, advertising, and product differentiation (Sraffa, 1926, in particular p. 545).

It became evident that a treatise on a part of these ideas and suggestions was compatible with a certain non-radical elaboration of the formal apparatus of neoclassical theory. Sraffa's 1926 article gave the principal impetus to the development of the theory of imperfect competition, which advanced in several places at the same time and which culminated in the well-known books of Joan Robinson and (independently of Sraffa) Edward Chamberlin (Robinson, 1972a; Chamberlin, [1948] 1962). Looked at in retrospect from the standpoint of PCMC, Sraffa's suggestions for details of the theory of price discrimination, inflexibility of prices and the like seem of course much less important than his new concept of competition. On the one hand, he turned resolutely against those who regard imperfect competition in a market with many suppliers and consumers as merely frictional losses. According to Sraffa, these market imperfections have rather a systematic character and, in certain circumstances, durable and cumulative effects, so that they are even capable of statistical analysis (Sraffa, 1926, p. 542).

If most firms under conditions of falling costs thus see their outlet limited by the market and practice price policies, that does not mean, on the other hand, that their monopolistic position in the markets of their original customers leads to the profits in different branches of industry or different enterprises being able to differ from each other to an indefinite extent. Rather, Sraffa discusses aspects of the process of diffusion of profits throughout the various stages of production, and the process of forming a *normal level of profit* throughout all the industries of a country (Sraffa, 1926, p. 550). He does so cursorily, of course, since his questions mainly concern the formation of individual prices.

The profits can thus be positive with imperfect competition and correspond to a normal standard in spite of imperfect competition. Profits may be in excess of the normal standard if barriers to entry are present (Sraffa, 1926, p. 549) but the standard of normality exists all the same – only its determination is not yet dealt with.

The central question from the point of view of PCMC – the extent of 'normal' profits and their compatibility with imperfect competition – was hardly discussed in the debates following Sraffa's articles. Sraffa took part only with a short contribution to the discussion[12] in the journals, since he had obviously privately already gone beyond the standpoint of the theoreticians of imperfect competition. By 1930, Sraffa's critique of Marshallian theory could culminate in the stark rejection quoted above, because, as is indicated in Sraffa's preface to PCMC, the basic propositions of his later theory had been elaborated in the late 1920s.

Notes

1 See Essay 3 below.
2 The reader should bear in mind that modern textbooks use the Marshallian conceptual apparatus almost exclusively for the analysis of the short period, partly in order to avoid a critique having its origin in Sraffa.
3 Modern terminology: increasing returns to scale.
4 Sraffa observes that the consumption of a good will similarly be associated with falling marginal utility simply because it is first used to satisfy the more urgent needs among the ones for whose satisfaction it can serve.
5 Compare Sraffa's discussion of Wicksteed's distinction between functional and descriptive curves (1925, p. 292).
6 This argument could also be used against the supply curve founded on the extensive margin in agriculture. But there, with given methods of production, fertility depends on natural conditions and is different for different soils. In industry, there are constant or increasing returns with a given state of technology as long as the effect of a scarce factor for the industry as a whole can be disregarded.
7 Sraffa (1925), p. 306: 'Il radicale cambiamento che (Principles of Economics produssero) nella sostanza delle leggi di variazione dei costi è passato quasi inosservato mentre la teoria del valore basata sulla "simmetria fondamentale" delle forze della domanda e di quelle dell'offerta, di cui quelle leggi sono premesse necessarie, remaneva immutata. In sostanza, sono state sostituite le fondamenta senza che l'edificio soprastante ne ricevesse una scossa, ed è stata somma abilità del Marshall far passare inosservata la trasformazione'.
8 There is a certain analogy of Sraffa's result with the modern 'non-substitution theorem' (Samuelson, 1966, p. 513 sq.).
9 In the letter quoted above Sraffa announces his work for an article which was published in 1926 in the *Economic Journal* (Sraffa, 1926).
10 Sraffa was also capable of transforming his polemics into trenchant mockery if the logic of his opponent was faulty and negligent. Compare Sraffa (1932) and a subsequent *Reply and Rejoinder*.
11 Sraffa (1926), p. 541. The allusion to the theory of Walras and Pareto occurs without mentioning their names. He had, however, worked on both and was, according to an oral report by Joan Robinson, the first to lecture on them in Cambridge towards the end of the 1920s.
12 In the Symposium on Increasing Returns and the Representative Firm, organized by Keynes ('Symposium', 1930) with a contribution in which he showed once again the logical impossibility of applying the Marshallian theory in the presence of internal economies.

Essay 2   Ricardo

With the rise of the utility theoretical determination of value in the second half of the nineteenth century the understanding for Ricardo's classical political economy vanished. In the appendix of his *Principles*, Marshall presents Ricardo as an ingenious but often awkward economist, with presentiments of his own utility-based value theory. E. Cannan's (Marshall, [1920] 1966, p. 624 sq.; Cannan, [1893] 1967) deviating interpretation was half-hearted, the Marxian interpretation too radical; Marshall's school dominated the English universities. In his essay of 1925 Sraffa had proved that thinking through Marshall's theory in a rigorous way reduced it to a vague Ricardian production-cost theory. The utility theoretical determination of value was basically superfluous. With this, however, Sraffa did not intend to show that Marshall could in fact claim to be a follower of Ricardo's. Rather, he proved that the Ricardian element in Marshall's theory was largely incompatible with the neoclassical and that only the former was economically relevant.

Ricardo's complete works – the production of which Sraffa, encouraged by Keynes, began in about 1930 – brought into prominence the rupture that Marshall had obscured. It therefore exerted an important impact upon the understanding of the history of theory and, beyond that, on the development of the modern theory of accumulation. Just as the theory of imperfect competition had been substantially inspired by Sraffa's first essays, Sraffa's introduction to Ricardo's *Principles* gave an important impulse to J. Robinson's work *The Accumulation of Capital* and other modern works concerning the theory of accumulation and distribution.[1]

Neoclassical theory, built on microeconomic foundations, had diverted attention from the problem of dynamic capital accumulation with its peculiar view of production as the use of factor supplies, transmitted by the market, to satisfy given needs. Keynes' *General Theory* with its introduction of the principle of effective demand, battered a hole in equilibrium theory, conceptually and materially, but it could overcome it only partially, leaving the traditional theory of value and distribution largely untouched. Now growth theory, which had awoken great interest after the war, required the theory of value and distribution to be thought through anew in the context of accumulation instead of stationary equilibrium. Thus economists – some consciously, some unconsciously – found their way back to the questions posed by the classicals, particularly by Ricardo.

The switch to a new specific paradigm, however, has not yet been fully accomplished. Attempts are still made to combine modern theory of growth with the neoclassical tradition. The alternative framework of the classicals is obscured by neoclassical approaches and views. [2]

Keynes is the spiritual father of one of these modern confusions, for he labelled Marshall and Ricardo alike as classicals in order to set himself apart from both as the discoverer of the principle of effective demand. Without confronting the classical period proper on a broader scale and in more depth, the theoretical clarity in the theories of value, distribution and accumulation cannot be improved. Because of his outstanding diligence and the exhaustive collection of references to parallel writings, contemporary circumstances, etc., Sraffa's Ricardo edition enables the committed reader to arrive at an understanding of Ricardo without being misled by interpretations based on the neoclassical paradigm. This edition also indirectly elucidates Sraffa's own relation to Ricardo. It was above all the general preface to the first volume that became famous. At first sight, it appears to offer not much more than bibliographic references to the genesis of the *Principles*. A closer look however, reveals important economic thoughts that anticipate PCMC. I will select two of them; other aspects of the Ricardian theory cannot be dealt with in our context.

Here we are concerned with the conceptual instruments that Ricardo developed to describe the historical development of the distribution of the national income among the classes, which he saw as the central economic problem. Sraffa concluded from allusions hidden in some of Ricardo's letters that Ricardo had constructed for his own use a – as we would say today – drastically simplified model to analyse the effect of accumulation on distribution. We are going to call this model the 'corn-corn model' and we shall present it in modern terminology, without too close a reliance on the original. Imagine an economically closed area. Let the land be of differing fertility and the property of aristocratic land-owners. They lease their land to tenants who organize the cultivation of corn by labourers. The labourers are a homogeneous mass, the wage rate is uniform and its level is determined by the workers' subsistence needs. The wage consists of corn. The tenants are capitalists who maximize profits on the capital advanced by them. Setting aside fixed capital, capital consists of a certain amount of corn for seed and an amount of corn for the wage fund, out of which a weekly wage is paid to the workers. Corn for seed and wage fund are in a fixed proportion to each other. They have to be advanced by the tenants at the beginning of the year so that at the end of the year the harvest can be brought in.

In the same way as competition among the workers leads to a uniform wage rate, competition among capitalists and landlords creates a uniform rate of profit on the land as a whole and a uniform rate of rent for each piece of land of a given quality. As a result of the equalization process, the landlord receives as his rent the difference between the total product and the marginal cost of production including profit. Every piece of land is cultivated with an intensity such that the marginal product (MP) of the last worker just yields the costs plus profit. Rent thus equals the average product (AP) of labour on a given land minus its marginal product, where the MP of the last unit of labour equals the cost for wages and seed in proportion to labour plus the profit (in proportion to the profit rate) obtained by the expenditure of this labour. This is immediately clear if we take, as Ricardo does, a piece of land with the lowest fertility that is only partially cultivated and therefore yields no rent. That piece of land is cultivated with the technique that yields the highest average revenue (AR) on this particular land. Marginal revenue (MR) and AR are equal. The profit rate on that last piece of land is simply equal to the surplus produced over and above the wage costs and costs for seeds, divided by these costs.

The land-owners of the more fertile land can now demand a rent that is just high enough so that their tenants obtain the same profit rate as is obtained on the last piece of land and the tenants cultivate the land with an intensity such that the MR of the marginal worker just covers the costs including profit.

The argument remains the same even if there is intensive cultivation of all lands, i.e. when the AR exceeds the MR everywhere. The mechanism of competition provides for the MRs to be equalized on all the lands; the differences in the AR accrue to the land-owners as rent. In any case, as a result, the rate of profit can be presented as the ratio of the surplus over the costs created by the last worker to the costs consisting of corn. The profit rate on each land thus is a ratio of physical magnitudes (two amounts of corn). If the corn consumption of the country rises, less fertile land has to be cultivated, so that, holding the subsistence wage constant, the surplus vanishes, i.e. the profit rate falls whereas the rent rises. Figure III.2.1 illustrates one step in this process.

The model can be supplemented by another element. We can assume, additionally, that luxury goods are produced in capitalist manufactures in which workers receive the same wages as land labourers. The luxury goods are consumed by land-owners and capitalists in country and towns, but not by workers. It remains true that the profit rate reached on the land can still be calculated as a ratio of corn surplus to corn wages on the last piece of land cultivated. This remains possible because the products manufactured in the towns do not affect the costs of production

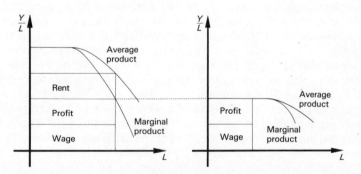

Figure III.2.1   *Corn (Y) as a function of labour (L) employed on relatively fertile and on marginal land*

of corn produced on the land, whereas, conversely, corn does affect the production of commodities produced in town via the costs for wages. Corn is the only 'basic commodity' in the sense of PCMC. Prices of luxury goods in the towns have to adjust in such a way that the profit rate of the capitalists producing in the towns (which is a ratio of money magnitudes) corresponds to the profit rate of the tenants on the land, which is a ratio of physical magnitudes and as such independent from prices and their changes, i.e. determined 'prior' to them.

Relative prices between town and country are already determined by the task of reproducing the given structure of commodity production and commodity exchange. There remains no place for 'supply and demand' in the sense of subjective consumer preferences except in so far as they have already entered the assumed data of reproduction.

For Ricardo, the value of the corn model lay in the possibility of proving with this heuristic simplification that the profit rate has to fall in the long run if the growing population requires the cultivation of increasingly less fertile land, resulting in an increase of the part of the surplus appropriated as rent in relation to profit. According to the logic of this model, the only possible way of counteracting this tendency was to gain access to fertile land outside England – hence his polemics against the high English corn taxes. Otherwise the methods of production had to be improved. Important progress in agricultural chemistry was hardly foreseeable in Ricardo's time.

The corn model, reconstructed by Sraffa,[3] had not been published explicitly by Ricardo, as Malthus had quite correctly pointed out that corn is neither produced solely by means of corn nor is it the only commodity to enter workers' real wages (Sraffa, 1951, p. xxxi). Corn is not the only 'basic commodity'. If, however, a great number of commodities appear both as means of production and as products, the question arises how the surplus can still be measured in such a way that the chosen standard can present the relevant starting point for the calculation of the profit rate and distribution of the product between social classes.

Social wealth is the result of human labour exerted on nature. It seemed natural to the classicals to define the value of commodities as labour time directly and indirectly embodied in it. Smith had shown that commodities are exchanged in the proportions of embodied labour time if the owners of those commodities face each other directly, i.e. 'before' capitalists and land-owners appropriate a surplus. To carry this determination of value over to capitalist relations is hindered by the fact that a general rise in wages seems to entail a general rise in prices without a change in the quantities of labour embodied in the commodities. In the Sraffian price system, prices of all commodities do in fact rise with a rise in wages if prices are expressed in terms of labour commanded, i.e. the quantity of labour time that is exchangeable at a given wage for a given quantity of commodities. But Ricardo was aware of the fact that if the prices of all commodities are expressed in terms of a standard commodity, e.g. gold, a general rise in wages leads to a fall in the profit rate such that not all prices, expressed in this standard, have to rise.

From this insight resulted a peculiar difficulty that heavily occupied Ricardo's mind. He discovered that the rise in wages affected the prices of commodities in different ways. The prices of commodities produced primarily with direct labour rose, whereas the prices of commodities produced primarily with fixed capital fell relative to them (Sraffa, 1951, p. xxxv). This effect, discussed in detail in Sraffa's PCMC, contradicts the immediate determination of prices through labour time. Despite this, Ricardo – occasionally hesitant (Sraffa, 1951, p. xxxix) – stood by this definition of value and considered the influence of changes in wages on prices merely as a 'modification' of the law of value, as Marx would put it. In order to take this into account conceptually, Ricardo constructed the notion of an invariable standard of value in the form of an average commodity for which the relation of direct to indirect labour could be given so that changes in the distribution of income or in the wage rate would not affect its price. In successive editions of his *Principles* and in an essay discovered and published posthumously by Sraffa, entitled *Absolute and Exchangeable Value* ([1823] 1966), Ricardo elaborated this idea in great detail without ever achieving a really clear view of the notion of 'invariability' of the standard of value. The standard of value had to be invariant vis-à-vis changes in distribution (Ricardo, [1821] 1951, I, p. 44). It also had to be invariant with respect to changes in production techniques over time (Ricardo, ibid., p. 44). He finally hoped that in the real world gold, at least as an approximation, would serve this purpose (Ricardo, ibid., pp. 45, 87).

The different functions that the standard of value was supposed to have were possibly distinguished more carefully by Sraffa in his Ricardo edition, in particular in the general index, than by Ricardo himself. At first sight the unchangeable standard of value seemed to be merely a question of definition. It appears to make sense, for example, to *define* labour as value and time as its measurement. Ricardo argues for such a definition when he writes: 'I may be asked what I mean by the word value, and by what criterion I would judge whether a commodity had or had not changed its value. I answer I know no other criterion of a thing being dear or cheap but the sacrifices of labour made to obtain it. Every thing is originally purchased by labour.' (Ricardo, [1823] 1966, IV, p. 397). He mentions in other places also that labour is the only real source of wealth of the nation (Ricardo, ibid., p. 213).

Fundamentally, therefore, Ricardo did not doubt that labour was the measure of productive power. This, to him, was almost self-evident. So we are saying that he *defined* value by labour. He was not concerned with looking for just any commodity with unchangeable price; for the price of each commodity is by definition equal to one and unchangeable if this commodity itself is used as a 'numéraire', i.e. to express all other commodities in terms of it, and is thus elevated by definition to a standard of value, as was done with gold socially. Given this freedom of definition, the question arises which one of the value definitions is meaningful – that of 'labour' or that of a single commodity – or how the definition of value by labour is compatible with the choice of a certain commodity as a standard of value.

The production processes of all commodities, including gold, apparently are subject to changes. When Ricardo was searching for the conditions that a commodity had to fulfil in order to possess invariable value he believed that by tracing the theoretical causes responsible for price changes of commodities he would be able to point out when a commodity was not subject to essential changes in prices. 'Is it not clear then as soon as we are in possession of the knowledge of the circumstances which determine the value of commodities, we are enabled to say what is necessary to give us an invariable measure of value?' (Sraffa, 1951, p. xli). Thinking about the 'invariable measure' therefore was thinking about the meaning and function of the definitions of value.

For Ricardo there are essentially two circumstances that determine price changes theoretically: first the labour (indirect and direct) expended for the production of the commodities; second, different production periods and different proportions of fixed capital to labour for different commodities, which consequently cause commodity prices to fluctuate because of changes in wages and profits (Ricardo, [1821] 1951, I, Chapter I, part V). The first point does not pose any theoretical problems. Looking at it in isolation and in abstraction from the second, each commodity produced with an ever equal amount of labour (once value is defined through labour) will make a good value standard. Such a commodity does not exist in reality; it is an empirical question, how far real commodities approach the conditions of constant amounts of labour necessary to their production (Sraffa, 1951, p. xli).

The second point, in contrast, does pose a theoretical problem: given production methods, wage changes influence prices. Because of this, the expended labour time for production can no longer express immediately the price of the commodity. The commodity price can still be related to the labour expended, though in a more complicated manner depending on the wage. The question arises, however, whether this can be done in any meaningful way (where 'meaningful' refers to theoretical consistency). Prices can be related in many ways to labour, taking into account wages for example as 'labour commanded by a commodity'. But if the wage changes relative to commodity prices without a change in the conditions of production this definition becomes deceiving (Ricardo, [1823] 1966, IV, p. 362).

Ricardo suggested choosing as a measure of value a commodity for which the relation between fixed and variable capital to labour and the length of the production period correspond to the average of the economy. He hoped to find such a commodity in gold (Sraffa, 1951, p. xliv). For he recognized the reason for the deviation of prices from the labour embodied in them in the different proportions and production periods of the commodities. This point was made clear in the essay *On Absolute and Exchangeable Value* (Ricardo, [1823] 1966, IV, p. 361). If all proportions and production periods were equal (in Marxian terminology: if all the organic compositions were equal) prices would have to be proportional to expended labour for every wage rate (Ricardo, ibid., p. 364). For those reasons, one had to conclude, a commodity *without* differences of proportions and production periods had to be regarded as invariable: the cause of price changes is *absent*. Ricardo apparently felt that this was the case for the commodity produced under average conditions. Sraffa added by way of interpretation that this standard of value is useful for those who are, like Ricardo, interested in the changes in distribution of surplus between the classes. The sum of all prices, expressed in the invariable standard of value, remains constant if wages change. With a different standard, the value of the aggregate would change with a change in wages, holding the physical surplus constant; the impact on profits of the change in wages would therefore be unclear (Sraffa, 1951, p. xlviii).

Ricardo was not able to work out his theory in a conceptually rigorous manner. It did not become clear how the 'invariable value standard' and the definition of value through labour were to be made compatible. However the ideas that I have selected from Ricardo's *Principles* and Sraffa's Introduction can be found in PCMC in a more thoroughly worked out and changed form. Sraffa introduces his standard commodity by analysing in the third chapter of PCMC the causes of price changes through wage changes and constructing an artificial commodity for which those causes are missing. It turns out that this is tantamount to finding the production process of a commodity for which the input and output are mutually homogeneous, as in the corn-corn model, so that the profit rate can be interpreted as a ratio between two physical magnitudes. With this, Sraffa finds an inherent unity in Ricardo's intellectual development, which represents a surprising and striking discovery. The value of the surplus or social product is not necessarily constant with changes in distribution, however, if measured in terms of standard prices (unless the economy is in standard proportions).

Since the main themes of PCMC are already present in Sraffa's interpretation of Ricardo, Sraffa's theory has recently often been labelled as 'neo-Ricardian'. Through the connection with Ricardo there are indeed important points of reference for the interpretation of Sraffa's theory over and above the theory of value, namely concerning the notion of prices, implicit ideas of competition, etc. It would, however, be naive to look at Sraffa as Ricardo's follower in every respect. This is not even true for the value theory, in which Sraffa, though connected to both, distinguishes himself from Ricardo as well as from Marx, for he does not determine value through labour directly. Rather he derives prices directly from the technical structure of production without relying on values. Relations between prices and labour expended are imputed only afterwards, by using the standard commodity.

Notes

1 See in particular Robinson (1956; 1973, p. 247 and passim). Further Kaldor (1956) and Pasinetti (1962).
2 One example only: the von Neumann model, with good reason famous since 1945, clearly implies the classical notion of surplus. The 'neo-neoclassicists' none the less interpret it as an element of their theory.

3 Hollander thinks (without doubting the didactic value of the corn-corn model) that Sraffa has over-interpreted Ricardo. See Hollander (1973), as well as the controversy between J. Eatwell and S. Hollander (Eatwell, 1975b). Since we are here more concerned with Sraffa than with Ricardo, we shall not pursue this point any further.

Essay 3   Critique of Neoclassical Theory

In the years immediately following the publication of Sraffa's book, only a few reviewers recognized its significance. In particular, the reviews by Joan Robinson (Robinson, 1961, 1965b, 1972) and Krishna Bharadwaj (Bharadwaj, 1963; modified version in Harcourt and Laing, 1971) offer valuable insights even today. However, many missed the point; the exact nature of the critique of the neoclassicists was at first completely obscure.[1]

Here, we will first attempt to characterize the difference between Sraffa's system and the neoclassical one in general terms and then discuss, or at least mention, a few specific critiques that have been brought up in scientific debates, following on from the results of PCMC.

One such critique consists of two statements, which are incomprehensible initially to those thinking in neoclassical terms. To begin with, prices are determined without any presumption about returns to scale; only characteristics of the system that are independent from variations in output and employment are mentioned. *Ex hypothesi*, variations in factor inputs (upon which the marginal productivity theory is based) cannot take place.

The separation of price determination from the determination of quantities produced is also the essence of Keynesian theory. This is generally acknowledged today for macroeconomics. Resistance to Sraffa's idea of price determination as being *subsequent* to the determination of quantities shows how little thought has been given to the impact that the Keynesian revolution ought to have had on so-called microeconomics. Sraffa's system 'lacks' equations for demand for and supply of 'factors' and 'consumption goods'. The starting point is a system that, assuming a certain profit rate, a corresponding wage rate and appropriate prices, is capable of ensuring its reproduction. It is the function of prices to make such replacement possible. Prices are introduced into the system without a surplus (PCMC, sec 1–3) as exchange ratios which reinstate the distribution of commodities as means of production necessary to repeat the production processes (separated by the division of labour) at the end of the production period.

We can imagine the reproducing system in terms of Sraffa's simple society, or as two closed societies trading with each other, where only commodities traded externally appear in the equations. Above all, each of the models discussed below that has a surplus can be transformed into one without surplus if the quantities of investment by capitalists and consumption goods bought by workers in each industry are known and can be imputed to the different processes on the same level as the physical inputs. This model serves the purpose of, and derives its value from, clarifying in general the function of relative prices in Sraffa's system. Relative prices are not introduced in the same way as by the neoclassicals, i.e. in order to bring into equilibrium quantities supplied and demanded according to subjective criteria. Rather, they represent the exchange conditions between physical goods that make reproduction within a given technical (methods of production) and social (distribution) framework *possible*. This definition does not exhaust the function of prices but it is sufficient as a basis of the intended critique of neoclassical theory (see also Essay 6 below).

If one is used to viewing the economy as a 'one-way street' from factors to consumption goods, the possibility of explaining prices by reproduction will seem strange, but its validity has to be acknowledged, because every economic theory taking its point of departure from these simple assumptions has to be able to explain the economy as a system that reproduces itself with labour (the only original factor) and capital, consisting of raw materials, produces the capital goods necessary for reproduction and the necessary consumption goods. The profit rate appears for the neoclassicals as the 'factor price of capital' and should therefore be positive.

The fact that relative prices are determined on the basis of these simple data represents the first approach of the critique, because it has traditionally been claimed that supply and demand in the subjective sense essentially determine prices. Now we find that they already follow from the circular character of production so that the impact of subjective preferences cannot find its expression primarily in prices.

In some sense this result can pass as an extension of the thesis in Sraffa's 1925 essay; it was shown there that, with Marshall's own assumptions, costs of production alone are essentially sufficient for the unambiguous determination of prices. The same result can be found here in an extended way. The watered-down notion of 'costs of production' is replaced by the conditions of reproduction. This is the basis on which the classical, in particular Ricardian, price theory rests. Marshall had seen in Ricardo's concept merely a theory of production costs, which he thought had to be completed by the element of the utility-determined demand curve. Sraffa, on the other hand, in his introduction to the Ricardo edition, shows that Ricardo was not interested in the notion of 'costs of production', which would have pointed in the direction of a one-way street leading from factors to consumption goods. Rather, he was concerned with the analysis of social reproduction, which under capitalism is determined in the first place by capital accumulation.

It might be objected that, since the quantities to be produced of all commodities depend on the quantities to be produced of all consumption goods, demand does in fact influence prices via the determination of production magnitudes. Sraffa himself impressively demonstrated such a price effect when presenting an increasing rent with increasing corn production (PCMC, sec. 88). The objection, however, misses the point. First it has to be noted that prices, presupposing the quantities to be produced and the distribution of income, are fully determined. It in no way follows from the fact that quantities produced are not explained by Sraffa that subjective preferences explain these magnitudes adequately.

The model would be closed according to the neoclassicals, with marginal productivity theory explaining the factor prices and demand theory (consumer sovereignty) explaining what is being produced. But it turns out that the pure neoclassical 'closing' of the model is not possible. The real problem is not demand (demand functions for consumption goods based on utility theory can perhaps even be accepted for the model, although some limiting remarks concerning this will have to be presented below); rather it lies in the formulation of the connection between 'factor supply' and 'factor demand'. The traditional explanations of this connection are manifold. Instead of submitting each one of them to a critique, Sraffa lets the profit rate vary, analyses the price changes resulting from this hypothetical variation of the profit rate and points out effects that are supposed to be incompatible with *all* neoclassical attempts to close the system. Since it is generally acknowledged that the model that serves as a point of departure presents a reasonable abstraction, the neoclassical theory is thereby being led *ad absurdum*. To prove this completely, as many analyses as there are versions of the neoclassical model would be necessary. Sraffa has renounced any attempt to carry out the critique which is to follow upon his 'prelude'. This implicit critical programme has not yet been fulfilled by the works written since the publication of PCMC. In this essay, I have to limit myself to indications of the debates that nevertheless have already taken place.

The central difficulty of neoclassical theory lies in the notion of 'capital'. 'How do you measure capital?' has been the battle-cry of the critics of neoclassical theory ever since Joan Robinson's famous article on the neoclassical production function, which opened the attack on the neoclassical theory (Robinson, 1953/4).

Under capitalism, produced commodities (which as such have a cost price) become *means* to produce other commodities, by employing labour, and to reproduce the real capital. This is because capitalists dispose of money capital with which real assets are bought. The price determination of real capital from the side of costs of production is contrasted with that from the discounted profits that are to be obtained with the help of that capital. But, in equilibrium, a capital good can have only *one* price, and according to neoclassical ideas of equilibrium this has to be such that on the one hand the profits are proportional to the capital advanced – following the general rate of profit – and on the other hand the price of the capital good is equal to the cost of production. The profit rate has to correspond to the interest rate and therefore, in neoclassical terms, is an indicator of the readiness of owners of the factor 'capital' to advance it to enterprises for the purpose of production. More generally, the neoclassical dilemma reads: How can the profit rate be determined by supply of and demand for the factor 'capital' when the profit rate itself enters into the price determination of real assets? As a first approximation one might say that the profit rate, in so far as it is supposed to bring supply of and demand for the factor capital to equality, is influenced by the expectations of the future yields (profits) to be earned from the factor. The profit rate, in so far as it enters into the determination of each capital good's cost, also determines the magnitude of value that represents a given quantity of real capital.

There results therefore a circular argument inasmuch as capital determines the profit rate and, as a magnitude of value, is determined by it. This circle was noticed long ago and there are basically two ways of getting around it. On the one hand, one can attempt to aggregate capital goods with some index without the profit rate entering into the index. For example, one can try to measure capital by the labour embodied in it. In this case the question arises whether the aggregate 'capital' constructed according to this index, which is *ex definitione* independent from the profit rate, is still a suitable theoretical tool to economically explain the rate of profit. *Or* one can attempt first to dispense with any notion of capital as an aggregate. Then the question arises how demand for and supply of capital goods in individual markets can be connected to supply of, and demand for, money capital and the interest rate.

The first approach seems to open a possibility for discussing accumulation in its development through time. The capital stock inherited from the past is a parameter today, and one can discuss how the supply of, and demand for, savings determine the interest rate, assuming that the capital stock increases by total savings (which, according to neoclassicals, are all invested). The problem of measuring the capital stock, which arises for the first approach, is avoided in the second by introducing an interdependent system of supply and demand functions of a Walrasian type. Formally this presents no particular problem, inasmuch as the supply and demand functions are connected to those for consumption goods. Each household decides according to its utility function which quantities of factors (labour, real assets and land, etc.) it is willing to advance for what prices and which consumption goods it wants to demand for what prices. Under reasonable assumptions the system of interdependent equations has one or several solutions. The difficulty enters when we ask what regulates the production of new (or the replacement of old worn-out) capital goods and the interest rate on saved capital. Assuming that the consumption alternatives for future periods are known for all agents, the production of capital goods is subordinated to this future consumption. But in this case it remains unclear why a uniform profit rate should be generated, because there are different conditions of scarcity for the 'inherited' stock of capital goods. Furthermore, to assume that consumption alternatives in future periods are generally known is unrealistic. However, if one attempts to represent an unspecified future within the model, savings and investments have to be matched as value magnitudes and not as disaggregated real capital, which would lead back to the first approach and its logical difficulties.

These connections have been presented in detail in a great many articles and books.[2] The discussion around the Walrasian version of neoclassical theory and the question of the extent to which it is affected by Sraffa's critique is still very open. In contrast, there is a general theoretical agreement (which is ignored in a scandalous way by most textbooks) about the untenability of neoclassical theories that take their point of departure from aggregate capital. I concentrate here on a summary of this second discussion; in the course of this, insight into Sraffa's method of critique by *reductio ad absurdum* will be provided.

After the Second World War, growth theory provided the framework within which neoclassicals attempted a macroeconomic determination of the rate of profit. Allusions to the problem of the aggregation of capital were made in theoretical formulations;[3] but the fact that the theory was subjected to innumerable methodologically insufficient empirical tests[4] proves a willingness to apply the marginal productivity theory of capital to an explanation of the distribution of income, even though some people today deny this.

In 1962 Samuelson attempted to support neoclassical growth theory by presenting a theoretical substantiation of the macroeconomic production function (Samuelson, 1962; also in Harcourt, 1972). At the beginning of his essay he asserts that disaggregated versions of neoclassical theory (meaning the Walrasian version) represent the actual strict theory, whereas his attempt to construct a production function is to be understood as an approximation only. However, he indicates a method by which a capital aggregate whose marginal product equals the profit rate can be deduced from a disaggregated model.

Samuelson was assuming that capital intensity is the same in all industries. As is shown in Essay 6, this is only possible if prices, expressed in terms of the net product or the standard commodity, are independent from the profit rate and equal to labour values.

To be able to compare different systems that produce the same net product we will make this the standard for prices. Since all prices in labour commanded (prices divided by the wage rate) increase monotonically with the profit rate, ranging from 0 to the maximum profit rate, there results, independently from the composition of the net product, a monotonically falling curve for the wage, expressed in terms of the net product, which is shown in Figure III.3.1. The per capita product y, calculated in these prices, equals wages plus profits per capita or $y = w + rk$, where k stands for capital intensity. Because y is independent from r, the capital intensity for each profit rate can be derived from the wage curve; it is equal to tan α in Figure III.3.1.

Now we assume that a large number of alternative production systems or techniques are given, all of which can produce the net product. All of these production methods are known. Then, for a given wage rate in a capitalist economy, those yielding the highest profit rate would have to be chosen. Assuming all wage curves to be linear, the configuration illustrated in Figure III.3.2 results. For very small profit rates, the technique would have to be chosen with which the highest per capita product can be reached (employing the highest capital intensity). For a falling wage rate and increasing profit rate, successively a shift towards techniques with lower capital intensity would take place; thus we would find that (as for the neoclassical production function) high profit rates are associated with low capital intensity and *vice versa*.

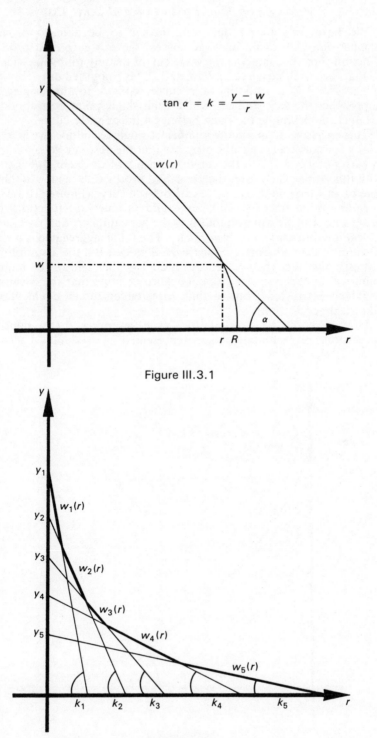

$$\tan \alpha = k = \frac{y - w}{r}$$

$w(r)$

Figure III.3.1

Figure III.3.2

We have only to go one step further to be able to prove, for Samuelson's case of linear wage curves, the existence of a production function. For this, imagine the wage curves densely following each other so that the envelope curve in Figure III.3.2 is smoothed out. Thus we get (Figure III.3.3) a smooth wage curve, convex to the origin, which approaches the axes and for which each single point corresponds to a production technique to which belongs a linear wage curve.

This envelope of an infinite number of single techniques we label $w(r)$. This wage curve $w(r)$ has the property that the absolute value of its slope at each point is equal to the capital intensity of the technique associated with this point. Therefore, the per capita product reached with the profit rate of this technique can be read from the curve (Figure III.3.3).

Both capital intensity and per capita product are functions of the profit rate. But we can also interpret the per capita product as a function of capital intensity, i.e. $y = f(k)$.[5] Then the aggregated production function is derived from a disaggregated model. But the assumptions are so restrictive that the constructed model neither allows for immediate empirical application nor presents cause to hope that the assumptions could be abstracted from so that an extended model could allow for empirical application.

First it should be stressed that, even assuming almost continuous successions of techniques, each represented by a similar linear wage

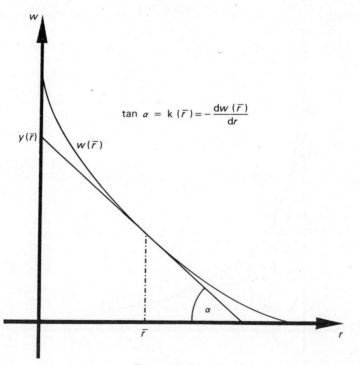

$$\tan \alpha = k(\bar{r}) = -\frac{dw(\bar{r})}{dr}$$

Figure III.3.3

curve, the production function obtained in this way cannot be interpreted in the sense of neoclassical equilibrium theory. For neoclassical equilibrium is supposed to be stable: if, for instance, the capital stock increases as a result of a transient act of saving, the profit rate should fall to a level such that the increase of capital stock, with increased capital intensity and a constant quantity of labour, can be demanded by firms in accordance with the factor prices that they face. Such a transition to a higher capital intensity causes no difficulty in a corn-corn model; but in a multiple-product model the shift to higher capital intensity means the introduction of new production techniques, possibly not just in one but in many industries. Even if, according to our assumptions, the composition of the net product remains constant, a shift to other basic commodities can thereby become necessary. Such a fundamental restructuring of production cannot be thought of as a smooth transition. The abstraction from the problem of effective demand is of course not correct, and even if we abstract from this by assuming, e.g., a Keynesian economic policy, the difficulty remains: although the demand function for capital (which is given by the equality of the marginal product and the profit rate) slopes down from the upper left side to the lower right side, neighbouring points can correspond to completely different production methods so that the picture of 'wandering' along this curve with increasing capital supply is illegitimate.

However, our considerations do not aim at this argument, but at a critique of the completely arbitrary assumption of a linear wage curve for each single technique, which comes about if and only if all sectors have equal capital intensity. It is somewhat ironic that the production function, the basis of the neoclassical theory of distribution, exists precisely when prices equal values according to the Marxian assumption (see Bhaduri, 1969; also Harcourt and Laing, 1971). If prices deviate from values, the construction can no longer be understood even as an approximation.

Let us recall that Sraffa in PCMC proves that the prices of two commodities for a given technique and any price standard may be equal for two different rates of profit and different for the rates of profit that lie in between. In his section 48, he hints at the critique that could be drawn from this: it is not possible to construct a concept of capital, e.g. with the Böhm–Bawerk production period, that is independent of the interest rate and yet appropriate for determining the interest rate. Sraffa further concludes in sections 92–94 that the wage curves of two systems that differ with respect to the production method for a basic good can intersect for two different rates of profit. If we express, deviating from Sraffa, the wage rate not in terms of the standard product of one of the systems but as before in terms of the net product common to both of them, it follows that the wage curve for each production system will not be a straight line unless the capital intensities in all sectors happen to be equal. The wage curves might be concave as well as convex to the origin; hence the possibility that the wage rates for two systems that differ only with respect to the method of production of a basic good are equal for two different rates of profit, as represented in Figure III.3.4. But if the

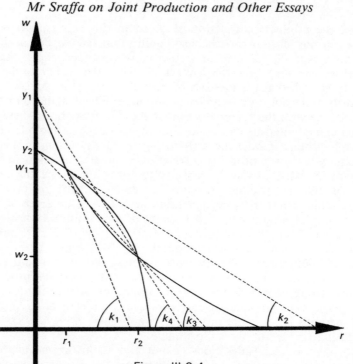

Figure III.3.4

first technique is advantageous for a low rate of profit, a second technique for the higher rate of profit, and the first technique again for the highest rate of profit, the assignment of specific capital intensities to specific rates of profit or continuous intervals in which the rate of profit varies evidently is not uniquely determined and the construction of the production function is impossible.[6]

The construction of the production function does not even require this refutation via the phenomenon of returning techniques ('reswitching'), because a production function for which the marginal product equals the factor price already becomes impossible if the wage curves of single techniques are not straight lines (except for a few unimportant cases; see Garegnani, 1970; also Hunt and Schwartz, 1972). Contrary to the usual interpretations today, the debate about the possibility of returning techniques is important not only because it proves that the production function with its marginal products is nonsensical, but because, on a more general level, it can be shown that a demand function for capital (see Figures III.3.5 and 6) cannot be defined.[7]

The essential difficulty of the critique of neoclassical theory lies in the proof that a demand function for capital is a necessary property of neoclassical theory claiming to explain the level of the rate of profit or rate of interest. We have to limit ourselves here to a few points:

(1)   Besides the macroeconomic production function, the conception of which stems from Clark and which has been proved and recognized to be

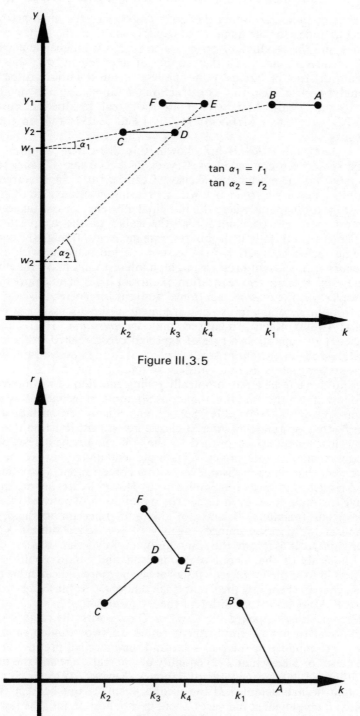

$$\tan \alpha_1 = r_1$$
$$\tan \alpha_2 = r_2$$

Figure III.3.5

Figure III.3.6

untenable, there are Böhm-Bawerk's and Wicksell's attempts to construct an index for the quantity of capital, based on the notion of dated labour and the production period, such that it is independent from the rate of interest, and such that supply of and demand for this capital explain the rate of interest none the less. From the above discussion it should be clear that this construction is untenable (for details, see Garegnani, 1970). Marshall's notion of real production costs (see PCMC, sec. 7 and Marshall, [1920] 1966, p. 282) falls in the same category.

As Garegnani (1964/5) has shown, this theoretical tradition has in some sense been continued by Keynes in the *General Theory*. Keynes thought that the marginal efficiency of capital for a single entrepreneur exhibits a decreasing tendency with increasing investment so that he will invest up to the point where the marginal efficiency of capital equals the interest rate. He concluded that the value of the aggregate of all investment goods falls as the interest rate increases. It might be correct to assume such a connection for the short period because, with constant revenues from current production, high interest rates make the financing of new investments and realization of current investments more difficult. However, for the reasons mentioned above it is incorrect, even abstracting from uncertainty, to use this argument in the discussion of the long period (which Keynes mentions only *en passant*). If the marginal efficiency of capital, as a rate of expected profit related to the costs of capital goods in current prices, is set equal to the interest rate, we get a price system that is like the Sraffian system, in that the value of capital does not have to be a monotonically falling function of the interest rate. It follows from this that the numerous attempts to reconcile Keynes with the neoclassicists (Hicks, MIT School, and others) rest on false assumptions − they postulate an interest-elastic investment function that would allow investment to be pushed to the full employment level with an adequate interest rate policy. This argument underlines Keynes' main statement that, in capitalism, even with a correct monetary policy, there is no tendency towards full employment. However, Keynes attempted to prove his main tenet even under the assumption of interest-rate-elastic investment functions. Because of this and other unsatisfactory compromises his position gained cogency of conviction among academic economists. It is from this ambiguity in Keynesian theory that the neoclassicals of the school of Samuelson and Solow could build on Keynes in their theory of growth, whereas the more radical interpretation of Keynesian theory by the Cambridge school (J. Robinson, Lord Kahn, Lord Kaldor) leads to a different theory of growth.[8]

Keynes himself opened the *General Theory* with the remark that the traditional theory of employment rested on two 'fundamental postulates': (1) equality of the real wage and the marginal product of labour (demand for labour); and (2) equality of the real wage and the marginal disutility of labour (supply of labour) (Keynes, 1936, p. 5). Keynes thought he had demolished the second postulate but he kept the first: 'Thus, *if* employment increases, then, in the short period, the reward per unit of labour in terms of wage-goods must, in general, decline and profits increase' (Keynes, 1936, p. 17).

Today we know that the first postulate 'in general' is as untenable as the second. In order to define the marginal product of labour, the other factors have to be held constant. If the term 'capital' is used in the sense of aggregate capital, the difficulty of defining the latter is transmitted to the definition of the marginal product of labour. If we hold the physical means of production constant and focus on the short period (which undoubtedly comes closer to Keynes' intention), we notice that the majority of plants work with over-capacity (which is to a certain degree planned) so that, if the wage is about half of value added, it constitutes only half of the marginal product of labour, as long as the profit margin on direct costs is constant (see Robinson, 1972b, p. 234). Thus, the notion of the 'marginal efficiency of capital' and the 'marginal product of labour' are elements of the neoclassical theory of value that survive in Keynes and have to be replaced.

(2) The majority of modern authors refer to the disaggregated Walrasian theory. As we have seen above, Sraffa took a stand against this from the very beginning because, even though Walras could dispense with Marshall's *ceteris paribus* clause, he had to avoid the problems connected with imperfect competition and accumulation under uncertainty conditions. Now the discussion concerns the logical consistency of the Walrasian theory inasmuch as it claims to serve as a basis for a theory of accumulation, at least in perfect competition.

The modern form of the Walrasian theory (Debreu) completely does away with the notion of aggregate capital. Walras himself has attempted to construct a connection between the money market and the markets for capital goods, but this side of his model encountered difficulties and is almost forgotten today. Debreu's mathematically sophisticated but economically abbreviated version of the Walrasian equilibrium does not deal with the tendency to the equalization of profits in all sectors. The phenomenon of the interest rate appears only in so far as physically equal commodities have different prices and different own rates of interest at different points in time. Debreu does not give conditions under which price variations of different commodities between two points in time, resulting in different own rates, can be reduced to a uniform discount rate (which in turn might be determined in a money market). The problem of explaining the money rate of interest is not even posed, let alone its relation to industrial profit. It therefore appears strange when, as a reply to Sraffa's critique, reference is made to Debreu who, far from offering an explanation of 'the' interest rate and 'the' rate of profit that could be criticized, offers none (or a plurality of interest rates).

The essential difficulties with Walrasian models (including Debreu) originate, as mentioned above, from the following assumption: they all take the quantities of the different capital goods as given from the beginning. If the lifetime of these capital goods were unlimited, capital goods would not have to be produced in a stationary system and could therefore produce a rent that was analogous to that of different types of land and labour. But because capital goods depreciate they have to be reproduced. Their prices of production have to contain interest according to a uniform rate of the money capital advanced for production.

Since the supply prices for existing capital goods, which depend on the conditions of scarcity and the potential uses of capital goods in production, do not stand in a genuine relation to prices of production of reproduced capital goods in the model, an ambiguous double price determination occurs. The modern Walrasians avoid this by allowing for different prices for already existing capital goods and those to be reproduced.

Therefore Debreu's economic equilibrium is a hybrid: except for capital, supply and demand in markets for goods and factors are in an equilibrium that could reproduce itself, with unchanged preferences and resources even beyond the time horizon intended for production. But for the means of production there exists an equilibrium only *within* this time horizon because the non-durable reproducible capital goods are used up within it; only imperishable resources such as land and labour power, which are reproduced outside the capitalistic process, will be left. Since the reproducible capital goods are consumed within the time horizon and the model deals only with the final demand for consumption goods, there is no place for the uniform interest payment on capital; neither is there an explanation of the unlimited reproduction of capital goods. To avoid the question of the reproduction of capital goods, it has to be assumed that the time horizon is far away so that a theory of demand for investment goods and saving 'in general' (i.e. without the intention of investing the savings in a particular investment project) can be completely forgone.

Such a simple escape, which allows the representation neither of long-run capital accumulation, nor its Keynesian short-run counterpart, did not satisfy Walras himself.[9] He was looking for an equilibrium in which each of the existing capital goods is lent out for productive purposes at a price that is equal to the interest on the production costs of a new capital good of the same kind plus the depreciation and insurance costs. The new capital goods are assumed to be produced in such quantities that this equilibrium relationship can hold and at the same time the total cost of the new capital goods (investment) corresponds to savings, which are dependent on the interest rate, among other factors (surplus of supply of productive services over demanded consumption goods). But at this point, as Garegnani has shown (1960, pp. 91–121, esp. p. 115), Walras got entangled in a contradiction that could only be avoided by aggregating the different capital goods to a physically homogeneous aggregate 'capital'.[10] This aggregation was impossible, however, because different conditions of scarcity for the capital goods exist initially relative to the requirement for the production of consumption goods. The production prices of the new capital goods are essentially determined by the methods of production. Therefore either the scarcity conditions of the initially existing different capital goods have to be variable (by transforming themselves into each other to become malleable, if they are to be fully employed capital), or else a uniform interest payment on capital becomes generally impossible.

None of the Walrasian systems explains how an accumulation process with self-reproducing capital goods and a uniform rate of profit comes about in an equilibrating process. Hence J. Robinson (1965b, p. 12) wrote already in her first critical review of PCMC:

> When we are provided with a set of technical equations for production and a real wage rate which is uniform throughout the economy, there is no room for demand equations in the determination of equilibrium prices.... [This] emphasizes a point which, both in its scholastic and in its political aspect, is of great importance; in a market economy, either there may be a tendency towards uniformity of wages and the rate of profit in different lines of production, or prices may be governed by supply and demand, but not both. Where supply and demand rule, there is no room for uniform levels of wages and the rate of profit. The Walrasian system makes sense if we interpret it in terms of an artisan economy, where each producer is committed to a particular product, so that his income depends on his output and its price. Each can have a prospective rate of return on investment in his own line, but there is no mechanism to equalize profits between one line and another.

The analysis of the artisan economy does not need the concept 'demand for capital'.

To summarize, it appears that the difficulties with the notion of capital arise as soon as the attempt is made to explain distribution in the context of neoclassical consumer preferences determining supply and demand relations. The discussion about this has not yet come to an end, among other reasons because each critique provokes the construction of new models. We have not been able to discuss all neoclassical versions. If the discussion is not to get lost in interminable details, one has first to decide about the legitimacy of the basic and most commonly used models. Much would be achieved if unanimity existed about the deficiencies of the versions of neoclassical theory discussed here. As for the rest, the same saying for theories applies as for medications: the greater the variety suggested, the higher the probability that none of them works.

Notes

1 Dobb (1973) provides an extensive historical overview.
2 See, in particular, the summarizing book by Harcourt (1972), the seminal opus on the history of the neoclassical capital theories by Garegnani (1960), as well as J. Eatwell's dissertation (Eatwell, 1975a), which gave me valuable ideas that were enriched by discussions with the author.
3 Clearly and honestly by Swan (1956; abbreviated in Harcourt and Laing, 1971).
4 The fact that the economic tests seemed to explain the existence of a Cobb–Douglas function must and can be explained – see Gahlen (1972).
5 For this we interpret the relations following from the construction: $k(r) = -\,dw/dr$ and $y(r) = w(r) + rk(r)$ as a parameter representation for the production function $y = f(k)$. The parameter representation is legitimate, since the derivatives do not vanish. It remains to be shown that the production function defined in this way has the properties normally required for a production function and that its derivative is equal to the profit rate so that the marginal productivity theory holds:

$$y(r) = w(r) - rw'(r)$$

$$\frac{\mathrm{d}y}{\mathrm{d}r} = \frac{\mathrm{d}f}{\mathrm{d}k}\frac{\mathrm{d}k}{\mathrm{d}r}$$

therefore

$$\frac{\mathrm{d}f}{\mathrm{d}k} = \frac{\mathrm{d}y/\mathrm{d}r}{\mathrm{d}k/\mathrm{d}r} = \frac{w' - w' - rw''}{-w''} = r.$$

It follows from this that the profit rate is equal to the marginal product of capital if one shifts from a production function dependent on capital intensity to a production function dependent on K and L, which can be defined by $Y = F(K, L) = Lf(k)$, $k = K/L$. From

$$\frac{\mathrm{d}^2y}{\mathrm{d}r^2} = \frac{\mathrm{d}^2f(k)}{\mathrm{d}k^2}\frac{\mathrm{d}k}{\mathrm{d}r} + \frac{\mathrm{d}f}{\mathrm{d}k}\frac{\mathrm{d}^2k}{\mathrm{d}r^2}$$

it follows further that:

$$\frac{\mathrm{d}^2f}{\mathrm{d}k^2} = -\frac{1}{w''(r)}.$$

Therefore, the production function constructed from the wage curve $y = f(k)$ has a positive but falling marginal product if $w''(r)$ is positive.

6   The phenomenon of 'returning techniques', though observed, had been treated as a mere curiosity previously to Sraffa (see Harcourt, 1971). In Sraffa's work it appeared as a case that seemed as normal as its opposite. But the concrete numerical example given by Sraffa related to non-basics. Samuelson's student Levhari thought that a return of techniques could not take place if the techniques are different in the methods with which they produce the basic products. An incorrect 'proof' – as Samuelson and Levhari soon had to admit – of this statement was published in the *Quarterly Journal of Economics* in 1966 (Levhari, 1966) and provoked the famous debate about 'reswitching'. The fact that it was only with the scandal of a published, incorrect proof that the untenability of the production function became generally known, sheds light on the conventional standard of scientific cogency in the formation of economic theory.

7   This may be illustrated in two ways. Figure III.3.5 shows which net product per capita is reached for which capital intensity when the rate of profit increases from 0 to its maximum, corresponding to the first of the two techniques presented in Figure III.3.4. The graph shows what remains of the production function. First the rate of profit is 0 and the per capita product y_1; the capital intensity is somewhat greater than k_1 (point A in Figure III.3.5). With increasing rate of profit and decreasing wage rate the capital intensity first falls without a switch in techniques to capital intensity k_1 (point B). With a constant rate of profit and wage rate, the second technique is introduced (point C). The capital intensity increases to k_3 (point D) and the first technique is reintroduced for the rate of profit r_2 and wage w_2 (point E). The capital intensity again falls until the maximum rate of profit is reached (point F). The direct relation between capital intensity and the rate of profit (to which, of course, a marginal product no longer corresponds) can be derived from Figure III.3.4. The resulting 'demand curve for capital' is presented in Figure III.3.6. It consists of three unconnected pieces, it

partly has multiple values and it runs partly from the lower left to the upper right side instead of the other way round as should 'normally' be the case.

8 See in particular Robinson (1956). Harrod's attempts to revive the Wicksellian theory of the natural interest rate in a Keynesian way, on the other hand, are a perfect example of the subtle attempts to make Keynes a neoclassicist.

9 See the third model in Walras ([1926] 1954; (the English translation is preferable to the French original because of Jaffé's critical apparatus).

10 Morishima's proof of the existence of an equilibrium solution in the Walrasian system does not contradict my interpretation because he does not prove that in each production period positive quantities are produced of all reproducible capital goods. As Eatwell has shown in his dissertation (Eatwell, 1975a) only those capital goods are reproduced whose initial supply is scarcest relative to the demand for the production of consumer goods. In this case, trivially, the supply price of the single reproducible capital good is linked to its price of production by a uniform discount rate (see Morishima, 1964).

Essay 4   Sraffa and Marx

The critique of neoclassical theory presented in Essay 3 does not imply that all elements of the neoclassical doctrine have become obsolete. Various models of consumer demand or of optimization in production remain valid in the appropriate context. But the broad subsumption of economic development under the notion of a neoclassical equilibrium has been questioned, i.e. the idea that the production and distribution of the net product can be explained by supply of and demand for goods and factors without taking the concept of surplus into account.

While the critique thus aims at the very core of neoclassical theory without, however, questioning the usefulness of many neoclassical techniques, the exact opposite – broadly speaking – can be said about the relation of Sraffian theory to classical theory. If one puts the 'classicals' – Smith, Ricardo, Marx – on one side as adherents of an 'objective' theory of value, and the neoclassicals on the other side as adherents of a 'subjective' theory of value, which is to some extent accurate from the standpoint of 'positive' economics, Sraffa should really be counted with the first group, for he explains prices through objective conditions of production, modified by the influence of distribution among the classes. However, he differs from the three classicals as regards the 'technique' of price determination, because he does not treat prices as somewhat modified labour values. He reduces price (as influenced by distribution) *and* labour value – which are independent of each other – to a third common element, namely the production process as specified by the physical inputs and outputs. The notion of 'natural price' or price of production does not seem to be affected; it remains to be distinguished from 'market price'. In this sense Sraffa seems simply to reinforce an old tradition and revive it by giving it a modern form with which he defends it against the neoclassical interlude.

This way of putting it has certain advantages if we draw upon the difference between subjective and objective value theory to distinguish the different schools, but other criteria will produce different distinctions. With respect to effective demand, Malthus and Keynes can be counterposed to Ricardo and Marshall. As regards Sraffa, it is obviously our task here to focus on the different ways of treating the notion of capital and the connection between income distribution and price formation. This viewpoint differentiates the classicals' positions; in particular, the relation between Sraffa on the one hand and Ricardo and Marx on the other becomes more contradictory than it might seem at first sight.

A vast literature has dealt with the extent of Sraffa's contribution to solving the Marxian 'transformation problem'; here we are going to discuss Sraffa's relation to Marx by mentioning some alternative positions that can be taken in this matter, without however expressing a preference for any one in particular.

Taking a closer look, the differences between Marx and Sraffa with respect to price theory are manifold. They start with different definitions of the basic functions of prices and end with differences in their treatment of rent and in explaining why a given technique can be superior to others. Sraffa's work contains analyses that Marx tends to avoid in *Das Kapital*, such as joint production. It goes without saying that Marx, on the other hand, deals with a multitude of economic problems and questions that Sraffa neither deals with nor even hints at. Many of these differences deserve to be discussed in detail. I will begin by listing some of Sraffa's results that are fundamentally opposed to Marxian statements or at least seem so in the eyes of some people. After enumerating some possible reactions to the resulting dilemma, I want to show by means of examples that the Sraffian theory, despite these differences, is useful for solving a number of problems concerning 'positive' Marxist economics. We shall see that the peculiar relationship between Sraffa and Marx – which is partly antagonistic and partly complementary – is closely connected with different methodological ideas.

The main contrasts are (Cogoy, 1974):

1   Sraffa specifies the production processes as the quantities of commodities or (to use the Marxian term) 'use values' that, together with a certain quantum of unskilled labour, enter into and leave production. Only the complex of these processes of production allows the simultaneous determination of labour values and, for a given profit rate, of prices of production. For Marx, on the other hand, constant capital enters into the process of value creation as a value magnitude together with variable capital; the latter is capable of producing surplus value. Value is engendered by labour; it is a 'substance' the quantity of which remains constant as long as there is no change in the productive forces. In the transformation of values into prices the surplus value, which is proportional to the variable capital in each sector, is distributed as profit in proportion to the total capital advanced in each sector. All sectors in the economy take part simultaneously in the process of redistribution. However, the constant capital entering into production is not simultaneously transformed from value into price, even though Marx admits that constant capital is bought for prices that deviate from values. Marx's procedure in the transformation thus does not refer explicitly to the use values that enter the different processes of production. He therefore cannot show how the prices of the elements of constant capital are to be calculated. He nevertheless stresses the necessity of deriving prices from values.

2   Accordingly, Marx formulates a notion of capital, exactly like some neoclassicals, which is given prior to income distribution in the form

of the rate of surplus value or the rate of profit. The fact that Marx takes capital as a relation of production does not alter the analytical shortcomings of his method.

3   Through the peculiar method of transformation without recourse to use values Marx arrives at the thesis that the total value of all produced commodities equals their total price and at the same time that total profit equals total (redistributed) surplus value. (The substance of value is redistributed and changes its form but not its quantity.) This statement is important in itself as a justification of the Marxian conception of profit. It is also important because, if total value equals total price and total surplus value equals total profit, the equality of the sums of constant capital and variable capital in values and in prices must hold, so that the same rate of profit is obtained by dividing either total profit by total capital measured in prices or total surplus value by the total labour value of capital. This identity is significant for the Marxian derivation of the tendency of the rate of profit to fall. It generally does not hold in a system where values and prices of production are calculated according to Sraffa.

From Sraffa's point of view, Marx's procedure is inadequate and faulty.[1] Sraffa's implicit critique of Marx's method is certainly not new in the debate about Marx. However, his contribution initiates a new type of discussion, because it offers at the same time a starting point for overcoming the transformation problem.

Marxists who take into account Sraffa's incontrovertible analytical results characteristically take one of the following positions:[2] Sraffian price theory can be substituted for Marx's value theory by giving up the labour theory of value; one can attempt to produce a coexistence of the two theories by combining them; or else one can argue that the Marxian analysis in terms of values allows the 'essence' of the capitalistic process of accumulation to be captured, while prices are 'surface phenomena' that do not need to be backed up mathematically by values. Unless it is linked with an imperative to strive for a new synthesis, the first position weakens and shortens Marx's theory, since it simply ignores the theory of the forms of value. In any case it is by no means clear how this could possibly be integrated with Sraffa's theory. The last position stands in admitted opposition to Marx's own intentions. He clearly saw the reduction of prices to values as essential for an objective foundation to the glittering notion of prices as well as to explain profits. This position also precludes empirical verification of statements derived on the basis of value theory. I am not going to deal with it here.

The middle position obviously has the greatest attraction for those who wish to reconcile Marxism with economic logic. Here, in numerous variants, attempts are made to combine the Sraffian method of starting from the physical structure of production with the Marxian analysis of value. Such attempts are not at first sight doomed, given that Marx distinguishes the work process from the process of 'valorization'. The processes of production as specified in Sraffa could be interpreted as representative of Marxian work processes. Sraffa's price theory would then reflect the results of the processes of valorization. Though it is impossible to take profit as redistributed surplus value in the sense of the above definition,[3] it can be proved that the rate of surplus value as a measure of exploitation is positive when the rate of profit is positive. Morishima (1973) therefore interprets the positive rate of surplus value as proof of the existence of a positive rate of profit and believes that this is the core of Marxian theory.

However, this position encounters the difficulty that the argument is circular: the answer to the question why labour value theory has to be dragged on is that it is necessary to prove exploitation; in order to answer the question how exploitation is to be proved, reference is made to the theory of value. If exploitation consists only of the definition and quantification of the notion of surplus labour, Sraffian analysis seems to grasp the phenomenon adequately. To defend Marx and avoid the circle it would have to be shown that the value theory is maintained because it is necessarily linked to other aspects of the Marxian analysis, such as the theory of the forms of value, a specific theory of money, the definition of capital, the description of exploitation as a *process* of extraction of surplus labour with specific implications for the character of technical progress, etc. But then the necessity of applying the theory of value and its compatibility with Sraffian price theory would also have to be tested each time.[4] Given the multiple functions that the theory of value has for Marx, it is no surprise that the literature on possible alternative explanations of the transformation process according to the 'middle way' seems artificial and does not satisfy anyone (Napoleoni, 1974). I will therefore not deal with this but consider other aspects of the Marxian position involved in the confrontation with Sraffa. The limited space available here allows only a few eclectic examples.

First, we notice that the Sraffian notion of the production process is defined in a broader way than Marx's work process. Marx introduces the production process as a goal-oriented human activity in which an object of labour, i.e. the raw material, is transformed by means of a tool (later a full-grown machine) into a product, which in turn becomes a commodity in a commodity-producing society. A similar conception is implicit in the main part of Sraffa's work. However, Sraffa begins more generally with a notion of production in which labour-time as such does not appear – in accord with the fact that the concept of labour, as opposed to leisure and creative activity, is itself a historical category.

If the farmer, whose household is self-sufficient, sells corn in order to buy metal tools and the blacksmith is self-sufficient except in so far as he sells metal tools in order to buy corn, the 'external exchange' between the two economic communities *can* be ruled by the labour embodied in the production of corn and iron respectively, but it does not have to be so. The exchange ratio is not very likely to stand in any kind of definable relation to the total labour of each household. Sraffa's exchange relations, as derived from the quantities of corn and iron wares produced and exchanged outside the household (but not from the hens and the vegetables produced and consumed within the household), therefore provide a more general approach for determining relative exchange relations, as we shall see in greater detail in Essay 6.

Sraffa also defines the process of production in a more general way when looking at the possibility of joint production. Marx's conception of the process of production as an activity oriented towards *one* goal means that the value of joint products is not explained except for special cases such as fixed capital (see section I.10). For Sraffa, it is definable, assuming that the number of processes of production corresponds to the number of commodities. On this assumption alone, values and prices can be determined. I do not wish to discuss the possible justification for this assumption here (it is obvious only in the case of fixed capital and rent; see sections I.11 and II.1). However, a number of effects suggest that capitalistic production does not function with the same simple rationality in the case of joint production as in single-product systems. The problem is interesting because of its historical component. Obviously modern enterprises produce more products under conditions of higher concentration than was the case in early capitalism where production was more clearly specialized. Insofar, it seems that the simple classical labour theory of value was more suitable for analysing early rather than later forms of capitalism.

This is even more true of the treatment of the wage. When Marx assumes a certain real wage, he does so in order to later discuss variations of the wage level. National differences of wages are mentioned but nowhere does Marx discuss the effect that gives modern capitalism its imprint and that was institutionalized ideologically and politically in Keynesian theory and economic policy – namely, the dynamic demand effect of money wages increasing with productivity. Wages had already begun to rise in the second half of the nineteenth century. Joan Robinson has, in her interpretation of Marx, attempted to connect this phenomenon with the fact that, in the discussion of the falling rate of profit in the third volume of *Capital*, the rate of exploitation essentially has to stay constant in order for the Marxian argument to hold. Marx therefore must have had in mind increasing wages as a systematic tendency. His argument implies this but we do not find any explicit analysis, presumably because the notion of labour power, which keeps its full meaning only in connection with the notion of an essentially constant real wage, prevents discussion of the dynamics of increasing wages. Nothing has been understood about developments since the Second World War (at the latest), if one believes it is possible to explain increasing real wages by the increasing cost of reproduction of labour power instead of focusing on the pressure of increasing nominal wages and their demand effects. Sraffa's 'nominalist' wage theory is helpful in linking the Keynesian analysis of the development of wages and its enormous political significance with a classical concept of surplus.

This does not remain without effect on the notion of money. The logic of the Marxian theory of the 'forms of value' is fascinating but obscure. At any rate, the equation of money and gold under early capitalist relations, which is an essential ingredient of the Marxian approach, is better regarded as a rough approximation or as a theoretical starting point. In view of the existence of the mine rent (even if problems of the world market and the differential wages in England and in the Californian gold mines are ignored) the price level could not be thought of as immediately determined by the given costs of production of gold. The equation of money with a commodity produced under capitalistic conditions with given costs of production is none the less a helpful auxiliary concept to illustrate why money always enters circulation with a certain purchasing power. For Marx, the main function of this theoretical assumption is to refute quantity theory and to replace it with the 'law of circulation', which indicates how much money the circulation can absorb for given absolute prices and how much has to be hoarded. However, it is actually only Keynes' introduction of speculative demand for money regulating the interest rate that yields a true explanation of how the 'law of circulation' manifests itself under developed capitalistic conditions. For Keynes the price level is essentially given with the level of money wages.[5] For a given price level and quantity of money, the interest rate adjusts because the money not absorbed in circulation is held by those who expect a drop in the prices of assets, so that it makes sense to hold money rather than assets. These reflections on the theory of money are a reasonable supplement to Sraffa's 'nominalist' wage theory. Marx, in constrast, basically cannot adequately explain why the quantity of hoarded gold money corresponds exactly to the quantity required by the 'law of circulation'.

Let us return to Sraffa's price theory. The wage curve makes it strikingly clear that the wage rate (i.e. per capita wages) and the rate of profit cannot fall at the same time. A new technique of production represents technical progress and is introduced if, for a given wage rate, it raises the rate of profit. For Marx, the increasing organic composition of capital is due to technical progress (more specifically to the production of 'relative surplus value'). It follows from this that the rate of profit can fall only if the wage rate rises. This conclusion – to which some Marxists by no means consent – follows inevitably if we exclude falling returns to scale in a Ricardian manner (which Marx at first did not have in mind).

In order to analyse the question of what type of technical progress causes an increasing organic composition, Sraffa's price theory is of great help. It reveals some paradoxes that can briefly be summed up as follows (see Schefold 1973, 1974). Since the rate of profit measured in price terms is different from that measured in value terms and since the fall in the rate of profit measured in prices represents the economically relevant incident, it makes sense to measure the organic composition in price terms. It then is the ratio of the sum of capital measured in price terms divided by the wage sum. The organic composition measured in prices is obviously dependent on the rate of profit. It is, none the less, an analytically useful instrument, because it is equal to the quotient between the sum of capital goods, measured in price terms and expressed in commanded labour, and total 'living labour'. This quotient obviously rises monotonically with the rate of profit for a given technique. The same is true for the relation between profits and wages, which is equal to the organic composition measured in price terms multiplied by the rate of profit. If one can prove that a change in technique causes the organic composition in price terms to increase for every imaginable rate of profit, the transition to the new technique implies that the actual rate of profit for given relations between profits and wages has to fall. The interaction of the rate of surplus value and the organic composition of capital, measured in value terms, with the rate of profit measured in value terms can thus be reproduced at the level of prices. However, it is necessary to show that certain forms of technical progress actually lead to an increase in the organic composition if one wants to prove that technical progress causes a fall in the rate of profit.

Three cases may be mentioned here. If the technical progress simply consists in shortening the labour-time expended in each production process, we assume, to present the argument in the purest form, that this reduction of labour-time advances equally in all sectors with constant physical inputs. The organic composition for a given rate of profit does not then change because the decrease of labour-time reduces the prices of all commodities in the same proportion as the unit wage-costs so that the quotient between capital and wages, which represents the organic composition, remains constant. Wage-rates will thus rise at a constant rate of profit. Only if wages are constant will the organic composition rise. In this case, however, the rate of profit rises as well. Thus the organic composition remains constant with a constant rate of profit even though, from the point of view of the Marxian value theory, the opposite might easily be expected because the amount of expended 'living labour' (in relation to the capital goods expended per product unit) has been reduced. If we assume on the other hand that the amount of raw materials expended per product unit decreases, while living labour remains constant, the organic composition *falls* because of a double effect: on the one hand, fewer raw materials per unit of product are required; on the other hand, the prices of capital goods fall.

This does not mean that the Marxian rising organic composition would not be encountered in this model. It can be shown that rising organic composition results if a process that produces, for example, 'cloth' by means of 'thread' and 'living labour' is replaced by two production processes, one of which produces a weaving machine with the use of raw materials already existing in the system while the other utilizes this weaving machine for the production of 'cloth', without a reduction of the amount of thread used per 'cloth' compared with the original process. The increase in the organic composition here is related to the fact that the physical surplus for this particular change in production methods is reduced, i.e. net product decreases relative to gross product. Therefore the maximum profit rate of the system falls. The transition to the new method of production is nevertheless possible because – again calculated per unit of product – much of living labour is saved. The possibility of a rising organic composition is therefore confirmed; with a constant ratio of profits to wages it must entail a falling rate of profit. However, the technical progress that leads to this rise in the organic composition is of a very specific character and will dominate only in particular historical epochs. We find again that the Marxian analysis is immediately applicable only to certain periods in the development of capitalism, while modern events have to be analysed in a different manner. The Sraffian theory of prices then turns out to be a useful instrument for building a bridge between the development of capitalism as analysed by Marx and its modern sequel.

The integration of Marxian analyses with those of the Keynesian school and those of Sraffa, which has been hinted at by means of subjectively chosen examples, may appear strange to those who are inclined to regard Marx as the critic of modern political economy because he shows the social genesis and the historical transitoriness of economic categories, while they reckon Sraffa among the uncritical political economists (see Brunhoff, 1972). But, as is shown in Essay 3, Sraffa should not be counted among the uncritical positivists, even if this reproach were justified in relation to the integration of the Sraffian theory of prices with the Marxian theory of accumulation which we have hinted at. However, this integration is, in my view, legitimate from the point of view of the critique of political economy, if it is interpreted in a modern fashion. What Marx meant by 'critique' is explained in volume I (Marx, [1867–92], 1972, vol. I, pp. 392–3) where it is said:

> Darwin has interested us in the history of Nature's Technology, i.e., in the formation of the organs of plants and animals, which organs serve as instruments of production for sustaining life. Does not the history of the productive organs of man, of organs that are the material basis of all social organisation, deserve equal attention? And would not such a history be easier to compile, since, as Vico says, human history differs from natural history in this, that we had made the former, but not the latter? Technology discloses man's mode of dealing with Nature, the process of production by which he sustains his life, and thereby also lays bare the mode of formation of his social relations, and of the mental conceptions that flow from them. Every history of religion, even, that fails to take account of this material basis, is uncritical. It is, in reality, much easier to discover by analysis the earthly core of the misty creations of religion, than, conversely, it is, to develop from the actual relations of life the corresponding celestialised forms of those relations. The latter method is the only materialistic, and therefore the only scientific one.

The highest task of a materialistic critique for Marx consists not in an enumeration of empirical counter-examples or in the *reductio ad absurdum* of the theory under consideration (in this example, religion), but in proving that the false theory has to spring necessarily from the given material conditions if the latter are understood correctly. According to this, the atheist would have a scientific argument for the understanding of religion if modern psychology explained religious need and modern sociology the canonization.

Thus, Marx's *Capital* is constructed so as to explain the 'genesis' of 'vulgar' economic conceptions about the origin of incomes of the main classes (rent, profit and wage) from the factors of production land,

capital and labour. Marx was confronted with vague conceptions rather
than with a theory, for the elevation of 'vulgar' economic thinking to the
neoclassical theory, which marked a sharp separation from the preceding
Ricardian ideas, developed only after about 1870. The process was partly
animated precisely by the desire to find an answer to Marxian economics.
It was only towards the end of the nineteenth century that neoclassical
theory acquired the systematic character that allowed Sraffa to pursue
the critique of it as *reductio ad absurdum*, the most academic form of
criticism.

Marx connects his critique of the as yet undeveloped vulgar economic
ideas – ideas at which the modern neoclassical smiles – with a critique
of a quite different nature of the Ricardian economy. He says (Marx,
[1861–3] 1968, vol. II, pp. 165–6):

> Adam Smith himself moves with great naiveté in a perpetual con-
> tradiction. On the one hand he traces the intrinsic connection existing
> between economic categories or the obscure structure of the bourgeois
> economic system. On the other, he simultaneously sets forth the
> connection as it appears in the phenomenon of competition and thus
> as it presents itself to the unscientific observer just as to him who is
> actually involved and interested in the process of bourgeois society. ...
> A. Smith's successors ... can always regard A. Smith as their basis
> whether they follow the esoteric or the exoteric part of his work or
> whether, as is almost always the case, they jumble up the two. But at
> last Ricardo steps in and calls 'stop!' to science. The foundation, the
> starting point of the physiology of the bourgeois system – for the
> understanding of its internal organic coherence and life process – is
> the determination of *value by labour time*. Ricardo starts with this and
> forces science to get out of the root, to render an account of the extent
> to which the other categories evolved and described by it ... correspond
> with the contradiction between the apparent and the actual movement
> of the system. ... Closely bound up with this scientific merit is the fact
> that Ricardo describes the economic contradiction between the
> classes. ... Carey ... therefore denounces him as the father of com-
> munism.

Thus, as we saw above, Ricardo's merit lies in his attempt at a
consistent analysis of the capitalistic system under the presupposition of
the determination (Joan Robinson would say 'definition') of value by
labour-time. Whether this definition of value is adequate to the object of
cognition is to be shown by the success of the analysis.

It was obvious that – however consistent Ricardo was in his thinking
in comparison with his antecedents – Ricardian economics is not carried
through in a completely consistent way. The determination of the value
of commodities through labour-time cannot be extended to those
fictitious 'commodities' that neoclassicists call factors of production.
The 'commodities' labour, land, capital are associated with prices,
namely the wage rate, rate of rent and rate of interest. No economic
system is consistently thought through either if one does not find the

same basis for the determination of value for 'real' and 'fictitious' commodities or if one is not able to prove why a unique law for real and fictitious commodities cannot hold, i.e. why commodities separate into real and fictitious.

Neoclassical theory subsumes real and fictitious commodities under the same law of supply and demand. It thereby follows the 'bad' tradition of Adam Smith. Sraffa shows the necessary inconsistency of this conception. (It may be remarked that the dissimilarity of the laws governing the exchange of commodities and the laws governing the exchange of the 'factors' is also proved by the fact that commodity markets precede capitalism whereas feudalism is marked by the characteristic that it does not have free markets for labour, land or capital, as was shown above all by Karl Polanyi, 1944.)

A different path was chosen by Ricardo. Whereas his notion of capital still has certain ambiguities, he takes a clear position vis-à-vis rent by proving through his specific law of rent why land has to be and can be exempted from the determination of value through labour, i.e. he shows why the exception 'land' does not disturb the value determination through labour of the produced commodities. Ricardo becomes significant for Marx because he attempts to extend the determination of value through labour to labour itself by explaining the price of labour, i.e. the wage, through the costs of reproduction. Here is the nucleus of Marxian analysis, but it still falters on conceptual grounds. 'Value of labour' is an irrational expression because, according to the definition, labour creates value. Thus it is not the *labour* that the worker sells to the capitalist, neither is it the work; it is not the activity but the right to use it: labour power. Value of labour power and wage for labour are by no means the same thing. If the product of a 12-hour work-day represents a value of 24 shillings and the necessary and surplus labour amount to 6 hours each, labour's wage has to be related to 12 hours and is equal to 12 shillings for the work-day, whereas the value of labour power is 6 hours or − expressed in money terms − 12 shillings as the equivalent of 6 hours work. This surprising paradox is resolved consistently only if the capitalists' command over labour is understood as productive consumption of the labour power in the production process, in complete analogy with the use of raw materials. Under this assumption the law of value holds for the production of labour power (even though labour power is not produced under capitalistic conditions but only under the conditions of simple commodity production in the household). It also holds for the consumption of labour power where labour power is the particular commodity that has the use value of producing value exceeding its production cost.

This is the admirable and logically irreproachable construction with which Marx frees himself from those unclear formulations through which Ricardo shows that he is caught in the Smithian tradition. But what next? Like Smith before him, Ricardo knows that the price of a commodity produced under capitalistic conditions generally deviates from the labour embodied. Again, Marx's achievement above all consists in conceptual clarification by carefully differentiating between price and value. He adds, to the known differentiation between market price and natural price, that between price of production and value. Ricardo, on the other hand, wavers between two contradictory needs. On the one hand he wished above all to progress to a quantitative determination of the price relation. For that he searched for auxiliary concepts such as the invariable measure of value, which was supposed to bring him to a theory of the development of the distribution of output in capitalistic production despite the heterogeneity of the commodities to be distributed. On the other hand, as we have seen, he was by no means inclined to give up his numerous attempts to reduce the determination of prices essentially to *labour*. He insisted on conceiving of the difficulties provoked by the existence of capital as *modifications* of the law of value.

Marx was faced with the task of specifying the 'modification' and chose a solution to the transformation problem that represented a critique of Ricardo. He did so by developing his theory with conceptual rigour, aiming at an explanation of the 'inverted conceptions' of 'vulgar economy'. With his transformation of values into prices, he intended to focus on the phenomenon of capitalistic production at two different levels, in much the same elegant way as the value of labour power was transformed into the wage of labour above. One level, that of values, was appropriate for generating an understanding of the inner dynamic of the system, while the other, the level of prices, was appropriate for grasping phenomena closer to the empirical world, which is the point of departure of 'vulgar' economic ideas.

With this transformation, the Ricardian system was closed. This is apparent in many little formal details such as the fact that the Marxian *average industry* is analogous to Ricardo's invariable measure of value, or the 'industry' that produces Sraffa's standard commodity. One result of Marx's reinterpretation of Ricardo is that profit has to be understood as redistributed surplus value, and thus as originating from the exploitation of labour power. This twist is based on Ricardo's thought but had not been grasped by him; it was a heavy blow to Ricardian political economy as an expression of bourgeois thought. Marx always describes Ricardo's mistakes (which he corrects) with friendly expressions such as 'insufficient analysis', 'failings', 'superficialities', etc. But in remedying the shortcomings he transforms the theory completely: the connection between Ricardo's economics and Ricardo's political standpoint was – or was supposed to be – demolished by Marx's critique.

As well as solving the transformation problem, the basis for an analysis of vulgar economic ideas was formulated. Prior to the transformation of values into prices, the system analysed in *Capital* appeared rational and coherent within certain limits. It is true that even at the beginning, in the discussion of simple commodity production, 'contradictions' are mentioned. Marx holds these responsible among other things for the genesis of money, and there results the vulgar economic 'paradox' when talking about the 'price' of labour. However, the contradictions – such as the fundamental one between concrete and abstract labour – are 'superseded' (aufgehoben) in the genesis of new categories like 'money', which, as gold, underlies a rational value determination, or 'surface' phenomena such as 'wage' are reduced to 'rational categories' like 'value of labour power'.

Thus it is only after the transformation that the realm of 'absurd forms' and 'mystifications' really begins (Besnier, 1970). Absurd forms (in German: 'verrückte Formen') are more literally translated as 'crazy' or 'displaced' forms. Above all 'interest', as the price of capital, is an 'absurd form'. This is mainly justified immanently – money is exchanged for money. However, it is also explained by the way in which interest is reduced to the rational categories of the value system. Interest, according to Marx, exists because capital – after the transformation from values into prices – is capable of yielding profit according to the general rate of profit. The 'absurdity', according to Marx, is threefold. First, following the logic of Marx's system, profit already represents a transformed (and thus mystifying its origin) form of surplus value. Second, the interest on a given capital by no means equals the profit on this capital according to the general rate of profit; on average it is a smaller sum, because profit is split into interest and the profit of the enterprise. There is no 'rational' law governing this split, in the sense that the rate of profit is derived from the rate of surplus value and organic composition. Third, it turns out that the rate of interest, though, as a category, derived from the division of the surplus value that springs from production, presents itself quantitatively as a monetary phenomenon. Its level is regulated by supply of and demand for money capital. Marx does not possess a general hypothesis to explain the supply of and demand for money capital as Keynes does in his theory of speculative demand for money. Rather, he gives numerous determinants of demand for and supply of money. The mystification engendered by the phenomenon of interest reaches its peak for Marx in the monetary crisis that occurs during an economic collapse, when the rate of interest paradoxically is high while the profit rate falls and everyone feels the need to realize their claims to wealth in cash. In the credit system, money is no longer simply gold, but in the crisis only gold is money. The contradictions hinted at even prior to the transformation from values into prices are no longer superseded by existing 'rational' categories. The inherently rational core of capitalism, crystallized for Marx in the law of value, disappears behind the smoke and fire of the exploding crisis.

Marx is completely misunderstood, however, if one believes that in his system an absolutely rational core is to be neatly distinguished from the description of the 'mystification'. The contradictions are present in his system from the very beginning. Indeed, the point of his exposition lies precisely in the fact that the 'rational' value system itself generates the crisis. Without wasting any time on the question of which are the original contradictions, we see that the derivation hinges upon the transformation where the mystified forms break through and the necessity of crisis is derived from the allegedly demonstrable tendency of the rate of profit to fall. The rationally acting law of value dissolves in a two-fold manner – on the one hand by periodically failing in a crisis in its function as a

regulator of capitalistic production; on the other, because its foundation
– competitive capitalism – undermines itself because of the concentration and centralization accelerated by the crises.

We have pointed to four aspects of the transformation: the foundation
of prices on values and, thereby, a theory of the capitalist economy based
on a supposedly operational law; the theory of exploitation as a
paradoxical result of 'thinking through' Ricardo's theory; the mystification of the law of value with the genesis of 'vulgar' economic forms;
and, finally, the self-dissolution of the system in its contradictions, which
again is two-fold: periodical (crisis) and secular (socialization through
concentration and centralization, i.e. supercession of the law of value
and of competition). Marx is thus to be regarded not only as a
theoretician of a capitalist system that in itself remains unchanged but
also as a theoretician of its inner modifications and as a critic of its
theoretical reflexions. The problem of the opposition between Marx and
Sraffa changes accordingly: the methodological aspect becomes para-
mount. The inner coherence of the Marxian exposition, which deals with
so many different problems like the positive theory of an object of
cognition, the critique of its forms of appearance and its inner modifications within a 'system', apparently is closely connected with the
dialectical method and exhibits a peculiar 'aesthetic' fascination. This
'dialectic', as is well known, has its traps – it introduces a dilemma into
the discussion about Marx because no accepted criterion exists to judge
when a contradiction in *Capital* represents an adequate reflection of the
contradictory object of cognition and when a contradiction represents a
logical error. This becomes particularly clear in some astonishing
interjections from Marx when he is dealing with the transformation
problem – these seem to be motivated partly by discomfort with the
deficiency of the analytical method, partly by pleasure at the manifest
ineptitudes of capitalism.

Here Sraffa intervenes for his part and calls 'stop'! He offers a scheme
of convincing logical coherence, which confirms that the transformation
is not solvable in the way outlined by Marx. The necessity of deriving
prices from values disappears through the reduction of both to a
common third element. Since the contradictions that provide the particular dynamic of the Marxian system are thereby extinguished, one is
forced to give up asking whether this or that element of the Marxian
theory – for example, the explanation of exploitation or the theory of the
forms of value – is compatible with the Sraffian results. A similar fate
befalls the Marxian method of dialectics and critique. Ricardo has been
dead for a long time, so the critique of his system is not urgent. Of more
importance today is the critique of the neoclassicists. For that, Sraffa's
reductio ad absurdum is more effective than a Marxian attempt to set a
neo-Marxian 'total system' against the neoclassicals who, as modern
positivists, no longer believe in the possibility of a 'total', i.e. comprehensive, theory. Looking at it this way, we see that Sraffa offers an
approach that allows modern economics and modern economists to carry
through an essential part of the critical programme that Marx sketched
out for the second half of the nineteenth century. Up to now, mainly

Joan Robinson has attempted to link Sraffa's and Keynes's achievements and to develop them as continuations of the Marxian theory. To the extent that Sraffa's theory is at all suitable for 'positive' economics (which, given its subtitle, is not clear from the outset), the major task is to integrate Sraffa's price theory into a general theory of capitalist development. A more limited task is the search for a theory of income distribution that would be compatible with the system and that would allow the determination of the remaining 'free' variable – the rate of profit.

Notes

1 To make Sraffa's approach commensurate with Marx's, the wage should actually be treated as advanced. Formally this does not cause any particular difficulties (see Roncaglia, 1975, p. 87). On the other hand, Sraffa's decision to take the rate of profit as a datum has further implications. The real wage becomes a dependent variable, which contradicts the notion of a given value of labour power in Marx.
2 For extensive references see Cogoy (1974), Roncaglia (1975).
3 Through a redefinition of the 'necessary labour-time' (applicable above all for modern capitalism) this can be reached even though the rate of profit measured in prices is not equal to the rate of profit measured in value terms (Schefold, 1973; Pennavaja, 1974).
4 Despite the transformation problem, it does not follow from the fact that Sraffa's theory (such as we seek to demonstrate) cannot be integrated organically into Marx's theory that the two are in principle incompatible. The situation is different from the case of neoclassical theory where an inconsistency in the theory was proved at a crucial point, and this inconsistency was not rectified without giving up the essential part of the whole theory. *Here* two levels of a theory (value and price), which for Marx are based upon each other, are treated as equals and are reduced to a common third level, whereby the originally basic level loses its supporting function. The statement that value theory thereby becomes altogether worthless or wrong can be neither proved nor contradicted in this way.
5 Price level and wage level do of course interact with each other and are influenced by other factors as well: but the modern result can be reached fastest by thinking of the price level as given by the wage level (expressed in terms of a sum of paper money) and viewing other influences as modifications of this point of departure.

Essay 4a Sraffa and Marx: Some Reflections on the Homogeneity of Labour

The next essay will be dedicated to outlining some contributions to political economy that may be combined with the Sraffian framework to give an idea of the modern form of classical theory. Some concepts are derived from Marxian ones, and close followers of Marx will frown upon such an attempt to treat *Das Kapital* as a quarry from which stones for a new building are taken, although this is what Marx did to his predecessors. They might argue that Marx was the first and only great theorist to give classical theory a logical, deductive form, which contrasts with the approaches of Smith and Ricardo whose main works (especially those of Ricardo) resemble more collections of miscellaneous essays than systematic treatises with an axiomatic basis. Only Marx seems to have shown that a complete, deductive system may be erected on the Ricardian foundation.

However, the Marxian system contains defects; the best known concerns the transformation problem. As we have seen, this is not only a question of a transformation of 'forms', the substance of which is 'value'. It is not possible to represent profits (to be divided into interest, entrepreneurial profit, etc.) with quantitative rigour as redistributed surplus value. The suspicion arises that the definition of the 'substance' itself as 'abstract labour' is questionable.

The problem of the definition of labour as a measurable quantity has already been mentioned in section II.20b. As is well known, Marx by no means invented the labour theory of value. As a tool, it had been used before him to explain the comparability of heterogeneous objects or commodities. The homogeneity of goods belonging to the same class of commodities may be defined through social conventions on the basis of objective properties. These properties define a class of commodities unambiguously (a metal: gold; a fruit: an apple). These heterogeneous objects are said to be equal as products of labour. Marx recognizes that concrete labour is different in the production of each industry (a metal worker, a peasant), but the commodities are equal to products of 'abstract labour'. But why should it be easier to understand that there is an underlying homogeneity of metal working and farming as 'abstract labour' than to understand the homogeneity of gold and apples as 'values'? What has been gained by having recourse to labour?

An equality between different types of concrete labour may be established through social norms. In a command economy, either one hour of forging or two hours of plucking may be required of certain workers. In a market economy, one ounce of iron may be exchanged for two sacks of apples by their respective producers. In a capitalist economy, the wage rate of the metal worker may be twice that of the farm labourer. In each case the existence of the norm needs to be explained because it is the norm that fixes the equivalence of the type of labour of Mr A and of type of labour of Mr B and therefore between types of labour A and B. On the surface, the equivalent to be given for labour (some entitlement, a commodity, a wage) seems to be the *explanans* that establishes the equality of A and B rather than the other way around, the *explanandum*. Why are A and B equal *a priori*?

When Marx, discussing capitalism, chose to take the homogeneity of abstract labour as the *explanans*, and the homogeneity of commodities as values as the *explanandum*, he followed the classical tradition. In Figure III.4a.1, the direction of the arrows indicates the Marxian logic of explaining value.

Marx gave a critical twist to the classical assumption of homogeneous labour with his theory of alienation, in which he followed a philosophical

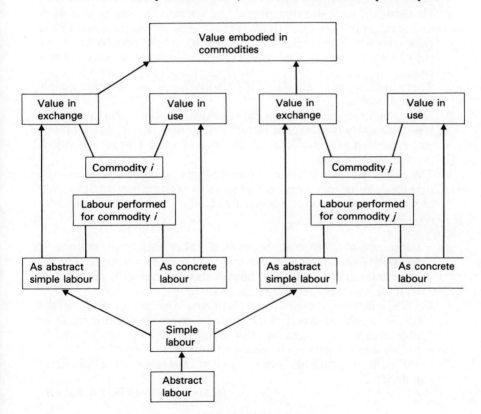

Figure III.4a.1

tradition going back to Hegel (who in turn had – like Marx – found one source of inspiration for his interpretation of the work process in Adam Smith). What Marx did not take from his classical predecessors, but took from more obscure sources, was the attempt to justify the homogeneity of abstract labour physiologically, having introduced it as a philosophical postulate (or, if one prefers, as an axiom).

The measure of abstract labour in Marx is not direct. The expenditure of equal amounts of abstract labour in different occupations in the same period defines, after abstracting from individual abilities and industriousness, 'average', 'simple' labour, if it is 'unskilled' (the explanation of wage differentials due to skills by the cost of production of skills may here be taken for granted). A given degree of 'intensity' of labour then defines normal effort. The intensity of labour rises with the rhythm of work. An increase in the intensity of work means an increase in productivity obtained without changing the methods of operation. Heterogeneous kinds of labour could for Marx therefore not only be aggregated but actually treated as equal (from the abstract point of view) and the effort expended could be measured – essentially because of five conditions:

1 He thought that it was meaningful and operative to distinguish work as instrumental human activity from other states of the human life (sleep, leisure, contemplation, interaction). The generalization from the content of each type of work is abstract labour performed in real time.

2 There are historical standards for normal work and they are simply taken as given.

3 In particular, there are historical standards for the intensity of work where intensity is measured in terms of muscle power, brain power, etc. expended. A physiological measure of the intensity of work is therefore postulated.

4 The capacity of work (labour power) is produced and consumed; the reproduction of labour power involves the restoration of the ability to work according to the normal standard of intensity. This is where physiology comes in:

> Labour-power, however, becomes a reality only by its exercise; it sets itself in action only by working. But thereby a *definite quantity* [emphasis added – BS] of human muscle, nerve, brain, etc., is wasted, and these require to be restored.
>
> This increased expenditure demands a larger income. If the owner of labour-power works today, tomorrow he must again be able to repeat the same process in the same conditions as regards health and strength. His means of subsistence must therefore be sufficient to maintain him in his normal state as a labouring individual.
>
> (Marx, [1867] 1954, pp. 167–8).

5 Greater intensity of work means increased expenditure of labour

power, hence the creation of more value in a given amount of time; this has to be compensated by a higher wage per unit of time. A shorter working day of greater intensity may produce more value:

> The first effect of shortening the working-day results from the self-evident law that the efficiency of labour-power is in an inverse ratio to the duration of its expenditure. Hence, within certain limits what is lost by shortening the duration is gained by the increasing tension of labour-power.
>
> (Marx, [1867] 1954, p. 387)

A longer working day, on the other hand, requires a higher wage:

> The value of a day's labour-power is, as will be remembered, estimated from its normal average duration, or from the normal duration of life among the labourers, and from corresponding normal transformations of organised bodily matter into motion, in conformity with the nature of man. Up to a certain point, the increased wear and tear of labour-power, inseparable from a lengthened working-day, may be compensated by higher wages.
>
> (ibid., p. 493).

> The amount of labour which a man had undergone in the course of 24 hours might be approximately arrived at by an examination of the chemical changes which had taken place in his body, changed forms in matter indicating the anterior exercise of dynamic force.
>
> (Grove, 'On the Correlation of Physical Forces', a physicist quoted by Marx in a footnote to the above quotation).

It follows that, for an unchanged working day, greater intensity has also to be compensated for by higher wages.

There is as much nineteenth-century prejudice as truth in each of these statements. It is true that there are conventional estimates regarding the relative intensity of different kinds of work, which are formed and transformed in social evolution, but it is wrong and contrary to the results of modern scientific research to assume a direct relationship between such social evaluations and physiological measurements of effort.

Since it is therefore not possible to explain the homogeneity of labour by providing an exact scientific basis for the conventions of intensity, one might fall back on the Marxian philosophy of work. But here, too, our views have changed. In the twentieth century we have learned a great deal about the importance of forms of human interaction that are not directly related to work: the social bonds in primitive society are primarily cultural and not defined through the organization of work (of which very little is needed — see Sahlins 1972) and the depths fathomed by psychoanalysis reveal an aspect of human existence that cannot be derived from man as a planner and toolmaker, i.e. as an intellectual or manual worker.

For Engels, however, the first humans had something to say to each other only because of the invention of tools, and for Marx the highest form of human activity was free and artistic work. He objected not to the pre-eminence of the role of work in modern society, but to the fact that work appeared under capitalist production only in alienated forms. Marx's method of exposition consisted in accepting the prejudice about the existence of alienated work as a matter of course in order to develop this assumption critically. The prejudice was that normal work was not a problematic concept; the normal worker had, after all, been 'produced' by historical circumstances. Hence it seemed plausible to readers in the middle of the nineteenth century that two different concrete activities like window-cleaning and shovelling could be compared directly from an abstract point of view (by measuring the length of labour-time), whereas the possibility of comparing two use values (jacket and table) in the process of exchange was an enigma and had to be explained. But I surmise that the average hunter and gatherer (a savage who may well be as intelligent as the average European) would not see the point of the exercise since work and the measure of work in terms of time would mean very little to him.

It follows that not only the proletariat, which sells homogeneous labour power and expends average labour at average intensity, but also abstract labour itself is a historical category. It transcends capitalism in its generality, yet it is capable of application within a narrow institutional framework. In Marx's own words:

> This example of labour shows strikingly how even the most abstract categories, despite their applicability − precisely because of their abstraction − to all epochs, are just as much the product of historical circumstances in the determination of this abstraction itself, and how they possess their full validity only for and within those circumstances.
> (Marx, [1857−8] 1974, Introduction, Section 3, my translation)

The labour theory of value therefore rests ultimately on an institutional basis. This concerns the concept not only of average labour, but of abstract labour itself. It is fairly obvious, on the other hand, that average labour, average intensity of work and the homogeneity of the proletariat result from definite historical processes, involving both free competition and coercion, and that the explanatory power of the labour theory of value would wither away if the majority of unskilled workers did not actually conform to this average with a − *sit venia verbo* − small standard deviation. The applicability of the labour theory of value in concrete circumstances presupposes that most unskilled workers are close to the average.

Marx was not simply an institutionalist, however. When he claimed to have been the first to develop the opposition between abstract and concrete labour *critically*, he meant that he had been the first to explain the contrast between the rich individuality of human creation and the cold rationality of capitalist accumulation by reducing it to the opposition between the individuality of concrete labour and the tendency to equalize all creation as abstract labour. The individuality of workers and the content of work was thought, under capitalism, to be irrelevant to accumulation in so far as it is governed by the law of value. Marx developed this point by showing its consequences for the transformation of the work process, the alienation of the worker, etc.

On the other hand, there was a rational kernel to the 'law of value'. Marx assumed that labour could be and was measured, and that this measure could become the basis of a rational system of planning. Forgetting both about the institutionalist basis and his critical purpose, he then spoke – as we have seen – of the expenditure of labour power as of the expenditure of human brain power and muscle power, and in the section on the intensification of work still more quotes can be found suggesting that he believed that the intensity of work could one day be measured physiologically and that the physiological measurement of intensity was not merely a 'façon de parler' for him.

However, whereas gold is indifferent to the measuring of its fineness, a worker is not indifferent to the evaluation of his productivity, particularly if the result of the measure will later serve as a norm. The vagaries of planning under socialism could, in a Marxist spirit, in part be explained as inevitable failures to predict and dictate human performance in the direction and execution of work processes, while the extreme ideology of central planning relates to a different kind of Marxism: that which forgets that abstract labour is a critical (and historical) category and treats the workforce as one disposable mass that is to serve one goal.

The cruelty of Stalinist primitive accumulation was in important respects similar to that in the West, among other things because an urban proletariat had to be created by force in both cases and vast numbers of people were made to migrate to the centres of development. Subsequent events have shown in either case that the working class did not conform to the unnatural requirement of homogeneity. Taylorism used differences in ability to increase productivity by introducing sophisticated techniques for paying wages according to performance. Workers were selected not only according to acquired skills, but also according to natural talents or talents acquired in the process of early socialization. As a result there were growing wage differentials, even among unskilled workers, and segmentation of the working class. In the planned economies, too, an increasing discrimination between different types of workers and their rewards became necessary.

Of course, the assumption of homogeneous labour related to a view of work as a mere instrument of accumulation is not confined to Marxism. Already the *idée fixe* of the late mercantilist and earlier classical economists had been to have a mass of homogeneous unskilled labourers at the disposition of capital. The slow traditional medieval artisans tied to the most diverse professions and labourers tied to the soil by manifold forces and customs were to be replaced by a mobile labour force of diligent unskilled workers who could as well be placed in a manufacturing industry as on a large agricultural estate. Petty's (1964) 'political arithmetic' involved an attempt to solve the 'calamity of Ireland' by transferring two-thirds of its population to England and Scotland as an addition to the indigenous labour force, and by abandoning the remainder of the population of Ireland to the raising of cattle. As is well known, Adam Smith gave reasons for differentiating wage rates, but his measure of value – labour commanded – remains a conceptual expression of something similar to what Petty wanted. The Malthusian and Ricardian subsistence theory of wages complemented the postulate of a disposable labour force by a reassuring law governing the reproduction of the working class: it was basically to regenerate itself according to the needs of the accumulation of capital, provided natural wages were paid. Ricardo thought that the Poor Laws were an economic threat to discipline.

Marx had a concept of what I should like to call 'strong homogeneity' of labour in that different amounts of simple or average labour could be added up as abstract labour, even if they corresponded to different kinds of concrete work. We have now seen that this raises more problems than it solves. Either we say that the measure of abstract labour is simply the amount of time spent by a worker working, in which case it does not explain value independently of evaluations of concrete labour because the works performed in different occupations can be equated only by adopting arbitrary norms corresponding to what the market does, to prejudice or to decree – 30 sacks loaded per hour equal 10 windows cleaned per hour. Or the expenditure of labour power has, as Marx stresses later, a two-dimensional measure – labour-time (extensive) and intensity – so that abstract labour is equal to the physiological effort. But this cannot be measured.

The classical notion of homogeneity in Smith and Ricardo is less pronounced; we might call it 'weak homogeneity'. They admitted the existence of wage differentials, which were in part explained by factors such as skill and which were not all thoroughly discussed. To accept market evaluations of different types of labour as determinants of value meant, in Marxian terms, that not just abstract labour-time, but also social evaluations of concrete labour entered the determination of value. The justification was, at the analytical level, that wage rates tended to move in parallel, in the opposite direction to that of the rate of profit.

On the other hand, a certain new social and economic homogeneity of the working class did indeed obtain during the long transition from feudalism to capitalism which called for a mobile labour force. The instrumental character of capitalist civilization led to the association of slow work with idleness, when in fact it may be done in a contemplative spirit and may in this sense be more meaningful than the efficient execution of a monotonous task. But such factors did not count when the work process began to be planned so as to allow the execution of a given task in a minimum amount of time in profit-making enterprises. This was the essence of the capitalistic spirit, which penetrated the industrializing nations at the time of the classicists. The relentless drive towards efficiency (Taylorism in particular) had not yet started then, but regular, coordinated, disciplined work had to be enforced from the beginning.

The concept of strong homogeneity, which Marx emphasized, seems to derive from this line of thought. In Marx's day, the real working class was more fragmented than his theoretical treatment would suggest and labour management has since tended to create new segmentations of the working class on the basis of new differentiations of natural or acquired talents at least as often as it has had to wipe such differences out.

If a physiological measurement of the expenditure of labour seems impossible to us today and if the 'historical and moral' elements in the determination of the conditions of reproduction of labour power determine everything and 'subsistence' determines nothing, the Marxian concept of strong homogeneity must be dropped; labour cannot be treated as a physical means of production. The underlying concept of intensity is, like cardinal utility, not measurable in an economically meaningful way, and there is some similarity between ideological attempts to show that they are.

Of course, not just labour is less predictable than the abstract conceptions of planning would have it, but so is the weather, organic nature and even materials: what are correct standards in the construction of nuclear power plants, or what should 'normal' standards be?

However, there is a reason for questioning the concept of homogeneous labour power, performing with given intensity, which is more fundamental than the uncertainty about the quality of material inputs. In order to understand it, it is necessary to compare the 'commodity' labour power with ordinary commodities such as steel, bread and apples. None of these is perfectly homogeneous; they are classed according to criteria that are in part under the producer's near-perfect control (e.g. the composition of bread) and reflect in part random natural influences (e.g. the weather in the case of apples). Yet, there is a large degree of substitutability between different classes as regards consumption, and the processes of production are similar for different classes of the same commodity and lead to similar costs of production.

The same might be said of labour power, because it is produced in one process of production (in the average working-class family) and because there is substitutability between unskilled workers in different jobs, in the same way as the same ton of steel can be used to build a bridge or to build a car.

But only the worker, not the steel, can alter his use value while the commodity is being productively consumed. It is true that the worker will have sold his labour power in accordance with a contract that regulates the intensity of the concrete work that is expected of him. We may even suppose here that the intensity of his activity as concrete work is measurable, e.g. in terms of a number of sacks of given weight to be loaded on a lorry, and that the worker is ready to fulfil the contract. But his readiness is not a sufficient basis to judge whether the intensity of his work is equal to that of other workers doing other jobs. Since no general measure of productivity exists across professions independently of prices, one might speak of equal intensity of work in all industries if there is free competition in the labour market for unskilled workers, but this would represent at best a definition of equal intensity (if free competition can be defined independently of intensity, e.g. by the absence of trade unions for specific professions) and a tautology otherwise; it is not the basis for a direct verification of whether intensities are uniform. It is indeed likely that the reward for equal hours of unskilled labour will be the same in different concrete applications because of competition, but it will not be possible to decide scientifically whether existing wage differentials (even if they are equal to unity, i.e. even if there are no differentials) express or hide differences of intensity. A precise and meaningful definition of intensity is possible only within professions, not across professions. As a short reflection shows, even that is possible only in those professions that are suitable for the payment of piece wages.

Since there is no physiological measurement of effort and since the result of the expenditure of effort cannot be measured by an objective standard across professions prior to the determination of prices (a measure based, for example, on human energy expended might theoretically be possible, but it would not be economically applicable), we seem to be thrown back on subjective evaluations of the work processes. This would appear to justify the neoclassical view of the matter, but if workers are different as individuals, but all have to accept the same wage rate and the same labour-time, they cannot all equate the marginal disutility of their work with the real wage. In fact, the conventions that determine the standards for various kinds of unskilled labour and that lead to the determination of wage differentials for, say, window cleaners and shovellers are inseparable from their institutional contexts. If we ask on the other hand why the wage differentials for different kinds of unskilled labour are in practice not large and why they do not tend to deviate much over time, we must admit that there is, after all, some vague content left in the Marxian notion of average labour of given intensity: competition will ensure that the effort demanded from shovellers will not be very much different than that demanded from window cleaners; as long as the wage differential is small, there are no barriers to entry and apprenticeship is negligible.

Thus, a norm is imposed on each type of unskilled work, defining its equivalence with other types. The measure may be one-dimensional (number of windows cleaned, number of pins pointed). If it is, the specification of these measures can be made independently of the categories of the market (i.e. value, price and money), but their fixation can never be thought of as deriving purely from objective technological or physiological necessity, however tiresome a job may be said to be, nor is it purely subjective. If it is then somehow agreed that the loading of 40 sacks is equivalent to the cleaning of 10 windows, and that it takes one hour to clean 5 windows or to load 10 sacks, it follows that one hour of window-cleaning counts twice as much as one hour of sack-loading, independently of prices – and this is how the equivalence between different types of work (weak homogeneity) can be defined prior to the operation of the market. Such ratios may also be set as norms by planners.

I apologize for having ultimately have to come up with so trivial a conclusion. The discussion was necessary, however, as long as there are on the one hand people who maintain that the problem of the determination of relative wages is analogous to that of capital goods and there are on the other hand those who accept the dogmatic view of the homogeneity of the working class without reflecting on the complexity of the historical forces from which wage differentials emerge. To admit the fundamental heterogeneity of work is, of course, only a necessary, not a sufficient condition for the improvement of the institutions governing the work process.

All this means that – quite apart from other difficulties with the Marxian form of the labour theory of value – it is better to abandon the concept of homogeneous labour power by introducing wage labour as an activity that gives entitlement to a share in the surplus in Sraffa's sense, which is rewarded according to given differentials. The abstractions involved in talking about the uniformity of (unskilled) labour are less well founded than those involved in assuming the uniformity of different types of commodities – although there is a great deal of product differentiation in the case of cars, there is little in the case of gold. This justifies Sraffa in starting from a closed system for the reproduction of commodities by means of commodities (where commodities are homogeneous), and introducing labour only later (where wage rates are used for aggregation). This systematic idea will be taken up after the essay on political economy.

Essay 5   Distribution, Prices and Competition

The most striking immediate result of PCMC undoubtedly is this: if only we know the profit rate, the complex of all prices is known on the basis of the given methods of production; and nothing is known about it if we do not know the rate of profit (or the wage rate or some other determinant of income distribution). The final proof that the system cannot be closed by equations for supply of and demand for 'capital', not even through Walrasian equilibrium conditions can only result from further complicated arguments. (As regards the Walrasian case, the argument has not yet been presented in a definitive form.) One might ask how the system can be closed through other forces. Assuming that the answer 'supply and demand' is unacceptable, the answer evidently has to point in the direction of 'power', 'conflict', 'history'. But how are these mediated?

Sraffa's only allusion in this respect (PCMC, sec. 44),[1] – that the rate of profit is influenced particularly by the money rate of interest – at first sight seems confusing. According to Marxian and Keynesian theory, high interest rates in an unregulated capitalist system indicate the beginning of falling profits and a recession, just as low interest rates may coincide with high profits during an evenly developing boom. Marx furthermore rejected any notion of a long-term average rate of interest as vague and non-operational for a closed theory.[2] Keynes is not fundamentally opposed to this when he thinks of the rate of interest in the long term as determined merely by conventions that in turn are subject to influence by the central bank ([1936] 1967, p. 204). Sraffa's mysterious phrase seems to make most sense if one assumes that it refers to a nearly stationary capitalist economy in which the banking system institutionally determines the interest rate and in which enterprises are heavily indebted to, or else closely interwoven with, the banking system so that their prices have to cover their interest debt. Real wages rise until the profits of enterprise are eliminated by entrepreneurs competing with each other such that prices are reduced to the costs of production including the interest on capital. Competition among capitalists thus explains not the level of profits but only the degree of uniformity of the rates of profit; furthermore it means that the profit rates do not exceed the rate of interest to any great extent. As long as demand for investment is low (as presupposed here), prices will not, because of demand effects, lie above these costs (including interest). The approach seems compatible with

Keynesian ideas,[3] if Keynes' notion of marginal efficiency of capital is replaced by that of the rate of profit. Garegnani (1964/65, p. 73) rightly adds that such a point of departure does not at all presuppose an almighty central bank, for banks do not operate in a vacuum but interact with other institutions, particularly with labour unions. They have to mediate between the rentier's interest in high interest rates and stable money value, the unions' interests in high wages and a low profit rate, and the entrepreneurs' interests in high profits.

But over and above the interest payable to the bank, the profits of enterprises normally contain an element that, as Marx points out, does not stand in any kind of fixed relation to the interest rate.[4] It is obvious that a boom can produce high profits of enterprise, at least in the short term. Moreover, we know that for long periods the main source of investment was enterprise profits and not money advanced by the bank. The 'central bank theory' of the rate of profit, therefore, at best describes a partial truth pertaining to periods with slow accumulation and a strong financial sector.

A different but (it seems to me) complementary theory is represented by Joan Robinson, Kaldor, Pasinetti and others.[5] This relates to a capitalist economy with buoyant accumulation in which firms finance themselves predominantly from retained profits. Investment is the independent variable. In the short run, profits rise if investment rises because production capacities are better utilized (with constant marginal costs, average costs fall) and/or because money prices rise faster than nominal wages as a result of high demand. Thus an increase in the share of investment causes an increase in the share of profit in the national income, which allows the savings necessary for investment to be generated. In this formulation, the thesis of the determination of the share of profit by the share of investment is still dependent on specific assumptions about capacity utilization of enterprises, price policy, etc.

A more abstract and general formulation can be reached by a modification of the Keynesian equations of the circular flow of income and expenditure. If the entrepreneurs retain all profits and if, on average, the workers do not save, net investment is equal to net profits in accounting terms where, according to the theory of effective demand, the level of investment, through saving behaviour, causally determines the level of profits, and not *vice versa*. Thus the rate of profit equals the rate of growth g. If the capitalists consume a proportion $1 - s_c$ of their profits P, investment can be expressed as:

$$I = s_c \cdot P$$

or, if we divide by the price of total capital K, the profit rate r becomes

$$r = P/K = I/(s_c \cdot K) = g/s_c.$$

The rate of growth of capital g, together with the capitalists' propensity to save, determine the rate of profit (Robinson, 1965b).

This model can be completed, without losing its character, by integrating the savings rate of the workers and the state. At a high level of abstraction it represents an essential contribution to the understanding of the accumulation process with modest inflation, as observed in the first two post-war decades in the western industrialized countries. However, the idea that the rate of profit is determined by the rate of growth is only legitimate if accumulation takes place evenly. Otherwise, changing rates of accumulation will cause fluctuations in the rate of profit, which in turn disturb the accumulation process.

The above formula, rather than presenting a complete theory of income distribution, should be understood (like the 'central bank theory') as a first approach or conceptual orientation. The rate of growth itself requires an explanation. The share of profits in national income (the 'rate of surplus value') codetermines it. Further, the nature of technical progress is significant. When we are dealing with time periods long enough that the influence of technical progress changes not only the production plants of single firms but customary techniques in whole industries, then the methods of production in Sraffa's sense can no longer be assumed to be 'given'. The attempt to create such a theory of accumulation along classical lines of thought was developed furthest by Joan Robinson.

This, however, is not the place to discuss in detail the theory of accumulation. Sraffa skilfully excludes questions of political economy by limiting himself to the pure logic of prices. One cannot expect the theory of accumulation to exhibit as much coherence and tightness as the price theory in PCMC. We will therefore carefully move along the boundary drawn by Sraffa and develop a few ideas about the conditions under which competition brings about a uniform rate of profit.

All entrepreneurial activity presupposes a close connection between prices and costs of production. No rational investment calculation is possible unless the prices of investment goods, both those bought by the entrepreneur himself as well as those bought by his competitors, stand in a 'normal' relation to the costs of production. The buyer, being dependent on tight calculations, is forced to run incessantly from one seller to the other in order to identify the most advantageous buy – unless he can hope that the sellers closest to him in the market in which he finds himself calculate prices on a 'normal' basis and earn no more than 'normal' profits. This idea of normal prices is also the basis of Marshall's description of the accumulation process. At this level of abstraction, they are nothing other than 'natural' prices or prices of production that result from competition. The classical theories of prices of production attempt to show how, as an outcome of competition, subjective ideas of normal prices can be reduced to the average rate of profit.

However, in single sectors as well as in the economy as a whole there may be disturbances of the accumulation process in which no unique rate of profit is imaginable, so that the idea of 'normality' breaks down. Even with steady accumulation, costs of production in oligopolistic industries fall faster relative to money prices than in others owing to special technical progress, so that profit rates are never uniform. A truly uniform rate of profit is well approximated through competition with some certainty only if the real wage is fixed and the technique of production is given, because changes of technology as well as of the real wage disturb normality. Finally, there are endogenous short-run disturbances.[6]

In this light Sraffa's theory of prices of production appears pre-Marxian and pre-Keynesian. He does not take into account either the possibility of a crisis or the effect of an extraordinary boom on the divergence of rates of profit. However, to imply that Sraffa meant to present capitalist development as perfectly tranquil would be naive.[7] Behind Sraffa's theory of prices of production must be hidden some idea other than that of a completely even process of accumulation as the normal case.

Let us recall that in his essay of 1926 Sraffa had shifted from a critique of Marshall's notion of equilibrium to a critique of the neoclassical notion of competition. For the neoclassicists, the criterion of competition is fulfilled if prices are given for buyers and sellers, which is assumed as soon as the number of buyers and sellers is large. Sraffa in contrast points out that, even in a market with many buyers and sellers, the unity of the market is not guaranteed. Each enterprise has a number of regular customers. In between there are customers switching back and forth between several enterprises. Thus enterprises are monopolies for the group of regular customers though forced to pay heed to the other enterprises because of the 'switching' customers. The market is not perfect. The modern theory of competition has emphasized the mechanisms of product differentiation, etc., in which the imperfection of such markets expresses itself. On the other hand, the theory of competition has overcome the idea that, if concentration decreases the number of competitors, a monopolistic situation prevails by necessity. The fear of potential rivals exerts competitive pressure on the seller even if there are but few competitors. The modern theory of competition[8] thus at times consciously, at other times unconsciously, deviates from the neoclassical notion of competition and returns to the classical notion.

In classical terms, competition was measured not according to whether single enterprises had an influence on prices but whether a specific market was open for the entry of new enterprises so that the rate of profit approached a general average. The tendency toward a uniform rate of profit in this case is identical with the assumption of competition in the classical sense.

As mentioned above, there are obviously sectors that take advantage of barriers to entry and thus regularly make profits above or below average as a consequence of specific growth, specific productivity development and specific locations, so that a permanent profit rate differential exists. However, since barriers to entry are never insurmountable, it is legitimate to abstract from this for many considerations.

Furthermore, capacity utilization changes in the short period so that the rates of profit fluctuate or cannot even be calculated in a meaningful way. Therefore the notion of prices of production is most relevant in the context of even conditions of accumulation for a long period in which an average capacity utilization can be identified. Then the notion of price of production may be realized in the following way. From the very beginning entrepreneurs include considerable overcapacities in their construction plans in order to be able to meet demand in the case of a real boom, which occurs rather rarely and is hard to predict. Prices are calculated so that, for a capacity utilization considered normal over a long-period average, the mark-up on the variable costs is just sufficient to cover the fixed costs and, in particular, depreciation as well as a normal net profit. Competition means that this normal profit corresponds approximately to the uniform general rate of profit. The rate of profit formed in this manner is an accounting magnitude (Roncaglia, 1975) that is not easy to compute, given the fact that the prices of production themselves are based on averages taken out of accounting magnitudes. Because of the increase in joint production in modern industrial production (which will be discussed below), the calculation of costs of production out of accounting magnitudes confronts increasing difficulties, and these add to the obstacles to the formation of a general rate of profit mentioned above. However, the actual prices charged correspond to prices of production to the extent that the latter are known, and varying market conditions are reflected not so much in varying market prices but rather in variations in capacity utilization.

This interpretation of prices of production may seem strange, for it leads to the impression that the profit has arisen from the entrepreneurs' arbitrary mark-up over variable costs. Taking a closer look, however, it turns out that the long-term average profit depends on the long-run capacity utilization of the enterprise, i.e. the level of production, and therefore, for all enterprises taken together, on the surplus, given the real wage. Taking average demand, i.e. the quantities to be produced (as in PCMC), as given, the rate of profit is objectively determined for a given wage rate despite the seemingly arbitrary mark-up. In accordance with the fact that the modern business cycle has become shorter and milder than before and that competition today is expressed less in price policy than in other marketing activities, the establishment of an average rate of profit occurs rather through the formation of averages for commodity inputs and outputs than by price fluctuations. Prices today are fairly stable relative to money wages and can therefore in principle stay close to the 'accounting prices of production'.[9]

It is thus perfectly possible, with some caution, to go beyond the esoteric task of theoretical critique and instead to integrate the Sraffian theory of prices of production into modern economics.

For this, however, a number of traditional ideas have to be abandoned. For those educated in the modern neoclassical tradition the main difficulty, despite Keynes' analogous procedure in macroeconomics, certainly lies in switching to Sraffa's method of taking the quantities demanded and the methods of production used as given, so that the problem of their determination is referred to a further analysis which Sraffa does not even sketch out. In my opinion this approach is extremely fruitful and it is the only one that makes it possible to talk about the accumulation process as a process of development. Applied economists argue more often than they are aware along the lines of classical economics.[10]

Of the two problems mentioned above – that of the determination of the rate of profit and that of the given technique – the latter seems more familiar at first sight, because a new production technique is obviously introduced into a system only if the other methods of production already exist. The new, lower-cost method yields a surplus profit to those enterprises that first introduced it. As soon as the majority of enterprises have switched to the new method, the price of production will decrease and the surplus profit will disappear. The enterprises lagging behind may keep the old technique for a while as long as the old machines yield a quasi-rent in the sense of Sraffa (PCMC, sec. 91; above, sec. II.17).

Up to here things look easy. It will not in practice always be as easy to find the price-determining technique (as Marx would say, the socially necessary technique) because the role of the price leader often falls into the hands of the largest enterprise independently of its relative technical advantage.

However, the more competition decreases and state intervention increases, the less can the technique naively be assumed to be given on the one hand by 'private inventors' and on the other by competition. This affects the price theory above all (but not only) if phenomena like joint production or rent are concerned.[11] To give a few examples. The difficulties begin with the social determination of the particular quality of a product, say the body of a car, that is uniquely determined neither by the taste of the public nor by technical conditions, though it affects the costs of production. Or if we take an enterprise's expenditures for purposes of representation: to what extent are they to be considered as costs of production and what determines them in the first place? A third example, again of a different nature, is presented by the 'rent of location' in the cities. The city administration defines the construction areas and thereby the most profitable technique; the height limits of construction thus depend upon a political decision, which is partly oriented to economic needs for which, however, there are no unambiguous economic criteria. The increase in joint production as a consequence of increasing economic concentration further complicates the rational choice of technique because of the problem of imputing overheads. 'Political' criteria have to be brought in when completely 'rational' economic decisions, i.e. decisions according to the principle of profit maximisation, cannot be made. To go yet a step further one should look at, say, energy research, which determines the techniques of tomorrow: it is clear that the choice not only between coexisting techniques but even between research priorities is shaped by political considerations. Sraffa's theory of joint production shows that, under conditions of equal numbers of processes and commodities, uniquely defined production prices exist that will eventually dominate even behind the book-keeper's back. To begin with, however, the production processes have to be given.[12]

Sraffa's assumption of given socially necessary methods of production therefore is not simply 'realistic'. It is based on an abstraction that suggests itself, on the one hand, because the determining causes of the 'socially necessary technique' are extremely complex and, on the other hand, because the assumption is sufficient to draw further conclusions. In other words, the point of departure is fruitful.

It is not so much the question of the origin of the method of production in Sraffa that irritates the neoclassicals as the assumption of given quantities of consumption goods demanded and, in connection with this, the assumption of a given level of production for each branch of industry. Sraffa is therefore cautious enough (significantly, he mentions Lord Keynes' name right at this point) to recommend that his readers first read his book with the implicit additional assumption of constant returns to scale, because then, according to what is ineptly called the 'non-substitution theorem', [13] for a given rate of profit prices are independent of demand.

The assumption of constant returns to scale, however, is by no means a necessary one. Ricardo had already shown with the example of rent how demand for corn with decreasing returns in agriculture is best analysed by examining how new land has to be cultivated if the social demand for corn rises. For this kind of partial analysis one may assume price elasticities of demand for the discussion of gradual or discontinuous changes of methods of production induced by the change in demand for a single commodity (PCMC, p. 88).

However, it seems as though greater generality is gained only if the conditions of demand are represented by downward-sloping demand curves for all consumption goods. If one returns to the Walrasian system of equilibrium, on the one hand one arrives at a contradictory idea of the accumulation process, as I mentioned above following Garegnani's proof; on the other hand, even though the social need for consumption goods may be *described* by demand functions, it is incorrectly or insufficiently *explained* by them. One should know, after Keynes, that the relevant problems of demand occur in connection with demand for investment goods, which is by no means dominated in an unambiguous manner by the demand for consumption goods because of uncertainty about the future. The demand for raw materials has to be taken into account in a specific manner, since it depends on special forces. From the point of view of macroeconomics, dependence of demand on prices is less relevant than that on incomes. Following Keynes one would not want to determine the level of national product by supply and demand.

Anyone who is interested in the special problem of the evolution of demand for different consumption goods and wishes to examine not only the facts but also their causes must venture into socio-historical analysis. The analysis of demand is similar to the problem of the definition of the socially necessary technique. Demand is determined by too many and too complex factors for one to hope to find a unified theory for it. In particular it is not determined by current relative prices and the incomes that are derivable from them. Demand functions or even utility functions are unable to produce a *general* theory of demand. Even here, therefore, Sraffa's point of departure is for most purposes the most fruitful. Assume as given the quantities to be produced and then observe the result of their variation. Or, if this standpoint does not seem acceptable, one might all the same think of the demand for consumer goods as determined by a neoclassical preference ordering. But the whole critique of Sraffa and Keynes culminates in the proof that price and employment of 'factors' in the short term and the long term cannot be determined by supply and demand in the sense of subjective preferences.

Despite that, there is nothing to be said against the usefulness of the concept of elasticity of demand, provided that it is used in the context of appropriate questions – and 'general equilibrium' does not belong in this category. The demand elasticity for cars does not *explain* the size of the American car industry; to determine this, one would have to discuss e.g. the determinants of the politics of infrastructure. But the demand elasticity for butter – an empirical magnitude – predicts the effect on sales of a relatively small change in the price of butter. The explanation of the different elasticities of demand in markets for raw materials and capital goods is a significant and fascinating theoretical problem. What I want to criticize here is therefore not the analytical instruments of the theory of demand, but the omnipotent position occupied by the law of supply and demand, as derived from subjective consumer preferences, in neoclassical theory and in that part of it which is still taught today.

It should be remembered that, because of the presupposition of given techniques and produced quantities, increasing external or internal returns in Sraffa's system do not cause any difficulties. The classical notion of the price of production still makes sense if the productivity of labour of steel plants increases sharply with the growth of the plant. Competition in the classical, but not in the neoclassical, sense can keep profits close to a normal 'level' even with increasing returns to scale.

With these remarks about income distribution, competition and price formation, I am now coming to the end. I have left the realm of strict analyses *more geometrico*, having changed the level of abstraction. This was the right thing to do as there is no better method. If a model is not adequate for an extended investigation, the modern theoretician does not hesitate to change the model. But there are no systematic criteria for doing this. Obviously one wishes to reconcile contradictory points of departure in a general model in which they appear as special cases so that the 'contradiction' resolves itself. But the 'complete' theory always remains utopian, and in most cases of such complex questions as the dynamics of the capitalist economy, one has to limit oneself. One has to renounce not only to complete but even to complicated models, and one has to find simple models that present the characteristics that are to be discussed in the simplest context. It is typical that some neoclassicals believe that, if only models are made complicated enough, they are resolvable in supermodels in which their consistency can be proved – possibly – on the basis of the theory of marginal productivity. [14] But how many mahogany desks does the board of directors need? The reader of PCMC will realize that the determinants of the method of production cannot be formalized on the same theoretical level as the price theory that follows as soon as these methods of production are given. To think that the capitalist economy could be summarized in a uniform system of laws is wrong and ahistorical. Sraffa refutes this idea by presenting a model that is open and at the same time logically closed, i.e. it does not allow substantive extensions. The connections with Marx, Keynes, etc. touched upon here therefore require 'thought bridges'.[15] The best that I have learned from Sraffa I learned when awkwardly attempting to construct these bridges.[16] Each of Sraffa's readers will confront the same task.

Notes

1   I should like to thank Piero Sraffa for many highly inspiring conversations. In my postscripts, especially in this part, I have tried as best as I could, maybe with no great success, to pay heed to his original comments, which were always aimed at teaching me to overcome the limits as set by formal assumptions of PCMC.

2   Marx ([1894] 1954), vol. III, p. 374. The long-term average interest rate must lie between zero and the long-run average rate of profit.

3   In this context I should like to mention that Sraffa (who was a close personal friend of Keynes) was part of the so-called 'circle' − a group of young Cambridge economists that included Austin and Joan Robinson, Richard Kahn and James Meade. Here he participated in working out the basic ideas of the *General Theory*. The work of the 'circle' is acknowledged in vols 13 and 14 of the Keynes edition (Keynes, 1971−9).

4   Concerning Marx's theory of interest see Marx ([1894] 1954), vol. III, part 5, in particular Chapter 23. Marx is entirely correct in not interpreting the difference between profit rates and interest rates as a risk premium (ibid., p. 220). The risk premium is a pure cost element.

5   This idea goes back to Kalecki (see e.g. Kaldor, 1956; Pasinetti, 1974). Pasinetti (1974) demonstrates how the theory of effective demand can be linked to the Sraffian price theory.

6   At least in part Marx supports this objection when, instead of speaking of a uniform rate of profit, he calls it average rate of profit.

7   In this context, Sraffa's first works should be noted, e.g. Sraffa (1922). It may also be remarked that his political views caused him to become an exile after the First World War. He was a friend of A. Gramsci (see Gramsci, 1968).

8   See the books of Bain (1956), Sylos-Labini ([1969] 1972) and others.

9   This construction is not far from the Marxian theory of prices of production. However, Marx argues the other way around. He starts with a surplus value proportional to variable costs and transforms the rate of surplus value into the rate of profit. The 'mark-up' of the surplus value on variable capital is presented as the objective datum (given labour value, given division of the working day). After the transformation of values into prices, the subjective profit expectations of the entrepreneurs are generated on this basis. Marx's point is accepted in so far as it turns out that the mark-up, sufficient for a profit considered 'subjectively normal' (Joan Robinson), in reality has to be in accordance with a general rate of profit determined by an objective law. For Marx, general deviations from the price of production seem to result above all from deviations of the market price from the price of production. He does not grasp the modifications of the cost situation occurring as a consequence of a change in capacity utilization.

10   The leading example of an eminent economist who argues on the basis of the

classical theory of prices of production while believing himself to be a Walrasian – as Joan Robinson has observed repeatedly – is W. Leontief.

11 C. Jaeger, to whom I am very much indebted for discussions concerning this section, has consistently drawn my attention to the importance of this set of problems and its historical dimension.

12 Von Neumann's model presupposes that goods can be catalogued completely so that it can be calculated which goods become commodities, i.e. have positive prices with prices resulting from a minimization of costs at a uniform rate of profit. The examples above show that this way of proceeding encounters substantial difficulties. Since the market does not decide on the basis of a complete list of goods and since the choice of which of the goods becomes a commodity with positive price, the selection of a list of goods is – economically speaking – quite arbitrary. It does not make much sense for a theory of capitalism to assume a given list of goods because of the large number of substances exchanged between the economic processes of production and the environment.

13 For its discovery see essay III.1.

14 See Kaldor (1966), p. 309–19:

> It is the hallmark of the neoclassical economists to believe that, however severe the abstractions from which he is forced to start, he will 'win through' by the end of the day – bit by bit; if he only carries the analysis far enough, the scaffolding can be removed, leaving the basic structure intact. In fact these props are never removed; the removal of any one of a number of them – as for example, allowing for increasing returns or learning by doing – is sufficient to cause the whole structure to collapse like a pack of cards.

15 On the other hand Sraffa's book is of interest only for those already posing such questions. Because of Italy's particular political and economic problems, PCMC has become the focus of a discussion there that until now has had only little effect, for example in the Federal Republic of Germany, for reasons that remain to be analysed.

16 It is not by accident that we close with a methodological remark. It was a major merit of Sraffa's that he was able to talk the obstinate Wittgenstein out of his positivistic position in the *Tractatus* and to stimulate his 'most consequential' ideas in the *Philosophische Untersuchungen*. These contain astonishing sentences like: 'The bourgeois position of the contradiction or its position in the bourgeois world: that is the philosophical problem' (Wittgenstein, 1975, p. 69; my translation – BS). See also the preface, ibid., as well as Malcom (1958) and Wright (1958).

Essay 6   Some Thoughts on the Foundation of Value in Sraffa and his Standard Commodity

This book has dealt extensively with the foundations of Sraffa's theory of prices from a formal point of view. But what is the conceptual basis of his theory of value? There is no explicit discussion of what constitutes the 'cause' of value in PCMC and very little of it elsewhere. I do not dare to venture here into a systematic discussion, but I want to indicate a possible line of argument.

Economics is concerned with the changing forms of material re-production of man, which are accompanied by changing forms of economic rationality. The modern organization of society has led to the problem of the allocation of scarce means for alternative uses being identified with economics, but this view is not helpful in understanding earlier social formations and represents only a partial truth today. Even the phenomenon of systematic monetary exchange (based on coinage), which has for a long time been considered as the economic phenomenon *par excellence*, arose only late in the seventh century BC – long after the oriental empires had developed; and economic rationality continued to be different from that prevailing in modern times in spite of the existence of monetary institutions throughout antiquity and the Middle Ages.

If economic rationality and economic institutions are historically specific, it ought to be possible to delineate conceptually the conditions under which certain economic institutions arise. In particular, it ought to be possible to found the fundamental concept of 'value' on a *proto-economic* theory. The *definiendum* is 'value', but the *definiens* must be taken not from economics, but from some other science.

Both the classical and the neoclassical school have – more or less explicitly – tried to do this. The neoclassicals refer to a psychological notion of wants relative to which there is scarcity. The classicals founded the concept of value on labour in the apparent belief that labour (in the sense in which it was used in the theory) was not in itself a category to be explained within the science of economics. Marx introduced 'abstract labour' in order to reduce absolute and relative value to labour as a proto-economic datum. Since labour was believed to be the activity that distinguishes man from other animals, it transcended economics or, at any rate, the economics of commodity-producing societies. The difficulty was to relate this kind of 'labour' – work in general – with wage labour.

An analogy may help us to understand the appeal to an extra-

economic foundation for economic theory. One approach to thermo-
dynamics is based on a special axiomatic system. This might be compared to an economic theory founded on self-explanatory economic
axioms. But there is also the theory that explains temperature and heat of
gases through statistical mechanics. This might be compared to an
attempt to found economic theory on extra-economic concepts.

The foundation of a theory may suggest specific uses to be made of it.
Many Marxists believe − or used to believe − that a planned economy
involves the allocation of homogeneous labour and that a planned
economy represents a social system that is supposed to be completely
different from capitalism. This corresponds to the idea that labour is a
proto-economic notion; the expenditure of labour power is supposed
to have an objective measure, which may be put to good use under
socialism while it is misused to exploit the worker under capitalism.

We have seen, however, that the homogeneity of labour that is thus
postulated as something potentially to be established independently of
the market mechanism, and that is so important for the Marxian version
of classical theory, has no foundation. Marxian attempts to 'verify'
abstract labour as a philosophical postulate by means of a physiological
measurement of the intensity of simple labour fail. The failure may also
be observed if we think of the allocation of 'homogeneous' labour as an
object of planning. Homogeneity can be achieved only by introducing
coefficients that define the equivalence of different kinds of labour, each
of which is performed according to its own standard of efficiency
(number of sacks loaded per hour, number of windows cleaned per hour,
etc.). The establishment of these coefficients is arbitrary since the
measurement of performance can be made objective at best for each kind
of concrete labour. The process by which the equivalence of different
kinds of labour is established can be made the object of a separate
enquiry, but it ultimately requires an explanation in terms of economic
theory or economic history; it is not proto-economic, rather it is
'proto-capitalist'. As such its introduction by the classicists was legitimate, but that of the Marxian notion of strong homogeneity was not. It
follows from this that processes that establish the weak homogeneity of
labour with its inherent arbitrariness under capitalism may also be
needed under socialism and reveal a profound similarity between capitalism and socialism.

The neoclassical school derives value from utility, and, more generally,
the sphere of economic action from the specific type of economic
rationality that individual utility maximization is thought to imply.
Economics is then not only to be founded on notions that are not in
themselves economic, but represents as such a transhistoric science. The
historical school criticized this − in my view quite rightly − as an
oversimplification of human motives, even within the economic sphere
of modern society. The Cambridge critique of neoclassical theory has
shown that it cannot be extended from its basis in subjectively rational
decision-making to a complete explanation of capitalist reality, including
distribution and the demand for capital (investment). If this critique
holds, other aspects, including a more complex representation of motivation, must come into the story (some were emphasized by Keynes).

The difference between classical and neoclassical economics represents the most important divide in the history of economic thought. There is also a different point of view, which allows us to speak of an 'age of ideology' in which the explanation of value through the metaphysical concept of abstract labour or, alternatively, subjective utility became unduly prominent; this period was preceded by an age of more pragmatic 'Ricardian' analysis and was followed by more technocratic approaches, with Leontief and Keynes each introducing tools for planning under capitalism.

Where is Sraffa to be located? His mode of discourse is certainly analytical rather than ideological and his introduction of the concepts of price might seem axiomatic, but I believe that a construction of an underlying concept of value on, as it were, proto-economic data is implicit in his presentation. I want to attempt a proof of this contention, albeit sketchy and provisional.

My interpretation starts from Sraffa's closed model (PCMC, secs 1–3):

$$\hat{\mathbf{A}} \to \mathbf{I}.$$

Considering the system first rather formally, we observe that there is no surplus, i.e. $\mathbf{e}'\hat{\mathbf{A}} = \mathbf{e}'$ where $\mathbf{e}' = (1, 1, ..., 1)$, and the system cannot be decomposed. Hence $\hat{\mathbf{A}}$ must be indecomposable, for if $\hat{\mathbf{A}}$ was decomposable (without being completely decomposable, i.e. without falling apart into two disconnected parts), we could write

$$\hat{\mathbf{A}} = \begin{bmatrix} \hat{\mathbf{A}}_1^1 & \mathbf{O} \\ \hat{\mathbf{A}}_2^1 & \hat{\mathbf{A}}_2^2 \end{bmatrix}$$

with $\hat{\mathbf{A}}_2^1 \neq \mathbf{O}$. Whereas Leontief would reject this possibility because the equation

$$\hat{\mathbf{A}}\hat{\mathbf{p}} = \hat{\mathbf{p}}$$

could then not be solved with $\hat{\mathbf{p}} > \mathbf{o}$, Sraffa would presumably reject it because he would consider $\hat{\mathbf{A}}_1^1$ as a basic system generating a surplus, and systems with a surplus are to be discussed at a later stage of his argument.[1]

$\hat{\mathbf{A}}$ is therefore assumed to be indecomposable, and the solution to

$$\hat{\mathbf{A}}\hat{\mathbf{p}} = \hat{\mathbf{p}}$$

yields a positive $\hat{\mathbf{p}}$, unique up to a linear factor (the dominant root of $\hat{\mathbf{A}}$ equals one). How do we get from this mathematical result to the concept of price?

Before we come to that, it should be noted that the closed model (here assumed to be of order $n + 1$) admits formally of a wide variety of interpretations. Anticipating the conceptual construction that is to be derived later we may think of $\hat{\mathbf{A}}$

(a)   as of the closed form of an 'open' single-product system

$$(\mathbf{A}, \mathbf{l}) \rightarrow \mathbf{I}$$

with a surplus $\mathbf{e}'(\mathbf{I} - \mathbf{A}) = \mathbf{s}'$. The system can be closed by writing

$$\hat{\mathbf{A}} = \begin{bmatrix} \mathbf{A} & \mathbf{l} \\ \mathbf{s}' & 0 \end{bmatrix}$$

with labour appearing as an additional commodity used as an input in all except the last process where it is produced by means of the whole surplus even if only part of the surplus goes to wages. We clearly have $\mathbf{e}'\hat{\mathbf{A}} = \mathbf{e}'$; relative prices (labour values) given by

$$\mathbf{A}\mathbf{p} + w\mathbf{l} = \mathbf{p},$$

are easily seen to be equal to the first n components of $\hat{\mathbf{p}}$ if we normalize $\hat{p}_{n+1} = w$. (We postpone the problem of the homogeneity of labour.)

(b)   Or we could introduce matrices $(d_i^j) = \mathbf{D}$, $(c_i^j) = \mathbf{C}$ where d_i^j (or c_i^j) is the amount of commodity j bought by the workers (or by the capitalists) in industry i so that

$$\mathbf{e}'(\mathbf{I} - \mathbf{A}) = \mathbf{s}' = \mathbf{e}'\mathbf{D} + \mathbf{e}'\mathbf{C},$$

with

$$\hat{\mathbf{A}} = \mathbf{A} + \mathbf{D} + \mathbf{C}.$$

If the usual price system is given

$$(1 + r)\mathbf{A}\mathbf{p} + w\mathbf{l} = \mathbf{p}$$

and if capitalists and workers buy commodities according to their revenues in each industry, i.e. if

$$\mathbf{D}\mathbf{p} = w\mathbf{l}$$

and

$$\mathbf{C}\mathbf{p} = r\mathbf{A}\mathbf{p},$$

we find that $\hat{\mathbf{p}}$ is proportional to $\mathbf{p}$ for the first n components.

(c)   The introduction of consumption proves that the coefficients of $\hat{\mathbf{A}}$ must not be thought of as being purely 'technically' determined (whatever that means in a modern world where what is technically necessary depends as much on design and advertising, needs for representation, safety conventions, conventions as to the intensity of work, etc., as on 'engineering requirements'). It is possible to construct a neoclassical free exchange model yielding equilibrium prices that coincide with the prices determined by the $\hat{A}$ matrix of commodities exchanged between agent i and j.

(d)   But it is also possible to think of the $n + 1$ activities of

$$\hat{A} \rightarrow I$$

as of separate economies pursuing a kind of 'international' trade. The nations (or 'units', as we shall call them in this context) are completely specialised as far as trade with the outside world is concerned, and they use the proceeds of their sales to buy inputs (the rows of $\hat{A}$) from other units. It does not matter whether the units are organized internally as communes without an internal exchange of commodities but producing and using a variety of objects that never become commodities or whether they function internally as capitalist economies using and partly producing the same commodities as those entering international trade, and some others besides. In the first case, we think of pre-capitalist communes trading according to principles of commodity exchange only with the outside world and producing and distributing goods internally according to different principles. (A familiar example is the peasant family selling wheat and buying ploughs on the market while it grows other products – which are not turned into commodities – only for its own needs.)

Sraffa's first 'extremely simple society' with only two units (iron = town, wheat = countryside) belongs to the last category (d), but his starting point would hardly yield an interesting theory of prices if the formal results did not apply in more general contexts, of which (b) is mentioned in PCMC, sec. 8. Sraffa's opening chapter must in fact be meant to explain what prices are (in the classical sense), since an economic theory of value that *presupposed* the concept of price could hardly be regarded as fundamental. But his explanation is, as usual, at best alluded to, not given in detail.

Sraffa's first, as it were 'axiomatic' or 'proto-economic', concepts are 'commodity' and 'single' as opposed to 'joint' production. The commensurability of diverse objects, which is the peculiar result of the existence of prices, is given rise to not by any structure of production, but (if what was said above is correct) primarily by the structure of indecomposable single-product systems. This contention looks odd to the theorist of joint production, but consider an example of cyclical reproduction in nature which seems at first to present analogies with economic production. It concerns the interaction of global chemical cycles such as the cycles of water, oxygen, etc., on the earth.

There are, for example, four 'units' or 'reservoirs':

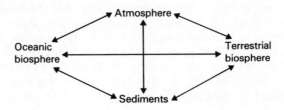

In order to establish the analogy with economic reproduction, we introduce matrices $\mathbf{A} = (a_i^j)$, $\mathbf{B} = (b_i^j)$ where a_i^j or b_i^j are the total mass of substance j (such as water, carbon dioxide, etc.) received or released by reservoir i (such as 'terrestrial biosphere', i.e. terresterial plants and animals), per period. The conversion of mass into energy in the sun drives the whole process but, ignoring such conversion on earth, we can say that the conversions in each of the four reservoirs are given symbolically by the four rows $\mathbf{a}_i \rightarrow \mathbf{b}_i$ or

$$\mathbf{A} \rightarrow \mathbf{B}$$

where matrices $\mathbf{A}$, $\mathbf{B}$ have as many columns as there are chemical compounds in global chemical cycles (a very large number).

We have

$$\mathbf{e}'\mathbf{A} = \mathbf{e}'\mathbf{B}$$

if each substance is in equilibrium. To begin with, we can measure each substance in a unit adapted to its physical and chemical properties and which expresses its mass: e.g. litres of water at given pressure and temperature or the number of molecules of carbon dioxide. Let p_j denote the mass of a litre of water if j denotes water or the mass of a molecule of CO_2 if j denotes CO_2 etc.; we then have, choosing a common unit of mass,

$$\sum_j a_i^j p_j = \sum_j b_i^j p_j$$

since the chemical 'processes of production' preserve the total mass in each reservoir and in each period, if there is again no accumulation. In vector notation,

$$\mathbf{A}\mathbf{p} = \mathbf{B}\mathbf{p}.$$

The analogy with a price system seems striking at first sight. Of course, if we had measured every substance in amounts of its mass in a common unit, we would get $\mathbf{p} = \mathbf{e}$; the equation

$$\mathbf{A}\mathbf{e} = \mathbf{B}\mathbf{e}$$

indicates the homogeneity of matter as mass, but similarly we could measure commodities in our basic Sraffa system

$$\hat{\mathbf{A}} \rightarrow \mathbf{I}$$

with

$$\mathbf{e}'\hat{\mathbf{A}} = \mathbf{e}', \qquad \mathbf{A}\hat{\mathbf{p}} = \hat{\mathbf{p}},$$

by introducing the diagonal matrix $\mathbf{N} = \operatorname{diag}\{\hat{p}_1, ..., \hat{p}_{n+1}\}$, $\bar{\mathbf{A}} = \hat{\mathbf{A}}\mathbf{N}$,

$\bar{\mathbf{I}} = \mathbf{IN}$, $\hat{\mathbf{p}} = \mathbf{Ne}$ so that

$$\bar{\mathbf{A}}\mathbf{e} = \bar{\mathbf{I}}\mathbf{e}:$$

all commodities are homogeneous as values.

The point, however, is that the above matrices of natural flows $\mathbf{A}$, $\mathbf{B}$ do not determine a *unique* right-hand vector $\mathbf{p} > \mathbf{o}$ such that $\mathbf{Ap} = \mathbf{Bp}$ since they have more columns than rows. If we now ask what values are and why they are unique in each system, we find that the analysis in Sraffa is structured so as to let the indecomposability of the self-reproducing society, and the absence of joint commodity production, appear as the conceptual origin of value.

By contrast, the homogeneity of chemical substances is defined and exists logically and historically prior to any particular geochemical cycle. Similarly, the attempts to found value on utility or on labour may have reflected the desire to define the concept of value prior to the establishment of any particular structures of reproduction (indirect labour is in fact not mentioned in the first chapter of *Das Kapital*).

Sraffa's theoretical edifice thus rests on the axiomatic introduction of 'commodities' and 'production' in a 'self-replacing' state. In so far as the definition of the homogeneity of goods and of the structure of interdependence (the chosen definition of basics) is based on extra-economic sciences, use is also being made of proto-economic concepts. An explicit reference to decision rules (maximization) is not required.

Prices should be derived. They have not been defined yet, except as mathematical magnitudes, and we do not know why we should interpret $\hat{\mathbf{p}}$ as relative or absolute values. But we can open Sraffa's initial closed model for any 'unit', say the first, which produces coal, and we can then interpret the coefficient u_i given by

$$u_i = a_i^2 u_2 + \cdots + a_i^{n+1} u_{n+1} + a_i^1, \qquad i = 2, ..., n + 1$$

as coal values (coal embodied) either using a dated reduction to coal inputs (the direct coal inputs to industry i are given by a_i^1, $i = 2, ..., n + 1$) or by applying the subsystems approach to 'coal embodied', as Sraffa does for labour embodied.

If one likes this sort of game, one can similarly define steel values, wheat values and finally labour values, opening for each commodity in turn. The concept of 'embodiment' can in this way be constructed as part of a 'proto-economic theory of production' and the concept of 'value' can be defined through 'embodiment'.

The 'exchange' of one commodity for another may then be explained in terms of the *replacement* of inputs to productive units. The output of each unit (say the first, coal) can be subdivided into parts such that each of the inputs to the coal sector embodies as much coal as one of those parts into which the output, coal, has been divided. Replacement according to such embodiments is now called 'exchange'. It is easy to show that the system of exchanges is consistent, in that triangular exchange yields as much as bilateral exchange. The ratios $\hat{p}_i/\hat{p}_j = u_i/u_j$ may be written as p_i/p_j; they are independent of the 'opening' chosen, and p_i/p_j has the dimension of 'quantity of commodity j divided by quantity of commodity i'. If the opening for unit j is made, p_i/p_j denotes the quantity of j embodied in a unit of commodity i. It may be called 'relative price' or 'price of commodity in terms of commodity j'.

Sraffa thus presents us with an approach to the definition of value and relative price that appears to be completely novel: the structure of reproduction of a system of single-product industries is by itself sufficient cause to give rise to a system of 'prices', and what prices are can be explained, albeit in so far only in a rudimentary fashion, in 'proto-economic' or 'technical' terms.

It will be objected that the determination of the structure of the system is an important economic problem which cannot be solved independently of the price system and/or not independently of the 'real causes' governing value. The neoclassical will argue that the quantities of matrix **A** depend on utility; the Marxist that, somehow, labour value rules the roost.

To this, it may be answered first of all that here a *generalization* of previous explanations of value has been discovered. The allocation of labour, or utility, or technical requirements and other forces may determine the input–output matrix. Given these, relative values may be derived. The axiomatic layer of this theory lies deeper than that of rival theories; it is – accordingly – more abstract.

The theory nevertheless stresses some properties of the economic system that distinguish it from seemingly analogous natural systems. Some of these points have already been mentioned in various places in this book.

1 The basic data are homogeneous commodities. Natural resources have already been reduced to the commodity form. Since commodities are not uniquely classifiable according to natural properties, they presuppose the imposition of social norms for the quality of the products. It is therefore thought that the goods are, as commodities, not treated as individualities like biological resources or works of art (or indeed almost any object in a primitive society), but are purposely reduced to standardized forms. (The opposite view, of course, would be that substitutability as derived from utility and objective properties of goods regulates the degree of homogeneity and diversification.)

2 The coherence of the system is assured through its being basic, not through the fact that every commodity is produced by homogeneous labour.

3 Processes are single-product industries; the derivation of the concept of value therefore rests on the assumption that commodities are produced singly, while goods are always produced jointly.

4 The number of commodities and processes is known and finite; nothing is said about the unknown variety of natural objects and processes that are indirectly involved in human production. Thus, the theory of economic production contrasts with representations of the reproduction of natural systems. The modern scientific view, which

isolates chemical cycles or the interaction of animal populations, exhibits a different structure. The view of economic production is, on the other hand, different from a morphological view of natural creation which denies homogeneity.

5   However, commodities do not by themselves 'know' where they have to go in the system of reproduction, which is not automatic but supported by the action of people. Nor does nature automatically conform to this system of reproduction. Sraffa speaks of 'self-replacement'. Reproduction may go on unchanged, but it may also be enlarged or disturbed. This results in uncertainty and the will of people to hang on to commodities, which guarantee survival through exchange.

To pursue the last point, we now have to go one step beyond Sraffa. If X_i, X_j are quantities of i and j, and if $X_i/X_j = p_j/p_i$, we may call X_i and X_j 'equivalents'. The system is driven by people's desire to obtain equivalents because commodities do not by themselves come to them in order to ensure reproduction. If commodities did go by themselves or were driven by natural external forces like the substances in a geo-chemical cycle, a monetary equivalent would be needed neither as a means of exchange nor as a store of value. However, since reproduction is complicated, the simplification of exchange through a medium of exchange is necessary, and since reproduction is precarious (so that the individual may improve or worsen its position within it), money is desired as a store of value.

Here we have a contradiction or – if one prefers – an inevitable break in the argument: the necessity of money, indeed what money is, can only be explained through admitting the disturbance (for better or worse) of the process of reproduction, but the equivalent can only be realized exactly if reproduction goes on perfectly undisturbed. It is therefore important for Sraffa to distinguish self-replacement (the possibility of reproduction) from reproduction itself (PCMC, p. 1).

An alternative representation of the introduction of money is as a clever and handy invention that reduces the number of relative prices that have to be known. However, this is not really an explanation of money as a tangible object, but rather of the convenience of having an abstract unit of account. The inadequacy of the explanation is revealed in the erroneous conclusions of the quantity theory of money, which is the usual outcome of this approach in which the other functions of money remain unexplained.

The uncertainty of reproduction can take different forms and thus give rise to different forms of money. To the uncertainty of a commodity-producing unit that wishes to realize the self-replacement of its inputs, there corresponds the desire to hold money in periods of crises. To the uncertainty of a sufficiently large planning unit that has to ensure replacement by establishing standards for different tasks, there corresponds the use of money as a means of enforcing discipline of workers through using money as the medium of paying wages tied to efficiency. Socialists have therefore nowhere been able to renounce the use of money in planned economies, contrary to Engels' expectations (Engels, [1894] 1972) as expressed in the *Anti-Dühring* (where even value was thought no longer to be needed). If we are to believe Polanyi (1968), lists of goods to be delivered according to the command of planning authorities in the old oriental empires represented the origin of accounting. If people were unable to deliver in an uncertain world what they had first been told to give, equivalences established by decree between different goods allowed them to substitute one tribute in kind by another in given proportions. Thus, even prior to the use of commodity-money, the use of units of accounts may be said to have been necessitated by uncertainty.

It might be possible to introduce money systematically into the system by developing the contrast between self-replacement and uncertainty, where uncertainty concerns exogenous forces (nature, free will) and endogenous causes rooted in the functioning of the economic system itself. In particular, gold as commodity-money could be introduced by distinguishing monetary and other uses of gold, if it is observed that gold is used as an ornament in definite quantities like other inputs in quantities determined by cultural needs. Instead of the quantity theory of money one then has the 'law of circulation': if too much gold circulates, gold prices rise and the value of gold falls below its cost of production. The production of gold is thus reduced while people are induced to hold more gold as ornament or treasure because these have become cheaper. The amount of gold in monetary circulation falls to the quantity required (1) by the value of transactions in the given structure of production and (2) by the velocity of circulation as defined by the conventions regulating the exchange of commodities. *Vice versa*, if the supply of money has to adapt to a shortage of monetary gold. Later, forms of money may be introduced and developed on the assumption that this archetype already exists. Liquidity preference and accommodating banking policies still ensure, given an exogenously determined price level, that the law of circulation holds rather than a quantity theory of money.

However, Sraffa sidesteps all arguments about money by ignoring uncertainty. Reproduction is assumed to be assured. His presentation can be rendered more explicit by giving the definitions of relative price, of steel values, coal values, etc., but the economic logic of money is more difficult to develop. A 'price' in Sraffa may therefore simply be defined as a relative price in terms of a unit of account. Its properties can be explained by using the concept of embodied value.

In order to interpret prices, the closed model has to be opened up so that a surplus arises. The symmetry between units of production then gives way to a distinction between commodities (produced in industries) and labour.

The homogeneity of labour presupposes the homogeneity of commodities, for – as we saw at the end of Essay 4a – different types of labour can be compared and defined as equivalent only by measuring their respective outputs (labour is not itself a proto-economic concept).

Sraffa, however, does not next open his closed model to introduce labour. Instead, he teases orthodox Marxists by opening up for profits first! He introduces the uniform 'rate of profits' as it were by a sudden revolution, but even a *coup d'état* requires silent preparation.

In fact, we are on familiar ground, so that a sketch suffices to show the way. We observe our units in a quiet process of commodity exchange: the commodity produced in any unit is given away ('sold') for money, and money buys commodities as inputs to production. The system is in a self-replacing state, which implies that each unit (which may be rich or poor in terms of self-made goods for home consumption) is able to afford the commodities as inputs required for its reproduction. But the reproduction of the units does not go on undisturbed in an uncertain world, and while some 'families' within a unit fall behind, produce less than expected and buy less (relative to the state of physical self-replacement), others will possibly gain. If commodity production is not complemented by its logical opposite, redistribution (through central authority or the help of neighbours), it becomes a matter of economic survival to produce more rather than less. Production of commodities for exchange leads to an acquisitive drive to produce more in order to get more, and to get more in order to produce more. It emerges as a tendency opposed to the traditional production of goods for use within families and units. This engenders the *surplus*.

The surplus does not only exist in commodity-producing societies, but the system of commodity production inherently tends to generate a form of competition leading to the growth of the surplus. This competition is something more specific than rivalry or the wish to excel. It follows from the measurement of success in commodity production in terms of money. Such measurement ('accounting') is a necessity in order to compare the increased (or diminished) product with the heterogeneous means of production. A comparison in physical terms with producers in the same unit ('industry') is feasible. But if a surplus is to be gained in one industry, a greater one is perhaps to be gained in another, and this requires a relationship between the value (in terms of commodity-money) of the net product and that of the means of production. Competition is *defined* as the drive of producers to seek the highest rate of profit. It is dictated by the necessity of survival. Other forms of economic competition are subsidiary to this. Competition regulates itself in that higher than average levels of profit lead to an increase in production in the corresponding industries beyond what will be bought by the others.

We thus arrive at Sraffa's second model with a uniform rate of profit

$$(1 + R)\mathbf{A}\mathbf{p} = \mathbf{p}.$$

The system with a surplus $\mathbf{e}'(\mathbf{I} - \mathbf{A}) = \mathbf{s}' \geqslant \mathbf{o}$ leaves room for a distinction between basics and non-basics or luxury goods. As a matter of fact, luxury goods are to be regarded as a first *raison d'être* of the surplus. In the previous model of the society that produced 'just enough to maintain itself', the means of production were composed of technical means of production and means of subsistence (these notions are to some extent elastic). A surplus arises at the level of the 'family', if an increase in production (obtained through increased productivity or restraint from consumption) is not transformed into a means of subsistence because it is a luxury good. This is the more likely to happen the more pronounced are the social divisions within the producing units. Luxury goods are then appropriated by one class of people, necessities by another.

Next, we may speak of growth. The part of the surplus that is not consumed as luxuries is accumulated; and if there is no luxury consumption, we may have balanced growth at a rate equal to the rate of profit. Yet, this 'proto-capitalist' form of production does not presuppose 'capitalist' wage labour – in fact, it is compatible with various forms of organization of labour and precedes capitalism both (though not in pure form) historically and (in Sraffa) conceptually.

Such proto-capitalist forms of production developed in different places and periods, but their evolution was, prior to the eighteenth century, always controlled through laws and traditions in – to some extent *conscious* – rejection of the threat of free capitalism to the established order. Their development was further impeded by the lack of supporting institutions and a pre-capitalist rationality, as Sombart (1916–27) and Weber ([1920] 1972) rightly emphasized. All three obstacles were reduced to a historical minimum under nineteenth-century liberalism. The precondition, of course, was the emergence of wage labour, which presupposed a break with familial or partriarchal links, bondage or direct personal coercion within producing units. The institution of wage labour provided the stimulus to raise output per head ('productivity') because the cost of labour could now be made dependent on the level of output (whereas the cost of a member of a family, a slave or a serf is a fixed overhead). The freedom of the worker was also the freedom of the capitalist to employ as much labour as was most profitable. It allowed the extension of the rationality of accounting to the measurement of the performance of the worker. Given this institution, the drive to maximize profits could also be translated into an incentive for workers to raise their productivity by making wages depend on output, so that the rise of the social product eventually depends on the self-interest not only of capitalists, but also of workers. It thus appears that the concept of labour should be derived from the concept of commodity production and not, as in Marx, the other way round.

The relationship between value, productivity and the rise of the surplus is, in classical theory, traditionally analysed in terms of the labour theory of value. I prefer to analyse simple commodity production not in terms of a labour theory of value, but along the lines sketched in this essay because the homogeneity of labour seems to me to be a problematic concept corresponding to a comparatively late historical development while the 'closed model' leads easily to the concept of a surplus and the rate of profit. Labour values, on the other hand, had no historical reality prior to capitalism (e.g. the work of artisans and serfs could not be compared and guilds were maintained among other things in order to keep work differentiated). But the labour theory of value still provides an excellent analytical tool as a preliminary to the analysis of capitalism. We therefore consider once more simple commodity production, but with homogeneous labour as an input, although homogeneous labour really means wage labour (i.e. a capitalist institution with given wage differentials, hence 'weak homogeneity'). The surplus is ascribed to labour; the profit-earning capitalists are assumed away.

We open the closed model for labour by defining homogeneous labour as in section II.20b, to obtain the system

$$\mathbf{Ap} + \mathbf{l} = \mathbf{p}.$$

We now find a new interpretation for prices. If $\mathbf{s}$ is the vector of the surplus with $\mathbf{e}'(\mathbf{I} - \mathbf{A}) = \mathbf{s}'$, we get

$$\frac{\partial s_i}{\partial s_j} = -\frac{p_j}{p_i},$$

i.e. p_j/p_i indicates by how much the amount of commodity i can be increased if one unit of commodity j is taken out of the surplus, with the surplus otherwise being unchanged, and with employment kept constant (assuming constant returns to scale).

Proof:

Let $\mathbf{s}$ be the surplus and $\mathbf{q}$ activity levels. We then have

$$\mathbf{s}' = \mathbf{q}'(\mathbf{I} - \mathbf{A}),$$

$$\frac{\partial \mathbf{s}'}{\partial s_i} = \frac{\partial \mathbf{q}'}{\partial s_i}(\mathbf{I} - \mathbf{A})$$

and (the total input of labour being unchanged)

$$\frac{\partial \mathbf{q}'}{\partial s_i}\mathbf{l} = 0,$$

therefore

$$\frac{\partial \mathbf{s}'}{\partial s_i}(\mathbf{I} - \mathbf{A})^{-1}\mathbf{l} = 0.$$

With $\partial s_i/\partial s_i = 1$, $\partial s_j/\partial s_i$ as unknown, $\partial s_k/\partial s_i = 0$, $k \neq i, j$, and $(\mathbf{I} - \mathbf{A})^{-1}\mathbf{l} = \mathbf{p}$, we obtain

$$\frac{\partial s_j}{\partial s_i}p_j + p_i = 0,$$

q.e.d.

The subsystems approach would yield the same result since p_i (p_j) is the amount of labour required to increase the net production of commodity i (j) by one unit. Private rates of exchange, social trade-offs in the surplus and the embodiment of one commodity in another all coincide in the present notion of relative price.

The possibility of expressing rates of exchange, social trade-offs and embodiment in one common unit is what gives significance to the choice of a unit of account. It is clear that we could formally also have opened up the model for a commodity and not for labour. But we shall now show that there is a specific reason for 'opening up' for labour. The distinctive role of labour values compared with commodity values derives exclusively from the fact that growth in productivity means growth in the productivity of labour, which is directed at an increase in the surplus per unit of labour. The open model is

$$\mathbf{Ap} + \mathbf{l} = \mathbf{p}$$

with surplus $\mathbf{s}' = \mathbf{e}'(\mathbf{I} - \mathbf{A})$; the closed model is

$$\hat{\mathbf{A}} = \begin{bmatrix} \mathbf{A} & \mathbf{l} \\ \mathbf{s}' & 0 \end{bmatrix}$$

with $\mathbf{e}'\hat{\mathbf{A}} = \mathbf{e}'$, $\hat{\mathbf{A}}\hat{\mathbf{p}} = \hat{\mathbf{p}}$. Then we have two theorems:

(a)   Changes of technique (or the method of production used in one industry) induce falls of all prices (labour values)

$$p_i = \hat{p}_i/\hat{p}_{n+1}, \qquad i = 1, ..., n,$$

if and only if the surplus can be produced with less labour. *Proof:* see above, section II.18.

(b)   If the method of production i is changed and the productivity of labour improves, the price of commodity i will fall relative to all the others, i.e. p_i/p_j will fall; $j \neq i$; $i, j = 1, ..., n$.

Proof: see Schefold (1978b).

Statement (a) proves that labour values are reliable indicators of gains in productivity; statement (b) proves that competition can operate through the lowering of *relative* prices. This is true even if progress takes place in the gold industry, which produces commodities of price 1 under a pure gold standard, because the gold prices of all other commodities will rise.

But commodity prices are, whether we think of gold prices or coal values, not important indicators of productivity gains. This may be exemplified by means of coal values (industry 1 produces coal).

If progress takes place in industry n, which produces steel, p_n/p_1 will fall (as will more generally p_n/p_j, $j \neq n$) so that the coal value (but also the copper value, wheat value, etc.) of commodity n will fall along with labour values, and this is the tangible, technical effect of what was observed above, i.e. that progress in sector n will reduce the price of n in terms of all other commodities. The fall of p_n/p_1 implies a fall in the absolute value of $\partial s_1/\partial s_n$ at a given level of employment. Hence, per capita consumption of steel can *ceteris paribus* be increased with a given reduction in the net output of coal if any progress takes place in the steel industry. If the coal value of steel falls, a given quantity of coal commands more steel.

In contrast, the amount of steel commanded by a given amount of coal will diminish if progress takes place in the coal sector! For progress in the coal sector implies that p_1/p_n falls, therefore that p_n/p_1 rises. This result ceases to look paradoxical if we bear in mind that progress in any industry i implies that its product can be obtained with increased productivity of labour and of all other commodities, but this means precisely that increases in the net product of these other commodities at a given level of employment will now require greater reductions in the net product of the first. The symmetry of both movements (p_i/p_j falls, p_j/p_i rises) explains why commodity values are of only limited interest: each gain in productivity (steel in terms of coal) is also *ipso facto* a loss (coal in terms of steel).

There is only one commodity in $\hat{\mathbf{A}}$ for which this symmetry, although formally still correct, does not exist economically, and this is labour. Formally, nothing changes. If we open the closed model for any commodity $j \neq i$ and keep the inputs of commodity j constant, we get $\partial s_i/\partial s_{n+1} = -p_{n+1}/p_i$. But $s_{n+1} = 0$, since labour is not contained in the surplus. If we now allow for progress in industry i, with a fall of $\hat{p}_i/\hat{p}_{n+1}$, less direct and indirect labour per unit of output is required. *But the opposite rise of p_{n+1}/p_i has to be interpreted not as a greater commodity cost in the production of labour but as an increase in the disposable surplus.* The rise of $\hat{p}_{n+1}/\hat{p}_n$ that accompanies technical progress in the production of steel is not a rise in the steel cost of labour (or labour power). This explains the conceptual pre-eminence of labour values as opposed to commodity values. Labour values become important precisely when it is not clear at the outset whether the increased productivity really implies an 'increase in the cost of labour', i.e. in wages, or whether the increase in the surplus is invested or consumed by somebody else.

This development of Sraffa's theory therefore allows us to show that labour values are ultimately of greater importance than commodity values, although the foundation of this theory of value is independent of the identification of labour power as a homogeneous commodity input.

Commodity values are useful for the conceptual foundation of price theory. They are measures of substitutions in the net product. However, they are poor indicators of absolute quantities consumed in the production of a given output, although they can be interpreted in terms of embodied quantities of each commodity.

A different definition is available and also applicable to labour. Since it is important to know the commodity intensity of various technologies (e.g. the oil or coal requirements of different methods of production), we include a discussion of this matter before returning to the main theme: the concept of value.

Consider the input–output matrix of the open system. The open system is the relevant frame of reference if changes of productivity leading to an increase in the surplus have to be analysed. Let $\mathbf{e}_i$ be the i'th unit vector, so that $\mathbf{q}_i$ is the vector of activity levels producing one unit of commodity i as the net product. This is again the subsystem approach as discussed above, but here we explicitly assume constant returns to scale:

$$\mathbf{e}_i = \mathbf{q}_i(\mathbf{I} - \mathbf{A})$$
$$\mathbf{q}_i = \mathbf{e}_i(\mathbf{I} - \mathbf{A})^{-1} = \mathbf{e}_i + \mathbf{q}_i\mathbf{A}.$$

It follows that we may interpret the element q_i^j of

$$\mathbf{Q} = (\mathbf{I} - \mathbf{A})^{-1}$$

as the activity level of the j'th industry in subsystem i, but, in a single-product system with the appropriate definition of physical units, q_i^j is also the amount of commodity j produced in subsystem i as gross output. We can therefore say that q_i^j is the gross amount of commodity j incorporated in one unit of commodity i. This amount will be of special interest if the process of production of commodity j is the process of mining it or otherwise extracting it from the soil. The resource is then finite. The economic system acts as if it was not, but it is of importance to know how long the process of extraction can continue, etc.

Suppose $j = 1$ and let commodity 1 again be coal. The coefficient q_i^1 will then be called the coal intensity of commodity i. The name should remind us of the fact that q_i^1 is at once a quantity of coal (gross amount required per unit of commodity i) and an activity level (of the coal industry in subsystem i). These two concepts will have to be differentiated in the case of joint production.

Suppose now that coal is extracted from the earth in one process. It must be process 1, which is coal producing. From $\mathbf{Q} = (\mathbf{I} - \mathbf{A})^{-1}$ we obtain $\mathbf{Q} - \mathbf{A}\mathbf{Q} = \mathbf{I}$ and $\mathbf{Q} = \mathbf{I} + \mathbf{A}\mathbf{Q}$, hence

$$\mathbf{q}^1 = \mathbf{e}^1 + \mathbf{A}\mathbf{q}^1$$

where $\mathbf{q}^1$ is the column vector of coal intensities and where $\mathbf{e}^1$ is the first unit column vector. This now means that the gross amount of coal incorporated in the output of each process is equal to the extraction of coal in each process *plus* the amount of coal incorporated in each input – an equation that is exactly analogous to

$$\mathbf{p} = \mathbf{l} + \mathbf{A}\mathbf{p},$$

which says that the amount of labour embodied in the output of each process is equal to direct labour plus the amount of labour embodied in the inputs of each process. 'Nature' contributes coal directly in the first process only; the workforce contributes labour in all processes. 'Intensities' are then a kind of 'price' as well as 'activity levels'.

The coal intensity of commodity i can thus also be given by

$$q_i^1 = \mathbf{q}_i\mathbf{e}^1$$

and the labour values of commodity i by

$$p_i = \mathbf{q}_i \mathbf{l},$$

$\mathbf{q}_i$ being activity levels of subsystem i and $\mathbf{e}^1$, $\mathbf{l}$ being the 'sources' of coal and labour respectively (though $\mathbf{e}^1$ denotes the produced coal, not the coal underground).

In vector form we have

$$\mathbf{q}^1 = (\mathbf{I} - \mathbf{A})^{-1}\mathbf{e}^1$$

and

$$\mathbf{p} = (\mathbf{I} - \mathbf{A})^{-1}\mathbf{l}.$$

The coal intensities have to be distinguished from the coal values considered above, which are given by $\hat{\mathbf{p}}/\hat{p}_1$, where $\hat{\mathbf{A}}\hat{\mathbf{p}} = \hat{\mathbf{p}}$. In particular, the coal value of a unit of coal is (by analogy with the gold price of gold and the labour value of labour) equal to one while the coal intensity of coal is greater than one.

Technical change, which invariably lowers labour values under present assumptions and which always raises a commodity value if it lowers its reciprocal, will on the whole tend to raise commodity intensities, because the increase in the productivity of labour through falls in components of l_i is most frequently attained through increased use of raw materials and, in particular, energy commodities. An increase in coefficients of $\mathbf{A}$ raises all intensities because

$$(\mathbf{I} - \mathbf{A})^{-1} = \mathbf{I} + \mathbf{A} + \mathbf{A}^2 + \cdots.$$

Matters are somewhat more complicated with joint production. Activity levels will still be given by

$$\mathbf{Q} = (\mathbf{B} - \mathbf{A})^{-1}$$

if we are dealing with joint production, but intensities will be different from $\mathbf{Q}$ and denoted by $\bar{\mathbf{Q}}$. We have

$$\bar{\mathbf{Q}} = (\mathbf{B} - \mathbf{A})^{-1}\mathbf{A} + \mathbf{I},$$

for $\mathbf{q}_i = \mathbf{e}_i(\mathbf{B} - \mathbf{A})^{-1}$ will still be the activity levels appropriate for subsystem i, and $\mathbf{q}_i\mathbf{a}^j$ will be the amount of commodity j used as an input in subsystem i, so that $\bar{q}_i^j = \mathbf{q}_i\mathbf{a}^j + \delta_i^j$ ($\delta_i^j = 1$ for $i = j$ and $\delta_i^j = 0$ for $i \neq j$) are the gross amounts of commodity j produced in subsystem i ($\mathbf{q}_i\mathbf{a}^j$ is the input, δ_i^j the net output of commodity j in subsystem i). The matrix of commodity intensities $\bar{\mathbf{Q}}$ will be equal to the matrix of activity levels of subsystems $\mathbf{Q}$ if and only if

$$\mathbf{Q} = (\mathbf{B} - \mathbf{A})^{-1} = (\mathbf{B} - \mathbf{A})^{-1}\mathbf{A} + \mathbf{I} = \bar{\mathbf{Q}}$$

or if and only if $\mathbf{B} = \mathbf{I}$. Coal intensities can hardly be interpreted as prices in analogy to $\mathbf{q}^1 = \mathbf{e}^1 + \mathbf{A}\mathbf{q}^1$ above, since the vector of sources for coal (above $\mathbf{e}^1$) cannot be identified with joint production. The relationship between commodities and labour values remains the same, however. The subsystems approach allows us to interpret

$$\mathbf{p} = (\mathbf{B} - \mathbf{A})^{-1}\mathbf{l}$$

as labour values as above, and relative labour values can still be interpreted as relative commodity values measuring the rate of substitution:

$$\mathbf{q}'(\mathbf{B} - \mathbf{A}) = \mathbf{s}', \qquad \mathbf{q}'\mathbf{l} = L$$

entails

$$\frac{\partial \mathbf{s}'}{\partial s_j}(\mathbf{B} - \mathbf{A})^{-1}\mathbf{l} = 0$$

and

$$\frac{\partial s_i}{\partial s_j} = -\frac{p_j}{p_i}.$$

The private rate of commodity exchange p_j/p_i (which ensures reproduction) is thus still equal to the social rate determining the 'exchange' of a certain amount of s_i for a unit of s_j.

In the case of joint production, the open model can again be closed. It suffices to consider the equations

$$\mathbf{A}\mathbf{p} + \mathbf{l} = \mathbf{B}\mathbf{p}$$

and

$$\hat{\mathbf{A}}\hat{\mathbf{p}} = \hat{\mathbf{B}}\hat{\mathbf{p}}$$

where

$$\hat{\mathbf{A}} = \begin{bmatrix} \mathbf{A} & \mathbf{l} \\ \mathbf{s}' & 0 \end{bmatrix}, \qquad \hat{\mathbf{B}} = \begin{bmatrix} \mathbf{B} & \mathbf{o} \\ \mathbf{o} & 1 \end{bmatrix}.$$

The interpretation of commodity values and of relative prices as rates of substitution remains the same; the point, however, is to use it for the explanation of negative values.

If all labour values are positive, commodity values are positive, too, and no problem arises. But if (and only if) the value of one commodity is negative, net output can be increased using less labour and producing more of the commodity in question. This has been discussed in Part II. It follows here from the fact that $\partial s_i/\partial s_j$ will be positive if p_j/p_i is negative. It may again be illustrated by means of an old machine with a negative price. Net output can be increased by shifting employment from the oldest to younger machines in such a way that net output stays constant. The old machine will then be overproduced and labour will have been saved thanks to the increased use of the relatively more efficient new machines. But one could similarly shift labour to younger machines keeping employment constant and increasing the production of any commodity X_i with a positive price. The oldest machine would appear in the net product and its increased production would be 'substituted' for the increased production of commodity X_i; the possibility of producing more of X_i would be 'bought' by the production of more of the old machine and reflected in the negative rate of substitution. The 'proto-economic concepts' discussed in this essay thus serve both as methodological tools for introducing value, relative price and absolute price, and as technical concepts in their own right which are useful for understanding the structure of production.

Not much attention has been paid to these concepts so far by other authors who have, when talking about Sraffa's theory of value, mainly been interested in the standard commodity. It is of course true that the standard commodity represents Sraffa's most fascinating single contribution to the theory of value because of the inferences that can be drawn from it, but it should not be overlooked that the standard commodity is systematically rooted in Sraffa's very peculiar method of laying new foundations for the classical theory of value, which is close to the Ricardian and Marxian tradition but not identical with either.

The standard commodity sheds light on the problem of distribution by means of a peculiar normalization of prices. We then combine the analysis of profits in the second model of this essay with an analysis of the model opened up for wage labour.

In the single-product Sraffa system

$$(1 + r)\mathbf{Ap} + w\mathbf{l} = \mathbf{p}$$

prices in labour commanded are equal to labour values at $r = 0$; they rise monotonically afterwards and diverge to infinity as r approaches the maximum rate of profit. They rise with different 'speeds', however. On the one hand, this causes the main difficulty in understanding the theory; on the other, it constitutes the basis of Sraffa's critique of the theory of capital. The standard commodity is supposed to render this movement transparent.

In order to introduce it, the equations for prices are normalized by taking net national product as the first standard of measurement. We then have

$$1 = \mathbf{e}'(\mathbf{I} - \mathbf{A})\mathbf{p} = w\mathbf{e}'\mathbf{l} + r\mathbf{e}'\mathbf{Ap}.$$

Wages $w\mathbf{e}'\mathbf{l}$ and profits $r\mathbf{e}'\mathbf{Ap}$ add up to unity. In order to understand the changes in prices caused by variations in the rate of profit, we differentiate the price equations and obtain

$$\mathbf{p}' = w'\mathbf{l} + \mathbf{Ap} + (1 + r)\mathbf{Ap}',$$

therefore (the prime denoting the derivative)

$$\mathbf{p}' = [\mathbf{I} - (1 + r)\mathbf{A}]^{-1}(w'\mathbf{l} + \mathbf{Ap}).$$

The latter expression can be developed into a series; one then obtains

$$\mathbf{p}' = (w'\mathbf{l} + \mathbf{Ap}) + (1 + r)\mathbf{A}(w'\mathbf{l} + \mathbf{Ap}) + (1 + r)^2\mathbf{A}^2(w'\mathbf{l} + \mathbf{Ap}) + \cdots.$$

Hence we obtain $\mathbf{p}' = \mathbf{o}$ and prices do not change if $w'\mathbf{l} + \mathbf{Ap} = \mathbf{o}$. From $w'\mathbf{l} + \mathbf{Ap} = w'\mathbf{l} + w\mathbf{A}[\mathbf{I} - (1 + r)\mathbf{A}]^{-1}\mathbf{l} = \mathbf{o}$ follows that $\mathbf{l}$ must be an eigenvector of matrix $\mathbf{A}$ in this case,[2] and, since vector $\mathbf{l}$ is positive, the equation $(1 + R)\mathbf{Al} = \mathbf{l}$ follows. One can conclude from this that all prices are stationary at a rate of profit at the same time if they are constant at all rates of profit and equal to labour values. And (unless matrix $\mathbf{A}$ has a very exceptional structure as in an irregular system – see section II.3) this will happen if and only if the labour vector is an eigenvector of matrix $\mathbf{A}$ – which can be the case only by an extremely unlikely coincidence. If prices are, as we shall now assume, not equal to labour values, we have $w'\mathbf{l} + \mathbf{Ap} \neq \mathbf{o}$ for all r.

The formula derived above for $\mathbf{p}'$ demonstrates that a component p_i' of vector $\mathbf{p}'$ will vanish *in first approximation* at a given rate of profit if $w' l_i + \mathbf{a}_i\mathbf{p} = 0$ obtains there where l_i is the i'th component of the labour vector and $\mathbf{a}_i$ the i'th row of matrix $\mathbf{A}$. In other words: the price of the i'th commodity is stationary in first approximation if at a given rate of profit

$$-w' = \frac{\mathbf{a}_i\mathbf{p}}{l_i}$$

holds. This relationship defines a 'watershed' between industries whose commodities rise in price with an increase in the rate of profit and others whose prices fall. The 'watershed' is not precisely the one mentioned by Sraffa, however. If the ratio of the price of the means of production $\mathbf{a}_i$ to labour employed l_i in an industry corresponds to the absolute value of the change in the wage rate, the price of the product of the industry will be stationary in first approximation; one may conclude from the same formula for $\mathbf{p}'$ that commodities of industries with

$$\frac{\mathbf{a}_i\mathbf{p}}{l_i} > -w'$$

will rise in price with a small increase in the rate of profit in first approximation and fall in the reverse case.[3]

If one considers the formula in which $\mathbf{p}'$ is expressed as an infinite series, one can see that p_i' will vanish in *first and second approximation* if not only $-w' = \mathbf{a}_i\mathbf{p}/l_i$, but also $-w' = \mathbf{a}_i\mathbf{Ap}/\mathbf{a}_i\mathbf{l}$ holds. The second of these equations means simply that not only the price of the means of production used directly in the industry to direct labour, but also the price of the raw materials used in the previous period and 'embodied' in the means of production $\mathbf{a}_i$ must be in the same ratio to 'embodied' labour of the previous period $\mathbf{a}_i\mathbf{l}$ as the 'watershed proportion' $-w'$ if p_i' is to vanish in first and second approximation. If it appears from the first approximation that the price of a commodity i must rise because $\mathbf{a}_i\mathbf{p}/l_i > -w'$, one may be deceived because it is possible that $\mathbf{a}_i\mathbf{Ap}/\mathbf{a}_i\mathbf{l} < -w'$ holds in second approximation. These complications are discussed by Sraffa in his section 20.

The exact calculation requires taking into account all higher terms

$$\frac{\mathbf{a}_i\mathbf{A}^2\mathbf{p}}{\mathbf{a}_i\mathbf{Al}}, \frac{\mathbf{a}_i\mathbf{A}^3\mathbf{p}}{\mathbf{a}_i\mathbf{A}^2\mathbf{l}} \text{ etc.,}$$

which indicate the proportions in which means of production and labour from periods of production lying still further in the past are 'embodied' in commodity i.

The price of commodity i would therefore be exactly stationary for all rates of profit between 0 and R if the infinite series of equations

$$-w' = \frac{\mathbf{a}_i\mathbf{p}}{l_i} = \frac{\mathbf{a}_i\mathbf{Ap}}{\mathbf{a}_i\mathbf{l}} = \frac{\mathbf{a}_i\mathbf{A}^2\mathbf{p}}{\mathbf{a}_i\mathbf{Al}} = \cdots \quad \text{for} \quad 0 \leqslant r < R$$

held (PCMC, sec. 21).

This is not the only possibility for a constant price. If commodity i served only as a standard of prices, its price would stay constant even if the infinite series of equations above did not hold. But the fulfilment of the infinite series of equations is the only condition under which changes in prices do not disappear trivially and artificially from the fact that the corresponding commodity is the standard of prices, but from the deeper-rooted proportions between means of production and labour employed, which are, as we have seen, really responsible for the changes of prices. If we can find a standard of prices for which the infinite series of equations holds, the corresponding w' denotes the 'watershed' or the equilibrium proportion discussed by Sraffa (PCMC, secs 17, 21 and 22).

We now assume that a commodity, or rather a combination of commodities, expressed by a vector $\mathbf{b}$ fulfilled the infinite series of equations; i.e. we should have

$$-w' = \frac{\mathbf{b}'\mathbf{A}^{t+1}\mathbf{p}}{\mathbf{b}'\mathbf{A}^t\mathbf{l}} = w\frac{\mathbf{b}'\mathbf{A}[\mathbf{I} - (1+r)\mathbf{A}]^{-1}\mathbf{A}^t\mathbf{l}}{\mathbf{b}'\mathbf{A}^t\mathbf{l}}, \quad t = 0, 1, 2, \ldots,$$

therefore:

$$\mathbf{b}'\{w\mathbf{A}[\mathbf{I} - (1+r)\mathbf{A}]^{-1} + w'\mathbf{I}\}\mathbf{A}^t\mathbf{l} = 0, \quad t = 0, 1, 2, \ldots$$

Matrix $\mathbf{A}$ is of order n. Since the vectors $\mathbf{l}, \mathbf{Al}, \mathbf{A}^2\mathbf{l}, \ldots, \mathbf{A}^{n-1}\mathbf{l}$ are linearly independent (except in the economically trivial case where $\mathbf{l}$ is an eigenvector of matrix $\mathbf{A}$, i.e. where prices equal values, and except for special cases of only mathematical relevance[4]), it follows that

$$w\mathbf{b}'\mathbf{A}[\mathbf{I} - (1+r)\mathbf{A}]^{-1} = -w'\mathbf{b}'$$

hence that **b** must be an eigenvector of matrix **A** where **b**, because of **b** $\geqslant$ **o**, must be the Frobenius eigenvector with eigenvalue $1/(1 + R)$. From

$$w\mathbf{b}'\mathbf{A} = \frac{w}{1 + R}\,\mathbf{b}' = -\,w'\mathbf{b}'\,[\mathbf{I} - (1 + r)\mathbf{A}] = -\,w'\left[1 - \frac{1 + r}{1 + R}\right]\mathbf{b}'$$

we obtain the differential equation

$$w + w'(R - r) = 0$$

which can be integrated

$$\int \frac{\mathrm{d}w}{w} = -\int \frac{1}{R - r}\,\mathrm{d}r$$

to yield

$$\ln\,w = \ln(R - r) + C.$$

If the constant is chosen so as to fulfil the initial condition $w(0) = 1$, we obtain the familiar formula for the wage in terms of the standard commodity

$$w = 1 - \frac{r}{R}.$$

By means of an argument quite different from that used in Part I, we have thus shown that the 'invariant standard of value' fulfilling the infinite series of equations must consist of basic commodities produced by a complex of industries that use the same basic commodities in the same proportions as inputs. The standard commodity is therefore like Ricardo's 'corn' produced by an industry whose inputs are physically homogeneous with the output. The initial condition $w(0) = 1$ implies

$$\mathbf{b}'(\mathbf{I} - \mathbf{A})\mathbf{p} = \mathbf{b}'\mathbf{l} = 1,$$

hence **b**' is equal to Sraffa's standard commodity, which was defined by $(1 + R)\mathbf{q}'\mathbf{A} = \mathbf{q}'$, where the definitions $\mathbf{e}'\mathbf{l} = 1$ for **l** and $\mathbf{q}'\mathbf{l} = 1$ for **q** were chosen as normalizations of **l** and **q** so that we had

$$1 = \mathbf{q}'(\mathbf{I} - \mathbf{A})\mathbf{p} = r\mathbf{q}'\mathbf{A}\mathbf{p} + w\mathbf{q}'\mathbf{l} = \frac{r}{R}\,\mathbf{q}'(\mathbf{I} - \mathbf{A})\mathbf{p} + w\mathbf{q}'\mathbf{l},$$

$$1 = \frac{r}{R} + w,$$

i.e. the linear relationship between the rate of profit and wages obtained by Sraffa in PCMC sec. 30.

Sraffa therefore bases his choice of the standard commodity on reasoning that is independent of the main result, which is derived later by means of the standard commodity, i.e. the linear relationship between the rate of wages and the rate of profits. His theory of price movements explains why the standard commodity may be justly considered as an invariant standard of value: the standard commodity is – according to our proof – the only 'commodity' for which (if it is used as a price standard) the prices of the means of production and of labour employed in the current period, and indirectly also in all previous periods, are always to be found in the same proportion. Thus the inequality of the proportions that is the fundamental cause of price changes, according to the reasoning given above, is *absent* for the standard commodity (and only for it). Only after this proof has been given is it shown further that the invariant standard of value has, like 'corn' in Ricardo's simple model, the property of being produced by an industry whose means of production are physically homogeneous with the produced product (PCMC, sec. 24), and in section 30 the linear relationship between wages and rates of profit is derived. It is therefore not correct if the meaning of the standard commodity is in the literature seen only in connection with the latter theorem.

The contrast between the three properties of the standard commodity can be made clearer if the assumption according to which the wage is paid only after the end of the period of production is replaced by the assumption of a wage paid in advance. The first two properties of the standard commodity (invariant standard of value in the sense of the analysis given above of an infinite regress to the means of production and labour embodied on the one hand; homogeneity of product and means of production on the other) will then be retained *mutatis mutandis*, whereas the relationship between the wage rate and the rate of profit turns out to be more complicated.

From

$$\mathbf{q}'(\mathbf{I} - \mathbf{A})\mathbf{p} = (1 + r)w\mathbf{q}'\mathbf{l} + r\mathbf{q}'\mathbf{A}\mathbf{p}$$

$$= (1 + r)w + \frac{r}{R}\mathbf{q}'(\mathbf{I} - \mathbf{A})\mathbf{p}$$

$$= (1 + r)w + \frac{r}{R} = 1$$

one obtains the relationship $w = (R - r)/[R(1 + r)]$. It represents one branch of a hyperbola that cuts the r axis at the maximum rate of profit and the w axis at $w = 1$, with $w'(0) = -[1 + (1/R)]$ (Figure III.6.1).

It is easily seen that the same reasoning applies to those joint-production systems that have a unique standard commodity such that the infinite series

$$\mathbf{p} = w[\mathbf{B} - (1 + r)\mathbf{A}]^{-1}\mathbf{l}$$
$$= w[\mathbf{I} - (1 + r)\mathbf{B}^{-1}\mathbf{A}]^{-1}\mathbf{B}^{-1}\mathbf{l}$$
$$= w\mathbf{B}^{-1}\mathbf{l} + (1 + r)\mathbf{B}^{-1}\mathbf{A}\mathbf{B}^{-1}\mathbf{l} + (1 + r)^2(\mathbf{B}^{-1}\mathbf{A})^2\mathbf{B}^{-1}\mathbf{l} + \cdots$$

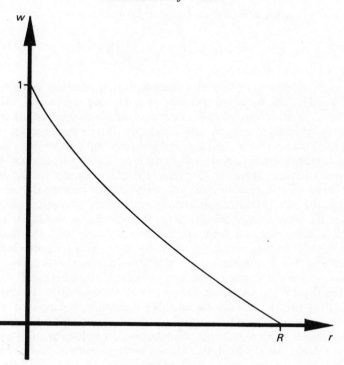

Figure III.6.1

exists and converges. This series was discussed in sections II.4 and II.6. For those joint-production systems that possess a standard commodity but cannot be expanded in such a series, the use of the standard commodity is restricted to providing the analogue of the corn model and the linear wage curve. Any attempt to interpret changes in relative prices caused by changes in the rate of profit in terms of a reduction to proportions between indirect inputs of means of production and labour then fails.

Standard prices are useful for intuitive reasoning because they may be interpreted as transformed labour values; their dimension is labour-time per unit of product. For the normalization $q'1 = 1$ means that the components q_i of the standard vector of q have the dimension of commodity i divided by the dimension of labour, a_i^j has the dimension of commodity j divided by that of commodity i, p_j has the dimension of labour divided by that of commodity j, and r (and R) are dimensionless (since time is divided into fixed periods) so that the equations, with w as a share,

$$1 = q'(I - A)p = rq'Ap + wq'1 = \frac{r}{R} + w$$

can be seen to be dimensionally consistent. Standard prices are equal, not just proportional, to labour values at $r = 0$; at positive rates of profit r they are equal to prices $\hat{p}$ in terms of labour commanded, multiplied by the corresponding fraction of the standard wage, *w*:

$$\mathbf{p} = w\hat{\mathbf{p}} = \left(1 - \frac{r}{R}\right)\hat{\mathbf{p}}.$$

The transformation of labour values to standard prices is such that the total value of the standard commodity $\mathbf{q}'(\mathbf{I} - \mathbf{A})$ is equal to total labour employed at all rates of profit. But this transformation of labour values is, as we have seen, not the one sought by Marx, since it does not allow total profits to be represented as redistributed surplus value. The interest in these transformed labour values derives, as with Ricardo's invariable measure of value, from the fact that labour values express the direct and indirect productivity of labour, and the standard commodity allows us to confer this interpretation on absolute prices by excluding the effect of 'unequal compositions of capital' in the numéraire commodity.

Sraffa constructs his standard commodity only with the pedagogical intention of making the logic of prices more transparent. There is no pretention that a monetary authority should ever try to devise a system of state-managed money that would imitate the effects of a standard commodity. Whereas Ricardo may well have hoped to understand capitalism better in order to improve economic policy, and may have sought for an invariable standard of value in order to find a real measure of the effects of progress and distribution on value, Sraffa's purpose is analytic and critical: the standard commodity is an expository device that renders his critique of capital theory more concise and allows the exposition of the book to be structured by stressing the importance of the standard system, and therefore the distinction between basics and non-basics, etc.

It follows, first, that the standard commodity – however prominent it may appear to be in the book – does not add to Sraffa's theory as a contribution to positive economics in the classical tradition in the same way as, say, the distinction between basics and non-basics, or the method of considering technology and distribution as given, are of immediate practical relevance by pointing towards an approach to applied economics that is an alternative to the neoclassical approach.

The standard commodity has led to a definition of absolute value that has nothing to do with absolute value in the real world, i.e. money. This is perfectly consistent with Sraffa's definition of value given in the opening chapter of his book. His point is to show that relative prices depend on the structure of the economy in a self-replacing state. There is no obvious necessary link between a theory of relative prices in this sense and a theory of money. The link between the proto-economic concepts introduced above and money, based on uncertainty, represents a trail not pursued by Sraffa himself. The gap left by this lack of a theory of money is filled by a theory of absolute values that really serves only to explain relative value.

It follows, secondly, that the standard commodity is not a very important element in a mathematical treatment of theories of prices of production of the type discussed by Sraffa. Mathematical methods allow the pattern of price movements to be grasped directly; the standard commodity is useful because it allows complicated mathematical relationships to be explained in economic terms and a firm analogy to be established between a system with many commodities (and indeed with joint production) and Ricardo's 'corn' model. These are the reasons why the standard commodity figures so much less prominently in this book – which may be regarded as a commentary on Sraffa – than in *Production of Commodities by Means of Commodities* itself.

Notes

1 The input matrix of a single-product system is indecomposable if and only if it is basic. It is here called basic if for every pair i and j a chain of coefficients $a_{i_1}^j, a_{i_2}^{i_1}, a_{i_3}^{i_2}, ..., a_i^{i_k}$ can be formed such that no element of the chain vanishes, for it is then clear that every commodity enters directly or indirectly the production of every other commodity, because an amount $a_i^{i_k}$ of commodity i_k enters the production of commodity i, an amount $a_{i_k}^{i_{k-1}}$ of commodity i_{k-1} enters the production of commodity i_k, an amount $a_{i_1}^j$ of commodity j enters the production of commodity i_1 so that commodity j enters the production of commodity i_1 directly and the production of commodity i indirectly. It is intuitively plausible, and can be proved rigorously, that a non-negative square matrix is indecomposable if and only if the matrix corresponds to an economic system in which every commodity is a basic commodity in this sense. The proof of this fact is to be based on the observation that the 'chains' that have been mentioned are elements of the powers $\mathbf{A}^2, \mathbf{A}^3 ...$ of matrix $\mathbf{A}$ the sum of which is positive if and only if $\mathbf{A}$ is indecomposable.

2 According to the theorem concerning the commutability of the elements of the matrix-ring generated by a matrix, one obtains

$$w'\mathbf{l} + w\mathbf{A}[\mathbf{I} - (1 + r)\mathbf{A}]^{-1}\mathbf{l} = w'\mathbf{l} + w[\mathbf{I} - (1 + r)\mathbf{A}]^{-1}\mathbf{A}\mathbf{l} = \mathbf{o}$$

therefore

$$\frac{w'}{w}\mathbf{l} = \left\{ \frac{w'}{w}(1 + r) - 1 \right\}\mathbf{A}\mathbf{l},$$

and hence after some steps by integration $w = 1 - r/R$, therefore the same relationship as will be derived below for the standard commodity.

3 From the formula $1 = \mathbf{e}'(\mathbf{I} - \mathbf{A})\mathbf{p} = w\mathbf{e}'\mathbf{l} + r\mathbf{e}\mathbf{A}\mathbf{p}$ we obtain for w' by differentiation

$$-w' = \frac{\mathbf{e}\mathbf{A}\mathbf{p}}{\mathbf{e}\mathbf{l}} + r\frac{\mathbf{e}'\mathbf{A}\mathbf{p}'}{\mathbf{e}'\mathbf{l}}.$$

The 'watershed proportion' $-w'$ therefore equals the labour value of capital employed divided by total labour employed at $r = 0$. It follows from this that the price of a commodity differs only a little from labour value at small rates of profit if the ratio of capital to labour, expressed in labour values, corresponds in this industry to the average of the economy. One might call this result – which we have obtained in passing – 'Marx's theorem' since he uses the relationship frequently, without, however, knowing that it is true only in first approximation.

4   If the system is not regular in the sense of the definition given above in Part
    II. The vectors

$$\mathbf{l}, \mathbf{A}\mathbf{l}, \mathbf{A}^2\mathbf{l}, ..., \mathbf{A}^{n-1}\mathbf{l}$$

will be linearly independent if and only if the corresponding system is regular
as was proved first in Schefold (1976a, c).

Bibliography

Abraham-Frois, G. and Berrebi, E. (1976), *Théorie de la valeur, des prix et de l'accumulation* (Paris: Economica). Transl. as *Theory of Value, Prices and Accumulation – A Mathematical Integration of Marx, von Neumann and Sraffa* (Cambridge: Cambridge University Press, 1978).

d'Agata, A. (1983), 'The existence and unicity of cost-minimizing systems in intensive rent theory', *Metroeconomica*, vol. 35 nos 1–2, pp. 147–58.

Arena, R. *et al.* (1982), *Etudes d'économie classique et néoricardienne* (Grenoble: Presses Universitaires de France).

Bain, J. S. (1956), *Barriers to New Competition* (Cambridge, Mass.: Harvard University Press).

Baldone, S. (1980), 'Fixed capital in Sraffa's theoretical scheme', in L. L. Pasinetti (ed.), *Essays on the Theory of Joint Production* (London and Basingstoke: Macmillan), pp. 88–137. Originally published as 'Il capitale fisso nello schema teorico di Piero Sraffa', *Studi Economici*, vol. 29, no. 1 (1974), pp. 45–106.

Becker, W. (1972), *Kritik der Marxschen Wertlehre* (Hamburg: Hoffmann & Campe).

Besnier, B. (1970), 'Le taux de profit et la "loi" de la valeur', *Annali dell' Istituto G. Feltrinelli* (Feltrinelli).

Bhaduri, A. (1969), 'On the significance of recent controversies on capital theory: A Marxian view', *Economic Journal*, vol. 79, pp. 532–9.

Bharadwaj, K. (1963), 'Value through exogenous distribution', *The Economic Weekly*, pp. 1450–4.

Bharadwaj, K. (1970), 'On the maximum number of switches between two production systems', *Schweizerische Zeitschrift für Volkswirtschaftslehre und Statistik*, vol. 106, pp. 409–29.

Bidard, C. ([1982]1984), 'Choix techniques en production jointe', in C. Bidard (ed.), *La Production jointe – nouveaux débats* (Paris: Economica), pp. 186–207.

Bomel, Ph. (1976). 'Théorie de la production et formes du capital productif', PhD thesis, University of Nice.

Brunhoff, S. de ([1972]1973), 'Marx a-Ricardien: Valeur, monaie et prix au début du capital', mimeo, Nice. Transl. and repr. as 'Marx as an a-Ricardian – value, money and price at the beginning of Capital', *Economy and Society*, vol. 2, pp. 421–30.

Cannan, E. ([1893]1967), *A History of the Theories of Production and Distribution from 1776 to 1848* (London: A. Kelley).

Cartelier, J. (1979), 'La théorie de la rente dans la logique ricardienne', *Cahiers d'Économie Politique*, vol. 5, pp. 11–20.

Chamberlin, E. ([1948] 1962), *The Theory of Monopolistic Competition*, 8th edn (Cambridge, Mass.: Harvard University).

Clapham, J. C. (1922), 'Of empty economic boxes', *Economic Journal*, vol. 32, p. 305–14.

Cogoy, M. (1974), 'Das Dilemma der neoricardianischen Theorie', in H.-G. Backhaus *et al.* (eds), *Gesellschaft, Beiträge zur Marxschen Theorie*, vol. 2 (Frankfurt/M.: Suhrkamp), pp. 204–63.

Debreu G. ([1959] 1971), *Theory of Value: An Axiomatic Analysis of Economic Equilibrium* (New Haven, Conn. and London: Yale University Press).

Dobb, M. (1973), *Theories of Value and Distribution since Adam Smith* (Cambridge: Cambridge University Press).

Eatwell, J. (1975a), 'Scarce and produced commodities', PhD thesis, Harvard University, Cambridge (Mass.).

Eatwell, J. (1975b), 'The interpretation of Ricardo's "Essay on Profits"', *Economica*, vol. 42, pp. 182–7.

Eatwell, J. and Milgate, M. (eds) (1983), *Keynes's Economics and the Theory of Value and Distribution* (London: Duckworth).

Engels, F. (1894), 'Herrn Eugen Dührings Umwälzung der Wissenschaft (Anti-Dühring)', *Marx-Engels-Werke*, vol. 20 (Berlin: Dietz Verlag, 1972), pp. 3–303.

Gahlen, B. (1972), *Der Informationsgehalt der neoklassischen Wachstums-theorie für die Wirtschaftspolitik* (Tübingen: J. C. B. Mohr (Paul Siebeck)).

Gale, D. (1956), 'The closed linear model of production', in H. W. Kuhn and A. W. Tucker (eds), *Linear Inequalities and Related Systems* (Princeton, NJ: Princeton University Press), pp. 285–303.

Gantmacher, F. R. (1966), *Matrizenrechnung II* (Berlin: VEB Deutscher Verlag der Wissenschaften).

Garegnani, P. (1960), *Il capitale nelle teorie della distribuzione* (Milan: Dott. A. Giuffrè). Transl. into French as *Le Capital dans les théories de la répartitation* (Paris: Presses Universitaires de Grenoble).

Garegnani, P. (1964/5), 'Note su consumi, investmenti e domanda effettiva', *Economia Internazionale*, vols 17 and 18. Transl. and repr. as 'Notes on consumption, investment and effective demand', *Cambridge Journal of Economics*, vol. 2, pp. 335–53 and vol. 3, pp. 63–82. Repr. in J. Eatwell and M. Milgate (eds), *Keynes's Economics and the Theory of Value and Distribution* (London: Duckworth), pp. 21–69.

Garegnani, P. (1970). 'Heterogeneous capital, the production function and the theory of distribution', *Review of Economic Studies*, vol. 37, pp. 407–36.

Gibson, B. and McLeod, D. (1980), 'Land, non-basics and joint production', mimeo.

Gramsci, A. (1968), *Lettere dal carcere*, 2nd edn (Turin: Einaudi). Transl. into English as *Letters from Prison* (London: Harper & Row, 1975).

Gregory, C. A. (1982), *Gifts and Commodities* (London: Academic Press).

Gröbner, W. (1966), *Matrizenrechnung* (Mannheim: Bibliographisches Institut Mannheim).

Guichard, J. P. (1979), 'Rente foncière et dynamique sociale', PhD thesis, University of Nice.

Harcourt, G. (1969), 'Some Cambridge controversies in the theory of capital', *Journal of Economic Literature*, vol. 7, pp. 369–405.

Harcourt, G. (1972), *Some Cambridge Controversies in the Theory of Capital* (Cambridge: Cambridge University Press).

Harcourt, G. and Laing, N. (eds) (1971), *Capital and Growth* (Harmondsworth, Middx: Penguin).

Hicks (1970), 'A neo-Austrian growth theory', *Economic Journal*, vol. 80, pp. 257–81.

Hollander, S. (1973), 'Ricardo's analysis of the profit rate 1813–1815', *Economica*, vol. 40, pp. 260–82.

Hollander, S. (1975), 'Ricardo and the corn profit model: Reply to Eatwell', *Economica*, vol. 42, pp. 188–202.

Hotelling, H. (1931), 'The economics of exhaustible resources', *Journal of Political Economy*, vol. 39, pp. 137–75.

Hunt, E. K. and Schwartz, J. G. (eds) (1972), *A Critique of Economic Theory* (Harmondsworth, Middx: Penguin).

Jevons, W. St. ([1871] 1970), *Political Economy* (Harmondsworth, Middx: Penguin).

Kaldor, N. (1956), 'Alternative theories of distribution', *Review of Economic Studies*, vol. 23, no. 2, pp. 83–100.

Kaldor, N. (1966), 'Marginal productivity and the macroeconomic theories of distribution', *Review of Economic Studies*, vol. 33, pp. 309–19. Repr. in G. Harcourt and N. Laing (eds), *Capital and Growth* (Harmondsworth, Middx: Penguin, 1971).

Kemeny, T. G., Morgenstern, O. and Thompson, G. L. (1956), 'A generalization of the von Neumann model of an expanding economy', *Econometrica*, vol. 24, pp. 115–35.

Keynes, J. M. (1971–9), *The Collected Writings of John Maynard Keynes* (London and Basingstoke: Macmillan).

Keynes, J. M. ([1936] 1967), *The General Theory of Employment, Interest and Money* (London and Basingstoke: Macmillan).

Kurz, H. D. (1977), *Zur neoricardianischen Theorie des Allgemeinen Gleichgewichts der Produktion und Zirkulation – Wert und Verteilung in Piero Sraffas 'Production of Commodities by Means of Commodities'* (Berlin: Duncker & Humblot).

Kurz, H. D. (1980/1), 'Smithian themes in Piero Sraffa's theory', *Journal of Post-Keynesian Economics*, vol. 3, no. 2, pp. 271–80.

Kurz, H. D. (1986), 'Classical and early neo-classical economists on joint production', *Metroeconomica*, vol. 38, pp. 1–37.

Leontief, W. ([1951] 1976), *The Structure of the American Economy 1919–1939 – An Empirical Application of Equilibrium Analysis*, 2nd edn (White Plains, NY: International Arts and Sciences Press).

Levhari, D. (1966), 'A non-substitution theorem and switching of techniques', *Quarterly Journal of Economics*, vol. 79, pp. 98–105.

Lippi. M. (1979), *I prezzi di produzione* (Bologna: Il Mulino).

Łoš, J. (1976), 'Extended von Neumann model and game theory', in J. Łoš, M. Łoš (eds) *Computing Equilibria – How and Why?* (Amsterdam: North Holland).

Malcom, N. (1958), *Ludwig Wittgenstein. A Memoir* (London, New York, Toronto: Oxford University Press).

Manara, C. F. (1968), 'Il modello di Piero Sraffa per la produzione congiunta di merci a mezzo di merci', *L'industria*, vol. 1, pp. 3–18. Transl. and repr. as

'Sraffa's model for the joint production of commodities by means of commodities' in L. L. Pasinetti (ed.), *Essays on the Theory of Joint Production* (London and Basingstoke: Macmillan, 1980), pp. 1–15.

Marshall, A. ([1920] 1966), *Principles of Economics*, 8th edn (London and Basingstoke: Macmillan).

Marx, K. ([1857–8] 1974), *Grundrisse der politischen Ökonomie* (Berlin: Dietz Verlag).

Marx, K. ([1867–94] 1972), *Das Kapital – Kritik der politischen Ökonomie*, vols I–III (Berlin: Dietz). Transl. as *Capital* (1954), vols I–III (London: Lawrence & Wishart, 1977).

Marx, K. ([1861/63] 1974), *Theorien über den Mehrwert*, vol. II (Berlin: Dietz). Transl. as *Theories of Surplus Value*, vol. II (Moscow: Progress Publishers, 1968).

Medick, H. (1973), *Naturzustand und Naturgeschichte in der bürgerlichen Gesellschaft* (Göttingen: Vandenhoeck & Ruprecht).

Mill, J. St. ([1848] 1970), *Principles of Political Economy* (Harmondsworth, Middx: Penguin).

Morishima, M. (1964), *Equilibrium, Stability and Growth* (Oxford: Oxford University Press).

Morishima, M. (1973), *Marx's Economics* (Cambridge: Cambridge University Press.).

Morishima, M. and Seton, F. (1961), 'Aggregation in Leontief matrices and the labour theory of value', *Econometrica*, vol. 29, pp. 203–20.

Napoleoni, C. (1974), *Ricardo und Marx* (Frankfurt/M.: Suhrkamp).

Neumann, J. von (1945/6), 'A model of general economic equilibrium', *Review of Economic Studies*, vol. 12, pp. 1–9. Originally published as 'Über ein ökonomisches Gleichungssystem und eine Verallgemeinerung des Brouwerschen Fixpunktsatzes', in K. Menger (ed.), *Ergebnisse eines Mathematischen Kolloquiums* (Leipzig: Franz Deuticke, 1935/6), pp. 73–83.

Newman, P. (1962), 'Production of commodities by means of commodities', *Schweizerische Zeitschrift für Volkswirtschaft und Statistik*, vol. 98, pp. 58–75.

Nuti, D. M. (1973), 'On the truncation of production flows', *Kyklos*, vol. 26, pp. 485–96.

Okishio, N. (1963), 'A mathematical note on Marxian theorems', *Weltwirtschaftliches Archiv*, vol. 91, pp. 287–99.

Parrinello, S. (1970), 'Introduzione ad una teoria neoricardiana del commercio internazionale', *Studi economici*, pp. 267–321.

Parrinello, S. 1982 'Exhaustible natural resources and the classical method of long period equilibrium', in J. A. Kregel (ed.), *Distribution, Effective Demand and International Economic Relations* (London: Macmillan), pp 189–99

Pasinetti, L. L. (1962), 'Rate of profit and income distribution in relation to the rate of economic growth', *Review of Economic Studies*, vol. 29, no. 4, pp. 267–79.

Pasinetti, L. L. (1969), 'Switches of techniques and the "rate of return" in capital theory', *Economic Journal*, vol. 79, pp. 508–31.

Pasinetti, L. L. (1973), 'The notion of vertical integration in economic analysis', *Metroeconomica*, vol. 25, pp. 1–29. Repr. in L. L. Pasinetti (ed.), *Essays on the Theory of Joint Production* (London and Basingstoke: Macmillan, 1980), pp. 16–43.

Pasinetti, L. L. (1974), *Growth and Income Distribution* (Cambridge: Cambridge University Press).

Pasinetti, L. L. (ed.) (1977), *Contributi alla teoria della produzione congiunta* (Bologna: Società editrice il Mulino). Transl. as *Essays on the Theory of Joint Production* (London and Basingstoke: MacMillan, 1980).

Pasinetti, L. L. (1980), 'A note on basics, non-basics and joint production, in L. L. Pasinetti (ed.), *Essays on the Theory of Joint Production* (London and Basingstoke: Macmillan), pp. 51–4.

Pennavaja, C. (1974), 'Die Rezeption der Werke Piero Sraffas in Deutschland. Zu einer Problematisierung des neoricardianischen Ansatzes', in H.-G, Backhaus *et al.* (eds), *Gesellschaft, Beiträge zur Marxschen Theorie*, vol. 1 (Frankfurt/M.: Suhrkamp), pp. 181–221.

Petty, W. (1964), *The Economic Writings of Sir William Petty* (edited by C. H. Hull), (New York: Kelley).

Pigou, A. C. (1922), 'Empty economic boxes. A reply', *Economic Journal*, vol. 32, pp. 458–65.

Polanyi, K. (1944), *The Great Transformation* (New York: Rinehart & Co.).

Polanyi, K. (1968), *Primitive, Archaic and Modern Economies – Essays* (edited by G. Dalton), (New York: Doubleday).

Quincey, Th. de ([1844] 1970), 'The logic of political economy', *Political Economy and Politics* (New York: Kelley).

Ricardo, D. ([1821] 1951), *On the Principles of Political Economy and Taxation*, in P. Sraffa (ed.), *Works and Correspondence of David Ricardo*, vol. I (Cambridge: Cambridge University Press).

Ricardo, D. ([1823] 1966), Absolute value and exchangeable value, in P. Sraffa (ed.), *Works and Correspondence of David Ricardo*, vol. IV (Cambridge: Cambridge University Press), pp. 357–412.

Robinson, J. (1953/4), 'The production function and the theory of capital', *Review of Economic Studies*, vol. 21, pp. 81–106.

Robinson, J. (1956), *The Accumulation of Capital* (London: Macmillan).

Robinson, J. (1961), 'Prelude to a critique of economic theory', *Oxford Economic Papers*, vol. 13, pp. 53–8.

Robinson, J. (1965a), 'A reconsideration of the theory of value', in J. Robinson, *Collected Economic Papers*, vol. III (Oxford: Basil Blackwell), pp. 173–81.

Robinson, J. (1965b), 'Prelude to a critique of economic theory' (extended version), in J. Robinson, *Collected Economic Papers*, vol. III (Oxford: Basil Blackwell), pp. 7–14.

Robinson, J. (1971), *Economic Heresies* (London and Basingstoke: Macmillan).

Robinson, J. (1972a), *The Economics of Imperfect Competition*, new edn. (London: Macmillan).

Robinson, J. (1972b), 'Capital theory up to date', in E. K. Hunt and J. G. Schwartz, *A Critique of Economic Theory* (Harmondsworth, Middx: Penguin), pp. 233–44.

Robinson, J. (1973), *Collected Economic Papers IV* (Oxford: Basil Blackwell).

Robinson, J. (1979), 'History versus equilibrium', in J. Robinson, *Collected Economic Papers*, vol. V (Oxford: Basil Blackwell), pp. 58–68.

Roncaglia, A. (1975), *Sraffa e la teoria dei prezzi* (Rome and Bari: Laterza). Transl. as *Sraffa and the Theory of Prices* (Chichester: Wiley, 1978).

Sahlins, M. (1972), *Stone Age Economics* (Chicago: Aldine – Atherton).

Salvadori, N. (1982), 'Existence of cost-minimizing systems within the Sraffa framework', *Zeitschrift für Nationalökonomie*, vol. 42, pp. 281–98.

Samuelson, P. A. (1962), 'Parable and realism in capital theory: the surrogate production function', *Review of Economic Studies*, vol. 29, pp. 193–206.

Samuelson, P. A. (1966), *The Collected Scientific Papers* (Cambridge, Mass.: MIT Press).

Schaik, A. B. T. M. van (1976), *Reproduction and Fixed Capital* (Rotterdam: Tilburg University Press).

Schefold, B. (1971), 'Piero Sraffas Theorie der Kuppelproduktion, des Kapitals und der Rente', PhD thesis, University of Basel.

Schefold, B. (1973), 'Wert und Preis in der marxistischen und neokeynesianischen Akkumulationstheorie', *Mehrwert – Beiträge zur Kritik der politischen Ökonomie*, vol. 2, pp. 125–75.

Schefold, B. (1974), 'Fixed capital as a joint product and the analysis of accumulation with different forms of technical progress', mimeo. Transl. in L. L. Pasinetti (ed.), *Contributi alla teoria della produzione congiunta* (Bologna: Società editrice il Mulino, 1977), pp. 195–299. Repr. in L. L. Pasinetti (ed.), *Essays in the Theory of Joint Production* (London and Basingstoke: Macmillan, 1980), pp. 138–217.

Schefold, B. (1976a), 'Relative prices as a function of the rate of profit', *Zeitschrift für Nationalökonomie*, vol. 36, pp. 21–48.

Schefold, B. (1976b), 'Different forms of technical progress', *Economic Journal*, vol. 86, pp. 806–19.

Schefold, B. (1976c), 'Eine Anwendung der Jordanschen Normalform', *Zeitschrift für angewandte Mathematik und Physik*, vol. 27, pp. 873–5.

Schefold, B. (1976d), 'Nachworte', in P. Sraffa, *Warenproduktion mittels Waren – Einleitung zu einer Kritik der ökonomischen Theorie* (Frankfurt/M.: Suhrkamp), pp. 131–226.

Schefold, B. (1976e), 'Reduction to dated quantities of labour, roundabout processes, and switches of techniques in fixed capital systems', *Metroeconomica*, vol. 28, pp. 1–15.

Schefold, B. (1977), 'Energy and economic theory', *Zeitschrift für Wirtschafts- und Sozialwissenschaften*, vol. 97(3), pp. 227–49.

Schefold, B. (1978a), 'Fixed capital as a joint product', *Jahrbücher für Nationalökonomie und Statistik*, vol. 192, no. 5, pp. 415–39.

Schefold, B. (1978b), 'Multiple product techniques with properties of single product systems', *Zeitschrift für Nationalökonomie*, vol. 38, nos 1–2, pp. 29–53.

Schefold, B. (1978c), 'On counting of equations', *Zeitschrift für Nationalökonomie*, vol. 38, nos 3–4, pp. 253–85.

Schefold, B. (1979), 'Capital, growth, and definitions of technical progress' in 'Festschrift für G. Bombach', *Kyklos*, vol. 32, nos 1–2, pp. 236–50.

Schefold, B. (1980), 'Von Neumann and Sraffa: Mathematical equivalence and conceptual difference', *Economic Journal*, vol. 90, pp. 140–56.

Schefold, B. (1981), 'Nachfrage und Zufuhr in der klassischen Ökonomie' in F. Neumark (ed), *Studien zur Entwicklung der ökonomischen Theorie I*, Schriften des Vereins für Socialpolitik, Neue Folge, vol. 115/1, pp. 53–91.

Schefold, B. (1985a), 'Cambridge price theory: special model of general theory of value?', *American Economic Review*, vol. 72, pp. 140–5.

Schefold, B. (1985b), 'Sraffa and applied economics: joint production', *Political Economy. Studies in the Surplus Approach*, vol. 1, no. 1, pp. 17–40.

Schefold, B. (1985c), 'On changes in the composition of output', *Political Economy. Studies in the Surplus Approach*, vol. 1, no. 2, pp. 105–42.

Schefold, B. (1985d), 'Ecological problems as a challenge to classical and Keynesian economics', *Metroeconomica*, vol. 37, no. 1, pp. 21–61.

Schefold, B. (1986), 'The standard commodity as a tool of economic analysis: a comment on Flaschel', *Journal of Institutional and Theoretical Economics*, vol. 142, pp. 603–22.

Schefold, B. (1988), 'The dominant technique in joint production systems', *Cambridge Journal of Economics*, vol. 12, no. 1, pp. 97–123.

Schefold, B. (1989), 'Joint production – a further assessment', forthcoming in *Political Economy. The Surplus Approach*.

Schumpeter, J. A. (1954), *History of Economic Analysis* (Oxford: Oxford University Press).

Schwartz, J. T. (1961), *Lectures on the Mathematical Method in Analytical Economics* (New York: Gordon & Breach).

Semmler, W. (1982), 'Competition, monopoly and differential profit rates', *Rivista internazionale di scienze economiche e commerciali*, vol. 29, no. 8, pp. 737–62.

Smith, A. ([1776] 1976), *An Inquiry into the Nature and Causes of the Wealth of Nations*, 2 vols, in R. H. Campbell and A. S. Skinner (eds), *The Glasgow Edition of the Works and Correspondence of Adam Smith* (Oxford: Oxford at the Clarendon Press).

Sombart, W. (1916–27) *Der moderne Kapitalismus: Historisch-systematische Darstellung des gesamteuropäischen Wirtschaftslebens von seinen Anfängen bis zur Gegenwart*, 3 vols, (Munich and Leipzig: Dunker & Humblot).

Sraffa, P. (1922), 'The bank crisis in Italy', *Economic Journal*, vol. 32, pp. 178–97.

Sraffa, P. (1925), 'Sulle relazioni fra costo e quantità prodotta', *Annali di economia*, vol. 2, pp. 277–328. Repr. in *La rivista trimestrale*, no. 9, 1964, pp. 177–213. Transl. into French and published as 'Sur les relations entre coût et quantité produite', in P. Sraffa, *Écrits d'économie politique* (Paris: Economica, 1975), pp. 1–49. Transl. into German and published as 'Über die Beziehung zwischen Kosten und produzierter Menge', in B. Schefold (ed.), *Ökonomische Klassik im Umbruch – Theoretische Aufsätze von David Ricardo, Alfred Marshall, Vladimir K. Dmitriev und Piero Sraffa* (Frankfurt/M.: Suhrkamp, 1986), pp. 137–93.

Sraffa, P. (1926), 'The laws of returns under competitive conditions', *Economic Journal*, vol. 36, pp. 535–50.

Sraffa, P. (1932), 'Dr Hayek on money and capital', *Economic Journal*, vol. 42, pp. 42–53.

Sraffa, P. (1951), 'Introduction', in P. Sraffa (ed.), *Works and Correspondence of David Ricardo*, vol. I (Cambridge: Cambridge University Press), pp. xiii–lxii.

Sraffa, P. (1960), *Production of Commodities by Means of Commodities – Prelude to a Critique of Economic Theory* (Cambridge: Cambridge University Press).

Steedman, I. (1975), 'Positive profits with negative surplus value', *Economic Journal*, vol. 85, pp. 114–23.

Steedman, I. (1979a), *Trade amongst Growing Economies* (Cambridge: Cambridge University Press).

Steedman, I. (ed.) (1979b), *Fundamental Issues in Trade Theory* (London: Macmillan).

Steedman, I. (1980), 'Basics non-basics and joint production', in L. L. Pasinetti (ed.), *Essays on the Theory of Joint Production* (London and Basingstoke: Macmillan), pp. 44–50.

Swan, T. W. (1956), 'Economic growth and capital accumulation', *Economic Record*, vol. 332, pp. 343–61.

'Symposium on Increasing Returns and the Representative Firm (D. H. Robertson, P. Sraffa, G. H. Shove)' (1930), *Economic Journal*, vol. 40, pp. 80–116.
Sylos-Labini, P. ([1969] 1972), *Oligopolio e progresso tecnico* (Turin: Einaudi).

Torrens, R. ([1821] 1965), *An Essay on the Production of Wealth* (New York: Kelley).

Varri, P. (1980), 'Prices, rate of profit and life of machines in Sraffa's fixed-capital model', in L. L. Pasinetti (ed.), *Essays on the Theory of Joint Production* (London and Basingstoke: Macmillan). Originally published as 'Prezzi, saggio del profitto e durata del capitale fisso nello schema teorico di Piero Sraffa', *Studi economici*, vol. 29, no. 1 (1974), pp. 5–44.

Walras, L. (1926), *Éléments d'économie politique pure ou théorie de la richesse sociale* (Paris: R. Pichon and R. Durand-Auzias/Lausanne: F. Rouge). Transl. as *Elements of Pure Economics* (Fairfield: Kelley, 1977).
Weber, M. ([1920] 1972), 'Die protestantische Ethik und der Geist des Kapitalismus', in M. Weber, *Gesammelte Aufsätze zur Religionssoziologie* I (Tübingen: J. C. B. Mohr) pp. 1–206.
Wittgenstein, L. (1975), *Philosophische Untersuchungen* (Frankfurt/M.: Suhrkamp).
Wright, G. H. von (1958), 'Biographical sketch', in N. Malcom, *Ludwig Wittgenstein. A. Memoir* (London, New York, Toronto: Oxford University Press), pp. 1–22.

Index